DATE DUE

GAYLORD			PRINTED IN U.S.A.

PSYCHOLOGY:

Henry Clay Lindgren, PROFESSOR OF PSYCHOLOGY, SAN FRANCISCO STATE COLLEGE

AN INTRODUCTION TO THE STUDY OF
HUMAN BEHAVIOR

AND *Donn Byrne,* ASSISTANT PROFESSOR OF PSYCHOLOGY, UNIVERSITY OF TEXAS

JOHN WILEY & SONS, INC.
NEW YORK LONDON

Drawings by *Abner Graboff*

Charts by *Jerry Allen Lewis*

Library of Congress Catalog Card Number: 61–5676
Printed in the United States of America

PREFACE

The central purpose of this textbook is that of aiding students to develop a better and more complete understanding of human behavior—their own behavior as well as that of others.

We have undertaken this project with two basic assumptions in mind. The first and perhaps the most important of these assumptions is the belief that of all the sciences, psychology has the most to offer in the way of a sense-making framework for understanding human behavior.

The second assumption that has guided us is the belief that any course or text, in order to be successful, must communicate with students. Unfortunately, a great many courses and texts in psychology, as in other subjects, fall short of attaining an adequate degree of communication because they attempt to answer questions that students not only have not asked, but have not dreamed of asking. On the other hand, students *do* have questions for which psychologists *do* have the answers. What we have tried to do in developing this textbook is to anticipate the questions that students are likely to ask and answer them in such a way that they might be led to ask some of the deeper and more significant questions that are of interest to the psychologist. To put this into other words, we have tried to write a book that begins with areas of interest that are common to beginning students as well as to psychologists and proceeds into areas which psychologists think are important for human understanding, but of which the layman has little awareness.

Although we feel that a successful textbook must take careful heed of the needs, motivations, and interests of students, we also feel it must take the next step of bringing the student beyond these initial interests. A course in psychology is of greatest value to the beginning student when it helps him gain new and broader perspectives regarding human behavior. However, these new perspectives must somehow become the student's perspectives and not just the perspectives of instructors and textbook authors. Even when the course is venturing into territory far removed from the "common-sense" concepts of everyday life, we must help the student keep in touch with his own experience, for if he decides that what he is being asked to learn has nothing to do with him or with reality as he perceives it, we have lost the struggle to promote intellectual growth, if but for the moment.

As far as most beginning students are concerned, they will never get a chance to become actively involved in the conduct of psychological research. [Even among psychology majors in college, only about one in ten goes on to graduate work and becomes a professional psychologist (Wolfle, 1955).] We want the student to develop an appreciation of psychological research, of course, but most of all we want him to develop what M. Brewster Smith (1951) calls "a scientific understanding of human nature." It is our feeling that he is helped to do this when he sees some relationship between psychology and his own experiences; hence we have drawn our illustrations from everyday life, as well as from psychological research. We hope, too, that the student will develop a kind of "enlightened skepticism," in that he will want to question the evidence when he hears "common-sense" statements such as these: "Television programs cause delinquency," "Too much attention will spoil a child," or "All any child needs is plenty of loving." Specifically, we have tried to present a sample of the relevant experimental data in the discussion of most concepts. Our aim in this textbook is not that of teaching experimental methodology to the beginning student, but rather that of acquainting him with the sort of evidence on which psychologists base their conclusions. If our efforts in this direction lead him to develop more scientific ways of thinking about and reacting to human behavior, we shall feel that the time and energy we have invested in writing this book have been amply rewarded.

We wish to express our appreciation to our colleagues in the Psychology Department of San Francisco State College, whose individual contributions to this book have been many and varied, but particularly to Dr. Ludwig Immergluck, who collaborated with the senior author during the early stages of the manuscript; Dr. Joseph J. Fortier, whose critical evaluation of the manuscript was of great aid in its revision; and Dr. Walcott Beatty, whose suggestions were worked into chapters dealing with human development, motivation, and personality theory. Thanks are also due to Fredi Lindgren, whose expert reading of the manuscript helped considerably to improve its clarity and organization.

Henry Clay Lindgren
Donn Byrne

San Francisco State College
The University of Texas
August, 1960

CONTENTS

Part One Introduction

1. Psychology as a science and a profession   **3**

"What is psychology, anyway?" Psychology as a form of manipulation. Psychology as a form of "magic." Psychology as perceived by psychologists. *Psychology as a science.* Science and "common sense." Psychology and "common sense." Behavior without awareness. Simple and complex explanations of behavior. All behavior is caused. The prediction of behavior. Factors affecting the predictability of behavior. Psychology as one of the newer sciences. The testing of hypotheses. The methods of psychology. The place of controversy in science. Psychology as a pioneering discipline. *Psychology as a profession.* The membership of the psychological profession. Fields of psychology. Interest patterns of psychologists. *Topical organization of this textbook.*

Part Two Human Development

2. Human development: infancy and childhood   **29**

Ways of perceiving the behavior of children. *Physiological bases of childhood behavior.* Primitive aspects of behavior. Beginnings of learning. Maturation and socialization. *Social development.* Social learning. The development of personality. Learning to conform to cultural demands. Expectations for a particular child. Consistency in childhood behavior patterns. *Directions of development.* Physical development. Social development. *Relationships between adults and children.* The "terrible two's." Problem behavior. Differences between strict and permissive homes. Disciplining children. *Psychological needs of children.* The need for love. Esteem needs. Self-actualization needs.

3. Human development: adolescence and adulthood   **53**

Defining adolescence. *Psychological needs and tasks during adolescence.* Basic needs. "Higher-level" needs. Developmental tasks of adolescence. *Physical development.* Changes. Early and late maturers. *Social development.* Relations with parents and peers. Independence vs. direction and control. The need for mutual understanding. *Emotional development.* Awareness of others. Growth in empathy. Self-concern. Anxiety and sex roles. Anxiety and cultural differences. Problems of sexual adjustment. *Adulthood. Psychological needs and tasks.* Basic needs. Developmental tasks. *Marriage and the family*. Recent interest in marriage and family living. Problems of marital adjustment. Emotional problems of adulthood. Maintaining psychological growth in later years.

Part Three Basic Principles of Behavior

4. Physiological processes 79

The reality of psychological processes. Relationships between physiological and psychological processes. Rationale of this chapter. *Physiological aspects of perception*. Vision. Hearing. Smell. Taste. The skin senses. Perception of internal stimulation. *The nervous system*. The integrating function of the nervous system. Peripheral nervous system. Central nervous system. The integration of sensory and motor activities. Brain waves. *The physiological aspects of response*. Voluntary muscles. Involuntary muscles. Duct glands. Ductless glands. *Physiological aspects of drives*. Homeostasis. Hunger. Thirst. Need for oxygen. Elimination. Sex. Sleep. Fear and anger. Pleasure. *Relationships between physiological and psychological variables*. Mind vs. body. Physiological variables may influence psychological variables. Physiological variables may be correlated with psychological variables. Psychological variables may influence physiological variables. Other physiological-psychological interactions. The multicausality of behavior.

5. The learning process 105

Behavior. An example of behavior. Stimulus. Drive. Response. Reinforcement. *Learning to respond to new stimuli*. Conditioning. Higher-order conditioning. Extinction. Generalization. Discrimination. *Learning new responses*. The learning dilemma. Trial and error. Insight. Imitation. Instruction. Learning and performance. Failure to solve a learning dilemma. *Other theories of learning*. Guthrie's contiguous conditioning. Tolman's sign-Gestalt theory. Skinner's descriptive behaviorism. *Additional factors in the learning process*. Testing for learning. Distribution of practice. Meaningfulness. Knowledge of results. Whole vs. part learning. Schedules of reinforcement. Transfer of learning. Anxiety and learning. Learning without awareness. Learning under democratic conditions. A final word of caution.

6. Perceptual processes 129

Some general principles of the perceptual processes. Perceptual functioning: Innate or learned? Sensory adaptation. Depth perception. Perception as an organized experience. Achieving environmental stability. Illusions: Normal perceptual inaccuracies. Subliminal perception. Sensory deprivation. Extrasensory perception. *Individual differences in perception*. Perceptual defects. Patterns of individual differences. *Factors influencing perception*. Attention. Set. Type of surrounding. Interests and values. Drives. Social pressures.

7. Motivation and emotional behavior 153

Internal forces underlying behavior. *Concepts of motivation*. Levels of motivation. Primitive biological motives. Instinct. Social motives. Satisfactions. Habits. Unconscious motivation. Selective perception. *Conflict. Emo-*

tional behavior. "Emotion" defined. Emotion as motivation. Varieties of emotion. Physiological aspects of emotional behavior. Changes in blood chemistry under emotional stress. Family backgrounds and emotional patterns. *Maturation of emotional behavior.* Control. Differentiation. Perceptual changes. Intensity.

Part Four   Individual Differences

8. The psychologist's use of statistics   175

Statistics of description. Measuring individual differences. Describing scores: The frequency distribution. Describing the central tendency of the scores. Describing the variability. Other descriptive statistics. Interpretation of a score. The relationship between two variables. *Statistics of inference.* Sampling. Probability. Significance. *Using statistics to evaluate a test.* Standardization. Validity. Reliability.

9. Intelligence and creativity   193

Mental testing. Binet-type scales. Group tests of intelligence. Clinical use of intelligence tests. *The nature of intelligence.* The validity of intelligence tests. Abstract or conceptual intelligence. *Environment versus heredity.* Effects of education on intelligence. Social stimulation as a factor in the development of intelligence. Implications of the heredity-environment controversy. *Changes in intelligence.* Personality factors in IQ change. Changes in IQ after adolescence. *Achievement and creativity.* The need for achievement. Studies of creativity.

Part Five   Emotional Factors in Behavior

10. Personality: the organization of behavior   217

The need for personality theory. Implicit theories of personality. Private theories of personality. *Psychological theories of personality.* The contributions of psychotherapists. "Personality" defined. Psychoanalytic theories of personality. Later psychoanalytic theories. The psychology of "the self." Research in the psychology of "the self." Are there "types" of personality? Trait theories of personality. Stimulus-response theory. *Psychodiagnostics.* The measurement of personality variables. Personality questionnaires. Reservations regarding personality questionnaires. Value of personality questionnaires. Projective tests. Other approaches to personality measurement. Cautions to be observed with respect to personality tests.

11. Personal adjustment and mental hygiene   237

Reactions to frustration and conflict. *Anxiety.* The nature of anxiety. Learning as a factor in anxiety. "Normal anxiety." Behavior mechanisms. *Everyday patterns of adjustment.* Self-deceptive mechanisms. Repression. Rationalization. Perceptual rigidity. Projection. *Adjustment through substitute behavior.* Fantasy. Compensatory behavior. Sublimation. Reaction formation. Displaced hostility. Conformity. *Less effective patterns of adjustment.* Regression. Behavior without choice. Alcoholism. Narcotics. Gambling. Hyperactivity. Shyness. Obsessive behavior. Phobic behavior. Psychosomatic disorders. *Psychotic patterns of behavior.* Schizophrenia. Paranoid disturbances. Affective psychoses. Organic psychoses. Interpersonal relations in psychosis. Sociological factors in mental illness. *Psychotherapy*. Group therapy. Play therapy. Occupational and recreational therapy. Nondirective methods. Specialists in psychotherapy.

Part Six   Social Factors in Behavior

12. The social matrix of individual behavior   267

The individual and other people. *The self and the group*. The question of identity. The unwanted self. Group affiliations and the self-concept. How groups change personal characteristics of members. *Masculinity and femininity*. Masculine and feminine identification. Masculine and feminine behavior in childhood. Cross-cultural studies of male and female behavior. The learning of sex-linked patterns of behavior. *The formation of personality*. Uniqueness and similarity. Social learning. The search for meaning. The cultural basis of meaning. The learning of meanings. *Characteristics of groups*. Norms. Roles. Reference groups. Homeostasis and self-structure. Group life and "the self." Status. *Social class*. The "Yankee City" study. Social-class differences in childrearing practices. Social class and authoritarian attitudes. Middle-class culture in America.

13. Communication   291

The essential human process. Communication as a social process. Communication and shared frames of reference. *Levels of communication*. Communication among nations. Inconsistencies in interpersonal behavior. Levels of communication in different cultures. *Interpersonal communication*. Communication and social learning. Empathic communication. Empathic communication and anxiety. *Stereotypes in communication*. How stereotypes develop. Stereotypes and defensive behavior. Stereotypes: Are they good or bad? Stereotypes may lead to "circular behavior." *Feedback*. "Feedback" defined. Feedback in social situations. Feedback and two-way communication. Correcting distortions in frames of reference. *Symbols*. Symbolic behavior. Symbols as abstractions. Abstractions of abstractions. Manipulation of symbols. The use of symbols in scientific research. The development of scientific terminology. Symbolic behavior and delinquency. Communication and psychopathology.

14. Group processes   311

The effect of the group on communication. Developmental stages in group awareness. Types of groups. Meeting needs in a group context. *Factors related to group effectiveness*. Group morale. Group cohesiveness. Group climate. *Leadership*. The role of the leader. Research supporting different theories of leadership. Leadership and communication. The need to share leadership. Social distance and leadership. *Competition and cooperation*. Competitive climates and group functioning. *Group structure*. Sociometric analysis of group structure. Inclusive and exclusive groups.

Part Seven   Applying Psychology to Human Problems

15. Selecting and learning occupational roles   333

Psychological motives in work. Occupational roles and social status. Dynamics of occupational choice. Vocational counseling. "Faith in people" as a variable. Interest tests. Factors that predetermine occupational choice. *The importance of the college years.* Differences between high school and college. Attitude changes during college years. College experiences and vocational success. College grades and extracurricular activities. "Under-achievers" and "over-achievers." What a college degree means. *Work as a source of satisfaction and dissatisfaction.* Vocational satisfaction. Differences among "white-collar" workers. Sources of vocational dissatis-faction. Conflicts between occupational roles and family roles.

16. Psychology in business and industry   355

The use of science in industry. Growth of industrial psychology. Differing objectives of psychology and business. *Selection.* Developing a selection program. Intelligence tests. Special aptitude tests. Personality tests. Forced-choice questionnaires. Interest tests. Situational tests. The problem of criteria. *Supervision and management.* Personnel development. The Hawthorne study. "Human relations" training. The International Harvester study. Ambiguities in the supervisor's role. *Engineering psychology. Public opinion sampling and marketing research.* The need to study opinions and attitudes. Motivation research. Sampling problems. Exaggerated claims.

17. Psychology and world affairs   377

The prevention of war. Psychological factors in international relations. "Common-sense" attitudes toward social pathology. Understanding the causes of war. Cross-cultural research. Frustration, hostility, and aggressive behavior. A psychological understanding of hostility. Catharsis as a means of coping with hostility. Prejudice as a source of chronic hostility. Authoritarian attitudes: The F scale. Pitfalls in questionnaire studies. *Psychological factors in propaganda.* Attitudes toward propaganda. The "Psychologist's Manifesto." Fear-arousing propaganda. Changing behavior through "group decision." Political participation.

Glossary   401

References   409

Index   425

PART ONE

INTRODUCTION

1

Psychology as a science and a profession

"What is psychology, anyway?" One of the more complex problems in communication that psychologists have to deal with from time to time is that of explaining psychology to laymen. Sometimes the question, "What *is* psychology, anyway?", comes from a chance acquaintance, like a fellow passenger on an airplane; sometimes it comes from a student who is puzzling over the problem of choosing a career; sometimes it comes from a member of a college faculty committee concerned with reviewing the basic courses required for graduation.

Trying to explain psychology to the layman is a difficult task for several reasons. For one thing, psychology covers an area of subject matter that is not readily definable in layman's terms. Although it is a science, it does not deal with phenomena that laymen have become accustomed to associate with science: rocks, plants, earth satellites, chemicals, electricity, insects, and the like. It is possible to say, of course, "Psychology is the science of behavior, especially of *human* behavior," but such an answer rarely satisfies an inquiring layman. Although he has no problem accepting the reality of human behavior, he does have difficulty in seeing how it can be studied scientifically. Human behavior is abstract and intangible: How can it possibly be measured? Every human being is different: How can there be anything that is true of human beings in general? Furthermore, why is it necessary to have a "science of human behavior" at all: Isn't psychology just a matter of being able to handle people?

Psychology as a form of manipulation. Let us first take up the last of these questions. In common, everyday usage, the term "psychology" *is* sometimes used to designate a kind of skillful

manipulation. Here is an example:

JEANETTE: How did you get the car for tonight? I thought it was out of the question, after the way your father acted last time.

MIKE: Last time I was real stupid. I just barged up to him as soon as he walked in the door and asked for the car. This time, I used *psychology* on him. I waited till he had a second helping of apple pie, then asked Mother, sort of offhand, if she knew how often the buses passed our street during the evening hours. She told me and then asked why I wanted to know. I said I was planning to take Jeanette to the show. Dad asked why I didn't take the car. It's wonderful what a little psychology will do.

When Mike says "I used psychology on him" what he means is: "I knew he would react better to an indirect approach than to a direct one, and I used this knowledge to manipulate the situation to my advantage." In other words, when we use the term "psychology" in this way, we mean "the technique of manipulating people successfully." Mothers say that they use "psychology" when they get infants to take cod-liver oil that has been blended with orange juice to disguise it. Salesmen say that they are using psychology when they ask a prospective customer "Would you rather take it with you or have it sent?" or "Which would you prefer—the model with the leather seats and the chrome trim or the stripped-down economy model?" The customer has not made a decision about buying the product at all, but by maneuvering him into making minor decisions that presuppose the major decision to buy, the salesman "clinches" the sale. It might be noted that such uses of "psychology" do not usually originate with the work of psychologists. Rather, they are interpersonal techniques that laymen have developed, techniques which sometimes work and sometimes do not.

Psychology as a form of "magic." All of us have at some time or other had the experience of manipulating others successfully and have thought or said: "In some ways, I'm pretty good when it comes to psychology!" When we use the term "psychology" in this way, we are really complimenting ourselves on our cleverness and good sense, but we also imply something beyond cleverness. We may be implying, for instance, that we have some "secret power" or "magic," that enables us to get people to do things without their being aware that they are manipulated. Most of us would of course deny any belief in magic, but there is something about our use of the word "psychology" in this context that implies or hints at some very special ability to control people. Although we think of ourselves as civilized and sophisticated individuals, free from the superstitions of past ages, most of us probably have some lingering remnants of childhood belief in magic that we have not quite eliminated from our thinking. The popularity of good-luck charms and newspaper horoscopes is but one indication of this common reluctance to give up our dependence on magic.

Because of this more-or-less unconscious desire to attribute magical or quasi-magical qualities to things we do not quite understand, we tend to regard scientists in general, and especially psychologists, as possessing powers that border on the supernatural. Psychologists are sometimes perceived, for example, as individuals who can hypnotise people and thus get them to do things against

their will and who can read a person's innermost thoughts by gazing steadily at him. Such ideas are of course less widespread among educated people, but it is nevertheless disconcerting for a psychology instructor to read comments like these when he asks his students to write an anonymous evaluation of the course:

"I liked the course, but every time you looked at me I felt you knew exactly what I was thinking."

"What I liked least about the course was having you stare at me and try to read my thoughts."

One gets the feeling that these students know that such anxieties and fears are baseless but that they cannot rid themselves of the idea that the psychologist is possessed of some kind of super- natural power.

A psychologist also finds it mildly disconcerting when he encounters the surprised and at times anxious responses of individuals at a social gather- ing who discover that they have been talking to a psychologist:

"Now you're not going to start psychoanalyzing me, are you?"

"I'd better be careful what I say to *you!*"

"Let me tell you about this dream my little boy had the other night, and see what you think I should do."

Part of the difficulty lies, of course, in the fact that the activities, concerns, and techniques of the psychologist are not readily comprehended by the lay public. Consequently there is a certain amount of uncertainty and apprehension about his abili- ties. Most of us have a reasonably clear picture of the professions or occupations with which we have frequent personal contact or which are widely publicized. It is difficult to imagine a teacher or a grocery clerk having much trouble in explaining his work to the public. But there are many other professions, psychiatry and law, as well as psychology, whose duties and responsi- bilities are not well known to the public. Some- times a degree of hostility creeps into our attitudes, particularly when we are afraid that our encoun- ters with members of the profession will lead to our being exploited or manipulated in some way without our being able to do anything about it. Lawyers, as well as psychologists and psychiatrists, are the common butt of funny stories and cartoons, whose hostile intent is often quite obvious.

In addition to these underlying feelings of re- sentment, there is often a degree of anxiety, as there is about any aspect of human experience that is shrouded in mystery. Not only is the work of these professions unfamiliar, but also a false image is widely held. Most lawyers do not take part in criminal trials, just as most psychologists do not treat patients in psychotherapy. Hence it is hardly surprising that psychologists are accused of doing or being able to do things that are beyond their powers, while, at the same time, some of their very real and potentially valuable contribu- tions to human welfare and understanding are ignored or belittled.

Psychology as perceived by psychologists. Another reason why psychologists have difficulty in explaining psychology to laymen has to do with the differing ways in which psychologists them- selves perceive psychology. Most psychologists would agree that psychology is a science, a body of knowledge, and a profession. Beyond this area of agreement, differences begin to present them- selves. Some psychologists are inclined to think of psychology primarily as a laboratory science devoted to the formulation of the basic laws of behavior. Such psychologists are, generally speak- ing, more concerned with the discovery of knowl- edge than they are with the practical application of the results of their research. Other psychologists are also interested in research, but their concerns grow out of the practical problems that are en- countered in human relationships: how to cure mental illness, how to make teaching and learn- ing more efficient, how to increase industrial pro- ductivity, how to improve international com- munication and understanding, and the like. Still other psychologists are primarily concerned with the application of psychological understanding and techniques in such areas as the treatment of mental disease, classroom learning, the testing and selection of job applicants or school applicants, and so forth.

Although psychologists might share some con- cepts about the nature of psychology and differ on others, it should be clear from the above that the layman's idea of psychology as a clever tech- nique for manipulating others or a kind of magic is far removed from any of the concepts held by psychologists. And perhaps this gap between the layman's and the psychologist's concept gives us the reason why psychology is so difficult to explain. In effect, laymen *already think they know* what psychology is, and, when the psychologist starts to describe what psychology means to *him,* lay- men cannot see any relationship between what the psychologist is saying and what they already know or think they know. In other words, the layman and the psychologist are using different frames of reference in their approach to psychology. Furthermore, each is drawing upon different experiences: the layman is thinking of psychology as applied to the problems he encounters in his everyday life, whereas the psychologist is thinking about the concepts and problems that are central to his professional specialty.

Psychology as a science

Science and "common sense." The layman's view of the universe, including human behavior in general, as well as his own personal experiences, is based on what we shall refer to as "common sense," which differs from the scientist's view of the same phenomena. Most of the areas of science have their counterparts in "common sense." In our manipulations of other people, we become, so to speak, "common-sense psychologists," just as we are also "common-sense physicists," every time we analyze a mechanical difficulty and decide that what is needed is a lever or a drop of oil and "common-sense doctors," every time we take some aspirin or recommend bed rest for some ailment.

Originally, "common sense" meant "understanding or knowledge based on the evidence of the senses," as opposed to mere suppositions, superstitions, or fancies, which could not stand up to a practical or empirical test. The meaning of "common sense" has become somewhat extended beyond this original meaning, although the idea of the empirical, practical test still remains. When a salesman tells us, "This blanket is fireproof—it will not burn even if you drop a lighted match on it," "common sense" prompts us to say, "Go ahead and prove it." In other words, "Show us evidence that we can evaluate with our senses." When we are faced by some obvious illusion, however, we rely on our general knowledge of the universe and deny the evidence of our senses. For instance, when we see a stage magician "saw a woman in half," we know that our senses are deceiving us. This does not cause us to lose faith in them entirely, because we know that if we could examine the equipment at close range, using our visual and tactile senses, the illusion would be dispelled. Hence our "common sense" (using the term in its modern, more extended meaning) tells us that the woman is not being sawed in half.

"Common sense" is a useful and often reliable guide to action in everyday life, so much so that it has come to be synonymous with "good sense." It has, however, certain rather marked limitations. In the first place, there are an infinite number of phenomena that are not available to the human senses, but which are just as real as anything that can be seen, heard, or felt. There are, for instance, sounds whose frequencies place them beyond the range of the human ear. Furthermore, it is possible for us to be affected by stimuli without being aware that the stimuli are present or that our behavior is at all being modified by them.

In the second place, "common sense" as we know and use it has been extended beyond "evidence that can be confirmed by the senses" or even "good sense." We make a number of judgments which presumably are based on "common sense" but which involve ideas that have not been tested empirically. We may say, for example, that "highway safety campaigns are good common sense" and appropriate millions of dollars for them annually. Yet we have no evidence to show that such campaigns reduce accidents at all. At least one research study has turned up the puzzling fact that fast drivers are more likely to believe in the value of such campaigns than are slow drivers. (Stewart, 1958*a*, 1958*b*.) Since fast drivers are themselves frequently the target of safety campaigns, this is a little like saying that the person who breaks laws has more confidence in their value than do the people who keep them. In other words, "common sense" has come to include a wide range of more or less unconscious assumptions, biases, and prejudices which could not stand empirical test and which we have no intention of putting to such a test.

Sometimes what we call "common sense" is based on a combination of prejudice and faulty evidence, as, for example, when we say, "Common sense will tell you that men are more intelligent than women; why, men outnumber women at least five to one in *Who's Who*." Or, "Common sense will tell you that women are safer drivers than men—they have far fewer accidents." Occasionally we permit folklore to dictate what we consider to be common sense. An older woman may tell her married daughter: "You shouldn't let that child read so much, common sense should tell you that too much reading is bad for the eyes."

Psychology and "common sense." Although "common sense" is sometimes an effective guide to action in everyday life, it is severely limited when it comes to understanding the more complex aspects of human behavior that have been studied by psychologists and other behavioral scientists.[1] This is particularly true when it comes to dealing with new concepts. The layman whose understanding of life is limited to "common sense" is inclined to dismiss the whole idea of studying human behavior scientifically as futile or senseless. The general tenor of such attitudes is shown by Table 1-1, which presents some of the results of a poll of high school students taken in 1957. Statements 4, 5, and 7 reveal a considerable degree of pessimism and skepticism with regard to the possibility of developing a scientific understanding of human behavior. Statements 1 and 6 indicate some feeling that the findings of psychologists are not related to the problems of everyday life, while Statements 2 and 3 show that a fairly large minority of students are hostile toward science.

[1] The term *behavioral sciences* is commonly applied to sociology, psychology, social anthropology, and those areas of other social sciences that involve the application of experimental and observational methods to the study of the behavior of man and the lower animals.

Statement 8, however, does receive some support from the students, although a strong minority state that they are opposed to applying scientific methods to the practical problems of everyday life.

Because of the limitations of "common sense," when it comes to dealing with the understanding of complex problems, and because of the hostility that laymen sometimes display toward any attempt to study behavior scientifically, many scientists are inclined to take this attitude: "Reliance on common sense is usually a confession that one has fallen back on prejudices which he refuses to examine." (English and English, 1958: 99.)

Behavior without awareness. Perhaps one of the reasons that psychology has overtones of magic for some people stems from the fact that much of it is concerned with stimuli and behavior that are "beyond awareness." There is little place in "common sense" for "behavior without awareness," since "common sense" assumes that we are completely aware of what we are doing and why we are doing it. A great deal of psychological research, on the other hand, has demonstrated that it is not only possible for people to be unaware of

Table 1–1 Reactions of a nationwide sample of high-school students to statements dealing with scientific activities. (After Heath, Maier, Remmers, and Rodgers, 1957.)

Statement	Percentages Replying		
	"Agree" or "Probably Agree"	"Disagree" or "Probably Disagree"	No Reply
1. Scientists who work in colleges and universities are so removed from everyday life that they have little to contribute to practical problems.	25	75	0
2. Scientists are more willing than nonscientists to sacrifice the welfare of others to further their own interests.	38	60	2
3. The willingness of the scientist to reject traditional beliefs may lead to confusion and disorder.	45	54	1
4. Since every person is different, it is impossible to establish scientific laws of human action.	57	40	3
5. Although science may be able to understand and control some things in the physical world, it can never hope to understand and control human action.	65	33	2
6. Scientific studies are conducted in the laboratory rather than in the actual world.	43	55	2
7. Science has its place, but there are many things that can never be understood by the human mind.	78	17	5
8. Scientific methods should be applied to human problems like segregation and poverty as well as to machines and modern conveniences.	59	38	3

their behavior and its causes, but also suggests that a great deal of everyday experience is "beyond ordinary awareness." For example, witnesses to a traffic accident will present conflicting versions of what actually happened, indicating that some of them are distorting the facts to some degree. Probably most of these distortions are unconscious. The tendency of people to present inaccurate reports has been tested many times by psychology instructors through classroom experiments like this one:

A student dressed in a striking way (loud tie, brightly colored shirt, etc.) enters the classroom after the hour has begun and goes up to the instructor, demanding redress for a low grade he received. The instructor asks the student to see him during his office hours. The student refuses, saying that the hours are inconvenient for him and that since he pays tuition, he is entitled to an interview at his convenience. The instructor counters with an irritable remark, and an argument ensues, culminating with the student throwing his books on the floor in a rage and stalking out of the room. The instructor then asks the members of the class to write down an accurate report of what they saw, describing the appearance of the student and the sequence of events. The accounts are invariably at odds with one another, and most of them contain errors of fact. Although some students feel tentative about their reports, others feel sure they have reported accurately and are hence completely unaware that they are distorting or misrepresenting the facts.

Most aspects of our society are, in fact, based on the general premise that people are rational, consciously motivated beings who know what they are doing at all times. We like to believe that we are completely free to be good or bad, to enter the occupation of our choice, to select friends, to make our own decisions on the merits of the candidate or issue when voting, and so forth. Because of the widespread belief that all choices or decisions are the result of rational, conscious processes, it is not surprising that psychological findings are disturbing and unpopular when they show that our decisions are to a large extent predetermined by forces beyond our awareness. An example of the kind of research that tends to refute "common-sense" notions of free choice in the selection of friends is a study by Festinger, Schachter, and Back (1950), who found that an important determinant of friendship patterns in a veterans' housing development was the propinquity factor—that is, veterans and their families were inclined to make friends with those who lived near them, and families who lived near the main arteries of traffic through the development tended to have more friends than those who lived in less traveled areas. Most people would rather believe that their friends were selected on some basis other than that of chance meetings on the way to the garbage can.

Simple and complex explanations of behavior. Laymen often express impatience with psychology because, as they say, psychologists make behavior unnecessarily complex. Sometimes they go so far as to imply that psychologists are "making a job for themselves" by finding or inventing fine gradations and dimensions of behavior that are not very relevant or important. Such an attitude is to a large degree based on the widespread but mistaken belief that human problems are essentially simple. This belief in turn is based on the hope that the problems of human existence can be solved by simple, direct remedies. Thus some mothers believe that all that is necessary to raise children properly is to give them enough love; some employers believe that all that is necessary to increase production is to offer bonuses for higher production; and some community leaders believe that juvenile delinquency can be eliminated simply by providing a sufficient number of recreational facilities for young people or by applying a sufficient number of "old-fashioned strappings."

The reason why such simple, direct solutions are doomed to failure is that they are based on oversimplified concepts of human behavior. To be sure, parental love is an essential ingredient in proper child development, employees need to be rewarded for their efforts, and some delinquency may be caused by a lack of adequate recreational facilities or a lack of parental discipline. But other factors, too, play important parts in the lives of children, employees, and young people, and to ignore such factors is to ignore important parts of the problem. Often the tendency to oversimplify the human problems is actually a kind of defense against developing any real understanding of them. We hope that if we can find the simple and direct solution to the problem at hand, we can solve it once and for all and will thus be saved the necessity of undertaking the detailed and ofttimes tedious research that unraveling the complexities of any human problem requires.

Generally speaking, most of us are neither prepared for nor interested in tackling the task of examining all the significant factors that may be involved in a given situation. Furthermore, in most instances there is just not enough time to carry on extensive research into all the elements that may be involved. Most problems we encounter in everyday life *do* call for immediate and direct solutions—for example, the problem of whether to have a cup of coffee with a friend and thus take a chance on being late to class, whether to ask the girl sitting in the next seat whether she would like to go to a show this evening, what to do when a child says, "I won't!", or the like. But many other problems, although they may be very pressing, cannot and should not be solved by split-second decisions. Hasty actions may even make matters worse. The problem of juvenile delin-

quency in a community, for instance, does not respond to simple, direct treatment, and it is in dealing with such problems that we need to invite the collaboration of psychologists and other behavioral scientists. Unfortunately, when direct solutions fail, as they often do, we tend to become impatient and irritable, blaming others for our failure and turning to drastic and ill-conceived measures, seldom thinking of looking critically at our own assumptions or methods to see whether they should be modified or improved. It is our tendency to assume that it is impossible for us to be mistaken, and to reject any tentative approach to studying a problem as a sign of weakness, that makes reliance on "common sense" a practice that is at times foolish and even dangerous.

All behavior is caused. Scientists make assumptions, too, but they are of a different order than the assumptions made by laymen. Whereas laymen's assumptions tend to have the purpose of eliminating the need for further inquiry in order to clear the way for prompt decision and action, scientists' assumptions are not intended to bypass inquiry, but to encourage it.

Psychologists as scientists make the following assumptions:

1. All behavior is caused.

2. Human beings are capable of studying, analyzing, identifying, classifying, and measuring these causes in order to develop generalizations that will enable them to predict behavior.

3. The principles or generalizations that govern and cause behavior are simpler than the original data on which they are based.

These assumptions are held by scientists in fields other than psychology and have been used to develop principles which make it possible to predict the movement of the planets, the activity of electricity, the effect of the pull of gravity on a free and falling object, the effect of vaccines on the probability of the development of a certain disease, and the like. Since the latter part of the nineteenth century psychologists have been working to develop similar principles to predict the behavior of living organisms. Even though psychology is a relatively new science and even though its task is probably the most difficult yet attempted by scientists, it is possible to predict a good deal of human behavior much more effectively than is possible using "common sense."

The prediction of behavior. Although most of us have learned to accept as valid predictions made by natural and physical scientists, many a beginning student in psychology has felt that the psychologist's claim of being able to predict human behavior is rather presumptuous, forgetting that everyone makes dozens of predictions regarding human behavior every day, some of them successful, some of them not. We predict that the morning paper will be at our doorstep when we arise; we predict that the soda-fountain clerk will hand back our correct change; we predict that if a student fails to attend class, he will fail the course. The predictions that psychologists make are less likely to be concerned with specific events in the lives of specific individuals. The psychologist as a scientist is primarily interested in measuring factors that can be used to predict the behavior of people in general, or, rather, the behavior under certain specified conditions of people characterized by certain specified qualities. As the result of certain research, he may predict, for example, that individuals making scores below a certain level on a specified college-entrance examination will have a 70 per cent chance of failing in college. Or he may predict that individuals scoring above a certain level will have a 50 per cent chance of making honor-roll grades.

Psychologists are able to predict the probability of certain events occurring under specified conditions because they have studied the conditions under which certain events occur, and have developed and tested hypotheses concerning the causation of these events. The assumption, then, that behavior has causes that can be measured has led psychologists to identify and measure these causes, and to formulate generalizations about them.

Factors affecting the predictability of behavior. It is true, of course, that psychologists, as contrasted with natural and physical scientists, are able to make firm predictions about a much smaller number of events. There are two reasons for this, each of which is interrelated. The task of predicting any behavioral event increases in complexity in proportion to the number of causal factors involved—in other words, the greater the number of factors that may affect a certain event, the more difficult the task of predicting it. It is relatively easier to predict events in the natural and physical world because it is easier to keep the factors or forces that would interfere with or invalidate the prediction at a minimum. The frog eggs observed by the biologist will not hatch if

they are eaten by fish or if someone drains the pond, but the biologist can easily take steps to prevent this from occurring. Iron placed in a crucible will not melt if someone forgets to turn on the power. This possibility, too, can be guarded against rather easily.

The number of factors that can interfere with the hatching of frog eggs and the melting of iron is *relatively* small, compared with the number that can invalidate the prediction of human behavior. A person may have a high score on a college-entrance examination, but it is extremely difficult to predict and control the factors that may interfere with his getting superior grades. He may have to work full-time in order to stay in college and consequently is unable to devote sufficient time to his studies. We may anticipate this difficulty and provide him with funds, thus making it unnecessary for him to work. But we do not foresee that he would become involved in an unhappy love affair toward the end of the semester, as a result of which he loses interest in his studies and does not even take his final examinations. Or perhaps he is a kind of person who is chronically unable to cooperate with instructors and other persons in authority and consequently gets grades that do not reflect his real potential. These are but a few of the many possible kinds of conditions or factors that make psychological prediction a difficult and hazardous undertaking. It is for this reason that psychologists predict *group* behavior more accurately than *individual* behavior. After allowance has been made for chance factors like those described, it is then possible to say that the chances of a certain high-scoring group getting superior grades are, say, 50 per cent. Such predictions are, of course, based on experiences in similar situations with similar groups and assume that the situation will not change markedly. The characteristics of groups tend to be more stable than the characteristics of individuals; the characteristics of an institution, like a college, are also quite stable. Because of these stable characteristics, it is possible to reduce the number of factors that would invalidate predictions.

Psychology as one of the newer sciences. The second reason why psychologists are able to make fewer predictions relates to the youth of psychology as a science. The natural and physical sciences have a history of hundreds or even thousands of years, depending on whether one thinks of them as beginning with the "Age of Reason" in the eighteenth century, with the Renaissance, or with the Greek philosophers. The beginning of psychology as a science, however, is customarily placed in the second half of the nineteenth century. William James began conducting psychological experiments at Harvard in 1875 and founded the journal *Mind* in 1876. A few years later, Wilhelm Wundt founded his psychological laboratory in Leipzig. About the same period of time, Charcot was doing pioneer work in psychiatry in France. It was not until the present century that psychology became well-established as a field of research in its own right. Although today most American and Canadian colleges and universities have independent departments of psychology, there are a few that have departments that still combine psychology and philosophy. In Russia, psychology is rather generally considered to be a branch of physiology, and a great many, if not most, of the universities of the world outside the United States and Canada do not even have departments of psychology. The point is that psychology, seen in terms of its historical development and the extent to which it is accepted by the other academic and scientific fields, is not only a very young science but also is one that is "still arriving."

The testing of hypotheses. Before the advent of psychology, the understanding of behavior was largely the concern of philosophy. Even today, psychology acknowledges a debt to philosophy, as do other branches of science, particularly with respect to its contributions to logical analysis and theory-building. Although "common-sense" usually looks with disfavor on anything "theoretical" as "impractical" or "idealistic," psychologists have found theory-development to be a necessary step in understanding human behavior. Scientific research usually begins with a problem to be solved or a question to be answered. Possible solutions take the form of hypotheses or "informed guesses." In actual practice, hypotheses usually grow out of various theories that are considered by the researcher as he searches for possible solutions to a problem.

A psychologist may, for example, become concerned with the problem of finding out whether it is possible to teach people foreign languages when they are asleep. Clinical research has indicated that it is possible to communicate with individuals when they are in sleeplike states induced by hypnosis or drugs. This suggests a theory that communication is also feasible during natural or normal sleep. He might also theorize that repeating certain meaningful combinations (such as foreign words paired with their English equivalents) might produce learning, basing his thinking on research in the field of human learning (e.g., Rock, 1958). This theorizing would lead him to construct the hypothesis that subjecting sleeping individuals to the phonographic reproduction of verbal material will result in measurable amounts of learning.

In order to test this hypothesis, he might pre-

pare a recording in which a vocabulary list of, say, German words are read slowly, each German word being immediately followed by its English equivalent. He then might run a "pilot" study with a few subjects to determine the volume at which the phonograph should be played in order to be clearly audible but not loud enough to wake up the sleeping subjects. The psychologist would also have to decide on some way of determining whether or not each individual actually is asleep during the experiment; perhaps he will decide on using readings from an electro-encephalograph (an instrument measuring electrical impulses from the brain) as an adequate criterion.

He would do well to choose subjects who (1) have no familiarity at all with German, and (2) are motivated to attempt this type of learning. The subjects would be divided into an "experimental group" (to be subjected to the German vocabulary at night) and a "control group" (to go through exactly the same procedure except that the recording would contain only pairs of English words). The two groups of subjects would be matched as closely as possible on variables that might influence their ability to learn, such as age, IQ, and years of schooling. Also the subjects would not be told whether they were in the experimental or control group because this knowledge might influence the results of the study.

The actual experiment might consist of giving every subject a pretest to determine how many German words he knew before the experiment, a week of nightly exposure to either the experimental or control recording, and finally a post-test to determine how many German words he knew at the close of the experiment. If the psychologist finds that the experimental group shows a significant increase in its German vocabulary whereas the control group reveals no change, he will probably conclude that sleep teaching is an effective device for teaching foreign vocabulary. He may even theorize that other kinds of material may be taught by the same method. Such theorizing may lead to the development of additional hypotheses to be tested. However, if he finds that his experimental subjects give no evidence of having learned any German, then he predicts that other subjects in similar circumstances will also experience no learning.[1]

[1] In actuality, experimental attempts to teach verbal material to sleeping individuals have met with *no* success. (Simon and Emmons, 1956.)

The methods of psychology. There are two characteristics that make psychology a science: scientific methods and scientific attitudes. Both are interrelated, of course. The proper use of methods must be accompanied by appropriate attitudes, and scientific attitudes lead to the development of appropriate methods.

The scientific attitude involves a good many components, including the assumptions discussed earlier about the predictability of behavior and the belief that ever more precise principles will be constructed, which will permit more accurate predictions. The scientific method is basically a way of testing hypotheses (or guesses) in as objective a fashion as possible. Ideally, all conditions are controlled except those that are under investigation. In a procedure, known as an experiment, these variables under investigation are manipulated in some way, and the results are carefully observed. Any description of a creative process such as research is to some extent artificial. However, we will attempt to describe the steps which usually take place in experimental investigations, using our imaginary sleep-teaching experiment as an example.

1. Phenomena are observed in the laboratory, in everyday life, in research reports written by other scientists, and even in literary writing. The idea for sleep teaching may have arisen from the discovery that communication is possible with individuals who are hypnotized or under the influence of certain drugs. Or we might have had the experience of talking to someone who was apparently asleep or perhaps sleep-walking. The idea could also have come from a science-fiction story such as Aldous Huxley's *Brave New World*.

2. Next, there is usually some explicit or implicit generalization about one's observation. The psychologist might say to himself, "I'll bet that anyone who is sleeping is able to perceive what is going on around him and remember it." In other words, he is saying that the reported or observed phenomena are not limited to a few isolated and special events; rather, he is betting that they are characteristic of human beings in general.

3. Not always, but often, at this point, the psychologist attempts to build some sort of theory which might account for such a thing happening. Perhaps he will suggest that our unconscious mental processes continue operating even during sleep. Perhaps he will guess that communication of this sort is possible only if the individual's rest is par-

tially disrupted. Or perhaps he will refrain from theorizing until he has checked on his original generalization to find out whether it is true or false.

4. At this point, the scientist makes a logical derivation from his generalization or his theory, and states it in such a way that verification will be possible. This derivation or postulate usually takes the form: if X is true, then Y should occur if Z is altered. In our experiment, we said, "if it is possible for a sleeping person to perceive and remember, then learning should occur if learning material is presented to him while asleep." Specifically, German vocabulary should be learned if pairs of German and English words are heard during sleep.

5. As was described, the experiment itself is planned in detail, trying to control as many extraneous variables as possible. The experiment is carried out and the results are subjected to statistical analyses. If possible, the entire procedure is repeated with other subjects to verify the findings.

6. If Y does occur, further generalization, theorization, postulation, and experimentation are undertaken in order to broaden our knowledge about the phenomenon and how it operates. If Y does not occur, as it did not in the sleep-teaching experiments, we can conclude that (1) there was something wrong with our experimental test of the hypothesis, (2) sleep teaching may be possible but not the teaching of German vocabulary, or (3) the whole idea should be rejected. In this instance, there have been a number of different studies of sleep teaching, none of which yielded positive results. While certainty is never possible in science, we *are* able to say that there is no evidence to support the notion that sleep-teaching is feasible.

Through countless repetitions of the total process of observation, generalization, theorizing, postulating, and experimental verification, psychologists and other behavioral scientists are able to formulate and reformulate their understanding of behavior in the form of generalizations or principles. And as these generalizations and principles develop greater validity, the scientist's ability to predict behavior improves.

The procedures outlined in these steps should be carried out as objectively and systematically as possible. The data and conclusions produced by the scientist should be free from and unaffected by personal bias; otherwise, questions could be raised as to their validity. Systematization is important in order to make it possible for other scientists to recreate the same conditions, re-do the experiments using the same techniques, and check to see whether they obtain the same results as the original experimenter.

The place of controversy in science. Science is, however, much more than objectivity and system, important as they are. As Conant (1951) points out, the history of science does not consist of a series of cold-blooded, methodical steps forward, progressively accumulating increasing quantities of knowledge about the universe. It consists, instead, of the stumblings and gropings of scientists through ". . . thickets of erroneous observations, misleading generalizations, inadequate formulations, and unconscious prejudice . . ." Although Conant's remarks were particularly concerned with the pioneers of science, a review of critical comment that appears in psychological journals (as well as in the journals of other scientific disciplines) will show that scientific endeavors are today still characterized by controversy and a considerable degree of emotionality.

Conant maintains that the essential nature of science is embodied not so much in its worship of objectivity and system as in its more dynamic qualities. He sees science primarily as an active process—as

. . . an interconnected series of concepts and conceptual schemes that have developed as a result of experimentation and observation and are fruitful of further experimentation and observation. In this definition the emphasis is on the word "fruitful." Science is a speculative enterprise. The validity of a new idea and the significance of a new experimental finding are to be measured by the consequences—consequences in terms of other ideas and other experiences. Thus conceived, science is not a quest for certainty; it is rather a quest which is successful only to the degree that it is continuous.[1]

Seen in this light, science is a growing, changing phenomenon, one that produces instability, confusion, and ambiguity in the sense that it is continually upsetting "established truths"—even "truths" that have been "established" as the result of previous scientific research.

A generation ago, John Dewey made this statement regarding ambiguity in science:

The scientific attitude may almost be defined as that which is capable of enjoying the doubtful; scientific

[1] Reprinted by permission.

method is, in one aspect, a technique for making productive use of doubt by converting it into operations of definite inquiry. (1929: 228.)

The concept of science as ambiguous and changing is almost the exact opposite of that which is held by the layman. In the public press (and unfortunately too often in the classroom), science takes on the aspects of accumulated facts, tested knowledge, and constituted authority, as personified by confident, white-coated men manipulating instruments and laboratory animals with an air of quiet certainty about the outcome of their inquiry. The essence of science is not the accumulation of authoritative facts but is, rather, contained in (1) the belief that the causes of behavior and other natural events can be identified and measured, and the behavior or event predicted, (2) the desire to develop valid principles or generalizations concerning behavior and other events, and (3) an understanding of the rules and procedures that govern the way in which principles or generalizations are developed and tested.

In attempting to develop these principles, scientists are continually encountering the unexpected, an experience which heightens the sense of uncertainty, ambiguity, and frustration, but which at the same time makes scientific inquiry one of the most exciting and rewarding of all fields of human endeavor.

"Common sense" is impatient with ambiguity and doubt and hastens to resolve it in ways that are often impulsive and arbitrary. Scientific progress, on the other hand, is fostered by the presence of unresolved and ambiguous problems. Indeed, one characteristic of the creative scientist, according to studies conducted at the Institute of Personality Assessment and Research at the University of California, is his enjoyment of and preference for ambiguous and "unstructured" situations. (Barron, 1958.)

Psychology as a pioneering discipline. It is important for the beginning student to keep the preceding paragraphs in mind as he embarks on his study of psychology. Whereas the natural and physical sciences, having a longer history than psychology and being concerned with the study of phenomena that are relatively more stable than human behavior, tend to speak with more assurance and authority, psychology is inclined to be more tentative. As Conant's analysis shows, however, this does not make it any less a science. And,

as the authors of this text attempt to show, studies conducted by psychologists have been most fruitful of new ideas which in turn lead to additional research in new fields. Whereas some areas of psychology, like animal learning and the measurement of intelligence, have been as thoroughly investigated as many areas of natural and physical science, research in most other areas, like mental illness and the behavior of groups, is still largely exploratory. Although the tentative nature of psychological findings may disturb those who expect science to be characterized by certainty, it should prove to be stimulating and exciting to those who are able to perceive science as a continuous series of forays and adventures into the unknown. A quality of this excitement is contained in the following quotation from a textbook on psychology written for laymen by an eminent psychologist:

The reader is here offered an opportunity to become initiated into certain aspects of what is almost a secret society. This society counts as its members those who have some modern scientific knowledge of the nature of mental life. Not a few former initiates into this society feel that their understanding of psychology has helped them personally acquire both a new stability and a new energy, and thus a greater power for constructive action than they would have had without a knowledge of this subject. (Carmichael, 1957: ix.[1])

Psychology as a profession

The membership of the psychological profession. If you were to ask what a psychologist is, you might think that the answer should be: "A person who uses the techniques and findings of psychology." Actually, however, most of the people who use psychological findings and techniques are not psychologists, but are members of other professions: social workers, teachers, psychiatrists, counselors and personnel workers in schools and in industry, advertising specialists, and so forth. To be sure, some of the individuals identified with these professions are also trained psychologists, but most of them are not. To a large extent, the psychological profession is a *source* of methodology and information—a kind of "consulting profession" for dozens of other occupations.

The principal characteristic that distinguishes

[1] Reprinted by permission.

psychologists from the members of the other professions who use psychological methods and information is the nature of their training. Persons who apply for membership in the American Psychological Association (referred to hereinafter as the APA) are expected to show evidence of having completed two years of graduate work in psychology or a master's degree in psychology plus a year of professional experience in psychological work. If they can meet these requirements, they may qualify for membership as "associates." In order to qualify as "members," they must present evidence of having received a doctor's degree (usually a Ph.D. or an Ed.D.) based in part on a psychological dissertation. The minimum standard for professional status in psychology as recognized by the APA is therefore the master's degree or its equivalent, and the preferred standard is the doctorate. Although the specific requirements differ from institution to institution, the usual professional preparation for psychology consists of courses in general, experimental, developmental, social, and abnormal psychology, together with courses in psychological statistics and testing, and history, theories, and systems of psychology. Some specialties, like experimental, social, developmental psychology, and educational psychology require considerable supervised experience in research, whereas other specialties like clinical, industrial, and counseling psychology require both research experience plus the satisfactory completion of internships, which consist of supervised experience in actual work settings.

Once members of the APA have accumulated five years of experience beyond the doctorate, they may apply for membership as "fellows," provided they can show that they have made outstanding scientific and professional contributions to the field of psychology. With five years of experience beyond the doctorate, clinical, counseling, or industrial psychologists may also apply for "diplomate status" in their respective fields, a process that involves the passing of written, oral, and practical examinations administered by the American Board of Examiners in Professional Psychology. The possession of a diploma issued by this board is taken as evidence of having attained a high degree of professional competence.

Something over half of the 18,000 members and associates in the APA now have the doctorate or its equivalent. In 1951, 46 per cent of the clinicians and 33 per cent of the counseling psychologists had this degree, as contrasted with 78 per cent of the experimental psychologists. By way of comparison, 24 per cent of the American Chemical Society and 45 per cent of the American Physical Society had the Ph.D. (Sanford, 1952.)

It naturally follows, as a result of this emphasis on graduate training, that psychology is a selective field. About 85 per cent of psychologists polled in one study stated that they were in the top quarter of their classes as undergraduates. (Clark, 1957: 117.) And a study of intelligence test scores of graduate students in various fields showed that psychology students had slightly higher scores, on the average, than students in the natural and physical sciences, who also scored very high. (Wolfle, 1955.)

In spite of this selectivity, the psychological profession continues to grow at a rate that seems extravagant when compared to that of other professions or scientific specialties. As Table 1-2 shows, the American Psychological Association increased the size of its membership 18.5 times between 1920 and 1950, a rate of growth that is unmatched by that of other professional organizations. In 1920, there were 3.7 psychologists for every million inhabitants in the United States; in 1950 the proportion had risen to 48.4 per million; and as this book is published, the ratio is well over 100 per million.

Table 1–2 Number of times the membership of various professional and scientific organizations increased in size between 1920 and 1950. (After Clark, 1957, p. 23.)

Association	Number of Times Membership Increased
American Psychological Association	18.5
American Historical Association	2.2
American Economics Association	3.3
American Statistical Association	4.4
American Sociological Society	3.9
American Political Science Association	3.9
American Anthropological Society	5.9
American Mathematical Society	5.5
American Physical Society	6.9
American Chemical Society	4.0
American Psychiatric Association	6.2
American Bar Association	3.5

Fields of psychology. In view of the fact that behavior is capable of an infinite number of complex variations, it is hardly surprising that psychologists have found it necessary to divide it up into special areas in order to make their study and research more effective. These areas range from those that are largely concerned with the solution of the practical problems of human existence ("applied research" and the application or use of psychological techniques) to those that are more concerned with exploring the underlying bases of behavior—what is sometimes called "basic research" or "pure research." Table 1-3 presents a system of classifying the major areas of psychology that was developed for the purpose of constructing a register of psychologists for the National Science Foundation, together with the number of psychologists working in each area. Table 1-4 gives some idea of where psychologists are employed. Although it is limited to psychologists who received their doctorate in 1950, it does give some idea of where the major concentrations of psychologists are. Most of them, as the table indicates, are in colleges and universities. Government, federal, state, and local, hires the next largest group. Relatively few are self-employed or in private practice, with a somewhat larger number being employed in business and industry. Table 1-5 presents the results of a study by Thorndike (1954), who administered a questionnaire to a sample of fellows (senior members) of the American Psychological Association. The respondents were asked to classify well-known psychologists according to their contributions to the

Table 1–3 Fields of specialization for 11,069 psychologists in the National Science Foundation Register. (After Ogg, 1955.)

Specialty *	Males	Females	Total	Percentage
Clinical	2,912	1,312	4,224	38
Counseling	1,056	269	1,325	12
Educational	635	218	853	8
School	113	162	275	2
Developmental	181	199	380	3
Human Engineering	149	6	155	1
Industrial	266	21	287	3
Personnel	766	70	836	8
Quantitative (tests and measurements, statistics)	332	65	397	4
Personality	306	51	357	3
Social	468	71	539	5
Experimental, Comparative, and Physiological	957	135	1,092	10
General and Nonspecialized	151	61	212	2
Nonpsychological	113	24	137	1
Totals	8,405	2,664	11,069	100

* Listed according to the order in which each specialty is discussed in the text.

Table 1–4 Where psychologists who received their Ph.D.'s in 1950 are employed. (After Clark, 1957, p. 143.)

Employer	Field of Specialty in Psychology					
	General	Experimental and Physiological	Personality and Social	Clinical	Educational and Developmental	Industrial
Number	52	64	44	211	55	14
College or University	58%	73%	69%	31%	74%	36%
Other educational institutions	5	—	—	2	10	—
Federal Government	16	13	10	40	5	14
Private industry, self-employed	—	—	5	7	—	—
Private industry, employee	9	5	7	2	2	43
Nonprofit organizations, including hospitals	9	7	10	7	2	7
State and local government	2	2	—	10	7	—

Table 1-5 Value systems of fellows of selected divisions of the American Psychological Association. (After Thorndike, 1954.)

Value Scales	Divisions of the American Psychological Association									
	General	Teaching	Experimental	Evaluation and Measurement	Personality and Social	SPSSI	Clinical	Industrial	Educational	Counseling
Global theorizing about behavior	—*	—*	—*	—*	—*	Hi*	Hi*	Lo*	—*	—*
Laboratory experimentation	Hi	Hi	Hi	—	—	Lo	—	—	Lo	—
Providing nonlaboratory research data (through tests and measurements)	Lo	Lo	Lo	—	—	—	—	—	—	—
Development of group measurements	—	—	Lo	—	—	Lo	—	Hi	Hi	Hi
Development of clinical techniques for studying the individual	Lo	—	Lo	—	—	Hi	Hi	—	Hi	Hi
Statistical analysis	—	—	—	Hi	—	Hi	Hi	—	—	—
Pioneering new areas in psychology	—	—	—	Lo	—	Hi	—	—	—	—
Disseminating psychological ideas	Lo	—	Lo	—	—	Hi	Hi	—	Hi	—
Administration in psychology	—	—	—	Lo	—	Lo	—	Hi	—	—

* "Hi" means that the fellows in this division rated these contributions significantly higher than did the average for the total group of psychologists; "Lo" means that the fellows in this division rated this contribution significantly lower; and "—" signifies a medium rating—fairly close to the average.

field of psychology. The ways in which the classifications were made provide an index to the interests or value patterns characteristic of each division of the APA. Members of the Divisions of General Psychology, Teaching of Psychology, and Experimental Psychology, for example, place a much higher degree of interest in laboratory experimentation than do members of the Society for the Psychological Study of Social Issues (SPSSI) and the Division of Educational Psychology.

As Table 1-3 shows, *clinical psychology* includes a larger number of psychologists than any of the other specialties. Although many clinical psychologists are employed in colleges, universities, and other educational institutions, an even larger number are employed by the Federal, state, and local governments, most of these being in Veterans Administration hospitals, mental hygiene clinics, and in administrative jobs relating to mental health. Only 7 per cent are in private practice.

Clinical psychology is largely concerned with helping individuals who have emotional or mental problems. The psychological techniques employed in this field are psychodiagnosis (which includes the use of intelligence and personality tests) and psychotherapy. In providing these services and in using these techniques, clinical psychologists often work closely with the members of the medical profession. Table 1-5 tells us something about the values of clinical psychologists: they appear to place high value on global (large-scale) theorizing about human behavior, the development of clinical techniques for studying the individual, and disseminating psychological ideas through writing, speaking, teaching, and other media.

Counseling psychology is also a major specialty. Although counseling psychologists use techniques (interviewing and testing) that are similar to those used by clinical psychologists, they are primarily interested in helping individuals with normal problems of everyday living—that is, problems of educational, vocational, or social adjustment—as contrasted with the diagnosis and treatment of disturbed or abnormal behavior. Most counseling psychologists work in universities, colleges and other educational institutions, although a great many of them are employed by Federal, state, and local governments and are concerned with employment interviewing and providing educational and vocational counseling for veterans. As Table 1-5 indicates, they tend to be more interested in group measurement techniques than clinical psychologists, and less interested in global theorizing, the clinical study of the individual, and in disseminating psychological ideas. Counseling and clinical psychologists together constitute about half the membership of the psychological profession.

Educational psychologists are concerned with problems relating to all aspects of education: classroom instruction, measurement of educational achievement, testing for selection, problems of school administration, etc. Like counseling psychologists, they place a great deal of importance on the development of group measurement techniques. They also place a high value on developmental research in tests and measurements, but not on laboratory research. Their research interests, therefore, appear to be concentrated in the "applied" area.

School psychologists, as the term implies, work in school settings. To some extent they function as clinical psychologists, providing psychodiagnostic and psychotherapeutic services for school children, but they may also counsel or advise parents, teachers, and administrators regarding psychological aspects of school problems. In some respects they resemble clinical psychologists; in other respects, educational psychologists. Although the number included in the study by Thorndike reported in Table 1-5 was too small to provide conclusive results, those who did participate gave high valuation to the gathering of data through tests and measurements, the study of the individual, and disseminating ideas, and low valuation to laboratory experimentation.

Developmental psychologists are concerned with studying the whole range of human development, particularly during childhood. For the most part they work in college and university settings doing research on developmental problems and teaching courses in child, adolescent, and developmental psychology. Their research interests tend to be less "applied" than those of the preceding groups. Only eight developmental psychologists replied to the questionnaire used in the Thorndike study referred to above, but their valuation tended to be high in global theorizing and low in group measurement and administration. In the National Science Foundation Register, they are one of the two groups in which women outnumber men, the other being the school psychologists.

Psychologists who identify themselves with *hu-*

man engineering, industrial psychology, and personnel psychology are for the most part employed by private industry, although many of them also do teaching and research in college and university settings. Another fairly sizable group works in governmental agencies. "Industrial psychology" is is a broad category that ordinarily includes both human engineering and personnel psychology. Human engineering is concerned with the design of equipment and the arrangement of the physical conditions of work in order to produce the maximum degree of efficiency, safety, and worker comfort. Personnel psychology, as the term implies, is concerned with personnel problems: selection, placement, promotion, supervision, morale, and employment procedures. It overlaps somewhat with counseling psychology and educational psychology, inasmuch as counseling and training are often included as functions of the personnel psychologist, and many of the problems with which the counseling psychologist or the educational psychologist must cope involve personnel even though they are in an educational setting. As Table 1-4 indicates, industrial psychologists, like educational and counseling psychologists, place high value on the development of group measurement techniques. Their interest in research is largely "applied," being based on the need to find solutions to practical problems arising in the employment situation. Perhaps as a consequence, they tend to place a low value on global theorizing. Their close relationship to management may influence the high valuation they place on administrative contributions.

Statistical or measurement psychologists are found in various branches of the profession, especially industrial, educational, and counseling psychology. For the most part, however, they are affiliated with the Division of Evaluation and Measurement of the APA. Their value pattern, as shown in Table 1-5, is high in statistical analysis, and low on clinical techniques for studying the individual, pioneering new areas, and administration. Although a great many of the problems studied by this group are of an "applied" nature, others involve "pure" research, particularly in the field of personality measurement.

Personality and social psychologists (commonly referred to simply as "social psychologists") also divide their interests between "applied" and "pure" research. On the one hand they are interested in the development of psychological methods

for dealing with social problems like race relations, crime and delinquency, and world peace, but on the other hand, they are also interested in the more basic relationships between individual behavior and social forces. A great deal of their research contributes directly or indirectly to the "applied" fields of psychology: clinical, counseling, educational, school, and industrial. Members of the Division of Personality and Social Psychology ranked the factors in Table 1-5 neither high nor low. This apparent "neutrality" may be due to the presence of interests in both "pure" and "applied" research. Most social psychologists work in colleges and universities, with a few working in government agencies, private industry, and nonprofit organizations.

A division of the APA that is allied in interests to social psychology is the Society for the Psychological Study of Social Issues (SPSSI). The value pattern of this group differs widely from the average of the total group of psychologists studied by Thorndike, showing especially high or especially low valuations for seven out of the nine value scales. Global theorizing about human behavior, clinical study of the individual, pioneering new ideas, and disseminating ideas are rated high by this group, and low valuation is placed on laboratory experimentation, group measurement, and administration. The general value pattern of this group most resembles that of the clinical psychologists, in spite of the fact that there is a much greater overlap in membership between SPSSI and the Division of Personality and Social Psychology, than between SPSSI and the Division of Clinical Psychology.

The psychologists who are most strongly oriented to "pure" research are those who identify themselves variously as *experimental, comparative, physiological, or general psychologists*. Many of the members of the Division on the Teaching of Psychology of the APA are also strongly identified with this group. Most of the individuals in these groups are employed by colleges and universities, with a few working in governmental agencies, private industry, and nonprofit organizations. Their values tend to be in sharp contrast to those of psychologists in the more "applied" fields. As may be expected, they place a high value on laboratory experimentation, an activity that is valued low by two of the "applied" groups. They have little interest in the development or use of measurements for studying groups or individuals, two activities that

EMOTIONAL NEEDS OF NEWBORN MONKEYS

Some psychological research produces findings that are of interest to specialists in a number of different fields of psychology, as well as to laymen. A recent study by Harlow (1958) was concerned with the developmental needs of macaque monkeys. As shown at the left (top), when newborn monkeys were kept in a cubicle with two kinds of mother substitutes, one made of wire and one made of sponge rubber covered with terry cloth, they preferred to spend the greater part of their time clinging to the "cloth mothers," even though milk was available only from the "wire mothers."

Harlow was able to test the strength of this preference in a number of ways. For example, he placed one of the "mothers" in an adjoining cubicle, where it could be seen through a window that opened whenever a lever was pressed by the monkey. Lever-pressing activity of 5-month-old monkeys was tested under three conditions: looking at the cloth mother, looking at the wire mother, or looking at an empty cubicle. As the graph shows, even at the end of a 6-month period of separation from their "mothers," the monkeys were still more interested in looking at the cloth mother than the wire mother. As far as the wire mother was concerned, they were no more interested in her than in an empty cubicle.

The infant monkeys also showed a marked tendency to turn to the cloth mother in stressful situations. In the presence of strange stimuli, like a toy bear (left), they would scurry to the cloth mother (below).

Harlow's study is of interest to experimental and comparative psychologists because it demonstrates the existence of drives or needs that have generally been ignored in previous research. It is also of interest to clinical and child psychologists, as well as to personality theorists, because of its implications for childrearing and personality development. Some psychological theories assume, for example, that a mother's ability to nurse the infant has an important influence on the emotional attachments that the child makes in later stages of emotional development, but Harlow's study suggests the possibility that later emotional attachments may be more closely related to the amount and kind of cuddling the infant receives, rather than the method of feeding. Harlow also suggests that if his findings are applicable to human beings, it would appear that men are quite as capable as women of giving infants whatever mothering they need for normal development.

Dr. Harlow and Dr. Zimmerman, his assistant, are shown at the right. Above, a small boy and his "security blanket"—evidence that the need for something soft to cling to is not limited to infant monkeys.

Photographs by Sponholz

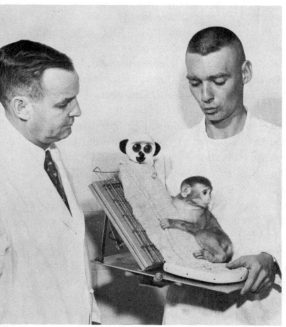

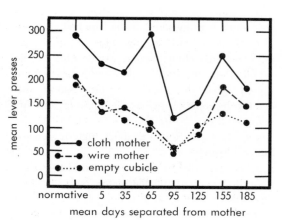

Relative attractiveness of cloth and wire mothers for infant monkeys.

21

Experimenting with animal behavior in a laboratory

**These photos depict three kinds of professional activities
performed by psychologists**

are valued high by some of the "applied" groups. They also tend to place a low value on disseminating ideas, an activity that is valued high by the "applied" groups. Indeed, all the activities that are valued high by the "pure" research group are valued low by some of the "applied" group, and virtually all the activities that are valued low by the "pure" research group are valued high by some of the "applied" group.

In his analysis of the data produced by his study, Thorndike pointed out that members of the Divisions of Experimental Psychology and Clinical Psychology represented the most extreme positions in terms of their pattern of values. These differences in values are very likely related to what Shaffer (1953) has termed "objective" and "intuitive" approaches to the collection and evaluation of psychological data. The "objective" approach, which would seem to characterize experimental psychologists, was associated with adjectives like

these: precise, methodical, hard-headed, logical, and thorough. The "intuitive" approach, which would seem more characteristic of clinical psychologists, was associated with adjectives like these: sensitive, sympathetic, understanding, and artistic. Evidence for there being some differences in early formative experiences in the backgrounds of experimental and clinical psychologists is offered by Carpenter (1954), who found that experimental psychologists were more likely to come from small towns and medium-sized cities and from the Midwest, whereas clinical psychologists were more likely to come from large cities. A higher proportion of clinical psychologists were foreign-born.

Interest patterns of psychologists. Clues as to the professional motivation of psychologists may be found in Table 1-6, which lists some of the items checked by a group of psychologists who were asked to indicate the factors they considered

Suzanne Szasz

Training students

Hays from Monkmeyer

Psychological appraisal of individuals

most crucial in their decision to enter the field of psychology. Almost half the respondents said that they became interested in psychology because of a desire to gain an understanding of human behavior, an interest that seems largely research-oriented. Being stimulated by a psychology teacher also seems to have been an important factor. Psychology courses themselves also contributed to their decision. Interests in applying psychology, as indicated by the desire to learn psychological techniques, help others, solve society's problems, and understand oneself, seem generally to be of somewhat lesser importance.

Some indication of the kind of people psychologists are is provided by the Strong Vocational Interest Blank for Men. When Strong (1943) administered the test to 285 seniors at Stanford, he computed coefficients of correlation between each of the scales. These intercorrelations provide some indications of the extent to which the interest pat-

terns that are typical of one profession resemble patterns that are typical of others. Strong's data indicate a fairly high degree of resemblance between the interest pattern that is typical of psychologists and those that are typical of artists, architects, physicians, dentists, mathematicians, physicists, chemists, musicians, and authors or journalists. The greatest differences were found between the psychologist's scale and those of the following occupations: public utility salesman, purchasing agent, office worker, banker, realtor, life insurance salesman, and sales manager. Such data suggest that the interests and values of psychologists most resemble those of persons in scientific, medical, and esthetic fields, but are the opposite of those that are characteristic of people in business occupations.

It is interesting to note that both the "objective" and the "intuitive" elements appear in the intercorrelations reported by Strong. Very likely those factors that are "intuitive" and most characteristic of clinical psychologists lead to substantial correlations with the artist, musician, and author-journalist scales, whereas those that are "objective" lead to substantial correlations with the mathematician, chemist, and physicist scales. The presence of these two somewhat opposing factors in the psychologist's scale would seem to support the idea that the "typical" psychologist is a person who responds to two sets of values: on the one hand he is a cautious, rigorous scientist, but on the other hand he wants to make contributions to human welfare. Some of this ambivalence may result from

Table 1–6   Factors considered as most important in leading to the decision to enter the field of psychology.* (After Clark, 1957, p. 112.)

Factor	Percentage Checking This Factor
Wanting to know more about human beings and their behavior	56
Being influenced by a particular teacher of psychology	54
Interest in human behavior as a field for scientific investigation	47
Becoming interested in the field through the content of courses in psychology	46
Becoming interested in the field through reading books in psychology	44
Interest in the application of psychological techniques in such areas as clinical, educational, or industrial psychology	43
Desire to work with individuals or groups	32
Courses were easy for me	29
Doing research in this field	25
Hearing or reading about research in this field	23
Need to understand myself	19
Desire to solve society's problems	16
The prestige of psychology	5
Having been helped in personal problems by a psychologist	4
Desire to enter a field which seemed to offer fairly lucrative rewards	1

* The group on which these data are based consists of 174 members of the American Psychological Association who received their doctorates during the years 1940–44.

the fact that most psychology students come from nonscience fields and are drawn to psychology because it is a field that deals with human problems. (Clark, 1957: 234.) As a result of their subsequent experiences and training in psychology these students do become scientists, but most of them retain a greater interest in solving the problems of humanity than is characteristic of most natural and physical scientists.

Topical organization of this textbook

The understanding of human behavior is a primary concern of this textbook, and the section that follows this introductory chapter attempts to indicate the scope and depth of this concern by presenting some of the more significant psychological events and problems that occur during the major stages of human development. Part 3, consisting of Chapters 4, 5, 6, and 7, deals with four of the principal dimensions of behavior studied by psychologists: the physiological, learning, and perceptual processes, and motivation. Parts 2 and 3 complement each other in several ways. Part 2 attempts to present human behavior in terms of its broader and more unified characteristics. There is a deliberate attempt to show, for example, how behavior in the various developmental stages is interrelated. Part 3, on the other hand, focuses on somewhat narrower aspects of behavior. Whereas the emphasis in Part 2 is more in the direction of personality and social psychology, the emphasis in Part 3 is experimental.

Individual differences are a concern of Part 4, which consists of two chapters, one dealing with statistical concepts that are basic to an understanding of psychological research and the other dealing with the intellectual-creative dimension of individual differences.

Part 5, consisting of Chapters 10 and 11, is concerned with emotional factors in behavior, personality, and problems of adjustment. Chapter 10 discusses some of the approaches psychologists have developed in order to make human behavior more meaningful, and Chapter 11 deals with the attempts that human beings make, some of them successful and some of them not, to adjust to one another, as well as to themselves.

The relationship between individual behavior and social forces is taken up in Chapter 12, which is the initial chapter in a part devoted to social psychology. Chapters 13 and 14 are concerned with the kind of forces generated in groups that not only affect their own behavior, but also the behavior of individuals and other groups as well.

The final section deals with the application of psychological techniques to three major areas of human endeavor. Chapter 15 is concerned principally with the individual college student and is devoted to a discussion of psychological factors in the selection and learning of occupational roles. Chapter 16 focuses on the problems of business and industry, and Chapter 17 discusses some of the ways in which psychology can contribute to an understanding of human behavior on a national and international scale.

Summary

It is difficult to explain what psychology really is. Although it is a science, it does not deal with phenomena that are associated with science in the minds of most laymen. Indeed, it is difficult for them to think of human behavior as a subject for scientific research. There is a tendency for laymen to associate psychology at times with the skillful manipulation of other people and at other times with hypnosis, mind-reading, and other quasi-magical techniques.

Psychologists perceive psychology as a science, a body of knowledge, and as a profession. The psychologist's approach to the understanding of behavior differs from that of the layman in that the layman is more inclined to base his conclusions on "common sense" and the psychologist on scientific research. Although "common sense" can be a useful guide to action in everyday affairs, its scope and value are limited. "Common-sense" conclusions may also be based on prejudice, bias, and folklore. One of the reasons why laymen have difficulty in understanding psychology is that much psychological research is concerned with phenomena that are beyond ordinary awareness and hence outside the scope of "common sense." Not only do the findings of psychologists often contradict what many people already think they know as the result of "common sense," but also they present concepts of behavior that are exceedingly complex. Most people would like to believe that human behavior is much simpler than it really is, in order that they may deal with it simply and directly. The simple, direct approach often works with some kinds of everyday behavior, but may get us into difficulties when it comes to dealing with behavior in which motivational factors are complex and which hence calls for more complete understanding.

Psychologists, like other scientists, assume that behavior is caused. It is the task of psychological research to identify and measure causal factors in order to be able to predict behavior. Measuring and predicting behavior is much more difficult in psychology than in the natural and physical sciences because the phenomena studied by psychologists are more complex and variable. Furthermore, psychology is relatively new as a science and has not as yet been able to explore its field as thoroughly as has been done in some of the older sciences. Psychological research is a controlled form of observation that is organized in such a way as to test hypotheses about behavior. These hypotheses stem from theories that have been constructed in order to account for various phenomena. The validity of any theory depends on whether the hypotheses derived from it are supported or rejected. Psychology is a science not only because it uses scientific methods, but also because it adheres to principles of objectivity and systematic procedure. In spite of its objectivity, systematization, and logic, psychology, like other fields of science, has its share of controversy and ambiguity. The layman finds ambiguity and controversy incompatible with his "common-sense" concept of science, but actually controversy and ambiguity help to stimulate research and scientific progress.

The minimum preparation for professional psychology consists of a master's degree in the field. About half the members of the American Psychological Association also have a doctoral degree. This percentage of doctorate holders is somewhat higher than that of other scientific societies. Although psychology is an intellectually selective field, the number of psychologists has increased much more rapidly than that of other professional fields.

Most psychologists are employed by colleges, universities, and other educational institutions. Somewhat smaller proportions are employed by governmental agencies, nonprofit organizations, hospitals, and private industry. Only a small percentage are in private practice. Psychology is divided into a number of fields that cover a broad range of interests with respect to "pure" research, "applied" research, and application of psychological techniques and principles to human problems. Clinical, counseling, educational, and industrial psychologists tend to be more interested in the application of psychology, whereas experimental, general, and physiological psychologists are more interested in "pure" or "basic" research. About half the psychological profession is in the fields of clinical and counseling psychology.

Most psychologists come to the study of psychology from nonscience fields and are attracted by the opportunity to work on problems dealing with human behavior. This background is reflected in the measured interests of psychologists, which are similar to those of the medical and the artistic-creative professions, as well as to those of natural and physical scientists. Psychologists' interests are quite unlike those of people in various business occupations.

Questions

1. Why is it necessary or desirable to study human behavior scientifically?

2. In what ways do "common-sense" and scientific methods differ?

3. Why is it sometimes dangerous to rely on "common sense" for decisions with respect to social problems?

4. Give some examples of "common-sense" thinking that are contradicted by scientific research.

5. Why are people sometimes anxious when they learn that they have been talking to a psychologist?

6. What are the chief differences between psychology as perceived by psychologists and psychology as perceived by laymen?

7. In what ways do psychologists agree among themselves in their approaches to psychology? In what ways do they disagree?

8. Give some everyday examples of "behavior without awareness."

9. What assumptions do psychologists make about behavior?

10. How can the testing of hypotheses contribute to the advancement of our understanding of behavior?

11. In what ways can psychologists be distinguished from nonpsychologists who use psychological techniques?

12. If you were going to refer someone to a clinical or a counseling psychologist for help with a personal problem, what qualifications would you look for?

13. What factors, do you suppose, account for the rapid growth of psychology as a profession?

14. Why do you suppose more psychologists are employed by colleges and universities than by business and industry?

15. What are the differences between clinical psychology and counseling psychology?

16. Whom do psychologists most resemble in their interests? Whom do they least resemble?

Suggestions for further reading

Cantril, H., *The "Why" of Man's Experience*. New York: Macmillan, 1950. A thoughtful, interpretive book that discusses some of the ways in which psychology aids in the understanding of human behavior. Written by an outstanding social psychologist.

Carmichael, L., *Basic Psychology: A Study of the Modern Healthy Mind*. New York: Random House, 1957. An interpretation of the science of psychology, written for the layman by a leading psychologist who is also the head of the Smithsonian Institution.

Clark, K. E., *America's Psychologists: A Survey of a Growing Profession*. Washington, D. C.: American Psychological Association, 1957. A review of a number of research studies referred to in the present chapter, dealing with a number of sociological and psychological characteristics of psychologists.

Murphy, G., *Historical Introduction to Modern Psychology*. New York: Harcourt, Brace, 1949. A review of the main currents in science and philosophy that led to the development of psychology as we know it today. Also contains a description and discussion of some of the current issues and controversies in psychology.

Ogg, E., *Psychologists in Action*. Public Affairs Pamphlet 229, New York: Public Affairs Committee, Inc., 1955. A brief, down-to-earth description of who psychologists are and what they do.

Skinner, B. F., *Science and Human Behavior*. New York: Macmillan, 1953. A discussion of the ways in which psychology can promote an understanding of human behavior, written by a leading and outspoken experimental psychologist.

Super, D. E., *Opportunities in Psychology*. New York: Vocational Guidance Manuals, Inc., 1955. A short pamphlet describing various aspects of professional psychology, written for the student who is thinking of entering the field.

The *Directory* of the American Psychological Association is also a useful source for anyone interested in learning more about the profession of psychology. It lists the names of all members of the Association, together with a summary of their professional training, their vocational history, and their professional interests. It also contains the by-laws of the Association.

PART TWO

HUMAN DEVELOPMENT

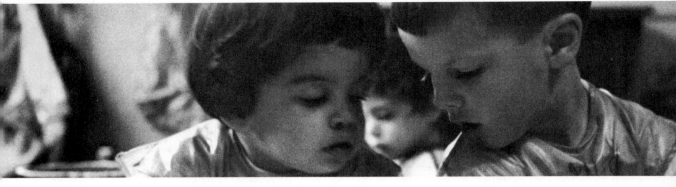

2

Human development: infancy and childhood

In this chapter and the one that follows, we shall attempt an overview of human behavior as it develops through the stages of infancy, childhood, adolescence, adulthood, and old age. Our purpose in putting these two chapters in an initial position in this textbook is to provide a broad background, against which may be plotted the more specific concepts and information to be presented in later chapters.

In the present chapter, we shall be describing in a very general way the sequence of processes and events that led up to our becoming the persons we are. Each of these processes and events is related to and affected by the processes and events that have gone before. One way of explaining current behavior is to relate it to antecedent behavior. For instance, the antisocial behavior of a delinquent is commonly attributed to improper training or experiences as a child, and our expectations of how individuals will behave in the future is to a large extent based on their past behavior. As we shall discover in future chapters, antecedent behavior is not the *sole* determining factor in current or future behavior, but it does provide some important clues that aid in understanding and predicting it.

Ways of perceiving the behavior of children. In observing the behavior of children, we often find ourselves using one of two approaches: one, that children are, in essence, "little adults," and the other, that children are completely different from adults. The first approach may lead us to expect too much from children—that is, we may expect them to be courteous and polite at all times,

29

to enjoy grand opera or professional football, to be interested in listening to adult conversation, or whatever our expectations of the moment happen to be. The second kind of approach sometimes leads us to overprotect children, to make decisions that they are capable of making for themselves, and to shut them out of participation in the adult world. These two contradictory ways of regarding children are most troublesome when we have to deal with adolescents: on the one hand, we criticize adolescents for not displaying more responsible and adultlike behavior, but on the other hand, we criticize them for claiming the right to adult privileges and freedoms.

People who are inclined to regard children as little adults are likely to use adult behavior as a kind of value standard, that is, if a child's behavior conforms to adult expectations, it is "good," if not, it is "bad." Needless to say, the application of such standards to the study of children's behavior will interfere with the objectivity of the observer. Hence, there is much to be said for adopting the point of view that children are beings completely unlike adults. Such a point of view enables the observer to make a fresh start, unhampered by preconception or bias. Studying children as children makes it possible to observe them in an uncritical way.

Although this second approach can yield valuable information, the observer does isolate himself from some valuable sources of information. Even though he may wish to ignore the relationship between childhood and adulthood, most children are keenly aware that their relationship to adults is a very close one. Much of their behavior is stimulated and modified by their interaction with the adults who play significant roles in their lives, and some of the developmental trends in childhood behavior can be explained in terms of children's attempts to copy the behavior of the adults they admire and respect. Furthermore, some of the motivation of children becomes more comprehensible if we start unravelling it from the adult end of the sequence. In other words, one of the ways of understanding children's behavior is to keep the behavior of adults in mind as we trace the patterns of childhood experiences. The understanding of both adult behavior and child behavior thus becomes an interactional affair: the more we find out about adult behavior, the more understandable child behavior becomes, and the more we find out about the behavior of children, the

better we are able to understand the behavior of adults.

Physiological bases of childhood behavior

Primitive aspects of behavior. We are all of us, first of all, animals. An understanding of the physiological or animal characteristics of man helps to explain some of the behavior he displays, although it is a mistake to assume that we are dominated by our physiology, any more than we can assume that our total behavior is dominated by thinking processes. Nevertheless, physiological factors do play an important part in predetermining our behavior, in some situations more, in others, less. As man has become civilized and more and more involved in the relationships and transactions that are the warp and woof of an urbanized culture, physiological processes have come to occupy less of his time and attention. There is, to be sure, a point beyond which physiological needs cannot be ignored, but this point varies with different individuals and with different situations. Some individuals must have eight hours' sleep in every twenty-four in order to maintain maximum efficiency; others can get by with four or five. A certain individual may normally stop work and go to lunch when noon arrives, but when he is at work on an absorbing project, he may forget about food altogether.

The point is that an adult human being is much more than an animal; or to put this in other words, only a minor portion of his behavior can be explained in purely physiological terms. An infant, on the other hand, is much more of an animal than an adult is, for a great deal of his behavior can be explained in purely physiological terms. The behavior of the newborn human infant is quite similar to that of the newborn of other mammals. He spends much of his time sleeping; when he is not sleeping, he is eating or squirming or crying. As a matter of fact, the newborn of many mammals—horses, cattle, deer, for example—are better able to care for themselves than is the human newborn.

As contrasted with humans, the lesser animals are simpler: they respond to a more limited range of stimuli and their behavior shows less variation. The prediction of infrahuman animal behavior is thus much easier than the prediction of human behavior. A rat placed in a maze is likely to set about the task of locating the food that has been placed at the end of one of its corridors. A human being in a similar situation might do the same,

The younger the child, the more primitive his behavior is likely to be.

but he also might be disposed to ask, "What kind of food is it?" or "What is the purpose of this?" The rat is likely to respond to the purely physical aspects of the experiment, whereas human subjects may respond to the personality of the experimenter, the relationship between them and the experimenter, and other aspects of the situation that would not have any effect on the rat's sensory apparatus.

Inasmuch as infants are more primitive in their behavior than are adults, it is to be expected that they, too, will respond to a narrower range of stimuli and will display behavior that is less variable and more predictable than adults. Both infants and adults will respond to loud noises, but noises that will annoy adults (the dripping of a water faucet, the fading in and out of an improperly tuned radio broadcast, or off-key singing) have no noticeable effects on infants any more than they have on the average house cat. To be sure, infants and even human fetuses can be conditioned to respond to certain sounds that they might otherwise ignore, but this type of learning is of a very elementary nature, being largely physiological.

The reactions of the newborn infant to external and internal stimuli are almost entirely physiological. When he is uncomfortable by reason of hunger, cold, or shock, he cries, and when he cries, he cries with his whole body. His activity may be thought of as "behavior without learning." No one has to show him how to suck, yet when the nipple is inserted, he responds appropriately. Nor does he have to learn how to sleep, breathe, or eliminate. His environment exists for him only to the extent that it affects him physically.

Beginnings of learning. It is difficult to say at what point learning begins. Perhaps it begins in the uterus, when the fetus comes to anticipate, or at least to develop a certain physiological readiness for, certain rhythms or patterns of movement, such as the mother's daily cycle of rest and activity. Or perhaps it takes place after birth, when the infant is in direct contact with the external environment and comes to anticipate certain significant events: being nursed, bathed, cuddled, handled, and so forth. Certain noises and patterns of stimulation become associated with these events and build up anticipatory states.

One example of such learning is the smiling response. When Spitz (1946a) studied the behavior of several hundred infants, he found that the appearance of a strange human face would call forth a smile on the part of 98 per cent of the infants aged 2 to 6 months, but only 2 per cent of infants aged 3 weeks to 2 months and 3 per cent between the ages of 6 months and a year. None of the infants under the age of 3 weeks responded with a smile.

What happens is very likely something like this: At first the infant is unable to make the sensory discriminations that enable him to distinguish faces from the rest of the environment, but by the end of a month or so he begins to be able to make the necessary discrimination. While he is learning to make this discrimination he evidently learns to associate the appearance of his mother's face with pleasant sensations—being fed, being changed from wet to dry clothing, and being comfortable. Or, it may be that the simultaneous appearance of the face and the pleasant sensations lead him to make the discrimination that he does. To put this in other words, being comfortable is essential to the infant's sense of well-being and he is more likely to be sensitive to events that accompany experiences of being comforted. Not only does he learn to make this particular perception (out of all the other perceptions that he might make), but he learns to express his pleasure through smiling. Between the ages of 2 and 6 months, he smiles indiscriminately at each face, since he has not learned to distinguish between familiar faces and strange ones, between potentially comforting faces and those that have nothing to offer. By the age of 6 months, however, he has learned to make this discrimination and has also learned not to respond indiscriminately.

Maturation and socialization. The learning and adaptation of the smiling response is also an example of the way in which interaction takes place between two major dimensions of growth and development—physical maturation and socialization. By physical maturation we mean the developmental changes that take place in the human organism, changes whose pattern and pace is set at conception. The *pattern* of maturation is general: changes like the transformation of cartilage into bone, the growth of pubic and axillary hair, and the eruption and loss of baby teeth are events that occur in the lives of *all* children between birth and maturity. The *pace* of maturation also has its general aspects. Six-year molars get their name from the tendency to appear in the mouths of children about the age of six, but some children get them as much as a year earlier or a year later. These variations in the pace of maturity are specific and individual. Although they may be affected by environmental factors, such as nutrition, they nevertheless are a function of each individual's unique arrangement of inherited characteristics.

Physical maturation is basic to learning. The child cannot respond to his mother's face until he has developed the physical coordination necessary to fix his gaze, and until his optic apparatus is able to sort out sensations. Most of the newborn's activity is diffuse and unorganized; smiling requires coordination. But coordination cannot take place unless the organism has reached a level of physical maturation that permits it. Anyone who observes infants during the latter months of the first year of life notices their vigorous attempts at locomotion and the excitement they display when they find they can move about under their own power. The appearance of crawling may, for example, be preceded by some weeks of random, excited wiggling which sometimes takes the form of swiminglike gestures. Occasionally an infant may, through such trial-and-error activity, accidentally crawl a few feet, but if he has not physically matured to the point at which he can sustain the coordination needed for crawling, he is unable to duplicate this feat until the proper time has come, perhaps as much as a month or two later.

Infants likewise make vigorous but random attempts to walk, but are unable to succeed until they have developed the physical strength and the neurological apparatus that are prerequisites for success. Learning to talk is not only dependent on the child's learning to imitate sounds and to utter them in the proper order, but is also dependent on his physiological development. Learning to talk depends, for example, on his ability to assume an erect position; his control of throat, tongue, and lip muscles; and the appearance of frontal teeth. (McCarthy, 1954.)

The processes of physical maturation function even in the absence of the kind of stimulation that "common sense" would prescribe as essential. One might think, for example, that the ability to walk would depend largely on the opportunity for vigorous, large-muscle activity. In our culture, we believe that the future physical development of the child depends on our giving him complete freedom to kick, squirm, and twist. Hence we would be inclined to think that restricting the movements of infants would retard their learning to walk. Observations made by Dennis (1943) among the Hopi Indians, however, point up the fallacy of this belief. Dennis noted that some families follow the practice, traditional among the Hopis, of strapping infants to cradleboards shortly after birth, wrapping them so securely that little movement of the arms and legs is possible. For the first three months, infants are removed from the board only for bathing and for changing soiled clothing. The board is rarely abandoned during the first six months and may be used during the entire first year. After the first six months, however, infants may spend some time each day away from the board, particularly if they resist being confined. Infants who have become accustomed to cradleboards have difficulty in going to sleep off the board and will cry if they are off the board for longer periods than usual.

At the time when Dennis made his observations

families in some Hopi villages had given up the cradleboard, although they still held to other Hopi practices in childrearing. Dennis compared the age at which walking was learned by infants who had been strapped to the cradleboard and those who had not and found that there was no difference, thus showing that physical maturation had not been impeded by the restrictions placed on activity.

Social development

Social learning. During the first two years of life, a child is largely preoccupied with developing a working understanding of his physical self and his physical environment. During this period he discovers the boundaries that separate him from the world around him; he learns that rugs and blankets are soft and that concrete sidewalks are hard; falling down, he finds, is easier than climbing up, but may hurt more; there are some things like chairs and toy autos that can be pushed around the room, but other things, like sofas, that cannot be moved. On the other hand, sofas are more fun to bounce on.

Note that all this learning takes place in terms of immediate, personal experience. Sofas, sidewalks, toys, and chairs are understood only in terms of their relationship with the child. In this respect, his learning relationships with his physical environment are not much different from his interaction with his social environment. There is, however, an important difference between his physical environment and his social environment. His physical environment is to a large extent inanimate and passive, whereas his social environment is active. His physical environment makes no attempt to modify his behavior, it has no interest in the kind of person he is or the person he will become. Not so with his social environment, which is populated with individuals who have a keen interest in his behavior, particularly when it does not conform to their expectations. Almost from the very beginning these individuals have been communicating—or, better still, *attempting* to communicate—their reactions to his behavior. Some of this communication is of a fairly direct nature:

"Learning to talk already. Now, isn't that just like a girl!"

"Boy, look at those leg muscles! *He'll* be a credit to the school team."

"Don't let his squalling bother you, folks—he just does it for exercise."

"Oh, murder! Haven't you had enough attention for one day?"

Although the exact meaning of such statements is of course lost on children of this age, communication of a very elementary nature does take place. In a New Mexico hospital where Zuñi Indians and white American babies were born, Kluckhohn (1949) classified them as "unusually active," "average," and "quiet." Although more white babies fell into the "unusually active" category, a certain number of Zuñi babies also displayed "unusually active" patterns of behavior. When the behavior of the white and Zuñi babies who had been classified as "unusually active" was compared two years later, the Zuñi children were much less active. When we consider that the Zuñi Indian culture is one that emphasizes restraint and self-effacement, it is evident that some of this way of life had been communicated to the children. It is highly probable that much of this communication was of a nonverbal sort, that is, the very activity and restlessness that are more characteristic of white Americans of all ages stimulated or supported hyperactivity, whereas the restrained atmosphere of the Zuñi home discouraged it.

The development of personality. The kind of person an infant is to become is based on layers or levels of factors. At the first level is *temperament,* a general pattern of emotional responsiveness that appears very early and is therefore considered to be largely inherited and physiological in nature. Newborn infants differ from one another in their reactivity and energy output, as Kluckhohn's study, cited in the paragraph above, shows. Some infants are noisy; others are quiet. Some take the nipple eagerly and feed with loud sucking noises; others feed so slowly that it seems almost as though they are absorbing milk instead of drinking it.

As Kluckhohn's study also demonstrates, this basic, more-or-less physical pattern of personality may be modified at an early age by the interaction between the family and the child. Such differences are of course more noticeable when the direction of influence is consistent within all the families of a certain cultural group, as it is with the Zuñis. The influence of the *culture* thus constitutes the second layer or level of factors influencing the kind of person an infant will become. Each culture has some rather characteristic ways of behaving toward children, and these patterns of behavior are based, in turn, on expectations or attitudes that

The attention and cuddling that we believe is necessary for proper child development is withheld from Balinese children when they are about 3 years old. A mother may even borrow a baby from a neighbor in order to shower attention on it and thus tease her own child.

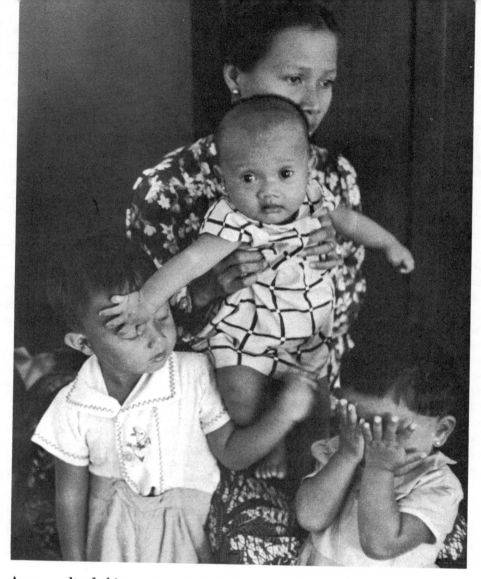

As a result of this treatment, the Balinese child learns not to depend on others for affection.

Photographs by Ken Heyman.

are "standard" or "normal" for that culture. In Italian families, a child may be alternately smothered with attention and ignored. From such behavior he learns that the attention he receives from his parents depends on *their* desires and feelings, rather than on his. He has little to say in the matter. Such early experiences prepare him for life in a family that is more authoritarian than the American family, in which life moves according to the desires of the parents and particularly the father.

A study by Bateson and Mead (1942) of child-rearing practices in a mountain village in Bali provides some interesting data on the close relationship between early childhood experiences and adult personality. Balinese infants are indulged and caressed during the first year or two and then are subjected to teasing. The mother refuses to pay any attention to the child's demands for attention and dramatizes her rejection by borrowing a child from a neighbor and caressing it in plain sight of her own child. This arouses frantic jealousy on the part of her own child, but the mother ignores his cries and screams of rage, smiling blandly as she goes on with her process of teasing. She deliberately arouses in her child the desire for attention, and just as deliberately she frustrates it. As an evident result of such experiences, Balinese children learn to withdraw and to find sources of satisfaction within themselves, rather than in close, warm relationships with others. They grow into adults whose behavior is characterized by withdrawn, passive detachment and dreaminess.

It is of course much easier to see the ways in which parents of other cultures interact with their children to produce the personality patterns that are characteristic of their culture. It is much more difficult to see how we shape the personalities of our own children, since the parent-child relationships that are characteristic of our culture seem to us to be "natural" and "normal." Gillin (1948) puts it very well when he says that ". . . a child in any society is encased in a sort of 'Iron Maiden' of socio-cultural pressures and channelized satisfactions which are intended to make him into the kind of person the members of the group want and expect him to be."

Learning to conform to cultural demands. During the first two years of life, children are unable to grasp the significance of a great deal of the behavior expressed toward them, partly because they are preoccupied with their physical selves and

their physical environment and partly because they have not reached a level of physical and social maturation that would enable them to understand what is expected of them and to respond accordingly. Many a parent has found that repeated scoldings and spankings have failed to discourage the vigorous exploring activity of the eighteen-month-old. Consequently most authorities recommend that the best way of preventing the destructiveness of children this age is to make rooms "baby-proof" (by placing breakable objects beyond their reach) or by keeping children out of rooms that are filled with valuable, fragile objects. It is not that children this age are unable to learn—Kluckhohn's observations imply that they can begin to learn a way of life—but rather that they cannot learn to make the specific kinds of discriminations that are second nature to adults and older children.

An eighteen-month-old child who is permitted to play with a gaily colored plastic toy cannot see why he should not enjoy the same liberties with an equally attractive Venetian glass ashtray. Even such basic differences as "yours" and "mine" seem lost on him. Although he has developed a good understanding of the boundaries between his physical self and the rest of the environment, his understanding of the boundaries of the social self (which includes such concepts as "yours" and "mine") has developed only to a degree. He knows that there is someone who is *his* mother (as distinguished from other people wearing dresses who are *not* his mother), but the idea of *objects* belonging to other people (and hence not available to him) is beyond his comprehension. Furthermore, he has trouble in inhibiting behavior once it has been stimulated. By eighteen months he has established control of his rectal sphincter to the point where he can be considered to be toilet-trained in this respect, although he still has difficulty in inhibiting the voiding of urine. But other forms of behavior, such as keeping himself from reaching for attractive objects or from putting things into his mouth, are beyond his control. On the one hand, he is unable to distinguish between things he is permitted to do and those he is not, but on the other hand, he probably could not keep himself from carrying out his impulses even if he could distinguish between appropriate and inappropriate behavior.

Expectations for a particular child. A third level or layer of factors that influence the kind of person the young child is to become, consists of those attitudes, expectations, and feelings that parents express toward a *particular* child, as distinguished from their expectations for children in general. In the American culture, children are expected to show a considerable degree of independence of thought and action at a fairly early age, as compared with other cultures, and this expectation applies with greatest emphasis to boys. The personality differences between men and women are very likely due largely to the different attitudes we express toward children of the two sexes.

The differences in personality between first-born children and their siblings have also attracted considerable attention from psychologists (for example, McArthur, 1956; Dreikurs, 1948). In a review of research relating to the relationship between order of birth and success, Jones (1954) found that the number of successful individuals who were first-born in their families considerably exceeded chance expectations. As Figure 2-1 shows, 64 per cent of individuals from two-child families listed in *Who's Who in America* were first-born, whereas the expectation according to chance would be only 50 per cent. Similarly, 52 per cent of the individuals from three-child families listed in *Who's Who in America* were first-born, whereas chance would lead one to expect only 33⅓ per cent.

First-born individuals also appeared in disproportionately large numbers among gifted children studied by Terman and others (1925), emi-nent men in a British study (Ellis, 1926), and persons listed in *American Men of Science* (Cattell, 1927).

Although Jones was unable to explain these findings to his own satisfaction, it seems likely the differing expectations that parents have for the oldest child in the family have much to do with his tendency to behave differently from his siblings. McArthur (1956) found that oldest children tended to be more adult-oriented, their behavior being characterized by such adjectives as *sensitive, good, conscientious, serious, fearful,* and *studious;* whereas second-born children tended to be peer-oriented, being characterized as *not studious, cheerful, placid,* and *easy-going.* When parents were asked if they had changed their methods of handling children between the first and second child, 65 per cent stated that they had "relaxed" more with the second, and only 3 per cent said they were stricter.

Koch (1955) asked teachers of five- and six-year-old children to rate them on a number of personality and behavioral characteristics. She found that when those children who were first-born in their family were contrasted with those who were second-born, the first-born were likely to be judged as showing more anger, being more intense emotionally, more easily upset by defeat, more inclined to "alibi," less responsive to sympathy and praise expressed by adults, and better able to articulate clearly when speaking. Male children who had younger siblings, contrasted

Figure 2-1. Percentage of first-born individuals among persons showing outstanding intellectual achievement. (Jones, 1954. Reproduced by permission.)

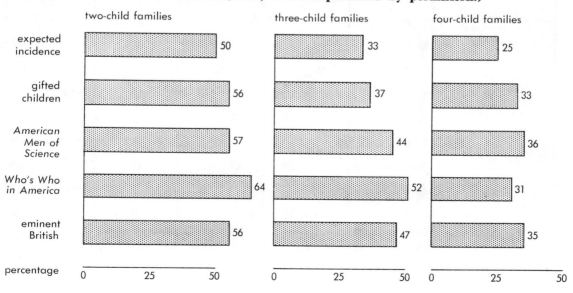

with those having older siblings, appeared to be more revengeful and more jealous and were more given to teasing. First-born children having siblings of the opposite sex, when contrasted with those whose siblings were of the same sex, were judged to be more self-confident, cheerful, kind, curious, tenacious, and decisive, and showed quicker recovery from emotional upset.

Although Koch's study dealt with a population dissimilar from that sampled by McArthur, it does, in a very general way, complement some of his findings, in that it shows first-born children, particularly males, to be more domineering and emotionally intense than their younger siblings,

and children who are younger siblings to be more sociable and pliable.

Consistency in childhood behavior patterns. In spite of the fact that the more-or-less physical orientation of the year-old child is subject to considerable modification during the preschool years, the general pattern of behavior or personality appears to possess a certain stability. Gesell (1954) made a motion-picture recording of the behavior of five children during the first year of life and repeated the process when they were five. The two sets of films were reviewed by independent observers, who ranked the children on fifteen different characteristics: energy output, motor demeanor, self-dependence, etc. As Figure

Figure 2-2. Persistency of behavior patterns between the ages of 1 and 5 for five children. (Gesell, 1954. Reproduced by permission.)

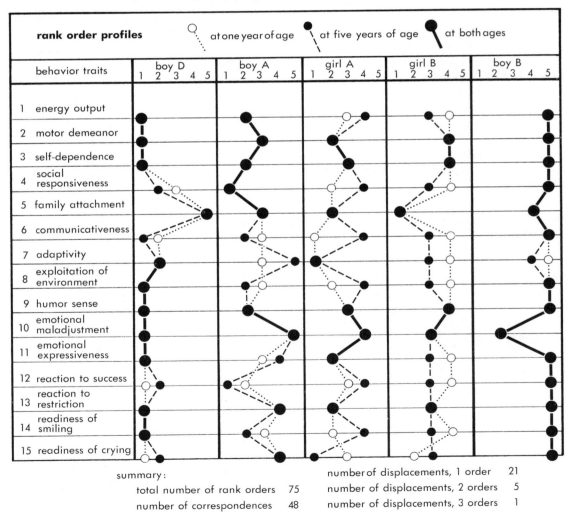

2-2 shows, there was considerable consistency in the rankings. Boy "D" rated the highest in energy output, self-dependence, sense of humor, emotional maladjustment, reaction to restriction, and readiness of smiling, and also showed the least family attachment. At the age of five, he received a different rating on only four of the fifteen variables, and even in these four instances changes were small. Both at one and at five he presents the picture of an active, vigorous, and independent child, who achieves both heights and depths in his emotional expressiveness. Boy "B" is even more consistent, showing little energy output and little emotional display. Both at one and at five he presents a picture of a child who is withdrawn, quiet, passive, unemotional, and apathetic. The remaining three children show less consistency than do the two children with the most extreme rankings, but most of the changes are relatively small, only six of the changes amounting to two or more rank differences.

Gesell's study appears to confirm what can be observed in everyday life—namely, that behavioral traits that are pronounced appear more likely to persist. Infants that are extremely energetic and active are likely to become active and energetic children, who, in turn, are likely to become active and energetic adults. Children with low levels of energy tend to become adults of the same type. There is no saying, of course, to what extent the traits that persist are due to physiological factors, cultural factors, the emotional climate of the family, or the attitudes that a given set of parents have toward a given child. Doubtless the contributions made by each of these sets of factors differ, from child to child. The point is, however, that whatever behavior pattern or personality pattern results from the interaction of these factors tends to have a kind of stability or persistence over a period of time, with changes, if any, tending to come slowly and gradually, rather than suddenly and dramatically.

Directions of development

Physical development. During the course of human development from conception to maturity, direction of behavior development is outward. The word "development" itself means "an unfolding," implying an outward movement. Regardless of whether the organism is in the stage of embryo, fetus, or newborn infant, its *central* areas are the first to develop a complexity of structure and function. During the first years of life, the central areas (head and trunk) keep well ahead of the development of the limbs. The infant develops considerable expertness with his lips and throat before he is able to pick up a toy with his fingers. The child masters the complex and intricate techniques

Figure 2-3. Patterns of play for children between the ages of 2 and 5, showing trend of increasing interest in others. (After Parten, 1932.)

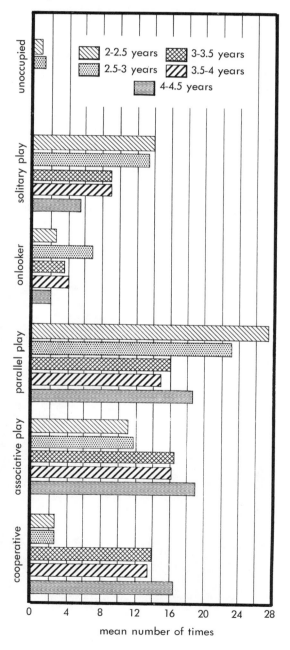

of speech before he develops comparable skill with his arms and legs.

Social development. The outward direction of development is also manifested in the social area. At first the child is preoccupied with himself. Then he becomes interested in the relations between others and himself, but almost entirely with respect to the way in which the relationship affects his welfare. In the second year of life he becomes aware of other children, perhaps sensing a similarity between him and them. Sibling rivalry, too, begins to make its appearance around this age, as he finds that he must compete with the other children in the family for the attention of his parents. The play patterns of children also reveal the outward trend of their development. At first they are quite content to play alone, even when other children are in the immediate vicinity. Or they may play independently in close association with another child (parallel play). After the age of three children tend to play more actively with others, sometimes in semi-independent fashion (associa-tive play) and sometimes in close collaboration (cooperative play). As Figure 2-3 shows, by the time they are four, they are, on the average, equally involved in parallel, associative, and cooperative play. (Parten, 1932.)

The tendency for children to shift their dependence from adults to their peers appears at a relatively early age. When Heathers (1955) compared the nursery-school behavior of two-year-olds with that of children four and five years old, he found that the older children spent less time in behavior concerned with getting attention, affection, or approval from the teacher and spent more time in seeking attention or approval from the other children.

Even though the shift from dependence on adults to dependence on one's peers may begin during the preschool years, children in this age group are inclined to be highly self-centered, relatively few of them making any lasting friendships. Real group relationships are virtually nonexistent at these ages—a kindergarten class is more a col-

Although children are emotionally dependent on adults during the middle years of childhood, they are also beginning to shift some of this dependence to other children.

Eugene Moses

Teachers find that children are more easily dealt with in large groups during elementary years than during preschool years.

lection of individuals than it is a real group, as many teachers have found when they try to get kindergarteners to "act as a group." During the primary years in school, group consciousness and close friendships begin to develop, and, by the time children reach the preadolescent stage of development, many of them are beginning to become deeply involved in group life. The gang, the clique, and the "crowd" play important roles in the lives of teenagers, and the importance of the family is likely to wane.

As the focus of the child's interest broadens to include his family, his playmates, and, finally, the peer group, he learns to develop the kinds of behavior that support this widening interest. In the earlier stages, he learns to play with other children, to share playthings, to give as well as take. In later stages, he learns to play the roles that are important to group activity—how to contribute to the goals of the group, how to express himself, and how to listen. He learns to inhibit or deny his own impulses or wishes in deference to the wishes of others and the needs of the group.

Relationships between adults and children

The "terrible two's." The child's first major difficulties in social learning are likely to occur during the third year of life, around the age of two and one-half. Children commonly go through a negative stage of development about this age as their impulses come to be more strongly opposed by the expectations of their parents. To be sure, many if not most parents make concerted attempts to modify the behavior of children under the age of two, but these efforts generally have little effect, largely because the child is unable to grasp what is

expected of him. By about two and one-half years, however, children have a better understanding of the expectations of others and, what is equally important, are able to exert some degree of conscious control over their behavior. Most children quite understandingly prefer to follow their own impulses, regardless of whether their behavior embarrasses, inconveniences, or upsets other people. A child is, however, very dependent on his parents' good will and acceptance, and when this acceptance turns into rejection or some other form of negative expression, he is naturally disturbed.

Evidently at two and one-half years he begins to see the relationship between his own behavior and the attitude of his parents and, as a consequence, learns that he must give up or inhibit his infantile impulses and direct his behavior into more acceptable channels.

In their attempts to cope with the child's misbehavior, parents are often unaware that problems of adjustment are creating as many, if not more, difficulties for the child as they are for his parents. The painfulness and difficulty of the period

Many psychologists are concerned about tendencies on the part of adults charged with the care and supervision of children to overvalue obedience and conformity.

probably are the result of the child's realizing that his parents can make him feel uncomfortable and upset by punishment or some other behavior that signifies rejection and the withholding of love and, furthermore, that he himself can bring about this rejection through his own misbehavior. Perhaps at first he struggles against the realization that his parents can have this much control over him; then he struggles to try to institute the behavior that will maintain an accepting relationship and avoid rejection. Most children achieve this state by a process of "identification," whereby they "identify" themselves with their parents and copy the behavior of their chosen models. The big lesson that the child first begins to learn at two and one-half is that conformity is the price of acceptance. This is a lesson that he must learn many times in his life, at school, in play groups, on the job, and in his relationships with society.

Problem behavior. The trials and tribulations that begin in the third year of life and continue in greater or lesser degree into adolescence and adulthood are not the exclusive concern of the child. Unhappiness is infectious: the discomfort of the child may upset parents or other adults in charge, even though they may feel that they are "doing the best thing" by punishing him or forcing him to conform. Or they may wonder whether they are being too strict or not strict enough. A child who is unhappy will usually express his unhappiness in some form of problem behavior. Some varieties of problem behavior, to be sure, are not especially annoying and consequently may be overlooked by adults. This is particularly true of behavior displayed by the child who withdraws from active contact with others or who adopts the defense of overconformity. Although such a child may be ignored, perceptive adults are aware that the behavior he displays is symptomatic of emotional disturbance.

The rebellious child is the one who is most likely to come to the attention of the adult in charge. Because rebelliousness and other nonconforming behavior disturb the orderly functioning of groups and are a direct challenge to adult authority, adults are of course forced to take steps to cope with the problem. When plagued by such difficulties, they are inclined to take the position that since too much freedom seems to be a bad thing, the safest course is to insist on complete obedience and conformity. They can hardly be blamed for taking this attitude, of course: obedient and conforming children *are* a great deal easier to handle.

Psychologists who work with children are, however, concerned about what seems to be an overvaluation of obedience and conformity. They are in general agreement that children must learn to conform if they are to live and work effectively in a world that is composed of other people, but they wonder whether conformity and obedience have not received an overemphasis in relations between adults and children and if conformity has not been secured at too great a cost. To a large extent, their concern about the insistence on overconformity has grown out of their clinical practice. More of the problems they encounter seem to be caused or aggravated by too much punishment and rejection and not enough freedom and indulgence, rather than the other way around.

This difference between the attitudes of psychologists and those of adults charged with the care of children is brought out in a study made a number of years ago by Wickman (1928), who asked 511 elementary teachers and 30 psychological workers to rank fifty kinds of problem behavior in order from the most to the least serious. The teachers were inclined to rank as most serious that behavior which challenged their authority, whereas the clinicians were inclined to consider behavior characterized by suspiciousness, withdrawing, unhappiness, and depression, as most serious. When Wickman's study was followed up twenty-five years later by Stouffer (1952), it appeared that the same basic differences of opinion still existed, although the two groups had moved a little closer together. The teachers had become somewhat more concerned about emotional factors, and clinicians had become somewhat more concerned about antisocial behavior.

Differences between strict and permissive homes. More recently the viewpoint of psychologists has been strengthened by a number of studies exploring various relationships between the behavior of children and their treatment by adults. One interesting study is reported by Watson (1957), who set out to compare the behavior of 50 children from "strict" homes and 50 from "permissive" homes.[1] Contrary to current folklore, he encountered great difficulty in locating the required number of "permissive" homes, and only after extending the study an extra year was he able to find 38 homes that were sufficiently permissive to be included in the study.[2] When Watson studied the behavior of children from the two types of homes, using psychological tests in a clinical setting, he found that children from permissive homes were:

1. More self-reliant and independent, and more inclined to display initiative.

2. More socialized and cooperative, and less negative or overcompliant.

3. More able to persist in the face of frustration when assigned tasks of increasing difficulty.

4. More inclined to express positive feelings toward others and less inclined to express hostility.

5. More likely to be highly creative, imaginative, spontaneous, and original in their thinking and general behavior.

He found no differences between the groups with respect to self-control, anxiety, passivity, and happiness. Ratings assigned by the children's teachers were somewhat inconclusive, although there was some tendency to classify children from strict homes either very positively or very negatively.

The results of Watson's study are remarkably consistent with the findings of other studies in this field. When Radke (1946) compared the behavior of children of nursery and kindergarten age who came from restrictive and autocratic (that is, strict) homes with the behavior of other children, she found them less aggressive, less competitive, more passive, more colorless, less popular, and less able to get along well with other children. However, children from homes that were less restrictive were more active, more competitive, more popular, and showed more consideration for others. Baldwin, Kalhorn, and Breese (1945) studied the behavior of children from a variety of home

[1] A "permissive" home is one in which children are allowed freedom of action and self-expression in order to permit the optimum degree of personal growth and development. As the word "permissive" is used by psychologists, it signifies a high degree of tolerance for a person's behavior, such tolerance being based on respect for the individual. In this regard, permissiveness differs from neglect, an attitude characteristic of individuals concerned only with their own welfare and therefore unconcerned with the behavior of others. Permissiveness also differs from indulgence, which is characterized by sentimentality and an inability to set limits. Indulgence is often accompanied by a strong need to overprotect and dominate others.

[2] Watson states that his difficulty in finding "permissive" homes could have been anticipated in the light of a survey by Whiting and Child (1953), who concluded, after reviewing childrearing practices in forty-seven cultures throughout the world, that only two cultures were as severe on the younger child as the typical American middle-class family, and no culture was *less* "permissive."

backgrounds over a three-year period. They found that children from homes that were "democratic" (that is, homes where the children had some equality of status and were treated with tolerance and respect) were more likely to show unusually large increases in measured intelligence and were also rated high on such qualities as originality, planfulness, patience, curiosity, and fancifulness. Children from homes where the attitude of parents was generally rejecting, restrictive, and autocratic tended to show only average gains in intelligence and were inclined to be rebellious, nonconforming, and quarrelsome.

In general, studies comparing democratic and permissive childrearing methods with methods that are restrictive and autocratic seem to come to similar conclusions. Children from strict families are likely to be conforming and obedient, but are handicapped when it comes to self-reliance, sociability, and originality. Extreme strictness may also produce a sizable minority of children who are chronic rebels and nonconformists. Democratic and permissive treatment seems to develop children who are both aggressive and competitive, but at the same time more popular and more considerate of others. Such children also seem to be more creative, original, self-reliant, and spontaneous.

Disciplining children. According to "common sense," the cure for delinquency is stricter discipline, that is, the application of more frequent and more severe punishment. However, a large-scale study of 500 delinquent and 500 nondelinquent boys by Glueck and Glueck (1950) found the parents of delinquents much more ready to invoke physical punishment. Approximately 60 per cent of the parents of delinquents used physical punishment, as contrasted with 35 per cent of the parents of nondelinquents. About 14 per cent of the parents of delinquents dealt with misbehavior through reasoning, as contrasted with about

26 per cent of the parents of nondelinquents. The differences between the two sets of parents in degree of control is shown in Table 2-1. The "common-sense" idea that the parents of delinquents are likely to be lax is given some support by these figures, but the idea that extreme strictness prevents delinquency gets no support at all, since three times as many of the parents of delinquent boys were overly strict. Some research by Shoben (1949) shows that parents of problem children (defined in terms of being referred for clinical help or being in the custody of juvenile authorities at least twice) were more inclined to approve of strict discipline and to insist on complete obedience than were parents of nonproblem children.

What do children learn when adults correct other children? Gump and Kounin (1957) collected and analyzed records describing incidents in which kindergarten children saw teachers correcting other children for some misbehavior. The behavior of the teacher was rated according to "clarity" (the use of statements like "Don't hit others," "We don't do that in kindergarten," or "Fold your hands and look at me"), "firmness" (actions which show "I mean it"—approaching, touching, or guiding the offending child; using emphatic speech or posture; "following through"); and "roughness" (actions showing irritation and hostility; overfirm physical handling of the child; angry words or looks). The researchers found that teachers' behavior characterized by a high degree of "clarity" helped to reduce misbehavior in the observing children, but that "firmness" was less helpful. However, when the watching child's behavior up to the time when he saw the misbehaving child being corrected showed that he, too, was misbehaving or showed tendencies that might lead to misbehavior, then a "firm" approach on the part of the teacher reduced his tendency to misbehave. Finally, the researchers found that cor-

Table 2–1   Percentage of homes of delinquent and nondelinquent boys classified according to the kind of control exercised by parents. (After Glueck and Glueck, 1950, Table XI, p. 23.)

Kind of Control	Delinquent Boys		Nondelinquent Boys	
	Mother	*Father*	*Mother*	*Father*
Lax	57	27	12	18
Overstrict	4	26	2	9
Erratic	35	42	21	18
Firm but kindly	4	6	66	55

rection characterized by "roughness" was likely to be followed by an increase in misbehavior on the part of the observing children.

Psychological needs of children

The discussion in the foregoing pages had showed the intimate relationship between parental attitudes and the kinds of behavior patterns developed by children. The relationship between the way a child is treated and the way he behaves is accepted so readily by most of us, that we seldom concern ourselves with the reasons for its existence. Why is it that the behavior of parents can have such a profound effect on their children? How does it happen—to pick a specific example—that a six-year-old child, who is perfectly capable of going by himself to the corner store to get an ice-cream cone, hangs back and loses confidence in himself when his mother says: "Oh, I guess you can go, if you want to, but if you'll just wait a half-hour till Daddy gets home, I'm sure he'll take you." Or to cite another example, why does the child who is being ignored continue to demand attention, even at the risk of being punished by an annoyed parent?

One way of explaining this close relationship between child behavior and parental attitudes is to refer the events of childhood to some kind of developmental theory. One such theory is the structure of "basic human needs" developed by Maslow (1954). Since Maslow's concept of basic needs is a useful formulation for classifying behavior, we shall be referring to it from time to time in this textbook. According to Maslow, all human needs can be classified under the following headings:

1. *Physiological needs:* The needs that must be satisfied if the physiological processes of the organism are to be maintained. These needs naturally assume a certain priority, inasmuch as the very existence of the organism depends on their satisfaction.

2. *Safety needs:* The needs to protect the organism against the dangers of the environment are second only to the physiological needs. The individual needs, furthermore, to feel some degree of security—to feel some kind of assurance that he will be protected from danger and that his physiological processes will be maintained.

3. *Belongingness and love:* The need to share some kind of a close, emotionally satisfying relationship with another person is an important one during the adult years. During the early years of development, the emphasis is on receiving, rather than giving love.

4. *Esteem needs:* These are the socialized needs—the need for self-respect, self-esteem, and the esteem of others, as well as the need to feel useful and necessary to others.

5. *Needs for self-actualization:* These include man's desire for self-fulfillment—that is, his need to realize his best potentials and to achieve the ideals and aims he has set for himself.

The need for love. Note that the needs in the list are arranged in ascending order from the most primitive to the most civilized, from the most simple to the most complex. The newborn infant must cope with needs only on the physiological and safety levels, but within a few weeks or months—no one can really say when—he develops a need for attention that appears to transcend merely physical considerations. It is not enough, in other words, for a child to be fed, kept clean and warm, and to be defended against dangers. A growing human being apparently needs stable and affectionate relationships with a single adult—not necessarily his own mother, but someone who will play a mother's role—a "mother figure." Spitz (1945, 1946b) has presented research to show that children who are deprived of this type of relationship experience a variety of developmental difficulties: they are listless, unable to speak, walk, and feed themselves. The mortality among such children, he claims, is quite high. Although Spitz's research has been criticized on a number of different grounds (Pinneau, 1955a, 1955b), his observations are at least partially supported by other authorities (for example, Bowlby, 1951; Ribble, 1943).

For children beyond the stage of infancy, the evidence showing a need for love and acceptance is more substantial. Widdowson (1951) studied the growth of children between four and fourteen years of age in two German orphanages shortly after World War II and reported that gains in weight were apparently more dependent on the amount of affection received than on the extent to which the children's substandard diet was enriched and supplemented.

Bender (1950) has this to say about the need for love:

The inherent capacity to identify with a mother can be realized only if the child actually experiences a relationship with a mother figure in the first two or

Physiological needs

A great deal of child behavior can be explained in terms of attempts to meet basic needs.

Safety needs

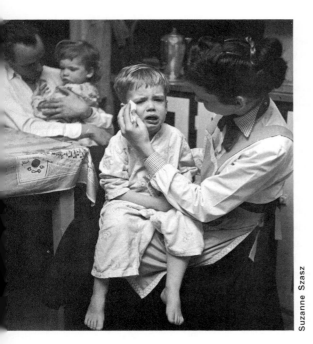

Belongingness and love

Needs for self-actualization

Esteem needs

three years of his life. If the child is deprived of this experience, his capacity to identify with any human or object relationship fails to develop and there is consequent failure or retardation in all aspects (or facets) of personality development. . . .

A large number of problem children have been brought to Bellevue Hospital, in New York City, from different childcaring institutions and foster home agencies because of profound inhibition in personality development. Children who have been in institutions for the first two or three years of their lives without parents or other relatives to visit, or take an interest in them, frequently show the most severe type of deprived, asocial psychopathic personality deviation. These children do not develop a play pattern, and cannot enter into group play with other children. They abuse children near them as frustrating objects to the satisfaction of their primitive impulses.

Bender goes on to say that these children have temper tantrums whenever they are frustrated or whenever any type of cooperation is expected from them. They are, she says, highly distractable, moody, unable to maintain satisfying human relationships, and likely to be intellectually retarded.

A study by Chambers and Zabarenko (1956) provides indirect confirmation to the findings of the preceding studies. They conducted an experiment with the intention of finding out whether the administration of glutamic acid would have any effect on the intellectual ability of mentally retarded and institutionalized boys. Their findings as far as glutamic acid was concerned were negative, because all the boys made gains regardless of whether they received glutamic acid or placebos (doses containing some neutral agent but resembling the experimental drug in appearance). They concluded that the gains must have resulted from the social stimulation and attention the boys received from being subjects of an experiment. The greatest gains were made by eight boys who had been transferred to an adult residence unit, where they became cottage favorites and thus received a great deal of personal attention.

In the light of such findings, it is hardly surprising that children are so responsive to the emotional factors in parental behavior. Children are vulnerable, where parents are concerned. The need for love and attention is particularly strong during the preschool years, and most children try to obtain as much as they can. In multichild families, this attempt to obtain one's share of love—and more than one's share, if possible—leads to sibling rivalry, a natural result of the competition for parental love and attention. Each child in a

family develops, without being aware of it, his own method of getting his share of attention. McArthur (1956) studied the personality traits of first- and second-born sons and found that the two groups showed some rather marked personality differences, which he concluded were the result of opposite roles or patterns of behavior that each boy is likely to develop in accordance with his position in the family. According to McArthur, the older son tends to seek attention and love through being responsible and diligent; whereas the second son is likely to compete for his share of attention by developing the qualities which his older brother possesses to a lesser degree: friendliness and warmth.

Esteem needs. The satisfaction of the esteem needs are also subject to considerable influence on the part of parents. The attitude a child develops toward himself is to a large extent dependent on the attitudes his parents have regarding him. As he goes to school and comes in contact with other adults and especially with children his own age, the influence of the home begins to become diluted. In general, the amount of influence exerted on a child's personality is in proportion to the importance to him of the individuals who are attempting to influence him. During his earlier years his parents have maximum influence, because their good will is all-important. During the preadolescent and adolescent years, as we shall see in the following chapter, the influence of the peer group may exceed the influence of the family, if the need to maintain the good will of the former becomes paramount, as it often does. Adolescents usually know where they stand with respect to the love of their parents, but are less secure about their acceptance by their peers. Hence the often frantic efforts to conform to the expectations of the peer group, a form of behavior that often leads to clashes with parental authority. By this age, however, the adolescent no longer feels that being accepted by his parents depends entirely on his willingness to conform to their desires; he feels, instead, that he can be defiant and rebellious and still count on them for as much love as he desires. Furthermore, he is not as dependent on them for attention as he was when he was a child and at times feels as though he would like less attention from them, rather than more. And by this age, of course, he has begun to look for other sources of love—the members of the opposite sex.

Despite the dominant position of the peer group,

There is a tendency, with each succeeding year of childhood, for children to become less dependent on their parents for acceptance and attention and to satisfy these needs in the company of their peers.

teenagers are inclined to take some of their cues from their parents, when it comes to self-regarding attitudes. Helper (1958) found a significant relationship between the self-evaluations of eighth and ninth graders and the evaluations of the same children by their parents. Interestingly, he found that the relationship was more significant for fathers than for mothers. Perhaps one could speculate that the love of mothers is likely to be given unconditionally, whereas the appreciation of fathers is hedged about by conditions and depends more on the behavior of the child.

Although parents have a significant effect on the behavior and personality of children, it should not be supposed that this influence is necessarily a conscious or even a deliberate one. Very likely neither parent nor child is consciously aware of the ways in which behavior is being modified or learned. Parents are often baffled in their attempts to change the behavior of their children, unaware that their very efforts may be aggravating the symptom they are trying to alleviate. A father may, for example, be upset by his son's cowardice and may spend a great deal of time and attention trying to show him how to defend himself against the physical attacks of other boys. But the more anxious the parent is that his son give a good account of himself, the more apprehensive the boy becomes. The anger and the irritation of the parent only seem to aggravate the problem. What neither is aware of is that the boy is learning to fear anger and aggression, irrespective of the source, and he cannot help having much the same

reaction to the hostility of his classmates that he has to the irritation of his father. And the more angry his father becomes, the more helpless the boy feels in the face of the anger of his classmates.

In other instances, the communication of attitudes and feelings will have a more positive effect. Self-esteem is based, at least in part, on the esteem of others. It is difficult for us to have a good opinion of ourselves, unless this opinion is substantiated and reinforced by the good opinion of others. We learn about ourselves through the evaluations of others. To be sure, we may also learn about ourselves through our own evaluation of our successes and failures and may eventually develop a set of opinions about ourselves that are somewhat different from those that others have for us. But a child has less opportunity to develop an independent evaluation of his conduct; hence his self-opinion is more dependent on the attitudes and feelings that others have for him. He is, in effect, *more vulnerable* with respect to the opinions of others.

Self-actualization needs. The need for self-actualization is a difficult one to assess. It touches on an area of psychology that is somewhat speculative and that borders on philosophy. It is to some degree a "hypothetical construct" that helps to explain why human beings, some of them at least, push beyond the first four levels of needs and become deeply involved in activity that appears to have nothing to do with maintaining physical and psychological comfort and security, into activity, in fact, that may actually increase personal discomfort and insecurity. The first four needs in Maslow's system are to a large extent homeostatic, that is, they are concerned with maintaining a physical, psychological, and social equilibrium. Any organism needs some kind of balance system in order to maintain its physical structure and processes and to cope with its environment. However, as von Bertalanffy (1956) points out, in an analysis of human growth and development, a great deal of human activity transcends homeostatic functioning. The organism is not, he says, a "responding machine" but is instead a "primary activity." Curiosity, play, creativity, and love of investigation are activities that are enjoyed for their own sake.

Although a respectable amount of research exists to show the importance of needs on the first four levels as conceptualized by Maslow, so far very little research has been conducted into the nature of the self-actualizing needs. It has just been in recent years, for example, that we have begun to investigate the nature of creativity. Nevertheless, the idea that we all have a need to fulfill ourselves, to realize our best potentialities, is an attractive hypothesis. It is a hypothesis that "makes sense"—it is consistent with what we already know about human behavior and helps to explain behavioral tendencies that cannot be readily explained by existing theory and research.

Summary

The understanding of adult human behavior may be aided by the study of the developmental process, because antecedent behavior provides many clues about current and future behavior. Children tend to be perceived either as "little adults" whose behavior may be examined in terms of its departure from adult standards, or as completely different beings for whom entirely different standards of behavior are appropriate. Both views have some degree of validity.

Human beings are members of the animal kingdom, and their physiological aspects are quite important. With adults, factors other than those which are purely physiological assume priority. However, with other animals and with new-born human infants, physiological variables are paramount. Infants respond to a narrower range of stimuli, and their behavior is less variable and more predictable than that of adults. It is difficult to pin-point the exact moment at which learning begins; perhaps there is some learning in the uterus, but learning obviously becomes an important factor shortly after birth. The two major dimensions of growth and development are physical maturation and socialization. Physical maturation involves developmental changes whose pattern and pace are set at conception. Socialization involves the changes dependent on learning. Most behaviors involve interaction between these factors; learning to respond to mother's face with a smile cannot take place until the physical maturation of the skills of coordination and vision is completed. Many aspects of maturation take place even without specific external stimulation; children grow, develop teeth, begin to make sounds, and even begin walking as a result of maturational processes.

A child spends his first two years learning primarily about his physical self and his physical environment. During the same period he begins to interact with his social environment, which in turn is simultaneously actively engaged in attempts to modify *his* behavior. An individual's personality is the product of the interaction of several levels of factors. Temperament is an individual's general pattern of emotional responsiveness, which is probably largely based on inherited and physiological factors. Cultural influences are reflected in the way that children are treated. Thus, certain broad characteristics are learned by most members of a given culture because children learn to conform to cultural demands. Finally, each child is affected by specific factors that are directed toward him as a particular child. Some of these influences are shared by broad classes of children such as males as opposed to females and oldest child compared to youngest child in the family; others are unique to a particular child in a particular family. In spite of all the factors that exert an influence on children in their preschool years, studies have found a certain stability of the general pattern of behavior or personality.

The direction of behavior development is outward; the head and trunk keep ahead of the limbs in developmental progress. Social development is also in an outward direction in that a child's center of interest moves from self to parents to peers.

Because children are dependent on adults both in terms of physical care and socialization, the relationship between a child and the significant adults in his environment is obviously of great importance. The child's first major social difficulties occur during the "terrible two's" when his desires and those of his parents begin to clash. Most children resolve this difficulty eventually by learning to identify with their parents and conforming to their demands in order to be accepted. The difficulties of this period can lead to two broad types of problem behavior. Some children withdraw from active contact with others and become overconforming, whereas others rebel and challenge authority. Most adults react with more concern to rebellious behavior than to overconformity, but psychologists regard both as problems requiring attention. Childrearing practices are thought to be of crucial importance in human development. One important dimension of childrearing behavior is that of strictness as opposed to permissiveness; many studies have found personality differences in children from the two types of homes. Strict discipline does not seem to justify the confidence that is often placed on it; for example, parents of delinquents tend to use more physical punishment than parents of nondelinquents.

One way of understanding the behavior of humans is through a consideration of psychological needs such as the five levels proposed by Maslow. The first two levels concern physiological needs and needs for safety. All of us must satisfy these two sorts of needs, but the newborn infant is motivated by them alone. Very quickly, however, it is clear that humans develop needs for belongingness and love; separation from a mothering figure seems to have a profoundly disturbing effect on infants. The fourth level of need, that of self-esteem, begins to assume importance as the child enters school and associates more intensively with his peer group. Both parents and peers may contribute to one's positive or negative feelings about his own worth. The highest level of human needs is concerned with self-actualization. A self-actualizing person is one who is able to engage in activities characterized by curiosity, play, and creativity, and enjoy them for their own sake.

Questions

1. What are some of the ways in which the behavior of children resembles that of adults, and what are some of the ways in which it is different?

2. In what way does the behavior of a six-month-old infant resemble that of a full-grown dog or cat?

3. List several childhood changes that appear to be largely the result of maturation, several that appear to be largely the result of socialization, and several which depend on both factors.

4. What are some of the personality factors that are determined by our culture but seem like "human nature" to us?

5. In what ways might family life be unique for the oldest child, for the middle child, and for the youngest child in a three-child family?

6. What differences might there be in peer-oriented behavior as opposed to adult-oriented behavior for young children and also for adolescents?

7. Describe some of the difficulties faced by children in their third year of life. What are some of the ways that different children resolve these difficulties?

8. What are some of the personality differences between children from strict homes and those from permissive homes?

9. What are some of the ways in which *you* are able to satisfy Maslow's five types of needs?

Suggestions for further reading

Baldwin, A. L., *Behavior and Development in Childhood.* New York: Holt, 1955. A well-written book that accomplishes the author's main objective—to make sense out of child behavior.

Bossard, J. H. S., *The Sociology of Child Development,* rev. ed. New York: Harper, 1954. A readable account of the forces within the family structure that shape the personalities of children.

Carmichael, L., editor, *Manual of Child Psychology,* 2nd ed. New York: Wiley, 1954. A monumental and encyclopedic review of research in the field. Particularly good in the physiological areas of child development.

Erikson, E. H., *Childhood and Society.* New York: Norton, 1950. A discussion of personality development in childhood from a point of view that combines Freudian psychoanalysis with cultural anthropology.

Martin, W. E., and C. B. Stendler, *Child Development,* rev. ed. New York: Harcourt, Brace, 1959. A standard textbook in the field that draws on contributions from a variety of fields.

Martin, W. E., and C. B. Stendler, editors, *Readings in Child Development.* New York: Harcourt, Brace, 1954. A collection of theoretical and research papers, emphasizing social factors in child development.

Watson, R. I., *Psychology of the Child.* New York: Wiley, 1959. A complete and well-developed treatment of the subject by a clinical psychologist.

3

Human development: adolescence and adulthood

Defining adolescence. Adolescence may be defined as that period or stage of development that comes between childhood and adulthood. Few people would quarrel with that definition. For one thing, it is rather obvious that children do not pass directly into adulthood; instead, they go through a stage in which they are neither children nor adults, but something else. And herein lies one of the problems of defining adolescence: it is easier to say what an adolescent is not than what he is.

Where does this stage we call adolescence begin and where does it end? This is another perplexing problem. Generally speaking, it is easier to identify the beginnings of adolescence than its final stages. It begins to show itself about ten, eleven, or twelve years of age with the changes in appearance and behavior that we call preadolescence. It makes its most obvious appearance at puberty, with the menarche (the beginning of the menstrual cycle) in girls and the first ejaculation of seminal fluid and/or the pigmentation of under-arm hair in boys.

The end of adolescence is harder to determine. Indeed, it is when we try to find the point at which adolescence ends and adulthood begins that we are forced to the realization that what we call adolescence is to a large degree an artifact of our culture. Adulthood is characterized by the playing of adult roles, roles associated with marriage, parenthood, vocational career, and civic and legal responsibilities. In some primitive cultures, like that of the Tuaregs of the Sahara, adolescence is short, and adulthood begins at about fifteen, because at fifteen boys and girls are able to take on the basic adult roles of their culture. In more urbanized cultures, such as ours, the roles of adult life are much more varied and complex. This produces two effects: (1) the period of adolescence is prolonged in order to permit the learning of a greater number of adult roles, and (2) the point at which an individual passes from adolescence to adulthood is less well-defined. The age of 21, voting age in most states, is sometimes thought of as the point at which one enters upon adulthood, but many individuals enter upon the adult roles of married life before that age, and military service may be begun as early as age 17. On the other hand, there are millions of individuals who are still attending school and financially dependent on their parents at the age of 21. Persons going into professions like law, dentistry, and medicine, may even extend this period of economic dependence until they have achieved full status as practitioners in their chosen profession, an event that may not occur until they are well into their thirties.

The problem of defining "adolescence" is further confused by differences among the subcultures that make up our larger culture. Adolescents from working-class families tend to play adult roles at a somewhat earlier age. They may drop out of high school, seek employment, marry, and start raising families—all before the age of 18. Individuals from working-class backgrounds are likely to be playing much the same roles at the age of 25 as they played at 18, but the roles played by most middle-class individuals at age 18 are likely to be quite different from those they will play at age 25.

One basis of this difference is the pattern of expectations that the subculture has for the individual and the individual has for himself. The working-class individual is more likely to expect that he will be independent of family ties at 18, whereas the middle-class individual at age 18 is more likely to expect that he will be playing the role of the student for the next few years. He may seek part-time or temporary employment in order to gain some measure of independence, but he does not expect that he will be doing the same kind of work or working at the same level at age 25. There are, of course, many variations on the basic patterns, some individuals attaining a large measure of adult status earlier, and others, later. These differences depend on a variety of factors: sex, family situations, personal characteristics, and the availability of opportunity. But the expectations that society has for us and which we consequently have for ourselves play a major role in determining when adolescence ends and adulthood begins.

Psychological needs and tasks during adolescence

Basic needs. In the previous chapter we discussed a hierarchy of needs starting from the most physiological and primitive to the most abstract and complex. (Maslow, 1954.) Infancy and childhood, we pointed out, were dominated by the first three levels of these basic needs; the need to maintain physiological processes, the need for safety, and the need for love and attention. These needs, of course, persist in adolescence, but they become less important as sources of concern. The first two needs are taken care of almost incidentally, through everyday routine behavior. The need for parental love and attention is not as crucial as it was in childhood—indeed, many adolescents feel, at times, as though they are receiving more attention than they need. Even those adolescents who grow up in families where love and attention are largely lacking generally know by this stage where they stand in this respect. During adolescence love needs may begin to change their character. The need to give or share love, particularly with respect to members of the opposite sex, may take on important proportions.

"Higher-level" needs. The "esteem needs" assume pre-eminence during the adolescent period of development. During the early years of the period, the adolescent begins to develop a sense of identity and selfhood that goes beyond the family circle. He wants to be more than "one of the Marshall kids" or "the oldest Schlaeger boy" and wants to be "someone in his own right." He seeks this primarily by gaining recognition and acceptance from his age-mates, but, as the years of adolescence go by, he may also look for recognition from other sources: teachers, employers, and members of the opposite sex. During the greater period of the adolescent years, however, the chief preoccupation is with securing and maintaining acceptance and status from the peer group, the gang, the crowd, the clique, the other fellows and girls. For many adolescents, seeking and maintaining the acceptance of their peers looms up with greater importance than maintaining an accepting attitude on the part of parents.

"Self-actualizing needs" may begin to make an

The automobile plays a unique role in the male teenage culture. Not only is it a symbol of adult status yet to come, but it seems to possess a kind of magnetic force that attracts youths and holds them together in a cohesive group.

appearance, particularly toward the middle and final years of adolescence. In our culture, "who we are" is dependent to a large degree on the vocation we have entered; hence, preparing for and succeeding in an occupation is likely to become a major consideration, particularly for middle-class teenagers. We also tend to find the major outlet for our creative energies in our occupational life.

Our ability to meet basic needs on the top two levels is to a large extent dependent on our level of emotional maturity. Some adolescents are unable to take the step of identifying with individuals and groups outside the home because they are unable to break away from their emotional dependence on their parents. A rather large number of individuals are able to develop satisfactory relationships with their peers but are unable to take the next step of developing a sense of identity and selfhood apart from the group. Self-actualization depends in part on our ability to be self-directive: to think for ourselves, make decisions of our own,

and to develop a life apart from our relations with the group. Individuals who are unable to take this step are what Riesman, Glazer, and Denny (1950) would term "other-directed" persons—that is, persons who are overly concerned about what others think of them.

Developmental tasks of adolescence. The course of human development may be seen in terms of a series of developmental tasks—problems, that is, which must be faced and solved by individuals at each stage in their development in order to be prepared for problems or tasks at the next stage. (Havighurst, 1953.) One of the developmental tasks of adolescence, for instance, is that of developing "emotional independence of parents and other adults." A teenager who is not able to resolve this problem successfully is likely to have difficulty with the tasks of adulthood: selecting a mate, learning to live with a marriage partner, managing a home, taking on civic responsibility, and finding a congenial social group. Here are nine basic developmental tasks which Havighurst maintains that each adolescent must face:

1. Accepting one's physique and accepting a masculine or a feminine role.
2. Achieving new and more mature relations with age-mates of both sexes.
3. Emotional independence of parents and other adults.
4. Achieving assurance of economic independence.
5. Selecting and preparing for an occupation.
6. Developing intellectual skills and concepts necessary for civic competence.
7. Desiring and achieving socially responsible behavior.
8. Preparing for marriage and family life.
9. Building conscious values in harmony with an adequate scientific world-picture.[1]

Havighurst rated the behavior of 30 children at ages 10, 13, and 16 and found a significant relationship between their accomplishment of developmental tasks at each of these ages. That is, children who were successful in coping with the developmental tasks of preadolescence tended to be successful with the developmental tasks of adolescence, and children who had difficulty with developmental tasks as preadolescents were likely to continue to encounter difficulties as adolescents. The trend was less noticeable over a span of six years, indicating that initial successes or failures became somewhat less important as time went on. Perhaps this was due, at least in part, to the varying rates at which adolescents achieve maturity. Nevertheless, the trends that Havighurst found were surprisingly stable, indicating what may be a certain consistency in the ability to make psychological adjustments: success tends to promote success, and failure tends to promote failure.

Physical development

Changes. The word "adolescence" means "the state of becoming an adult." It is during the period of adolescence that the physical changes take place that enable each individual to take on the form and functions of the adult of his sex. For males this means the deepening of the voice, the growth of the beard, and the ability to produce semen. For females, this means the development of breasts, changes in the uterine and general pelvic areas, and the menarche. For both sexes it means the growth of body hair, particularly in pubic and under-arm areas, increases in height and weight, changes in the contours of the face and body, and the eruption of new teeth. Most children demon-

[1] Reprinted by permission.

strate what is called a "prepuberal growth spurt," a marked increase in height and weight that occurs during the months prior to the menarche in girls and the growth of pubic hair and the first ejaculation of semenal fluid in boys. Since girls mature on the average about two years earlier than boys, this means that there will be a period of a few months when girls are likely to be a little taller and heavier than boys. The average girl is growing most rapidly at 12.6 years, as contrasted with 14.8 years for the average boy. (Shuttleworth, 1939.) The differential rate at which boys and girls mature is shown in Figure 3-1.

As you examine Figure 3-1, note that the differences in maturation rate *within* each sex are as striking as the differences *between* the sexes. At 11½ years, one-fourth of the girls have entered the puberty cycle; two years later, at 13½, one-sixth still have not reached this point in their development. In the meantime, two-fifths of the boys have begun the puberty cycle by 13½, but by 15½, one-tenth have not entered this stage. These statistics demonstrate one of the chief characteristics of adolescents: their variability. In a certain seventh-grade class, half the girls have entered the puberty cycle, the other half not. Bonnie, at age 13 is practically a young woman: her physical appearance leaves no doubt on that score, and she "goes steady" with a boy from the ninth grade who could pass for her younger brother. In class, she sits next to Eloise, who is also 13, but looks, in contrast to Bonnie's full-blown womanhood, as though she were four or five years younger. Eloise makes a show of talking about *her* boyfriends, when actually she is still a child who enjoys an occasional hour of playing with paper dolls.

Early and late maturers. The relationship between sexual maturity and social behavior is brought out in the research conducted at the Institute of Child Welfare at the University of California in Berkeley, where the growth, development, and behavior of a group of individuals has been studied from infancy to adulthood, covering a period of some thirty years. From observations made during the adolescent period of development for these individuals, H. E. Jones (1943) reports some interesting facts about the behavior of boys who mature earlier or later than their age-mates. The early-maturing boy, he found, has a decided advantage. He tends to be tall for his age and muscular, and is likely to be assigned to positions of leadership and responsibility. This may create more problems than he is

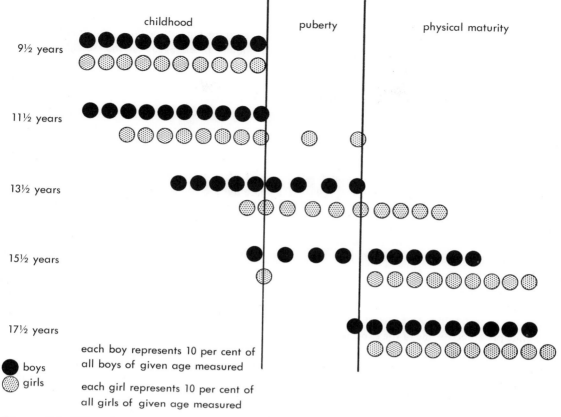

childhood puberty physical maturity

9½ years

11½ years

13½ years

15½ years

17½ years

● boys
◉ girls

each boy represents 10 per cent of
all boys of given age measured

each girl represents 10 per cent of
all girls of given age measured

Figure 3-1. When boys and girls mature. (After Keliher, 1938.)

ready to handle, just at a time when he is struggling to adjust to a new body-image, an enlarged physical structure, and new interests and impulses, but he generally finds more assets than liabilities in his situation. For one thing, he gets an opportunity to learn adult roles earlier than the rest of his age-mates. Furthermore, unlike the early-maturing girl, whose eventual height, Jones found, is usually below average, he is likely to reach average adult height.

The late-maturing boy, however, tends to be out of step with his age-mates. Still prepuberal at the age of 15 or 16, he is likely to be ignored or slighted by both boys and girls and, because of his small size and lack of strength, is unable to participate in most sports on an equal basis with other boys. Since some degree of success in sports is a prized attribute of the male role during the adolescent years, he is inclined to develop feelings of inferiority. Some late-maturing boys react to this situation by withdrawing from competition and becoming submissive and self-effacing; others "compensate" for their feelings of inferiority by "small-boy behavior"—that is, by making noisy and mischievous bids for attention. This behavior seldom gains them the acceptance

they long for, but usually heightens the hostility of both age-mates and adults. However, like many other individuals who for some reason find themselves rejected by their group, they would rather suffer teasing, criticism, and other forms of negative attention than be ignored.

Although H. E. Jones found early-maturing girls rating low in prestige and leadership, subsequent studies by M. C. Jones and Mussen (1958) and by Faust (1960) found them rating higher than late-maturing girls. Some confirmation of H. E. Jones's findings appears in Faust's observation that early-maturing girls lack prestige in the 6th grade, although she also observed that they excel in junior high school and high school. In sum, the research appears to indicate that early-maturing adolescents have a considerable advantage over late-maturers. M. C. Jones and Mussen report, for example, that early-maturers of both sexes tend to be more independent and surer of themselves and have better relations with their parents than do late-maturers.

In trying to account for the differences between early- and late-maturing adolescents, there is a temptation to explain them physiologically—to assume, in effect, that early-maturers are dominant and well-adjusted principally because of the presence or absence, say, of some glandular secretion. It is possible, of course, that such secretions may indirectly stimulate some aspects of more mature behavior. For example, hormone injections will produce changes in the social status of chickens. The chicken that has been dominated, pecked, in other words, by the other chickens in the flock will assume a position of dominance in the pecking order if it is injected with male hormone. (Allee, Collias, and Lutherman, 1939.) Hence the capacity for leadership displayed by the early-maturing boy may be the partial result of the release of a greater amount of male hormone in his blood stream.

However, to conclude that the behavioral changes of adolescence are due primarily to physical changes is to overlook the importance of attitudes and expectations. As adolescents change in size and appearance, some of the expectations that adults have for them also change. The more an adolescent resembles an adult, the more we will expect him to behave like an adult. These expectations are communicated to him directly, by such remarks as: "You're too old a boy to be doing that, aren't you?" or "You may look like a nine-year-old, but do you have to behave like one?" Or the expectations may be communicated more indirectly. Appointing one boy to a position of leadership and placing another in a subordinate position communicates the expectations of the adult in charge more effectively than any words.

Social development

Relations with parents and peers. During the adolescent and preadolescent years there is, as we have pointed out, a general shift in interest and involvement from the family to groups outside the family. This shift in interest does not necessarily take place gradually and peacefully. Boys and girls very commonly have misgivings about the changes that are taking place in their interests and may experience conflicting feelings. On the one hand, they may enjoy some aspects of the dependent relationship they have with their parents, but, on the other hand, they also find their associations with their peers satisfying. The peers usually win out, partly because they offer greater opportunities for esteem and status. At home, a teenager is in a subordinate status, whereas his friends are much more willing to accord him a position of equality. Parents, too, often complicate the problem by intensifying certain demands. As they realize that the relationship between them and their children is beginning to change, that their children are becoming more distant in their manner, more rebellious, less responsive, and less involved in the life of the family, they may feel threatened. Parents perceive children as psychologically an extension of themselves, and permitting them to slip away into the outside world is like losing a part of oneself. Such a loss is, of course, an inevitable part of approaching old age, a prospect which parents are understandably reluctant to face. Furthermore, being the parent of a teenager calls for a different kind of role than that played during the prepuberal years, and many parents are unwilling to make the necessary changes in attitudes or behavior or are unaware that changes are needed or are desirable. As teenagers become more independent and self-sufficient, they have less need of care, direction, and attention on the part of their parents. Parents not only need to face this fact and accept it, they must also find new interests and new roles to occupy their time and energy. The emotionally insecure parent especially has great difficulty in making these changes.

For his part, the teenager may at times feel the need for parental love and direction, but he is often too proud to admit or accept such feelings, looking upon any form of dependence as a sign of weakness. Hence many an adolescent experiences a conflict between wanting love and direction and at the same time wanting to be strong and self-sufficient enough not to need love and direction. Some adolescents resolve this conflict by making decisions that are not in their best interests and defending them stubbornly in the face of all adult opposition. Here is an example:

Georgia, a high school junior, often talked of a career in music. She had an excellent voice, took private lessons, got good parts in high school musicals, and was in demand as church soloist. Because of her music teacher's recommendation, she was awarded a summer's scholarship to a well-known music school several hundred miles away from home. However, accepting the scholarship would mean giving up her plans to teach swimming for the Red Cross during the summer, a job she shared with three of her closest friends. In spite of all the arguments and entreaties of her parents and her teacher, she refused to consider the scholarship. When her mother asked her whether a summer with her friends was more important to her than her musical career, she answered: "I know this sounds ridiculous, but spending the summer at the pool with Ruthie and the rest of the gang is the most important thing in the world to me right now."

Insecure and unsure of themselves, many adolescents reject the attention and direction they need so badly from adults, perceiving any form of dependence as a sign of weakness.

It is quite understandable how a division in loyalties between family and peer group might arouse tensions and anxieties and aggravate differences between the adolescent and his parents. For their part, parents are for the most part unaware of the struggle that goes on within their adolescent child as he tries to live according to a double standard composed of the expectations of his parents and those of his friends. The adolescent's air of truculence, superiority, and self-assurance is to a large extent a mask that serves to conceal his very real self-doubts from friends, family, and even from himself.

Independence vs. direction and control. Some of the opinion polls conducted among high-school students by Remmers and his associates (1952) indicate the rather consistent gap that exists between the self-appraisals and aspirations of adolescents and the appraisals and expectations of their parents. As Table 3-1 shows, students generally believe in less adult control and greater opportunity for independence, whereas parents

believe in greater direction and control on the part of adults and less independence on the part of adolescents. A comparison between the responses of ninth graders and twelfth graders show that the older adolescents believe in even greater autonomy, and there is a tendency for the parents to go along with this, although they are inclined to approve less freedom than the students want for themselves. Note, however, that there is an inconsistency in the replies. Although students generally want less direction and control than their parents think desirable, at the same time they are somewhat more approving than are their parents of the kind of assignment in which students are told what pages to read in the textbook. This kind of inconsistency is rather characteristic both of adolescents and their parents: adolescents want more independence but also want adults to tell them what to do; parents want more direction and control for their adolescent children, but at the same time want them to learn how to think and act for themselves.

Table 3-1 Differences between responses given by 9th- and 12th-grade students and their parents to questions dealing with the extent to which schools should control and direct pupils or permit and encourage independence. (After Remmers, Horton, and Scarborough, 1952.)

| | Percentage Giving Each Response | | | |
| | Students | | Parents of | |
Question	9th Graders	12th Graders	9th Graders	12th Graders
How much time should the school give to self-government?				
More	45	56	40	45
Same amount as at present	48	41	51	48
Less	7	3	9	7
Do pupils have their character improved by being required to sit still, walk in line, and keep quiet?				
Yes	46	46	63	62
No	35	40	21	26
Don't know	19	14	16	12
What should the main purpose of art instruction be for most pupils?				
Teach them to draw or paint well	24	17	24	24
Allow them to express their own ideas and feelings	64	74	62	63
Undecided	12	9	14	13
Which of the following best describes the way a classroom should be:				
A place where pupils are given facts and asked to recite about a subject	23	18	31	28
A workroom in which the pupils can study, look at extra materials, and experiment in the subject	68	77	59	64
Undecided	9	5	10	8
Should a school be a place where pupils are				
Taught to believe what the people of the past have decided was best and proper	15	7	18	15
Given the facts and experiences by which to decide for themselves what is best and proper	77	89	72	78
Undecided	8	4	10	7
Pupils cannot learn very much in a class when the teacher does not have strict order and discipline				
Agree	60	62	69	75
Disagree	29	31	22	18
Undecided	11	7	9	7
Which kind of assignments are better for pupils?				
Assignments for which pupils find their own material in encyclopedias, books, and other places	50	62	59	66
Assignments in which the teacher tells the pupils what pages to read in a textbook	37	27	28	19
Undecided	13	11	13	15

The need for mutual understanding. Many of the difficult problems that arise between parents and their adolescent children could be resolved if both parties had some kind of sympathetic understanding of the problems being faced by each other. Such understanding could be fostered if it were possible for teenagers and parents to find some way of discussing their mutual problems. Unfortunately attempts to clarify issues through discussion usually end in heated arguments as each party tries to defend some fixed point of view.

The following statement by a college freshman woman expresses how many teenagers feel about their relationships with their parents:

I have never been able to discuss my problems with my mother and she has always made me feel that I was a nuisance to her. She was always telling me to have outside interests so when I became interested in dramatics in my senior year in high school, I thought she would be happy, but no, she disapproved of my staying out at night for rehearsal. She even made me break up with the boy I was going steady with at the time. I still have this feeling of resentment about my mother and I guess I will always have it. I just dread going home on the weekends because I know we will have an argument about something even though I try to prevent it. I think that more parents should take psychology. I think it should be required in all colleges and maybe even required before you get a wedding license.

Usually, the later stages of adolescence are not as turbulent as the early teens. Parents are more inclined to be resigned to accepting more independence of thought and action on the part of their children. And adolescents, too, tend to be more relaxed and secure. This comes about partly because they have been able to work out some roles for themselves, and partly because through greater maturity they have been able to gain a deeper understanding of other people's feelings. Here is a statement by a college student that reveals his growing understanding:

I recall one evening when I came home from my part-time job feeling depressed and really wanting to take it out on someone or something. That someone happened to be my mother. Even when I was arguing with her, I realized that I was acting like a child and that she wasn't responsible for my troubles. Because I could account for my actions, I felt ashamed and guilty about the whole thing. At the time, I wished that I didn't understand my actions because I would have felt justified then in fighting with her.

The importance of positive family relationships is demonstrated by a study conducted by

Lindgren

Parents and their adolescent children might forestall needless friction if they could engage in serious attempts to understand each other's needs and problems.

Warnath (1955), who interviewed a number of ninth-grade boys, each of whom had been rated by his classmates on his general effectiveness in the group. He found that the boys who were held in greatest esteem by their classmates engaged in more activities with other members of their family, gave more examples of warm and friendly feelings of family members for one another, were permitted to engage more freely in activities outside the home, and tended to conduct themselves more like adults than most of their classmates. The implication of Warnath's study seems to be that teenage boys who are forced by family friction and tension to search for social satisfactions outside the home are actually less likely to be effective than those boys who find home a pleasant place. The teenager not only needs opportunities to become effective outside the family, he also needs to find emotional support and acceptance within the family.

Emotional development

Awareness of others. The adolescent's growth in the ability to interact with and respond to others is accompanied by two somewhat conflicting developments. On the one hand he becomes more aware of the needs and feelings of other people, but on the other hand he also develops a kind of anxious self-concern. Let us consider first the changes that take place in his attitudes toward others.

Harris (1957) conducted a questionnaire study of several hundred children and adolescents ranging in age from 10 to 18 years. He found a steady increase in responses indicating acceptance of social responsibility. The older the adolescent, the more likely he was to respond favorably to items like these:

At school, it is easy to find things to do when the teacher doesn't give us enough work.
If it is worth starting at all, it is worth finishing.
People can count on me to get things done, without checking on me.
It is more important to work for the good of the team than to work for your own good.

The differences between preadolescents and adolescents that Harris found are in the expected direction—that is, we would expect an age span of eight years to make a difference in the social attitudes of youngsters. This is a difference that can be confirmed by everyday observation, although we are often more inclined to notice the *lack* of responsible attitudes on the part of adolescents, rather than their presence. One of the problems, of course, is the difficulty that all of us—adults and adolescents alike—have of living up to our ideals. Even when we want to do the right thing, we sometimes are unable to find ways of carrying out our good intentions.

Growth in empathy. Behaving in ways that are considerate toward others involves, among other things, the ability to empathize—the ability to put ourselves into another person's shoes and see things as he sees them. Empathy is an ability that takes emotional maturity: it requires a willingness to value and understand the feelings and attitudes of others, as well as a willingness to admit that there may be a number of different points of view on a given subject. The adolescent who is successful in developing satisfactory relations with his peers is bound to develop a certain measure of empathy, for his success in getting along with the group will depend on his ability to be aware of and to respond to their attitudes and feelings. When it comes to relations with adults, adolescents tend to show a great deal less empathy. This may be due to a certain feeling on their part that it is more important for adults to understand adolescents than for adolescents to understand adults, or it may be a result of the limited experience adolescents have had with adult roles. Empathy is further blocked by the common tendency of adults and adolescents to be "on the defensive" against each other, an attitude that is hardly conducive to mutual understanding.

Real gains in empathy are made when teenagers begin to play adultlike roles. As they take positions of responsibility, particularly in paid employment, they begin to have experiences that provide some bases for understanding an adult frame of reference. Furthermore, looking ahead to the adult roles they will be playing a few years hence also helps to understand the viewpoint of adults. Naturally, this understanding must be fortified by the major prerequisite for empathy: the *desire* to understand another person's point of view. Unfortunately, too many teenagers see adults not so much as people who need to be understood, but as people who must be coped with—challenged, obeyed, tolerated, put in their place—but not necessarily understood.

For their parts, parents and other adults ordinarily contribute little by way of setting an example. If adolescents play the role of the antagonist, it is partly because adults put them into that role. Often, parents permit their personal problems to interfere with their relations with teenagers. The father who is discovering at the age of 40 or 45 that he will never attain the vocational goals he has set for himself, but must instead play a lesser role, may take out some of his frustrations by trying to dominate his children. Perhaps he tries to do their vocational and educational planning for them, telling them that he does not want them to make the mistakes he did. Or perhaps he tries to compensate for his feelings of failure and inadequacy by insisting on absolute and instantaneous obedience. As long as parents are concerned principally with their own needs, it is difficult for them to empathize with their children. Naturally, a great deal of parental self-interest masquerades under the guise of altruism, as witness the familiar: "Mind you, I'm only telling you this for your own good."

Self-concern. There is, as one might expect, an inverse relationship between self-concern and empathy—that is, the greater the self-concern, the less the empathy. The individual who is preoccupied with his own needs and problems has little time or energy to devote to understanding of the frames of reference used by others. In contrast to teenagers, adults generally have greater ability to put their self-concerns aside and to em-

Too many teenagers see adults not as people who need to be understood, but as people who need to be challenged.

pathize with others. Of course, one can possess this ability and not use it, and it is on the whole more difficult to be tolerant and objective about members of one's own family than toward those less closely related.

The teenager has, however, sufficient reason to be preoccupied with self. He is likely to feel a great deal of insecurity in his relations with others, and particularly with adults. Part of growing up is the learning of new roles, new ways of behaving and new expectations for oneself. The teenager who is beginning to look like an adult is expected to behave like one. More than that, he is especially eager to display adult behavior. The difficulty is, he is not exactly sure what kinds of adult behavior are appropriate or how it *feels* when one is behaving like an adult. Perhaps the problem would be simplified if there were standards of teenage behavior that were different from adult standards

and which were accepted by society, but society has no special standards for the behavior of this group. In effect, society hopes and expects that teenagers will behave like adults, but not *too much* like adults. This is not much help for the teenager who is, figuratively, "feeling his way" into adulthood and who often has no way of knowing whether he has gone too far or not far enough. Furthermore, he has two audiences to satisfy: teenage society and adult society. Very often the behavior that satisfies one group enrages the other.

As a result of this self-concern, adolescence is likely to be an anxious period. Some of the problems that plague teenagers, as revealed in a nation-wide poll of high school students reported by Remmers and Radler (1957), are listed in Table 3-2. A review of the problems most commonly reported shows that self-concern heads the list. The six problems that teenagers said were the most bothersome are direct evidence of the rather wide-spread feeling of personal inadequacy that is characteristic of this period of development. Some of this anxiety evidently begins to diminish toward the end of the high school years. Of the 103 different problems covered in the entire survey, 55 were reported more often by ninth graders, 33 were reported more often by twelfth graders, and the remainder were reported by the members of both grades with equal frequency.

Anxiety and sex roles. Girls are evidently more anxious than boys. Sixty-two of the problems were reported more frequently by girls, whereas boys reported only 35 more frequently.

This difference.may be due partly to the fact that society is somewhat more tolerant and accepting of boys' attempts to "act out" their conflicts and tensions more directly. For example, we tend to expect a great deal more aggressiveness and rebelliousness in boys than in girls. That is, we may *punish* boys for rebelliousness, but we nevertheless *expect* a certain degree of rebelliousness to be normal and "typical" of boys. Furthermore, boys are expected to engage in vigorous, body-contact sports like football, wrestling, and boxing, activities that enable them to work off a great many different kinds of negative feelings.

Girls have fewer such outlets available to them,

Table 3–2   Some of the most common problems reported by teenagers. (After Remmers and Radler, 1957.) *

Problem	All Boys	All Girls	All 9th Graders	All 12th Graders
Want people to like me more	47%	60%	55%	52%
Want to make new friends	45	56	52	46
Get stage fright before a group	46	59	54	47
Want to gain (or lose) weight	49	56	54	51
Wish I were more popular	36	47	50	32
Seldom have dates	48	39	50	32
Have a "crush" on a friend of the same sex	34	47	48	29
Do things I later regret	38	43	42	36
Can't help day dreaming	29	41	35	34
Worry about little things	26	44	32	40
Feel I'm not as smart as others	30	37	36	28
Want to improve my posture and body build	42	33	40	32
Concerned about improving my figure	7	41	26	21
Want to get rid of pimples	33	33	31	33
Don't have a girl friend (or a boy friend)	41	30	38	30
Need to develop self-confidence	31	40	33	41
Ill-at-ease at social affairs	26	25	26	23
Easily excited	14	32	23	23
Trouble keeping my temper	27	38	34	32
Often feel lonesome	16	24	19	20
Easily hurt	19	39	28	30
Hesitate to assume responsibility	21	15	16	19
Want to discuss my personal problems	19	29	24	27
Should I go steady?	19	25	20	22
Unsure of myself	20	26	21	26
How far should high school students go (on a date)?	24	26	24	24
Bite my nails	26	24	28	23

* From *The American Teenager* by H. H. Remmers and D. H. Radler, copyright © 1957, used by special permission of publishers, The Bobbs-Merrill Company, Inc.

and such outlets as they have are of a more abstract, socialized nature. They may, for example, compete for grades or enter essay contests, or they may enter into the complex maneuvers that characterize competition for social status. Competitive sports are more available to girls today than they were a generation or more ago, but this area of activity is still considered to be primarily a masculine field. Although society tolerates a certain amount of aggressiveness and competitiveness from girls, such qualities are considered to be primarily masculine, rather than feminine, traits. This means that girls generally have less opportunity to express tensions resulting from conflicts and frustrations in ways that are immediate, direct, and satisfying, and hence may feel forced to block expression of negative feelings or to contain them in some way. Therefore, girls may be aware of a great many more unresolved tensions and conflicts than boys and thus may experience more anxiety.

Another anxiety-provoking situation faced by girls is the change in status that ordinarily takes place during the adolescent years. In elementary school girls have a favored position in the classroom. They are generally better behaved than boys, are more successful in completing classroom assignments, and are, from an adult point of view, more likable and more responsive than boys. As they begin to approach adulthood, however, they begin to participate in a world that is largely male-dominated, that is, a world in which males have greater freedom of movement and choice than females, in which the decisions and wishes of males count for more than the decisions of females, and in which males are expected to attain higher levels of status and to earn greater material rewards. The problems girls face of adjusting to the transition from a social environment in which they had a preferred status to one in which they are ex-

pected to play secondary or supporting roles may very well aggravate feelings of insecurity and anxiety.

Anxiety and cultural differences. An examination of other data gathered by Remmers and Radler (1957) also shows that rural teenagers are twice as likely as urban teenagers to report higher percentages of problems. The rural teenager is subject to certain pressures that do not affect the city-dweller. The general trend in population movement is from the country to the city, and many a rural teenager has to make up his mind whether he will spend the rest of his life on the farm or move to the city where opportunities for advancement are greater. In effect, the choice of "Who am I going to be?" may be more anxiety-provoking for him. The city youth has to face the problem of self-identity, too, but he usually resolves it by remaining in the more familiar atmosphere of the city or its suburbs, whereas the country boy who decides on a career in the city must move into a new and sometimes unfriendly environment.

Children from lower-income families also show a higher incidence of problems and for much the same reasons. The trend in our culture is for children of lower-income families to attain middle- and upper-income levels. Hence the person from lower-class surroundings has to decide whether he will advance or remain where he is. To advance means that he will increase the social and economic distance between himself and his parents, but not to advance may mean the achievement of less than he is capable of. Both the rural youth and the youth from lower-income background have to resolve a problem that is for them rather ambiguous, a problem that aggravates self-concern and anxiety.

Another factor in the greater number of problems reported by these two groups lies in the character of our school system. Our schools are largely middle-class, urban institutions. Children from lower-class surroundings and from rural homes do not feel as much at home in them as do children from city homes or from middle-class backgrounds. A large number of studies have shown that on the average children from rural and/or lower-class homes have fewer friends, are less likely to become involved in school activities, have less academic ability, and get poorer grades. In effect, they are more likely to feel like outsiders, like people who do not fit in. Quite naturally they would be inclined to be self-conscious and to report feelings of inadequacy. Often problems of adjustment at school are aggravated by problems at home. In a study of childrearing practices, Sears, Maccoby, and Levin (1957) confirmed a finding reported by other researchers to the effect that lower-class parents tended to be less interested than middle-class parents in their children's education and were inclined to be more punitive and restrictive.

Problems of sexual adjustment. One of the most obvious areas of tension and anxiety in adolescence is that concerned with sexual behavior. Most individuals are physically ready by the time they reach their middle teens to perform the sexual functions of adults, yet society expects and demands that sexual expression be postponed until marriage. However, society does not speak with one voice, nor does it always speak clearly. Sex is an awkward subject in our culture; we have difficulty in speaking of it without embarrassment, derogation, or attempts at humor—all indications of the anxiety it arouses. Hence it is often difficult for an adolescent to get any clear answer to the questions and problems that plague him. Adults, too, frequently give public support to a particular standard of behavior and violate that standard in their private lives. Sometimes these inconsistencies engender a kind of cynicism that makes it difficult for adolescents and adults alike to respond to some of the more positive values in the standards society sets for sexual behavior.

The male sexual drive is strongest during the teens and gradually declines after the twenties, whereas the female sex drive reaches its height during the twenties and is maintained near its maximum level well into middle age. (Kinsey *et al.,* 1948, 1953.) Furthermore, females are not as readily aroused sexually as males and apparently do not feel the need for sexual expression as often. Very likely these differences are biologically de-

termined, but the pattern of sexual activity differs widely from individual to individual and from culture to culture.

Whether the heightened male sex drive during the teens is the result of biological or cultural factors, the fact remains that the need to express sexual drives rather generally creates a problem for adolescent boys. Although the desire for sexual activity is at its height during these years, there is no culturally approved way in which it can be expressed. Virtually all males, men and boys alike, get some relief through masturbation (sexual satisfaction through self-stimulation), and probably half to two-thirds of women engage in this activity at some time or other. Kinsey and others (1948) found that more than one-third of the 5300 men they interviewed had engaged in homosexual practices. Premarital intercourse is even more common. However, an interesting social pattern emerged from the Kinsey data when they were classified according to educational level. Adolescent males who had not gone beyond the eighth grade were about seven times more likely than college students to engage in premarital intercourse. College students, on the other hand, were much more likely to find outlets for sexual expression in masturbation and "petting to climax." These contrasting figures point up the fact that modes of sexual activity are to a large extent culturally determined.

Of all the biological drives, the sex urge is probably the most complex. Since it is not necessary for personal survival, it can be channeled into a wide variety of activities—work, sports, art and other forms of creative activity—or it can be repressed, perverted, and exploited. It probably acts as a subtle influence in much of our dealings with members of the opposite sex and indirectly affects a broad range of our everyday activities. Sigmund Freud referred to the sex urge as "libido" and identified it as the primary drive of life. The state of an individual's mental health, he believed, depended largely on the way in which he had learned to express, frustrate, or channelize this life force. Although most psychologists today would take issue with some of Freud's theories, they would probably agree that he rendered humanity a service in directing attention to the importance of the sex drive and in helping make it a legitimate subject for research and discussion. Today, although we are a long way from solving the sexual problems of adolescence, our better understanding of their dynamics has opened the way for the adoption of attitudes that are more sympathetic and helpful. Furthermore, the adolescents of today are better informed about sex and are better able to discuss sexual problems objectively and frankly than they were a generation or so ago.

Adolescence, as we have stated previously, is a period of life in which individuals make their first major attempt to learn adult roles. The sexual role is a crucial one, partly because it involves a shared and intimate relationship with another person, and partly because sexual adequacy carries a high degree of symbolic value in our culture. One indication of its importance is the great stress we place on being happily married and having children. Adults who do not marry, or who marry but do not have children, are at times made to feel in more or less indirect ways less than adequate, different, or atypical. The adolescent is aware of the value placed on sexual adequacy, and he is very naturally concerned about his ability to qualify. At the same time he is aware of internal or external pressures that tempt him to test his sexual adequacy. Such experimentation, as we have noted, is officially forbidden by society. If he yields to temptation, he is likely to be plagued by guilt feelings; if he resists temptation he will be plagued by feelings of frustration.

The extent to which this dilemma produces anxieties was examined by Powell (1955) who measured the reaction time of individuals between the ages of 10 and 30 to stimulus words dealing with various areas of adjustment. The method he used was that of asking subjects to give the first word that came to mind when they were presented with a stimulus word. His results, as shown in Figure 3-2, demonstrate that words dealing with heterosexual relations ("dance," "kissing," "marriage," "hugging," and the like) caused his subjects to hesitate longer before giving a response. Such hesitation, or "blockage," is usually considered to be an index to the amount of conflict or anxiety produced by the word in question. As Figure 3-2 shows, males experience the greatest conflict at age 15 and females at 16. However, females not only show greater conflict, but experience it earlier. The results are consistent with the findings of Remmer's poll of high school students reported in Table 3-2—namely, that girls tended to have a higher level of anxiety than boys.

ADULTHOOD

Psychological needs and tasks

Basic needs. During the early adult years, the self-actualizing needs begin to come into prominence. This is the period in which most individuals make their entrance into the areas of life which appear to offer the best opportunities for expression of their interests and talents. For some persons, this means the culmination of a long period of preparation that started in early childhood; for others, this may mean a drawn-out series of trial-and-error experiences, whereby first one job is tried, then another, and another, in an attempt to find the career or the position that is suitable. Many women find satisfying answers to the need for self-actualization at least three times in their lives: first, during their early twenties, when they go to work after graduation; later, during their late twenties and thirties, as mothers and wives; and finally, during middle age, when they return to paid employment.

Adult life offers opportunities for self-actualization in great variety: community service, vocational career, parenthood, religious activity, and leisure-time activities of various sorts. Most people avail themselves of more than one of these outlets. Such variety is characteristic of the adult years. Whereas general behavior patterns are most predictable during infancy and childhood, and become less predictable during adolescence, they are

Figure 3-2. Conflict in certain areas of adjustment as expressed in the amount of time required to react to stimulus words. (Data from Powell, 1955. Reproduced by permission from Pressey and Kuhlen, 1957, p. 345.)

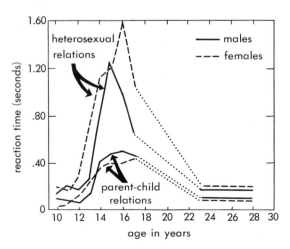

Many adults find themselves unable to cope with the developmental tasks of old age.

most variable and least predictable during adulthood. This is the period in which physical and mental powers are at their prime and in which the individual has the greatest freedom and opportunity to develop the widest variety of behavior. Toward the end of the adult period, as physical capacities start to decline, and as the individual suffers loss of status, loss of income, and a restriction of opportunities for self-expression, behavior is likely to become once again less variable and more predictable. Whereas during the early and middle adult years, needs for esteem and self-actualization are paramount, older individuals are likely to become preoccupied with needs lower on the hierarchy. The individual who is retired is faced by the need to find other social relationships, other ways of maintaining self-esteem. As

children grow up and move away, the needs to receive attention and express love become more acute. Furthermore, as the scope of interests and activities becomes narrower, needs for personal comfort and security become more prominent. And as physical self becomes more feeble, more vulnerable to disease, and less effective, the need to maintain physical processes becomes a major source of concern.

Developmental tasks. It is perhaps odd to think of individuals' having to cope with developmental tasks after they have become adults. People commonly think of childhood and adolescence as *the* periods of development, with the adult years being a kind of static condition or plateau, on which one remains until the declining years of old age. In reality, the onward drive of development continues through most of the adult years, although the rate of change is markedly slowed down. Even the older years, which are commonly looked upon as a period of deterioration and decay, have potentialities for development, potentialities that are to a large extent blocked by society's prejudice against the aged.

Many adults are, of course, unable to cope adequately with developmental change, partly because its gradual nature masks its approach, partly because of an unwillingness to face the approach of old age and death, and partly because each developmental change poses a task, a task that must be resolved through the learning of new roles, new adjustments, and new modes of conduct. Some adults are flexible enough to face these problems and to undertake the necessary learning, but many are unable or unwilling to learn and consequently are overwhelmed by the problems which they refuse to face and are thus forced into narrow and restricted lives. The major problems or developmental tasks of the adult years are listed in Table 3-3. They are largely concerned with marriage and family living, vocation, social relations and responsibilities, and adjusting to a changing physical self.

Marriage and the family

Recent interest in marriage and family living. During the last generation or so, there has been a general increase in interest on the part of the lay public in the psychology of marital adjustment and family living. This is not to say that people have not always been interested in these problems. What has happened, rather, is that problems dealing with marriage and the family have moved closer to the center of general interest, as revealed in topics of everyday conversation, as well as by the content of magazine articles, radio, television, movies, and the like. This change is the product of a number of forces. One is the higher status of women. In the American family of today, wives carry much more weight in the making of decisions than they did, say, fifty or one hundred years ago. This increase in status has given them the right to demand that more attention be given to those problems that were traditionally the primary responsibility of women—that is, problems of home management and childrearing. Marital adjustment is today seen as a *mutual* problem, a problem shared by both husband and wife. For example, when Tasch (1952) interviewed 85 urban fathers, she found evidence pointing to a pronounced trend in the direction of husband-wife relationships based on equal status. Whereas childrearing has traditionally been considered a woman's role, these men saw it as part of their role as fathers. Although husbands today still must divide their interests between their careers and their families, families come in for considerably more attention than in previous generations. William W. Whyte, Jr. (1956), in his critical book, *The Organization Man,* complained of the disappearance of the pre-World War II college graduate who was willing to devote the major part of his time and energy to furthering his vocational ambi-

tions. Instead, he says, business organizations are being staffed by young men who object when business interferes with family life and who, partly out of consideration of their families, value security more than opportunity for promotion. This conflict between interest in the home and vocational ambition will be discussed further in Chapter 15.

Problems of marital adjustment. It is possible that the greater public attention given problems of marriage and family life stem in part from the rather prevalent idea that a great deal of progress has been made in solving these problems psychologically. It is true that psychologists, together with other behavorial scientists, have been able to identify some of the major reasons for maladjustment, and that it is much easier to secure treatment for emotional problems today than it was a generation ago. Although this progress has been encouraging, it by no means justifies the rather extreme optimism expressed by some of the writers of popular psychology, who seem to have fostered the rather widespread idea that psychological problems can be solved by "being intelligent about them." The following quotation from the paper of a college student is characteristic of this attitude:

I have come to the conclusion that the way to achieve a happy marriage is to be sensible. I do not plan to get married until I know my future husband very well and for a long time. There will be no six

Table 3–3 Developmental tasks of adulthood. (Havighurst, 1953. Reprinted by permission.)

Tasks of Early Adulthood	Tasks of Middle Age	Tasks of Later Maturity
1. Selecting a mate.	1. Achieving adult civic and social responsibility.	1. Adjusting to decreasing physical strength and health.
2. Learning to live with a marriage partner.	2. Establishing and maintaining an economic standard of living.	2. Adjustment to retirement and reduced income.
3. Starting a family.	3. Developing adult leisure-time activities.	3. Adjusting to death of spouse.
4. Rearing children.	4. Assisting teenage children to become responsible and happy adults.	4. Establishing an explicit affiliation with one's age group.
5. Managing a home.	5. Relating oneself to one's spouse as a person.	5. Meeting social and civic obligations.
6. Getting started in an occupation.	6. Accepting and adjusting to the physiological changes of middle age.	6. Establishing satisfactory physical living arrangements.
7. Taking on civic responsibility.	7. Adjusting to aging parents.	
8. Finding a congenial social group.		

weeks' courtship and then get married like I have seen many of my friends do. For me there will be no getting married before I even know what life can be like. Almost everyone has an ideal man in mind, but too many settle for less and then think that everything will work out. These marriages almost always end in divorce. After I marry, I am going to wait four years before having children so that I can really know my husband. It might be that I had the wrong impression of him and would want to get a divorce. Too many couples stay together because of the children and are unhappy all their lives. I would not want to get caught in a situation like that. In fact, I think that I will insist that my fiance go with me to a marriage counselor and take some tests to see whether we are really suited for each other. Then we can be sure.

Actually, there are many good points to what this young woman has in mind. It is wise not to rush into a marriage, and visiting a qualified marriage counselor might be very helpful. However,

1860

1960

it is doubtful whether she will be able to follow through on the rather coldbloodedly rational plan she has set out for herself. If she does, she will find, as many others have before her, that the problems of marriage, like other problems that involve the relations between human beings, are not so simply solved. Even with the best of tests and the best of counseling, one can never achieve certainty. Although psychologists and sociologists have devised measures for predicting marital happiness that are successful in a very general kind of way, their results are based on research with *groups* of people—that is, it is possible to say that the *percentage* of people achieving a happy marriage is so-and-so-much higher with one kind of background than with another. Terman and others (1938), for instance, surveyed some 800 couples and found that those whose childhood discipline was "firm," but not "harsh" were on the average happier than those whose discipline was very strict, very permissive, or irregular. The point is that these findings held true *on the average*. After interviewing a prospective couple whose discipline as children was "firm but not harsh," we might say that they *probably* would be happier than couples with other kinds of backgrounds, but we could not say for sure whether they would fall into the majority who would be happy or the minority who would not. Marital success depends on a number of factors, many of which cannot be anticipated before marriage. Although premarital counseling may help by giving a couple a head start on dealing with certain problems and by clearing up certain false impressions, it is by no means a cure-all.

If anything, counseling is probably of greater use during the course of a marriage, when problems occur. Married people often have difficulty in facing and resolving problems because of an inability to discuss emotionally charged issues. At such times, qualified marriage counselors may be helpful in opening up channels of communication. One study of married couples found that 83 per cent of those who experienced the least amount of internal conflict resolved their problems through discussion, whereas this method was used by only 29 per cent of those who had the most conflict. Those who had the most conflict tended to use arguing in an attempt to settle differences, whereas only a small minority of those with little conflict tried that method. (Ort, 1950.) It appears likely that the ability to communicate without arousing

One of the ways to maintain psychological growth during the later years of life is to develop new interests within a socially stimulating context.

hostility or anxiety helps to promote better inter-personal communication and understanding.

In reviewing the problem of evaluating success in family life, Stott (1951) pointed out that there was no single "best way" of characterizing the successful marriage. A relationship that works successfully in one marriage would promote un-happiness in another. He did come to a conclusion that is consonant with the concept of continuous human development, namely, that happiness de-pends on continued growth in "facility to func-tion." It is not enough, he said, for people to function at a dead level of effectiveness, for human satisfaction normally depends on *developmental progress*. Each new developmental task provides the opportunity for growth and progress. If the challenge is not adequately met, then dissatisfac-tion and unhappiness may eventually result. The problems posed by growing children are a case in point. The happiness of the couple depends on the success they are able to achieve in helping their children develop mature and adequate personal-ities. As children leave the home to go their sep-arate ways, the couple must go through another period of adjustment and must find new outlets for their creative energies. People who are not able to solve this developmental task and make psycho-

logical progress at this point may look for ways to prolong the dependency relationship between their children and themselves. Or they may lapse into forms of behavior that arrest further develop-ment and permit senility and decay: apathy, de-pression, resentment, or the more serious forms of psychopathology.

Emotional problems of adulthood. One of the difficulties in developing any kind of organ-ized analysis of adult problems is their very di-versity. As individuals mature, the variety of be-havior, both adjustive and maladjustive, increases. Nevertheless, there are some ages at which certain kinds of social and psychological pathology are more likely to become evident. During late adoles-cence and young adulthood there is a sharp peak in the number of arrests, as young men find anti-social ways of working off feelings of frustration and rebellion. This increase is largely, but not en-tirely, a lower-class phenomenon. Middle-class youth is more likely to express hostilities through competition and through finding other outlets for the expression of frustration, but sometimes frus-trations aggravate feelings of bitterness, resent-ment and discouragement which eventually find their outlet in delinquent behavior.

Even the so-called "normal" or "average" adult

Human development: adolescence and adulthood | 71

has his share of emotional problems. A study of the worries of the members of two middle-class groups, businessmen and psychologists, indicates that worries during their early twenties are of the self-oriented type encountered in adolescence (concern about appearance and making a good impression on others) and sexual morality. Economic worries reach their peak during the thirties. In the late thirties and the forties come concerns about political convictions, health, and mari-

tal difficulties. (Dykman, Keimann, Kerr, 1952.) A somewhat similar pattern of worries was found by Van Zelst and Kerr (1951) in a survey of 236 building trades union leaders in Illinois. Eighty-one per cent of the men reported economic worries of some kind. Those who were 60 and over reported two ages at which economic worries were dominant: one at age 30 and another at age 55. At the latter age they also reported worries about loss of work efficiency, health, death, peace of

Figure 3-3. Ages of greatest worry for 236 union leaders (percentage of possible respondents at each age level expressing worry). (After Van Zelst and Kerr, 1951.)

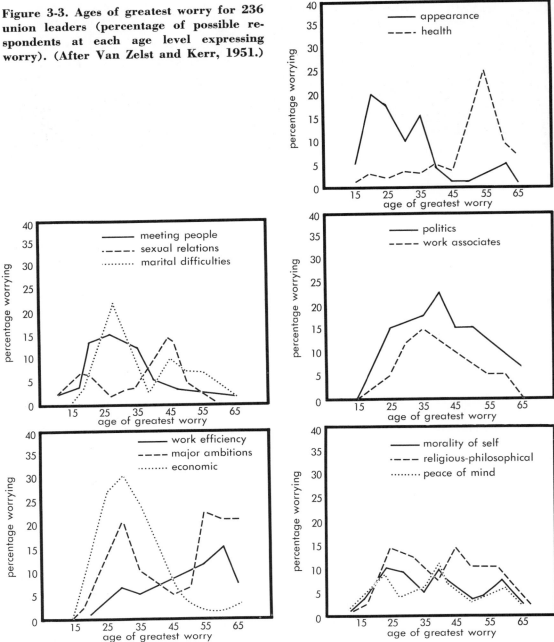

mind, and giving up major ambitions. For these men, worry about appearance reached its peak at 20; worry about meeting people was high at age 30. There were two peaks for marital difficulties, one at 30 and another at 45. Worry about sexual relations were also at their greatest height at 45. Worry about having to give up major ambitions reached a peak at 30, dropped off, and then reached a new and higher peak at 55. The general trend in both of these studies is for there to be a period of concern about oneself and one's relations with others during the twenties, followed by a period between the ages of 30 and 40 when worries are predominantly vocational, with a return to worries about self-adequacy after 40. (See Figure 3-3.)

Although the years between 30 and 40 tend to be worrisome years, they may also be highly productive. Studies of the productivity of outstanding scientists, writers, philosophers, artists, and composers by Lehman (1953) show that they tended to make their most significant contributions between the ages of 30 and 40. For most fields there was a sharp rise in productivity between the ages of 20 and 30, with a peak in the early thirties, followed by a more gradual dropping off.

Maintaining psychological growth in later years. The problem, of course, is how to maintain some level of creativity or, to use the concept suggested by Stott, how to keep growing. There are, of course, no formulas or recipes for this, but there may be some clues in some of the research that has been done comparing older and younger people. It may be hypothesized that the person who continues to face and cope with the problems of life is less likely to deteriorate psychologically. The question is, do older people have the ability to cope with the problems of everyday living? Are they, for example, able to cope with the problems they meet at work?

An analysis of foremen's ratings of 3660 employees at time of leaving found that older workers were less likely to be discharged as incompetent. As Table 3-4 shows, workers in the 61-and-over bracket were rated by their foreman slightly higher than workers in other age groups, and were considered desirable for rehiring. (Smith, 1952.) Another study by Bowers (1952) showed that workers 45 years of age and over were likely to be rated higher by their foreman on attendance, steadiness, and conscientiousness. On the other hand they were also rated as being somewhat slower than other workers, and somewhat less able to learn. However, on a number of other ratings, including efficiency and initiative, there was no difference between older workers and younger ones. Morale of older employees is likely to be better, too. Even when there is an over-all tendency for morale to deteriorate with length of service, older workers are inclined to have better morale, as Figure 3-4 shows. Hence, in answer to the question posed in the foregoing paragraph, the older worker who remains on the job is apparently able to cope adequately with the problems he faces. Although he may learn more slowly than the younger worker, he tends to be more dependable, and the value of his economic contribution is at least equal if not better than that made by workers many years his junior.

So far there have been no comparable studies of older workers in professional and other white-collar fields, but there is no reason to assume that they should be considered any less able. Owens (1953) compared the scores made on an intelligence test by a group of college students in 1919 with scores made on the same test by the same individuals 30 years later. Not only was there a consistent gain, but those who had completed five years of college showed greater increases than those who had completed only four years. It is quite possible that college preparation, the kind of work college graduates perform, or the kind of life they lead stimulates mental development.

Table 3–4   Ratings of workers according to age group. (Data summarized from Smith, 1952.)

	Age at Leaving Company			
	16–30	*31–45*	*45–60*	*61 and Over*
Average percentage rated by foreman as "excellent" or "good" in ability, attendance, or attitude	59	61	57	65
Percentage considered worthy of rehire	50	42	36	52

Another study of college graduates was conducted by Strother, Schaie, and Horst (1957). When they conducted tests of 25 men and 25 women aged 70 to 88, they found that although there was some decline with age, mental ability held up generally well through the middle seventies.

Still another bit of evidence dealing with the relationship between education and general competence during the later years of life is to be found in the survey of admissions to mental institutions in New York State conducted by Malzberg (1956). There is a striking difference between persons who had a high-school education and those who did not. Individuals with less than high-school education were three times more likely than high-school graduates to be admitted to hospitals with a diagnosis of one of the mental diseases associated with senile deterioration. Again, this may be evidence that education either provides some basis for resisting the decay of senility or prepares people for the kind of life that in turn helps them to resist it.

Summary

Adolescence is a period that begins at puberty, the age at which sexual maturation gets underway. Adolescence ends when the individual begins to play adult roles, but the age at which this occurs varies greatly among cultures, social classes, and individuals. The expectations of one's society have considerably more influence on the nature and duration of adolescence than do biological processes.

In the adolescent years, physiological and safety needs move to the background, and the need for parental love is less crucial. Esteem needs become all-important, and a good deal of the behavior of adolescents is centered around gaining the recognition and acceptance of their peers. As these needs are met, self-actualizing begins, usually in terms of vocational planning and preparation. In addition to satisfying these needs, the adolescent must face and solve a series of developmental tasks such as gaining independence from parents and seeking a marriage partner.

Figure 3-4. Morale scores of workers in various age groups according to length of service. (After Hull, 1939.)

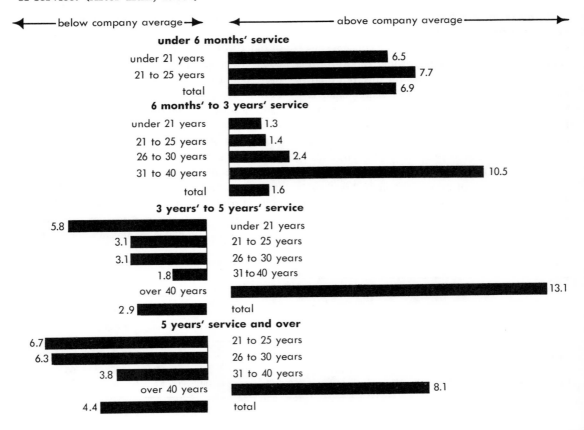

The physical aspects of adolescence involve general growth and, specifically, sexual development. Members of both sexes begin developing the secondary sexual characteristics of adults, and parenthood becomes biologically possible. Girls tend to mature about two years earlier than boys, but there are also vast individual differences within each sex. Studies have found that late-maturing adolescents face considerably more interpersonal complications than is true of early-maturing adolescents.

A major aspect of adolescent social development is the shift in interest and involvement from the family to outside groups. The conflicts that are aroused by this shift make life difficult for both the teenager and his parents. Adolescents tend to want more independence while parents tend to believe in more direction and control by adults. Many problems that arise between parents and their adolescent children could be resolved if mutual problems could be discussed in order to reach an understanding. Fortunately, the interaction between parents and offspring becomes easier and more relaxed as the later stages of adolescence are reached.

During adolescence, the individual's involvement with other people leads to two sorts of conflicting behavior. On the one hand, there is the development of empathy or the ability to see things from the point of view of other people. Probably the greatest difficulty lies in adolescents' and adults' inability to achieve empathy for each other. Conflicting with empathy is the development of increasing self-concern in adolescence, based in part on insecurity. It is not surprising that adolescence is usually an anxious period filled with a variety of problems. More anxiety is reported by girls, by rural teenagers, and by adolescents from lower-income families. Sex is an anxiety-provoking subject in our culture, and adolescents must work out their sexual adjustments in the face of embarrassment, inconsistencies, and cultural disapproval of all forms of adolescent sexual expression. Masturbation and heavy petting are common solutions, but premarital intercourse and homosexuality are also quite common in our culture.

In adulthood, the self-actualizing needs find their expression in community service, vocations, parenthood, religion, and avocations. Toward the end of the adult period, lower-level needs often resume their importance. As with adolescents, adults also face a series of developmental tasks, such as starting a family, achieving civic responsibility, and adjusting to old age.

In recent years there has been an increasing interest in the problems of marital adjustment and family life. Some people have become overoptimistic about the help which psychological tests and counseling can give in selecting a mate and in solving marital difficulties. The greatest help which psychologists can offer at the present time is through counseling during the course of marriage, part of the task being to help open channels of communication between husband and wife. Adults must face a series of emotional problems, with each period of life bringing characteristic types of difficulties. The later years tend to pose a special challenge for which education seems to be an invaluable resource.

Questions

1. In what ways is the adolescent period different for individuals in different social classes in this country?

2. What are some of the specific ways in which adolescents fulfill needs for self-esteem and for self-actualization?

3. What sorts of interpersonal relationships might arise in a typical junior high school class in which there are early- and late-maturing boys and girls?

4. The problems involved in achieving independence are difficult for both teenagers and their parents. How might families solve some of these difficulties?

5. Discuss the ways in which adolescents reveal the presence or the absence of empathy in their interactions with others.

6. Why would there be an inverse relationship between empathy and self-concern?

7. List some of the problems common to teenagers and suggest several alternate ways to go about finding a solution for each.

8. Discuss the pros and cons of the statement, "Our culture should provide an adequate way to handle the sex drive in adolescence."

9. In what ways do the opportunities for self-actualization differ at different periods of adult life?

10. Indicate some of the factors that contribute to marital happiness and to marital unhappiness.

11. What are the typical concerns of adults in their 20's, 30's, and after 40? Why do these concerns differ at various age levels?

Suggestions for further reading

Jersild, A. T., *The Psychology of Adolescence*. New York: Macmillan, 1957. One of the best of the several standard textbooks in this field.

Levy, J. and R. L. Monroe, *The Happy Family*. New York: Knopf, 1938. A warm and human book about the problems and experiences of married life. Sane, balanced, and readable. Written for a lay audience.

Pressey, S. L. and R. G. Kuhlen, *Psychological Development through the Life Span*. New York: Harper, 1957. Surveys the span of life from birth to old age under a variety of headings. Organized and written in such a way as to facilitate the understanding of the continuity of behavior.

Remmers, H. H. and D. H. Radler, *The American Teenager*. Indianapolis: Bobbs-Merrill, 1957. The attitudes, problems, and feelings of high-school students polled by Remmers and his associates during the years since World War II.

Strang, R., *The Adolescent Views Himself*. New York: McGraw-Hill, 1957. A textbook based in part on reports written by teenagers, describing themselves.

Wattenberg, W. W., *The Adolescent Years*. New York: Harcourt, Brace, 1955. Another good textbook in this field. Contains case material. Particular stress on the social factors in development.

White, R. W., *Lives in Progress: A Study of the Natural Growth of Personality*. New York: Dryden, 1952. Case studies of three normal adults, studied first as college students and again five to ten years later.

PART THREE

BASIC PRINCIPLES OF BEHAVIOR

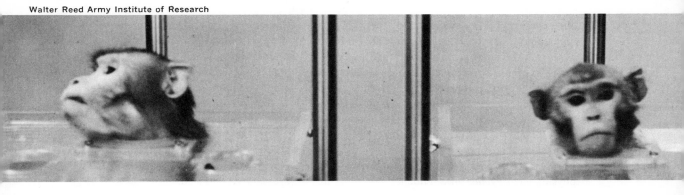

4

Physiological
processes

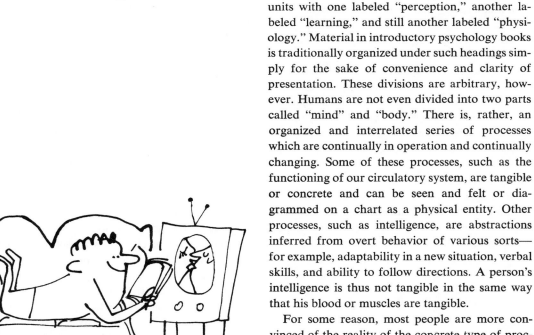

The reality of psychological processes. Most psychologists conceive of each aspect of human behavior as resulting from the more or less organized functioning of the entire organism. Man is not made up of a series of separate and distinct units with one labeled "perception," another labeled "learning," and still another labeled "physiology." Material in introductory psychology books is traditionally organized under such headings simply for the sake of convenience and clarity of presentation. These divisions are arbitrary, however. Humans are not even divided into two parts called "mind" and "body." There is, rather, an organized and interrelated series of processes which are continually in operation and continually changing. Some of these processes, such as the functioning of our circulatory system, are tangible or concrete and can be seen and felt or diagrammed on a chart as a physical entity. Other processes, such as intelligence, are abstractions inferred from overt behavior of various sorts— for example, adaptability in a new situation, verbal skills, and ability to follow directions. A person's intelligence is thus not tangible in the same way that his blood or muscles are tangible.

For some reason, most people are more convinced of the reality of the concrete type of processes than of the abstract. In fact, natural sciences which deal with "real" subject matter like chemicals, planets, atomic bombs, and anatomy usually attain greater public recognition and prestige than the behavioral sciences which deal with "theoretical" and abstract subject matter like culture, political beliefs, inflation, and creativity. It is obvious to scientists, however, that all events that can be objectively observed and measured are equally real and equally appropriate for scientific study. In physics, energy that is inferred from various observable events is as real as a lever, which may be perceived directly. In psychology, memory, which is inferred from certain sorts of behavior, is as real as the brain, which may be perceived directly.

However, these cultural biases lead to "common sense" misunderstandings and confusions. For example, most people are well aware that physiological events may influence our thinking, our mood, and our general outlook. The feelings that accompany a toothache, nausea, fever, or extreme hunger leave us with little doubt of the reality and importance of our physiological processes. Yet, the idea that feelings or thoughts can influence physical processes commonly meets with disbelief, incredulity, and skepticism. Although most of us can accept the evidence provided by specific examples like those in the following section, the general concept that psychological processes may have physiological effects is so much at odds with "common sense" that we have difficulty in accepting it.

Relationships between physiological and psychological processes. Sawrey and Weisz (1956) put rats in a situation where for one month they were subjected to an anxiety-provoking conflict each time they wished to eat. As a result, the rats developed the painful holes in the lining of their stomachs that we call gastric ulcers. A dentist applies force to a diseased tooth and yanks it out of the mouth of a wide awake patient, but there is no pain because the patient was given a posthypnotic suggestion under hypnosis that he would feel nothing. Two asthma patients reacted with attacks of asthma when they inhaled air containing grass pollen and house dust via an inhalation apparatus in the laboratory. In the course of further experiments, it was found that the substitution of pure oxygen would also cause asthmatic spasms. After a while, all the experimenters had to do to induce asthmatic attacks was to fit the inhalation mouthpiece on the patients and pretend to connect it. (Dekker, Pelser, Groen, 1957.) Consider the cases of a pair of identical twins, men in their mid-forties. Both have similar backgrounds, physiology, and personality patterns; both are shy, anxious, and inclined to depend on others. One of the twins has had a serious ulcer for the last eight years; the other has none. The twin with the ulcer began developing symptoms when his wife had an

affair with another man, experienced a severe nervous breakdown, and threatened to kill their children. Although his difficulties with his wife are somewhat diminished, they still persist, as do the ulcer symptoms also. The other twin married a woman who manages the family and accepts his need to depend on her. (Pilot and Lenkoski, 1957.) It would seem from the foregoing examples that such "intangibles" as anxiety, false perception, suggestion, frustration, and hypnosis are very real indeed.

Disbelief in the reality of psychological processes has considerable influence when it comes to the approach that is used in understanding human behavior. Many individuals, including some scientists, believe that since man's most basic and essential needs are physiological it must therefore follow that his behavior is dominated by a need to maintain physiological processes. According to this point of view, any understanding of man's behavior must be based on a knowledge of physiological functioning and must be described in physiological terms. However, as we demonstrated in the two preceding chapters, man's needs begin at a very early point in his development to extend beyond the merely physical. To use an analogy, the proper functioning of an engine is a basic need —a need that must be met—if an automobile is to be used as a means of transportation. Yet it is possible to gain a good working understanding of a good many aspects of an automobile without having much knowledge of how its engine functions. It is quite possible, for example, to learn how to drive an automobile, to teach others to drive, and to understand the regulations governing the operation of motor vehicles without ever having lifted the hood and looked at the engine. A knowledge of mechanics is a useful, but not an essential, skill for the automobile driver.

Nevertheless, any understanding of human behavior is necessarily incomplete without some knowledge of the way in which physiological processes are related to other aspects of our experience. Human behavior does not exist in isolation from bodily processes. Each behavioral act has physiological as well as psycho-social aspects. At times the physiological aspects dominate the scene; at other times they seem far removed.

The way in which these various aspects of behavior interact is indicated by some research into the causes of duodenal ulcers—ulcers of the upper part of the intestine, where it connects with the

Ronnie approaches the kitchen stove, opens the oven door, feels a blast of hot air,

breaks into tears,

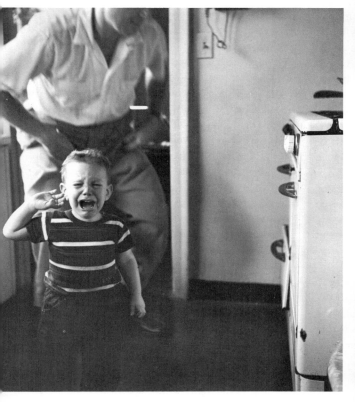

and is comforted by his father, who tells him that children should stay away from stoves.

How can we classify these events? Are they physiological? Psychological? Or are "physiological" and "psychological" merely different aspects of any given behavioral event?

Photographs by Suzanne Szasz.

stomach. A study was made of 2073 army inductees, and the 63 having the greatest amount of gastric secretion and the 57 having the least amount of secretion were identified. The two groups were then subjected to x-ray and psychological testing. X-ray examination showed that nine individuals, all of them in the first group, had active or quiescent ulcers. Psychological tests showed that these men also experienced a high degree of emotional conflict over dependency—that is, over problems related to their psychological need to be dependent on others. The researchers concluded that three factors were necessary to the development of ulcer: a high rate of gastric secretion, a particular kind of personality pattern, and some kind of situation that would prove to be upsetting and frustrating to the emotional needs of the individual concerned. (Weiner, Thaler, Reiser, and Mirsky, 1957.)

Rationale of this chapter. The major part of the discussion in this chapter will be devoted to a description of various aspects of human physiological structure and function. It is obvious, of course, that only a very brief overview of this area of physiology is possible within the space of one chapter. Nevertheless, we have tried to touch at least on those aspects which are of greatest importance in understanding human behavior.

We have organized our discussion according to the stimulus-drive-response schema to be presented in Chapter 5. In other words, we shall consider in sequence the physiological processes that are involved in receiving stimulation, the nervous system that integrates connections between stimuli and responses, and the muscles and glands that are involved in responding to stimuli. The physiology of motivation will then be discussed briefly as a way of drawing together these three areas of functioning. The chapter closes with a review of the ways in which physiological and psychological factors interact to produce various kinds of behavior.

Physiological aspects of perception

Man's only contact with his environment takes place through the activity of certain specialized cells located in various parts of the body. Cells forming the back layer of our eye and which are sensitive to certain wavelengths of light enable us to see. Other cells lining our inner ear, sensitive to certain frequencies of air molecule vibration, enable us to hear. Other cells, more widely scattered, react to particular types of molecular activity, and thus make it possible for us to feel temperature changes. These and other perceptual activities are transmitted to our central nervous system, and we attempt to make the appropriate response. Without the ability to perceive, living organisms would be isolated islands of tissue incapable of any sort of interaction with one another or with their environment. Life, as we conceive it, is not possible without perception, and perception depends on the functioning of our sense organs.

Vision. Although the characteristics and behavior of light are far from completely explained by physicists, one point of view that is commonly held considers it to consist of radiant energy possessing wavelengths within a certain range. Light that is visible to the human eye (within the visible spectrum) has a wavelength between 400 and 800 millimicrons.[1] Just beyond the visible spectrum are ultraviolet and infrared rays. Although they cannot be seen, their presence can be registered on various kinds of devices. Figure 4-1 shows how a ray of white light can be passed through a glass prism, which breaks it down into a full range of wavelengths of radiant energy, which we then perceive as the color bands of the visible spectrum. As each wavelength impinges on our optical apparatus, we perceive it as a color, and the various hues and shades that we perceive in our

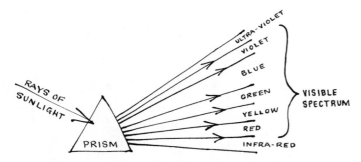

Figure 4-1. Refraction of white light into its component wavelengths. White light (e.g., sunlight) can be broken down into separate wavelengths by passing it through a glass prism. The prism accomplishes this by bending the shorter waves (e.g., the violets) more than the longer ones (e.g., the reds).

[1] A millimicron (mμ) is one-thousandth of a millimeter, a millimeter is one-thousandth of a meter, and a meter is 39.37 inches.

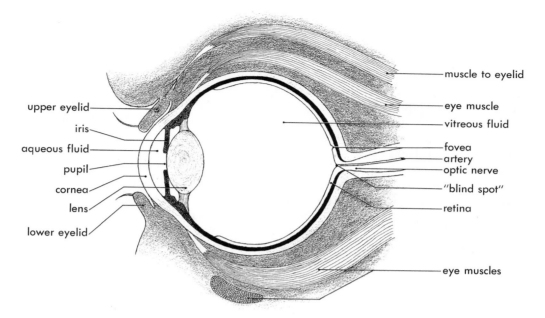

Figure 4-2. The human eye. (After Schifferes, 1960.)

physical environment consist of various mixtures of wavelengths.

The human eye is one of the most highly developed light receptors in the animal world. Light energy passes first through the cornea, then through an adaptable hole in the iris called the pupil, and is focused by the lens on the sensitive back surface (the retina) of the eyeball upside down and backwards. This perceptual information is then passed to the brain by way of the optic nerve. Figure 4-2 presents a diagram of the human eye.

The fovea is a small depression in the retina where the light rays are focused; it is thus the point of clearest and sharpest vision. Cells of a particular type, termed *cones,* are found concentrated at the fovea and in lessening numbers in the more distant portions of the retina. Cones are sensitive to all light and are essential to color or chromatic vision. Cells of a second type, termed *rods,* are more numerous in the distant portions of the retina. Rods respond to brightness but not to color and hence give us achromatic vision. In daylight or in a bright room we respond mainly to stimulation received by the cones; in darkness it is rod vision that we utilize. This is the reason that it is easier to see an object at night if we look slightly to one side so that the rods may be used, rather than straight at it, which places the burden on the cones.

Hearing. As with vision, man is not able to perceive all possible frequencies of sound waves. We are able to hear vibrations ranging from about 20 to 20,000 cycles per second. Other organisms have different auditory ranges. There are special whistles (known as Galton whistles) that emit frequencies beyond 20,000 cycles; a dog may respond eagerly to this noise while its owner hears no sound at all. There are instruments that enable us to extend our auditory range. For example, very sensitive microphones have been developed which pick up extremely faint sounds. And as all mystery fans know, even an inverted water glass placed against a wall will make the sound in the next room perceptible.

The part of the body that we commonly refer to as "the ear" is only the crudest and most external portion of our complex organ of hearing. Sound waves are trapped by the external ear, pass through the auditory canal of the outer ear, and reach the middle ear. There, vibrations are set up in the thin membrane of the ear drum which in turn puts several tiny bones (with the descriptive names "hammer," "anvil," and "stirrup") into motion. Their vibrations are then transmitted to the liquid-filled inner ear through the oval window. The transformed sound waves next reach the cochlea which contains the Organ of Corti where minute hair cells of varying lengths (somewhat like a harp) constitute the primary receptors of auditory stimulation. They transmit the signals to tiny nerve fibers and thence to the auditory nerve which leads to the brain. A diagram of the ear is shown in Figure 4-3.

The exact manner in which these vibrations are translated into our experience of sound is not entirely clear. Whatever the mechanism, the process is rather astounding when one considers that minute hair-like cells bathed in liquid are able to translate vibrations of air molecules into an experience that can be recognized as a presidential address, a Tchaikovsky concerto, or the shivering sound of chalk squeaking across a blackboard.

Smell. There has been considerably more research done on vision and hearing than on any of the other sense modalities. Hence our knowledge of the sense of smell is comparatively limited. It is interesting to note that our language similarly contains a much larger proportion of terms having reference to visual and auditory experiences. Try to describe a smell or a taste. Usually, we are limited to comparisons. "It smells like rotten eggs," or "It tastes a little like chicken."

Smell is largely a matter of being able to perceive changes in odors. Odors are transmitted through any gaseous entity, such as air. We are unable to smell an odiferous liquid, for example, if our nostrils are filled with it; and, ability to smell is curtailed by a head cold when mucus fills the nasal cavities. At the upper regions of the nose lie the olfactory receptors which transmit impulses directly to the olfactory bulb of the brain.

Taste. Most of what we commonly believe to be taste is really smell. When the nostrils are blocked, it becomes clear that our perception of taste is limited to salt, sour, sweet, and bitter. Subjects who have their nostrils clamped shut and are blindfolded are unable to identify foods placed on their tongue; a raw potato and a raw apple are indistinguishable. Other aspects of the taste of food may be traced to their feel. If you have ever eaten a soggy cracker, dried bread, or spicy enchiladas, or drunk cold coffee, you know that a variety of factors influence our perception of taste.

The taste receptors consist of cells known as taste buds, arranged on the sides of several small crevices or papillae of the tongue. In order for a substance to be tasted it must be soluble, so that it can reach the taste cells hidden in these crevices. Nerves carry the impulses to various parts of the brain. The taste buds seem to be arranged on the tongue according to the nature of the taste experi-

ence they transmit. Those on the back of the tongue respond to bitter, those at the tip of the tongue are most sensitive to sweet, and sour is perceived along the sides. Sensitivity to salt is a property of buds all over the tongue. It has been found that the total number of taste buds decreases with age. This is one of the reasons why older people often lose interest in eating, want more salt in their soup, and feel that "food just doesn't taste as good as it used to."

The skin senses. Tiny receptors scattered all over our body are sensitive to the energy changes that we experience as coldness, warmth, pain, and pressure. A good deal of work has been done to map the exact spots on the skin where these four types of receptors lie. Pain spots seem to be fairly stable in their location on the skin, but the other three appear to move about.

Psychologists have tried to identify particular types of cells that correspond to particular types of skin perception. The findings are far from simple, but certain generalizations are reasonably accurate. Pain seems to be transmitted by free nerve endings. Where these structures are absent (as in the brain) we are unable to feel pain even though the tissue may be cut or pinched. Pressure is received and transmitted by Meissner corpuscles, cells which lie close to hair follicles and by Pacinian corpuscles. The precise cells responsible for sensitivity to cold and heat are unknown. It is possible that they are on the walls of blood vessels or that free nerve endings transmit thermal changes. Further research is needed to clarify the precise way in which we are able to perceive variations in warmth and coldness.

Perception of internal stimulation. Another type of perception consists of our ability to be aware of the positions of various parts of our body without having to look at them. You are able to touch the tip of your nose with your finger even though your eyes are closed. You can walk without having to look to see which leg is up and which is down. This type of perception is called *kinesthesis.* Receptors that yield the kinesthetic experience consist of cells lying in various muscles, tendons, and joints. Movement of these body parts results in pressure on the receptors, which send their messages to the central nervous system.

We also know whether we are right side up or upside down, whether we are moving and in which direction. This perception is termed static sensitivity. Within the inner ear lie structures called

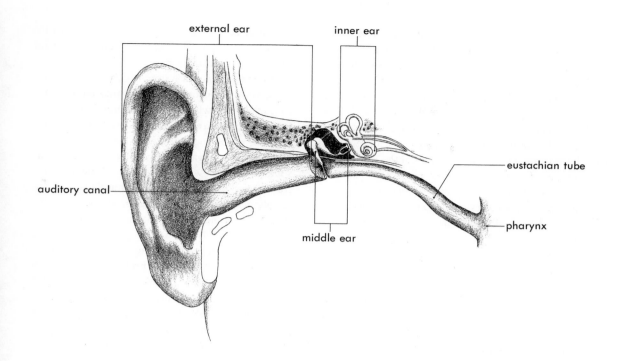

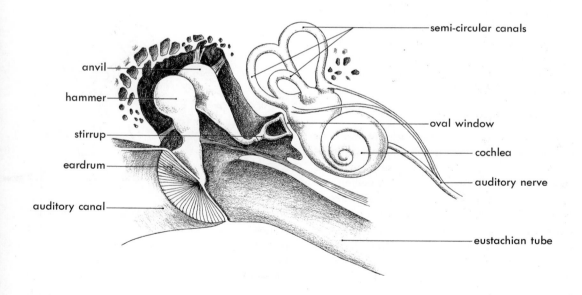

Figure 4-3. The human ear. (After Schifferes, 1960.)

the semicircular canals and the vestibule. There are three semicircular canals, each lying approximately at right angles to the others. Tiny hairs at the base of each canal are bent by sudden movements of the head; associated nerve fibers carry the message to the brain. The vestibule is lined with hairs weighted with tiny stone-like particles called *otoliths*. Up-down, front-back, or right-left body movement produces otolith movements which, in turn, arouse nerve impulses. Prolonged stimulation of the semicircular canals and vestibule may lead to dizziness and vomiting, especially if the individual is not accustomed to the activity. It is this disturbance which results in sea sickness, car sickness, and the "sinking feeling" in the pit of one's stomach brought on by the rapid descent of an elevator.

Some of the most important, and unfortunately, least understood perceptual processes are those occurring deep inside our bodies. We have been able to amass some data concerning the kinesthesic and the static senses, but what about the internal stimulation that results in headaches, stomach cramps, thirst, hunger, sexual craving, pressure in the bladder and colon, nausea, or the aching misery of a cold? While the receptors for deep pain undoubtedly mediate some of these experiences, there are probably other sorts of receptors involved. We might suppose that our understanding of behavior will be greatly advanced when we know more about these various sorts of internal stimulation and their perception.

The nervous system

The integrating function of the nervous system. No sense organ is able to function independently. We may say that we "smell with our nose" or "hear with our ears," but smelling and hearing involve far more of our physical structure than the organs that receive the stimuli that we recognize as odors or sounds. The characteristic impulses that each sense organ collects stimulate nerve endings which in turn transmit their "messages" along the nerve fibers that connect them with the central nervous system. Visual information is received by the eye and transmitted to the brain by way of the optic nerve; sound waves are translated into impulses traveling over the auditory nerve to the brain; pain is sensed when free nerve endings are stimulated and the impulses are sent through the spinal cord and up through the lower brain centers. These facts sug-

gest that part of the function of an organism's nervous system is the reception and transmission of stimulus information.

It is man's nervous system which makes possible the coordination or integration that enables him to respond as a whole. The human nervous system has been compared to an intricate telephone network in which incoming messages are picked up by the sense organs, relayed to the brain and spinal cord from which new "action" messages are transmitted to the appropriate muscle tissue. The telephone analogy is an appropriate one for relatively simple neural activity such as that which causes your leg to jerk when a physician taps your knee with his rubber hammer. However, most of the functioning of man's brain is too complex to be explained simply as a relay switchboard. Rather, it is like an electronic computer, only more complicated than the largest computers yet built. The nature of our own electronic circuits, storage units, etc. is being studied intensively in an effort to understand just how they operate.

The brain itself is a mass of nervous tissue. The information that is constantly being received from the sensory outposts is interpreted, analyzed, stored away, and, if appropriate, acted upon.

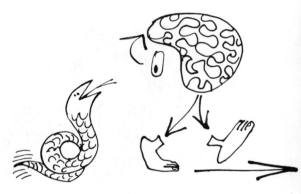

Nerve impulses are sent out to muscle tissue which responds accordingly. Certain stimulus-response patterns, called reflexes, are built-in and seem to be mediated by nerve centers in the spinal cord rather than in the brain. You touch a hot saucepan on the stove; the heat stimulus activates temperature and pain receptors in the fingers, and the message is sent at a rapid speed along nerve fibers to the spinal cord. The message is then transmitted to another set of nerve fibers which lead to muscles in the arm and fingers; the appropriate muscles contract, and your hand pulls away from the hot pan. When the message passed through the spinal cord, an auxilliary set of impulses passed upward to the brain, and you became conscious of the pain. The speeds involved in this neural activity are so rapid that it seems as if all of these events take place instantaneously. Reflexes are inherited stimulus-response patterns which serve to protect the organism: objects approaching our eye stimulate the blink reflex, pain stimulates a withdrawal reflex, loss of balance stimulates a complicated reflex in which we try to right ourselves, and so on. Other stimulus-response patterns that apparently operate in an almost identical way are the product of well-learned associations. An experienced automobile driver steps on an imaginary brake with his right foot in an emergency even when someone else is driving; a good athlete learns a series of reflexlike activities, such as diving for a fumbled football or rotating a tennis racket for a backhand shot, and an adult in our culture automatically shakes hands when presented with the stimulus of another person's outstretched arm.

Most of our stimulus-response patterns, however, are not reflexive in nature. Stimulus impulses are transmitted to our higher brain centers, where they set up cerebral activity which may or may not lead to an overt response. There may be a long delay before the response occurs, and the particular response evoked may vary from one situation to another. The exact physiological processes that occur in the brain when we perceive, consider, decide, learn, remember, and perform any of the other myriad cerebral activities are still matters of controversy. (Köhler, 1958.) A friend asks you what you plan to do this evening. You think about studying or going to a movie or bowling or cleaning out your closet. Finally you decide that you would like to read the new science fiction book you bought at the drug store. You say: "Oh, I guess I'll stay home and read tonight." It should be clear that this behavior sequence was *not* simply a reflex; much more complex sorts of processes were involved. It is just this type of complex process that distinguishes us from the other animals and makes our intellectual ability infinitely superior to even the most intelligent members of any other species.

Peripheral nervous system. Our nervous system consists of about ten billion highly specialized cells called *neurons.* There are three somewhat different types of neurons which serve different functions. Sensory neurons lead from the organs of perception, association neurons transmit information within the brain and spinal cord, and motor neurons transmit outgoing messages to muscles and glands. The three types of neurons are depicted in Figure 4-4. The length of these cells varies from a fraction of a millimeter to well over three feet. Hundreds and even thousands of the sensory and motor nerve fibers are bundled together in a sort of insulated cable which we call a nerve.

The peripheral nervous system consists of those nerves that lie outside of the spinal cord and brain. It is made up of sensory and motor neurons. The motor neurons are divided into those leading to the skeletal muscles (such as in the arms and legs) and those that lead to the visceral muscles (such as in the intestines) and glands. The second type of neurons make up what is called the *autonomic nervous system.* The autonomic is a "primitive" system, which functions automatically, more or less beyond our conscious control. It regulates the processes necessary to maintain blood pressure and body temperature, digestion, salivation, as well as those involved in sexual orgasm, perspiration, etc. This system is divided into the sympathetic and parasympathetic divisions both of which have fibers leading to most organs and which have somewhat opposite effects. The sympathetic system tends to operate in stress situations, whereas the parasympathetic governs regular activity. For example, the sympathetic increases heart rate when danger threatens; the parasympathetic slows down the heart for normal functioning.

Central nervous system. The central nervous system is made up of association neurons, which form the spinal cord and brain. The spinal cord is a long tube, the narrow hollow center of which is filled with spinal fluid. The spinal cord becomes larger as it passes the neck, and its upper portion is called the brain. The lower part of the brain is known as the *brain stem,* made up of the *thalamus* (a sort of relay station for all sensory information except smell) and the *hypothalamus* (the highest center for such reflex behavior as temperature control and for certain activities like sleep and hunger). The *cerebellum* functions to coordinate and integrate many sensory and motor activities; probably it serves other functions as well, but further research is needed to determine what they are. Finally the *cerebral cortex* is the familiar folded, wrinkled brain tissue that is essential for human intelligence, learning, foresight, planning, worry,

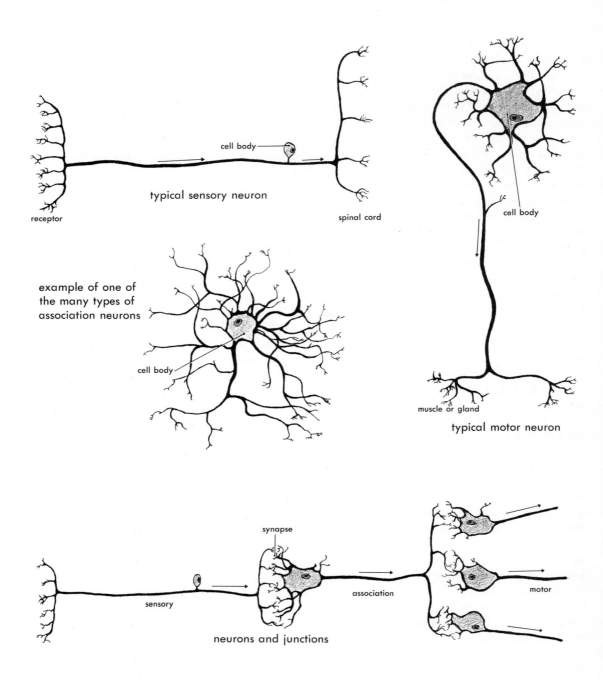

Figure 4-4. The three types of neurons. (After Munn, 1951.)

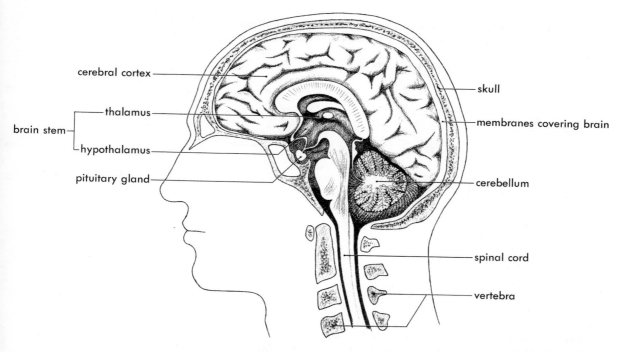

Figure 4-5. The human brain. (After Schifferes, 1960.)

creativity, and so on. Figure 4-5 shows a diagram of the human brain.

Discovering the precise functions carried on in various portions of the cerebral cortex has been a slow and difficult process, a process that is far from complete. A variety of research methods have been utilized. Nerve pathways have been traced into the brain in order to find out which area of the cortex receives fibers from the optic nerve, for example. Specific brain regions of experimental animals have been destroyed in order to discover which aspects of their subsequent behavior are affected. Similar observations are made of humans who have accidentally lost portions of the cortex through accident or disease. Finally, electrical stimulation has been applied to specific brain areas in both man and lower animals in order to determine what sort of behavior results. Through such research, physiologists and psychologists have been able to locate specific areas of the cortex which deal with vision, hearing, speech, the skin senses, motor control, reading, smell, etc. Most of the connections between the cortex and bodily functions involve opposite sides of the body; movement of the right hand is controlled by a portion of the left side of the cerebral cortex.

The integration of sensory and motor activities. The smooth coordination and integration of human activity is a function of the constant interaction of sensory, neural, and motor processes. In general, stimulus information is picked up by receptors in all parts of the body and is relayed to both the cerebral cortex and the cerebellum. "Messages" directing the appropriate response originate in the cerebral cortex and are sent on to the relevant muscles by way of the cerebellum. This detour is an important one, because it allows the "message" to be altered to whatever extent coordinated functioning requires. The cerebellum is receiving continual feedback or "reports" about the ongoing activity from receptors in the muscles. Thus it maintains a constant control over the appropriateness of the "orders" from the cerebral cortex. Figure 4-6 illustrates some of the nerve pathways that make this coordination and integration possible. An injury to the cerebellum would obviously result in profound disruptions in muscle tonus, coordination, and equilibrium. It occasionally happens that individuals who have suffered damage in this area of the central nervous system have been mistakenly arrested for drunkenness.

Figure 4-6. Patterns of interaction linking the cerebellum, the cerebral cortex, and various muscles, organs, and sensory nerves. (After Snider, 1958.)

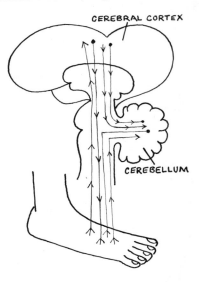

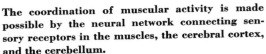

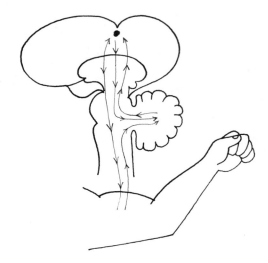

The coordination of muscular activity is made possible by the neural network connecting sensory receptors in the muscles, the cerebral cortex, and the cerebellum.

A similar sequence of neural interaction coordinates the sensations of touch, hearing, and vision. Circuits like these become activated when we engage in any activity requiring the coordination of touch and movement, such as searching for a coin in a pocket, feeling for a keyhole on a dark night, or testing the texture of various kinds of cloth.

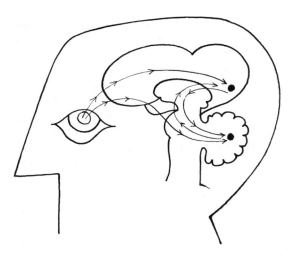

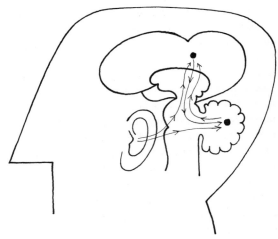

Feedback is particularly important in the many complex activities involved in vision. We turn our eyes toward an object we wish to see and follow it with our eyes as it moves about. We blink when anything approaches our eyes or when a speck of foreign matter comes in contact with our eyeball. The shutters of the iris close down when the light becomes bright, and we squint in order to protect our visual apparatus from being injured by too much light.

Hearing also causes us to look toward the source of the stimulus. A horn blast causes us to jump out of the way of a moving car. This diagram shows data from the auditory nerves being relayed to the cerebellum and to the hearing center of the brain.

Brain waves. An electronic amplifying system attached to the head of a human being will show that the brain is constantly generating waves of electrical energy. The machine that detects this activity is called an electroencephalograph, or EEG machine. The nature of brain waves differs during sleeping and waking, in childhood and adulthood, in healthy and diseased brain tissues. When brain waves were first discovered, some people were excited about the possibility of isolating "thought waves," but actually brain waves seem simply to reflect changes in the electrical potential of brain cells. They have proven useful primarily in the diagnosis of certain pathological conditions such as epilepsy. A few brain wave patterns are shown in Figure 4-7.

The physiological aspects of response

Voluntary muscles. Part of the motor neurons lead to the *skeletal* (striated, striped) or *voluntary* muscular system. The axons of these nerve cells branch out as they reach the muscle tissue, and each tiny hair-like portion of the end-brush leads to one muscle fiber. These muscle fibers are gathered together in tough elastic bundles which contract in length when the fibers receive a nerve impulse. When the muscles are contracted, the bones to which they are attached are moved. As

we voluntarily contract our left biceps muscle, our left forearm bends upward. The opposite motion of straightening the arm takes place when we send nerve impulses to the triceps on the back of the arm; these muscles contract and pull our arm straight again. Muscles act only in this contracting or "pulling" motion; they are unable to "push." Such sets of opposing voluntary muscles are located throughout our body and make it possible for us to use our arms, hands, and legs, to turn our head and trunk; and to speak when we choose to do so. It should be noted that the contraction of these muscles may be involuntary at times—as in the knee jerk.

Involuntary muscles. The most primitive of our muscles are the *visceral* (nonstriated, smooth) or *involuntary* ones. They contain strands that change shape and cause the muscle to contract. These muscles are found in such places as the stomach, intestines, arteries, and veins. Their action is automatic, and we are usually not even aware of their activity. These muscles are involved in the rhythmic contraction of our stomach during digestion, the activity of our intestines, vomiting, the contraction or dilation of blood vessels in cold or heat, etc. A third type of muscle, the *cardiac* or heart muscle, is really an intermediate type because it represents a special class of striated

Figure 4-7. Electroencephalogram records at different levels of excitation. The deep, regular waves with the narrow valleys and sharp spikes are the "alpha" waves, characteristic of a brain at rest. When the brain responds to sensory input, produced by opening the eyes or by touching something, the wave pattern changes. Changes also take place when the subject is asked to concentrate on a problem. (After Eccles, 1958.)

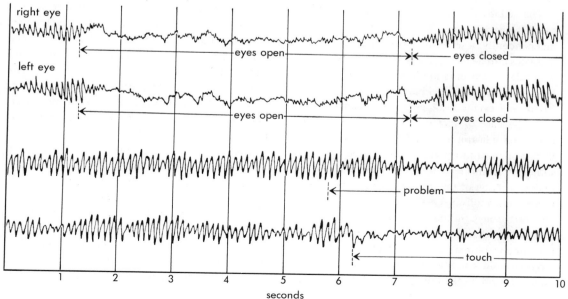

muscle, but one which is not under voluntary control. The rhythmic contraction and relaxation of this muscle keep the blood circulating throughout the body.

Duct glands. Some of the motor neurons go to glands rather than to muscle tissue. As with muscles, there are two types of glands. The *duct glands* empty their contents through small tubes or ducts into various body areas. The salivary glands pour saliva into the mouth; this secretion acts to moisten food and to digest carbohydrates. Other duct glands pour gastric juices into the stomach; the acid breaks down protein and thus makes it available for use in our body cells. The gall bladder empties its contents into the intestines and breaks down fatty foods. These and other duct glands serve an important purpose in maintaining human functioning. However, the second type of gland is even more important.

Ductless glands. The *ductless* or *endocrine glands* pour their secretions directly into the blood stream. Each endocrine manufactures a specific chemical product known as a hormone, and most secrete more than one hormone. These secretions, even in minute quantities, regulate and influence many bodily activities, including the functioning of other endocrine glands. The interactions between these glands is quite complex and not entirely understood at present. Some hormones act to inhibit or speed up the work of certain enzymes; these enzymes in turn act as catalysts that help bring about various chemical activites of the body such as the breakdown of glucose into a form that our cells can burn to obtain energy.

The *islands of Langerhans* are tiny glands located in the pancreas. They operate more or less independently in secreting insulin, a hormone that regulates blood-sugar level. When insulin secretion is deficient, as occurs in diabetes, the blood-sugar level rises and the individual feels depressed, confused, and eventually lapses into a coma.

In the base of the neck is the *thyroid* gland. It secretes a hormone called *thyroxin*, which contains a high proportion of iodine; diets that lack sufficient iodine lead to thyroid deficiency. The major function of the thyroid gland is the regulation of metabolism. Overproduction of thyroxin (hyperthyroid condition) results in an accelerated metabolism characterized by weight loss, nervousness, and insomnia. Underproduction of thyroxin (hypothyroid condition) slows down the metabolic rate and leads to the gaining of weight, slug-

gishness, fatigue, and a general feeling of weakness. Thyroid activity is measured by the basal-metabolism test, which determines the rate at which a resting individual uses oxygen. Thyroxin also influences heart rate and is important in growth.

Embedded in the thyroid but independent of it are the four *parathyroid* glands. The hormone from the parathyroid regulates the level of calcium and phosphorus content in the blood. Either a severe dietary deficiency in calcium or parathyroid disfunction results in severe convulsive seizures and eventually death. A mild deficiency in calcium may lead to irritability, extreme tension, and antisocial attitudes. (Podolsky, 1955.)

Just above each kidney lie two endocrine glands, the *adrenal medulla* and the *adrenal cortex*. The medulla secretes adrenalin when the individual is strongly disturbed emotionally; this hormone, along with the activity of the sympathetic nervous system, interrupts digestion, increases blood pressure, steps up the liver's output of sugar, speeds the heart rate, constricts blood vessels, causes the blood to clot more rapidly, and relaxes the intestinal muscles. The adrenal cortex produces at least twenty different hormones. Some regulate carbohydrate metabolism; an excess of these hormones is sometimes helpful in fighting disease and also leads to a feeling of well-being and to overactivity. Underproduction leads to exhaustion and a depressed feeling. Other hormones of the cortex regulate our salt balance, and deficiency in this hormone results in an abnormal craving for salt. Sex hormones are also secreted by the adrenal cortex; overproduction can lead to the very early development of puberty or to the development of the secondary characteristics (voice, facial hair, body shape, etc.) of the opposite sex. When the adrenal cortex is removed, less food and water are consumed, temperature drops, there is a lower basal-metabolism rate, pulse rate slows down, the body loses salt, and the individual experiences a general muscular weakness.

The *gonads* or sex glands have different locations in the two sexes. In females, the *ovaries* are located above the womb deep inside the body. The *testes* in males are located outside of the body cavity in a loose sack lying behind and below the penis. The gonads produce the reproductive cells (ova or sperm, as the case may be), as well as the hormones that regulate the sex drive, body shape, voice pitch, and the growth and pigmentation of

The measurement of brain
waves with an electroencephalograph.

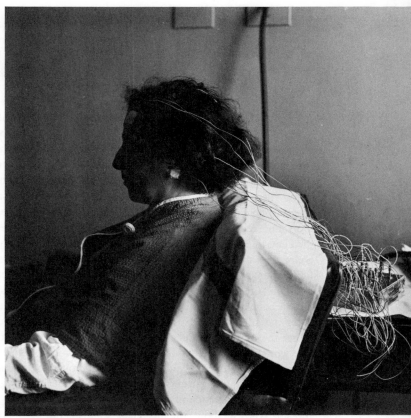

Suzanne Szasz, Medical Press

body hair. The male sex hormones also seem to contribute to aggressiveness, strength, a feeling of well-being, and some forms of baldness. Hormones from the ovaries regulate the complex female sexual functions of ovulation, menstruation, and pregnancy. Malfunctioning of the gonads may result in impaired development of sexual characteristics or development of inappropriate secondary sex characteristics.

At the base of the brain lies a small gland called the *pituitary* or "master gland." This organ is extremely important, and its functions are still being unravelled by physiologists. The anterior lobe of the pituitary produces at least six hormones. One hormone regulates the growth processes; its deficiency in childhood causes the individual to develop as a dwarf, whereas overproduction results in the person becoming a "giant" (as tall as eight or nine feet). Several of the pituitary hormones act to control other endocrine glands; one stimulates the adrenal cortex, another the thyroid, another the islands of Langerhans, and still another the gonads. The remaining pituitary secretions seem to regulate our water balance, metabolism for carbohydrates, proteins, and fats; still another regulates milk production in the mammary glands. Less is known about the posterior lobe of the pituitary, but its hormones seem to have an influence on metabolism, blood pressure, smooth muscle tonus, and water excretion.

Physiological aspects of drives

Homeostasis. Drives are aroused by either external or internal stimulation. The operation of many of our physiological drives can best be understood as functions that maintain a constant internal environment. Each of us is equipped with an interacting set of regulatory mechanisms that enable us to maintain body temperature, water balance, blood sugar, oxygen supply, blood salinity, and the like, at a relatively constant level. For example, when the external temperature goes up, we automatically perspire and are cooled by the evaporation of this liquid; the blood vessels near the skin dilate and release internal heat. When the external temperature goes down, we shiver and this muscular activity is slightly warming, blood vessels contract and conserve internal heat. This maintenance of constancy and equilibrium in our physiological world is called *homeostasis*.

Hunger. We know what it feels like to be hungry, but what are the physiological activities within our bodies that stimulate this feeling? Cannon and Washburn (1912) studied the stomach activity of subjects before and after meals and compared the stomach movements of individuals with their subjective statements about their hunger. The experimenters used two techniques: x-ray observation and a direct measure of stomach motion recorded by a swallowed balloon connected to a recording device. It was found that the sensation of hunger occurred when the stomach was contracting. However, later studies with both humans (Wangensteen and Carlson, 1931) and rats (Tsang, 1938) suggest that hunger is present even when the stomach has been surgically removed; it seems that the contractions of our stomach accompany hunger, but this is evidently not the only physiological stimulus for hunger. Possibly the level of sugar in the blood stream is related to the sensation of hunger, but the evidence is somewhat contradictory. (Morgan and Stellar, 1950.) Evidence for the existence of some sort of "hunger hormone" was found by Luckhardt and Carlson (1915), who discovered that they could cause stomach contractions in a fully satisfied dog simply by giving him a transfusion of blood from a starving dog. Probably the most important physiological factor in hunger is the activity of the hypothalamus; this portion of the brain regulates the amount of food taken into the body in relation to the amount of energy expanded. Damage to the hypothalamus of rats results in excessive overeating and obesity. (Brobeck, 1946.) It should also be obvious that in man more is involved in hunger than physiological activities. A tempting magazine advertisement or television commercial or even a vivid imagination may stimulate hunger. We also learn to like and dislike a variety of specific foods; we may find ourselves ravenously hungry for pizza but disgusted at the thought of grasshopper pie.

Thirst. It is a rather remarkable fact that a relatively constant water balance is maintained in our bodies even though we lose liquid through perspiration, respiration, and elimination and gain it through drinking quantities of fluid that may vary widely from time to time, depending on the occasion. Participating in a stimulating social gathering may increase fluid intake several hundred per cent, and involvement in an interesting task may cause one to overlook or ignore the need for fluids. The most immediate condition that stimulates our desire to drink is the dryness of our mouths and throats. However, many experiments have shown that this dryness is not the factor that regulates the amount of liquid taken in. When a sufficient amount of water is placed directly in the stomach (bypassing the mouth and throat) of a thirsty dog, after a 15-minute waiting period the dog will not drink water that is offered to him. (Bellows, 1939) The physiological factors which are responsible for the regulation of thirst and rate of urination seem to include hormones from the pituitary gland, the activity of the hypothalamus, and cellular dehydration. As with hunger, external factors, such as hearing a song about "cool, clear water," can operate to stimulate thirst. And, we may learn to prefer ice water rather than water at room temperature, or we may even bypass water when we are thirsty in favor of iced tea, lemonade, soda pop, or beer.

Need for oxygen. Our drive to maintain a constant level of oxygen and carbon dioxide in the blood is seldom frustrated; hence most of us rarely even think of this drive. Oxygen is plentiful, and few of us get into situations in which we run the risk of suffocating. However, this is obviously a vital bodily need. Again, a homeostatic process maintains constancy. If the oxygen level rises, receptors in the carotid artery and aorta are affected, and breathing slows down. If the carbon dioxide level rises (as when we are running), a portion of the brain stem is activated, and breathing is accelerated.

Elimination. Urination and defecation are, in their more primitive states, reflex mechanisms triggered by the presence of a sufficient quantity of material in the bladder or colon. We know very little about the specific stimulus receptors in those organs or the precise mechanisms that operate to activate elimination. We do know that certain species of animals inherit tendencies to eliminate in specific places and in specific ways. A cat, for example, prefers loose sandy soil in which to bury its body products. In spite of the reflexive nature of elimination, learning can modify the responses greatly in both humans and among lower animals. The difficulty we encounter in toilet training children and housebreaking dogs is convincing evidence that we are attempting to alter strongly fixed stimulus-response patterns.

Sex. The human sex drive seems to be stimulated by three classes of events: the presence of sex hormones, external stimulation, and cerebral activity (imagination, memory, etc.). Although castration or ovariectomy serves to diminish or eliminate the sex drive in lower animals, such operations apparently reduce sexual appetite of humans only if the individual is convinced that they will do so. Possibly glands other than the testes or ovaries produce sufficient kinds and quantities of sex hormones to maintain the sexual drive unimpaired. Tactile stimulation of erogenous zones (for example, genitals, lips, breasts) and visual stimulation (for example, nakedness, pornography, romantic movies) may also trigger the mechanisms that arouse sex drives. Anticipation, imagination, and memory may heighten sexual responsiveness or perform much the same function as direct stimulation.

The ways in which sexual drives are stimulated, inhibited, or expressed differ so widely among cultures and individuals that it is difficult to assign any relative weight to physiological or psychological factors. It is clear, however, that a great many aspects of sexual behavior (type of activity, choice of partner, frequency, subsequent feelings of guilt or satisfaction, etc.) are greatly influenced and modified by learning.

Sleep. The drive for sleep is a strong physiological need which increases and decreases with regularity. There seem to be individual differences in the amount of sleep needed per day. It is possible to learn certain sleeping habits such as taking naps opposed to sleeping at night only, or sleeping on a hard rather than a soft mattress. However, it is not possible to learn to do without sleep any more than it is possible to learn to do without food. As common and necessary as sleep is in our lives, there are many unanswered questions about what is involved in sleeping. We know that body activity decreases, perceptual thresholds increase, there is a loss of consciousness, and strong stimulation interrupts it. Even with decreased activity, however, we seem to remain still only about 11 minutes at a time (Johnson, Swan, and Weigand, 1930), our autonomic activities continue, brain waves change, and thinking continues in the form of dreams. The physiological basis for sleep is not entirely known. Evidence for chemical changes in the blood that induce sleep is somewhat contradictory and far from established. (Morgan and Stellar, 1950.) There seems to be a sleep center and a waking center in the hypothalamus; Ransom (1939) destroyed a portion of the hypothalamus of monkeys and caused profound sleepiness. It also seems that the activity of the cerebral cortex regulates these sleeping and waking centers to some extent; people with a damaged cortex are unable to stay awake for very long. (Davison and Demuth, 1945.) We are able to exercise some conscious control over staying awake or going to sleep, but outside stimulation is also important; sleep is not impossible amid loud noises and bright lights, but it is certainly difficult for most people.

Fear and anger. Two of the strongest emotional states, fear and anger, may also be considered as drives. They are somewhat different from the preceding drives in that they do not represent needs that increase with deprivation or which serve a homeostatic function. Rather, they are aroused by external stimuli or the thought of them and are highly subject to learning both with respect to the cues that evoke them and the way in which they are expressed in behavior. Perhaps there are also innately determined stimuli, such as the sensation of falling or of being frustrated, that trigger the emotions of fear in one case and anger in the other. Whether learned or innate, anger and fear arousal begins with the perception of drive-arousing stimuli; the autonomic nervous system is activated, and adrenalin is secreted into the blood. Several physiological changes then take place. Ax (1953) studied 43 subjects who were frightened on one occasion and angered on another. He found many physiological similarities such as increase in heart rate and some differences such as an increase in respiration rate in fear but not in anger. It seems that adrenalin is present in both emotions, and that, in addition, noradrenalin is present in anger. Other studies have found evidence to suggest that certain portions of the cerebral cortex are centers for increasing rage whereas others inhibit it. For example, cerebral operations can make cats so placid that it is impossible to get them angry, while other operations turn them into ferocious beasts who will attack anything. (Bard and Mountcastle, 1947.)

Pleasure. As important as is the drive for pleasure, there has been little systematic physiological study in this area. It is possible that pleasure results from the process of the reduction of any of the other drives. Complete satisfaction of a drive is not particularly pleasurable and may even be painful. However, pleasure is attained while the drive is being reduced; we feel pleasure while we are drinking when thirsty, eating when hungry, obtaining sexual satisfaction, drifting off to sleep, and so on. There are, of course, many learned pleasures such as listening to classical music or watching a basketball game, that may involve the stimulation and the reduction of acquired drives. Recent studies (Delgado, Roberts, and Miller, 1954; Olds and Milner, 1954) have shown the effects of electrical stimulation of the brain on motivation. Electrodes are implanted in specific areas of the brain, and the effects of stimulation on learning can be carefully studied. Among other findings, a pleasure center was discovered in the septal region of the brain; a rat will press a treadle in order to give himself a split second of electrical stimulation in this area. Some rats stimulated themselves as often as 5000 times per hour. Other studies have shown that prolonged stimulation (continued, steady impulse rather than intermittent ones) of this brain area leads to an avoidant drive, and the animal will push another device to stop the stimulation.

Relationships between physiological and psychological variables

Mind vs. body. An old problem that used to bother physiologists, philosophers, and psychologists was that of the effect of mind upon body and of body upon mind. The mind (or soul) was conceived as a mysterious force which involved such activities as thinking and imagination and memory, while body consisted of the anatomical structures. There was much speculation about these two entities; Descartes even conjectured that their point of contact was the pineal gland at the base of the brain.

Since those days, ideas have changed greatly. Psychology is no longer considered the science of the mind, but rather the science of behavior. Psychologists no longer speak of the mind as separate and distinct from the body. Instead, they recognize that all human functions are to some extent physiological, whether one considers the digestion of meat by gastric juices in the stomach or the solving of a complex problem by creative imagination. All human functions involve the activity of the central nervous system and the electrical charges that we call nerve impulses. Human functioning can also be described in nonphysiological terms like "attitude," "latent hostility," and "honesty." It is not that the mind has an attribute called "attitude about food" and the body an attribute called "hunger;" instead, these are different ways of viewing specific aspects of human behavior. Humans function as whole organisms: the division between "mind" and "body" takes place only in our *descriptions* of behavior.

What exactly does the man in the street mean, then, when he says "mind over matter," "the spirit is willing but the flesh is weak," or "my sore leg makes me irritable?" Basically, most people still use the mind-body dichotomy. Psychologists use this dichotomy as well, when they speak of "psychological" and "physiological" causes of behavior. In other words, some variables or characteristics such as acquired fear, IQ, and political values may be conveniently classified as "psychological," whereas other variables such as rate of thyroid secretion, brain tumors, and muscular strength may be classified as "physiological." There is nothing wrong with this division of variables as long as we keep in mind that it is fairly arbitrary. Although thyroid secretion is usually conceived in a physiological sense, and learning in a psychological sense, we *could* consider thyroid secretion as a behavioral act and learning as an alteration in electrical circuits in the brain. Real difficulties in classification arise at times. When certain circulatory changes occur, our faces turn white, and we pass into unconsciousness in a process known as fainting. This is easily classified as a behavior resulting from alterations in physiological variables. However, when we find that women faint more than men, that women fainted more frequently a hundred years ago than today, and that cultures are found where it is the custom for men to faint rather than women, we begin to wonder if psychological variables are not equally important. Furthermore, it is quite reasonable to study fainting behavior and its many causes without concerning ourselves with making a distinction between psychological and physiological characteristics.

Physiological variables may influence psychological variables. It was pointed out at the beginning of this chapter that the effect of physiological variables upon psychological ones is familiar to most people and rather easy to accept. Each of us has experienced a bad head cold, stomach cramps, or a severe headache and has found that our ideas, our general mood, and our overt behavior were greatly influenced by these conditions.

Many extreme physiological effects are the result of disease, anatomical irregularities, and other malfunctioning of various organs. For example, when the thyroid gland of infants fails to secrete a sufficient quantity of thyroxin (because of dis-

ease, injury, iodine deficiency, etc.), a condition known as cretinism develops. Cretins have very small, thick bodies, with stubby arms and legs, and large heads. They fail to mature sexually and are mentally deficient. However, early treatment of the thyroid condition can result in completely normal development.

Almost any factor that disrupts the functioning of the nervous system may profoundly affect human behavior. When polio makes it impossible for motor neurons to function, the resulting paralysis is extremely disruptive both in terms of helplessness and of the victim's reaction to this unfortunate situation. Even more disruptive are disorders of the brain itself. One of the possible aftereffects of syphilis is the slow destruction of brain tissue by spirochetes. The resulting disorder is called paresis and is characterized by speech disturbances, tremor, forgetfulness, carelessness, intellectual impairment, immorality, and gradually increasing personality deterioration. Brain tumor and brain injuries may cause a wide variety of behavior changes: depression, irritability, visual impairment, memory disruption, confusion, restlessness, fearfulness, loss of self-control, poor judgment, and so on.

Even in these fairly clear-cut instances in which physiological variables influence psychological ones, the nature of the resulting behavior is quite varied and quite dependent on past learning. For example, there are vast individual differences in response to polio, and there are also wide variations in response to brain damage.

Physiological variables may be correlated with psychological variables. There are instances in which relationships have been found between physiological and psychological variables but where it is so far impossible to determine whether one causes or even influences the other. For example, Levy (1942) developed an interview which could be used to classify the maternal behavior of women as high, low, and medium. He found a rather high positive correlation (.58) between the tendency to behave in a maternal way and the average duration of menstrual flow—in other words, women classified as having high degree of maternal behavior tended to have a prolonged menstrual period, whereas women demonstrating a low degree tended to have a short period. Landis (1957), in a study of 200 college girls, found that feelings of depression were common just before and just after the beginning of menstruation each month. It is not possible to state, of course, whether the depression was a direct result of endocrine changes or of learned cultural reactions to this biological process.

A good deal of interest has centered on studies that find physiological differences between normal individuals and mental patients diagnosed as schizophrenics. When compared with normal people, schizophrenics have been found to have a lower basal metabolism rate, more severe malfunctioning of sexual glands, lower blood pressure, and a lower degree of static sensitivity, as shown by the fact that they are *less* unsteady than normal people following rotation. (Hoskins, 1946.) When we consider such findings we are faced with the chicken and egg problem; which came first in schizophrenia—the physiological changes or the psychological changes?

It is, of course, possible that the tendency to develop schizophrenia may be due to the presence of inherited physiological traits. (Kallman, 1946.) It is also possible that environmental factors are the major factors producing both schizophrenia and the physiological changes (noted above) that are associated with this disorder. Psychologists face a similar problem when they try to account for patterns of behavior that are termed "antisocial" or "psychopathic." Diethelm and Simons (1945) found that individuals displaying such symptoms, when contrasted with normal people, were more likely to have abnormal brain-wave patterns, but it is difficult to say whether (*a*) the abnormal brain-waves caused the antisocial behavior; (*b*) the antisocial behavior caused the abnormal brain-wave patterns; (*c*) both the antisocial behavior and the brain-wave patterns were caused by inherited physiological characteristics; (*d*) both the antisocial behavior and the brain-wave patterns were caused by environmental factors; or, (*e*) inherited physiological factors and environmental factors interacted to produce both the antisocial behavior and the abnormal brain-wave patterns.

Some relationships have been found between the physical characteristics an individual has and his personality characteristics. Sheldon and his co-workers have suggested that fat, round individuals tend to be sociable and love comfort; that strong, muscular individuals tend to be energetic and aggressive; and that lean, fragile individuals tend to be inhibited and prefer solitude. (Sheldon and Stevens, 1942; Sheldon, Stevens, and Tucker,

1940.) The findings concerning these relationships have been somewhat inconsistent, and cause-and-effect explanations are far from certain. (Fiske, 1944; Child, 1950.) Perhaps a physiological tendency to fatness, for example, *does* produce friendliness or sociability, but an equally likely possibility is that the behavior tends to tailor itself to the limitations set by physique—that is, ". . . a fat boy has to be good-natured because he can't fight and he can't run." (Shaffer and Shoben, 1956: 383.)

Another way in which physiological differences can become related to psychological ones is through what we call social expectancy. That is, if people *expect* certain physical characteristics to be related to certain psychological characteristics, they will treat individuals in such a way as to bring about that which they expect. If parents believe that long fingers indicate musical talent as a pianist, they are more likely to give a long-fingered son a toy piano, piano lessons, and trips to piano concerts. It would not be very surprising under such circumstances if he developed an interest in and talent for the piano.

Psychological variables may influence physiological variables. At the beginning of this chapter, examples were given of psychological variables affecting physiological ones: contact with an inhalator mouthpiece setting off an asthma attack, conflict and frustration of dependency needs creating an ulcer, and hypnotism preventing pain. Other examples of this relationship are so obvious that we seldom think of them. For example, reading the newspaper headline, "Radioactivity of Drinking Water Increased by Freak Rainfall," immediately triggers a series of thoughts, accompanied by an increase in autonomic nervous system activity. We can also bring about physiological reactions by seeing an all-too-realistic horror movie, remembering an embarrassing and humiliating incident, taking a ride on a carnival loop-the-loop, or appearing in a school play.

Most of the research in this field, however, has been concerned with the effect of psychological variables on disease. Hinkle and Wolff (1957) studied almost 3000 individuals in order to find out what sorts of illnesses they had experienced and under what circumstances. They observed that illnesses are more likely to occur when an individual is having difficulty in adapting to various life problems. Illnesses do not occur randomly in people's lives, but appear in clusters which seem

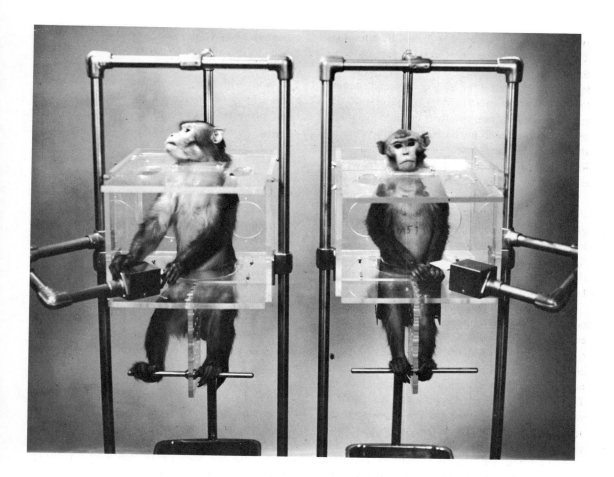

The two monkeys in the photograph above are in "restraining chairs," which permit them to move their heads and limbs, but not their bodies. Each animal receives a mild shock on the feet every 20 seconds. The monkey at the left is in an "executive" situation, because he can prevent the shock by pressing a lever. The monkey at the right also has a lever to press, but it is a dummy. The executive monkey learned very quickly that pressing his lever would prevent his being shocked; the other monkey tried pressing the lever at first but gave it up when he found it did no good. The experimental regimen consisted of 6 hours of intermittent shock and 6 hours of rest.

After 23 days of a continuous 6-hours-on, 6-hours-off schedule, the executive monkey died, even though he had seemed to be in good health. A post-mortem examination revealed a large perforated ulcer in the wall of the duodenum—the upper portion of the small intestine where it joins the stomach, a common site of ulcers among human beings. An examination of the other monkey showed it to be in perfect health. A second experiment, following the same procedure, produced much the same results—the executive monkey developed ulcers in the stomach and duodenum, and the control monkey developed no abnormal symptoms.

Although the experimenters are still investigating the various factors that produced the ulcers, it seems quite likely that a limited amount of freedom to control the environment increased the degree of emotional stress, which in turn brought about physiological changes resulting in the ulcers. (Brady, 1958.)

related to what is happening in the life situation. The most healthy people in their sample were those who were well-adapted to the circumstances in which they found themselves. Ill health seems to appear when an individual has excessive demands placed on him or when he fails to satisfy his drives and reach his goals. It should be noted that researchers in the field of psychological medicine do not attempt to deny the physiological causes of disease. For example, it seems clear that a virus (or a family of related viruses) is responsible for the common cold. Yet, most of us in any given week are probably exposed to this virus at least once; why do we catch a cold sometimes and fight it off at other times? It is in this latter realm that psychological factors (along with nutrition, fatigue, etc.) are probably of most importance.

One of the growing fields of medicine is that concerned with psychosomatic illness. Increasing evidence has shown that many well-known physical ailments result rather directly from emotional conflicts. Examples are gastric ulcers, asthma, migraine headaches, neurodermititis, and colitis. These disorders seem to appear and disappear in various individuals, in apparent relationship to the amount of stress to which they are subjected at various times. Probably several factors interact to determine whether a person develops a certain disease at a given time. Some people interpret the notion of influence by psychological variables as meaning that these diseases are "imaginary"; yet a hole in the stomach lining or a bleeding colon are quite real and may even lead to death if neglected. The most effective treatment seems to involve medical treatment of the diseased tissue combined with psychotherapy to help resolve the underlying conflicts.

Even more surprising than these findings dealing with lowered resistence to disease and psychosomatic illness are the recent studies of such physiological dysfunctions as cancer and heart disease. By the use of the Rorschach ink blot personality test, Fisher and Cleveland (1956) were able to differentiate breast cancer patients from those who had developed cancer in the cervix; the former individuals tended to view their bodies as a barrier against the world whereas the latter saw their bodies as easily penetrated or permeated. These and other studies led some workers to speculate that possibly physiological and psychological factors interact to determine an individual's susceptibility to cancer, the part of the body in which cancer is likely to develop, and the tendency of cancer to spread rapidly or to be sealed off and rendered harmless.

A study with rats gives evidence that hardening of the arteries (the precursor of heart attacks, high blood pressure, and stroke) depends on two factors: (a) stress and (b) a diet that contains a high fat content. Stress alone (in the form of intermittent electric shocks over a period of 10 months) did not increase hardening of the arteries, nor did a high-fat diet alone. However, when the two conditions were combined, the incidence of artery disease in the experimental rats was 400 per cent higher than in the control rats. (Friedman, 1958.)

Friedman and Rosenman (1959) also studied cardiovascular disease in three groups of men that were matched with respect to total calorie and fat intake, amount of physical activity, age, height, and weight, but differed in respect to psychological characteristics. Coronary artery disease was seven times more frequent in the group characterized by intense ambition, competitive drive, preoccupation with schedules and deadlines, and a sense of time urgency than it was in the other two groups.

Other physiological-psychological interactions. The types of food and liquid that we learn to take into our bodies may also have a striking influence on both physiological and psychological variables. A more balanced diet, for example, seems to account for the fact that Japanese born and raised in the United States are taller than their parents and other relatives raised in Japan. It has been found that even a slight vitamin-B deficiency (which may be characteristic of the diet of many families) over a period of six to eight weeks led to irritability, moodiness, uncooperative behavior, and vague fear. (Williams, Mason, Wilder, and Smith, 1940.) Harrell, Woodyard, and Gates (1955; 1956) found that the diet of mothers during pregnancy and breast feeding had a significant effect on the IQ of their children; women given an enriched food supplement had more intelligent children than those given a placebo (an inert substance which is used as a control).

Other sorts of influence on human functioning are brought about by drinking alcohol. Even a small percentage of alcohol in the blood stream slows down the functioning of the higher brain centers, and apparently lessens the amount of inhibitory control. The individual's anxiety level is

Although marijuana is popularly considered to be a stimulant, it is actually a depressant that has an effect similar to alcohol in the impairment of coordination and the removal of inhibitions. One of the chief sources of marijuana is Mexico, where this photograph was taken.

reduced, he usually feels happier, more friendly, and more adequate. He is more impulsive in his behavior, while his thought processes and motor coordination are impaired. With an increased intake of alcohol, unconsciousness and even death may result.

Nicotine has a variety of effects when it is introduced into the body. It apparently makes the smoker feel somewhat more relaxed and at ease. Many smokers suggest that the activities associated with smoking, such as lighting a cigarette, filling a pipe, etc., are the real reason for smoking because "it gives you something to do with your hands." However, the comparative sales figures of regular cigarettes and those with the nicotine removed gives overwhelming evidence that the drug itself is a major goal in smoking. In fact, the continued use of nicotine seems to create a craving

that is to some degree physiological. In recent years, the discovery of the relationship between lung cancer and smoking has added another problem. Although some controversy still exists, there is fairly convincing evidence that some of the elements in tobacco, such as tar, will, if taken regularly in large quantities over a long period of time, markedly increase the probability of cancer. An interesting sidelight to this problem was reported by Festinger (1957); he found that nonsmokers are more likely to believe that the relationship between smoking and lung cancer is a proven fact than are heavy smokers.

Although evidence is so far lacking with respect to the physiological damage caused by prolonged use of opium and its derivatives (heroin, morphine, codeine), there is no question but that addiction to these drugs has extremely serious psychological and sociological consequences. These drugs act to remove pain, give a feeling of relaxation and happiness, increase drowsiness, decrease sexual desire, and induce a pleasant sort of daydreaming state. After a few hours the pleasantness wears off and the individual feels "low." Continued use leads to a physiological craving for the drug, an increased tolerance level (more of the drug is needed in order to obtain the same effect), and severe, painful withdrawal symptoms if the drug is stopped. Similar results may obtain from a chronic overuse of barbiturates. Another drug, cocaine, acts as a stimulant and speeds up thinking, increases the sex drive, and prevents sleep. The continued use of cocaine can become habit forming in a *psychological* sense, but it does not cause a *physiological* craving, for there is no increased tolerance, and severe withdrawal symptoms are absent. Marijuana, usually smoked in cigarette form, is similar to cocaine in that it does not produce a physiological craving. However, it is a depressant which acts somewhat like alcohol in the impairment of coordination and the removal of inhibitions. The dangers, however, are many. Lack of impulse control may lead to reckless driving, immorality, and violence. A final danger is that many individuals are induced to try heroin while under the influence of marijuana because judgment is lacking.

We have stressed the negative aspects of drugs in the foregoing paragraphs, but they have many helpful purposes as well. The derivatives of opium are used medically to reduce pain, and barbiturates, to induce sleep and relaxation. Furthermore, the last few years have seen the development of tranquilizing drugs, which are used in various forms to reduce anxiety in normal individuals, as well as in individuals suffering from severe and chronic mental or emotional disturbance. When such drugs are used in mental hospitals, it appears that they often make it easier to aid patients through psychotherapy. This not only helps speed up the treatment for some patients, but also it enables psychiatric personnel to "reach" other patients who have so far resisted any attempts to help them. The new drugs are not a "cure" for mental illness, but they often are helpful in making patients amenable to psychological treatment.

The multicausality of behavior. So far in this chapter we have been largely concerned with the "mind-and-body" causes of behavior. We might also wonder about cultural or sociological causes.

When we see Harry, a nineteen-year-old who is addicted to heroin, what can we point out as the cause of his addiction? Is it the fact that he had learned to go along with the crowd and not be different from the group? Is it the fact that his father was too busy and his mother too anxious to give him sufficient love and closeness at home? Is it the fact that our law enforcement agencies have not been able to eradicate the traffic in narcotics? Is it because our society provides no very acceptable role for a nineteen-year-old, including no really appropriate way for him to reduce his sexual drives, meet his dependency needs, or express his hostility? Is it because he, like others in our society, fears that one day a war will come roaring from the sky in the form of guided missiles? Is it because the experience that heroin produces is so pleasant that its repetition is a strong temptation? Is it because the continued use of the drug leads to changes in cellular chemistry that make heroin a bodily need as strong, or stronger, than the need for food? Or is his addiction due to all of these causes and a dozen more besides? Thus it should be clear why psychologists avoid talking about *the* cause of a specific behavior and why the question of whether a cause is physiological *or* psychological is often not very meaningful.

Summary

Most psychologists think of human functioning as taking place in an integrated, organized way. Among the many processes that constitute man's behavior are physiological ones. Physiological structures and functions are actually no more real or basic than inferred processes such as those associated with intelligence, inasmuch as any event that can be objectively observed and measured is a real event and is appropriate for scientific study.

Perception takes place through the activity of certain specialized cells located in various parts of the body. The eye is a highly developed organ that makes it possible for us to perceive certain ranges of light waves. Images are focused by the lens on the retina, and information about size, shape, movement, and color are transmitted to the brain. A whole series of structures are necessary to carry the vibration of air molecules into our inner ear where hairlike cells in the cochlea receive it and thus allow us to perceive sound. Odor is transmitted through the air and stimulates receptors at the upper end of the nose. We taste only salt, sour, sweet, and bitter; most of what we call taste is really smell. When soluble substances are in the mouth, they stimulate taste receptors, which are in tiny crevices spread over the tongue's surface. The skin senses respond to coldness, warmth, pain, and pressure. We are also sensitive to many kinds of internal stimulation. Awareness of the movement and location of our bodily parts is made possible by kinesthetic receptors. In the inner ear, the semicircular canals and the vestibule contain receptors for static sensitivity; we know when our entire body is in motion, the direction of the motion, and whether we are right-side-up or not. Less is known about the perception of other internal stimulation such as headaches, hunger, and nausea.

The nervous system acts to integrate all bodily activity. Impulses are transmitted from sense organs to the brain and spinal cord, and then other messages are carried back to muscles and glands where responses are made. Reflexes consist of relatively simple stimulus-response patterns that are mediated by the spinal cord and lower brain centers. However, most stimulus-response activity goes through the brain where the activity is extremely complex. Nerve cells, or neurons, are divided into sensory, association, and motor types. The peripheral nervous system is divided into the voluntary and autonomic divisions; the voluntary system controls the skeletal muscles and the autonomic, the visceral muscles. The central nervous system consists of the brain and spinal cord. The brain is divided into the stem (thalamus and hypothalamus), cerebellum, and the cerebral cortex. Various experimental methods have yielded much information about the specific functioning of different portions of the brain, but much is still unknown. Brain waves reflect the electrical activity of brain cells and are recorded by the electro-encephalograph.

Motor impulses lead to muscles and glands where responses are made. Muscles are divided into voluntary and involuntary types. The former are under conscious control and enable us to move our limbs, trunk, and vocal apparatus. The involuntary muscles act automatically in carrying out the necessary movements in the stomach, intestines, circulatory system, etc. The cardiac or heart muscle is an intermediate type. Glands are also divided into two types, duct and ductless. The duct glands, such as the salivary gland, empty

their contents through small tubes into various body areas. The ductless or endocrine glands pour their secretions directly into the blood stream, exerting a powerful influence on many body functions. The endocrines and some of the functions they affect are the islands of Langerhans—blood-sugar level; thyroid—metabolism; parathyroid—calcium and phosphorus levels; adrenal medulla—emotional behavior; adrenal cortex—carbohydrate metabolism, salt balance, sexual characteristics; ovaries—female sexual functions; testes—male sexual functions; and, pituitary—growth, secretions of other glands.

Many of our physiological drives may be conceived as functions that serve to maintain a constant internal environment; this tendency toward internal constancy is called "homeostasis." The hunger drive seems to originate in a number of sources: stomach contractions, blood-sugar level, a hunger hormone, the activity of the hypothalamus, external stimulation, and learning. The maintenance of a fairly constant water balance is a remarkable bodily process; our experience of thirst is regulated by local dryness in the mouth and throat, pituitary and hypothalamus functioning, cellular dehydration, external stimulation, and learning. Our oxygen–carbon dioxide balance is regulated by still another homeostatic process. Urination and defecation are reflex mechanisms that can be modified by learning. The human sex drive depends on hormones, external stimulation, and cerebral activity. Apparently the hypothalamus contains a sleeping and a waking center that are influenced somewhat by impulses from the cortex. Fear and anger are strong emotions that may also be thought of as drives. There are several physiological similarities in their operation, probably because adrenalin is secreted in both emotions; in anger, noradrenalin is also present. Not much is known about the physiological aspects of pleasure; perhaps it is the accompaniment of any drive-reducing activity. Recent animal studies have located an area of the brain the stimulation of which seems to be pleasurable.

The mind-body problem is an old one, somewhat resolved by modern psychologists who conceive of all human functions as physiological but also recognize that nonphysiological concepts are often more appropriate in describing and predicting behavior. Psychologists often divide the determinants of behavior into psychological and physiological categories, even though they know that the division is fairly arbitrary and that many problems arise if the classification is made too rigid. Many studies show that physiological factors influence psychological factors. Thyroid deficiency, for example, may cause cretinism, and disruption of the nervous system may cause marked behavioral changes. Other studies find relationships between the two types of variables, but are unable to show which is cause and which is effect. For example, schizophrenics and normal people are often found to differ in physiological characteristics, but it is not known whether the physiological changes or the bizarre behavior appears first. The influence of psychological on physiological factors has been studied mainly with respect to the causes of certain diseases, including lowered resistance for disease in general, psychosomatic illnesses, and even such problems as cancer and heart trouble. Other studies have dealt with the effect on behavior of dietary deficiency, alcohol, tobacco, narcotics, and tranquilizers. It was concluded that any one behavior has a whole series of causes; finding these relationships is more important than classifying the causes as physiological, psychological, or sociological.

Questions

1. Give some everyday examples of the interaction between physiological processes and psychological processes.

2. List man's sense modalities and for each indicate the location of the body cells that make this sort of perception possible.

3. A small boy steps onto a hot sidewalk with his bare feet. Indicate the neural activity that takes place from the moment his foot touches the pavement until he has safely escaped the pain.

4. Draw a rough diagram of the human body, indicate the location of each endocrine gland, and label your drawing. What are the functions of each of these glands?

5. Choose one of the primary drives and suggest what sorts of physiological activities occur from a point of satiation to deprivation and back to satiation again.

6. What is meant by the mind-body problem? How is this issue usually resolved by psychologists today?

7. Discuss some of the research findings that show that psychological variables may influence physiological variables and vice versa.

8. Suggest some of the psychological and physiological factors that might induce an individual to smoke cigarettes.

Suggestions for further reading

Beach, F., *Hormones and Behavior.* New York: Hoeber, 1958. A survey of research dealing with the influence of hormones on behavior.

Cannon, W. B., *The Wisdom of the Body,* rev. ed. New York: Norton, 1939. A well-known book in which homeostasis is treated as a central concept in the understanding of behavior.

Dunbar, H. F., *Emotions and Bodily Changes,* 4th ed. New York: Columbia University Press, 1954. A standard reference work on the psychosomatic factors in illness.

Hebb, D. O., *The Organization of Behavior.* New York: Wiley, 1949. A presentation of a well-organized theory of the functioning of the brain.

Hebb, D. O., *A Textbook of Psychology.* Philadelphia: W. B. Saunders, 1958. A short, well-written introductory text which presents the viewpoint that psychology is a biological science and is neither a social science nor a profession.

Morgan, C. T. and E. Stellar, *Physiological Psychology,* 2nd ed. New York: McGraw-Hill, 1950. A somewhat difficult but fairly complete text which covers all of the major topics of physiological psychology.

Penfield, W. and T. Rasmussen, *The Cerebral Cortex of Man.* New York: Macmillan, 1950. A description of the effects of electrical stimulation of the human brain, including interesting case-history material.

Pfeiffer, J., *The Human Brain.* New York: Harper, 1955. A popular discussion of current knowledge and research dealing with brain functioning.

Stevens, S. S., Editor, *Handbook of Experimental Psychology.* New York: Wiley, 1951. See section on psychological mechanisms for thorough and scholarly discussions of the nervous system, sensory and motor mechanisms, and homeostasis. The section on sensory processes is equally thorough and scholarly.

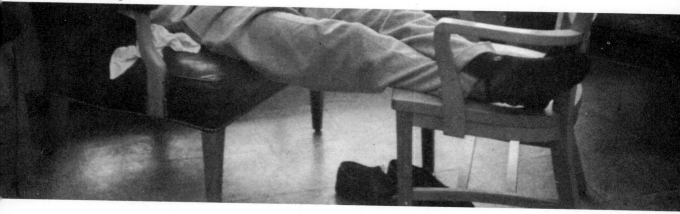

5

The learning process

Most of us tend to think of learning in terms of formal learning situations such as college lectures, dancing classes, or swimming lessons. It is obvious, however, that we were not born knowing the English language, how to button our coats, the difference between Brubeck and Brahms, or that gentlemen are expected to allow ladies to enter a doorway first. In some manner not altogether clear to most of us, we learn these and an infinite array of other behaviors.

Some learning is universal. For example, we all learn that the sun rises and sets daily. Some learning, such as the beliefs and rituals of a particular religion, we share with groups of people. Finally, some learning is unique for each individual, such as the skills and thoughts and feelings that characterize only one Albert Schweitzer and only one you. Even the spontaneous exclamation of "ouch!" when we prick our finger is learned; a Japanese may exclaim "itai!" while a Hawaiian responds with "aué!"

Learning is not only a universal phenomenon; it is the central problem in psychology. Most of the behavior that we perceive has been developed or modified through learning. Even the more obviously physiological varieties of behavior can be, as we have shown in the preceding chapter, markedly affected by attitudes, feelings, and other learned patterns of behavior. The possibilities that might develop from an understanding of learning are breathtaking, if we can conceive of its ultimate scope. If behavioral scientists can construct satisfactory laws of learning, we should be able to predict, and perhaps alter, such diverse phenomena as the behavior of rats in a maze, the development of neurotic defenses, the blind prejudice that some people feel against others of a different culture or appearance, and the hate that impels one nation to attempt the annihilation of another.

Instinctual behavior (inherited patterns of complex responses) becomes less important as life progresses up the evolutionary scale. The behavior of a garden spider is largely "built in"; she will spin her intricate web, trap and poison flies, and lay eggs like all others of her species, even if born and raised in complete isolation from other spiders. Contrast the instinctive activity of a spider with that of a cat who has considerably more freedom to learn and hence considerably more individuality. However, when you watch a cat stalk a toy mouse, clean its fur, or strengthen its shoulder muscles by scratching the living room furniture, it is clear that many of its behavioral patterns were inherited rather than learned.

A newborn baby is virtually helpless, except for its ability to cry, wriggle, make sucking movements with its mouth, and eliminate body wastes. Most of the subsequent behavior we display as children and adults is the result of learning. This fact gives mankind a marvelous freedom and range of behavior and a capacity for uniqueness that is unmatched by any of the other animals. It is man's tragedy that this freedom has brought both the Einstein theory of relativity and the Nazi cremation ovens. If psychology is able to achieve understanding of the learning process, perhaps it will be possible for the world to have more Einsteins and fewer Hitlers.

Behavior

In their attempts to analyze the learning of behavior, psychologists have found it convenient to construct what might be called a "theoretical model" of the process that occurs when learning takes place. This building of theoretical models enables them to identify various aspects and conditions that prevail at various stages of the process, as well as to conduct experiments, manipulating various factors in order to test the validity of their theories. Unfortunately for the beginning student in psychology, psychologists have not settled on any one theory regarding the nature of the learning process. They are still in the stage of theory-building and theory-testing.

There is, however, one major theory that in one form or another constitutes the basis for a large proportion of the laboratory experiments in psychology. This is a learning theory that is commonly called a "stimulus-response" (S-R) or "reinforcement" theory. Because it has played such a large part in the development of psychology as a science, we shall use a reinforcement type of S-R theory as a starting point for our discussion of learning. Perhaps we can best see how it works by applying its principles to the analysis of a bit of "real-life" behavior.

An example of behavior. Samuel Andrews is employed by a large manufacturing firm. As he sits working at his desk, various physiological changes take place in his body; his stomach begins a rhythmic contraction and there are various chemical alterations in his blood stream. Outside, the 12:00 o'clock whistle sounds. Across the room his office mate says, "Let's eat, Sam." and begins to unwrap a pungent salami and cheese sandwich. At this point, Sam stops writing, pulls open a desk drawer, grasps a paper bag, removes some of its contents, and begins to eat.

This simple scene contains all the elements of a complete behavioral act. Life is made up of an interconnected series of such acts. In each instance there is a stimulus or a set of stimuli that evoke a drive within the organism, which in turn leads to some sort of response. If the response leads to a reduction in the strength of the drive, the behavioral act is reinforced. Figure 5-1 presents these concepts schematically.

Stimulus. Behavior begins with a stimulus. A stimulus is any event that modifies behavior by producing activity in a sense organ. We live in a world of continuous stimulation, some internal and some external. A toothache is a stimulus and so is a stop sign. We respond to the smell and sound of frying bacon and to the thought that we owe a letter to a friend. A particular pattern of notes played on a piano acts as a stimulus and so does a newspaper headline. It should be noted that behavior is always the result of stimulation, but not all changes in the environment that might be expected to produce stimulation actually do so.

Drive. Most stimuli can be directly measured, but a drive cannot. Instead, a drive is a logical scientific construct. It is a hypothetical state which we infer from observing the behavior of an organism. The drive concept does not refer to an observable entity any more than do the concepts "gravity," "electron," or "intelligence." In addition to "drive," many terms have been used to label a motivational construct, such as "need" or "motive" or "energy." It was stated that a stimulus is necessary for a behavior to occur. The same statement could be made about drive but somewhat less convincingly. Perhaps psychologists could do without the concept of drive, but it has been a very convenient and useful idea.

Drives are usually classified as "primary" and "secondary." Primary or innate drives refer to motivations that are part of the biological equipment of the organism. Examples are hunger, thirst, sex, fatigue, need for oxygen, and avoidance of heat, cold, and pain. The first five are directly related to length of deprivation. Thus a man who has been without liquid for 48 hours has a stronger thirst drive than a man who has been deprived for 12 hours. The strength of the last three drives depends directly on the strength of the heat, cold, or pain stimulus. Dollard and Miller (1950) suggest that one of the functions of society is to protect man from the discomfort and compelling urgency of strong primary drives. Contrast the relative strength of these primary motives for a cave-dwelling Neanderthal man and for a modern suburbanite.

One of the differences between humans and the lower animals is in the number and variety of secondary or acquired drives that man learns. We are born with a hunger drive, but we must learn to desire paper money, the applause of an audience, and a daily bath. Perhaps we also have to learn to seek security and to want to enhance our self-esteem. Secondary drives are often defined in terms of an individual's tendency to approach or to avoid an object or an activity. Therefore, an attempted list of all possible secondary drives would be infinitely long.

The concept of "drive" is somewhat controversial in psychology in that it lends itself to several interpretations. The fact that it cannot be measured directly has led some psychologists (for example, Estes, 1958) to propose a stimulus-response theory in which stimuli are the only source of drive. This is basically the sort of model presented in this chapter. A second, and not inconsistent, possibility is the proposition that stimuli evoke drives, but only if the appropriate conditions are present. For example, the sight of water evokes thirst only after the organism has been deprived of liquids for several hours. This proposition is most useful in dealing with primary

drives, which increase in strength under conditions of deprivation. Another somewhat different possibility is that stimuli serve only as cues. Whenever a particular cue and a particular drive occur at the same time and lead to a response that is reinforced, the probability increases that this particular cue-drive combination will lead to that

Figure 5-1. A behavior sequence showing the relationships among stimulus, drive, response, and reinforcement.

A. Diagram of a behavior sequence

B. Diagram of Samuel Andrew's behavior

By reinforcing the desired responses, it is possible to get some animals to perform extremely complex feats. These pictures show the skill of a dolphin who has learned to dribble a basketball across the pool and shoot for the basket. The dolphin liked to bounce balls off its nose, and the trainer rewarded it—that is, reinforced this behavior—by giving it a piece of fish every time it made a basket. Thus the dolphin learned to do what was expected of it.

Photographs by Marine from Monkmeyer.

5 and a 4 into an adding machine each day for a week, and the answer will invariably be 9. Ask a friend each day for a week what 5 plus 4 equals, and his responses may vary from "Nine" to "What is this, a joke?" to "Go away, I'm busy." It is possible, nevertheless, to classify the responses of an organism in a particular situation according to their probability of occurrence. Such an arrangement is called a response hierarchy. The response that is most likely to be evoked by a given stimulus has the highest position in the hierarchy and those responses least likely to occur are at the bottom. Another way of stating this is to say that the connection is strongest between a given stimulus and those responses that are high on the hierarchy but is weak between the same stimulus and those responses that are low on the hierarchy. For example, the most probable response to the sound of a doorbell is to walk to the door and open it. A considerably less likely response to that stimulus would be that of turning on the water in the shower. It should be noted that some response hierarchies seem to be innate, such as an infant's tendency to cry in response to hunger pangs or the contraction of the pupil of the eye in response to bright light. However, most response hierarchies are the result of learning.

Reinforcement. We may define reinforcement as any event that strengthens the tendency for a response to be repeated. When an organism responds to a stimulus and that response is reinforced, it is very probable that the same response will be repeated the next time that stimulus occurs. A hungry dog is coaxed to "Stand up! Stand up!" as his food dish is held in the air. Eventually he balances himself precariously on his back legs. As a reward or reinforcement, he is allowed to eat his food. The next time he hears "Stand up!" and sees his dish being held, he is very likely to repeat the previously reinforced behavior of standing. Responses are not repeated indefinitely unless they are reinforced; new responses are not learned unless they are reinforced.

Most psychologists agree that the reduction in the strength of a primary drive is a reinforcing event. Activities that reduce thirst or relieve pain, for example, are reinforcing. Psychologists are not in agreement as to whether all reinforcement involves drive reduction. Most of the disagreement arises in regard to behaviors in which the evoked drive is a secondary rather than a primary one.

The major controversies revolve around two

same response on subsequent occasions. Which, if any, of these various formulations will eventually prove most useful to learning theorists is far from clear at the present time.

Response. When a stimulus evokes a drive, the organism makes some kind of response. By response we mean any perceivable activity of the organism. We are responding to stimuli when we scratch an itching foot, or when we say "Yes, I'll have a second helping of cake." Each response may also serve as a stimulus to other individuals and to oneself. A tickling sensation in your nose may result in a sneeze, which serves as a stimulus to a friend who responds with "Gesundheit!" which is a stimulus for your response of "Thank you," and so on.

Living organisms do not, of course, react in a mechanical, robot-like manner. A machine in good working order will always yield a particular output in response to a particular input; punch a

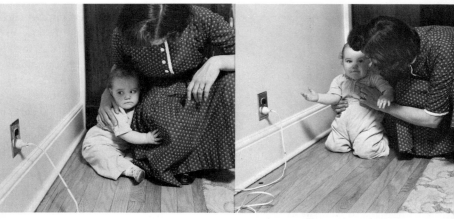

By pulling the baby's hand from the electrical outlet again and again, this mother hopes to "condition" the child to avoid the outlet instead of yielding to his impulse to explore and investigate it.

questions: (1) Are all drives the outgrowth of primitive biological drives? (2) Must secondary drives be periodically reinforced through the reduction of associated primary drives?

In any event, it is clear that behavior may be reinforced by secondary or learned reinforcements such as money or praise. Wolfe (1936) found that chimpanzees would learn to work for poker chips that could later be inserted in a vending machine to obtain grapes. They learned to distinguish food chips (white) from nonrewarded ones (brass), grape chips from water chips, and double-value from single-value chips. And, like their more advanced cousins, the chimpanzees learned to hoard the tokens in order to work less, to compete for them, and even beg for them.

Learning to respond to new stimuli

Conditioning. About 1904, a Russian physiologist named Ivan Pavlov (1927) began a series of conditioning experiments that were to have a tremendous influence on the psychology of learning. Although only a few psychologists have taken the extreme position that all learning is based on conditioning, most agree that a great many of our responses are conditioned.

A typical conditioning experiment might be set up in the following way: A dog is attached to a special apparatus that measures the amount of fluid his salivary glands produce (Figure 5-2). It is known that the presence of a small amount of weak acid in a dog's mouth will stimulate the ac-

tivity of these glands. In other words, salivation is high on the dog's response hierarchy (probably innately), when the stimulus is acid in the mouth. In this experiment, however, each time the acid is placed in the dog's mouth, a tuning fork is struck, giving off a ringing, bell-like sound. When these stimuli have been paired a number of times, learning takes place. At this point the tuning fork alone is sufficient to produce salivation, and a new stimulus-response connection has been learned. Previously, salivation was low on the response hierarchy associated with the sound of the tuning fork; now it has been moved to the top of the hierarchy, and the connection between it and the tuning fork has been strengthened.

A special terminology has grown out of conditioning studies. The "unconditioned stimulus" (for example, acid) that evokes the "uncondi-

Figure 5-2. Laboratory apparatus to measure conditioning in dogs.

tioned response" (here salivation) is replaced through learning by the "conditioned stimulus" (that is, sound of the tuning fork being struck), which now evokes the "conditioned response" (salivation to the striking of the tuning fork).

Conditioning is by no means confined to the laboratory. A small infant reaches out and touches a hot radiator. The heat stimulus evokes pain avoidance, which leads to the instant removal of the hand and the child's backing away from the radiator. Very often, one painful or frightening experience may be sufficient to produce conditioning. The sight of the radiator on the following day leads to a pulling back of the hand and avoidance of the stimulus. Both the laboratory and the everyday conditioning are shown in Figure 5-3. It is through conditioning that we learn to salivate at the sight of a juicy steak, to smile at the sound of the theme music of our favorite television comic, or to feel a touch of anxiety if a policeman on a motorcycle appears in a rear-view mirror when we are driving.

Higher-order conditioning. It is possible for the new stimulus-response connection to be used as a base for further conditioning. In the experiment mentioned above, the dog learned to salivate when he heard the tuning fork. If a flashing light is now presented each time the tuning fork is sounded, the dog will learn to salivate when he sees the light. This process is called second-order conditioning. Third-order conditioning (such as might be attempted through pairing a buzzer with the light) is very difficult to achieve, and conditioning beyond third-order is not possible with dogs. (McGeoch and Irion, 1952.)

Extinction. Earlier in the chapter it was proposed that reinforcement is a necessary condition if a particular stimulus-response connection is to be maintained. For example, the reinforcement of the acid-salivation behavior sequence is the reduction of pain through dilution of the acid by the saliva. But when the dog learns to salivate when he hears the tone produced by a tuning fork, what is the reinforcement for this bell-salivation behavior? Actually, there is no primary reinforcement; with repetition, this stimulus-response connection will grow weaker and eventually disappear. This process is known as extinction. Whenever a stimulus-response connection no longer leads to reinforcement, the response extinguishes. Extinction can be prevented by occasionally bringing back the original stimulus (for example, acid)

when the conditioned stimulus (the tone) is presented. Presumably, this procedure strengthens the learned stimulus-response connection (tone-salivation) by reintroducing the primary drive (that is, pain avoidance) and the reinforcement properties of the response.

After extinction has taken place, the extinguished response will sometimes return spontaneously after a rest period. For example, when the sounding of the tuning fork no longer leads to salivation, on a test trial some days later the dog may salivate when he hears the tone. The strength of this response is usually less than in the original learning trials. Although this phenomenon, called "spontaneous recovery," is not fully understood, it suggests that extinction does not eradicate a response but rather shifts its position downward in the response hierarchy.

It may be supposed that our positive response to money is the result of its countless associations with such reinforcements as food and entertainment. However, even our response to money can be extinguished when it no longer leads to reinforcement, as in the South after the Civil War.

Figure 5-3. Learning to respond to new stimuli: Conditioning.

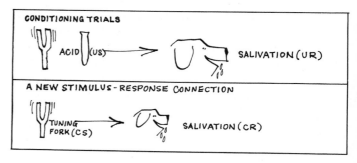

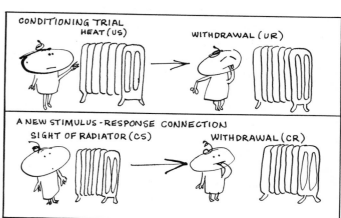

It should be noted that some psychologists have argued that an acquired drive does not need to be repeatedly paired with a primary reinforcement to be maintained. Allport (1937) holds that secondary drives may become functionally autonomous of their physiological origin. For example, Clyde Evans may take up stamp collecting as a way of reducing tension brought about by the need to remain in bed during a long convalescence after a serious illness. After he is back on his feet again, he continues to collect stamps. Stamp collecting is no longer related to any of the physiological needs that developed as a result of his illness and convalescence, but it has become a new source of pleasure for him. We may say that he has developed an acquired drive for collecting stamps, and the patterns of behavior related to stamp collecting have functional autonomy. An alternative explanation is that the secondary drive of stamp collecting is maintained by a variety of primary and secondary reinforcements such as the drive-arousing aspects of stamps needing to be sorted and placed in their proper places in the album, the stimulation that comes from socializing with other stamp collectors, the rest and relaxation associated with evenings set aside for working with stamps, the satisfaction of hearing other collectors comment favorably on his collection, and so on.

Generalization. When we learn to respond to a new stimulus, we are also acquiring a tendency to respond to all stimuli similar to it. Even though a dog learned to salivate to the sound of a particular tuning fork, it has been found that the salivation response will then be elicited by tuning forks having higher or lower pitch. The more similar a new stimulus is to the conditioned stimulus, the more likely it is to evoke the conditioned response. In other words, there is a "gradient of generalization" for each stimulus. A hypothetical generalization gradient is depicted in Figure 5-4.

An eleven-month-old boy who was conditioned to fear a rat, subsequently showed fear in the presence of a rabbit, a dog, a fur coat, cotton wool, and even Santa Claus whiskers. The similarity of these stimuli, which lay in their wooliness or furriness, evoked the conditioned response—fear. (Watson, 1924.)

If it were not for our ability to generalize we would have to repeat the learning process each time there was the slightest alteration in the stimulus. It is our ability to generalize, for example, that enables us to make the same response regardless of whether a sign says NO PARKING, or *NO PARKING.* Generalization has its disadvantages, too, as with the child who had developed the generalized fear. Similarly, we generalize from one individual to an entire group on the basis of stimulus similarity. Secord, Bevan, and Katz (1956) found that both prejudiced and nonprejudiced subjects assigned various stereotyped personality and facial characteristics to pictures of Negroes more than to pictures of whites. This was true even though the Negro pictures were selected to represent a considerable range of "Negroidness." It might be hypothesized that this same generalization process could cause us to react to anyone possessing a Russian accent in the same manner in which we would respond to Russians with pronounced Communist views.

Discrimination. Generalization may be counteracted by another process, discrimination. If responses to similar stimuli are *not* reinforced, although the responses to the original stimulus *are* reinforced, the organism learns to discriminate between the stimuli. If tone A is always paired with the acid, and tones B, C, and D are never paired with the acid, the dog will eventually learn to salivate only to tone A. The tendency to respond to the other three stimuli will extinguish.

We all must learn a vast number of discriminations, sometimes fairly subtle ones. A mother learns to discriminate the cry of her child from that of her neighbor's child. A little girl learns that aunts are not all alike. A small boy learns that bathroom functions may be discussed with his parents but not with his grandparents. A pilot in wartime learns to discriminate among the silhouettes of friendly and unfriendly planes.

Figure 5-4. A hypothetical gradient of stimulus generalization. (After Underwood, 1949, p. 252.)

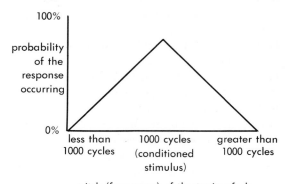

pitch (frequency) of the tuning fork

Learning new responses

The learning dilemma. As long as the responses of an organism are being reinforced, there is no reason to expect any dramatic behavior change. Through conditioning and generalization the organism learns to respond to new stimuli, but the dominant responses in its various response hierarchies should remain relatively static. However, certain questions arise. How were the responses learned in the first place? How can they be altered? How does an organism behave in a novel situation?

New responses occur when a stimulus evokes a drive and the drive leads to behavior which is not successful in reducing the drive. The organism is faced with a learning dilemma and must learn a new response. The situations that lead to a learning dilemma are frustration, conflict, and monotony.

With frustration, a barrier interferes with the goal-directed behavior. There are external physical barriers such as a refrigerator door that is stuck, external verbal barriers such as a sign which says, "Picnics Not Allowed," and internal barriers such as a conviction that raw oysters are not edible. (See Figure 5-5.) The organism's task in this type of learning dilemma is to find a way to bypass the barrier and thus gain satisfaction or drive reduction.

When stimuli simultaneously arouse two drives that impel an individual to make two or more incompatible responses, he experiences a condition which psychologists term *conflict*. A small girl with a penny to spend must choose either the lime or the peppermint candy. We want to jump to the last chapter of the murder mystery and find out who the murderer was, but at the same time we do not want to spoil the story for ourselves. We shall have more to say about conflicts in Chapter 7, and we mention them here principally because of their importance for learning. Resolving conflicts involves making a choice (unless some external force intervenes and thus makes the choice for us), and choice-making situations are learning situations.

New behavior will sometimes occur in the absence of frustration or conflict. Even though a response leads to drive-reduction, sheer repetition of a particular stimulus-response sequence may cause an organism to alter its behavior. It may be that organisms have a need for variety. Krechevsky (1937) set up a checkerboard maze for rats in which there was a short, fixed path leading to the goal and a longer, variable path also leading to the goal. Normal rats chose the second, more "interesting" pathway, whereas rats with brain lesions chose the former. Denny (1957) arranged a T-maze so that hungry rats were fed twice as many times on one side as on the other.

Figure 5-5. Frustration: A barrier interferes with goal-directed behavior.

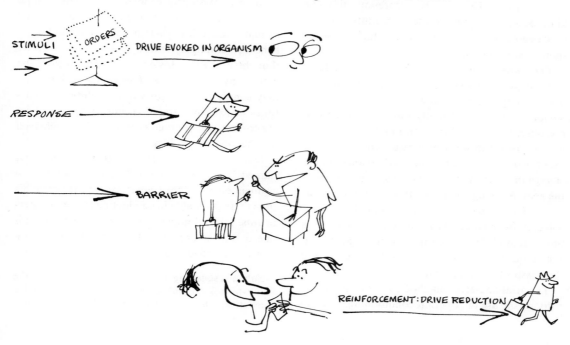

Like rats, even human beings choose the long way around for variety's sake at times.

When they were later given free trials in which they could go to either side, they showed a preference for the *less* frequently visited side. One intrepretation is that the rats responded in such a way as to obtain the greatest variation in stimuli. Moon and Lodahl (1956) found that monkeys would press a lever simply to change the illumination of their environment. The drive here seems to be some sort of need for variety or change.

In each type of learning dilemma there are usually some responses (or a response) that will solve the problem and then be reinforced. Dollard and Miller (1950) propose that radically new solutions to problems are rare because of the low probability that the correct combination of responses will occur. There are at least four somewhat distinct ways for new responses to occur in order to solve a learning dilemma; each is discussed below. They do not represent different kinds of learning. Rather, they constitute a means of categorizing several ways in which new responses are elicited.

Trial and error. The most primitive and least efficient problem-solving technique is for the organism simply to respond with trial-and-error behavior until he accidentally hits on a successful response. When we place a rat in a complex maze with correct pathways arbitrarily chosen by the experimenter, the animal has little choice but to engage in a trial-and-error behavior until he finds the goal. A young child usually attacks a mechanical puzzle in this same way; eventually he may solve it by chance. Trial-and-error behavior is most often elicited when there is no logical solution to the problem or when the solution is beyond the grasp of the organism.

The trial-and-error method may be channeled through the use of "operant conditioning," a tech-

nique refined by the psychologist B. F. Skinner. Essentially, the subject responds with trial-and-error behavior, and the experimenter rewards those responses that lead to the desired behavior. For example, a rat is taught to climb a miniature ladder to get food by rewarding him first if he happens to walk near the ladder, then if he smells it, then if he puts his paw on the bottom rung, etc. Parents reward an infant's chance babbles of "ma ma" with attention, laughter, hugging, and this particular response becomes more likely to occur along with "da da," "please," and "cookie." Azrin and Lindsley (1956) used an operant conditioning technique to develop cooperative behavior between children. A candy machine was designed in such a way that it took two children to work the apparatus. Hence whenever they happened to cooperate, the behavior was reinforced.

Insight. With greater intellectual ability, some of the more advanced organisms, such as the primates, are able to carry out their trial-and-error behavior implicitly through the use of their thought processes. Instead of going through the actual physical motions of solving a problem, we may simply think about various solutions, sometimes at extremely rapid speeds, until we hit on the correct one. We then say that we have achieved insight into the problem.

During World War II, a German psychologist named Köhler was interned by the Spanish government on one of the Canary Islands. He spent his time there profitably in conducting learning experiments, using chimpanzees as his subjects. Here is one of his experiments, conducted with a chimpanzee he called "Sultan."

Sultan is squatting at the bars but cannot reach the fruit which lies outside by means of his only available short stick. A longer stick is deposited outside the bars, about two meters on one side of the objective and parallel with the grating. It cannot be grasped with the hand, but it can be pulled within reach by means of the small stick. Sultan tries to reach the fruit with the smaller of the two sticks. Not succeeding, he tears at a piece of wire that projects from the netting of his cage, but that, too, is in vain. Then he gazes about him (there are always in the course of these tests some long pauses, during which the animals scrutinize the whole visible area). He suddenly picks up the little stick once more, goes up to the bars directly opposite to the long stick, scratches it towards him with the "auxiliary," seizes it, and goes with it to the point opposite the objective (the fruit), which he secures. From the moment that his eyes fall upon the long stick, his procedure forms one consecutive whole, without hiatus, and, although the angling of the bigger stick by means of the smaller is an action that could be complete and distinct in itself, yet observation shows that it follows, quite suddenly, on an interval of hesitation and doubt—staring about—which undoubtedly has a relation to the final objective, and is immediately merged in the final action of the attainment of the end goal. (Köhler, 1925: 174-175.[1])

Humans, of course, use insight a great deal to solve problems. In deciding on the shortest route to the football stadium, you do not have actually to try out each of a dozen alternatives. Insight is possible when all of the elements of the solution are within the grasp of the individual. The solution often involves a repatterning or restructuring of relatively familiar elements. In thought, sometimes

[1] Reprinted by permission.

without being aware of it, a person tries out various solutions until he hits on a correct one. The usual sudden success has led to the labeling of insight as the "aha!" experience. It seems reasonable to hypothesize that man's most novel solutions, most creative ideas, and most radically new inventions owe their origin and development to insight. Perhaps overt trial and error procedures could yield the same eventual results, but with considerably less efficiency. Jonathan Swift satirized such an idea in *Gulliver's Travels* when he described the great academy of Lagado, where scholars wrote books by randomly shuffling all the words in their language and extracting phrases whenever they hit on one that made sense.

Harlow (1949) has added to our knowledge about insightful behavior through his work on learning sets. In essence, he is studying the way in which organisms *learn* to learn. For example, he finds that both monkeys and children get much better at solving discrimination problems as they have experience in solving such problems. The learning process becomes increasingly a matter of insight rather than blind trial and error. As with any other behavior, when insightful behavior is elicited and reinforced, it becomes a more likely response in subsequent learning dilemmas.

Imitation. When we perceive the way in which another individual solves a problem, we do not have to work out our own solution through either trial and error or insight. A boy sees how a good

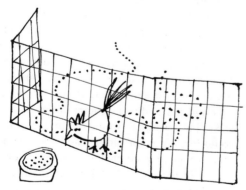

Differences between levels of intellectual functioning among infrahuman animals are illustrated by these sketches. A chicken placed behind a wire barrier is unable to perceive that food can be reached by going around the ends of the fence. Instead, it wanders about at random and finds the food by accident, if at all. A chimpanzee in the same situation does not have to resort to such trial-and-error learning but will go directly to the food. (After Munn, 1957.)

Sometimes the ability of infrahuman animals to use insight in order to solve
learning dilemmas displays itself in unexpected ways. Instead of using the pole
to knock down bananas hung out of his
reach, this chimpanzee has used it even
more effectively as a ladder.

tennis player holds his racket and moves about
the court, a freshman in high school notices the
way a popular senior handles a difficult social
situation, a teenage girl watches to see how a television actress accepts a date on the telephone, a
child hears his mother correct his father's gram-
mar: "It's not 'between you and I,' it's 'between
you and *me!*'"

Miller and Dollard (1941) have presented a
good deal of evidence to support the idea that
the tendency to imitate is itself a learned response.
If imitative behavior leads to reinforcement, the
individual will be more likely to continue to
imitate. They taught a "leader" rat to run toward
whichever end of a T-maze had a black card over
it. A "follower" rat then was placed in the maze
pathway behind the leader. He was fed only when
he went the same direction as the leader. The follower gradually learned to imitate the leader.
Other rats were successfully taught to go in a
direction opposite to that taken by the leader.
The experimenters also were able to teach children to imitate the behavior of another person
by rewarding imitative behavior. With both rats
and humans, the tendency to imitate persists when
the situation changes and when a different leader
is substituted.

Imitation can never lead to novel responses, but
it seems to be an effective way of learning problem
solutions when the behavior is readily observable
and there is an experienced model to follow. If
you came upon a bicycle for the first time and had
never seen one in use, try to imagine the difficulty
in figuring out its function and mastering its operation through the use of either trial and error or
insight! It should be noted that imitation can also
lead to unsuccessful behavior when the model is
deficient in some way. For example, some parents
make depreciating remarks about individuals of
other races, religions, or national origins; or, a
hoodlum may become the hero of the neighborhood.

Instruction. Man's ability to manipulate symbols gives him one final and extremely valuable
method for solving a learning dilemma. Someone
can tell us the correct behavior. As with imitation,
instruction does not lead to novel solutions, but
our complex society could not function without it.
Culture may be conceived as a storehouse of solutions. (Dollard and Miller, 1950.) Without symbols and the ability to communicate with them,
each man's behavior would be limited to what he
could figure out for himself and what he noticed
that his nearby companions were doing. It is
primarily the method of instruction that has allowed us to leave our caves and develop such phenomena as democracy, literature, and jet travel.
Of course, it has also allowed us to develop brainwashing, radioactive fallout, and the electric chair.

Learning and performance. In each of the
learning situations that were described (conditioning, trial and error, insight, imitation, and instruction), a stimulus-response connection (that is, a
"habit") is strengthened. Whenever a certain stim-

ulus is presented again, the response that has been associated with it is more likely to occur. An almost infinite number of such stimulus-response connections or habits are learned by a complex organism such as man. Some are used frequently, and some only on rare occasions. The acquiring of these habits is the "learning process," and their appearance in behavior is known as "performance."

For example, most of us have learned our own telephone numbers rather well. However this habit is not used except when we must call our homes or give our numbers to someone else. The distinction here is between the multitude of S-R connections that we have learned and the relatively limited number of S-R connections reflected in our behavior at any given time.

Failure to solve a learning dilemma. Not all attempts to solve problems lead to successful solutions. Sometimes the problem is not of vital importance. Bob wants to finish the crossword puzzle but finds himself stumped. He may get angry, feel slightly depressed, or say that he does not like crossword puzzles anyway. Nevertheless, the drive to complete the task remains unsatisfied. Or, the learning dilemma may involve the barrier to a vital drive, but still a solution is not found. A child is trapped in an abandoned refrigerator and is unable to open the door or attract help; without a successful response to solve the dilemma, the outcome is death.

In between these extremes the organism may be faced with an unsolved dilemma of greater concern than a crossword puzzle but which also does not involve a fatal outcome. Both psychological and physiological functions are often disrupted. A woman is in conflict about whether to choose the embarrassment of divorce or the embarrassment of remaining married to an unfaithful husband. She delays finding a solution and develops extreme anxiety and nervousness. When Pavlov forced dogs to make perceptual discriminations beyond their ability, they broke down. The animals whined and barked, salivated at the sight of the experimenter or the apparatus, could no longer make even easy discriminations, and tried to escape. They had developed experimental neurosis. When rats were placed for 30 days in an unresolvable conflict (hunger and thirst *vs.* shock), they developed gastric ulcers. (Sawrey and Weisz, 1956; Sawrey, Conger, and Turrell, 1956; Weisz, 1957.)

Susan Greenburg

The teaching of dancing, like the teaching of many other skills, depends for its success on the ability of students to learn through the process of imitation.

Two types of responses frequently elicited by an unsolved learning dilemma are aggression and withdrawal. Aggression may be constructive. For example, a weekend gardner may decide that the time has come to remove a stone that spoils the appearance of his lawn. As he digs down, he finds that the stone is much bigger than he thought. All attempts to pry it out with pick and crowbar fail. Frustrated, irritated, and thoroughly aroused, he borrows a sledge hammer and spike from a neighbor and, by dint of an afternoon of vigorous work, splits the stone into pieces and triumphantly carts it off. Even more frequently the frustration engendered by an unsolved learning dilemma

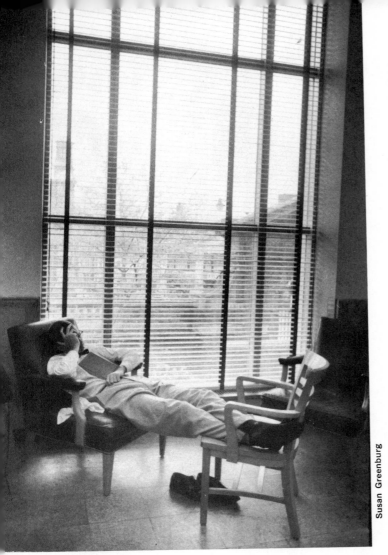

Susan Greenburg

One response that may result from failure to resolve a learning dilemma is withdrawal, which in this case takes the form of sleep.

leads to hostile behavior that does not solve the problem but does serve as an outlet for the individual's feelings. Many a teenager whose parents have refused him permission to carry out some cherished desire has reacted to the situation by stalking out of the room and slamming the door.

Withdrawal, on the other hand, can involve actual physical flight, psychological withdrawal and apathy, or depression. Some teenagers respond to parental thwarting by feeling "low" or going for a walk to get away from the problem. Barker, Dembo, and Lewin (1941) reported that when highly interesting toys were taken away from a group of preschool children and placed out of reach behind a wire screen, some of the children tried to get around the screen, some asked the ex-

perimenter for help, and some tried to withdraw from the room. When they then turned to the less desirable toys that remained, their play patterns of behavior regressed about a year and a half—that is, their play became less constructive and imaginative and more like the play of children a year and a half younger.

The foregoing examples have shown how failure to find adequate solutions to learning dilemmas can create difficulties. Learning is therefore a key process in our ability to adjust ourselves to our environment and to cope with the problems of existence. The remainder of this chapter will review some additional theories that psychologists have developed in order to explain the learning process, and will then consider various factors that influence the learning process and that may provide clues to the ways in which learning dilemmas may be resolved.

Other theories of learning

The preceding discussion of learning has been based in part on the writings of Clark L. Hull (1943) and the exposition and extension of his work by Dollard and Miller (1941, 1950). We have used this approach partly to provide consistency and clarity to our discussion and partly because it is a theoretical framework that a good many psychologists have found useful. There are, however, other theories of learning that have widespread acceptance and that differ in a number of ways from this sort of approach. In spite of these differences, they each have many elements in common. Although an extensive discussion of these theories is not appropriate in an introductory textbook, we will take a brief glimpse at some of them, in order to give the reader an idea of the different ways in which the problem of explaining the learning process may be approached.

Guthrie's contiguous conditioning. Edwin R. Guthrie has proposed a S-R theory of learning that does not involve reinforcement as an essential ingredient. He and his followers hold that all learning takes place simply through the *association* of stimuli and responses. Any stimuli that accompany a certain response will tend to evoke that response in the future. Drive reduction (or any other form of reinforcement) is not a necessary condition for learning to occur, according to this theory.

In Guthrie's system, learning is believed to take place at full strength when the stimulus and response occur together. Practice is necessary in order to link all the cues in the situation to all the appropriate responses. A complex task such as that of hitting a golf ball involves a multitude of little habits. A golfer must learn to associate each stimulus in that situation with the correct muscle movement. Faulty responses have to be unlearned. Guthrie does not believe that extinction takes place in the manner described in the first part of this chapter; unlearning is a matter of learning *new* S-R connections—connections incompatible with the old ones. To break a bad habit one simply has to make new responses in the presence of the cues to that habit. For example, if gum were chewed every time a stimulus suggested the smoking of a cigarette, theoretically the new S-R combination would replace the old.

In experiments involving the behavior of cats in "puzzle boxes," Guthrie and Horton (1946) found that the animals tended to repeat, in a markedly stereotyped manner, whatever they had learned in similar situations. The problem involved getting released from the puzzle box. All that was necessary was for the animals to touch the center pole. Each cat first solved the problem by trial-and-error method, when it happened to back into the pole, roll against it, bite it, or whatever. In subsequent trials the cats continued to use whatever maneuver (backing, rolling, biting, etc.) had preceded their release on the first occasion. Their behavior was somewhat like that of humans who develop superstitions. An unemployed worker may, for example, find a job on a day that he put his left shoe on first instead of his right one, and may forever after believe that putting his left shoe on first in the morning will bring good luck. Other superstitions, like knocking on wood and throwing salt over the left shoulder may have similar origins in the history of our culture.

Tolman's sign-Gestalt theory. Edward C. Tolman proposed a learning theory that is in many ways different from the S-R approaches of Hull and Guthrie. He believed that organisms learn "signs," rather than specific responses. Learning, according to Tolman, consists of acquiring what he terms a "cognitive map," rather than a series of muscular movements. This map acts as a guide that allows the organism to form various expectancies with respect to his environment.

This approach to learning makes a good deal of sense, particularly at the human level of functioning. Tolman would say that an individual does not learn a series of responses when faced with the problem of getting about in a new town. Instead, he adds information to his cognitive map. (This kind of behavior is explained by S-R theorists in terms of symbolic responses in learning and thinking.)

In an experiment with rats in a maze, Tolman, Ritchie, and Kalish (1946) pitted a movement habit against a space-orientation habit, in order to see which would be more effective in promoting learning. When rats were placed in a cross-shaped maze, those to be trained by the "movement habit" method could find food only by making a right turn regardless of which arm of the cross served as their starting point. The "place-learning" rats could find food only in a certain arm of the cross (always the same arm); locating this arm sometimes involved a right turn, sometimes a left. Tolman and his co-workers found that the "place-learning" rats were more successful in learning their way to the food. This study appears to support the idea that even rats acquire a kind of map or floor-plan of a situation more readily than a muscle habit.

Skinner's descriptive behaviorism. B. F. Skinner has proposed a theory in which the appearance of a response does not depend on a stimulus. He believes that some behavior (which he terms "respondent") is of the S-R type, but that other behavior ("operant") appears independently of known stimuli. He suggests that most human behavior is of the latter variety. However, it also appears in lesser animals. For example, if a rat is rewarded with a pellet of food for pressing a lever, he may continue to push the lever fifty or sixty times until the response is extinguished. However, periodic or intermittent reinforcement (discussed in the following section) will make the response resistant to extinction. Skinner uses the number of unrewarded responses that occur before extinction as a measure of the strength of operant behavior.

We have already discussed operant learning earlier in this chapter, but the Hullian notion considers such learning to be the result of reinforcing S-R connections, whereas Skinner considers it to be more a matter of rewarding responses, the stimuli for which are often unknown or unidentifiable.

Additional factors in the learning process

Testing for learning. How do we know whether an organism has learned a particular stimulus-response connection? How do we know the rat learned to follow a leader in the maze, that Sultan learned to rake in the long stick to get a banana, or that a first grader has learned to spell "cat?"

Recall is the most usual test for learning and is the most difficult for the subject. The same stimulus situation is presented on a subsequent occasion, and the examiner ascertains whether the correct response is repeated at this time. Presumably this response should be made more quickly and with fewer errors than in the original learning situation. We are testing to see whether he remembers the correct behavior or whether he has forgotten it.

Instead of testing recall, we can present the correct solution along with some alternative incorrect solutions and ascertain whether the subject can recognize the right answer. Recognition is easier for the subject, and it yields evidence of learning that the recall method overlooks. For example, students who are unable to recall an answer on an essay test can often identify the correct answer on a multiple-choice test.

Finally, the most sensitive test of learning is relearning. If the subject can learn the solution more quickly the second time, it is presumed that the increased speed indicates the effect of the previous learning.

Distribution of practice. Experimental results are fairly consistent in reporting that distributed practice is more efficient than massed practice. Ulrich (1915) found that rats given one trial a day in a problem box solved the task in 17 trials; rats given 3 trials a day took 25 trials to solve it; and rats given 5 trials a day needed 33 trials. It might be guessed that the student who studies six hours the night before a final examination will not learn as well as the student who studies an hour a night for six nights.

Meaningfulness. Rote learning does not appear to be as effective as learning that involves an understanding of the principles. The number 3612244896192 is rather difficult to memorize and even harder to remember over a period of time. However, the principle that it begins with 3 and then doubles each successive number is easy to learn and to remember. In a classic experiment, Judd (1908) gave two groups of boys practice in shooting at underwater targets. One group learned by trial and error while the other group learned about the refraction of visual images in water. When the depth of the water was changed, the second group showed superior skill in hitting the targets.

Knowledge of results. Does the knowledge of the results of one's attempts at the solution enhance the learning process? Apparently so. Angell (1949) compared freshmen chemistry students who learned their test results immediately after an examination with a matched group who got their results at the following class meeting. The former group did significantly better on the final examination. In other situations, knowledge of results is not just helpful but is essential. As an illustration of this, try to imagine the problems involved if one learned to bowl blindfolded and with ear plugs.

Whole vs. part learning. There are two possible approaches to the learning of a complex solution. An individual may try to solve the problem in small parts or as a whole. A person may attack the problem of memorizing a poem by learning it as a whole or line by line. In general, experiments have shown that the whole method is more efficient for more intelligent subjects, after they have had practice in its use, providing that material to be memorized is meaningful and that practice is distributed rather than massed. Obviously, various characteristics of the particular material to be learned (such as length) will influence the relative advantage of the whole opposed to the part approach to learning. (McGeoch and Irion, 1952: 501–507.)

Schedules of reinforcement. It has been emphasized several times that without reinforcement, behavior will not be learned. Does this mean that every time the stimulus-response sequence occurs it must be reinforced? The answer is not only "No," but also, as we pointed out in our discussion of Skinner's work in this field, learning actually seems to be more resistant to extinction when the response is reinforced only part of the time. The term for this sort of reward schedule is "partial reinforcement." Finger (1942) reinforced a running response in one group of rats after each of 16 trials; the second group was reinforced on only eight of the 16 trials. It took almost twice as long to extinguish the running response in the second group. Brackbill (1958) compared the effects of regular reinforcement (that is, reinforcement on every trial) with intermittent reinforcement on eight different occasions of the smiling response of eight infants, three and one-half to four and one-half months old. The reinforcement consisted of responding to their smile with smiling, soft words, jostling, and patting for 30 seconds. Four of the infants received this reinforcement every time they smiled; the other four were rewarded only intermittently. The smiling of the infants who received intermittent reinforcement was considerably more resistant to extinction.

There are three general ways of varying the reinforcement schedule. On a fixed-ratio schedule, reinforcement is administered after a given number of responses (such as, every five responses). Workers who are paid on a piecework basis are on such a schedule. On a fixed-interval schedule, reinforcement is given after a certain period of time (such as, every five minutes). Workers who are paid by the hour, week, or month are rewarded on a fixed-interval schedule. But the reinforcement schedule that is most resistant to extinction is the variable-interval schedule. Here the response occurs randomly. Salesmen working on a commission are rewarded on this basis.

We can also hypothesize that one factor that keeps gamblers at their task is the fact that they are on a schedule of variable-interval reinforcement. An occasional pay-off by a slot machine is sufficient to maintain the behavior during long periods. A parent's infrequent or occasional capitulation to a child's temper tantrum may be reason enough for the child to continue to use this approach to getting his own way, even though he succeeds, say, only one time out of twenty. The temper-tantrum behavior is thus on a schedule of variable-interval reinforcement.

Transfer of learning. All learning involves transfer. Learning at home transfers to the school setting. Some of the learning that takes place in grade school and high school transfers to college, and it is hoped that learning in college transfers to later life. It is stimulus generalization that makes transfer possible.

We can justify the tremendous expenditure of time, money, and energy that we put into instruction and learning in our schools and colleges only if we can assume that transfer of training takes place—that is, if we can assume that learning in one situation will facilitate learning in other situations. "Common sense" maintains that such transfer takes place automatically, that students who take two years of high-school French, for example, will be able to converse in French when they visit France or the Province of Quebec, or when they encounter a Frenchman. However, as almost

Transfer of training takes place when the subject is able to use a concept or a relationship he has learned in one situation and apply it to the solution of a problem in a different situation. An elephant was trained at the Zoological Institute in Münster, Germany, to discriminate between various pairs of symbols. The training apparatus consisted of two wooden boxes whose lids bore various symbols. One of the boxes contained a piece of bread; the other did not. Once the elephant learned to choose a certain symbol, it was able to "transfer" the concepts it had learned to other choice situations. For example, once it had learned to choose the box whose lid bore three dots, instead of the box with four dots, it was able to distinguish three-dot patterns from four-dot patterns, no matter what the position of the dots happened to be. In other words, the elephant learned the concepts of "threeness" and "fourness" in this kind of design and was able to transfer it to other situations. (Rensch, 1957.)

everyone who has tried to use his high-school French will verify, such an expectation has little foundation in fact. During World War II, the U.S. armed forces developed methods of teaching servicemen to converse in foreign languages after a few weeks of instruction. The difference between the usual high-school method of instruction and that used in the armed forces lies in the fact that the latter approach was deliberately designed to be functional, that is, to promote maximum transfer of training. But attitudes and practices that are well fixed by tradition are difficult to change. The functional method of teaching foreign languages developed by the armed forces has been rather

Rollie McKenna

The vast amounts of time, money, and energy we expend on education make sense only if we believe in "transfer of training" —that is, if we believe that what is learned in the classroom will "transfer" to activities outside the classroom. Belief in transfer of training also appears in our expectation that skills learned through training on automobile tires will improve performance on the playing field.

Susan Greenburg

generally rejected by teachers in high schools and colleges in favor of retaining the more conventional grammar-translation approach.

Other "common-sense" notions regarding transfer hold that skills learned in one school subject automatically transfer to other subjects. Difficult subjects, like mathematics and Latin, presumably subject students to a "mental discipline" that improves their ability to reason. Such notions persist today among the lay public and even among some professional educators, in spite of the negative findings of research conducted over a generation ago. Thorndike (1924), for example, found that high school students who had taken courses in mathematics made slightly superior gains in reasoning ability, as compared with students who had taken dramatics, biology, and home economics, but that this slight difference could be explained on the basis of the fact that mathematics was more often elected by the brighter students. He concluded that the reason that people assumed that good thinkers were developed by certain studies was that good thinkers tended to take those subjects. He wrote:

When the good thinkers studied Latin and Greek, these studies seemed to make good thinking. Now that the good thinkers study physics and trigonometry, these seem to make good thinkers. If the abler pupils should all study physical education and dramatic art, these subjects would seem to make good thinkers.

Probably the two factors that make transfer possible are transfer through identical components in the two situations (stimulus generalization) and transfer through the understanding of principles (meaningfulness of the materials). Experimental results suggest that transfer is likely to be positive when the new stimuli are similar to the old ones and the response remains identical. (Bruce, 1933.) After learning to drive a Plymouth, it is easy to learn to drive a Chevrolet. However, when the new stimuli are highly similar, but the desired responses different, negative transfer may result. In switching from a conventional automobile to one with automatic transmission, negative transfer is obvious in the movements of the left foot toward the nonexistent clutch pedal.

Anxiety and learning. What is the effect of anxiety on the process of learning? Is it a stimulant or a deterrent? Anxiety may be defined as a drive, similar to fear, that is evoked by threatening stimuli. There have been several approaches to the measurement of anxiety, and the relationship between learning and anxiety depends somewhat on the measurement that is used.

A good many studies have employed the Manifest Anxiety Scale, or MAS (Taylor, 1953), which consists of a series of statements to be answered true or false. Whether this test really measures anxiety, or some other complex of emotional factors, is a matter of some controversy. In general, it has been found that individuals with a high degree of anxiety, according to the MAS, are more successful on simple tasks, and those with a low degree are better with complex tasks. (Spence, Taylor, and Ketchel, 1956.)

Another sort of study compares learning under stressful and presumably anxiety-provoking situations with learning under neutral conditions. Sarason, Mandler, and Craighill (1952) found that low-anxious subjects improved performance under stress conditions (not given time to finish), whereas high-anxious subjects did not.

The measurement of anxiety has also been approached physiologically. The sweat glands of the human body are extremely responsive to anxiety; it is common knowledge that the damp, perspiring palm is indicative of the amount of stress, tension, and insecurity being experienced by an individual. It is not as commonly known, however, that tissues actually generate infinitesimal amounts of electricity, which vary according to the amount of emotional strain. These two kinds of changes, termed electrodermal response (EDR) or galvanic skin response (GSR) can be measured by a sensitive galvanometer and are often used as an index of emotionality or anxiety. Holmes (1958) found that the spelling ability of college students was positively related to GSR. This could mean that anxiety is helpful in learning to spell or that some common factor influences both anxiety and spelling ability. In some ways the effect of anxiety on learning may be similar to the effect of muscular tension. In a well-planned study, Courts (1939) had subjects grasp a dynamometer at various fractions of their maximum grip while they learned nonsense syllables.[1] He found that learning improved under increased tension up through 25 per cent of maximum grip. Beyond this point, learning efficiency began to decline, and at 75 per cent of maximum grip, learning was less efficient than under normal conditions.

Perhaps a tentative summary of the anxiety-learning relationship would be that moderate levels of anxiety or tension enhance learning whereas a high level of anxiety or tension interferes with the learning process.

Learning without awareness. At the beginning of this chapter it was pointed out that most human learning does not necessarily involve a formal classroom type of setting. At this point, we will go further and propose that during most human learning, the individual is not even aware that any learning is taking place. A learning dilemma arises, new behavior occurs and is reinforced, responses are altered, and the learner is unable to say what happened. We all learn without awareness. Can you remember and put into words exactly what the circumstances were when you learned to comb your hair, when you decided on your political affiliation, when you learned to be talkative or shy, when you learned the location of the water fountain at school? Can you even remember the processes whereby you learned the names of your college instructors this term?

Laboratory evidence clearly indicates that verbal awareness of the learning situation or of the new responses is not at all necessary for behavior to be altered. Greenspoon (1955) asked subjects to say all the words they could think of

[1] Many studies of verbal learning have used nonsense syllables, devised by Ebbinghaus. Usually, they consist of two consonants with a vowel in between such as MOK, TUD, etc. Their advantage in experiments is that they are equally familiar to all subjects.

in 50 minutes. The experimenter sat behind the subjects and uttered "mmm-hmm" (an assenting murmur) every time a plural noun was spoken. With other subjects, the experimenter murmured "huh-uh" (dissenting) when plural nouns were spoken. Most of the subjects were unable to see any connection between the behavior of the experimenter and the words they were saying. Nevertheless, "mmm-hmm" increased the number of plural nouns that were said, and "huh-uh" decreased the number of plural nouns.

Verplanck (1955) carried this operant conditioning of human behavior a step further. He had his students go out and reinforce the verbal behavior of unsuspecting friends, roommates, etc. during ordinary conversations. They talked normally for 10 minutes, then the experimenters reinforced (agreed with or paraphrased) every opinion stated by the subject for 10 minutes, whereupon there was no more reinforcement for 10 minutes. The rate of stating opinions increased with reinforcement and decreased with nonreinforcement. None of the subjects (including Verplanck) were aware they were subjects of an experiment or that they were learning anything.

In addition, several studies have been undertaken in which subjects were asked to learn a particular task and then tested on another, supposedly irrelevant one. For example, nonsense syllables are placed individually on colored cards and subjects are asked to learn the words. After the syllables are memorized, the cards are removed and the subjects asked to recall the colors. Incidentally, this particular type of learning is rather difficult to explain in terms of drive reduction as reinforcement. We would have to postulate that an acquired drive for attending to irrelevant stimuli was learned on the basis of past rewards. If you find yourself having to eat dinner downtown, you may know there is a cafe on the corner and eat there without remembering just how or when you learned its location.

A convincing demonstration of the unconscious aspects of learning and behavior comes when we move from one house to another. Suddenly, the light switches are in the wrong places, the faucet turns the wrong way, doors fail to open in the expected direction, etc. With a few learning trials and a few reinforcements, the new house straightens itself out again.

Learning under democratic conditions. A final factor, which is an extremely important one for individuals in our culture, concerns the conditions under which the learning takes place. The best way to teach, according to "common sense," is to tell the learners the right answers and promise them a reward for making correct responses and punishment for making wrong responses, grades being used in most instances as symbolic rewards and punishments. As we have tried to show in our discussion of some of the factors involved in learning, it is not as simple a process as we would like to believe. There is a great deal more to inducing learning than presenting learning problems and assigning rewards and punishment. Much of the research we have presented deals with learning that is associated with physiological processes or that involves abstractions (like nonsense syllables) of a relatively simple order, whereas most of the learning situations encountered in the classroom involve skills, attitudes, and concepts that are far more complex and abstract.

Methods that are based solely on the reward and punishment of responses learned through instruction or imitation have the disadvantages of (*a*) ignoring attitudes and feelings that are likely to have a significant effect on learning and (*b*) stifling creativity and originality. Essentially, such methods are autocratic or authoritarian, in that they focus attention on the person or institution that rewards or punishes, rather than on the learning process or the resolution of learning dilemmas. One critic of such practices has been Rogers (1951), who entertains grave doubts about the value of teacher-directed learning: "I have come to feel that the only learning which significantly influences behavior is self-discovered, self-appropriated learning." (Rogers, 1952.) Support for Rogers' viewpoint is supplied by Culbertson (1957) who found that subjects who took part in role-playing to act out the problem of whether Negroes should be permitted to move into white neighborhoods changed their attitudes more than either observers or control subjects.

Levine and Butler (1952) studied the most effective way of teaching industrial supervisors to rate their workers accurately. One group of supervisors was given no instruction, another group was instructed through the use of lectures, and a third group participated in a group discussion. Only the last supervisors significantly changed their method of rating in the desired direction.

A final word of caution. The material covered in this chapter should serve as an introduction to some of the concepts and experimental findings important in understanding the learning process. At a number of points in our discussion we introduced examples from everyday life in order to illustrate the concepts being presented. However, our use of examples drawn from life does not mean that carefully controlled experiments have been conducted to support each illustration mentioned. For example, it was suggested that the sight of a policeman's motorcycle in a rear view mirror is a conditioned stimulus resulting in a fear response. Though this is a reasonable and logical extension of learning concepts, to our knowledge no one has actually studied the conditioning of this specific response.

It should be noted that psychologists do not claim to have developed a complete science of human behavior. Even the most proficient learning theorist or laboratory psychologist has not reached the point where he is able to show convincingly how his conclusions or findings should be used in solving such ordinary but complex life problems as finding the best way to manage a classroom full of pupils, raising children to think for themselves, or unlearning maladjustive forms of behavior. Nor are the psychological data we now have of much use in explaining such phenomena as apparently spontaneous variations in behavior, "free will," wide individual differences, martyrs who willingly suffer torture for an ideal, or rats who continue to solve maze problems even when fully satiated. Questions relating to these and many other behavioral phenomena are being asked and answered daily through application of experimental techniques and the scientific method to the study of behavior. But most of the research in the field of learning is concerned so far with studying small segments of behavior in order to examine a few factors or variables at a time. Hence the evidence so far accumulated provides the answers to only a few of the endless number of questions we would like to pose. Experimentation and theory in the field of learning do, nevertheless, provide an important starting point for scientific study of the whole range of human behavior.

Summary

Since almost all human behavior is learned, psychologists consider the learning process to be the core of their science.

The term "behavior" refers to any observable response of an organism. Behavior sequences are initiated by stimuli which, in turn, evoke either primary (innate) or secondary (learned) drives that impel the organism to respond. If the response is reinforced (rewarded), the behavior sequence is ended.

Organisms learn to respond to new stimuli by the process of conditioning in which a new stimulus is paired with an old one until either is sufficient to evoke the response. Pairings of this new stimulus with still newer stimuli lead to higher-order conditioning. Whenever a stimulus-response (S-R) connection no longer leads to reinforcement, the response is extinguished. The tendency to respond to all stimuli similar to the original stimulus is called generalization. Differential reinforcement can counteract generalization, and the organism may learn to discriminate between similar stimuli.

New responses are learned when the organism is faced with a learning dilemma. Such a dilemma is created by frustration (blocking of goal-directed behavior), conflict (arousal of incompatible drives), or monotony (continued repetition of a particular behavior sequence). The most primitive way for new responses to occur in order to solve the learning dilemma is through random trial-and-error behavior. Insight refers to the outcome of a higher-level, more intellectual trial-and-error behavior which takes place covertly— that is, "mentally." We can also learn new responses through imitating the behavior of someone else. Finally, instruction may be used by human beings as an efficient way of solving a learning dilemma. Failure to find a solution can lead to psychological and physiological disruption, aggression, or withdrawal.

The explanations of the learning process we have used in this chapter have been based on the writings of Clark L. Hull, as expounded and extended by Dollard and Miller. Somewhat different theories of learning have been developed by Edwin R. Guthrie, Edward C. Tolman, and B. F. Skinner. Guthrie stresses the factor of association in S-R learning; Tolman explains learning in terms of "signs" and "cognitive maps;" and Skinner is more interested in operant behavior whose origin is not directly referable to external stimuli.

Learning may be measured by testing for recall, recognition, or the ability of the subject to relearn. A number of factors affect the learning process. In general, learning is more efficient when practice is distributed rather than massed, the material to be learned is meaningful, the subject knows the results of his efforts, the whole problem is attacked at once rather than part by part, and when reinforcement is intermittent rather than consistent.

When old learning is transferred to a new situation, it may either aid new learning or interfere with it. A moderate level of anxiety seems to help learning, but a high level is disruptive. Learning may take place without an individual's being aware of the process. Although "common sense" leads us to prefer "direct" methods of instruction, more democratic and self-directed approaches to learning have often been found to be superior.

Inasmuch as learning theory, as it exists today, is based on rather limited segments of behavior, it cannot and should not be readily applied in uncritical fashion to some of the more complex problems of everyday life. Studies in the field of learning do, however, provide the basis for future scientific research into all aspects of human behavior.

Questions

1. Select a behavioral act in which you were recently engaged and diagram it in terms of stimulus, drive, response, and reinforcement.

2. Think of a stimulus situation (such as hearing a cry for help inside a house which you are passing) and list a hierarchy of your possible responses in decreasing order of probability.

3. An infant learns to open his mouth and make sucking noises when he sees his bottle. How might this response have been conditioned? Label the unconditioned stimulus, unconditioned response, conditioned stimulus, and conditioned response.

4. Give some examples of stimulus generalization and discrimination.

5. What do psychologists mean by "frustration," "conflict," and "monotony"?

6. Name some of the advantages and disadvantages of each of the four ways in which new responses are learned.

7. Think of several occasions in which you failed to find a solution to learning dilemmas. What was the result?

8. Using the classroom situation, give specific examples of the three ways in which learning may be tested.

9. Name some of the variables which affect the learning process and indicate the nature of their effect.

10. Choose several college courses and suggest what sort of transfer of learning is expected from them. Do you believe that this expectation is fulfilled?

11. Describe several situations in which learning without awareness occurs.

Suggestions for further reading

Bartlett, F. C., *Remembering*. Cambridge, England: Cambridge University Press, 1932. A discussion of memory as a dynamic process, including experimental reports.

Dollard, J. and N. E. Miller, *Personality and Psychotherapy*. New York: McGraw-Hill, 1950. A clear presentation of the Hullian stimulus-response theory of learning and its application to personality theory and the psychotherapy process.

Guthrie, E. R., *The Psychology of Learning*. New York: Harper, 1935. A very readable exposition of Guthrie's "contiguous conditioning" learning theory.

Hilgard, E. R., *Theories of Learning,* 2nd ed. New York: Appleton-Century-Crofts, 1956. A description and discussion of all of the major theories of learning.

Köhler, W., *The Mentality of Apes*. New York: Harcourt, Brace, 1925. The Gestalt point of view presented with a description of Köhler's work with chimpanzees.

Rogers, C. R., *Client-Centered Therapy*. New York: Houghton Mifflin, 1951. Chapter 9, "Student-Centered Teaching," makes a very strong case for the democratic approach to learning in the classroom.

Tolman, E. C., *Purposive Behavior in Animals and Man*. New York: Appleton-Century, 1932. Tolman presents his learning theory and describes a variety of experiments dealing with animal learning.

6

Perceptual processes

Man's awareness of energy changes in the external world and within his own body is made possible by virtue of the functioning of those processes we know as perception. In Chapter 5 we presented a concept of behavior as a series of stimulus-drive-response sequences, and in Chapter 4 we discussed the physiological functionings of the sensory receptors that permit the organism to become aware of stimulation, that is, to perceive. In this chapter perception will be considered from a somewhat different viewpoint.

Life as we know it and the ability to perceive are synonymous. Try to imagine existence without sight, hearing, smell, taste, the skin senses, and without organic sensitivity. The only way of characterizing such a state would be death or a very deep coma. The importance of perception is never so sharply dramatized for man as when he loses even one of his channels of stimulus reception. A world suddenly devoid of sight or of hearing is a different world and a less pleasant one. Even the relatively minor malfunctioning represented by color blindness or tone deafness affects the way in which individuals react to their environment. Other perceptual differences are based on learning and various personality factors. An exhibition of modernistic sculpture may look quite different to two different viewers, and "rock-and-roll" music may be perceived in a variety of ways. Sometimes perceptions mislead us, as when we see a mirage on the desert. Or perceptions may change, as when we acquire a taste for olives. It should be clear that a knowledge of perceptual processes and the variables that influence them are essential ingredients in a science of behavior.

129

In everyday life, we are inclined to think of perception in terms of our inner experiences. Thus the internal event of awareness that takes place when we hear Dixieland jazz or see a Van Gogh painting or smell coffee percolating becomes for us our perception of these stimuli. However, psychologists are unable to study perception defined in this way, because such experience is in the nature of a private event. As behavioral scientists, psychologists must limit their research to events that can be observed and verified. Hence research in the field of perception is concerned not with awareness of stimulation as such, but with the observable responses that accompany or follow stimulation. In other words, psychologists cannot study your *experience* of "redness," when you see a red traffic light ahead of you on the road, but they can study your verbal response of "It looks red to me," or the speed with which you apply your brakes.

There are several ways of approaching the study of perception. In Chapter 4 we have already taken a brief look at the anatomical and physiological aspects of perceiving. In this chapter we discuss some of the ways in which we learn to perceive and consider some of the general laws or principles of perception that psychologists are constructing as a way of understanding and predicting perceptual behavior. Then we discuss some rather consistent individual differences in perception that are found whenever perceptual responses are measured. Finally, we consider several of the factors or variables that determine which of a given range of stimuli will be perceived and how they will be perceived.

Some general principles of the perceptual processes

Perceptual functioning: Innate or learned?

Certain aspects of perception are the result of inherited, physiological attributes. Our ability to perceive sound, color, and balance is dependent on our possessing the appropriate anatomical structures. Certain phenomena such as sensory adaptation (discussed in the following section) seem to be physiologically based. Also, some perceptual preferences appear to be innate. Newborn infants prefer sugar to quinine and warm milk to that which is either very hot or very cold. (Hilgard, 1951.) Certainly the instinctive behavior of animals depends on built-in responses to particular patterns of stimulation. Bees perceive the dance-like movements of a scout bee and are thereby informed (without any learning having occurred) which direction to go to find flowers and how far they are from the hive. (Von Frisch, 1955.) Tinbergen (1948) constructed a silhouette of a flying bird, shown in Figure 6-1. The model was suspended on wires and moved over the heads of several species of game birds in cages. When the model was moved in one direction, it caused fright; movement in the other direction did not. Presumably, one of the movements made the silhouette look like a hawk, and the other made it appear to be a harmless goose.

The navigating ability of migratory birds has intrigued many a scientist. Sauer (1958) has accumulated evidence that appears to indicate that birds respond to the patterns and configurations of the stars. He found that on clear nights during the appropriate seasons, caged migratory birds

Figure 6-1. Bird silhouette used to study reactions of game birds. (After Tinbergen, 1951.)

Moved to the left, it looked like a goose and did not frighten other birds.

Moved to the right, it looked like a hawk and frightened other birds.

pointed themselves in the direction in which their species is accustomed to migrate. During cloudy nights, however, the birds were disoriented. When the birds were released in a darkened planetarium which reproduced the stars as they appear on various dates in different parts of the world, the birds, after some short exploratory flights, took off in the appropriate direction. Figure 6-2 shows how they responded under various sky patterns.

On the learning side, there is a good deal of evidence that human beings must learn much of what seems to be "natural" perception. Senden (1932) reviewed the research dealing with the vision of persons born blind who gained sight through surgical operations. It was found that these subjects had to learn to perceive even fairly simple figures; the patients could see that a square and a circle were different, for example, but were unable to identify which was which. "Common sense" tells us that what we *feel* as a round ball with our fingers would be *seen* as round by our eyes without our having to learn the similarity, but work with blind persons who have recovered their sight indicates that this is not so. Several re-

Figure 6-2. How birds navigate by the stars. (After Sauer, 1958.)

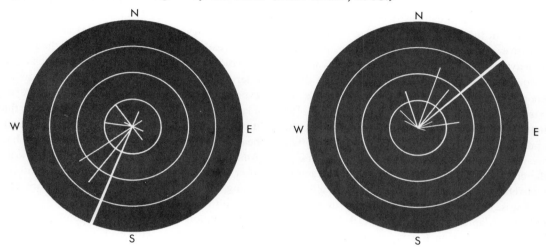

The above diagrams show the directions taken by (left) a garden warbler under a fall sky and (right) a blackcap under a spring sky, both skies being reproduced in a planetarium.

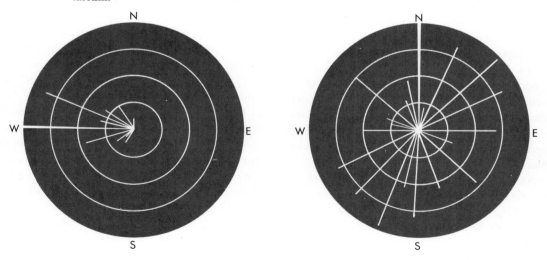

When the planetarium reproduced a sky several thousand miles to the east of the white-throat warbler's normal habitat, the bird took the courses indicated above left. The last diagram shows the course taken by the bird when no stars were projected on the planetarium dome.

ports suggest that primitive people who see a black-and-white snapshot for the first time are unable to perceive anything but a confusing pattern of grey color. They have to learn that the small, motionless, two-dimensional, achromatic card is depicting large, moving, three-dimensional, chromatic objects in the real world.

Sensory adaptation. There is an old saying to the effect, "You can get used to anything except a rock between your toes." Psychological evidence supports this proposition. In most of man's sensory modes, continued activity of a sensory organ leads to adaptation.

When we enter a dark theater we are unable to see at first, but we gradually become accustomed to the dimness and can easily find our way to an empty seat; this process is called dark adaptation. The reverse process, light adaptation, occurs when we leave a darkened theater in the daylight and are suddenly faced with the blinding glare of the afternoon sun. During dark adaptation the pupils dilate, and the retina becomes more sensitive to light. During light adaptation, the pupils contract, and the retina becomes less sensitive to light, often accompanied by a momentary painful feeling if the change is a sudden one. At least two factors interfere with one's ability to become adapted to darkness. First, a vitamin-A deficiency in the diet impedes adaptation, sometimes leading to night blindness. In addition, Clark, Johnson, and Dreher (1946) found that exposure to bright sunlight for several hours a day interfered with dark adaptation and hence with night vision. They suggested that Navy personnel wear polarized sunglasses during the daylight hours; this procedure significantly improved the ability to see at night.

Adaptation to auditory stimuli takes place in that we "get used to" most sounds. The noise of a busy street, the roar of a factory, the cries of the neighbor's newborn infant can each be extremely disturbing when first experienced. With continuing stimulation, however, these noises seem to fade into the background as sensory adaptation takes place.

Almost everyone is familiar with olfactory adaptation. One quickly becomes accustomed to even a fairly pungent odor. For example, a housewife cooks fish for dinner, but the smell is not noticeable to her family after the first few minutes. However when guests drop in after dinner they are confronted at the door with a gust of air laden with odiferous seafood. Taste adaptation is also a common experience. Lemonade tastes surprisingly sour right after peppermint candy. Apparently the taste buds for sweet have become adapted, so that the sourness of the lemonade is perceived without the usual accompanying sweetness. Other taste adaptations occur, too. Grapefruit juice tastes quite sweet if it follows bitter medicine, the second bite of dill pickle is not as shocking as the first, and the strange taste of water in a new town eventually goes unnoticed.

Among the skin senses, only pain adaptation appears not to take place. A person really does not get used to a rock between his toes, a toothache, or stomach cramps. Often an injury is painless for a short period, but this phenomenon seems to be the result of a temporary numbing of the nerve endings. Adaptation to heat and cold take place readily. Walking from a warm house into the cold outside air is most uncomfortable at first; after becoming adapted to the cold, the house is experienced on our return as hot and stuffy. A frog adapts so well to slight changes in temperature that it will sit undisturbed in water which is gradually heated, even after the boiling point is reached. Adaptation to mild pressure takes place easily; after a brief period we fail to notice our clothing, a ring, the feel of eyeglasses, the pressure of a chair on which we are sitting, etc.

Adaptation to internal stimulation has not been studied extensively. However, continued stimulation of the inner ear mechanisms leads to adaptation, as shown by two types of evidence. First, it is possible for most people to become accustomed to motion; the new sailor and the new merry-go-round operator are more likely to get dizzy or sick than are the old salt or the experienced carnival worker. Second, after a long period of this stimulation, such as takes place on a sea voyage, when port is reached the streets and houses now seem to roll and sway.

Depth perception. We live in a three-dimensional world and are able to perceive it as such largely because of the particular arrangement of our two eyes. Even when we use one eye there are cues that we learn to employ in ascertaining the distance of objects such as their relative size, the position of one object in front of another, texture, the presence of shadows, etc. A motion-picture screen shows only two dimensions, but looks somewhat three-dimensional because we utilize these sorts of cues. However, more important in real depth perception is the fact that our two eyes are a short distance apart and view the world at slightly different angles. Each time we view a scene, our brain receives two somewhat different pictures which are perceived as one three-dimensional image. Various attempts have been made to gain this depth quality in photographs and movies. The method is that of taking two pictures of each scene, at angles similar to those of the human eye. Then one of the pictures is shown to the right eye and one to the left. This task is accomplished either by separating the two pictures as with the old fashioned stereoscope or by superimposing them and then separating the images for the two eyes with glasses constructed in such a way that the left lens screens out the picture for the right eye and vice versa. The second technique was used to bring about a brief boom in three-dimensional movies in the early 1950's, but the inconvenience of the glasses and the mediocre quality of the movies involved soon ended the experimental venture.

Depth perception of a sort is possible in the auditory realm also. As sounds reach our two ears, we are able to perceive their direction with some accuracy, and our general tendency is to turn our head to face the sound. Traditional sound transmission and reproduction has ignored the depth factor. Now, stereophonic techniques utilize two recordings, one made on the left and one on the right side of the recorded event. When they are played back through two speakers, the same left and right positions are maintained, thus producing the effect of auditory depth.

Perception as an organized experience. One school of psychologists, known as the Gestaltists,[1] has been much interested in conducting research based on the idea that perception is not the result of separate, distinct impressions but of wholes. When we recognize a friend's face, we do not react to a pair of eyes and eyebrows, a mouth, a chin, a nose, cheeks, etc. Instead, we perceive his face-as-a-whole. If the parts are noticed at all, they are seen in relationship to the whole face.

The Gestalt psychologists point out that perception is based on figure and ground. When attention is focused on a particular object, it is seen as the figure, while the remainder of the perceptual field is relegated to the background. Figure 6-3 suggests a few aspects of figure-ground perception.

[1] From the German word "Gestalt," which means "form, shape, pattern or configuration."

Figure 6-3. Figure-ground relationships.

Some figure-ground perceptions seem to be absolute.

The man is seen as the figure while the remainder of the scene is background.

Labels influence figure-ground perception.

TENNIS BALL ON VELVET

The white circle is seen as the figure standing out from a black background.

BLACK DOOR WITH HOLE

The black surrounding area is seen as the figure standing out from a white background.

Some designs, usually rather ambiguous ones, are spontaneously reversible.

The face-vase illusion

Figure 6-4. Perceptual grouping.

Proximity influences grouping.

x x x x x x x x x

The letters are seen as a row of nine objects.

xxx   xxx   xxx

With proximity differences introduced, they are seen as three groups.

xxxx   x   xxxx

Another shift in proximity leads to a somewhat different perception of the nine stimuli.

Stimulus similarity influences grouping.

● ○ ● ○ ● ○
● ○ ● ○ ● ○
● ○ ● ○ ● ○
● ○ ● ○ ● ○
● ○ ● ○ ● ○
● ○ ● ○ ● ○

Most people see six vertical columns rather than six horizontal rows. Stimulus similarity sometimes leads to perceptual grouping on the basis of rather superficial characteristics such as skin color.

Continuity influences perception.

Which lines go together? Most people see a jagged line intersecting a wine glass rather than a combination of the two drawings on the right.

Closure influences perception.

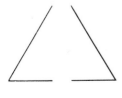

Bobbitt (1942) found that subjects tended to perceive the top figure as a triangle, but the bottom one as two separate angles. It was necessary for approximately 68% to 72% of the triangle to be present for the closure effect to operate.

Another feature of organized perception is the patterning or grouping of stimuli. Again, the general point is that the world is not perceived as a series of unrelated energy changes, but in an organized manner. In 1915, Köhler conducted a classic experiment on responses to patterning. Chickens were trained to respond to the darker of a pair of grays. When the gray to which they had been trained to respond was paired with a new and still darker gray, they chose the latter. (Allport, 1955: 62.) Although other theoretical explanations of such studies have been proposed, the Gestalt interpretation is that organisms respond to relationships, as well as to specific stimulus values.

In addition, certain stimulus characteristics tend to influence the way that we organize them in perception. Examples are shown in Figure 6-4. We tend to group stimuli on the basis of their *proximity;* objects that are close together tend to be perceived as part of the same group. There is also a tendency to group on the basis of *stimulus similarity.* A third principle of perceptual organization is that of *continuity:* stimuli that seem to form continuous patterns are perceived as wholes. Finally, there is *closure:* stimuli which form part of a recognizable whole tend to be perceived together.

Achieving environmental stability. Hilgard (1951) suggests that one of the major goals of perception is the achievement of environmental stability. Or, we might postulate that the need for stability is a strong acquired drive. We can tolerate a certain amount of change and instability, but too many rapid and violent changes in the perceptual field lead to anxiety, confusion, and severe stress. Environmental changes such as moving from town to town or experiencing a number of markedly different cultures in rapid succession can become uncomfortable. There has been some speculation that one of the greatest difficulties in space travel is going to be the human element; how will man react to a completely unfamiliar perceptual world in which the earth is a round object in the sky, gravity is absent, and the concepts of up and down are meaningless? Even minor changes in the stimulus characteristics of familiar objects are upsetting. An experiment was performed in which a group of subjects ate what under other circumstances would have been a delicious dinner, the food of which was colored in unfamiliar ways through the use of tinted lights. After a meal of

The back wall of this specially constructed room actually slants backward on the left side. However, it looks like a normal room and the figures consequently appear to be of different sizes. The usual cues to distance have been deliberately altered by the experimenters.

green meat, blue milk, and red potatoes, many of the subjects felt rather ill. The food "just didn't taste right."

Environmental stability is achieved in two general ways. First, "common sense," as based on our perceptions, tells us that the surrounding world is fixed and stable. We quickly learn that even though we move our heads or our eyes, the world about us is solidly anchored. Today, almost five hundred years after Magellan demonstrated the roundness of the world, most people still think of the earth as a solid, relatively flat expanse. We may know intellectually that we are spinning about the solar system on a round speck of matter, but still the sun seems to rise and set over an immovable world. It is not surprising that even mild earthquakes may be extremely disturbing events— they forcibly remind us of the instability of the earth on which we live.

A second major way in which we achieve environmental stability is through perceiving objects as having a constant shape, size, and color. Even though an object is perceived from many different angles, we tend to see it as having only one shape. From the side, the image of a framed picture which falls on our retina may have a decidedly trapezoidal shape, but we see it nevertheless as rectangular. A coin tossed in the air presents a variety of shapes to us; still we perceive it as round, not as elliptical. Size constancy is another phenomenon that aids us in maintaining a stable perceptual field. A man seen from a distance is perceived as man-size, not as some strange, tiny creature. And, from a tall building the cars down below may give us the momentary impression of a

toy shop, but we nevertheless realize that they are regular-size cars. Color constancy is similar in its operation. We see an apple as red whether it is in the bright light of the vegetable market or the dim light of our kitchen at night.

The constancy principle probably is the result of numerous learning experiences that we encounter as we grow up. The infant in his crib reaches for the moon but finds that it eludes his grasp. Some years later he learns to see it as a huge body of matter over 200,000 miles away. The fact that our ability to perceive a given object as possessing the same size, irrespective of its distance from us is a learned skill, rather than a quality inherent in the objects themselves or a biologically inherited ability, is demonstrated by a study conducted by Holway and Boring (1941). They discovered that the fewer the cues to an object's distance, the less their subjects tended to react in terms of size constancy and the more the perceived size was judged in relationship to that of the image on their retinas.

Illusions: Normal perceptual inaccuracies. When most human beings perceive a particular set of stimuli in an incorrect manner, we say that they are responding to an illusion. Some illusions are the result of misinformation that we incorrectly interpret as accurate. The studies conducted (Lawrence, 1949) at the Hanover Institute show that learned cues are exceedingly important in our interpretation of the perceived world. The two pictures on this page depict a room which was constructed in a very distorted fashion. We are accustomed to rectangular or square rooms. Therefore, the two men standing at the corners of the

Figure 6-5. Visual illusions.

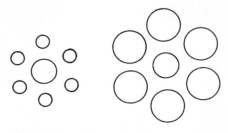

The center circles are the same size.

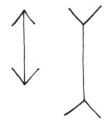

The Müller-Lyer illusion: The two vertical lines are the same length.

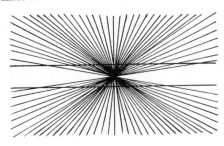

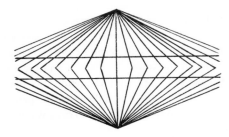

Hering's illusion: The horizontal lines are parallel.

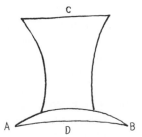

The distance between A and B is the same as the distance between C and D.

room are not accurately seen as being of equal size at different distances, but rather as a very small and a very large person. Even when they reverse positions, the illusion continues to fool us because of our well-learned habits of perception. In other words, our ability to perceive size constancy has broken down in a situation where we are fed misinformation about distance. Other studies with objects of unusual size (such as extra large playing cards) reveal that subjects are unable to judge correctly how far away they are placed. We have learned that playing cards are a particular size, and any changes in such a familiar object requires new learning on our part before accurate perception is possible.

Other sorts of illusions seem to be based on physiological factors rather than on learning. When two nearby lights are flashed in rapid alternation, they are seen as one light moving rapidly back and forth. This principle is called the "phi phenomenon" and is used in thousands of neon signs in the form of moving arrows, bubbling beer, running figures, etc. The phi phenomenon also underlies motion pictures. A long series of still pictures are projected on the screen in rapid succession, and our perception supplies the illusion of movement. An incorrect perception that has been noticed for centuries is the moon illusion; near the horizon the moon looks larger than when it is directly overhead. It was found that the overhead moon appears smaller only if we have to raise our eyes to see it. The illusion depends on peculiarities of our perceptual and cognitive processes rather than on any characteristics of the stimulus.

There are other illusions that seem to depend on the interaction between physiological and experiential factors. They are the familiar visual tricks which abound in such places as Ripley's *Believe It Or Not*. A few examples are shown in Figure 6-5. In each instance the eye seems to be fooled or tricked by certain characteristics of the stimulus.

Subliminal perception. The word *limen* is the Latin term for "threshold." Much of the early laboratory work in psychology was concerned with establishing perceptual thresholds in various sense modalities. For example, if a very dim light is projected on a movie screen, subjects say that they see nothing. If the light is projected again and again at increasingly higher intensities, there is a point at which subjects will say, "I can see it."

Similarly, all subjects with normal vision are able to see a very bright light, and a gradual decrease in intensity leads to a point where subjects are unable to see any light at all. The average of several such ascending and descending trials yields a threshold of visibility. We are able to see stimuli brighter than this threshold value and unable to see dimmer stimuli.

It would be a reasonable assumption that organisms are able to respond only to stimuli that lie above their perceptual thresholds. Very early studies revealed, however, that people are influenced by stimuli that are below their threshold (subliminal). For example, Sidis (1898) held up a series of cards at a sufficient distance from the subjects that they were unable to see what was printed on them. When asked to guess whether each card depicted a letter or a number, however, the subjects "guessed" correctly more accurately than chance would allow. It has also been found (Williams, 1938) that subjects could guess better than chance whether a circle, triangle, or square was projected on a ground-glass screen even though they said that they could see nothing. Coyne, King, Zubin, and Landis (1943) reported that subjects could discriminate (at better than chance) auditory stimuli presented at intensities below the determined minimal threshhold. These and other studies lead us to the conclusion that there are two perceptual thresholds. The traditional one is really a conscious threshold; subjects give verbal evidence that they perceive the stimulus. Evidently there is a much lower threshold of actual physiological reception of the stimulus. Between these two points lies the area of "subliminal" perception in which individuals are not aware of perceiving the stimulus even though their responses are affected by it.

The possibility that subliminal stimulation can be manipulated to influence human behavior is a rather disturbing one. It has been found that one of two identical lines will be judged longer than the other providing that the arrows of the Müller-Lyer figure are subliminally present. (Hollingworth, 1913.) The presence of an unpleasant subliminal odor on women's hose caused subjects to decide the hose were inferior to identical pairs that did not exude the subliminal olfactory cues. (Laird, 1932.) Smith, Spence, and Klein (1959) found that the type of description given of a drawing of a face can be determined by the rapid subliminal superimposition of descriptive words. Flashing the word "happy" led to descriptions of the face as pleasant; the word "angry" led to unpleasant descriptions. Byrne (1959) found that college students could be made more hungry by flashing the word "beef" at $\frac{1}{200}$ of a second superimposed on a classroom motion picture film. The subjects were not aware of anything unusual about the movie, but a rating scale indicated that they were significantly more hungry afterward than control subjects who saw the film without the subliminal message.

Subliminal stimulation was brought to the attention of the general public by Vicary's 1956 report (Brooks, 1957) that he could cause theater patrons to buy certain products. He flashed the phrases "Eat Popcorn" and "Drink Coca-Cola" at $\frac{1}{3000}$ of a second on the screen during regular movies and claimed that popcorn sales rose over 50 per cent and Coca-Cola sales rose 18 per cent. This demonstration was lacking in many experimental controls, but public concern ran high that subliminal messages would influence much of their behavior without their being aware of it. Various claims and fears have gone beyond the known facts, but data are being slowly accumulated. More research is necessary to determine the sorts of behavior influenced by subliminal stimulation and the conditions under which such influence is possible.

Sensory deprivation. Earlier in the chapter it was suggested that life without perception is inconceivable. What would happen, though, if an individual was placed in a situation in which the amount and variety of incoming stimulation were reduced to a minimum? Bexton, Heron, and Scott (1954) studied the behavior of individuals insulated from normal sensory stimulation. Each subject was confined for a period of several days and nights in a small, sound-proofed room. Except when he was eating or when he went to the toilet, he lay on a bed and did nothing. Each subject wore frosted glass goggles that admitted light but did not permit normal, pattern vision. His ears were covered by a sponge-rubber pillow in which were embedded small speakers, which enabled the experimenters to communicate with him. A microphone hung nearby. His hands were covered with gloves; cardboard cuffs covered his forearm and extended beyond his fingertips, permitting free motion but little tactual perception. One might suppose that a quiet, stimulus-free environment like this would have allowed one to relax, make

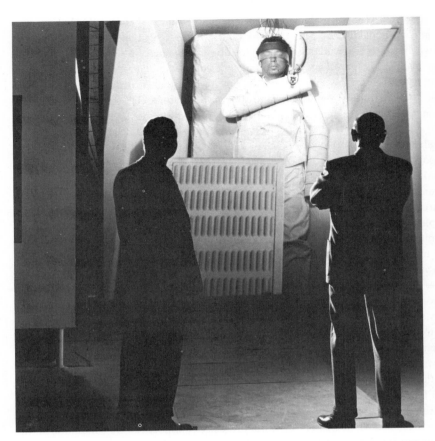

The men in this picture are looking at the blown-up photograph of a subject in an isolation chamber, insulated from normal sensory stimulation for experimental purposes. (Bell System Science Series TV Film "Gateways to the Mind.")

plans, and think quietly. Actually, however, the deprivation of sensory input had a profoundly disturbing effect on the subjects, all of whom were college students, paid to participate in the experiment. During the stay in the cubicle, there was a decline in their ability to solve simple problems. Some of them complained about an inability to concentrate; they were bored to the point of looking forward eagerly to working on the next problem, but when it was presented, they found themselves unable to make the effort to solve it. Subjects took intelligence tests before and after their stay in the cubicle; results showed a significant loss during the period of the experiment. Nearly all the subjects reported hallucinations, some of them quite vivid. Others became so confused that they had difficulty in finding their way home after they left the laboratory. It may be hypothesized that normal human functioning requires regular contact with the external world.

When man is cut off from normal perception of the ouside world (through sensory deprivation experiments, sleep, or some types of mental illness), his thinking becomes confused, disorganized, and useless for initiating adequate behavior.

It was mentioned in the chapter on learning that one sort of learning dilemma is monotony, or repetition of particular stimulus-response sequences. With the results of the sensory deprivation experiments in mind, we can propose that organisms not only desire variety in their behavior but also that varied incoming stimulation is a necessity. For normal functioning it seems that man must live in a range of stimulation in which he achieves environmental stability but at the same time avoids unchanging monotony. One of the so-called "brainwashing" techniques is that of isolating prisoners in dark cubicles, cut off from normal stimulation. The need for perceptual contact is so strong for most people that after a period of time most people agree to almost anything, even if it means accepting an ideology they have hitherto rejected, or confessing to crimes they never committed.

Extrasensory perception. Extrasensory perception (or ESP) refers to the intriguing possibility that man's perceptual activity is not limited to the known senses. Perhaps there is another, somewhat mysterious sense which allows certain individuals to send and receive thoughts (mental telepathy), gain awareness of objects or events not within range of the usual senses (clairvoyance), and to influence the movement of physical objects without physically contacting them (telekinesis).

Experiments with ESP phenomena have been concerned with the transmission of mental images, the ability to guess which one of five symbol-bearing cards is being turned up, and the possibility of controlling the numbers that come up on dice. Earlier research in this field has come in for a great deal of criticism on the grounds that proper experimental controls were lacking, statistical errors had been made, and attempts at repeating the experiments did not produce the original findings. More recent studies by Schmeidler, a clinical psychologist, and McConnell, a physicist, appear to have benefited by these criticisms. One of their more significant findings, as confirmed by Gardner Murphy, is that people who believe in ESP tend to score a little above chance expectation on a card-guessing task, whereas those who disbelieve score below chance. Other research has produced evidence that seems to demonstrate differences in personality patterns between high- and low-ESP scorers. (Schmeidler and McConnell, 1958.)

Many ideas such as ESP, dreams that foretell the future, reincarnation, and magic hold a real fascination for scientists and Sunday-supplement readers alike. These beliefs probably are manifestations of very strong wishes for supernatural knowledge and power. However, with such topics scientists are caught in a sometimes painful conflict. On the one hand it would be sheer stupidity to pretend that our present knowledge of mental and perceptual processes is complete. We should not repeat the mistakes of the nineteenth-century obstetricians who scoffed at the idea of washing their hands before delivering a baby or the well-meaning seventeenth-century church fathers who forced Galileo to renounce his "foolish notion" that the sun, rather than the earth, is the center of what we now know is the solar system. On the other hand, it is not necessary to accept naively every new idea which is presented *unless* there is convincing experimental evidence that supports it. Although ESP research findings are in contradiction to presently held theories in psychology and physics, Warner (1952) found that only 10 per cent of a group of psychologists surveyed believed that ESP is an impossibility. On the other hand, less than 3 per cent felt it to be an established fact. In short, it is prudent to keep an open mind and also to retain a healthy skepticism about unproven notions. The burden of proof is on those who put forth the hypotheses, not on those who doubt.

Individual differences in perception

Individual differences are found in every physical and psychological attribute ever studied. Whenever we speak of man's height or the age at which children begin to talk or the intelligence of physicists, we are speaking of averages around which individuals vary. With perceptual thresholds, for example, there are continuous fluctuations for each person as well as variations among different people. When we consider the effects of physiological differences, motivational differences, and differences resulting from learning experiences, it is clear that laws of perception must be extended to include individual differences as well as individual similarities. As Klein (1951: 328) said at the 1949–1950 Clinical Psychology Symposium at the University of Texas, "Our target is a theory which would lead to laws of *perceivers*, not laws of *perception* . . ."

Perceptual defects. Considering the delicate and complex mechanisms that make possible the functioning of man's highly specialized sensory receptors, it is not surprising that there are many physical defects that interfere with various aspects of the perceptual processes. As important as the defect itself are the reactions of the handicapped individual and of other individuals to the situation.

Vision is especially subject to difficulties. The wonder of visual perception is especially obvious in its absence, either in the blindness of others or ourselves. The loss of sight is especially disturbing when it comes later in life. However, adjustment to sightlessness is quite possible, and tremendous strides have been taken by our society in pursuing the establishment of educational facilities and occupational opportunities for the blind. Society's outlook is markedly different when vision is not absent, but simply weak. Nearsightedness, or *myopia,* is very often the subject of ridicule; "four-eyes" is a familiar children's taunt while adults laugh at Weakeyes Yokum, Mr. Magoo, and the bespectacled young man in the movies who always loses the girl to a hero with 20/20 vision. Thornton (1944) found that whether or not a person wears glasses affects judgments made about him, at least first impressions. Subjects estimated several personality traits of an individual who wore glasses as he sat in front of one group and went without glasses for the other group. When wearing glasses, the person was judged to be more intelligent and industrious, but with a poorer sense of humor.

Farsightedness or *hyperopia* is less common in youth, but a special form (*presbyopia*) often appears in later life as part of the aging process. Reading becomes more difficult, and many older people will hold reading matter at arm's length to take advantage of distance vision. Sight is also distorted by irregularities in the surface of the lens of the eye, a handicap known as *astigmatism.* A fairly small proportion of individuals, mostly males, are unable to distinguish certain hues and are said to be color blind. Many such people do not realize their difficulty because they have learned that objects with a particular brightness are called red, others green, etc. The Ishihara Test is useful in detecting color blindness because it consists of a series of plates depicting two numbers in colored dots; one number is set apart by hue differences and another by brightness differences. The color-blind individual responds to the latter, and his defect is revealed.

Even more than vision, defects in hearing give rise to resentment and ridicule. The ear trumpet, the verbal misunderstandings made by the hard of hearing, and even electrical hearing aids have long been standard comic devices. Thus, in a somewhat more profound manner than the blind, the deaf or partially deaf individual finds himself isolated from his fellow man. In spite of these rather cruel and thoughtless reactions, the public also holds great admiration for individuals who succeed in overcoming handicaps, the most notable example being Helen Keller who was stricken deaf, dumb, and blind as an infant and yet was able to become a successful writer, linguist, and publicist.

The other perceptual modalities are also subject to defects but are less well known. Complete lack of olfactory sensitivity is called *anosmia.* There are also wide individual differences in ability to perceive various odors. Temperature and pain sensitivity may be destroyed by the disease *syringomyelia.* Individuals may first notice this disease when they scratch their hand, or burn it, but feel no pain. The sensation of touch or pressure is maintained, but the other three skin senses are lost. When syphilis destroys parts of the brain stem or spinal cord, kinesthetic perception is blocked. The person must then watch his legs in order to walk or climb stairs, has difficulty in standing upright when his eyes are closed, and may be unable to touch his nose without the use of sight. Dizziness and nausea similar to sea-sickness may be produced by a variety of diseases which affect the semicircular canals and vestibule of the ear.

Patterns of individual differences. Klein (1951) suggests that each individual has a series of particular perceptual attitudes, or personal outlooks on the world. If we were able to identify and measure these attitudes, we should be several steps closer to a predictive science of human behavior. Such differences in perceptual behavior may very likely be the result of differential learning experiences, but experimental evidence has not yet been accumulated that would confirm or deny this proposition.

In research he has conducted at the Menninger Foundation, Klein's approach has been that of following up various leads in experimental data, hunches, intuition of subjects, and other suggestions. Three of the perceptual attitudes he was able to isolate in this manner are as follows:

1. *Leveling* vs. *sharpening of differences.* When a stimulus is altered (such as the size of projected squares), some subjects tend to keep up with the changes (sharpening) whereas others lag behind and see the stimulus as if it were unaltered (leveling). It is suggested that the latter subjects tend to deny or ignore differences in a search for stability whereas the former group is better able to perceive the stimuli as they really are, even when changes occur. Personality studies then found that the leveling group tended to avoid competition, to seek relationships in which they could be dependent on others, and to be self-oriented, self-abusing, and passive. The sharpening group tended to be competitive, exhibitionistic, and to have high achievement needs.

2. *Tolerance* vs. *resistance to the unstable.* We previously described the phi phenomenon as a

tendency to see movement when two or more nearby stimuli such as two neon arrows are flashed in rapid succession. However, individuals differ in the ease of perceiving this movement. The difference seems related to the ability of the subject to let himself go in fantasy and imagination, to tolerate any sort of instability, and to behave in a flexible manner.

3. *Physiognomic* vs. *literal perception*. Novelists often attribute lifelike qualities to inanimate objects; houses may "crouch menacingly beside a dark road," a landscape may be "overcast with an aura of loneliness," and fountains may "sparkle with gaiety and laughter." Again, subjects differ in the extent to which they perceive the world in this physiognomic way as opposed to matter-of-fact perception. Klein hypothesizes that physiognomic or imaginative perception is characteristic of individuals who are empathic or able to perceive the world from another's viewpoint. At the physiognomic extreme are found young children and some mental patients whereas the literal extreme includes the narrow concreteness of the brain-damaged person.

Another way in which individual patterns of perception can be identified and measured is that of presenting subjects with anxiety-provoking stimuli in the same context as neutral stimuli. For instance, sexually toned words and neutral words are flashed on a screen, one at a time, first with exposures so brief that the words cannot be recognized and then with increasing amounts of exposure until the subjects recognize the word. The length of exposure interval the subject requires to recognize a word, usually a fraction of a second, represents his perceptual threshold for that word. Some people take a considerably longer exposure than most to recognize the sexually toned words; hence we say that their perceptual threshold is higher for words of this sort—a form of "perceptual repression." Others perceive such words considerably faster than most people; we say that they have a low threshold for such words—"perceptual sensitization." Either a particularly high or low threshold is considered to be a form of *perceptual defense*. In one instance the individual is in effect trying to protect himself from perceiving the anxiety-provoking word; in the other instance the individual is so sensitive to the implications of words of this sort that he is overready to perceive them. Lazarus, Eriksen, and Fonda (1951) found consistencies in the behavior of

psychoneurotic patients with respect to their reactions to both sexual and hostile stimuli as measured by recognition of partially intelligible sentences on a wire recorder, responses to a sentence completion test, case history material, and behavior in an interview. For example, patients having a low threshold for understanding aggressive sentences were more likely to express hostile ideas openly on the sentence-completion test and showed a greater tendency in everyday life to deal overtly with hostility either in behavior or intellectually.

Witkin and his associates conducted two kinds of experiments to determine the ability of each of their subjects to sense (*a*) whether what he *saw* was in an upright position, or (*b*) whether *he* was in an upright position. The photographs on the following page depict the rod-and-frame experiment, which was performed in total darkness, with only the luminous rod and frame being visible. When the rod, the frame, the subject, or all three were placed in tilted position, the subject was asked to return the bar to an upright position. He accomplished this task by giving directions to the experimenter, who turned a crank that changed the position of the bar. In another set of experiments the subject found himself in a tilted room and was faced with the task of bringing himself back to an upright position.

Witkin found that some subjects tended to depend heavily on the visual environment for their cues. The girl in the picture, for example, says that she is upright because she is looking at a room (not shown in the photograph) which is tilted at the same angle as her position. However, she is considerably in error, as is indicated by the position to which she has brought herself, which may be compared with the true upright, as shown by the arrow at the vertical arrow above her head. Witkin found that persons who depended on the visual field for their cues to uprightness (field-dependent) differed in personality from those who were able to make judgments primarily according to their bodily cues (field-independent). Field-independent children tended to make higher scores on those portions of intelligence tests concerned with analytical competence. When home backgrounds of the children were analyzed, field-dependent children were found to have mothers who were more restrictive, more concerned with dominating and controlling the behavior of their children, and inclined to discourage curiosity and to encourage

Witkin's rod-and-frame experiment.

Photographs by David Linton

conformity. The mothers of field-independent children tended to encourage individuality, responsibility, exploring behavior, and independence. In other studies, Witkin and his associates (1954) found that adults who were field-dependent were inclined to be passive and submissive to authority, to be afraid of their sexual and aggressive impulses, and to be in less control of them. They were more anxious and had a low estimation of themselves. Field-independent individuals tended to be independent in their social behavior, rather accepting of their hostile and sexual impulses and better able to control them. They were less anxious, more self-confident, and more self-accepting.

Factors influencing perception

Man's perception is neither 100 per cent accurate nor 100 per cent representative of the stimuli impinging on his receptors. Again we are reminded that man is not a smoothly functioning machine but is, instead, a fallible living organism that perceives and misperceives stimulus information coming from both outside and inside its own body. In Chapter 5 we discussed learning as the process of connecting particular stimuli with particular responses. However, the way in which certain stimuli, rather than others, are selected out of a learning situation demands further study. Thinking back to the conditioning studies, why did the dog learn to respond to the sound of the tuning fork as a conditioned stimulus rather than to the sight of the experimenter or the smell of the laboratory or the ticking of the wall clock? The fact that perception is selective rather than all-inclusive leads us to an examination of various factors that influence perception.

Attention. Out of the infinite variety of stimuli bombarding our receptors at any one moment, we seem to perceive only one particular set of stimuli —those to which we are attending. Sitting on a bench on the campus lawn, Charles is engaged in lively argument with Vivian. He sees her face and listens to her words. These stimuli engage his attention while a host of other stimuli are ignored. Unless something happens to draw his attention away from his companion, Charles fails to perceive the pressure of his shoes on his feet or of the bench on his back and thighs, the conversation of passing students, the sounds of traffic several blocks away, the warmth of the sun on his exposed arm, or the faint fragrance of perfume from Viv-

ian's neck. It is possible to shift attention, of course, but at any given moment one's attention is directed to a relatively narrow range of stimuli.

Several variables that influence attention have been isolated. Many of the studies come from the field of advertising in which attention is all-important. Unless the customer's attention is caught, the advertising message is ignored. A large stimulus is more likely to attract attention than a small one; in a landscape a large tree or mountain is more likely to catch your eye than a small bush or rock. The intensity of a stimulus affects attention; for example, a very bright light, a pungent odor, or a loud noise. A stimulus that is repeated, such as a ringing telephone, is noticed more than a single stimulus. Finally, contrast is extremely important in determining attention; even a very tiny moving object stands out if all the other objects are stationary. The photographs on the next two pages depict some examples of attention-determining factors.

Set. We perceive what we expect to perceive. In interacting with our environment, we become familiar with the world and learn what to expect from it. Alterations in our familiar surroundings are often missed because we are "set" to perceive certain stimuli. Students often misread questions on examinations and answer the question they expected to receive rather than the one that is actually used. Here is another example, one of the words in this paragraph is misspelled; did you notice it? Or were you set to perceive properly spelled words?

There are countless other examples of the influence of set on perception. An old word game goes something like this: "What's a president's name that rhymes with an uncle's wife?" "Grant." "What's a president's name that rhymes with the title of a man who runs the mile?" "Tyler." "What's a president's name that rhymes with the word for the white of an egg?" And most people reply "Polk" before realizing that they have been led to a misperception through the operation of set or expectancy. The magician and the card sharp often rely on this factor to fool their audiences; they report that children are more difficult to deceive than adults presumably because they have built up fewer expectancies about the world. Siipola (1935) flashed a series of words rapidly on a screen; among them were six nonsense syllables. Half the subjects were told that the words had to do with animals or birds, and half were

Susan Greenburg

Intensity

Susan Greenburg

Variables determining attention.

Size

Gene Cook

Repetition

Lindgren

Contrast

145

told that the words concerned travel or transportation. The nonsense syllables were seen quite differently by the two groups because of their different sets. Table 6-1 gives samples of the differing responses.

The influence of set on perception is not all a matter of leading us to make mistakes and misperceptions, however. Much of the smooth functioning of everyday perception and everyday behavior is undoubtedly the result of our being set to perceive certain stimuli. One of the upsetting features of a new environment such as a new house or new city or new job is that many of our old sets are no longer appropriate.

Type of surrounding. Many individuals express the general notion that pleasant surroundings are desirable. A great deal of thought and planning is given to decor both in the home and in the business world. The idea seems to be that people feel happier and work better if the general perceptual background is pleasant and attractive. Thus, industrial concerns often paint their walls in soft colors, hang curtains on the windows, and play pleasant music during the work day.

Maslow and Mintz (1956) studied the effect of background beauty and ugliness upon people by comparing the behavior of subjects in a beautiful room (indirect lighting, mahogany furniture, rug, paintings, bookcase, sculpture, etc.), an ugly room (a naked overhead bulb, torn lampshade, straight-backed chairs, tin-can ashtrays, dirty, torn window shades, etc.), and an average room (a clean, neat professor's office). Each of the subjects was asked to rate the energy and well-being of faces depicted in ten negative-print photographs. Neither the examiners who administered the pictures nor the subjects were aware of the experiment's purpose. The type of room significantly affected the subject's perception of the faces; the ratings in the beautiful room were highest and in the ugly room lowest. A follow-up study was concerned with the reactions of the examiners who had each spent three testing sessions in the ugly room and three in the beautiful room. It was found that the examiners' "practice" ratings of the photographs followed the same pattern as those of the subjects. Furthermore, each examiner finished the testing faster when in the ugly room. Observational data revealed that in the ugly room the examiners experienced monotony, fatigue, headache, sleepiness, discontent, irritability, hostility, and a desire to avoid the room. The feelings in the beautiful room were ones of comfort, pleasure, enjoyment, importance, energy, and a desire to continue working in the room. (Mintz, 1956.) It seems that surroundings do influence our perceptions and other behavior as well.

Interests and values. When a specific stimulus is of special interest or importance to the individual, it appears that he is able to perceive that stimulus more easily than other similar stimuli. For example, what about an entire page of names —does *your* name stand out from the rest? Or, an individual decides that he is going to attend a particular university; suddenly the name of that university seems to appear much more often in the newspaper headlines than it did before. For that individual the name of his university now stands out. A woman takes up a new hobby and immediately afterward begins to notice magazine and Sunday supplement articles dealing with that hobby.

Postman, Bruner, and McGinnies (1948) were able to demonstrate that personal values are determinants of an individual's perceptual selectivity. They measured the value orientation of twenty-five students with the Allport-Vernon Scale of Values. Then words representing the six values measured by the test were rapidly flashed one at a time on a screen with increasingly longer exposures until they were recognized by each student. Their general finding was that the higher the value represented by a word, the more rapidly the subject was able to recognize it. In another study, Bruner and Goodman (1947) found that values may exert other sorts of influences on perception. They asked ten-year-olds from wealthy and poor families to guess the size of coins of various denominations (1, 5, 10, 25, and 50 cents) by varying the diameter of a circle of light. Both groups overestimated the size of the coins, but the poor children did so much more than the rich ones. (See Figure 6-6.)

Table 6–1 Nonsense-syllable perception influenced by set.

Nonsense Syllable	Animal or Bird Set	Travel or Transportation Set
chack	chick	check
sael	seal	sail
wharl	whale	wharf
pasrort	parrot	passport
dack	duck	deck
pengion	penguin	pension

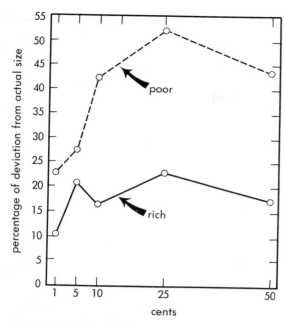

Figure 6-6. Estimates of size of coins made by children from poor and rich families. (Bruner and Goodman, 1947. Reproduced by permission.)

Drives. As we pointed out in Chapter 5, stimuli evoke drives. However, the reverse relationship is also true; many studies have found that an aroused drive increases the tendency to perceive objects related to that drive. Levine, Chein, and Murphy (1942) presented subjects with pictures of various objects distorted behind a ground-glass screen; those who had gone 3 to 9 hours without eating saw more food objects than did subjects who had eaten 45 minutes to 2½ hours before the experiment. A psychological state characterized by extremely high drive may even lead to the perception of stimuli that do not exist, as when the man on the desert dying of thirst thinks he sees a waterfall cascading into a lake of cool water. McClelland and Atkinson (1948) deprived Navy men of food for periods ranging from 1 to 16 hours. The experimenters pretended to flash faint pictures on a screen but actually projected nothing. They found a steady increase in the frequency of food "perceptions" as hours of deprivation increased; the apparent size of the food objects also increased as hunger increased. Murray (1933) had a group of young girls describe the picture of a man both before and after they played a game of "murder." After the game the girls saw much more maliciousness in the man's face than before.

Rogers (1951) has emphasized that a strong need for self-consistency also influences perception. If for example, an individual has learned to regard homosexual behavior as an abnormality "too disgusting for nice people to consider," his occasional experiencing of homosexual desires is denied perception because "decent human beings just do not feel that way." Or, a girl who has learned to think of herself as unintelligent and inadequate learns that she got an "A" on a midterm; this perception is inconsistent with her self-picture and hence she feels it must be distorted. "It wasn't a very hard test," she says. "I was probably just lucky, and besides I could never do it again."

Social pressures. The only way of ascertaining whether our perceptions are correct or incorrect is through constant checking with other people. Finding such agreement is termed *consensual validation.* Most of us build up a strong drive to acquire such validation. One probable reason that the sensory deprivation experiments we mentioned earlier are so disorganizing is that the subjects are isolated and thus unable to check their perceptions with anyone. Consensual validation does not, of course, mean that the percept or concept is necessarily correct. A hundred years ago, Indians were generally feared and despised. "The only good Indian is a dead Indian," was a common saying. People who had positive feelings toward Indians were likely to be regarded as sentimental, queer, or "affected." Today the attitude of society toward Indians is much more accepting, and many people are proud of their "Indian blood."

The need for constant validation of our perceptions makes it reasonable to expect that social pressures strongly influence our perception. One set of studies that supports this idea are those by Sherif and others dealing with the autokinetic effect. A subject is placed in a pitch-black room, the only visible object being a small stationary dot of light. After a brief period, most people indicate that they see the light move. It has been found that when subjects are alone they vary widely in their estimation of the imaginary movement; in small groups, however, the estimates of each subject fall much closer to the average estimate of the group. (Sherif, 1935.) Asch (1956) conducted a series of experiments in which subjects were given the simple perceptual task of judging which of three lines (Card B in Figure 6-7) was equal in length to a standard line (Card A in Figure 6-7). The photograph shows the way in which the tasks were presented. In the experiment portrayed, the group

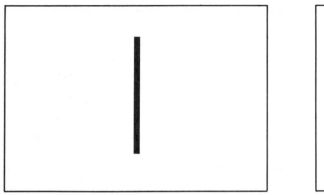

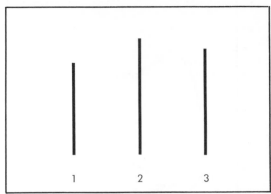

A   B

Cards used in Asch's study of group pressures on individuals.

Scene from Asch's study.

Figure 6-7. Asch's study of group pressures on individuals. (Asch, 1955. Reproduced by permission.)

consists of one naive subject (sixth from the left) and six "stooges," who had been instructed to give a wrong answer for a number of cards. All subjects are in agreement on the first two trials. Then, on the third trial, the naive subject finds himself in disagreement with the others. The strain of disagreeing with the group shows in his face.

Asch found that an average of 37 per cent of his subjects accepted the wrong judgments of the majority on each trial, whereas when they were not under group pressure, they made incorrect judgments less than 1 per cent of the time. Three-fourths of the subjects yielded to the majority on at least one of the twelve trials, only one-fourth consistently refusing to yield. The size of the group arrayed against the subject was also important. The graph in Figure 6-8 shows that when naive subjects were opposed by one member, an average of only 3.6 per cent of them gave the wrong reply, but when they were opposed by a majority of three, the errors jumped to 31.8 per cent. Asch

Figure 6-8. Effect of size of majority on judgments made by naive subjects. (Asch, 1955. Reproduced by permission.)

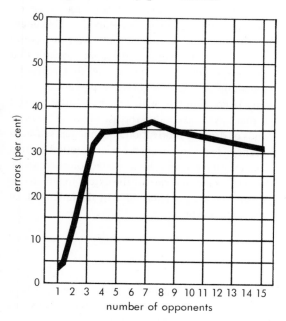

"Errors (per cent)" refers to the percentage of errors made by the naive subjects in conformity to the calculated misjudgments of the accomplices of the experimenter, and "number of opponents" means the number of accomplices in each group instructed to make calculated misjudgments.

also experimented with situations in which the naive subject had the support of a group member instructed to give the correct answers. Under such conditions, the proportion of wrong answers dropped to one-fourth. The reactions of the subjects to the "partner" were very interesting. The feeling was generally that of warmth and closeness, and he was perceived as someone who inspired confidence. However, the subjects rejected the idea that the presence of the "partner" somehow inspired them to behave more independently.

One of the incidental but significant findings in Asch's study was the fact that the subjects were unaware of the extent to which their judgments were being predetermined by the group. Even though they behaved in an "other-directed" fashion, they still clung to the idea that the replies they gave were the results of their own decisions. Indeed, when many of the subjects found that their perceptions differed from the other group members, they attributed this difference to some defect or deficiency within themselves, which they strove to hide at all costs by merging with the majority.

The disquieting conclusion that emerges from Asch's work, then, is the suggestion that our perceptions are readily modified or predetermined by the judgments of other people without our being aware of it. And since our perceptions form the basis of our attitudes, opinions, and actions, it seems that even when we think we are being independent and are making our own decisions we are ofttimes merely following the patterns of behavior set by those around us.

Summary

Energy changes in man's internal and external environment are made known to him through his perceptual processes. Though perception is often defined in terms of an experience, scientists are able to study only those observable responses that accompany or follow stimulation.

Perceptual functioning is based in part on inherited, physiological attributes of the organism, but there is a good deal of evidence that perception in human beings is based largely on learning. Sensory adaptation occurs when there is continued activity of a sensory organ. Dark adaptation involves an increased sensitivity to light stimuli, whereas light adaption is the reverse process. In other sensory modes, continued stimulation leads to decreased sensitivity for sound, smell, taste, pressure, temperature, and motion; a pain stimulus, however, continues unabated. Visual perception of depth is made possible partly through two-dimensional cues such as relative size of objects, whether one object is in front of another, texture, shadows, etc. However, true depth perception is the result of having two eyes that register pictures of the world at slightly different angles; auditory depth is possible because our two ears receive sound waves from right and left sides of an event.

Gestalt psychologists stress the fact that perception is an organized experience. Their work has dealt with perception of figure and ground, response to relationships, and with the principles of stimulus grouping or patterning: proximity, similarity, continuity, and closure. Our need for environmental stability is met through a tendency to perceive the surrounding world as fixed and a tendency to perceive objects as having a constant shape, size, and color. The perceptual inaccuracies known as illusions are the result of false stimulus information, physiological factors, and interaction between physiological and experiential variables.

Perception is called subliminal if the stimulation lies below the threshold of awareness and yet influences behavior. It has been found that "guesses" about subliminal stimuli are of greater-than-chance accuracy, and that subliminal stimulation also has a measurable effect on certain other behaviors. Experiments on sensory deprivation find that individuals isolated from sensory input may suffer interference with perception and with intellectual functioning. A few research workers are studying extrasensory perception, which includes mental telepathy, clairvoyance, and telekinesis. Although recent research has avoided some of the several methodological flaws of earlier studies, most psychologists still entertain doubts about the validity of these phenomena.

Individual differences are the rule in psychology, including the perceptual processes. Perceptual defects are not unusual, and problems arise both in the interference with stimulus reception and in the reaction of the individual and of society to his handicaps. A list of perceptual defects would include blindness, nearsightedness, farsightedness, astigmatism, color blindness, deafness, anosmia, disruption of static sensitivity, and loss of temperature, pain, and kinesthetic sensitivity. In measuring most perceptual tendencies, patterns of individual differences have been discovered that seem to be related to various personality differences, tolerance as opposed to resistance to an unstable environment, physiognomic opposed to literal perception, the perceptual defenses of sensitization opposed to repression, and field-dependent compared to analytic perception.

Perception is neither completely accurate nor completely representative of the stimuli impinging on an organism's receptors. Attention is a term that describes the selective nature of perception; among the stimulus variables influencing attention are size, intensity, repetition, and contrast. We tend to perceive what we have learned to expect; psychologists term this tendency "set." The esthetic qualities of one's perceptual environment have been found to exert an influence on several aspects of an individual's behavior. Stimuli that hold a special interest for us, or that represent something we value highly, are perceived differently from stimuli in which we have little interest or that have a low value for us. Likewise, various kinds of drive or motivation, like hunger, self-consistency, fear, and a need for consensual validation, may have a considerable effect on perception. Most of us are unaware of the extent to which our perceptions are predetermined by the judgments of those around us.

Questions

1. List all of the perceptual activities in which you are engaged at this moment.
2. What is meant by sensory adaptation? Think of a few examples from your everyday life.
3. In what ways do individuals respond to relationships rather than to specific stimulus values?
4. How is perceptual stability achieved? Give some examples of situations which involve changes in the perceptual field. What responses are made to this instability?
5. Explain what is meant by subliminal perception. Do you believe that subliminal cues influence any of your everyday behavior?

6. What are the similarities between the behavior of subjects in sensory deprivation experiments and our tendency to dream at night?
7. Why do you think a phenomenon like ESP stirs up strong feelings both pro and con?
8. How do most people react to slightly defective vision or hearing in others? Why?
9. Describe some of the patterns of individual differences in perception that psychologists have studied.
10. Discuss the various factors that probably influenced your recent perception of an individual, a situation, or an object.

Suggestions for further reading

Allport, F. W., *Theories of Perception and the Concept of Structure*. New York: Wiley, 1955. A description of the major theories of perception.

Blake, R. R. and G. V. Ramsey, Editors, *Perception, An Approach to Personality*. New York: Ronald Press, 1951. A series of papers by several psychologists dealing with the relationship between perceptual processes and personality variables.

Ellis, W. D., *A Sourcebook of Gestalt Psychology*. New York: Harcourt, Brace, 1938. Translation of German articles by Gestalt psychologists with an emphasis on perceptual studies.

Geldard, F. A., *The Human Senses*. New York: Wiley, 1953. An advanced book dealing with the structure and function of human sensory receptors.

Lawrence, M., *Studies in Human Behavior*. Princeton: Princeton University Press, 1949. A description of interesting laboratory demonstrations of depth perception and other phenomena.

McConnell, J. V., R. L. Cutler, and E. B. McNeil, "Subliminal stimulation: an overview," *The American Psychologist,* 13: 229–242; 1958. An article that reviews a half century of subliminal stimulation experiments from the early laboratory demonstrations to recent advertising applications.

Witkin, H. A., H. B. Lewis, M. Hertzman, K. Machover, P. B. Meissner, and S. Wapner, *Personality through Perception*. New York: Harper, 1954. A report of the studies relating performance on the rod-and-frame test and tilting-chair-tilting-room test to personality variables.

7

Motivation and emotional behavior

Internal forces underlying behavior. Both psychologists and laymen alike have an interest in understanding why people behave as they do. Indeed, it was this desire to probe the causes of behavior that led to the development of psychology as a science. The internal aspects of this causal background of behavior may be generally and perhaps vaguely referred to as *motivation*—the forces and conditions that impel behavior, that predispose us to one kind of behavior rather than another.

Although no field of psychology is more important with respect to the understanding of behavior, motivation remains an area that has so far been insufficiently explored. It is an area that is so vast and complex that our rather extensive efforts to understand it so far leave it largely unexplained. The attempts to develop some understanding of motivation have largely taken two main routes, one of which might be termed the "laboratory" approach and the other, the "clinical" approach.

The first of these approaches grows out of the scientific tradition of the nineteenth century, a tradition characterized by an intense and persistent curiosity about the nature of all varieties of natural phenomena. It was inevitable that the scientists of this period would become interested in human behavior, and they studied it by selecting some particular aspect, like pain, color vision, or taste, and subjecting it to intensive analysis. The experimentation that had its origins in the nineteenth century and resulted in modern psychological research has been surveyed briefly in the preceding chapters. It has produced a very respectable body of information regarding the nature and functioning of sensory organs and has led to an immense amount of research into some of the fundamental processes involved in human behavior—particularly learning, perception, and the functioning of the central nervous system.

The second approach has been equally concerned with understanding human behavior, but has been motivated principally by the need to *solve human problems*—not that scientific curiosity has been lacking in this approach, but rather that the desire to relieve human suffering has taken precedence over purely experimental considerations. Of the two approaches, the "clinical" approach has been considerably more productive of theories that attempt to explain the *totality* of human behavior and thus provide some kind of guide to therapeutic management and treatment of psychological disturbances. In Chapter 10 we shall give special attention to the theories that have been developed by this approach to the understanding of human behavior.

The "laboratory" approach, then, has been principally concerned with experimentation and analysis in different areas or aspects of behavior, rather than with studying behavior-as-a-whole. Both approaches are, of course, necessary. A thorough grasp of any one aspect of behavior not only contributes to the understanding of the whole, but also is essential. Although an understanding of the process of learning cannot explain human behavior as a whole, human behavior as a whole cannot be understood without an understanding of how humans learn. To use an analogy from botany, an understanding of how a plant uses mineral elements from the soil does not explain the totality of plant functioning, but an understanding of plant functioning would be incomplete without an understanding of how minerals are incorporated and used.

Similarly, motivation needs to be understood if human behavior as a whole is to be understood. It is not clear, at this point in the development of psychology as a scientific field, whether motivation can actually be studied separately from other aspects of behavior. Perhaps eventually it will be assimilated by other fields, such as learning or perception. So far, motivation has been studied largely as a theoretical field, with its major concepts drawn from research in the psychological laboratory.

Concepts of motivation

Levels of motivation. There are several ways of conceptualizing the motivating forces of human behavior. Most systems place the various kinds of motives on a continuum that ranges from the most rudimentary, biological, and primitive to the most complex, socialized, and abstract. At the primitive-biological end of the continuum are drives that help maintain bodily processes; at the socialized end are attitudes toward oneself and others.

As we pointed out in Chapter 5, motives may also be classified as "primary" and "secondary." Primary motives or drives have a strong physiological component. Tissue needs for nourishment, water, and air, as well as needs for elimination, physical comfort, and erotic stimulation, come under this classification. Secondary motives or drives are acquired through learning and socialization. Behavior beyond the most primitive level may be thought of as "goal-directed"—that is, directed toward whatever is required to satisfy the need that initiated the behavior. Motivation may also be seen as an on-going process produced by the interaction of internal and external forces.

The choice of which approach or system to use in studying behavior is to a large degree based on the interests of the researcher. The psychologist who is interested in reducing behavior to the smallest measurable unit is likely to think in terms of drives and goals—what is sometimes called the "molecular" approach. The psychologist who wants to study behavior in terms of its larger, more organized, and more integrated aspects tends to think in terms of needs, forces, and expectations —what is sometimes called the "molar" approach. At the present stage of the development of psychology as a science, the relationship between the findings of molecular and molar approaches is not very clear. We are not sure, for example, how the motivation for learning that is being studied in the laboratory (molecular) is related to the motivation for learning that is being studied in classroom settings (molar).

Primitive biological motives. The structure or hierarchy of needs [1] developed by Maslow

[1] Although the language of the experimental laboratory tends to limit the term "need" to "tissue needs," such as those that figure in hunger, thirst, etc., many writers use the term "need" to cover "drive," "tissue needs," and "motives in general," as Maslow does. Maslow, in fact, uses "need" to refer to the deficiency which initiates goal-directed behavior, as well as whatever is sought to satisfy the deficiency.

(1953), which we introduced in the chapters dealing with human development, may be used here as a framework for classifying and analyzing motives.

At the first level are the primitive-biological motives that are universal—motives that can be identified in the behavior of every human being and all forms of animal life. Within this level, the most primitive needs are the homeostatic mechanisms: the physical changes and adaptations that maintain body temperature at an optimal level, keep a proper concentration and balance of mineral salts in the blood stream, help us recover from disease and injuries, and so forth.

Next in order of complexity come the forms of behavior that have the purpose of maintaining the physical self, but which are more or less consciously undertaken. Under this heading we find behavior functioning to reduce tensions relating to hunger, thirst, and sex. Needs for rest, sleep, and the voiding of wastes are also included in this category.

Up to this point, motivation is rather obviously concerned with body maintenance. Now we come to behavior that is less obviously concerned with the physical self, but which is nonetheless a universal phenomenon among humans and the higher animals. The drive to explore and become acquainted with one's physical environment can perhaps be explained in terms of an interest in safety or security, but exploring activity, even in infrahuman animals, often goes beyond mere safety needs. Maternal motives also may be universal. However, like other forms of human behavior, even at the primitive-biological level, such motives can be markedly modified by social learning. There is a possibility that such behavior can be stimulated by glandular secretions during and after childbirth, but its tendency to persist for long periods of time and to appear even in the absence of child-bearing raises questions as to whether it is more "psychological" or "social," than "biological."

Instinct. Some psychologists, particularly during the earlier years of the development of psychology as a science, attempted to explain behavior resulting from exploratory and maternal drives as "instinctive." This approach led to the development of elaborate systems of instincts which were thought to be basic to all forms of human activity. Further research, however, has disclosed that the behavior that appears at first glance to be instinctive actually varies widely from culture to culture and individual to individual. Hence the concept of instinct has in general received little attention in recent years as a basis for studying human behavior, although it still has value in studying the behavior of animals. The migrating and nest-building habits of birds are common examples of instinctive behavior. Even with animals, however, psychologists find that they must exercise caution in classifying behavior as instinctive or learned. Some behavior, commonly thought to be instinctive (and hence invariable) turns out to show unexpected variation when studied scientifically. Although the mice-killing behavior of the Norway rat (the common brown rat) might be thought instinctive, Karli (1956) found that some rats killed mice, but others did not. As contrasted with Norway rats raised in captivity, more of the wild rats were killers, but there were no indications of why some killed and others did not. Even when faced by starvation, a condition that might be thought certain to bring out the instinctive response, rats that had not killed mice previously tended not to kill the mice placed in their cages.

The motives associated with needs at the third level of Maslow's hierarchy—the belongingness or love needs—may also have some physiological basis. As the research we reported in Chapter 2 suggests, young children may have a need to receive care and attention above and beyond that concerned specifically with nourishment and physical protection. However, such needs may be determined or modified by the culture. For example, Balinese children cry bitterly when ignored or teased by adults, and their behavior may show the presence of a need for love, but they learn to grow up without it and, as adults, appear to have little need to give or receive affection. (Bateson and Mead, 1942.)

Social motives. At the next level of complexity are the motives that are more obviously social in character. The drive to associate with others appears to be well-nigh universal. The satisfaction of this drive may not be essential as far as physical maintenance is concerned, but observations of a few human beings that have grown up in a wild state, away from human society, indicate that the qualities that make us "human" are derived from our associations with others. There is a large degree of self-concern inherent in much of our behavior that brings us into contact with others. According to Maslow, there is a need for self-esteem, recognition, and approval—even a need to be needed. Ashley Montagu (1953), an anthropologist, maintains that cooperation is also a basic drive, taking priority over such egocentric motives as competition. Other students of the subject would probably say that cooperation and other forms of apparently altruistic behavior have their self-oriented aspects.

Motivation may assume a kind of "functional autonomy," that is, it may be satisfying for its own sake, irrespective of the original need it was intended to satisfy. Eating presumably has the purpose of satisfying tissue needs for nourishment, but, as Hebb (1949) points out, eating a few salted peanuts not only does not satisfy the need for peanuts, but also it stimulates the need for *more* peanuts. Here is a need that has nothing to do with the survival of the organism, but which we deliberately stimulate (by taking the first handful of peanuts) in order to experience the pleasure of satisfying it again and again.

Maslow maintains that the needs at the complex-socialized end of the hierarchy tend to possess functional autonomy to a high degree. This is particularly true of self-actualization, which has no apparent survival purpose but which may be a dominant force in behavior. Some persons with a strong drive for creativity or self-expression will endure physical danger, hunger, thirst, and other forms of privation in order to find satisfactory expression for this drive.

Although we ordinarily think of the more basic drives as having precedence over the more complex-socialized drives, this relationship may be reversed, depending on the maturity of the individual. A small child who discovers that he is thirsty during a church service proclaims this fact at the top of his voice, much to the embarrassment of his parents who seek to distract and quiet him. Given a similar situation ten years later, the same child may display a little restlessness, but will postpone the satisfaction of the need for fluids till services are over. Learning may also affect the way in which a need is satisfied. An individual may have learned to prefer a cola drink and may not wish to quench his thirst with mere water, or he may not want to quench his thirst at all unless he can sit down with his drink at a table and socialize with a friend. Or he may be hard at work solving a difficult but interesting problem and may not be aware of his need for fluids.

Satisfactions. There is a marked tendency for us to organize our behavior in such a way that satisfactions are maximized, that is, we try to satisfy as many needs as possible with a single behavioral act and, when faced by a choice, we will select the behavior that satisfies the greater number of needs. Drinking with a friend satisfies both tissue and social needs. A father may want to enjoy the company of his wife and children after supper (that is, to express love needs), but instead he attends the meeting of a committee for civic improvement, thus satisfying his need for self-actualization and self-esteem, and indirectly satisfying needs to express love by helping to make the community a better place for his family to live in.

Human behavior is highly variable not because human needs are variable, but because satisfactions or goals are variable. There are, for instance, an infinite number of ways in which human beings satisfy their needs for nourishment, fluids, sociability, and creativity. To a large extent, this variability is a function of culture. For instance, the American ordinarily meets some of his needs for fluids by drinking water. Continental Europeans, particularly in the middle and upper classes, prefer to meet this need with something other than ordinary water—mineral water, wine, beer, or some brand of soda pop. Americans who travel in Europe frequently complain about the difficulty of getting ordinary water served with their meals. Many Americans traveling in Europe also find the Continental breakfast (which consists of rolls and coffee) quite inadequate, feeling that they need much more in the way of nourishment with which to face the day. We tend to regard breakfast as a fairly substantial meal, a meal that may be eaten in haste, perhaps, but not a meal to be slighted. Europeans in the countries bordering on the Mediterranean, however, find the Continental breakfast quite adequate and often "take it on the run." The French gentleman depicted in the adjoining photograph is eating his breakfast off a railway baggage cart while waiting for his train at Nice. For him, this breakfast is just as satisfying of his needs for nourishment as the traditional ham-and-eggs breakfast is for most Americans. These are just two minor instances of the ways individuals in different cultures learn to seek different kinds of satisfaction for their needs.

Satisfactions vary with individuals, as well as with cultures.

The French find that rolls and coffee are all they need in the way of nourishment with which to start the day.

One Friday night, Mr. Matson asked his family if they wanted to go on a picnic the following day. Philip, the oldest, said he would go. He actually wanted to stay at home and work on his speedboat, but he felt that if his father was willing to devote his Saturday to the family, the least he could do would be to cooperate. George, the second boy, greeted the idea with cheers. He saw it as a chance to get out of mowing the lawn, cleaning the basement, and doing his homework. Ted, the youngest, objected. He had just received a large packet of stamps and he had planned to spend the day sorting them and putting them in his collection.

Here are three boys, members of the same family and close together in ages, each with the same basic needs, but with different ways of satisfying them. Philip finds satisfaction in making things, but he also finds satisfaction in supporting his father's suggestions. As an oldest son, he feels a certain responsibility for the solidarity of the family group. George takes as much satisfaction in avoiding responsibility as Philip finds in seeking it. Going to the picnic appeals to him primarily as an opportunity to escape from his chores. Ted finds satisfaction in collecting things, particularly

things that can be sorted and classified. Each boy responds differently to the situation because he perceives it in a different way, and his perception is based partly on the kind of satisfaction that is important to him.

Individual patterns of development also create variability in satisfactions. Although the need for sleep is universal, some individuals get along on five or six hours of sleep in every twenty-four, and others may require nine or ten. Again, the culture may create variations in how this need is satisfied. In the United States, most people get their quota of sleep between ten o'clock at night and six or seven o'clock in the morning, whereas in Southern Europe, a common pattern is midnight to 6 A.M., with a one- or two-hour nap in the middle of the afternoon, after the main meal of the day. Nor is there any universally standard schedule for satisfying the need for nourishment. Among Western peoples, regular meal times are the rule, but in Indonesia, evening meals may be eaten at haphazard hours. Differences in attitudes toward when meals should be taken have sometimes led to difficulties in conferences attended by delegates from Indonesia and Western countries. When delegates from Indonesia become interested in a discussion, they are likely to want to go on indefinitely, irrespective of when they have eaten last, whereas Western delegates become increasingly irritable and tense as the hours past their regular mealtime start to lengthen.

Habits. The term "habit" is often used to refer to organized and learned response patterns that are used repeatedly or automatically. Taking one's meal at a predetermined hour is an example. Presumably habits have the purpose of enabling us to meet our needs and to cope with the demands made on us by our physical and social environment. Civilized man has the habit of wearing clothing—presumably as a way of coping with extremes of heat and cold. The bushman of Australia has not developed the habit of wearing clothing and copes with the problem of protection in other ways. Any culture may be viewed as a complex organization of habit patterns which functions partly to meet basic human needs, but which has the added effect of creating a "way of life." Cultures can be described in terms of habitual patterns of eating, dressing, body care, child-rearing practices, working, recreation, conducting relations between the sexes, and so forth, *ad infinitum*. And each of these patterns expresses itself in the personal habits of the individuals who are members of the culture.

A habit can develop symbolic value to the extent that it is more than a way of satisfying this or that need, and becomes a means of relating oneself to the culture-at-large. American smokers habitually hold their cigarettes between the second and third fingers; in some European countries cigarettes are held between thumb and first or second finger. The method of holding a cigarette is learned from other members of the culture; once it is learned it becomes one of an infinite number of ways of participating in the cultural group. The individual who conforms is in effect communicating his acceptance of the group and its culture; the individual who does not conform may be symbolizing a desire to place conditions and reservations on his participation with other members of the group.

Within any culture, there are, of course, individual variations. But even these variations are expected to fit with some general, over-all framework prescribed by the culture. The culture may, for instance, prescribe a range of habits to cover certain situations. In the American culture, habitual patterns of coping with tension include gum chewing, playing golf, and watching television. Americans are not likely to cope with their tensions through chewing betel nut, playing bocci, or watching long drawn-out, slow, stylized dances.

In Chapter 5, we spoke of the way in which some motives assume a kind of functional autonomy, in that they do not have to be reinforced by their original associations in order to be maintained, but develop almost a kind of independence in their ability to initiate and reinforce themselves. For example, smoking may be learned by an individual as a way of demonstrating adult status or as a means of socializing with other smokers. Perhaps it comes to have value as a tension-reducer as well. After smoking has become habitual, the individual may enjoy smoking when he is alone, that is, when there is no need to use it as an aid to socialization—and may even want to smoke in situations that are ordinarily relaxing, rather than tension-producing. The satisfaction of smoking a cigarette to reduce tension is such that the individual experiences a mild tension in order to have the pleasure of reducing it through smoking. Casual reading is another habit that may assume functional autonomy.

Alex Flock has learned the habits of social intercourse that are characteristic of our middle-class culture. He can engage in the give-and-take of conversation and, most of the time, enjoy it. But if he should happen to pick up a magazine, he is likely to become engrossed in it, ignoring the others who are in the room. He feels somewhat guilty when he does this, but when his wife berates him later, he is likely to make excuses, saying, for example, that his curiosity was intrigued by the announcement on the magazine cover of an article on a subject in which he was much interested.

Unconscious motivation. Alex's defensive reaction to his wife's criticism illustrates one important aspect of motivation: most of it functions outside the ordinary limits of our awareness. Although we usually have little difficulty in explaining why we do what we do, such explanations do not take into account all the factors involved in our motivation. When we explain our behavior, we are usually more interested in providing an explanation that is socially acceptable, rather than one that gets at the basic factors in our motivation. In the example just given, perhaps Alex does not want to admit that he was bored or that the others were not giving him the attention he thought he deserved. Or maybe there is no really "reasonable" explanation of why he feels compelled to pick up and read any magazine that is lying close at hand. Nor are we usually aware of the cultural aspects of habit: we believe that we do things in a certain way because it is the "proper" way to do it—it would not be "right" to do it otherwise. Or we may think that we "want" to do certain things, unaware that participation in our culture has left us little choice to do otherwise.

Certain aspects of our motivation may be charged with so much anxiety or guilt that we may unconsciously overlook them.

Pearson (1949) describes the case of a fourteen-year-old boy who was doing failing work in school in spite of a superior level of intelligence. The boy blamed his difficulties on laziness, talking too much in class, inattentiveness, the unfairness of his teachers, and a change in high schools. In describing his personal life, he said that he kept doing things that caused trouble—like taking his mother's car (he was forbidden to drive by his parents and had no license) and having a minor accident. He reported a number of other incidents in which he had openly and flagrantly defied his parents and other people in authority. When asked to describe his plans, he said that he expected to complete high school, attend college, and enter the business that his father was building up for him. His real ambition was to become a band leader, but he knew that taking up such a career would hurt his father's feelings.

Subsequent investigation showed that his poor grades in school were the result of what appeared on the surface to be a refusal to do what was expected of him. Even when he was getting a passing grade in a course, he would go out of his way to miss examinations. He would not finish assignments, or, if he did finish them, would not hand them in. He was often late to school, and sometimes he cut classes.

After detailed analysis of the case material, Pearson concluded that the boy had an unconscious need to be caught and punished. This was deduced from the fact that he committed infractions openly and made no attempt to avoid punishment. Yet he was unaware that he was deliberately courting punishment by his behavior. He did not dare to differ openly with his father regarding the plans for his future. Instead, he unconsciously sabotaged these plans by failing in school. Being expelled from school would prevent his going to college and entering his father's business, whereupon he would be forced by circumstances (but not by his own conscious wishes) to become a band leader.

"Repression" is the term that is commonly

used by psychologists to designate the process whereby we unconsciously "forget" certain disturbing events, attitudes, or feelings. In the anecdote, the boy repressed any feelings of guilt and anxiety he had with respect to the conflict between his father's plans for his future and his own aspirations. We all use repression to some extent: it is one of the common mechanisms of adjustment that is discussed in Chapter 9. It constitutes one of the several ways in which we conceal certain aspects of our motivation from ourselves. Not only do we keep these aspects from our general awareness, but also we are even unconscious that we are repressing anything.

Selective perception. In the previous chapter we discussed the processes whereby we "select" certain aspects of our environment to respond to and ignore others. Much selectivity goes on more or less consciously, but much more takes place unconsciously. The boy in the case just cited perceived many factors in his situation but somehow overlooked the significant relationship between his failure at school and the examinations he was missing. Sometimes the kinds of things we notice about our own behavior are predetermined by our personal problems, as they were with the 14-year-old boy. He could not perceive the fact that he was doing things that would bring about his own failure, because the idea that he would do such a thing was incompatible with his concept of himself. To have faced this fact and accepted full responsibility for his behavior would very likely have produced more anxiety than he could manage. Everyone is to some degree inconsistent in his behavior, yet we tend to think of ourselves as consistent, conveniently overlooking the inconsistencies. We do this because it is somehow *important* to us to be consistent; hence we per-

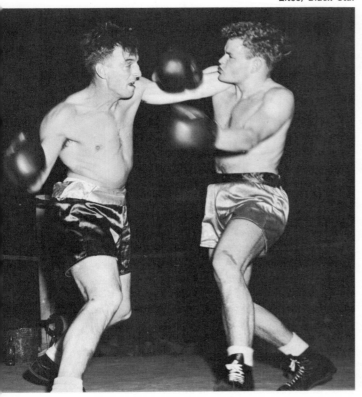

Thanks to cultural learning, we are able to enjoy watching boxing and other "body-contact" sports without the slightest awareness that our motivation is in any way bloodthirsty or sadistic.

ceive a great deal more consistency than actually exists.

Sometimes our perceptions of our motivation are guided by our culture, which tells us, in effect, why we behave as we do. When the people of the Middle Ages burnt and tortured heretics, any perception of themselves as possessing cruel or sadistic motives was effectively blocked by their confidence that what they were doing was in the best interest of the victims. Although the situation is not directly comparable, the twentieth-century individual who enjoys wrestling and boxing matches on television has similar defenses against perceiving any bloodthirstiness in his motivations.

It is important for the student of psychology to keep in mind that people are generally unaware of most of the motivational forces that are operating to produce the behavior they are displaying at any given moment. This point is important because "common sense" tells us that everyone is completely aware of his motives. The belief that peo-

ple are ordinarily aware of the significant factors that underlie their behavior is a common source of misunderstanding and false prediction in everyday life, and even produced many false leads during the earlier years of psychological research. As our explanations of our behavior are generally more concerned with "making sense" in terms of socially or individually predetermined concepts than they are with identifying the "true causes" of behavior, it is evident that they are not likely to be very revealing with respect to the more significant motives underlying the behavior in question.

Most of the research conducted by psychologists, particularly in the fields of personality and social psychology, deals with attitudes, feelings, and patterns of behavior that are "beyond awareness" to a greater or lesser degree. This is true even of research done with self-report questionnaires. Although we are certainly aware of the responses we make to questionnaire items, responses that are of necessity based on our awareness of our own experience, we are not aware of the relationship among the various items nor of our position with respect to other people on the matter being tested. To give a specific example, an individual filling out a questionnaire that measures, say, "social sensitivity," is not likely to be aware (if the questionnaire is properly constructed) of what the items measure, and even if he were aware, he would not be able to say, with any degree of accuracy, how much "social sensitivity" he has.

Conflict

When two motives oppose each other, when we are, so to speak, pushed and pulled in two different directions simultaneously, we experience what is termed *conflict*. Kurt Lewin (1935) identified three different ways in which motives can come into conflict with one another: *approach-avoidance, approach-approach,* and *avoidance-avoidance*.

Approach-avoidance conflicts are experienced when we are attracted and repelled by the same goal. Here is an example. The celebration for Frank's tenth birthday consisted of a trip to an amusement park in the company of his father and four other boys his age. As they passed the entrance to the roller-coaster, the boys clamored to be permitted to ride it. Frank's father agreed to take them if they would behave themselves and not do anything wild. Actually, Frank was frightened, but he pretended to be as interested as the others. He wanted to impress his friends and his father that he was growing up and "not a sissy." He wanted to go with the group and impress them with his maturity (approach), but at the same time he was frightened (avoidance).

Being faced with two attractive choices produces an *approach-approach* type of conflict. Consider the situation faced by Hal Rehbock, who cannot decide whether to ask the campus beauty queen or the fraternity sweetheart to go to the spring prom with him.

Avoidance-avoidance occurs when we are faced with two distasteful alternatives. We must spend two anxious hours taking a difficult final examination for which we are not adequately prepared or else fail the course. Neither of these alternatives is attractive: we do not want to take the examination (avoidance), but neither do we want to fail the course (avoidance). As is characteristic with conflicts of this sort, we vacillate. We think: "Is it really so bad to fail a course? On the other hand, maybe the examination is not as hard as we think it is." And we ponder ways whereby we can escape —"leave the field" as Lewin puts it. We think: "Perhaps we can drop the course. No, the instruc-

tor would fail us if we dropped now. Perhaps we can drop out of school altogether and come back next semester and make a fresh start. Is a college education really worth putting up with conflicts like these? Wouldn't life be simpler if we got a job checking groceries?"

Approach-approach conflicts may also be perceived as *double-approach-avoidance* conflicts. Hubert is finishing his junior year in college and is making excellent grades. He has received a very attractive job offer that he is reluctant to turn down. There is no assurance that he will be able to get as good a job as this one if he waits till he has graduated. On the other hand, if he quits college and takes the job, he will be giving up the college degree he planned for all his life. On the surface, it appears as though he faces an approach-approach conflict, the choice between two desired goals—the college degree and a good job—but actually each of these rewards carries a penalty with it: if he selects the goal of the college degree and continues in college, he runs the risk of never getting an opportunity like this one, but if he takes the job and quits college, he will probably never get the degree he has hoped for.

Conflicts evoke feelings of exasperation and

Figure 7-1. Conflict: Two drives impel the organism toward two incompatible goals or responses.

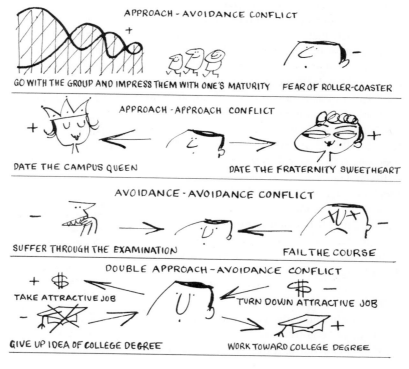

frustration. No matter what we decide, we must give up something. Ten-year-old Frank must give up either his self-respect and the good opinion of others or he must give up the security that comes from having both feet on the ground. No matter which girl Hal takes to the dance, he gives up the opportunity to take the other. Those of us who are faced by the difficult examination must give up our peace of mind (if we decide to take the examination) or our self-respect (if we decide not to take the examination and fail the course). No matter what decision we make we will experience feelings of frustration and possibly irritation or anxiety.

Like other motivational phenomena, conflicts can take place beyond the level of ordinary awareness. That is, we can be aware of the feeling of frustration or anxiety caused by the conflict, without being aware of what is causing it. In the case of the fourteen-year-old boy, cited a few pages back, his rather inadequate behavior was in part the result of a conflict between wanting to be a band leader (approach) but not wanting to hurt his father's feelings by refusing to finish his schooling and enter the family business (avoidance).

Emotional behavior

"Emotion" defined. Although we commonly think of ourselves as being generally reasonable and rational, actually only a relatively small part of our behavior results from rational activity—the end product, that is, of the deliberate and conscious process of reasoning. We live in a culture that places a high value on reasoning and thinking; hence we are inclined to think of ourselves as primarily rational individuals and consequently overlook the nonrational factors in our behavior and in the decisions we make. One of the classes of behavior that tends not to be based on rational decisions is that we call "emotional."

Psychologists prefer to speak of "emotional factors" or "emotional behavior," rather than of "emotion." "Emotion" is a very difficult word to translate into behavioral terms. That is, it is possible to classify one kind of behavior as more "emotional" than another, but when it comes to identifying "emotion" as a separate entity or "thing," there are bound to be difficulties.

The forces we call "emotions" may lead to activity or inhibit activity; they may also have attractive or unattractive characteristics. Hebb (1958) points out that the common factor characterizing the various forms of emotional behavior is this: the individual's motivation is somehow in a special state—that is, he is moved, for the moment, to act in a more or less unusual way. Hebb points out that "emotion" is a layman's term, having an everyday, "common-sense" value, but not very useful in scientific investigation: it is a term that refers to the individual's motivation in general, but not to any particular motivational process.

Behavior may be characterized as "emotional" if it departs somehow from an internal state of relative equilibrium. From one point of view, such behavior consists of bodily changes. In extreme emotional states the heart pounds, the skin is cold and clammy or heated and flushed, breathing is rapid and shallow, pupils of the eyes are dilated—all depending on the variety of emotion that is being expressed. Even minor changes in emotional behavior produce physical changes. The reaction of a subject to an interview or a motion picture film can be measured by a polygraph, an apparatus that registers changes in respiration, heart beat, palmar sweating, and so forth. From another point of view emotional behavior consists of more or less conscious disturbances in impulses and feelings, either pleasant or unpleasant. The milder, dilute versions of such behavior appear as preferences or aversions, irritation or enjoyment; the more intense forms appear as panic, rage, hilarity, or sexual passion.

Emotion as motivation. The point of view traditionally taken both by psychologists and laymen is that emotional behavior is essentially disorganized or disorganizing behavior. However, Leeper (1948) makes the point that all emotional behavior essentially has an organizing effect, that what appears to be disorganization is actually the result of motivational forces operating at cross purposes with one another. He states:

Emotional processes are one of the fundamental means of motivation in the higher animals—a kind of motivation which rests on relatively complex neural activities rather than primarily on definite chemical states or definite receptor stimulation, as in the case of bodily drives or physiological motives such as hunger, thirst, toothache, and craving for salt. In lower animals, such as a clam, there probably are no such emotional processes, but merely the physiological motives. . . . The discussion of emotion belongs in the field of motivation. When we omit it from this field we may be doing justice to the motivation of clams, but we are not doing justice to the motivation of human beings

. . . We need to see that emotional functioning is . . . one of the primary needs of human life.[1]

The idea that emotional behavior is disorganizing probably stems from incidents like these. A taxpayer who expected to get a five-dollar refund for overpayment of income tax was surprised to get a check for a million and five dollars in the mail. It turned out that a love-sick clerk had inadvertently both punched a wrong key in making out his check and omitted punching a key for a check to be sent to a large corporation, and the errors balanced. The errors should have been caught by the accountant in charge of the office, but he had just concluded an angry telephone conversation with his wife. Emotional factors certainly had disorganizing results in these two events—not because love or anger are inherently disorganizing, but because they organized the two individuals for something different than what they were doing. The clerk was emotionally organized for activities related to being with her boy friend, and the accountant was organized to do battle with his wife. In both instances they were organized for activities at cross purposes with their assigned responsibilities.

Varieties of emotion. Although psychologists differ with respect to what they consider to be the basic varieties of emotional behavior, most of them do, in some way or other, identify these: fear, rage, and elation. To this list we would add one more: depression. One way of characterizing these varieties of emotion is by viewing them in terms of the implied direction of the behavior.[2] Fear implies movement *away from* the source of the stimulus. The frightened person may not actually move away, but he senses a desire to escape from or avoid the threatening situation. Rage implies a movement *against* the situation. The angry person may not actually attack the source of his anger, but he senses a desire to destroy or injure whoever or whatever is producing the threatening stimulus. Elation also implies a movement in the direction of the source of stimulation, but a movement *toward* rather than against it. Whether the individual wishes to approach the source of the stimulus, to have it approach him, or merely to remain in its proximity will depend on how he per-

ceives the situation. In any event, the attitude is one of perceiving or wanting a sense of closeness or identity with the source of stimulation. Depression is a withdrawing type of response and in this sense it resembles fear. Unlike fear, however, it calls for a *cessation of activity,* a withdrawing into oneself, and a feeling of resignation, apathy, or hopelessness.

Physiological aspects of emotional behavior. Physiologically speaking, the different varieties of emotion possess both similarities and differences. Fear and rage are symptomatically the most similar. When an infant is disturbed, it is difficult to determine whether he is afraid or angry. If his cries are the result of a loud noise, we assume that he is frightened, but if they are the result of having his bottle removed from his mouth in the midst of feeding, we assume that he is angry. Nevertheless, in making this judgment, we are depending on *our* perception of the situation. Bridges (1932) found, in a study we will discuss later in this chapter, that she could not distinguish between fear and anger in the behavior of infants during the first few months of life. Even with adults there is some simliarity between fear and anger. In Chapter 4, we referred to a study by Ax (1953) who measured changes in heart beat, respiration rate, conductivity of the skin, and face temperature, while his subjects experienced two kinds of situations, one kind producing anger, and the other, fear. Of the fourteen varieties of physical changes measured, four were significantly associated with anger, and three with fear. Differences between fear-producing and anger-producing situations were insignificant as far as the other seven kinds of changes were concerned. Under anger-provoking situations, Ax found that his subjects were more likely to demonstrate these symptoms: slower heart beat and increased diastolic blood pressure.[3] When subjects were frightened, heart rate and respiration rate increased. Muscle tension and skin moisture increased under both fear and anger-provoking situations, but the pattern of increases was different under the two kinds of conditions.

Although Ax was able to show some measurable differences between states of fear and anger, his

[1] Reprinted by permission.
[2] The idea of classifying behavior according to its direction, that is, movement *toward, against,* or *away from* appears in Horney (1945).

[3] Diastolic blood pressure is read when the heart has expanded and is filled with blood and is thus contrasted with systolic blood pressure, which is read when the heart has contracted and has forced blood out into the circulatory system.

Toward (love)

Emotional behavior may be classified according to the implied direction.

Against (anger)

World Health Organization

Susan Greenburg

Away from (fear)

Immobilization (depression)

Susan Greenburg

Ted Russell (photo posed by professional model)

research leaves some question regarding the basic differences between fear and anger. However, more recent research by Funkenstein, King, and Drolette (1957) sheds greater light on the problem. These researchers subjected volunteers to two stressful situations. In one situation, subjects were asked to do computation problems which initially were easy. As the problems became difficult, the subjects were hurried, insulted, and otherwise harassed by the experimenter. In the other situation, subjects were asked to retell a story as rapidly and accurately as possible. As they started to tell the story, however, they found themselves speaking into sonic confusers, microphones that relayed the sound of their voices to their ears after a delay of one-fifth of a second. This caused stammering, slurring, and other difficulties in speaking, accompanied by a marked tendency to slow down. The more rapidly the subjects spoke, the greater the stammering induced by the sonic confuser, and the greater the amount of stammer-

ing, the more they tried to slow down. Whenever they stopped or slowed down, they were punished with a mild electric shock. This produced an avoidance-avoidance conflict, which aggravated the stress. Stress was also heightened by the fact that in both the problem-solving and the sonic-confusion situations subjects were tested lying on their backs, strapped down by the ballistocardiograph equipment that was used to measure the movement imparted to the body by the heart beat.

Funkenstein and his associates found three main patterns of reaction to these stress-provoking situations:

1. *Anger-out:* the subject reported his feelings as mostly that of being angry, irritated, or annoyed.

2. *Anger-in:* the subject reported himself as angry, but turned this feeling toward or against himself.

3. *Severe anxiety:* the subject reported that he was made anxious, apprehensive, frightened, or panicky by the experiment.

When the researchers examined the ballistocardiograph reports of their subjects, they found that the three kinds of reaction listed above produced different patterns. (See Figure 7-2.) A comparison of prestress and poststress patterns for the "anger-out" subjects shows the least change. "Anxiety" subjects show the most change, with "anger-in" subjects being somewhat in between. It appears that "anger-out" subjects were least disturbed by the experience, and that "anxiety" subjects were the most disturbed.

Changes in blood chemistry under emotional stress. Confirmation of these different patterns of responding to stress showed up in an analysis that was made of the blood content of the subjects. "Anger-in" and "anxiety" states were accompanied by increases in the amount of epinephrine or adrenalin in the blood. Epinephrine is a substance that stimulates metabolic activity: faster heart beat, muscle tension, rapid breathing, and so forth. "Anger-out" was accompanied by the release of *nor*-epinephrine (or nor-adrenalin), a substance that produces a low level of metabolic activity and little physiological disturbance.

Funkenstein and his associates point out relationships between their findings and other research in this field. Chemical analyses of the adrenal tissues of animals that depend on aggressiveness for survival (lions, whales, dogfish sharks) show a high concentration of nor-epinephrine, whereas

Figure 7-2. Prestress and poststress ballistocardiograph tracings typical of subjects characterized by three kinds of emotional reactions to stress. Although there is some disagreement as to what ballistocardiograph waves actually measure, evidence seems to indicate that they reflect variations in cardiac output, that is, the amount of blood being forced out of the heart. (Funkenstein, King, and Drolette, 1957. Reproduced by permission.)

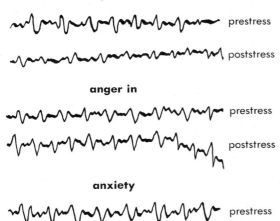

anger out

prestress

poststress

anger in

prestress

poststress

anxiety

prestress

poststress

similar analysis of animals that depend upon flight for survival (rabbits, guinea pigs) show a high concentration of epinephrine. Analyses of the adrenal of the human fetus and the newborn infant show a preponderance of nor-epinephrine, with epinephrine increasing as the child develops.

Family backgrounds and emotional patterns. Funkenstein and his co-workers were as concerned with the psychological aspects of emotional behavior as they were with its physiological aspects. An analysis of the background of their subjects (all of whom were Harvard students) indicated that the relationship they had with their parents had some bearing on the kind of emotional behavior they displayed under stress. Individuals whose characteristic response was "anger-out" described their father as a figure of authority, stern and difficult, often angry and seldom showing affection, whereas their mother was described as having little authority in the family but showing a great deal of affection and understanding. Despite the difficulties with the father, "anger-out" subjects admired him more than the mother and described him as having the same kind of attitudes and feelings that they saw in themselves. As Figure 7-3 shows, "anger-out" subjects looked upon their father as a source of authority and as a model for their own behavior, but did not see him as a source of affection. Their mother was perceived as a source of affection, but not as a source of authority or as a model for their own behavior.

Although "anger-in" students were characterized by a variety of patterns of relationship with their parents, the commonest pattern was one that resembled the "anger-out" group to some degree. In this pattern, the mother was perceived as being more affectionate than the father, but the relationship with the father was also an affectionate one. There was not the sharp contrast between the perceptions of the mother and father roles that was characterized by the "anger-out" group. The fathers of the "anger-in" students tended to share some of their authority with the mothers, and the mothers shared some affection with the fathers.

The "anxiety" group was characterized by family relationships in which the mother was perceived as being the main source of authority and affection and was also the prime model for the individual's behavior. The fathers of more than half the students in this group were missing because of death or divorce.

The data from the several parts of this study

"ANGER-OUT"

"ANXIETY"

"ANGER-IN"

Figure 7-3. Schematic presentation of relationship to parents according to individual's predominate pattern of emotional reaction under stress. (After Funkenstein, King, and Drolette, 1957.)

strongly support the idea that emotional behavior is *both* physiological and psychological. The way in which an individual responds to stress is evidently related to the amount of epinephrine and nor-epinephrine secreted, as well as to response patterns learned in childhood through interaction with his parents. Although at birth we tend to be largely nor-epinephrine or "anger-out" types of individuals, some of us develop reaction patterns characterized by epinephrine and "anger-in" or "anxiety" reactions to stress. Which one of the three patterns we develop seems to depend on the kinds of roles played by our parents and our relations with them. The "anger-out" individual apparently identifies with a stern, difficult, and angry father and hence learns to perceive frustrations imposed by his environment as calling for an "anger-out" type of response. The "anger-in" individual also models his behavior after that of his father, but whereas the "anger-out" individual describes his relationships with his father as difficult, the "anger-in" individual describes them as close and affectionate. His family relationships in general are described as being better balanced and more cooperative. Such an atmosphere, coupled with friendly relations with his father, would be conducive to his learning to make the kind of perceptions that would discourage "anger-out" reactions and encourage the development of the self-control necessary for "anger-in" reactions. It is interesting to note that "anger-in" responses were much more characteristic of students from upper social classes. The "anxiety" type of student grows up in a family in which the mother is the dominant figure. She is perceived as an emotionally disturbed person, being frequently angry or depressed. In view of the fact that "anxiety" individuals tended to identify themselves with their mothers, it is hardly surprising that they learned to perceive the stresses of their environment as anxiety-provoking.

Maturation of emotional behavior

Control. One of the changes that comes with maturity is greater control of the emotions. As Funkenstein and his associates state:

Anger-Out is a more primitive and less civilized response than Anger-In or Anxiety. As the child becomes socialized and learns to be a civilized person, he must learn to curb hostile impulses. This results in either turning the anger on the self or having conflicts about hostile impulses. Certainly, the curbing of hostile impulses so that self-related emotions result causes a great deal of suffering to a person. He, rather than his opponent, must suffer. Such suffering is in Freud's words, "The price paid for civilization." [1]

Another change that comes with maturity is the greater stability of emotions. Anyone who has observed the behavior of an infant knows that changes from one emotional state to another may come very rapidly. When an attractive toy is removed, smiles dissolve into cries of rage and frustration, but joy can be restored when the toy is returned. Feelings of frustration and elation are freely expressed; there is no brooding or restraint.

[1] Reprinted by permission.

Figure 7-4. Emotional development during the first 2 years of life. (After Bridges, 1932.)

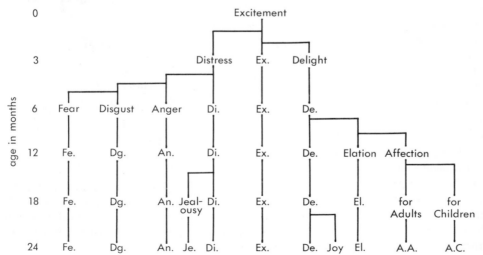

The psychological boundaries between infants and their environment are easily penetrated: they can be easily distracted, and their behavior can be easily affected by changes in temperature, noise level, and visible phenomena.

Differentiation. The most detailed study of infant and child emotional responses was made by Bridges (1932) who conducted daily observations of the behavior of 62 infants at the Montreal Foundling and Baby Hospital. Bridges found that the only emotion evidenced at birth was a generalized excitement, expressed by such behavior as a tensing of the muscles, breathing more quickly, and opening the eyes. By the time infants were three weeks old, Bridges was able to distinguish a pattern of behavior associated with distress. A few weeks later, behavior characterized by evident feelings of delight appeared. As the infants grew into childhood, the process continued—simpler, generalized emotional behavior became differentiated into more specialized patterns of emotional behavior. For example, at about seven or eight months after birth, elation and affection appeared as variants of the "delight" pattern. The "affection" sub-pattern became further differentiated in terms of affection for adults and affection for other babies. (See Figure 7-4.)

Perceptual changes. This pattern of development apparently continues throughout childhood and into adulthood, as we learn to respond to different situations in different ways. It is quite likely that what we recognize as the development of new patterns of emotional behavior are the result of the emergence of new patterns of perception on the part of the child. A 9-year-old boy standing in a cafeteria line at school is pushed from behind. Almost as if by reflex, he turns around and shoves the child behind him. When the same thing happens to a 18-year-old, he is irritated and is tempted to shove back, but instead stops to see why he is being shoved and finds that some horse-play is going on about eight places up the line, whereupon he is no longer angry at the person just behind him but at the individuals who are the causes of the difficulty. Instead of taking direct action, as a 9-year-old might do, he hesitates and considers. If there is no more shoving, he will probably contain his anger or limit it to calling out: "Watch what you're doing!" or some such admonishing phrase.

Emotional responses also change in other ways. Small boys traditionally dislike movie scenes in-

Robert Overstreet

Through interaction with one another, and under the guidance of adults, children learn the degree and kind of emotional responses that the culture considers to be appropriate for various situations.

volving a great deal of affectional display, unless the object happens to be a horse or a dog. A few years later they watch the same kind of scene with much more interest. The adolescent who is punitive, moralistic, and self-righteous as a member of the student court in high school grows up to become an adult who is considerably more tolerant and considerate of others and more judicious.

Intensity. There are changes, too, in the intensity with which emotions are expressed. Infants and small children are easily panicked or enraged and just as easily transported into ecstasies of delight. Children of school age are not aroused as readily or as frequently as younger children; they are somewhat less inclined to deviate as frequently or as widely from their usual emotional state. As contrasted with adults, however, they are more likely to experience extremes of depression and elation, anger and fear. An adult in our Western middle-class culture strives to keep his emotions from exceeding what are considered to be conventional bounds. He likes to be amused and he tolerates a certain amount of irritation, but he seldom experiences the excitement of genuine elation and joy, and he tries to keep from losing his temper. He achieves this state of relative balance by learning not to be unduly elated or upset by minor occurrences. Getting a raise in salary may give him a glow of satisfaction, but he does not

As we become more mature, our emotional behavior tends to become less intense.

jump about with pleasure and excitement as a small boy does who has just found a quarter. Nor is he thrown into a state of panic at the prospect of going downstairs into a dark cellar.

We also keep our emotions under control by avoiding situations that are likely to arouse extremes of emotional behavior. Hebb (1955) points out that it is easy to be scornful of children or of primitive people for their superstitious fear of dead bodies. When he asked his students how many of them had actually had much experience with dead bodies, less than half of them were able to reply in the affirmative. One of the ways in which we keep our emotional life on a relatively even keel, then, is by developing a culture that organizes our environment in such a way that the opportunities for marked emotional stimulation (particularly with respect to fear and anger) are kept to the minimum.

Summary

Interest in understanding the forces that impel behavior and the causes of differential behavior has led to the concept of motivation. Psychologists have studied motivation from both the experimental and the clinical approach. The experimental method has been concerned primarily with developing principles to predict specific aspects of human behavior, based on careful experimentation. The clinical method involves, primarily, an attempt to solve the emotional difficulties of individuals, with theories to explain human behavior evolving as a by-product.

Motivation can be conceptualized as occurring at different levels. Primary drives consist of inborn motives with strong physiological components, whereas secondary drives are acquired. Some psychologists approach the study of motivation in a "molecular" way in terms of specific drives and goals. Others adhere to a "molar" approach to behavior-as-a-whole. Our most primitive biological needs have to do with homeostatic processes; higher level primary drives are concerned with maintaining the integrity of the physical self. Drives such as those for exploration and maternal behavior seem physiologically based, but they can be extensively modified by learning. Early psychologists attempted to explain a great deal of human behavior as instinctive, but the discovery of wide cultural variations has not supported the idea that much of human behavior is based on instinct. Needs to belong and to be loved have some physiological basis but are greatly influenced by learning. Social motives are quite varied in their nature and can become relatively independent of physiology. The ways in which human beings learn to satisfy their needs are infinite. Behavior tends to be organized in such a way that as many needs as possible are satisfied by any one behavioral act. There are both cultural and individual differences in the learning and organization of need satisfaction.

Learned patterns of response are called habits. Besides the satisfaction of needs, habits come to have their own special meaning in terms of an individual's relationship with his culture. There are variations in habits within a culture, but the types of accepted variations are culturally prescribed.

Many of our motives are unconscious ones; we tend to give socially acceptable explanations for our behavior and hide the real motives even from ourselves. Anxiety causes us to repress the memory of various events and feelings. A good deal of our perception is selective, based on self-consistency and culturally determined patterns of behavior.

When two incompatible motives are aroused simultaneously, we are in a state of conflict. Conflicts may be categorized into approach-avoidance, approach-approach, avoidance-avoidance, and double approach-avoidance types. Conflicts are anxiety-provoking, and we may be involved in conflicts of which we are unaware.

Emotional factors may have integrating or disintegrating effects on behavior. Behavior is emotional if it involves internal disequilibrium. Human emotions may be divided into fear (moving away from a situation), rage (moving against), elation (moving toward), and depression (cessation of activity). Fear and rage are the most similar physiologically. It has been found that individuals respond to stress with one of these patterns: "anger-out," "anger-in," or "severe-anxiety" reactions. The latter two states are accompanied by epinephrine increases in the blood stream whereas nor-epinephrine accompanies anger-out responses. Family patterns also show differences; "anger-out" individuals tend to have stern, authoritarian fathers, "anger-in" subjects tend to have parents who share their authority and who are both affectionate, and the "anxiety" group tend to come from families in which the mother is the main source of authority.

With increasing maturity, we learn to exercise greater control over our emotions. Our emotional behavior becomes more stable, and we learn to respond to different situations in different ways as we grow older. Infants and small children reveal much more intense emotional states than adults. Adults in our Western middle-class culture strive to keep emotions within prescribed bounds both by internal control and by learning to avoid situations that might arouse extreme emotional behavior.

Questions

1. What is meant by the term "motivation"? Discuss the two major approaches to the study of motivation.

2. List several of your needs. Are they innate or acquired? If the latter, how did you acquire them? What sort of behavior satisfies each one?

3. Select a few fairly common needs such as safety, self-esteem, and love. Name the different ways in which various individuals have learned to satisfy these needs.

4. Why should any of our motives be unconscious? Are there any advantages to be gained in making such motives conscious?

5. Suggest several examples to illustrate each of the four types of conflict.

6. How is emotional behavior different from other behavior?

7. Describe the four basic varieties of emotional behavior. How do you go about identifying these emotions in yourself and in others?

8. Discuss some of the differences between an "anger-out," an "anger-in," and a "severe-anxiety" response to stress. Which way do you respond?

9. How does emotional behavior change from infancy to childhood to adolescence to adulthood?

Suggestions for further reading

Carmichael, L., *Basic Psychology: A Study of the Modern Healthy Mind*. New York: Random House, 1957. See the chapters on emotion and on drives and motives.

Funkenstein, D. H., S. H. King, M. E. Drolette, *Mastery of Stress*. Cambridge, Mass.: Harvard University Press, 1957. A report of the study that identified the "anger-out," "anger-in," and "anxiety" patterns of behavior.

Hebb, D. O., *The Organization of Behavior*. New York: Wiley, 1949. Chapters on motivation and emotional disturbances contain an interesting and provocative analysis.

Heyns, R. W., *The Psychology of Personal Adjustment*. New York: Dryden, 1958. Chapters on motivation and emotions show how these two aspects of behavior are interrelated.

Lindgren, H. C., *Psychology of Personal and Social Adjustment,* 2nd ed. New York: American Book, 1959. Chapter 3 discusses unconscious factors in motivation; Chapter 4 discusses emotion in terms of need satisfaction and the perception of threat.

McClelland, D. C., Editor, *Studies in Motivation*. New York: Appleton-Century Crofts, 1955. An unusually well-selected and interesting collection of papers on this subject.

Reymert, M. L., Editor, *Feelings and Emotions*. New York: McGraw-Hill, 1950. A collection of papers on this subject by a group of eminent psychologists. An excellent source book for those interested in theoretical aspects.

Shaffer, L. H. and E. J. Shoben, *The Psychology of Adjustment,* 2nd ed. Boston: Houghton Mifflin, 1956. Chapters 2, 3, and 4 deal with motivation, frustration, and conflict.

8

The psychologist's use of statistics

For a good many persons, the mere mention of such words as "mathematics," "formula," or "equation" evokes mild feelings of anxiety. College students faced with the prospect of taking a course in statistics (or even the task of reading a chapter dealing with the subject) often seem overwhelmed by the frightening possibilities. Yet the subject matter of statistics does not need to be as nightmarish as students seem to expect.

In fact, many statistical concepts are already familiar to most people. Each day, we deal with a variety of statistics. We read that a football team has *averaged* three touchdowns per game this season. We note that the *range* of yesterday's temperature was from a low of 58 to a high of 75 degrees. We hear that further evidence has been found to show that incidence of lung cancer is *related* to the number of cigarettes smoked per day. We learn that women have a *longer* life span than men. We are told that the *chance* of rain today is 30 per cent. Each italicized word suggests the use of an important statistical concept. Each of them will be discussed in this chapter.

There are two major uses for statistics in the science of psychology. Statistics are used in *describing* masses of data and in drawing *inferences* about the meaning of data. Words like "average" and "range" and "relationship" come from the statistics of description. Words having to do with odds and probablility and significance of differences are from the statistics of inference. In this chapter, both uses of statistical tools will be described, as well as the statistical evaluation of tests.

Statistics of description

Measuring individual differences. The basic assumption that underlies the development and use of psychological measuring instruments is that people differ. As mentioned in previous chapters, individuals differ in every physical and psychological attribute ever studied. That is, if any group of people is measured with regard to any factor, differences are found among them. Actually, there would be no need to name an attribute unless there *were* individual differences in it. Height is important only because people are not all equally tall. Anxiety is important because it varies from person to person and from time to time for any one person. It would not be worthwhile to measure intelligence if everyone had the same IQ. The fact that human attributes *vary* for different people is one reason that psychologists use the term *variable.* Thus, height, anxiety, intelligence, income, age, pulse rate, grade-point average, and finger dexterity are all variables.

Perhaps it seems trite and obvious to say that people differ. Yet, a great deal of "common sense" thinking is based on the assumption that people do *not* vary. Possibly you have heard (or even made) statements like these:

"People are the same the world over."
"Women drivers are all alike—they signal for a left turn and then go to the right."
"All Negroes are musical."
"At heart, everyone is kind."
"Oh, he's one of those dumb football players."
"Artists are so temperamental."

The basic assumption that underlies these statements is that people (at least people in certain large groups or categories) do *not* differ. These notions imply a uniformity of people in general, women drivers, Negroes, football players, and artists. If we are alert and unbiased in our observations, we can obtain data that indicate that such sweeping assumptions are false. A great deal of the research that psychologists have undertaken has been motivated by the desire to put such assumptions to the test. However, ideas like these are durable; they seem to be well able to withstand the impact of damaging evidence. For many persons, such beliefs are able to satisfy certain motives, such as the need to explain away or rationalize some irrational behavior or to justify an unwarranted attitude of superiority.

Our main point, though, is that individuals do differ. Once this is accepted, statistics become in-valuable tools for anyone who wishes to work with the science of human behavior.

Describing scores: The frequency distribution. The first step in describing a series of scores is to convert them into a form in which it is possible to comprehend them as a whole. After a group of individuals have been measured on any variable, the result is a series of numbers: the "raw scores." In order to illustrate the process of describing a set of measurements, we will use data from a study dealing with humor. (Byrne, 1956.)

Forty-five neuropsychiatric patients were presented individually with a stack of 32 cartoons mounted on heavy cardboard. Earlier, a group of psychologists had agreed that 16 of the cartoons depicted the expression of hostility and 16 were neutral in content. Each subject was told to divide the cartoons into two equal piles. In one pile he was to place those cartoons in which "insults, anger, teasing, or meanness" was expressed, and in the other pile those cartoons in which these factors were not present.

The variable being measured might be labeled "the ability to judge hostile content of magazine cartoons," and each subject's accuracy would be shown by his "hostility-judging score." It was decided to give a score of one for each cartoon placed in the correct pile. It was assumed that individuals would differ on this variable. Theoretically, scores could range from 0 (no cartoons correctly judged) to 32 (all cartoons correctly judged). The actual scores are presented in Table 8-1 as they appear on the data sheets of the author.

One glance at the 45 scores in Table 8-1 shows

Table 8–1 Raw scores made by 45 neuropsychiatric subjects in judging hostility in cartoons.

1. 14	16. 22	31. 22
2. 20	17. 20	32. 14
3. 28	18. 14	33. 14
4. 28	19. 28	34. 20
5. 26	20. 16	35. 14
6. 22	21. 12	36. 22
7. 16	22. 28	37. 12
8. 12	23. 20	38. 14
9. 20	24. 12	39. 14
10. 24	25. 24	40. 30
11. 22	26. 20	41. 22
12. 24	27. 26	42. 30
13. 24	28. 18	43. 28
14. 30	29. 18	44. 28
15. 30	30. 24	45. 32

why statistics of description are necessary. It is very hard, if not impossible, to make sense out of this array of numbers. Accordingly, the first step to be taken in describing the characteristics of a group of people on any variable is that of making a frequency distribution, such as is shown in Table 8-2. The scores are arranged in order, grouped, and tallied. Although a frequency distribution is a far from perfect description of the group, with respect to the variable being measured, it is much easier to form a picture of the patients' ability to judge hostility in cartoons by inspecting Table 8-2 than by trying to make sense out of Table 8-1.

Describing the central tendency of the scores. One of the simplest and most familiar ways of describing a group's characteristics on a variable is the *average*. We speak of the average weight of American women, the average yearly rainfall in Oregon, and the average score on the mid-semester examination. The statistical term equivalent to average is the *mean*. To obtain the average or mean, you simply add all the scores and divide by the total number of scores. When the mean score is obtained, it gives us a convenient way to express just where a given group stands on a particular variable. The mean hostility-judging score of the 45 patients is 21.29 (958 ÷ 45). In other words, the average subject classified approximately 2 out of 3 cartoons correctly.

A book listing the height of every man in this country would be much more difficult to understand than a sentence saying "The mean height of the American male is 5 feet 8½ inches." Knowing the mean also makes comparisons possible. If we are told that the mean height of American women is 5 feet 4 inches, we can comprehend at a glance that men tend to be taller than women and by how much. We call the mean a measure of central tendency because it tells us something about where the center of the frequency distribution lies. It is a useful shorthand way of describing a group.

Although the mean is the most commonly used measure of central tendency, two other measures are sometimes employed. The *median* is the midmost score; half of the individuals in a distribution score below the median, and half score above the median. In most instances, the mean and the median are the same or almost the same score. That is, in the usual situation a group's average score and midmost score tend to fall at about the same place. We found that the mean of the scores in Table 8-2 is 21.29; the median is 21.56. Why then, would the median ever be used? It is because the median usually gives a better picture of central tendency than does the mean when a few extreme, unrepresentative cases are included in the distribution. As a hypothetical example, Table 8-3 presents the annual incomes of the 21 residents of a Gulf Coast village. The village houses a handful of poor fishermen, craftsmen, and tradesmen. In addition, resident 21 is a wealthy manufacturer who lives in semiretirement in a mansion on the hill. His annual income of $400,000 represents an extreme, unrepresentative case in this distribution. The town's *mean* annual income is a very comfortable $21,254.76 ($446,350 ÷ 21) but a more realistic figure is the town's *median* annual income of a meager $2500 (the midmost score, resident 11). In situations such as this, the use of the mean as an indication of central tendency is both inappropriate and misleading.

A third, little used, measure of central tendency is the *mode* or score which the largest number of individuals obtain. In most situations this will not be greatly different from the mean and median; in Table 8-2 the mode is the center of the 21–24 category, or 22.5. Sometimes the modal score is often not representative of the central tendency, and there may be more than one mode, in which case the distribution is called bimodal, or trimodal, etc. The mode would never be used in preference to the mean and median, but is sometimes included as an additional descriptive device.

Table 8–2 Frequency distribution of the cartoon hostility judging scores.

Scores	Tallies	Frequency
29–32	ⵏⵏⵏ	5
25–28	ⵏⵏⵏ ///	8
21–24	ⵏⵏⵏ ⵏⵏⵏ /	11
17–20	ⵏⵏⵏ ///	8
13–16	ⵏⵏⵏ ////	9
9–12	////	4

Table 8–3 Annual income of residents of an imaginary Gulf Coast village.

1. $750	8. $1800	15. $3000
2. $900	9. $2000	16. $3100
3. $1000	10. $2000	17. $3100
4. $1500	11. $2500	18. $3500
5. $1500	12. $3000	19. $3550
6. $1750	13. $3000	20. $3600
7. $1800	14. $3000	21. $400,000

Describing the variability. Merely knowing the central tendency of a distribution of scores is not as informative as also having some knowledge about how scores are spread out around this point. The simplest measure of variability is the *range* from the lowest to the highest. Thus, the cartoon hostility-judging scores ranged from 12 to 32, and the annual income in the Gulf Coast village ranged from $750 to $400,000. Knowing the range gives you the limits between which all the scores fall.

However, scores may be located in a variety of ways between the bottommost and topmost limits. They may bunch up around the mean or they may be spread evenly throughout the range, and one extreme score (as in the village) may extend the range far beyond the remainder of the scores. It would be helpful to know where most of the scores fall. The most useful statistic for this purpose is the *standard deviation*. When the standard deviation is computed,[1] we then know a great deal more about the variability of our scores. In a theoretically normal distribution, slightly over two-thirds—68.27 per cent—of all the scores fall between the limits set by one standard deviation below the mean and one standard deviation above the mean, 95.45 per cent between two standard deviations above and below the mean, and almost all the cases—99.73 per cent—between plus and minus three standard deviations.

The student may wonder what the use is of such information. First of all, the standard deviation is useful in understanding just how the scores of a particular variable are distributed. When you learn that in the group on which the Stanford-Binet Intelligence Scale was standardized (that is, the "standardization group") the mean IQ was 100, and the standard deviation was 16, you know a great deal about the distribution of IQ in the population. A moment's calculation will show you that 68.27 per cent of the standardization group (and presumably the general population) had scores falling somewhere between 84 and 116 (100 ± 16), that 95.45 per cent fell between 68 and 132 (100 ± 32), and almost all IQ's fell between 52 and 148 (100 ± 48). It can be seen that the mean and standard deviation are very important tools in describing and understanding a

[1] The standard deviation is equal to the square root of the sums of the squared deviations (differences or D) of scores from the mean, divided by the total number (N) of scores: S.D. $= \sqrt{(\text{Sum of } D^2)/N}$.

distribution of scores. The second value of the standard deviation is that it makes the meaning of a particular score much more clear. An IQ of 132 is no longer just a number hanging in the air. With a statistical knowledge of the distribution you know that an individual attaining an IQ of 132 rates higher in intelligence than 97.7 per cent of the population. Figure 8-1 shows a normal distribution of scores with the locations indicated for the standard deviation points.

Another measure of variability commonly employed, but less useful to psychology, is the *quartile deviation* (third quartile minus first quartile divided by 2). The first quartile is the score below which one-fourth of the cases fall. The third quartile is the score below which three-fourths of the cases fall. Incidentally, the second quartile (below which half the cases fall) has already been discussed under a different name—the median. Like the median, quartiles are most useful in describing distributions that contain extreme scores. A similar measure, and one which is used very frequently, is the percentile. Knowing the percentile of a given individual's score tells you what percentage of the group scored below him. In fact, the first quartile is the twenty-fifth percentile, the median is the fiftieth percentile, and the third quartile is the seventy-fifth percentile. If you learn that your score on a college admissions test fell at the seventy-ninth percentile you know that 79 per cent of the persons who took the test when it was standardized received a score lower than yours.

Other descriptive statistics. For most purposes, a knowledge of the central tendency and variability of a distribution of scores is sufficiently descriptive. However, for many advanced statistical purposes it is necessary to know whether the distribution is *normal* or not. The normal distribution was first discovered by an English mathematician, DeMoivre, about 250 years ago. The normal or bell-shaped curve is shown in Figure 8-1. Scores on a wide variety of variables are found to be normally distributed if enough cases are collected. For example, normal distributions have been found for college entrance examination scores, weights of horses, IQ's, baseball batting averages, etc. The way in which W. J. Youden, a statistician in the National Bureau of Standards, both depicted and praised the normal curve is depicted in Figure 8-2.

Without going into the statistical tests that indi-

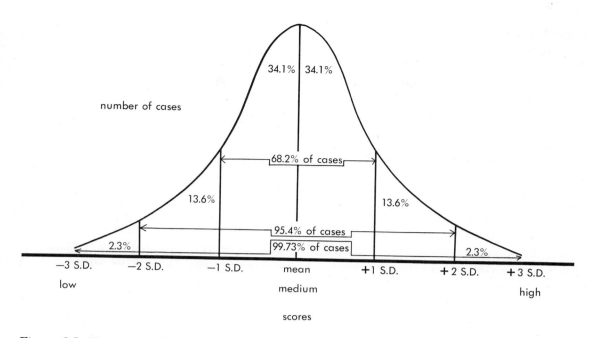

Figure 8-1. The standard deviation in a normal distribution of scores.

THE

N O R M A L

LAW OF ERROR

STANDS OUT IN THE

EXPERIENCE OF MANKIND

AS ONE OF THE BROADEST

GENERALIZATIONS OF NATURAL

PHILOSOPHY ◆ IT SERVES AS THE

GUIDING INSTRUMENT IN RESEARCHES

IN THE PHYSICAL AND SOCIAL SCIENCES AND

IN MEDICINE AGRICULTURE AND ENGINEERING ◆

IT IS AN INDISPENSABLE TOOL FOR THE ANALYSIS AND THE

INTERPRETATION OF THE BASIC DATA OBTAINED BY OBSERVATION AND EXPERIMENT

Figure 8-2. In praise of the "normal curve." (Youden, 1950. Reprinted by permission.)

cate whether a given distribution is normal or not, we will mention two relevant descriptive measures indicative of normality. When the distribution is such that the cases do not fall evenly about the mean, it is said to be a *skewed* distribution. For example, the tendency of pedestrians to wait for a green light at an intersection yields a very skewed distribution. As shown in Figure 8-3, Britt (1940) found that most pedestrians wait on the curb when the light is red and a traffic policeman is watching, but a few step off the curb, still fewer walk to the middle of the intersection and wait, and a very small number ignore the light and cross anyway. In a normal distribution, the amount of skew is zero. In an unbalanced distribution, skew to the right is expressed as a positive number, and skew to the left as a negative number. Examples are given in Figure 8-4.

A second measure that describes the normality of a distribution is *kurtosis*. This measure indicates the extent to which the distribution is flat or peaked. As with skew, a normal distribution is indicated by a zero degree of kurtosis. Positive kurtosis indicates a steep or peaked distribution and negative kurtosis reveals a flat-topped distribution. Figure 8-5 gives two examples.

Interpretation of a score. John received a score of 45 on a leadership test. What do you know about him that you did not know previously? Virtually nothing. To say that a person has a score of 72 on the final examination, or that his yawn has an intensity of 8, or that he can complete a certain task in 92 seconds does not really tell us very much. What we need to know is: how does this score compare with the scores made by others? In other words, where does John's score fall on the distribution of scores made by the general population, by other college students, or by senior men—whichever is appropriate? Is he above average, below average, about average, in the top 2 per cent, or what?

In order to understand John's leadership score of 45, you will need to know the answers to four questions: (1) With what group of people is he being compared? (2) What is the average or mean leadership score of that group? (3) What is the variability or standard deviation of the scores? And, perhaps, (4) what is the general shape of the distribution of scores—that is, do they form a normal distribution curve or not? Figure 8-6 presents a distribution of scores on a sociometric leadership rating scale. (Lindgren, 1953.) When

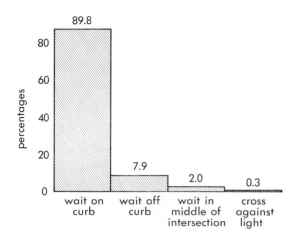

Figure 8-3. Skewed distribution: Pedestrians at a traffic light. (After Britt, 1940.)

141 male and female undergraduate students were asked to rate one another on a scale of leadership ability, their mean score was 33.9, and the standard deviation was found to be 5.6. Superimposed on the distribution of their scores in Figure 8-6 is a "true" normal curve. It will be noted that the actual scores tend to follow the general shape of the normal curve, and we may assume that as more cases are collected, the data will more and more take on that shape.

What can we say *now* about the meaning of John's leadership score of 45? In the light of the statistical data presented in Figure 8-6, we may say that he is at the upper end of the distribution of leadership among college undergraduates, that is, he has a marked tendency to be perceived by other students as a leader. His score places him almost 2 standard deviations above the mean; he is thus in the top 2 per cent of this group of students. It should thus be clear that a raw score of 45 on a leadership test has meaning only when we have the necessary information about the distribution of all the scores.

The actual way that the distribution is presented may take a variety of forms. The data of Figure 8-6 are presented in three alternate ways in Figure 8-7. No matter what sort of presentation is selected, the important point to remember is that unless the four questions above are answered, you cannot possibly interpret the full meaning of any score, regardless of whether it is an IQ, a basal metabolism rate, the speed at which an individual runs the hundred-yard dash, the weight of a newborn infant, or your score on an aptitude test.

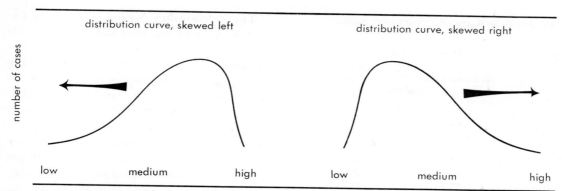

Figure 8-4. Skewed distributions.

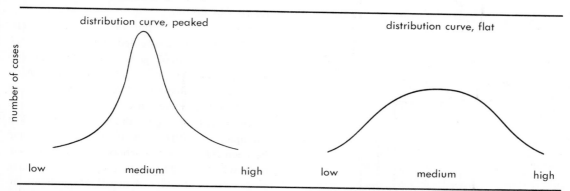

Figure 8-5. Kurtosis.

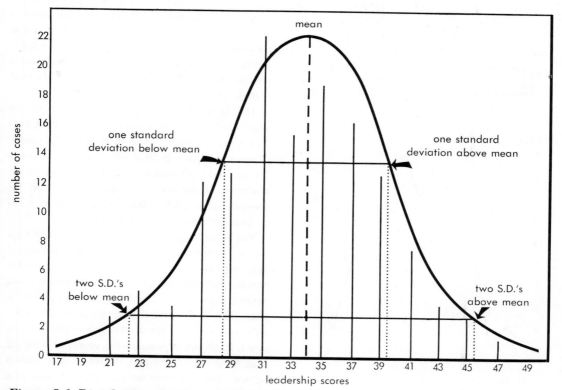

Figure 8-6. Distribution of scores made by 141 college students on a sociometric leadership rating scale. (Lindgren, 1953.)

Figure 8-7. Ways of presenting data.

1. Frequency Distribution Table

Leadership Scores	Frequency (Number of Individuals)
47	1
45	3
43	4
41	10
39	14
37	18
35	20
33	16
31	20
29	13
27	12
25	3
23	4
21	3

2. Histogram

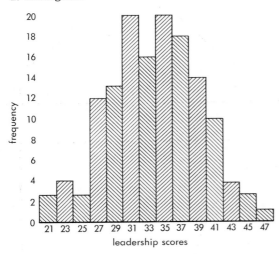

3. Frequency Polygon

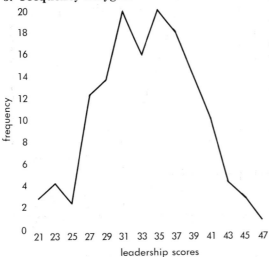

The relationship between two variables.

Among the most important and most frequently asked questions in psychology, as in other sciences, are those having to do with relationship. Is frequency of delinquent behavior related to monthly income of parents? Are the number of hours spent in practice related to the performance score later achieved in a certain kind of task? Is there a relationship between the number of times television commercials are presented and the subsequent sales of the advertised products? The direction and magnitude of such relationships are expressed by a single statistical measure, the *correlation coefficient*.

When we speak of the "direction" of the relationship, we are concerned with whether high scores on one variable go with high scores or with low scores on a second variable. A positive correlation indicates that high scores on variable X tend to go with high scores on variable Y, and that low scores on X tend to go with low scores on Y. For example, a positive correlation is usually found between IQ scores and school achievement: students with high IQ's tend to get better grades than students with low IQ's. A negative correlation indicates that high scores on variable X tend to go with low scores on variable Y, and high scores on variable Y tend to go with low scores on variable X. For example, a negative correlation is found between number of hours of practice on a typewriter and number of typing errors made on a test; individuals who have had more practice tend to make fewer mistakes.

The "magnitude" of a relationship indicates the *degree* to which two variables are related. A perfect positive correlation is indicated by a coefficient of $+1.00$, a perfect negative correlation is -1.00, and 0.00 indicates a complete lack of relationship between the two variables. Table 8-4 presents some relationships in which various degrees of correlation have been found.

The relationship between any two variables on which a group of individuals have been measured may be plotted on a "scatter diagram." Figure 8-8 presents several scatter diagrams demonstrating various degrees of relationship between two variables. The Y, or vertical, axis represents one variable, and the X, or horizontal, axis represents the other. Each dot represents the scores of a single case. When there is a high degree of relationship between the two variables the dots fall close to a diagonal line. The less the pattern made by the dots resembles a diagonal line, the less the relationship and the lower the correlation.

Knowing the correlation between two variables tells you whether it is possible to predict one from the other with better-than-chance accuracy; the higher the correlation (the closer to ±1.00) the more accurate the prediction. For example, if the correlation between aptitude test scores and work output on an assembly line were +1.00 or −1.00, prediction would be perfect; the test score of a new job applicant would tell you exactly how much work he would be able to turn out. A correlation of zero between the test and work output would mean that the test gave you absolutely no help in predicting job performance.

A word of caution is in order at this point. There is a common tendency to assume that a high correlation between two variables implies that one variable *causes* the other. For example, we would very likely find a fair amount of correlation (perhaps +.25 or more) between annual income and the hour in the morning that individuals regularly arrived at work (that is, the later the hour the higher the income), but we would be mistaken if we assumed that the amount of income was the *result* of the hour at which each person begins his work. In order to explain the relationship, we would need to find a third factor—in this case, the occupational level of the work. This is the really significant variable in predicting both income and the beginning hour of work, because both depend on the occupational level of the individual. In general, factory workers and other "blue-collar" employees start working earlier in the morning and receive less income than professional and managerial workers.

Table 8–4 Variables yielding correlations of different magnitudes.

First Variable	Correlation Coefficient	Second Variable
Form "L" of 1937 Stanford-Binet Intelligence Scale correlates	.92	with Form "M" of 1937 Stanford-Binet (Terman and Merrill, 1937)
Artists' Vocational Interest Scale correlates	.85	with Architects' Vocational Interest Scale (Strong, 1943)
Cartoon Hostility Judging Score correlates	.75	with IQ measured with four subscales of the Wechsler Adult Intelligence Scale (Byrne, 1956)
Ability to pick abstract meaning of a word correlates	.60	with adequacy of social interaction of schizophrenic patients (Flavell, 1956)
Height of fathers correlates	.56	with height of sons (McNemar, 1955)
Otis Self-Administering Intelligence Test correlates	.56	with productivity of bookkeepers (Hay, 1943)
Empathy Test scores correlate	.44	with sales records of automobile salesmen (Tobolski and Kerr, 1952)
Amount of hostility expressed on the TAT (a personality test) correlates	.44	with rapid recovery of T.B. patients (Moran, Fairweather, Fisher, and Morton, 1956)
Officer Candidate School final grades correlate	.17	with combat proficiency ratings of Marines (Williams and Leavitt, 1947)
Anxiety measured by Taylor Manifest Anxiety Scale (MAS) correlates	.00	with anxiety measured by amount of perspiration on hands (Lotsof and Downing, 1956)
Number of children in family correlates	−.18	with intelligence (Anastasi, 1956)
Sexual Deviation Scale correlates	−.59	with MMPI (a personality test) scale that measures attempt to fake psychological health (Peck and Storms, 1956)
Wholesale price of cotton correlates	−.70	with number of lynchings in the South, 1882–1930 (Hovland and Sears, 1940)
Office Workers' Vocational Interest Scale correlates	−.79	with Artists' Vocational Scale (Strong, 1943)
Physicists' Vocational Interest Scale correlates	−.83	with Life Insurance Salesmen's Vocational Interest Scale (Strong, 1943)

Figure 8-8. Scatter diagrams showing various degrees of relationship.

1. Perfect positive correlation. Earnings of a student assistant during one semester. (Hypothetical.)

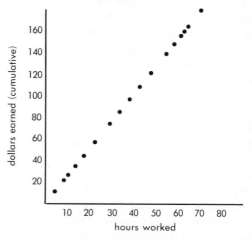

2. High positive correlation. (McNemar, 1955.)

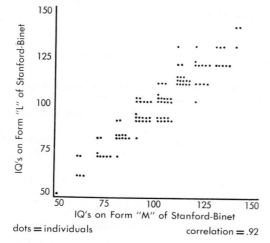

dots = individuals   correlation = .92

3. Moderate positive correlation. (Byrne, 1956.)

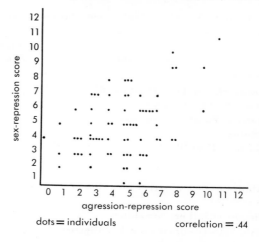

dots = individuals   correlation = .44

4. Zero correlation. (Byrne, 1956.)

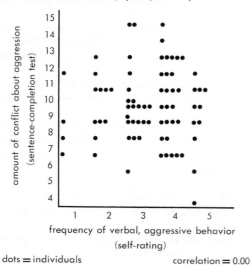

dots = individuals   correlation = 0.00

5. Negative correlation. (Byrne, 1956.)

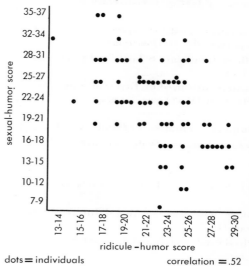

dots = individuals   correlation = .52

Statistics of inference

Sampling. Psychologists are continually trying to answer questions about human beings. Is massed practice more efficient than distributed practice in learning? Do mothers of schizophrenic patients have different childrearing attitudes than mothers of nonschizophrenics? Is there a relationship between scores on an IQ test and grades in school? What is the relationship between stomach contractions and the subjective feeling of hunger? Does the activity of the leader have a bearing on the performance and morale of the group? If it were possible to study every human being in the world, we would not have to be concerned with the statistics of inference. We might find, for example, that distributed practice is twice as efficient as massed practice for 75 per cent of the population, equally efficient for 15 per cent of the population, and one third as efficient for the remaining 10 per cent, and that would be that.

However, we never deal with the entire world's population and almost never deal with an entire group (such as *all* seniors in *all* colleges, or *all* Southern Baptists). Instead, we take *samples* of various sizes from the groups in which we are interested. We usually assume that the sample is random and try to select it in a manner that will eliminate biases (such as picking every tenth patient admitted to the hospital in the preceding year if we are interested in studying the hospital population). Or, we may try to make our sample match certain known characteristics of the total population we wish to study. For example, if you were trying to study Maryland adults, you might decide ahead of time to build a sample containing the same proportions of individuals with certain characteristics such as sex, marital status, age, income, area of residence, etc., as will be found in the total population of the state. Within these limitations, the selection of subjects is still on a random basis, of course.

As an illustration, let us say that you hypothesize that twelve- and thirteen-year-old American girls have a greater interest in love and romance than boys in the same age group. You decide that a convenient measure of interest would be the number of romantic stories read during a six-month period minus the number of other types of stories read. You might get a group of judges to rate a list of current stories as to whether they deal with romance or not. You develop a brief ques-

tionnaire about reading. Then comes the problem of selecting subjects. Ideally, you would march every twelve- and thirteen-year-old child in America into a mammoth auditorium and pass out your questionnaires. This is, of course, impossible; hence the problem of sampling arises. It might be possible, although not very feasible, to pick every one-hundredth or every five-hundredth eligible subject across the country. More probably, you would have to limit yourself to picking the four junior high schools in your city and surveying as many of the thirteen-year-old pupils there as possible. Let us say that you are able to reach 500 boys and 500 girls. You find that the mean romantic minus nonromantic reading score for girls is +12 and for boys is −8. Can you conclude that thirteen-year-old girls in the total population read more romantic stories than boys? What if the mean scores were +12 and +11; would your conclusions be the same? What if you had surveyed only 2 girls and 2 boys and found mean scores of +12 and −8; would you be as sure of your finding as with 500 girls and 500 boys? If you repeated the study in another town with other subjects, would you find the same sex difference? In short, how sure are you that your findings may be generalized to all thirteen-year-olds in the country? How sure are you that your sample did not yield these findings simply by chance? In order to answer these questions, we must turn to the statistics of inference.

Probability. Although the mathematics of probability is a highly specialized field, almost everyone has some familiarity with the general idea of probability. The chances are 50–50 (probability = .50) that a tossed coin will come up heads. Figures show that 97.5 per cent of the infants born in this country live to be a year old, so

The rules governing games of chance are based on the statistics of probability.

the chances are 97½ out of 100 (probability = .975) that a particular infant will survive the first year. The weather bureau says the chance of rain next Thursday is 40 per cent (probability = .40). We are certain the sun will rise tomorrow (probability = 1.00).

If these probability figures are correct, it means that you should be able to make a number of fairly accurate guesses about the events involved. Your best bet would be that a coin tossed 4000 times would come up heads 2000 times, that 25 out of every 1000 American babies will die in their first year of life, that 100 such weather predictions will be followed by a rainy day 40 times and a dry day 60 times, and that the sun will rise 300 out of every 300 days. Psychologists must make exactly these sorts of bets and guesses about whether experimental findings are applicable to the entire population.

Significance. The inferences that psychologists make about their experimental results with samples of the population are expressed in terms of *levels of significance*. If a psychologist reports that he performed an experiment to test problem-solving ability and found that in his sample the mean score of boys was higher than the mean score of

girls at the 5 per cent level of significance, he is indicating that the chances are only 5 out of 100 (probability = .05) that these same findings would not hold true in the total population, and 95 out of 100 (probability = .95) that they *would* hold true. In other words, if in the total population boys and girls really do not differ in problem solving ability, 100 such experiments with 100 samples would have found a sex difference of that magnitude only 5 times by chance alone. There is no way to know absolutely and positively, of course, whether boys and girls *really* differ or whether this particular sample simply yielded a chance finding which is not true for the total population. The best a scientist can ever do is make an estimate or bet. If the mean difference is found to reach the 5 per cent level of significance, the odds are 95 to 5 (or 19 to 1) that the difference is a real one. If the difference reaches the 1 per cent level of significance (probability = .01), the odds reach 100 to 1. At the 0.1 per cent level (probability = .001), the odds are 1000 to 1 that the finding is a true one. Obviously, the better the significance level, the more certain we can feel about the results.

It should be clear that scientific facts are never

a complete certainty unless the total population is available for study. It should be clear that the repetition of experiments becomes important, because duplicate findings lend strong support to the original ones. If ten experimenters with ten different samples find that the mean score of boys on a problem-solving task is higher than that for girls, we are considerably more confident that this represents a real, nonchance difference between the sexes in this particular ability.

Statistical inference is also important in evaluating the correlation coefficient. If a relationship is found between two variables in a given sample of the population, what are the chances that this same relationship holds true for the total population? Again, the mathematical procedures will be omitted, but it is sufficient to say that the significance level of correlation coefficients is also reported by experimenters. How big must a correlation be in order to reach significance at the 5 per cent level, or at the 1 per cent level? The answer depends on the number of subjects for whom the correlation was computed. Table 8-5 indicates the magnitude which a correlation coefficient must reach in order to be significant at the 5 and 1 per cent levels. It can be seen in the table that the larger the sample, the smaller the correlation coefficient may be and still reach statistical significance. For example, with three subjects, the correlation must be perfect before the coefficient reaches the 1 per cent level of significance. Yet, with 1002 subjects the 1 per cent level of significance is reached with a correlation coefficient of

only .08. Of course, a correlation as small as .08 is not very useful for prediction; its significance simply tells us that it is probably a real relationship, although a slight one.

Using statistics to evaluate a test

Standardization. A few pages back the point was made that in order to understand the meaning of an individual's raw score it is necessary to know (1) the group of persons with whom he is being compared, (2) the mean score of that group on the variable being measured, (3) the standard deviation of the scores, and (4) the shape of the distribution of scores. What happens, then, when you sit down alone in a counselor's office and take a test of vocational interest, an aptitude test, or an intelligence test? In order to interpret the meaning of your score, there must be a comparison with a group, but what group?

One of the criteria used in evaluating a test is the kind of *norms* available for it. If a particular test is supposed to be used with college freshmen, the test author should administer the instrument to a large randomly selected sample of college freshmen; these individuals than make up the *standardization* group. The test manual will include the information about this standardization group, including the mean and standard deviation of their scores on the test. The interpretation of any score obtained on this test in the future will involve the comparison of the individual's score with the test norms, that is, with the scores made by the standardization group. The test will be used properly if the testee is similar in most respects to the individuals in the standardization group and if the test is given under the same conditions as it was given to that group. For example, a test standardized on college students is not likely to be appropriate for farm workers; a test standardized with individual administration (that is, given to one person at a time) is not appropriate if given to individuals in a group setting.

Validity. Data other than those covered by test norms are also essential for proper interpretation of a given score on the test. Thinking back to a specific test, that of leadership discussed earlier, other questions arise. Just because the test was labeled "leadership," how do we know that it measures this attribute? Is it *really* a test of leadership? What will performance on this test tell us about the leadership behavior of an individual? These are questions concerning the *validity* of the

Table 8–5 Size of the correlation coefficient necessary to reach significance for various numbers of subjects.

Number of Subjects	Size of Correlation Coefficient Necessary to Reach 5% Level	Size of Correlation Coefficient Necessary to Reach 1% Level
3	.997	1.00
10	.63	.76
20	.44	.56
30	.36	.46
52	.27	.35
92	.20	.27
302	.11	.15
502	.09	.12
1002	.06	.08

test. We are asking whether this scale can be accepted as a valid measure of leadership. There are four types of validity, each concerned with slightly different uses to which a test may be put. (American Psychological Association, 1954.)

If the test, or other instrument of measurement represents a sample of particular kinds of behavior on which the individual is being measured, we would expect that it would contain a variety of items related to this behavior. The *content validity* of a test is concerned with the extent to which its items sample subject matter or behavior appropriate to whatever is being measured. A leadership test should contain items concerned with such matters as the leading of a group, dominance, independence of action, etc. A test of intelligence should contain items having to do with problem-solving, memory, verbal skills, learning ability, etc. And we would expect a test which purported to measure aptitude for manual skills to include tasks involving finger dexterity, familiarity with tools, visual-motor coordination, etc. If a test of intelligence contained items dealing with running ability, and a manual aptitude test dealt with music appreciation, they would not have content validity. The test authors would have to present very unusual and convincing evidence to support the use of such items in their scales.

The *predictive validity* of a test is evaluated by showing the accuracy with which one can make predictions with it. Usually, predictive validity is indicated by presenting the correlation between scores on the test and some subsequent criterion. Thus, scores on a leadership test should be correlated with such variables as the number of leadership positions actually attained in the year following the test, scores made subsequently on other tests of leadership, or the like. Scores on a valid intelligence test should correlate with school grades. Performance on a secretarial aptitude test should be correlated with subsequent supervisory ratings of secretarial ability. If substantial correlations of this sort are reported for a test, we can assume that the test is useful for prediction. If a test does not predict anything, it is not a useful test.

When a test is used to estimate an individual's present standing on some variable, we would be interested in its *concurrent validity*. Students who are campus leaders should score higher on a leadership test than their fellow students. A test that is supposed to measure abnormality of behavior according to accepted diagnostic categories would be expected to agree with a psychiatric diagnosis of mental patients. If a test was supposed to measure aptitude for architecture, it should be possible to show that successful architects achieve higher test scores than successful lobster fishermen. Again, a sufficiently large correlation coefficient would indicate the validity of the test.

Finally, there is *construct validity*. This last use of validity is most often employed when the psychologist wishes to infer the degree to which an individual possesses some trait or quality for which there is no single criterion variable. In measuring a behavior like typing aptitude, we have a specific behavior in mind that we hope to predict: ability to type. In measuring qualities such as leadership, intelligence, anxiety, or hostility, we are measuring a psychological variable that should be reflected in a variety of behaviors but not *perfectly* in any single one. We might be able to find correlations between leadership test scores and tendency to initiate conversations with strangers, scores on a dominance test, number of elective school offices held, the tendency to assume leadership in a group discussion, etc. All of these behaviors are *relevant* to the construct or quality which we think of as leadership, but no single one is *exactly equivalent* to what we mean when we say, "He has leadership qualities." An intelligence test should show construct validity by being related to school grades, teachers' ratings of intelligence, and ability to learn new material. All of these variables are relevant to intelligence but none is exactly equivalent; in fact, an "intelligence" test which correlated close to 1.00 with school grades would probably not be considered a good intelligence test (even though it might be a very useful school aptitude test).

In order to gain an adequate understanding of what a test measures, it would be essential to know about all four types of its validity. It should be clear that the gaining of a real understanding of a test involves much more than reading the title printed on its front cover; the important thing is to gain information about its validity. Keeping the problems of standardization and validity in mind you can imagine how psychologists feel about the scores obtained on the "tests" and "quizzes" that appear in magazines and newspapers. Another sort of test about which more information would be useful is the traditional classroom examination, which is supposed to measure the learning that has taken place in a given course. Many instructors would be surprised to learn how ineffective their examinations really are, if the latter were given the rigorous evaluation to which most widely used psychological tests have been subjected.

Reliability. In evaluating a test, the one final but important characteristic that must be determined is its *reliability*. It is necessary to know the extent to which it can be depended upon to yield consistent results. A consistent test is a reliable test, and an inconsistent one is unreliable. As with validity, there are four types of reliability.

A test should be stable over a period of time; this quality is expressed as its *coefficient of stability*. You would expect, for example, that a cloth or steel tape measure would give the same results in measuring your height each day for a week; its consistency makes it a reliable measuring instrument. A rubber tape measure would be unreliable because it might inform you that you are 5 feet 8 inches in the morning, 6 feet 2 inches at noon, and 5 feet 1 inch in the afternoon. Psychological tests, too, must be stable if they are to be of any use in prediction. If any intelligence test measured a student's IQ at 80 one day and 140 the next, it would be difficult to come to any realistic conclusions as to whether the student could do college work. Stability of a test is indicated by the correlation between scores made on a test given on two different occasions, hence it is sometimes called "test-retest" reliability. There is no set figure for the size that the reliability coefficient should be, but obviously a test-retest correlation below .80 or .90 leaves something to be desired in terms of stability. Sometimes problems are created when the variable that is being measured changes over a period of time: the height of a child changes over the years, abnormal behavior may improve or worsen, learning experiences may alter performance on an achievement test. A test must yield stable results at least over a short period of time in order to make prediction possible, but long-range stability is often not a test goal because of the alterability of psychological characteristics.

Psychologists are entitled to expect that two forms of a test should yield the same results; this form of reliability is expressed in terms of the *coefficient of equivalence*: the correlation between the two forms. One would not expect much discrepancy if height were measured the same day by a tape measure and then by a yard stick. A test that has two or more alternate forms is reliable if the forms are found to be equivalent. For example, it was reported in Table 8-4 that Form L and Form M of the Stanford-Binet Intelligence Test correlated .92. Would you conclude that each of the two forms of the test measured the same thing if the correlation had been .04?

If a test is measuring one variable, it is supposed that all of the items in it are consistent; thus, a third reliability figure is the *coefficient of internal consistency*. The first 18 inches of a yard stick should be able to measure height just as well as the second 18 inches. In a reliable psychological test, there is a high correlation among the items which compose it. Usually, a correlation is run between the odd and even test items. The test is, in effect, split in half, and the relationship between the two halves is measured.

A fourth type of reliability is a problem only in instances where the scoring of the test requires subjective judgment. One would expect different judges to be able to agree on each subject's score. That is, a test should have high *interjudge consistency*. On some types of test, there is no problem of judges disagreeing: the answers on an arithmetic test are clearly either right or wrong. On other tests, interjudge consistency is high, but considerable training is necessary to achieve this standard; clinical psychologists show good agreement in scoring the vocabulary items on the Stanford-Binet after extensive training and experience. On some tests, interjudge consistency is hard to obtain; as we shall discover in Chapter 10, projective tests of personality often yield different results for different psychologists because of divergencies in scoring and interpretation and consequently have low reliability.

A good test demonstrates all four types of reliability. It is stable over a period of time; if it has more than one form, each yields the same results; it is internally consistent; and different judges agree in scoring it. It should be noted that a test can not be valid unless it is reliable. However, a test may be highly reliable and yet be invalid; that is, a "driver aptitude" test may give very consistent results and still fail to be a valid measure of driver aptitude. Reliability is a necessary, but not a sufficient, condition for validity.

Summary

Although the idea of studying any sort of mathematics is often frightening to the student, it was pointed out that statistical concepts are acually common currency in our everyday lives. In psychology, statistics are used in describing masses of data and in drawing inferences about the meaning of experimental results.

The assumption underlying the development and use of psychological tests is that people vary on psychological attributes. The first step in describing a series of raw scores is to lay out a frequency distribution. The next descriptive step is to compute the measures of central tendency: the mean, or average; the median, or midmost score; the mode, or score with the highest frequency. It is also important to know the variability of the obtained scores. Variability is described by the range, the standard deviation, and the quartile deviation. The shape of the distribution is also an important factor in describing it. A normal curve is found for a wide variety of physical and psychological variables; skewness and kurtosis are two of the measures that indicate the normality of a particular distribution. In order to understand the meaning of any individual's score it is necessary to know (1) the group of individuals with which he is being compared, (2) the mean score of that group, (3) the standard deviation of their scores, and (4) the shape of their distribution of scores. The data about a distribution may be presented in a frequency distribution table, a histogram, or a frequency polygon. The relationship between two variables is described by the correlation coefficient, which may range from +1.00 to −1.00. The size of a correlation indicates the degree of accuracy with which one variable may be used to predict another, but a correlation does not imply that one variable causes another.

Statistical inference is important because psychologists study samples of the total population and must guess or infer how accurately their results may be generalized beyond the subjects in the sample. Probability refers to the frequency with which a particular event will occur over several occasions; a probability of .60 for a particular event means that it should occur on 60 out of every 100 occasions. The results of psychological experiments are reported in terms of levels of significance; for example, the 5 per cent level of significance indicates that a given difference between means or a relationship between variables is very likely to be a real one; the probability is only .05 that the difference or relationship was due to chance.

Test evaluation is one of the major uses of statistics in psychology. In order to interpret the meaning of test scores, the test must have been given to a standardization group of known characteristics so that each testee's score can be compared to the norm scores. The validity of a test indicates whether it measures what it purports to measure. The four types of validity are *content validity* or the extent to which the test samples the appropriate subject matter; *predictive validity* or the accuracy with which the test predicts other variables; *concurrent validity* or the accuracy with which the test estimates present standing on other variables; and *construct validity* or the degree to which it measures a trait for which no single criterion is available. Test reliability indicates the extent to which a test is consistent in what it measures. The four types of reliability are *stability,* or the extent to which scores are consistent over time; *equivalence of forms,* or the degree that two forms of a test yield the same results; *internal consistency,* or the correlation between two halves of the same test; and *interjudge consistency,* or the ability of judges to agree on scoring the test. It was pointed out that to be valid a test must be reliable, but a reliable test is not necessarily valid.

Questions

1. Using any available raw data (class scores on a midterm examination, weights of football players, price of text books, etc.), construct a frequency distribution. What does this distribution tell you about the data?

2. Compute the mean, median, and mode for your data in Question 1. Which would you be most likely to report and why?

3. Can you think of any specific situation in which the median would be superior to the mean as a measure of central tendency?

4. Look through several back issues of your local newspaper and find the classified advertisements for used automobiles. Record the prices of used Plymouths, Fords, Chevrolets, and Ramblers for models of the past several years. How do the mean prices compare? What can you conclude from your study? How valid are your conclusions? (For example, if the mean price of Chevrolets is $900 and the mean price of Plymouths is $1150, does this mean that used Plymouths typically sell for more than used Chevrolets?)

5. If the mean score on a college entrance test is 150 and the standard deviation is 30, how are the scores grouped about the mean?

6. What does it mean if your score on a civil service examination places you at the sixty-sixth percentile?

7. Did the data you collected in Questions 1 and 4 form a normal curve? If not, in what ways were the curves not normal?

8. On an "Artistic Talent Test" you receive a score of 152. What does this score tell you about your talent as an artist? What further information must you obtain in order to interpret this score?

9. Plot a scatter diagram for some convenient data (class scores on midterm and on final, height and weight of class members, etc.). Does there seem to be a relationship between the variables? If you want to compute the correlation coefficient, consult any statistics textbook or the workbook accompanying this text.

10. If you read that a psychologist using 100 college sophomores found distributed practice a more efficient technique for learning German vocabulary than massed practice at the .05 level of significance, what would this mean to you?

11. What is meant by the term "standardization group"?

12. Choose one of the short quizzes from a magazine or newspaper. If you wanted to use this device as a test, what would you need to know about its validity and reliability? How would you go about determining these characteristics?

Suggestions for further reading

American Psychological Association, "Technical recommendations for psychological tests and diagnostic techniques," *Psychological Bulletin,* 51: 201–238; 1954. A technical report indicating in detail what material should be included in a test manual.

Brose, I. D. J., *Design for Decision.* New York: Macmillan, 1953. An introduction to the logic of statistics that requires no special mathematical training.

Edwards, A. L., *Statistical Analysis,* rev. ed. New York: Rinehart, 1958. A simply written, standard elementary textbook in statistics.

Huff, D., *How to Lie with Statistics.* New York: Norton, 1954. A useful and often amusing exposition of the misuses of statistics.

McNemar, Q., *Psychological Statistics,* 2nd ed. New York: Wiley, 1955. A sound, high-level statistical text which is probably too difficult for the student with only a casual interest in statistics.

Wallis, W. A. and H. V. Roberts, *Statistics: A New Approach.* Glencoe, Ill.: The Free Press, 1956. A clear and comprehensive presentation of statistical methods and their underlying reasoning written in a way that requires no special knowledge of advanced mathematics.

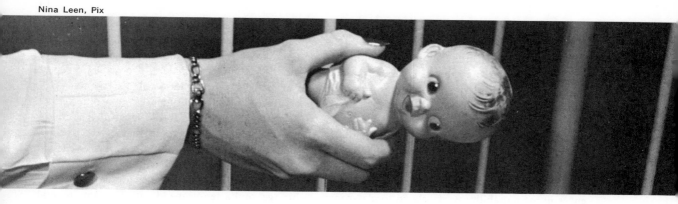

Nina Leen, Pix

9

Intelligence and creativity

It was through intelligence testing that psychology first came to the attention of the general public. More than a million American men took the Army Alpha, a group intelligence test administered to recruits during World War I. About the same period, the research of Lewis Madison Terman with the Stanford-Binet tests of intelligence attracted a great deal of attention in the popular press. Indeed, if you had asked the man in the street during the period between World War I and World War II what psychologists do, he probably would have replied "Give IQ tests." Few psychological terms have been accepted into popular speech more readily than the term "IQ," and even today it is commonly used as a synonym for "intelligence."

The intelligence test was a preliminary step to the development of various branches of applied psychology. The growth of educational psychology as an applied field was to a large degree stimulated by the fact that educators saw in the intelligence test a way of helping them group children in an attempt to make teaching more effective. Personnnel managers in business and industry saw in the intelligence test a means of keeping less efficient workers off the payroll. Today the applied psychologist is still concerned with the administration and interpretation of intelligence tests, but his role has expanded to include far more functions, as we shall see in the chapters that follow.

Mental testing

To the nineteenth-century psychologist, intellectual ability was only one of the many human

faculties that offered intriguing research possibilities, and the crude intelligence tests he developed were not concerned with the solution of practical problems. As a matter of fact, popular belief of the day held (as it still does to some extent even today) that school success is entirely a matter of putting forth enough effort. The idea that there might be individual variations in ability was given very little consideration by the general public and particularly by parents. Educators, however, were somewhat more aware that differences in mental ability were related to classroom performance.

Binet-type scales. In the year 1904 the French Minister of Public Instruction became concerned about the children in the schools of Paris who were unable to profit from the usual instruction. A plan was devised whereby such children could be helped in special schools, but before they could be assigned to such schools it was necessary to identify them. School authorities were reluctant to leave the responsibility of identifying candidates for the special school to the teachers because of the possibility that teachers might be inclined to make their decisions on the basis of the amount of trouble a pupil gave them. Thus a relatively bright child who was a trouble-maker might be nominated to the special school, whereas a dull child who was pleasant and cooperative might be retained. On the other hand, the authorities did not want to leave the decisions up to juries or panels of experts, since it was difficult to get agreement. What was needed was an *objective* measure of intelligence.

In order to get help with their task, the authorities turned to Alfred Binet, a psychologist, who had been studying individual differences and mental ability for a number of years. In 1905, Binet produced a list of 30 tasks, ranging from such simple tasks as following a moving object with the head and eyes and pointing to the head, ear, and nose on request, to such complex tasks as mentally calculating what time it would be if the small and large hands of a clock placed at 4 minutes to 3 were reversed and then explaining why it would be actually impossible to reverse them. Binet and his co-worker, Simon, set up norms or standards for this test based on the records of children at ages 3, 5, 7, 9, and 11 years.

Although this first intelligence scale or test was found to be quite useful, it was admittedly crude, and in 1908 Binet and Simon published a revision consisting of 59 items. Each age level from 3 to 13 was represented with three to eight items. Each item was assigned a certain number of months' credit, thus making it possible to report each child's score in terms of his "mental age," expressed in years and months. A mental age of 8 years and 6 months would mean that a child's mental ability was equal to that of the average child aged 8 years and 6 months. A six-year-old who achieved a mental age of 8 years and 6 months would be considered quite advanced for his age, and a ten-year-old with the same mental age would, of course, be considered retarded.

The 1908 version of the Binet-Simon scale received widespread attention and was translated into a number of languages within a very few years. In America, the scale was tested by Lewis Madison Terman, who found it useful, in spite of

Table 9–1 Reference points for establishing the meaning of an IQ. (After data summarized by Cronbach, 1949.)

IQ	Level of Competency
120	Needed to do acceptable work in a first-class college with normal effort.
114	Mean or average IQ of children from white-collar, skilled-labor families, living in a Midwestern city.
107	Mean IQ of high school seniors.
104	Minimum level for satisfactory or "average" work in high school, in an academic curriculum.
100	Average IQ in unselected population (theoretical).
93	Median IQ of children in eight one-teacher rural schools in Texas.
91	Mean IQ of children from low-income, socially depressed homes, living in a Midwestern city (see IQ 114).
90	At this level, a child can get through eight grades with some retardation. With persistence, can complete high school with some difficulty.
70	At this level, an adult can set and sort type, do farm work.
70	A child with this IQ may do work at the fifth-grade level.
60	An adult at this level can repair furniture, paint toys, harvest vegetables.
50	An adult at this level can do rough painting, simple carpentry, domestic work.
50	A child above this level can profit from special classes in regular schools and need not be segregated.
40	An adult at this level can mow lawns, handle freight, do simple laundry work.

a number of defects, and set about developing a revision that could be used with an American population. The result was the Stanford Revision of the Binet Scale—commonly called the "Stanford-Binet"—which he and his associates published in 1916.

Terman extended Binet's concept of mental age a step further by developing the "intelligence quotient" or "IQ," which he derived by dividing a child's mental age by his true or chronological age and multiplying the result by 100, i.e.,

$$IQ = \frac{MA}{CA} 100.$$

Over the years the IQ has proved to be a very useful index of intellectual functioning. How IQ's at various levels may be translated into competencies is indicated by Table 9-1. Table 9-2 lists IQ classifications commonly used by psychologists. The lowest classification, "mentally defective," is sometimes subdivided into three classes as follows: *Moron*—IQ 50–70; *Imbecile*—IQ 20–50; *Idiot*—IQ below 20.

The idea of having a single measure to represent an individual's level of intellectual functioning was very attractive both to laymen and professional psychologists. Within a few years, the term "IQ" had entered popular speech, and all intelligence tests were called "IQ tests" by the lay public, regardless of whether or not their scores were reported in terms of IQ. As new tests of intelligence were developed, authors provided conversion tables that enabled scores to be interpreted in terms of IQ, even though some of the tests were for adults and hence made no attempt to measure "mental age."

Group tests of intelligence. Shortly after the publication of the 1916 version of the Stanford-Binet, the United States entered World War I. Military authorities were faced by the problem of classifying hundreds of thousands of inductees in order to determine who should receive special training and who should be given assignments as commissioned and noncommissioned officers. The American Psychological Association placed its facilities at the disposal of the War Department, and a group of psychologists, using some unpublished research of A. S. Otis, developed a verbal test known as the Army Alpha and a nonverbal test (for illiterates and persons unable to read English) known as the Army Beta. About one and three-quarter million men were tested during the ensuing months—the first large-scale intelligence testing program. This experience with the Army Alpha demonstrated the practicality and the value of group intelligence testing and opened the way for dozens of tests of similar design.

During the 1920's the public schools were looking for some way to improve the efficiency of education. The new group tests of intelligence seemed to be a quick, easy, and efficient method of classifying students according to ability. Test results could thus be used as a basis for assigning students to fast, average, and slow sections. Theoretically, curriculum and methodology might then be adapted to each kind of class according to the ability of the students. In spite of the fact that this idea has not worked out as well in practice as it did in theory, the use of intelligence tests did introduce teachers to the concept of individual differences in ability and helped them develop better understanding of their students. As a result, intelligence testing at various age levels is standard procedure in most schools.

Although intelligence tests do in fact permit

Table 9–2 IQ classifications commonly used by psychologists. (After Merrill, 1938.)

IQ	Percentage	Classification
160–169	0.03	
150–159	0.2	very superior
140–149	1.1	
130–139	3.1	
120–129	8.2	superior
110–119	18.1	high average
100–109	23.5	
90–99	23.0	normal or average
80–89	14.5	low average
70–79	5.6	borderline defective
60–69	2.0	
50–59	0.4	
40–49	0.2	mentally defective
30–39	0.03	

the identification of individual differences in ability, the intent behind their use, as we have described it up to this point in our discussion, is *group*-centered or *institution*-centered rather than *individual*-centered. To put the same idea in different words, the purpose is one of *selection* rather than that of providing clinical help. Binet's scale was used to identify slow learners who could then be assigned to special classes. The concern here was with the welfare of the group of normal children whose progress would presumably be hindered by the presence of retarded learners, as well as with the welfare of the retarded learners who could then be put into classes designed to meet their special needs. It was expected that this arrangement would enable the school to operate with greater efficiency on behalf of *all* students. The Army Alpha was used to select individuals for officer billets or for special training. The concern here was not for the individuals selected, but for *the needs of the larger group*—the needs of the Army and a nation at war.

Clinical use of intelligence tests. About the time that the group-centered uses of intelligence testing were becoming widely accepted, a small but growing number of psychologists were developing an interest in the way in which intelligence tests could help them understand the intellectual behavior of individuals. They found that some of the responses of individually administered tests like the Stanford-Binet provided clues that aided in the diagnosis of various types of emotional and intellectual malfunctioning. Although the Stanford-Binet provided only a single measure—mental age—clinicians using the test noticed that individuals with certain kinds of emotional and intellectual disturbances tended to do better on some items than on others. This kind of information seemed to be helpful in psychodiagnosis, and a need was expressed for a test that would provide a larger number of measures or scores than the Stanford-Binet. Another shortcoming of the Stanford-Binet was the inadequacy of its norms for use with adults. Terman's research had led him to conclude that intellectual growth slowed down at age 13 and stopped altogether at age 16, and all adult IQ's computed on the basis of his test assumed a chronological age of 15. The material contained in the Stanford-Binet was selected to appeal to children and was criticized as appearing "babyish" to many adults. Furthermore, the heavy emphasis on verbal material in the Stan-

ford-Binet seemed to make it an unfair measure for individuals who were not verbally inclined but who appeared to be intellectually competent.

One of the tests devised to meet these criticisms of the Stanford-Binet was the Wechsler-Bellevue Intelligence Scale,[1] developed by David Wechsler, a clinical psychologist at Bellevue Hospital in New York City. The Wechsler scale is a lineal descendant of the Binet-Simon scales and consists of six verbal and five nonverbal or "performance" subtests, as follows:

VERBAL SCALE

1. *Information subtest.* Consists of questions, arranged in order of increasing difficulty, formulated to measure the range of information possessed by the subject. Examples of the kinds of questions asked: "How many inches in a foot?" "Where is the Amazon River?"

2. *Comprehension subtest.* Consists of questions designed to measure general understanding. An example of the kind of question asked: "Why are coins made of metal?"

3. *Digit-span subtest.* Tests the ability to repeat series of numbers, starting with three digits and going up to nine digits. For the second part of this subtest, the subject is asked to repeat a different series, but in reverse order. For instance, if the examiner says 8-4-3, the subject is to say 3-4-8. Although this subtest correlates rather poorly with "general intelligence," Wechsler found that it did discriminate rather well at the lower levels of intelligence.

4. *Similarities subtest.* The subject is asked to describe the way in which certain objects or abstractions are similar. At the beginning of the subtest are items like this: "In what way are 'table' and 'chair' alike?" At the end of the subtest will be found items like this: "In what way are drowsiness and excitement alike?" This subtest has turned out to be one of the best in the entire scale.

5. *Arithmetic subtest.* A test of reasoning, consisting of ten problems in mental arithmetic increasing in difficulty.

6. *Vocabulary subtest.* The extent of an individual's vocabulary is one of the most reliable indexes to his intelligence. This subtest consists of a list of 42 words, arranged in order from easy words, like "table," to difficult words like "odometer."

PERFORMANCE SCALE

1. *Picture-arrangement subtest.* Each item consists of a collection of cartoon-like drawings which make a story when arranged in proper order.

[1] Form I of the Wechsler-Bellevue Intelligence Scale was superseded by the Wechsler Adult Intelligence Scale, commonly referred to as the WAIS, in 1955. The Wechsler Intelligence Scale for Children (aged 5 to 15), commonly referred to as the WISC, was introduced in 1949.

This child is taking the block design portion of the Wechsler Intelligence Scale for Children. Photographs by The Psychological Corporation.

2. *Picture-completion subtest.* This subtest consists of a series of pictures which are presented to the subject one at a time. An important part is missing from each picture and must be identified by the subject. This test is very useful in picking out mental defectives.

3. *Block-design subtest.* The subject must arrange a collection of vari-colored cubes in such a way that they reproduce certain printed designs. One of the best of the subtests, but discriminates against individuals over 40.

4. *Object-assembly subtest.* Three jigsaw type puzzles are presented to the subject one at a time and in order of increasing difficulty.

5. *Digit-symbol subtest.* The subject is required to match each one of a series of printed digits with an appropriate symbol, using a prescribed code.

The performance of the individual taking the test is reported in terms of the number of points for each subtest and scaled scores for each subtest. The total scaled scores obtained on "verbal" and "performance" sections of the test may be converted into IQ's based on the norms for per-sons his age, and an IQ can be obtained from the total scaled score of the test. Figure 9-1 reproduces a portion of the face sheet of the WAIS, showing how these various measures are computed.

Although Wechsler suggested that certain patterns or signs should be used as indicative of certain kinds of mental disturbance, subsequent research has not been able to demonstrate their validity. On the other hand, skilled clinicians are able to get a great deal of important information from the test, very often from the comments of the subjects, rather than from the scores themselves. Here is an example of the answer of a patient who arrived at a correct conclusion but through a reasoning process that is decidedly schizophrenic:

EXAMINER: How far is it from New York to Paris?
PATIENT: I don't know.
EXAMINER: Try to figure it out.
PATIENT: Well, it takes about a week to get from Paris to New York. There are seven days in a week

Figure 9-1. Face sheet of Wechsler Adult Intelligence Scale (WAIS), showing computation of subtest scores, scales scores, and IQ's. (Reproduced by permission.)

WAIS RECORD FORM
Wechsler Adult Intelligence Scale

Name JOHN SMITH
Birth Date 8 14 21 (MO. DAY YR) Age 32 Sex M Marital: S (M) D W (CIRCLE ONE)
Nat. ENGLISH-GERMAN Color WHITE Tested by Brown
Place of Examination CLINIC Date 10-17-59
Occupation CLERK
Education 1 YEAR OF COLLEGE

TABLE OF SCALED SCORE EQUIVALENTS*

Scaled Score	Information	Comprehension	Arithmetic	Similarities	Digit Span	Vocabulary	Digit Symbol	Picture Completion	Block Design	Picture Arrangement	Object Assembly	Scaled Score
19	29	27-28		26	17	78-80	87-90					19
18	28	26		25		76-77	83-86	21		36	44	18
17	27	25	18	24		74-75	79-82		48	35	43	17
16	26	24	17	23	16		76-78	20	47	34	42	16
15	25	23	16	22	15	67-70	72-75		46	33	41	15
14	23-24		15		14	63-66	69-71		44-45	32	40	14
13	21-22	21	14	19-20		59-62	66-68	18	42-43		38-39	13
12		20		17-18	13	54-58		17	39-41	28-29	36-37	12
11	17-18	19	12	15-16	12	47-53	58-61	15-16		26-27	34-35	11
10	15-16	17-18	11	13-14	11	40-46	52-57	14	31-34	23-25	31-33	10
9	13-14	15-16	10	11-12	10	32-39	47-51	12-13	28-30	20-22		9
8	11-12	14	9	9-10		26-31	41-46	10-11	25-27	18-19	25-27	8
7	9-10	12-13	7-8	7-8			22-25	35-40	8-9	21-24	15-17	22-24	7
6	7-8	10-11	6	5-6	8	18-21	29-34	6-7	17-20	12-14	19-21	6
5	5-6	8-9	5	4		14-17	23-28	5	13-16	9-11	15-18	5
4	4	6-7	4	3	7	11-13	18-22	4	10-12	8	11-14	4
3	3	5	3	2		10	15-17	3	6-9	7	8-10	3
2	2	4	2	1	6	9	13-14	2	3-5	6	5-7	2
1	1	3	1		4-5	8	12	1	2	5	3-4	1
0	0	0-2	0	0	0-3	0-7	0-11	0	0-1	0-4	0-2	0

SUMMARY

TEST	Raw Score	Scaled Score
Information	19	12
Comprehension	22	14
Arithmetic	13	12
Similarities	21	14
Digit Span	9	7
Vocabulary	72	16
Verbal Score		75
Digit Symbol	63	12
Picture Completion	19	14
Block Design	37	11
Picture Arrangement	31	13
Object Assembly	28	9
Performance Score		59
Total Score	134	

VERBAL SCORE 75 IQ 114
PERFORMANCE SCORE 59 IQ 112
FULL SCALE SCORE 134 IQ 114

*Clinicians who wish to draw a "psychograph" on the above table may do so by connecting the subject's raw scores. The interpretation of any such profile, however, should take into account the reliabilities of the subtests and the lower reliabilities of differences between subtest scores.

and twenty-four hours in a day; so multiply 24 by 7 and you get 161 which equals the hours in seven days or one week. Now there are twenty blocks in a mile, so multiply 161 by 20 and this gives you 3,220. The distance from Paris to New York is 3,220 miles.[1] (Wechsler, 1944.)

The nature of intelligence

In everyday life, few of us have any difficulty in understanding the term "intelligence"—it is the quality that "intelligent" or "sensible" people possess. But each of us would actually *define* "intelligence" somewhat differently, and we would probably disagree among ourselves to some extent if we were asked to rate a number of people according to their intelligence. Furthermore, generally we are not aware that what we call "intelligence" is actually a very complex phenomenon. Like many other everyday phenomena that have been investigated by psychologists, it is not as simple as it appears at first glance. The problem of definition becomes very important when we set out to measure a given phenomenon, because we want to be sure that we are measuring what we are supposed to be measuring and not something else.

The problem of defining "intelligence" caused difficulty almost from the very beginning of the intelligence testing movement. Binet (1909) thought of intelligence as comprising such capacities as comprehension, inventiveness, persistence, and critical analysis, but after trying in vain to measure each of them separately, he decided to test them in combination. Starting out with the idea that some children are bright and some are dull, he looked for tasks that would discriminate between bright children and dull children. He found that children who were best on tests of judgment also did well on tests of attention, memory, vocabulary, and so forth, thus demonstrating an interrelationship among these skills or capacities. What Binet actually did in developing his scale was to measure the amount of intelligent behavior demonstrated by children. The more intelligently a given child behaved the more "intelligence" Binet ascribed to him.

This basic approach has been followed by psychologists who have followed Binet. A child may appear bright and intelligent, but if he cannot complete and solve problems that can be solved by at least 50 per cent of the children his age,

the psychologist is unable to rate his intelligence as "average." Conversely, the child who appears to be dull, but who is able to complete tasks that are ordinarily completed by children two years older than he will be rated high on intellectual ability. As far as psychologists are concerned, intelligence, like other psychological qualities and attributes, exists only to the extent that it can be operationally defined—that is, only to the extent that it appears in actual behavior. For this reason, psychologists and laymen often come to different conclusions as to who is intelligent and who is not. For instance, a teacher might rate as "above average in intelligence" a child who is pleasant, cheerful, cooperative, and eager, whereas a psychologist, basing his judgment on an IQ of 85, would rate the same child as "low average."

The validity of intelligence tests. In the preceding example, there is a possibility that both the teacher and the psychologist may be right. Each is responding to a different aspect of the child's behavior. The teacher is judging the child's ability to get along with others—what might be termed "social intelligence"—whereas the psychologist is judging the child's ability to solve abstract problems—"test intelligence" or "conceptual intelligence" or "abstract intelligence."

In selecting personnel to fill "sensitive" military positions during World War II, the Assessment Staff of the Office of Strategic Services (1948) found it convenient to identify three varieties of mental functions: *mechanical intelligence* (the ability to deal with things), *social intelligence* (the ability to deal with people), and *conceptual intelligence* (the ability to deal with ideas and symbols). This scheme of classification is similar to that developed some twenty years previously by Thorndike (1920), who classified intelligent activity into three types: *social intelligence, concrete intelligence,* and *abstract intelligence.*

The advantage of such systems lies in their ability to make sense out of perplexing problems of classification like the one described above. In other words, we do not have to become involved in a fruitless debate whether or not the child who gets along very well with others but who has an IQ of 85 is "intelligent." Instead we can agree that he shows more capability in social situations than in paper-and-pencil tests. Another common situation is that of the individual who is "clever with his hands," but who does rather poorly on

Although intelligence may be classified into a number of different categories, there may be a general factor (or factors) that underlies each of them.

paper-and-pencil tests of intelligence. Such an individual usually scores higher on the "performance" or nonverbal scale of intelligence tests than on the "verbal" scales.

The disadvantage of such systems of classification is this: they may exaggerate differences between different kinds of intelligence. Research with intelligence tests does not support the idea that these varieties of intelligence are as "different" as they seem at first glance. Tests of verbal and mechanical or concrete intelligence tend to correlate between .25 and .45, with average correlation in the low .30's. Although such correlations are fairly low, they do indicate the presence of common factors. The ability to succeed in social situations is also related to intelligence measured by paper-and-pencil techniques. Liddle (1958) studied a group of 273 tenth-graders and

found a substantial interrelationship among such variables as measured intelligence, leadership ability, and personality test scores, even after socio-economic status had been "partialled out," that is, eliminated, as a factor. Very likely the amount of "general intelligence" an individual possesses is in turn related to the amount of ability he is able to demonstrate in several different directions.

Abstract or conceptual intelligence. Although recognizing the existence of several varieties of intelligence enables us to evade controversies regarding the classification of this or that individual as "more intelligent" or "less intelligent," it does not particularly help us in understanding the meaning and importance of a considerable body of research that has accumulated in the field of intelligence. Most of the work done by psychologists in intelligence testing has been concerned with abstract or conceptual intelligence, and most of the intelligence tests that are available are of this type.

For one thing, it is easier to validate a test of abstract or conceptual intelligence than a test of social, concrete, or mechanical intelligence, particularly in situations involving classroom learning. Perhaps this is because such learning situations are more standardized and consistent—more "structured"—than are situations that call for the exercise of social or mechanical intelligence, and this structured quality reduces some of the variability, thus making prediction easier. Or it may be that learning ability is actually a skill that is more readily identifiable and measurable than social or mechanical ability. Whatever the reason for the higher validity of tests of abstract intelligence, the fact remains that persons scoring high on such tests are able to learn more rapidly and efficiently than those who score low. Unfortunately, intelligence tests in general are not yet so effective in predicting success *beyond* the period of education or training, but this may merely be evidence that intelligence is only one of several factors involved in on-the-job success. It can be argued that social or mechanical intelligence should be an important factor in vocational success; tests that attempt to measure these capacities are generally no better than tests of abstract intelligence in predicting success after graduation. A major consideration here, of course, is the fact that employment situations are more variable (and hence less predictable) than school situations.

When we say that tests of intelligence do not do as well in predicting on-the-job success as school success, we do not mean that they are worthless. Actually, there is some relationship between measured intelligence and success in the world outside the classroom. As a check on this, try the following experiment. Rank the following ten occupations in terms of the amount of intelligence you think is required. Give the occupation that requires the most intelligence a "1," the occupation that demands the second highest amount of intelligence a "2," and so forth:

Blacksmith	Locomotive Fireman
Postal Clerk	Radio Repairman
Farm Worker	Laundry Machine Operator
Draftsman	Statistical Clerk
Hospital Orderly	Machinist

Even the solution of concrete or mechanical problems involves the ability to conceptualize or to think abstractly.

Now look at Figure 9-2 on page 202 and check your ratings. This figure presents some of the results obtained by the Army in testing more than twelve million inductees during World War II. The average scores obtained by individuals grouped according to various occupations rather generally conform to the estimates of intelligence that most of us would make. Such agreement between the test and what may be ordinarily observed can be accepted in this instance as evidence of validity.

The relationship between measured intelligence and leadership was studied by Flint and Bass (1958), who found that individuals who showed superior leadership in small group problem-solving exercises also had higher intelligence, as measured by the American Council of Education Psychological Examination. Another study of leadership conducted by Palmer and Greer (1956) showed that military personnel perceived as leaders by their peers scored higher on the Army General Classification Test. Still another study, using financial and vocational success as the criterion, found that Cleveland, Ohio, high school students who had been classified as "gifted" (IQ 125 or higher) between 1938 and 1952 reported far more than average success when queried in 1953. Over half the employed respondents were in professional or managerial work, as contrasted with a figure of less than twenty per cent for all employed persons. (Barbe, 1956.)

The second reason why tests of abstract or conceptual intelligence are preferred as research instruments by psychologists has to do with their statistical reliability. Tests of this type are much more reliable than tests of mechanical or social ability —that is, their scores are much more consistent and dependable. Perhaps this means that we need to find new and better ways of measuring social and mechanical competence, or perhaps the measurement of these two kinds of ability is complicated by a larger number of unidentified or uncontrolled variables. It may be that the degree of mechanical or social ability that is expressed is far more dependent on the kind of situation in which the individual finds himself. Whatever the reason, tests of abstract intelligence do their job much more precisely than do existing tests for mechanical or social ability.

A third reason for the preponderance of research with abstract or conceptual intelligence is the feeling on the part of many psychologists that the ability to use abstractions—symbols, concepts, ideas, and so forth—is the *essential* factor

Figure 9-2. Army General Classification Test (AGCT) scores for civilian occupations. (After Stewart, 1947.)

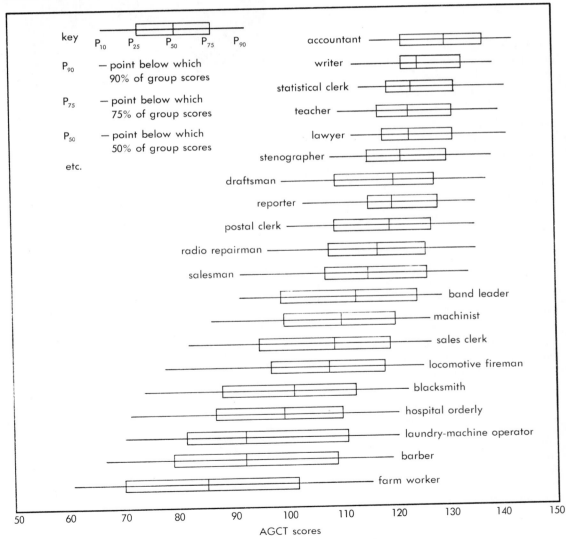

in intellectual functioning, a factor that may be basic to *all* forms of intellectual functioning. If so, measured differences between what appear to be varieties of intelligence may be due to such variables as motivation, cultural background, and attitudes toward oneself.

Environment *versus* heredity

An issue that has evoked considerable disagreement among psychologists is the question of the relative influence of environment and heredity on intelligence. Few psychologists, if any, would deny the importance of one or the other of these two factors, but the "environmentalist" would say that observed differences in IQ's are largely due to differences in environment, whereas the "hereditarian" would say that they result from differences in inherited potential.

The evidence in favor of the hereditarian point of view comes from the studies with twins. Nontwins from the same family tend to correlate about .50 in IQ, as well as in height. Fraternal twins correlate about .65 in each of these variables, whereas identical twins correlate about .90 in IQ and .95 in height. When the IQ's of identical twins reared apart are compared, the correlation in height is about the same, but the correlation in IQ drops to a little less than .80. (Newman, Freeman, and Holzinger, 1937; Woodworth, 1941.) From these data it would appear that the greater similarity of inherited traits that is characteristic of identical twins promotes a similarity in intellectual ability. Such a conclusion would leave unexplained, however, the differences between fraternal twins on the one hand and nontwin siblings on the other. The inherited traits of fraternal twins are no more similar than the inherited traits of nontwin siblings. If so, why should the IQ's of fraternal twins be more closely alike? The environmentalist would argue that the psycho-social environment of fraternal twins is likely to be more similar than the environment of siblings (brothers and/or sisters) born one or more years apart. The arguments of the environmentalist are also supported by some aspects of the research performed on identical twins raised apart. In 5 out of 19 pairs of twins there was a difference in education of four or more years. In each instance, the twin who had received the larger amount of education had a higher IQ; the five twins with better education scored an average of 16 IQ points higher than their cotwins. Three

other twins averaged 12 IQ points higher than their cotwins, and in each instance the educational advantages were estimated to be higher. (Newman, Freeman, and Holzinger, 1937.) The correlation between discrepancies in education and the discrepancies in IQ was very high: .79.

Effects of education on intelligence. The importance of schooling as an environmental variable is demonstrated by other research. A study by Gordon (1923) of children raised on British canal boats, relatively isolated from contact with other persons and receiving only occasional schooling, showed a decline in IQ over an age span of 6 to 18 years. The average IQ of children in the 4-to-6-year-old group was 90, whereas in the oldest group, it averaged only 60. Home surroundings were satisfactory from the standpoint of health and cleanliness, but many of the parents were themselves illiterate. When Gordon compared canal-boat children, who attended school only 5 per cent of the normal amount of time, with gypsy children, whose attendance was 35 per cent of normal, he found that the latter had higher IQ's. Although the IQ's of gypsy children also declined with age, the decline was not as marked as with canal-boat children. Apparently the greater amount of social interaction and the greater amount of time spent at school resulted in a higher IQ.

In a study of Tennessee mountain children, Wheeler (1942) found that IQ's in 1940 were considerably higher than they were in 1930. He attributed the difference to better schools, greater school attendance, and wider contact with the outside world through better roads. Sherman and Key (1932) found that children living in isolated spots in the Blue Ridge Mountains had lower IQ's than children living in villages in the same general area. Although the IQ's of both groups of children declined with age (as is common with children from families where educational standards are low), the decline was more marked with the mountain children, whose opportunities for schooling were much more restricted.

Still another study that indicates some relationship between intelligence and education is a comparison by Tuddenham (1948) between the scores made on the Army Alpha by inductees in World War I with those made in World War II. A group of 768, selected as representative of the entire population of enlisted men in World War II, made a median score of 104, whereas the

The hereditarian point of view regarding intellectual development is supported to some degree by the fact that differences in abilities of various kinds begin to appear very early.

At the age of three months, the average child ▶ is able to raise his head;

at four months, he is able to play with his hands;

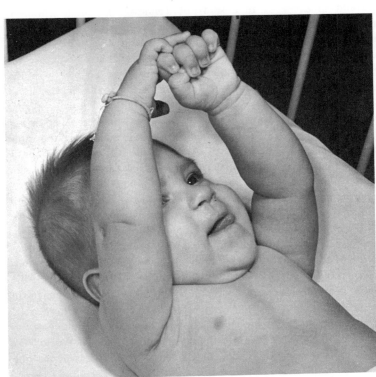

Photographs by Nina Leen, Pix.

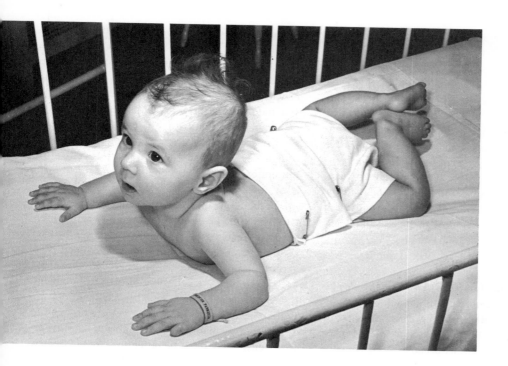

at six months, he can reach for ▶
things. But these norms are merely
averages; some children develop
rapidly and attain these skills
sooner than others, whereas others
attain them later. However, the
correlations between tests of ability
administered during the first two
years of life and those given during
the later years of childhood are
quite low. Perhaps what we later
come to recognize and measure as
"intelligence" during school years
cannot be measured during infancy. Or perhaps environmental
forces produce drastic modifica-
tions of initial patterns of intellectual development.

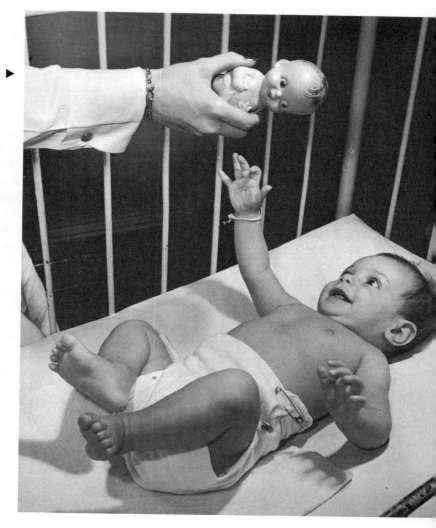

median score for soldiers during World War I was 62. A score of 104 corresponds to the eighty-third percentile on World War I norms. In other words, 83 per cent of the soldiers in World War I scored below the score achieved by at least half the soldiers in World War II. It is possible that the difference was partly due to the greater familiarity of World War II inductees with objective tests or to the improvement in nutrition and general health that took place between the two wars. But a more valid explanation seems to be the educational difference between the two groups: the average soldier in World War I had completed 8 years of schooling, whereas the average amount of schooling of the World War II inductee was 10 years.

Social stimulation as a factor in the development of intelligence. It is sometimes pointed out that individuals with a greater number of years in school would be expected to attain higher scores on intelligence tests because the latter contain items that are either drawn from school curricula or experiences or require skills that are similar to school tasks. Undoubtedly school experience is a factor in achieving success in intelligence tests. There is, for example, a very high degree of correlation between school achievement tests (tests that measure how much subject matter has been learned in school) and intelligence tests, even though the intelligence tests attempt to measure basic ability or aptitude and not the amount of subject matter or knowledge that has been acquired. Nevertheless, there is some evidence that indicates that scores attained on intelligence tests are affected by factors over and beyond the number of years of schooling completed.

For example, a recent survey of Illinois high school students found that measured intelligence varied according to the distance from the nearest town of 25,000 or more population and the distance from the nearest operating coal mine. Since the students covered in the survey had completed approximately the same number of years of schooling, we must find other variables to explain differences in their performance. It is suggested that students living in or near large towns and cities and away from coal mines experienced a higher degree of social and intellectual stimulation. (Mohandessi and Runkel, 1958.)

Studies with animals also support the importance of social stimulation in intellectual func-

tioning. For instance, Melzack and Thompson (1956) raised 21 dogs in a restricted environment and compared their behavior with 16 dogs raised in a free environment, that is, as pets in private homes or in the psychological laboratory. When dogs from the two groups were brought together in a competitive situation, dogs that had been raised in the restricted environment showed a high degree of ineptitude. The restricted dogs did not exhibit "the sustained, well-oriented curiosity toward other dogs" characteristic of dogs raised in a normal environment. Furthermore, they were unable to escape from an experimenter who approached them with noisy, aggressive, stamping steps. The investigators concluded that "restriction of early social and perceptual experience has a definite retarding effect on the emergence of normal, adult, social behavior in dogs." Other research with these dogs reported by Hebb (1955) shows that they were unable to learn from experience, paying little attention to an object that produced an electric shock and repeatedly thrusting their noses into a flaming match.

The extent to which intellectual functioning is dependent on social stimulation is suggested by the research by Hebb and his associates that we presented in Chapter 6. You may recollect that when college students were isolated from contact with the outside world for periods of two to three days, they experienced a marked loss in their ability to do simple problems. Furthermore, they made lower scores on the intelligence tests they took after emerging from isolation, as contrasted with scores made before commencing the experiment. (Hebb, 1955; Bexton, Heron, and Scott, 1954.)

Implications of the heredity-environment controversy. Although the weight of evidence at the present favors the environmentalist point of view, the issue is by no means settled. Studies of intelligence and its correlates have raised more questions than they have answered. Whenever a group of children is tested, there is always some unexplained variation among their IQ's, no matter what their inheritance and their environmental background.

However, the relative importance of environment and heredity on intelligence is of more than academic interest. For one thing, the kind of educational system that is developed depends on the weight that is given to one over the other. The environmentalists assume that intelligence is largely a product of the kind of environment in which one grows up: the more stimulating the environment, the higher the level of intelligence, and the more intellectually impoverished and sterile the environment, the lower the intelligence. He is also inclined to take the position that the child who enters school with a low IQ can, if stimulated adequately, develop a higher level of intellectual competence. Thus the environmentalist believes that the quality of tomorrow's leadership depends on how intellectually stimulating the schools are today for *all* children.

The person who is inclined to take the hereditarian point of view believes that little can be done to modify the intelligence a child is born with. Therefore he is inclined to favor school programs that emphasize *selection* and to put proportionately less stress on providing intellectual stimulation for all children equally, for he sees little point in providing a great range of stimulation for children who are not intellectually endowed. The quality of tomorrow's leadership, according to this viewpoint, does not depend so much on whether the school has been able to stimulate all or most children, but on how well it has been able to identify, select, and, of course, train those children who have the greatest amount of intellectual endowment. In general, the environmentalist point of view has been more characteristic of the philosophy underlying American schools, whereas the hereditarian point of view has characterized European schools.

Changes in intelligence

The IQ is said to be relatively stable. Theoretically, a child aged 4 with an IQ of 100 would be expected to have approximately the same IQ at ages 8, 12, or 16. In other words, a child of "average intelligence" would be expected to remain a child of "average intelligence." However, as we have seen from the foregoing discussion, there are some factors that prevent some children from maintaining a constant IQ. For example, we would expect that children growing up in an environment that is not intellectually stimulating to experience a decline in IQ. And there are other factors or conditions that cause IQ's to change. Honzik, Macfarlane, and Allen (1948) tested the intelligence of 252 children 14 times between the ages of 6 and 18 and found that the IQ's of almost 60 per cent of the group changed 15 points or more. Nine per cent showed changes of 30

points or more. The changes tended to be in the direction of the educational and socio-economic status of the family. In other words, children with high IQ's growing up in low-status families tended to experience reduction in IQ, and children with below-average IQ's growing up in high-status families tended to show increases. The children whose scores fluctuated the most also tended to have a greater number of disturbing experiences in their life situation—severe illnesses, loss of a parent, etc.

Sontag, Baker, and Nelson (1958) administered Stanford-Binet tests to 140 children at various intervals between the ages of 3 and 12. Only a small percentage of the children showed any tendency to make the same IQ's over the nine year period. There was even an inconsistency in the patterns of change, some individual's reversing the trend that they had been apparently following. Some of the less stable patterns are reported in Figure 9-3. The authors were of the opinion that the high degree of variation among the mental growth curves was a strong argument for environmental rather than hereditary causes of IQ change.

Personality factors in IQ change. One pattern of change identified by the authors was a tendency for the IQ's of girls to decline. Of the 35 children showing the most increase in IQ, two-thirds were boys, and of the 35 showing the most decline, two-thirds were girls. As Figure 9-4 shows, even the 13 boys in the second group tended to better their scores after they entered school. The poorer record made by girls is an interesting contrast to their success in school. A number of studies have found that girls tend to get higher grades and to have fewer difficulties in school. This discrepancy very likely is due to such factors as the greater rapidity and ease with which girls learn both the social skills that are involved in getting along with classmates and teachers, and the linguistic skills basic to reading, writing, and speaking. Another factor is indicated by the finding of the authors that girls whose IQ declined tended to rate high on "femininity." In another report based on the same body of research data, but covering ages from 3 to 15, the authors report that all the individuals whose IQ's dropped off at the end of the period were girls. They explained this tendency as a "flight into femininity," by which they meant that "competition and achievement are of primary importance only in

Figure 9-3. Illustrations of variability in IQ between the ages of 3 and 12. (Sontag, Baker, and Nelson, 1958. Reproduced by permission.)

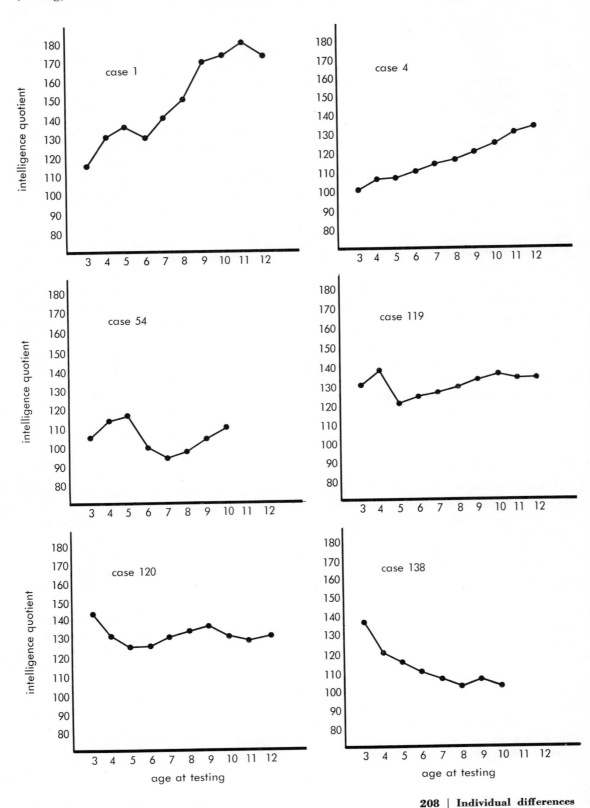

being more feminine, more charming, more subject to admiration." (Sontag, Baker, and Nelson, 1955.) For such girls, intellectual attainment had evidently lost its value.

The authors also tried to identify the personality traits associated with an *increase* in IQ. Each child was rated at age 6 and at age 10 in terms of a number of variables, some of which were found to be significantly related to increases in IQ. When children whose IQ's increased during the four years were compared with children whose IQ's decreased, the former were more inclined to demonstrate the following behavior patterns: (1) they were more competitive; (2) they were less emotionally dependent on their parents; (3) they preferred to solve problems rather than avoid them; (4) they were not particularly well-behaved at home; (5) they engaged in activites they themselves had initiated; (6) they did not have to be prodded or urged by their teachers; (7) they found satisfactions in their work rather than in the praise of others; and (8) they were inclined to express hostility toward their brothers and sisters.

Changes in IQ after adolescence. The question of changes in intelligence after adolescence has been explored by a number of researchers. Terman concluded that intellectual growth stops about age 16. The researches of Jones and Conrad (1933), Miles and Miles (1932), and Wechsler (1944) depicted a growth curve in intelligence that reaches a peak during the mid-twenties and drops off gradually thereafter. The conclusions of these three studies are based, however, on tests administered at the same point in time to individuals of varying ages. Inasmuch as individuals at age 40 scored lower than individuals at age 25, and individuals at age 60 and 70 scored lower still, it was assumed that the lower scores were due to a decline in intelligence associated with increased age. In no case did the researchers test the same individuals over an extended period of time.

In recent years, however, additional research points to fallacies in conclusions based on these earlier studies. In Chapter 3 we referred to a study by Owens (1953), who in 1949 and 1950 administered the Army Alpha to 127 men who had taken the same test in 1919 when it was used as an entrance test at Iowa State College. Instead of a decrease, the group showed a significant increase. Other evidence of growth in intelligence after the twenties is found in a study by Bayley and Oden (1955) of scores on intelligence tests given twelve years apart to highly gifted individuals and their spouses, who ranged in age at the time of initial testing from 20 to almost 60. All age groups in this study showed significant gains. A more recent study by Bradway, Thompson, and Cravens (1958) compared IQ's of indi-

Figure 9-4. Mean IQ points gained and lost by children who demonstrated the greatest gain or the greatest loss. (After Sontag, Baker, and Nelson, 1958.)

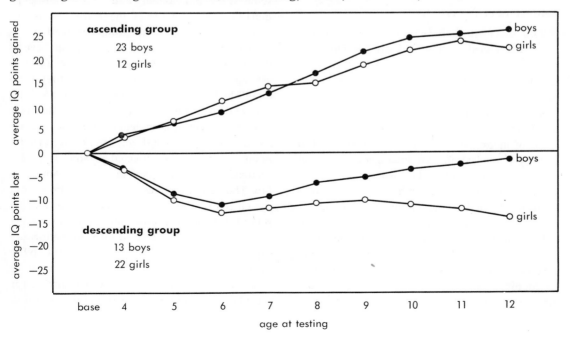

viduals tested in 1931 (when they were between 2 and 5 years of age), in 1941, and in 1956. Although the average IQ—113—of the individuals tested did not change significantly between childhood (1931) and adolescence (1941) it rose to 124 in 1956. For these individuals, the period of late adolescence and early adulthood appears to have been one of accelerated intellectual growth.

There is, of course, insufficient evidence in these studies on which to base a claim that mental growth can be *routinely* expected in individuals beyond the ages of 50, 25, or even 16. Data from Owens' study suggest that the amount of growth depends on the amount of intellectual stimulation. Such a hypothesis would certainly be consistent with existing research on intellectual growth of children. Since the groups studied in these reports are considerably above average, as compared with the general population, one might wonder whether the ability to respond to intellectual stimulation of adults depends on the initial level of intelligence.

There is, however, a study by Charles (1953) that indicates that positive changes may also occur in groups at the opposite end of the intellectual spectrum. After a lapse of 15 years, Charles retested 24 individuals who had been classified as subnormal in intelligence. The mean IQ of the group as tested in 1935 was 58; in 1950 it was 72. Every individual showed some gain in IQ with the exception of one person who achieved an IQ of 68 on both testings.

Achievement and creativity

The need for achievement. Although psychologists tended, during the early "developmental" decades of mental testing, to be concerned largely with identifying and measuring intelligence as such, in recent years they have turned to some of the broader and more complex areas of intellectual functioning. The broadening of the scope of investigation has been brought about in part by a realization that intelligence does not exist in isolation from other aspects of an individual's life. We have shown how it can be stimulated or inhibited by the amount and kind of social interaction experienced by the individual. Other evidence shows that the individual's own aspirations and need for achievement play a large part in the level and quality of his intellectual functioning. A study by Sewell, Haller, and Straus (1957) found that the IQ's of high school seniors were more closely related to their vocational and educational aspirations than to the social status of their families. Students with high IQ's from low-status families were twice as likely to have high occupational and educational aspirations for themselves as were low IQ students from high-status families.

The need to achieve sometimes brings an individual into conflict with the group. Group members often do not look kindly on the efforts of a single member to achieve production or recognition above that of the group norm. College students, for example, sometimes make caustic comments about the motives of individuals who consistently receive the highest marks on examinations. Some unions actually take steps to protect their members against "over-achievement" by specifying in their contracts what a "normal day's work" should be and by inflicting fines on members who exceed this norm. It is understandable, of course, that groups should feel threatened by the unusually high achievement of a few members. Such achievement is felt to reflect on the adequacy of the other members and raises the question of whether a higher level of production should not be expected from everyone. Just as membership in a group serves to restrain antisocial nonconforming behavior, it also serves to inhibit nonconforming behavior that is in no way antisocial.

The advantages of group membership are many; hence we more or less willingly sacrifice some of our individuality and right to self-determination. But sometimes the price that is demanded is too high. Some groups demand an excessive amount of conformity, going far beyond the observance of ordinary conventions and tolerating no deviation from the norms they have established. Although we usually associate excessive demands for conformity with totalitarianism, the citizens of even democratic states are not immune. As Riesman, Glazer, and Denney (1950) point out, the "other-directed person" is an exceedingly common phenomenon in American life. The "other-directed" individual differs from the citizen of the totalitarian country in that he is not forced into his conformity by any externally imposed decrees, but instead turns to conformity eagerly. He has a rather highly developed ability to find out what others expect of him in order to conform to their expectations. This makes for great flexibility and ease in personal relationships,

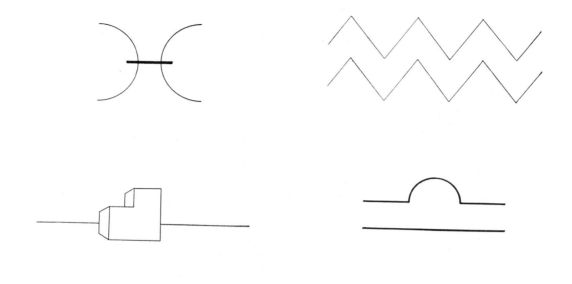

Figure 9-5. The Welsh Figure Preference Test requires that subjects express a preference, or lack of preference, for abstract line drawings on cards. Subjects chosen at random tended to prefer drawings such as the four shown at top; creative subjects, drawings such as the four at bottom. (Consulting Psychologists Press. Reproduced by permission.)

but may be detrimental to individual development and creativity if it is carried to an extreme or if it becomes the dominant pattern of behavior.

Studies of creativity. One of the most comprehensive attempts to study the characteristics of creative individuals consists of a series of studies that have been under way for some years at the Institute for Personality Assessment and Research of the University of California at Berkeley. Although most of the studies are at this moment still in progress, some of the preliminary findings suggest that creative individuals, both artists and scientists, are far more independent in their judgments and are far more tolerant of ambiguity, irregularity, and disorder than most individuals. For example, when an unselected group of subjects was asked to find words to describe the drawings in Figure 9-5, they tended to use terms that indicated preference for the more or less conventional drawings at the top. A group of some 80 painters, however, showed a marked preference for the lower four drawings. When similar pairs of drawings were presented to two groups of university doctoral candidates who had previously been classified by their instructors as "more original" and "less original," the "more original" candidates demonstrated preferences similar to those of the 80 artists. When subjects were given a large number of small, colored squares and were asked to use them in constructing a mosaic, those students who had been judged more creative constructed mosaics like those on the top of the facing page, whereas other students constructed conventionalized mosaics like those on the bottom. (Barron, 1958.)

One of the studies conducted at the Institute consisted of a three-day assessment of a group of 100 professional men. Among the tests to which they submitted was a situational test designed to measure tendencies to conform to inaccurate group judgments, somewhat similar in nature to the experiments conducted by Asch (1956) described at the end of Chapter 6. When the assessment staff compared the results of interviews and test records of the conforming with the nonconforming subjects (without any prior knowledge of the degree of conformity expressed), they found that the nonconforming individual tended to show the following characteristics:

Is an effective leader.

Takes an ascendant role in his relations with others.

Is persuasive; tends to win other people over to his point of view.

Is turned to for advice and reassurance.

Is efficient, capable, able to mobilize resources easily and effectively.

Is active and vigorous.

Is an expressive, ebullient person.

Seeks and enjoys aesthetic and sensuous impressions.

Is natural; free from pretense, unaffected.

Is self-reliant, independent in judgment; able to think for himself.

Men who were high in conformity were characterized as follows:

Is submissive, compliant and overly accepting with respect to authority.

Is conforming; tends to do the things that are prescribed.

Has a narrow range of interests.

Overcontrols his impulses; is inhibited, needlessly delays or denies gratification.

Is unable to make decisions without vacillation or delay.

Becomes confused, disorganized, and unadaptive under stress.

Lacks insight into his own motives and behavior.

Is suggestible; overly responsive to other people's evaluations rather than his own.[1] (Crutchfield, 1955.)

Although the results of research on conformity and creativity are so far largely exploratory and cannot be considered conclusive, they do suggest that the ability to function competently on an advanced level, intellectually speaking, depends to a large degree on an individual's willingness to tolerate or seek out situations or experiences that are unusual or even irrational, that do not conform to the routine of everyday living. As Barron (1958) suggests, the kind of unbalanced approach to life that is evidenced by the creative individual may actually be more healthy than unhealthy. "The truly creative individual," he says, "stands ready to abandon old classifications and to acknowledge that life, particularly his own unique life, is rich with new possibilities. To him, disorder offers the potentiality of order." [1]

[1] Reprinted by permission.

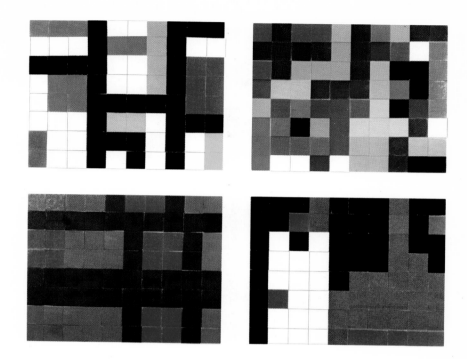

MOSAICS

constructed by
creative subjects

contrasted

with

those done by
members of an
unselected group

Hall, 1958. Reproduced by permission.

Summary

It was through intelligence testing in the Army during World War I that psychology first came to the attention of the general public. The term "IQ" became an accepted popular term, and intelligence testing spurred the development of various applied branches of psychology.

Although intelligence measures were one of the research interests of nineteenth century psychologists, the first practical use of such tests was in France at the beginning of this century. A psychologist named Binet developed an objective test to select the less capable school children who should be placed in special schools. This test was revised several times, and an American revision by Terman became the widely used Stanford-Binet. Other tests for both children and adults soon were developed. In order to aid in the classification of service personnel during World War I, psychologists developed the Army Alpha and Army Beta group tests of intelligence. Similar group tests were utilized by educators. The armed services, schools, and industry used tests for the benefit of the institution, rather than that of the individual—that is, the aim was to select individuals for specific purposes. At the same time, other psychologists began using intelligence tests to help them in understanding individuals; this clinical use of the tests led to a need for tests that measured a variety of intellectual functions. Among the tests that answered this purpose were those developed by Wechsler. His tests, for both adults and children, are divided into a series of specific verbal and performance tasks. Clinical psychologists use such tests not only to measure intelligence but also as a source of clues about personality functioning.

The definition of intelligence has been a difficult problem, but most psychologists agree that individuals who do well on tasks involving judgment, attention, memory, vocabulary, etc., are intelligent. Somewhat different types of skills are involved in social intelligence (the ability to deal with people) and mechanical intelligence (the ability to deal with things). Most intelligence tests concentrate on conceptual intelligence (the ability to deal with ideas and symbols) and have greater predictive validity than tests measuring the other two areas. Intelligence tests are best at predicting school success, but there is also a relationship between an individual's intellectual level and the type of occupation in which he is employed, leadership ability, and financial and vocational success. Tests of conceptual intelligence are also found to be more reliable than the other two, and many psychologists feel that conceptual ability is the essential factor in all forms of intellectual functioning.

An issue in psychology has been the controversy about whether environment or heredity is a more important determinant of intelligence. Studies of identical and fraternal twins suggest that intellectual ability is determined partially through heredity, but that environmental factors are extremely important in influencing intellectual development. Studies show that opportunity to attend school leads to higher IQ's, and individuals living in restricted environments actually show a decline in IQ as they grow older. School experience probably leads to higher test scores both because some test items are related to school experiences and because school provides both social and intellectual stimulation. Studies with animals also suggest that social stimulation is a vitally important factor in intellectual functioning. The heredity-environment issue has important implications, because an extreme position favoring the hereditarian point of view would lead to school selection of only those children with innate ability, whereas an extreme environmentalist position would favor intense educational exposure for all children to develop their abilities. The environmentalist doctrine underlies the philosophy of American education, and a more hereditarian notion is characteristic of European schools.

Theoretically, the IQ is a stable measure which does not change for an individual over the years. Although this is generally true, some factors do operate to raise and other factors to lower IQ. High IQ's tend to decline in lower socio-economic families; and low IQ's tend to increase in families of higher status. Intelligence has also been found to decline after disturbing life experiences; also, girls reveal more decreases in IQ than boys, and various personality factors contribute to changes in measured intelligence. Longitudinal studies have found that intellectual growth is possible even after adolescence, probably depending on the amount of intellectual stimulation available.

It has been found that the level and quality of an individual's intellectual functioning is partly dependent on his need for achievement. The aspirations of individuals to succeed sometimes come in conflict with the resentment of the group toward someone who stands out from the rest. There are many advantages to group membership, but complete conformity to group demands is a high price to pay. Studies of creative and conventional individuals have found many personality differences that are related to the dimension of creativity. In general, the creative individual is more inclined to seek out unusual situations and experiences that do not conform to the routine of everyday living.

Questions

1. For what purpose were intelligence tests originally devised?

2. Why is the term "IQ" not an appropriate one for describing the results of all intelligence tests?

3. How does the group-centered or institution-centered use of intelligence tests differ from clinical use?

4. Before reading this chapter, what did the term "intelligence" mean to you? Has your concept been changed in any way by the chapter?

5. If you wanted to construct a test to measure social intelligence, how would you go about it?

6. If a friend asked you, "Is intelligence determined by heredity or environment?" how would you answer his question?

7. What factors are related to increases and decreases in IQ?

8. What is meant by "need for achievement"? Do you believe that achievement or conformity is more important? Why?

9. How do psychologists judge the creativity of individuals? How do highly creative people differ from less creative ones?

Suggestions for further reading

Anastasi, A. and J. P. Foley, Jr., *Differential Psychology,* rev. ed. New York: Macmillan, 1949. A very complete survey of the psychology of human differences.

Cronbach, L. J., *Essentials of Psychological Testing,* 2nd ed. New York: Harper, 1960. For those who want to learn more about the theoretical and technical aspects of psychological testing, this is an outstanding textbook.

Freeman, F. S., *Theory and Practice of Psychological Testing,* rev. ed. New York: Holt, 1955. A standard textbook in this field; particularly good in its coverage of intelligence and intelligence testing.

McClelland, D. C., J. W. Atkinson, R. A. Clark, and E. L. Lowell, *The Achievement Motive.* New York: Appleton-Century-Crofts, 1953. The report of a five-year research program, making use of phantasy material, concerned with the need to achieve, a motive basic to creativity.

McClelland, D. C., A. L. Baldwin, U. Bronfenbrenner, and F. L. Strodbeck, *Talent and Society: New Perspectives in the Identification of Talent.* Princeton: Van Nostrand, 1958. A collection of papers, consisting of research reports from a committee of the Social Science Research Council.

Tyler, L. E., *The Psychology of Human Differences,* 2nd ed. New York: Appleton-Century-Crofts, 1956. A very readable textbook in the field of differential psychology.

Wechsler, D., *The Measurement and Appraisal of Adult Intelligence,* 4th ed. Baltimore: Williams and Wilkins, 1958. A discussion of the theory underlying the development of Wechsler's intelligence scales for adults, together with information regarding their standardization and application to problems of psychodiagnosis.

PART FIVE

EMOTIONAL FACTORS IN BEHAVIOR

10

Personality: the organization of behavior

The need for personality theory. In our everyday dealings with other people, many of us are occasionally aware of the feeling that while human behavior is varied, interesting, and even fascinating at times, it is essentially irrational. A community very obviously needs a new high school, yet its citizens vote down the bonds that would have provided the money to build it. A handsome and otherwise intelligent woman "throws her life away" by marrying an alcoholic. A debt-ridden family adds to its already staggering monthly payments by buying an expensive automobile. At such times we are inclined to say such things as: "Now *why* do a thing like that? It doesn't make a bit of sense! I guess there's just no way to figure people out."

What such statements mean, of course, is that the observed behavior does not fit our concepts of rational and logical human behavior. Our ideas have led us to develop certain expectations regarding human behavior, and these people are not behaving according to our expectations. Actually, it is not that other people are irrational, but that they do not fit *our* idea of rationality. If we are to understand the actions of others—that is, if we are to make better predictions of their behavior— what we obviously need are some ways of looking at human behavior that will produce better results than the "common-sense" principles that most of us use in analyzing people and predicting what they will do. Perhaps we could improve our understanding and predictions if we would modify our attitudes toward human behavior: instead of assuming that it is *irrational,* let us assume that *all behavior has a certain logic or rationale*. If we can make such an assumption, our problem becomes one of understanding what that logic or rationale might be. If we are successful in doing this, we will have developed some new ways of looking at human behavior—some ways that will improve our understanding and enable us to make better predictions.

One approach that assumes an implicit logic in human behavior, and is concerned with developing an understanding that will permit the making of better predictions, is what psychologists call "personality theory." A personality theory is an attempt to create a hypothetical structure or model that explains why people behave as they do.

Implicit theories of personality. Although the word "theory," as far as many college students are concerned, has connotations of extreme abstractness, vagueness, complexity, and impracticality, there is nothing mysterious or impractical about using theories, for we use them all the time without being aware of it. In our everyday relationships with others we are making predictions continually about their behavior. If we were unable to make such predictions, we would have no basis on which to interact with others and would always be in a state of complete confusion as to what we should do or say next. Hence we organize what we have perceived and learned about people according to some kind of an interrelated framework into which we fit our perceptions of each new person we encounter. Our decisions as to how we will behave toward the other individual and our predictions of how he will react to our behavior are based on our perceptions and the way in which they fit into our framework. This framework is what Bruner and Tagiuri (1954) would call our "implicit theory of personality"—*implicit* because the theoretical elements we are employing may be deduced or *implied* from the responses we make and evidently expect from others.

Generally speaking, of course, we are not aware that we are using a frame of reference or are making predictions at all—these aspects of our behavior function unconsciously, beyond the limits of ordinary awareness. The person who rather consistently argues and disagrees with others may be expressing or responding to an implicit theory that says, in effect: "Other people are stupid—even the best of them. Most of them don't know what they're talking about, and those that do know, talk without thinking." The hypercritical individual therefore takes upon himself the enlightenment of these foolish people. Chronic arguing and disagreeing may of course be the result of other kinds of implicit theories regarding other people, but the point here is that interpersonal behavior that has any kind of pattern and consistency (like chronic arguing and disagreeing) is based on structured assumptions and expectations regarding other people. We develop such implicit theories as a way of coping with the interpersonal relationships in our lives.

Whyte (1955) points out that a great many of the difficulties in communication that occur between management and labor are due in part to the perceptions and the expectations that many individuals in managerial positions have regarding people in general. Management personnel tend to believe that any individual, if faced by a choice, will select the alternative that is to his greatest economic advantage; that people respond separately and individually to all stimuli; and that employees can be treated as impersonally as machines. The natural result of such beliefs is the piecework system in industry, whereby each individual is paid according to the amount he produces, rather than by the hour. Many individuals in management are unaware that they subscribe to such implicit personality theories, and may maintain, for example, that good human relations are more important than production, but their insistence on piecework as a basis for employment is a much more accurate index to their motivation. Presumably the belief held by many working men that employers are interested only in exploiting their employees operates as an implicit theory for them as well.

Private theories of personality. To a large extent the implicit theories of personality that we use as a basis for our reactions to others are learned from our culture—that is, we learn from others what to perceive and how to interpret what we perceive. However, we also respond to more individualized theories and expectations that develop as a result of our own unique experiences.

Frank Zimmer got a "C" in World History, although he thought he should have received at least a "B." To Frank, the reason for his getting the lower mark was obvious: the instructor took a dislike to him because Frank had objected to the way his mid-term examination had been graded. The reason Frank got a "C" was also obvious to Mr. Gorson, the instructor.

Earlier in the semester, he, too, had thought that Frank would get at least a "B," but like a lot of otherwise intelligent students, Frank did not study hard enough. In Frank's world, instructors are usually against him; hence he was disappointed but not particularly surprised that he got a "C." In Mr. Gorson's world, students seldom study as hard as they should; hence he was disappointed but not particularly surprised that a promising young man like Frank should get a "C."

There is a danger, of course, in pushing too far the analogy between the layman's attempts to explain and predict everyday behavior and the psychologist's attempts to explain and predict behavior-in-general. The layman and the psychologist are, after all, trying to do two quite different things. Frank Zimmer and Mr. Gorson, for instance, develop their implicit theories or concepts of human behavior in an attempt to make some sense out of the events in their lives. Their theories and concepts are developed unconsciously and indirectly and are very much a part of their personal experiences, whereas the theories and concepts that psychologists develop are arrived at consciously and deliberately in an attempt to find unifying relationships among the diverse phenomena that go to make up human behavior. Furthermore, psychologists are continually testing and revising their theories.

Psychological theories of personality

The contributions of psychotherapists. Psychological theories of personality have for the most part developed from the work of clinicians or psychotherapists: psychoanalysts, clinical psychologists, and psychiatrists. The individual who fills the professional role of psychotherapist is struck by the fact that the everyday "common-sense" theories and concepts of human behavior have little value when it comes to aiding individuals who are variously labeled as "mentally or emotionally ill," "mentally or emotionally disturbed," "neurotic," "psychotic," or simply "maladjusted." Although "common-sense" theories may be more or less satisfactory in helping one cope with everyday problems, they are of little use in shedding any light on emotional maladjustments. As we have indicated previously, the idea that behavior may be motivated by forces or factors that are beyond the scope of individual awareness is inconsistent with "common sense," which holds that each individual is fully aware of the reasons for his behavior. Another reason why

"common-sense" formulations are not helpful is that they do not give adequate consideration to the emotional factors in motivation. As we indicated a few pages earlier, a great deal of stress is placed in our culture on being rational. Generally speaking, feelings and emotions are considered to be a less valid basis for behavior than thinking and reasoning. It is all too easy for us to take the next step—that of assuming our own behavior is more reasoned and rational than it actually is.

In their search for pattern and structure in the behavior of their patients, the pioneer figures in the field of personality theory tended to consider the behavior of the person as a whole—the totality of human behavior, rather than its individual components. In this, their approach has differed from that of the psychological experimenters in the laboratory, whose research into the nature of learning, physiological processes, perception, motivation, and so forth, consists essentially of attempts to study and explain behavior through an analysis of its elements. The initial contributions to personality theory stemmed from the clinical observations of Charcot, Janet, Freud, and Jung —all of them physicians specializing in the care and treatment of patients with nervous disorders. Further contributions came from social psychology, from individuals like McDougall, as well as from Gestalt psychology, an approach that conceptualized behavior as organized into wholes. Leaders in the Gestalt school include Köhler, Koffka, and Wertheimer.

All of these early contributors to personality theory were much impressed with the essential unity of all behavior and were inclined to believe that a study of its separate elements would not prove as enlightening as a study of the broader dimensions of behavior. In recent years, however, a number of psychologists have attempted to find some common ground between laboratory research findings and personality theory. Research with psychological tests and with physiological processes is also beginning to make some contributions. In general, the closer relationship between experimentally minded researchers and the clinically minded developers of personality theory has helped to put the latter on a sounder, more scientific basis. (Hall and Lindzey, 1957:2.)

"Personality" defined. The term "personality" is a difficult one to define, partly because psychological usage is different from everyday usage, and partly because the concept of per-

Ordinarily when we use the term "personality," we are referring to only the superficial aspects of what psychologists call "personality."

sonality differs according to the theory under consideration. When used psychologically, the term "personality" generally refers to the *total* behavior of the individual, whereas in everyday usage it usually applies to the *external* or socially oriented aspects of behavior—how the individual affects other people. This latter aspect of personality is termed "stimulus value" by psychologists, because people usually *do* make a value judgment in responding to a person's behavior, and this for them becomes his "personality." We say, "He has a pleasing personality," or "What she needs to do is improve her personality." It is this outer layer of personality that the so-called "charm schools" seek to modify. Unfortunately, we commonly fall into the trap of assuming that this superficial aspect of personality is the "real person," forgetting that most people develop a kind of "social self" that they slip into or out of, depending on whether they see themselves as being under public scrutiny. Personality as conceived by the psychologist is much broader and much deeper than the popular concept. It includes such other qualities as "character" (the characteristic way in which an individual behaves on crucial issues) and "temperament" (the basic emotional patterns characteristic of an individual). Personality, used in the psychological sense, cannot be changed by a few weeks in a "charm school" or even in a "leadership development course." It may be changed over a period of time under the impact of changed circumstances (for example,

under prolonged psychotherapy), but such changes are seldom, if ever, accomplished easily and may even involve considerable psychological pain and anxiety. Even under such conditions, the basic pattern of the personality is seldom modified, although fundamental changes in attitude may be accomplished.

Psychoanalytic theories of personality. Progress in the field of personality theory is marked, as it is in other scientific fields, with the continual development of new theories and the modification of old ones, as research produces data that older theories fail to accommodate or explain. The history of psychoanalysis is an example of this kind of development. Freud's original formulations were revised by him a number of times during his long career, and his basic concepts have been reworked and extended. Some of his contributions, like unconscious motivation and the importance of emotional experiences in childhood, are principles that have rather wide acceptance among personality theorists, whereas other concepts, like the centrality of the sex drive, have met with mixed reactions.

Freud's concept of the casual factors underlying human development and behavior constituted a major departure from "common sense." Freud did not object to the "common-sense" concept of man as a reasoning animal, but he made it clear than man's capacity to think and reason did not necessarily make him a rational animal. We are, he pointed out, much more guided by our feelings and emotions than we are aware. Our behavior is to a large degree irrational, being motivated by internal forces and stresses, the true nature of which is unknown to us. According to Freud, the psychological life of the individual is a struggle between "id" (primitive, instinctual, infantile drives), "ego" (the conscious, organizing self, in contact with reality), and "superego" (the conscience, the source of guilt feelings). Figure 10-1 consists of a "cross-sectional diagram" of Freud's concept of the personality. It presents a picture of man as basically a creature of primitive, savage drives (the id) held in check by a thin veneer of "civilization" (the ego and superego). The unconscious area of the personality also constitutes a reservoir of forgotten experiences. The memories of painful and embarrassing experiences, according to Freud, are forced from the conscious into the unconscious area of the personality by "repression," an unconscious process, which he distinguished from "suppression," the *deliberate* attempt to force an annoying or unwelcome thought from consciousness.

Freud's work with his patients in Vienna led him to conclude that neurosis [1] in adults was largely the result of badly confused or inadequate child-parent relations. Freud theorized that a boy during his preschool years quite normally develops a strong attachment for his mother, sometimes even to the point of wanting to get rid of his father, so that he can have her all to himself. This sexually tinged longing for the mother and hatred for the father, which Freud labeled "Oedipus complex" (after Oedipus, the hero of two of Sophocles' tragedies, who unwittingly killed his father and married his mother), is repressed from consciousness but may continue to create neurotic difficulties throughout life if not adequately resolved.[2] Adequate resolution consists in the boy's coming to develop positive feelings toward his father and to identify with him, recognizing the irrationality of the Oedipal feelings. According to "classical" psychoanalytic theory, the Oedipus complex is the central or "nuclear complex" of all neuroses.

Freud's formulations aroused a storm of attack and controversy, which has still not completely abated. The idea that the sex drive is central to all behavior was only slightly less shocking than his concepts of infantile sexuality. The thought that a normal child could both love and hate his father was of course incompatible with the formulations of "common sense."

Freud's methods of treatment were also unorthodox. Instead of following the "common-sense" practice of telling his patients to take hold of themselves and force themselves to forget their ridiculous quirks and irrational fears, he encouraged them to talk about their problems and their feelings. However, this was not easily accomplished. After trying hypnosis, as a way of getting his patients to discuss their difficulties and to recall events and memories of their childhood, he

[1] Both neurosis and psychosis are terms that are applied to chronic mental or emotional disturbance. Psychosis is much more severe and disabling, commonly leading to hospitalization. Neurosis is milder in character.

[2] Girls, according to Freud, develop an attachment for their fathers and a hostility toward their mothers. This development is specifically called the Electra complex, although the term "Oedipus complex" is commonly broadened to cover both types of relationships.

turned to the technique of "free association." This method calls for the patient to relax and to say whatever comes to mind, without any effort to organize or direct his thinking. Thoughts and feelings thus produced are analyzed by the psychoanalyst and interpreted to the patient. The patient's dreams also form part of the material thus analyzed and interpreted. The purpose of this process, called "psychoanalysis," is that of locating focal points of conflict and maladjustment and aiding the patient or "analysand" to reorganize his thoughts, feelings, attitudes, and eventually his personality in order to bring about a better adjustment. The basic problem to which psychoanalysis is directed is that of helping patients to accept their emotions and feelings and the demands and limits of society.

Psychoanalysts are individuals who have themselves been psychoanalyzed and who have had special training in conducting psychoanalysis. Most of the psychoanalysts in the United States are psychiatrists (medical doctors specializing in

Figure 10-1. The psychoanalytic concept of personality. (Healy, Bronner, and Bowers, 1930. Reproduced by permission.)

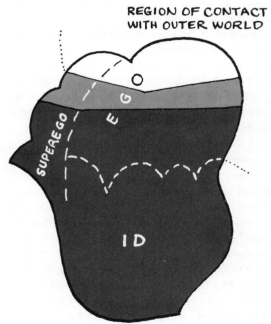

The heavily shaded portion represents the area of personality at the unconscious level of awareness, the lightly shaded area is preconscious, and the unshaded area is conscious. The id is entirely unconscious; the ego and superego function at all three levels.

the treatment of nervous and mental disease), but a few, termed "lay analysts," do not have medical degrees. Although there are less than one thousand qualified psychoanalysts in this country, their influence is far greater than their number would indicate.

Many lay persons think of psychoanalysis as being synonymous with psychotherapy, and some even confuse it with the whole field of psychology. Actually, the term is used to designate psychoanalytic psychotherapy, as well as the body of doctrine produced by Freud and his followers.

Later psychoanalytic theories. As psychoanalysis grew as a theory and as a form of therapy, it developed a number of different schools or schisms, each of which produced variations on Freud's basic theories. Adler and Jung are the best known leaders of these schools. Adler developed a concept of psychological development based on the idea that self-development and personal progress are the result of attempts made by the individual to compensate for feelings of inferiority and inadequacy. Both Adler and Jung placed less emphasis on the sexual nature of man than did Freud, both conceived the "self" as playing a much larger role in behavior than Freud's "ego," and both were far more concerned than Freud was with the cultural factors in man's environment. Adler's concepts have made large contributions to modern thinking in the field of social psychology. Jung's writings have had more appeal to individuals outside the field of psychology, partly because the subject matter of some of his research, theology and religion, lies outside the professional area of most psychologists.

Adler, particularly, has been the forerunner of a group of "neo-Freudians"—notably Sullivan, Horney, and Fromm—who have reacted against Freud's lack of concern with cultural differences. Freud assumed that the psychodynamics conceived by him were universally prevalent in human behavior, whereas subsequent anthropological research has shown that different cultures produce different patterns of personality development. The Oedipus problem, for example, seems to be largely characteristic of family life in cultures that are paternalistic and authoritarian and hence is less likely to appear in matriarchal societies like that of the Trobriand Islanders in the Western Pacific. (Malinowski, 1927.) Whereas the "classical" Freudian approach places a great deal of importance on instinctual strivings, the writings of the neo-Freudians emphasize the importance of cultural patterns and interpersonal relations as determining factors in personality development and adjustment.

The psychology of "the self." In recent years a body of personality theory has been developing around the concept of "the self." To some extent these theories merge and overlap with some of the more recent Freudian and neo-Freudian thinking, a branch of which is termed "ego psychology." William James (1890) laid down some of the concepts which form the basis of present-day thinking about the self, and contributions have also come from Adler, Jung and Rank. The psychology of the self is also influenced by social psychologists like Lewin, who applied concepts from the physical sciences to the study of human behavior and developed a branch of psychology known as "field theory."

The theories of Snygg and Combs (1959) may serve as an example of the work of psychologists interested in the psychology of "the self." Snygg and Combs lean very heavily on what might be called a "perceptual approach" of explaining human behavior. According to their theory, behavior occurs in terms of how an individual perceives himself and his surroundings. The individual's view of himself is his "self-concept"—"who he is." The part of the environment in which the individual is more or less personally involved is called the "phenomenal self." The phenomenal self includes the self-concept, but it also includes those aspects of life that are not a part of the "real self" but are in some way related to it: one's family, career, home, school, clothing, and the like. The environment that the individual perceives or notices is termed the "phenomenal environment." As Figure 10-2 demonstrates, the phenomenal environment includes both the phenomenal self and the self-concept, but it also includes an area of life outside those aspects in which the individual feels personally involved. The college we attend is to some degree a part of our phenomenal self: it is "our college." A college in a nearby city is likely to be in our phenomenal environment: we are aware of its existence and may have various kinds of attitudes about it, depending on our values and our experiences. If we happen to be reading a newspaper and we encounter an item about our own college, we are likely to stop and read it, because it is, in a sense, about "us." An item about the college in the nearby city might be read or not, depending on our interest in the college. An item about a college we have never heard of might be overlooked, unless the facts in the story were in themselves interesting (that is, bore some relationship to ourselves). Such a college would be likely to be outside our phenomenal environment, because there would be nothing about it that would arouse our interest in it.

What Snygg and Combs call our "phenomenal field" is called by other psychologists "personal field," "behavioral field," "psychological field," or "life space." (Koffka, 1935; Lewin, 1935.) Probably "private world" would be a good everyday term for it. (Frank, 1939.) Snygg and Combs make the point that this phenomenal field or private world is *reality* for each individual, that is, each of us acts as though what he perceives and how he perceives it is the "real world." This helps to explain why two persons in the same situation may behave differently—that is, they behave differently because they perceive the situation differently. An adult walking down the street sees an automobile at the curb with the keys in the ignition. If he notices it at all, it may be only to think that the owner is taking unnecessary chances. A teenager who is looking for thrills and who has a need to rebel against the restrictions of society may perceive the same scene quite differently. He may, for instance, see the situation as an

automobile "asking to be borrowed," or as an opportunity to go joy-riding that cannot be passed up. He may, in fact, feel *compelled* to take the car.

This theory helps to explain a great deal of behavior that otherwise seems completely irrational. The paranoid mental patient perceives what he thinks is a slightly metallic taste to his food and immediately assumes he is being poisoned. Seen in this frame of reference his threats to kill the cook take on a certain degree of coherence: he is only acting in self-defense. It sometimes happens that a student taking an objective-type, machine-scored examination will use an ordinary lead pencil to mark his answers on the special answer sheet, even though the directions stated very clearly that *only* the special pencil is to be used. Such behavior seems somewhat senseless until we remember that examinations rather commonly arouse anxiety and that anxiety reduces or narrows the perceptual field. A person can respond only to the reality he perceives, and if his perceptual field is narrowed to the point that he actually sees the instructions but does not *perceive* the statement regarding the special pencil, then he quite understandably behaves as though the statement is not there.

Research in the psychology of "the self." The theories concerned with the psychology of the self have been very productive of research. Tests have been devised, for example, to measure attitudes toward the self, as well as toward other significant individuals in the phenomenal environment. The "Q-sort" technique calls for the subject to sort statements into categories on a continuum in terms of the extent to which they apply to himself. In the categories at one end of the continuum he places the statements that he feels are most descriptive of him, and the statements that are least descriptive he places in categories near the opposite end. Each statement can then be assigned a score in terms of where it is placed. If nine categories are used, the statement placed in the "most like me" category would be given a score of "9," the statement placed in the next group would be given a score of "8," and so on, with the statement in the "least like me" category being scored as "1."

Each statement's score can then be compared with the way it is scored by others or by the same person in other situations. The subject might, for instance, be asked to sort the items again, this

Figure 10-2. Diagrammatic representation of the "self-structure." (Snygg and Combs, 1959. Reproduced by permission.)

Sometimes our self-concepts may vary somewhat from reality as perceived by others, but each individual behaves as though his self-concept is reality.

time referring them to his *ideal* self, the person he would like to be or the person he believes that he ought to be. The two sortings can then be compared numerically, and a coefficient of correlation worked out, reflecting the similarity between the individual's "real self" and his "ideal self." Presumably, the less the relationship between the two selves (and the lower the coefficient of correlation), the greater his problems of adjustment. The individual who is continually behaving in ways that are contrary to his ideals or his expectations is likely to be plagued by feelings of guilt, inferiority, and anxiety. Differences between the way in which an individual perceives himself and how he is perceived by others can be measured by asking people who know him to sort the same statements into the same number of categories in terms of the extent to which they believe the statements are descriptive of him. Their ranking of the statements can then be compared with his ranking and a coefficient of correlation computed to indicate the degree of similarity. A certain amount of disparity is always to be expected, of course, but large differences (as reflected in low correlations) raise the question of whether an individual really does "know himself."

Still another method of using the Q-sort is to ask the subject to sort the same group of statements according to his perceptions of his father and mother. This makes it possible to find clues as to the influence of his father and his mother on his psychological development. Or, a married couple can sort statements for themselves, for their perceptions of each other, and for the way in which each of them thinks the other will rate him, or her. The differences between these ratings may provide clues as to the accuracy of their interpersonal perceptions, their self-knowledge, and their empathy—their awareness of each other's feelings.

Q-sorts are also used in research in psychotherapy. Differences between an individual's self-concept and self-ideal are computed at various stages in the therapeutic process. If therapy is successful, it usually results in a closing of the gap between the two, as the individual develops greater self-confidence and a better opinion of himself and a less extravagant and unrealistic self-ideal. The therapist, too, can check up on his perception of the patient by trying to predict the way in which the latter will rate himself. (Rogers and Dymond, 1954.)

Measures of attitudes toward the self can also

be used to explore various aspects of psychodynamics in groups. Bruce (1958) asked sixth-grade children to evaluate themselves on a scale designed to measure self-acceptance, which he defined in terms of the degree of similarity between self-concept and ideal-self. He found that children rating high in self-acceptance also rated low on anxiety and displayed classroom behavior indicating a lower degree of emotional insecurity than children who rated low in self-acceptance. However, students who had been enrolled for a two-year period in an experimental program designed to develop more understanding of their own and others' behavior showed less anxiety and insecurity than children in other groups studied in the course of the research.

Are there "types" of personality? In our everyday attempts to understand the behavior of others and to create some workable pattern of responding to their behavior, we are inclined to categorize them in one way or another. Frank, we say, is a shy person, George is open-minded, Gladys is pessimistic, Nora is quick-tempered. When we have a speech to be made, we are not likely to call on Frank; we are inclined to ask George's advice on problems; we tend to discount whatever Gladys says; and we are particularly careful in what we say to Nora. This categorizing or stereotyping has a certain practical value, because it enables us to work out ways that are more or less effective in dealing with the individuals concerned.

There is, however, also a danger in this process, because we are inclined to lose sight of other important personal characteristics of the individuals and think of them only in terms of what is for us their outstanding characteristic. We may, for instance, fall into the habit of thinking of Frank as "the shy one," ignoring the fact that he is intelligent, open-minded, and interesting. Or we may assume that he is shy in every situation, whereas he may only be shy in speaking up before a strange group. Or he may not be shy at all, but merely reluctant to talk on subjects with which he is unfamiliar.

When we label people as "shy," "open-minded," "pessimistic," and so forth, we also assume a kind of typology, that is, we think of "shy people" and "out-going people," people with open minds and people with closed minds, and so forth, as though people tended to divide themselves into two groups according to whatever trait we happened

to be using. This tendency to type people influenced psychology, too, during its early years. Kretschmer (1925) found a relationship between body build and certain types of mental illness and built a theory of personality around his findings. A similar approach was used by Sheldon and others (1940, 1942, 1954) more recently. One of the difficulties of the systems developed by Kretschmer and Sheldon is the eagerness of the authors to believe in a certain priority of body structure, to believe, that is, that body structure *causes* personality patterns. The greatest weakness in such systems, however, is their artificiality. For instance, when Sheldon's system was subjected to careful scrutiny, it failed to hold up. (Ekman, 1951; Tyler, 1956: 444.)

The labels "extravert" and "introvert" that have become so much a part of everyday speech are the contribution of Jung, who actually was more concerned with describing attitudes than types of individuals. He described introversive attitudes as hesitant, reflective, reticent, and cautious, and extraversive attitudes as accommodating, open, relaxed, venturesome, confident, and friendly. These formulations fit in readily with the popular tendency to classify individuals according to types—shy, withdrawn individuals being characterized as "introverts" and affable, friendly, outgoing individuals being classified as

"extraverts." However, when people are measured according to their introversive and extraversive tendencies, they do not fall into two separate groups, as "common-sense" type theories would have us believe. Instead, most of them fall around the middle of a scale ranging from "extremely introverted" to "extremely extraverted." This tendency of people to group themselves in a normal curve, between the extremes of whatever trait is being measured, demonstrates the artificiality of classifying people into "types." Such a finding is in keeping with Jung's formulations, inasmuch as he held that both types of attitudes were present in every person, although one type of attitude might take precedence over the other.

Trait theories of personality. Another difficulty with the "type approach" to personality is the tendency of individuals to vary from the type, that is, they display so many diverse kinds of behavior that it is difficult to classify them as belonging to one type or another. The concept of "type" has been found too broad and too crude and has given way in recent years to the more precise "trait" approach to the measurement of personality, which is an attempt to break down personality into aspects or dimensions, each of which is based on observable behavior. Although the "introvert" and the "extravert" did not stand scrutiny as demonstrable types, it might be possible to single out the kinds of behavior that would characterize introversion and extraversion. For example, it might be possible to identify and measure behavior according to scales like these: talkative *vs.* silent and introspective; adventurous *vs.* cautious; trustful *vs.* suspicious.

One of the first difficulties encountered by psychologists in their attempt to identify traits that comprised personality was the large number of labels that can be used to describe various kinds of behavior. A review of any dozen pages of the dictionary will bear this out. Many of these labels have overlapping definitions; some cover so many aspects of behavior that they are too imprecise for scientific research. The problem is that of reducing several thousand trait names to a few that could be readily identified and measured. R. B. Cattell (1946) was able to produce a list of 171 trait names by eliminating obvious synonyms. He then secured ratings of the behavior of a sample of 100 persons. Each person was rated on all 171 traits as "above average" or "below average" by someone who knew him. By combining those

traits that appeared to be related to one another, he reduced the total number to 35, which was then reduced through further statistical manipulations to 12, which Cattell termed "the primary source traits of personality." Here are some of them:

General mental capacity *vs.* defect
Emotionally mature, stable character *vs.* demoralized general emotionality
Sensitive, anxious emotionality *vs.* rigid, tough poise
Trained, socialized, cultured mind *vs.* boorishness
Positive character integration *vs.* immature, dependent character

Although Cattell put a great deal of time and effort into the statistical manipulation of his data, his research has been criticized on other methodological grounds. Other researchers have produced lists of traits which differ from that of Cattell, thus raising the question of whether it is really feasible to produce a brief list of traits that is at all comprehensive and descriptive of the infinite variety and totality of human behavior.

Nevertheless, the identification and measurement of traits has much to recommend it. It provides us with a way of studying personality in a more precise way than is possible, say, through the interview. The interview may tell us a great deal about the person-as-a-whole, but it is difficult to make comparisons among individuals on the basis of interviews. Such comparisons can be made more readily with the results of easily scored, readily quantifiable personality questionnaires, many of which are attempts to measure traits.

Stimulus-response theory. Although most theories of personality have their roots in clinical practice or in naturalistic observations, the stimulus-response theory of personality owes its origin to experimental work in a laboratory setting. At the Institute of Human Relations at Yale University, Hull's learning theory was broadened into a conceptual framework useful in studying various aspects of psychology, sociology, and anthropology. The major aspects of this theory have already been discussed in Chapter 5, where a stimulus-response model of learning was presented.

Essentially, personality is viewed from this approach as a more or less integrated collection of habits. The way in which these habits are acquired, the way they function, and the way in which they disappear are specified in terms of such concepts as drive, reinforcement, conditioning, extinction, generalization, discrimination, etc.

Even though these concepts were developed in laboratory experiments dealing primarily with rats as subjects, they have been extended to human behavior as well.

The emphasis of stimulus-response theory has been on empirical research rather than on more subjective speculation about human functioning. For example, Miller (1948) taught two rats to stand on their hind legs and fight each other by subjecting them to electric shock until they made this response. Once this behavior was well learned, a small doll was substituted for the second rat. Using the concept of stimulus generalization, it was predicted that the rat would begin fighting with the doll when the shock was felt. The prediction was accurate; the rats responded to this substitute object, and the aggressive response was displaced to an available target. Does the same sort of process occur with humans? Miller and Bugelski (1948) used questionnaires to measure the attitude of a group of boys in summer camp toward Mexicans and Japanese. In the middle of the questionnaire process, the boys learned that they would miss a desirable social event. The experimenters compared the boys' attitudes toward the minority groups before and after the frustration and found significantly more negative attitudes afterward. The hostility that was aroused by the psychologists was displaced to the minority groups. These sorts of experiments demonstrate the way in which stimulus-response theorists concentrate their attention on the prediction of behavior in particular situations rather than on a classification of types of behavior.

Since learning has such an important effect on behavior, it might be guessed that this personality theory is vitally concerned with the problems of childhood learning and cultural influences on habit formation. It is assumed that the way in which habits are learned and function is universal, but what specifically is learned depends on the unique experiences of each individual.

Another feature of this theory is that its major proponents view a theory as a tentative generalization to account for the facts. As new data are obtained the theory is revised to account for the new information. Thus, stimulus-response theory has been more open to modification than many personality theories not as well founded in experimental research.

Stimulus-response theory has tended to borrow many hypotheses from other sources such as psychoanalysis. It is felt that any hypothesis that is consistent with known facts and that is experimentally testable may legitimately be translated into S-R terms and verified by research. In this way, a learning theory that began in the animal laboratory has been extended so that it has encompassed such diverse phenomena as racial prejudice, counseling, treatment of mental illness, child-rearing practices, and response to humor.

Psychodiagnostics

The measurement of personality variables. The major function of personality theories is to allow us to make accurate predictions about human behavior. In order to utilize theories in this way, we must develop instruments to measure those variables with which a theory is concerned. It should be clear that the way in which a psychologist measures personality is somewhat dependent on the particular theory he holds.

For example, projective techniques have often been used to measure psychoanalytic concepts. Working from Freudian theory, Blum designed the Blacky projective test in which subjects respond to cartoon drawings of dogs depicted in various scenes of psychosexual conflict (sibling rivalry, castration anxiety, Oedipal jealousy, etc.). As suggested above, self-theorists have relied heavily on the Q-sort technique to explore various aspects of the self-concept of individuals. Proponents of Sheldon's type theory have utilized both direct measurement of physical characteristics and depth interviews. Psychologists interested in the Jungian concepts of introversion and extraversion have developed various questionnaires to measure this dimension. Trait theorists have utilized both rating scales and paper and pencil tests to tap what they consider the basic personality traits. Since stimulus-response theory is somewhat broader in its use of psychological variables, any test that accurately measures some aspect of human behavior is potentially useful to this approach.

Personality questionnaires. In spite of these divergent approaches to personality, most personality tests fall into the category of either questionnaire or projective technique. The most elementary variety of personality questionnaire is a self-report type of instrument that asks the subject to respond to questions such as these:

Yes   No   Do you find that other people are prone to give you more advice than you need?

Yes No Do you enjoy driving faster than the law allows?

Yes No Do you find it difficult to "get going" in the morning?

Yes No Do you often find that you are tired for no accountable reason?

Yes No Do you often have the feeling that other people do not like you?

By classifying the responses to such questions, it is possible to find clues to the kinds of problems the subject is facing and the ways in which he is coping with them.

Responses to the California Test of Personality can, for example, be scored on the following scales:

Personal Adjustment:	Social Adjustment:
Self-reliance	Attitudes toward social standards
Sense of personal worth	Social skills
Sense of personal freedom	Antisocial tendencies
Feeling of belonging	Family relations
Withdrawing tendencies	Occupational relations
Nervous symptoms	Community relations

The test is scored by comparing the number of "good adjustment" responses made by an individual with the test norms—a scale based on the responses of the people on which the test was standardized. It is thus possible to specify the extent to which an individual's adjustment is better or poorer than that of the norm group. It is also possible to identify those areas of life in which he has achieved his best and his poorest adjustment.

Reservations regarding personality questionnaires. An impressive amount of research and statistical work has gone into the development of most of the widely used personality questionnaires, yet their results cannot be accepted without some reservation. One problem relates to the obvious or "transparent" nature of the items included in most of the questionnaires. Few of us, for instance, would have any difficulty in giving the "well-adjusted" responses to the five personality-test items listed a few paragraphs above. This transparency makes it possible for many subjects to answer the questions in such a way as to present a favorable or unfavorable psychological picture of themselves, depending on which alternative happens to appeal to them or is to their advantage. An individual who is applying for a job, for example, may be tempted to present a "well-adjusted" picture of himself,

whereas a prisoner who is trying to avoid assigned tasks by getting into the hospital may see an advantage in presenting a picture of a "sick" person and hence would be tempted to respond to the same items negatively.

Test makers have attempted to build controls into their tests in order to compensate for tendencies to slant responses positively or negatively. Some tests, like the California Personality Inventory (CPI) and the Minnesota Multiphasic Personality Inventory (MMPI) have special "validating scales" to check on "faking," and are constructed of empirically tested items (e.g., items to which emotionally disturbed and normal people respond differently) which are not obvious, rather than items based on largely "common-sense" concepts. Most personality questionnaires, however, particularly those that are used in huge quantities by schools and by business and industry, have no such controls. It is obvious that the value of the results obtained from such testing programs will depend in part on the situation in which the tests are given. For instance, if the individual feels that the results are going to be used to help him, he is more likely to give honest, straightforward answers, but if he thinks the results might be used to discriminate against him, then he would be more likely to slant his answers in the direction he thinks would give him the best advantage. Even if the situation encourages cooperation, however, it is still possible for individuals to slant their answers unconsciously.

Value of personality questionnaires. Assuming that a personality questionnaire contains adequate controls for faking and is given under optimal conditions, does it have any value as an index to personal adjustment or to personality patterns? The answer to this question depends in part on the use made of the results. The use of such tests can be most readily justified if they are to be used in research studies where investigators are interested in exploring various dimensions of personality. In such situations, the average score made by a selected *group* of individuals is compared with the scores made by other selected groups. If a personality test like the California Test of Personality were to be given to mental hospital patients, patients at a mental hygiene clinic, and "normals" (nonpatients), the average adjustment score would increase with the "normality" of the group, the hospital patients having the lowest average score and the nonpatients having the highest. There would, however, be considerable overlap in scores among the three groups. As Figure 10-3 shows, the scores made by patients at the mental hygiene clinic would overlap those made by both the hospitalized and the nonpatient groups, and some of the hospitalized patients would get better scores than quite a few nonpatients. Although some of this overlap is undoubtedly caused by misclassification (for example, some of the nonpatients ought to be patients), most of it is caused by the fact that the personality test is only a rough index to personal adjustment. Or, perhaps stated differently, even at its best it measures only a few of the factors that are involved in adjustment. Inasmuch as the typical research study is primarily interested in *generalized* personality patterns as they apply to certain selected groups, a certain amount of overlap is expected and tolerated, but the application of test results to the analysis of an individual raises a different question. Take, for example, the individual who makes a score of 100 on the theoretical personality test whose norms are displayed in Figure 10-3. Should he be considered a suitable candidate for out-patient treatment at a clinic, because his score is the equal to the average for that group? Or is his score typical of the one-sixth of the nonpatients who scored at or below that point? Or is it typical, rather, of the one-sixth of the hospitalized patients who scored at or above that point? These are questions that can be answered only after a detailed study of many other factors bearing on his case.

Figure 10-3. Theoretical distribution of scores made on a 200-item personality test by patients in a mental hospital, nonhospitalized patients at a mental hygiene clinic, and nonpatients.

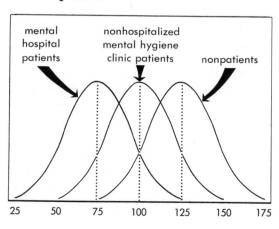

One shortcoming of many personality tests is their tendency to focus on rather superficial levels of behavior. The subject is asked to respond to the questions in terms of how he views his behavior—a somewhat biased source of information, if interpreted literally. (Such information, may, of course, be useful if one is doing research on how people evaluate their own behavior.) Some tests like the CPI and the MMPI, mentioned above, are constructed in such a way that subconscious levels of behavior can be explored without the knowledge of the subject, but most personality tests accept the subject's report at face value. There are some occasions, however, when self-reports can be useful. For instance, when an individual visits a guidance center of a clinic for help with his personal problems, it is often very useful to get a picture of how he sees himself and his problems. At such times it is naturally very important for answers to questionnaire items to be given candidly and honestly.

Projective tests. One of the reasons for the conscious or unconscious "faking" that takes place with certain personality questionnaires is that the subject knows what answers are expected of a well-adjusted individual and slants his replies accordingly. The projective test meets this problem by presenting the subject with stimuli which are more or less ambiguous and for which there are no obvious answers. Since the stimulus has no particular meaning in and of itself, the subject is forced to "project" something of himself into the process, and his response provides some clues as to the way in which he responds to his environment or organizes his perceptions. His responses thus supply clues as to the basic trends and characteristics of his personality, as well as to the focal points of conflict in his life.

One of the most used of the projective devices is the Rorschach test. The subject is presented sequentially with ten cards, each of which bears the reproduction of an ink blot. The subject is asked to state what he sees on each card—what each blot might resemble or represent. His responses, when recorded, classified, and analyzed, constitute a psychological picture of the way in which he perceives his environment, his relations with others, his emotional tendencies, and so forth.

The Thematic Apperception Test, or TAT, is another projective device in common use. The subject is presented sequentially with a series of

A Rorschach test may be very helpful in revealing personality patterns and trends.

pictures and is asked to say who the individuals are in each picture, what is going on, what led up to it, and what the outcome will be. Because the subject matter of the TAT is more "structured" than that of the Rorschach, it is possible to get reactions to certain situations and relationships that are common to the experience of everyone. The examiner is thus able to get a picture of the subject's attitudes toward himself, members of the opposite sex, his parents, and the like.

Another variety of semi-structured projective test is the Incomplete Sentences Blank, or ISB, sometimes termed the Sentence Completion Test, or SCT. The subject is asked to write a number of sentences, each of which is to begin with one of a series of "stems" which must be used as the opening words. Standardized forms of the SCT have been prepared by Rotter and Rafferty (1950) and Rohde and Hildreth (1947), but numerous other versions have been constructed by psychologists to meet local situations or to test various kinds of hypotheses. Here are some "stems," together with some completions that suggest the presence of rather severe emotional problems. The "stem" portion is in italics.

What I like is to take my knife and cut, cut, cut, cut.
My father I wish he would die a horrible death.

I am under the control of a world-wide conspiring of hypnotical scientific agents that can lucidate anything whatandever into our recesses and crevasses.
I wish I was dead.

Other projective tests call for subjects to draw houses, trees, and persons; to arrange small models of houses, people, and buildings; to complete drawings; and so forth. The possibilities for projective testing are infinite: people reveal something of themselves in their responses to almost any kind of stimulus situation.

Rosenzweig's Picture-Frustration Study is a good example of the ingenuity that goes into the construction of some projective tests. The subject is presented with 24 cartoonlike pictures involving two central characters, one of whom is involved in a frustrating or annoying situation. The other character is depicted as saying something that adds to the frustration of the first character or helps to define the nature of the frustration. The subject is asked to supply the reply that would be made by the first character in each cartoon. Figure 10-4 gives an example of the kind of situation used in the test. Responses are scored in terms of whether they indicate a tendency to express aggression against the environment or toward the self, or whether the subject

Photographs by Suzanne Szasz

tries to gloss over or belittle the frustration. Responses may be scored on other scales that reveal personality characteristics.

One of the chief advantages of projective tests is their ability to "get beneath the surface" of behavior and to reveal motivational patterns that are largely unknown to the subjects. For example, an 18-year-old college student who had threatened suicide seemed unaware that his suicidal intent had rather pronounced elements of a hostile gesture directed at his mother who, he believed, was exercising an intolerable amount of control over his life. During counseling interviews, he denied that he had any hostile feelings toward his mother, professing to have nothing but love and respect for her. When he was asked to tell stories for each of the TAT pictures, however, he responded to each picture containing the figure of an older woman in a manner that revealed a great deal of latent hostility. The older women in the stories were witches, or were dominating, possessive women who were trying to ruin the life of the boy in the picture.

Although the ability of projective tests to probe unconscious depths of behavior and to present a broader and more complete picture of the subject's personality than is possible with most personality questionnaires is a distinct advantage, there are some disadvantages to their use. Administration, scoring, and interpretation calls for a high degree of training and sophistication, as well as for the investment of a great deal of time. The most commonly used tests, the Rorschach

Figure 10-4. Example of situation used in Rosenzweig Picture-Frustration Study. (Rosenzweig, 1948. Reproduced by permission.)

and the TAT, are preferably given to one subject at a time, whereas personality questionnaires can be given not only to hundreds of subjects simultaneously, but also may be scored by machine. The scoring and interpretation of a single Rorschach protocol may take hours. The projective method of assessing personality is obviously an expensive one.

An even greater problem than the expense is the rather high degree of variability among trained experts. Baughman (1951) investigated the scoring of 633 Rorschach protocols by 15 examiners, all of whom used the same system of administration and scoring. In 16 out of 22 scoring categories he analyzed he found significant differences among the scorers. Interpretations of the results obtained on the Rorschach and other projective tests are characterized by even greater variability. The clinician must often fall back on his "general clinical experience" in making interpretations. (Anastasi, 1954: 624.) Research studies of the relationship between projective test results and the "real-life behavior" of subjects have proved generally disappointing. In the lack of such objective data, the clinician has no choice but to use subjective methods in evaluating projective test protocols.

Despite these shortcomings, projective techniques are a valuable research tool for the psychologist who wishes to study aspects of personality that are not accessible by more direct means. Some of the cross-cultural studies using the Rorschach have confirmed its value in this respect. DuBois (1944) administered Rorschach tests to Alorese, inhabitants of a Pacific island. A "blind" analysis of her records gave results that closely corresponded to her analysis of the Alorese personality. Kaplan, Richers-Ovsiankina, and Joseph (1956) found that Rorschach records from four cultures (Spanish-American, Navaho, Zuñi, and Mormon) could be identified on "blind analysis" with a fair degree of accuracy. Another approach that appears to have possibilities is that of comparing the responses of successful and unsuccessful individuals in various roles. For instance, Symonds and Dudek (1956) found four general trends in Rorschach records that distinguished superior teachers from inferior teachers.

The TAT is also proving to be a highly useful research tool. McClelland and his associates (1953), for example, have used the TAT extensively in measuring the need for achievement and correlating it with a wide variety of trends and behaviors. Their success has stimulated other researchers, who have found the need for achievement, as measured by the TAT or similar tests, to be correlated with the rate of learning of nonsense syllables (Hurley, 1957), incidental learning (Karolchuck and Worell, 1956), and the ability to recall interrupted tasks (Atkinson and Raphelson, 1956), to list a few of the many studies in this field that have appeared in recent years. A review of this research leads one to the conclusion that psychologists have barely begun to exploit the potentiality of projective techniques in the study of personality.

Other approaches to personality measurement. While the term "personality test" is usually applied to the type of instruments just discussed, many other types of personality measurement are utilized by psychologists. For example, tests of aptitude, intelligence, and interest may be thought of as measures of specific aspects of personality. Various perceptual tasks, such as the rod-and-frame method discussed in Chapter 6, have been found to be related to personality variables. When we use interviews or behavior observations or situational problems as measuring instruments, we are really employing special types of personality tests. Since personality refers to the organization of the total behavior of individuals, there are obviously an infinite number of approaches to its measurement. The measurement of any aspect of human behavior is, in a sense, personality measurement.

Cautions to be observed with respect to personality tests. In evaluating the results of scores made on personality tests, there are three points to keep in mind: (1) a score made by an individual on a personality test may have very little meaning in the absence of other data; (2) decisions regarding the psychological treatment of an individual should be made on the basis of much more data than a personality-test score; and (3) evaluation of personality-test scores is a complex job, full of pitfalls for the unwary and is best done by trained and experienced persons.

Even trained psychologists have to be extremely cautious when using the results of personality tests. It is all too easy to assume that scores on, say, a test of "conformity" are significantly related to the degree of conforming behavior that individuals actually express. Unfortunately, many studies have reported discouraging

Projective tests may also be used experimentally to study personality traits and characteristics. These drawings were done by two fourth-grade girls, rated high in anxiety and low in anxiety, respectively, according to scores on various personality questionnaires. (Fox et al., 1958.) See if you can tell which pair of drawings was done by the girl rating high in anxiety and which was done by the girl rating low. Then check your guess by looking at the bottom of the following page.

results. The findings of Applezweig and Moeller (1958) are not unusual. They attempted to predict the extent to which a number of college students would conform in an experimental situation involving social pressure, basing their predictions on certain scales in the personality tests the students had taken previously. Unfortunately for their hypothesis, only 2 of the 27 measures on which their predictions were based proved to have any value. The study of hostility presents equally perplexing problems. When Lindgren (1960) compared the responses of American and Canadian school teachers to an incomplete sentences blank designed to measure attitudes toward authority, he found that Canadian teachers made significantly more hostile responses, even though their outward behavior toward authority figures was more "accepting" than that of the American teachers. Such discouraging results do not mean, of course, that there is never any relationship between personality test scores and behavior in real life, but they do show the need for a cautious and conservative approach to making interpretations of personality test scores even for groups of individuals.

Summary

It is difficult to understand and predict human behavior; however, the psychological approach using personality theory is superior to "common-sense" notions. In order to be able to deal with others, everyone utilizes some sort of personality theory, usually an implicit one. Most often, these theories are supplied by one's culture, but we also develop private theories on the basis of our own unique experiences. The psychologist's personality theories differ from the layman's in that they are arrived at consciously and are subjected to experimental verification.

Most personality theories have been developed by psychotherapists engaged in the treatment of patients. In recent years, this clinical interest in the functioning of individuals has been merging with an experimental interest in scientific verification of hypotheses. The term "personality" as used by psychologists refers to the total behavior of a person; in everyday usage, "personality" usually means just the external, socially oriented aspects of behavior. It is a very difficult and sometimes even a painful process to bring about major changes in the personality of an individual.

While most psychologists do not accept all aspects of Freud's personality theory, his work was an important psychological milestone. Concepts such as unconscious motivation and the importance of childhood emotional experiences are generally considered as vitally important. Freud viewed human behavior as determined largely by irrational forces. The ego, he maintained, has to integrate the demands of the primitve id, the superego or conscience, and the outside world. Childhood experiences and their outcome, such as love for the opposite sex parent and rivalry with the parent of the same sex (Oedipus conflict) were seen by him as crucial factors in each person's development. Both Freud's theories and his use of free association and interpretation in psychotherapy met bitter criticism at one time. Psychoanalysts, usually M.D.'s, are psychotherapists who have received special psychoanalytic training. Some analysts developed theoretical differences with Freud, particularly in terms of decreased emphasis on sexuality and increased emphasis on cultural influences and interpersonal relationships.

Another sort of personality theory has come from psychologists interested in the concept of the self. According to self theories, behavior is determined by the way an individual perceives himself and his surroundings. This phenomenal field of each individual constitutes reality for him. A great deal of behavior that appears to be irrational actually becomes logical and consistent when seen from the viewpoint of the individual's own perception of the situation. Some of the research dealing with self theories has utilized the Q-sort technique in which subjects sort a series of statements with respect to the way in which they perceive themselves, their ideal selves, other people, etc. This technique is also used to study changes that take place during the course of psychotherapy and to investigate group interrelationships.

Type theories of personality have a long history and conform to our rather common tendency to type other people. In psychology, a few theorists have tried to relate body types to specific personality characteristics, but research evidence has not been very supportive of these notions. Jung postulated extravert and introvert types, but these

The two drawings on the preceding page that consist of single figures are the work of the girl rating high in anxiety.

characteristics seem to represent extremes on a continuum with most individuals showing some of each characteristic. A more precise outgrowth of type theory is represented by trait theories of personality. Cattell has isolated what he believes are the 12 primary source traits of personality, but other trait theorists offer somewhat different lists of the primary traits.

The stimulus-response theory of personality originated in animal experimentation but has broadened to include many aspects of psychology, sociology, and anthropology. These theorists have emphasized experimental research; attention is concentrated on theory building and theory testing. Stimulus-response theory has borrowed many hypotheses from other sources, translated them into S-R terms, and subjected them to experimental verification.

In order to utilize a personality theory to predict behavior, it is necessary to develop measures of the variables with which a theory is concerned. Thus, the type of personality measure used by a psychologist is somewhat dependent on the theory he holds. Although many types of personality measurement have been attempted, most personality tests fall into one of two categories: questionnaires and projective techniques. The most primitive type of questionnaire is of the self-report variety in which subjects respond directly to questions about themselves. Such tests are often transparent and thus fakable. A more sophisticated form of the questionnaire (represented by the MMPI and CPI) uses empirically derived scoring keys that are often impossible for the subject to outguess; in addition, they contain special keys to detect lying and faking. As with all tests, questionnaires are better at predicting the behavior of groups than of individuals. Furthermore, their scores must be interpreted by experts.

One attempt to get at "deeper" levels of personality functioning and to avoid "transparency" has been the development of projective personality tests. These devices utilize ambiguous stimuli for which there are no obvious answers. Examples are the Rorschach, Thematic Apperception Test, the incomplete sentences tests, and Rosenzweig's Picture-Frustration Study. Such tests attempt to uncover unconscious motives, which are "projected" onto the ambiguous stimuli. Interpretation of projective tests is a lengthy, difficult task, and agreement among experts is not very impressive. In addition, research has shown that the predictive validity for most uses of projective instruments is far from adequate. However, Rorschach cross-cultural studies, among others, have yielded interesting results. The TAT has also proved to be a highly useful research tool.

Even though the term "personality test" is applied primarily to questionnaires and projective devices, there are many other approaches to the measurement of human behavior. The measurement of any aspect of behavior is, in a sense, personality measurement. It is important to keep in mind that personality test scores are only *indicators* of behavioral trends. They should not be taken as infallible indices of the degree of emotional adjustment characteristic of an individual and should always be evaluated in relationship to other data.

Questions

1. What are some of the theories of personality that you commonly use? In other words, what sort of hypotheses do you usually offer to explain the behavior of yourself and others?

2. Where have most psychological personality theories originated? Do you have any suggestions as to why this is so?

3. Is the psychological meaning of the term "personality" the same as the layman's meaning? If not, how do the two meanings differ?

4. What is your reaction to Freud's ideas about personality functioning as they were presented in this chapter? How could you find out whether his ideas are valid or not?

5. Describe some of the research that is being conducted on "self" theories of personality. How do you think your self-concept, your ideal self, and other people's perception of you differ one from the other?

6. How are trait and type theories of personality similar and how are they different?

7. When you answer a personality questionnaire, what are your reactions to it? What are the advantages and disadvantages of questionnaires?

8. What is the general rationale behind projective tests? Describe the advantages and disadvantages of such tests.

Suggestions for further reading

Brand, H., editor, *The Study of Personality*. New York: Wiley, 1954. A well-organized compilation of readings concerned with theory, methods, and problems in the field of personality research.

Dreikurs, R. R., *Fundamentals of Adlerian Psychology*. New York: Greenberg, 1950. A brief book, written for popular consumption, giving an overview of Adler's theories.

Fromm, E., *Man For Himself*. New York: Rinehart, 1947. A brief, but cogent statement by one of the leaders of the neo-Freudians.

Horney, K., *The Neurotic Personality of Our Time*. New York: Norton, 1937. A readable presentation of the theoretical position held by a leading neo-Freudian.

Langer, W. C., *Psychology and Human Living*. New York: Appleton-Century-Crofts, 1943. A discussion of the problems of everyday life, written for teenagers and their parents, drawing rather heavily on Freudian psychology.

Hall, C. S. and G. Lindzey, *Theories of Personality*. New York: Wiley, 1957. Probably the most balanced and objective review of the major theories of personality.

Mullahy, P., *Oedipus, Myth and Complex*. New York: Nelson, 1948. A review of psychoanalytic theory, both Freudian and neo-Freudian, together with the three Oedipus plays of Sophocles. Available also in soft cover as an Evergreen book, published by Grove Press, New York.

Munroe, R. L., *Schools of Psychoanalytic Thought*. New York: Dryden, 1955. A thoughtful analysis of the Freudian and neo-Freudian theories of personality.

Murphy, G., *Personality: A Biosocial Approach to Origins and Structure*. New York: Harper, 1947. An attempt to integrate and organize psychological theory and research findings in terms of their meaning with respect to personality and its development.

Rogers, C. R. and R. F. Dymond, editors, *Psychotherapy and Personality Change*. Chicago: University of Chicago Press, 1954. A group of research papers concerned with changes in self-concept taking place in psychotherapy.

Snygg, D. and A. W. Combs, *Individual Behavior*, rev. ed. New York: Harper, 1959. A clear and stimulating presentation of a theory of psychology organized around the individual and his perceptions of himself and his environment.

Sullivan, H. S., *The Interpersonal Theory of Psychiatry*. New York: Norton, 1953. Selections from Sullivan's lectures, organized and edited posthumously. Difficult reading at times, but interesting and thought-provoking.

Symonds, P. M., *The Ego and the Self*. New York: Appleton-Century-Crofts, 1951. A brief presentation of the results of experimental findings and indications from clinical experience concerning the ego and the self—central concepts in a number of theories of personality.

Thompson, C., *Psychoanalysis: Evolution and Development*. New York: Nelson, 1950. Another review of Freudian and neo-Freudian theories, written for lay readers.

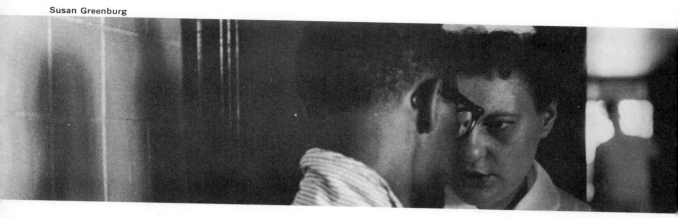

11

Personal adjustment and mental hygiene

Reactions to frustration and conflict. The process of adjusting to our environment inevitably results in what psychologists term "learning dilemmas"—problem situations in which desired goals cannot be reached through responses that were formerly effective. If we are unable to resolve such dilemmas, we very commonly react with some degree of emotional disturbance.

Each of us develops certain characteristic patterns of responding to frustrating situations, such as are experienced in learning dilemmas and conflicts. Such situations may be termed "threatening" because they are perceived by us as "threats" to our self-concept or to our ability to adjust or adapt ourselves to the demands of our environment. The degree to which we are able to resolve or not resolve the learning dilemmas and conflicts we encounter may be considered to be an index to our level of adjustment, and the characteristic patterns of behavior that we use in responding may also provide clues regarding our personalities, particularly with respect to the ways in which we have learned to perceive ourselves and our environment. Here are examples of two ways of responding to a threatening situation:

When Loren Cartwright opened the mail box one Saturday morning in April, he found a letter from Harrison University. Loren did not have to open the letter; he knew what it contained: a notification that Harrison had accepted him as a freshman student. It did not occur to Loren that the letter might contain anything different: he had always expected to go to Harrison when he graduated from high school. His father had gone to Harrison, and several of his friends were either attending Harrison or were planning to go.

237

And so he might have left the letter unopened on the mantel with the rest of the mail. But he began to wonder when he was supposed to appear on campus the following September, so he opened the letter and began to read.

The letter was short and to the point. "We regret to inform you . . ." it began. The second and final paragraph said something about ". . . an unprecedented number of applications . . . ," but Loren did not bother to read it. He rolled the letter up into a ball and hurled it into the empty fireplace, then ran downstairs to the basement where he kept his gym equipment, and gave his punching bag such a vicious drubbing that it broke loose from its moorings and crashed through a window.

A similar letter was received the same morning by Mike Garcia, who attended the same high school as Loren, but who lived on the other side of town. As he read it over, the first idea that occurred to him was: "It isn't fair! They're doing this to me because my name is Mike Garcia and not Loren Cartwright or Lowell Witherspoon." Then came a soberer and more depressing thought: "No, it must have been the grades. I didn't think they were too bad, but I guess they weren't good enough."

A day or so later, Mike talked the problem over with his mother and said: "I think what I'll do is go to junior college here in town for a year or so. If I really dig in and study, I should get the kind of grades that will get me into Harrison. After all, Ted Panakis got in that way, and his high school grades were worse than mine."

Here are two different kinds of reactions to frustrating situations that have certain similarities. When Loren throws the letter in the fireplace and gives his punching bag a beating, he is reacting aggressively, turning his hostility against the environment. Mike is angry, too, at first, but he swallows his anger and tries to think of some way whereby he can salvage the situation. For both Loren and Mike, attending Harrison was very much a part of their self-concept—a part of the self-that-was-to-be—and the letter from the university threatens this concept of themselves. Loren reacts to the threat with "anger-out," whereas Mike reacts with "anger-in."

Mike did not arrive at the solution of his problem painlessly. He did not even tell his mother of the letter until two days after it arrived. During this period, he alternated between depression and irritation. Some of the time he was irritated at the college for what looked like discrimination, but mostly he blamed himself for not studying hard enough in high school. He felt much better, however, when he had worked out his plan for getting into Harrison via the junior-college route.

During the two days, Mike was experiencing a kind of double approach-avoidance conflict. He was faced with choosing between two concepts of himself: a concept of himself as a young man who was going to attend Harrison University and be a success in life, and a concept of someone who was an "academic reject." He was forced to "avoid" the first possibility because the letter from the university had robbed it of its validity. The second concept, though somewhat more realistic, was equally unacceptable, because he could not bring himself to think of himself as a failure. Until he had found a third and reasonably satisfactory alternative, his behavior was characterized by anxiety—an emotion that often results from conflict situations and that is a common cause of depression and irritability.

Anxiety

The nature of anxiety. Anxiety is an emotion that resembles fear. Fear is a more dramatic and intense emotion, evoked by a threatening situation that is perceived as immediate and potentially overwhelming. Anxiety is likely to be more diffuse and vague and is usually of lower intensity than fear. Anxiety is commonly aroused by situations that are ambiguous, whose meaning is not clear. Inasmuch as one of the characteristics of unresolved conflicts is ambiguity, it is understandable how conflicts can generate anxiety. Anxiety is also aroused by concern about the future and the extent to which other people are accepting us. To a large extent, our ability to continue to meet our needs and satisfy our drives depends upon what lies ahead of us in the future, as well as on the good will of others. To a greater or lesser degree we can plan, manipulate, and arrange matters so that we can have some degree of security about the future and about our relations with others, but we can never be completely sure, because we can never control all the variables. There is always a note of ambiguity and uncertainty in the future and in our relations with others that is a constant source of anxiety.

There may also be a certain degree of irrationality in behavior that is prompted by anxiety. Because the threatening situation has a quality of ambiguity or abstractness, we are likely to have difficulty in knowing exactly what we should react to or what we should do to resolve the situation. Furthermore, since anxiety is a painful emotion, we are often more concerned about reducing or eliminating the *feeling* of anxiety than we are about eliminating the *situation* that is producing the anxiety. For instance, during Mike Garcia's two-day period of brooding over his rejection by Harrison University, he became embroiled in a couple of arguments with his mother over rather trivial matters. Arguing with his mother was irrational, in the sense that it did not resolve the conflict he was facing, but it did help momentarily to get rid of some of his pent-up feeling. However, after the arguments, he felt guilty, and that made matters worse.

On a scale of psycho-physical development fear and anger are more primitive than anxiety. Frustration of basic physiological processes is more likely to produce fear or anger, whereas frustration of socialized needs is more likely to produce anxiety. Animals are inclined to react to frustration with fear or hostility, but man is more prone to respond with anxiety. An important qualification is in order, however. The tendency to respond to threat or frustration with fear and anger or with anxiety depends on the experience of the organism—that is, what the organism has learned. By small (but not painful) electric shocks, Liddell (1954) was able to produce anxiety in sheep to the point that any small noise would produce a rapid acceleration in heart beat. When Maier (1949) placed rats in a "conflict" situation and subjected them to *repeated* frustration, they reacted with convulsions and other forms of behavior characteristic of severe anxiety.

Learning as a factor in anxiety. Similarly, man's reaction to frustration, conflict, and other forms of threat is determined by the way he has learned to react. In our culture, the middle-class child characteristically learns to contain his hostile impulses and to turn them upon himself ("anger-in"). Even though adults may treat him in a "permissive" manner, he may still learn what kinds of response should be controlled or inhibited by copying their behavior. A moderate amount of anxiety is characteristic of middle-class life; it serves as a controlling force to keep behavior within the bounds specified by society. Some individuals learn their lessons all too well and develop what Funkenstein and his associates (1957) would call the "anxiety" or "severe-anxiety" pattern of reacting to stress. Lower-class behavior is characterized by more frequent emotional outbursts and less anxiety. (Davis, 1948.) Although lower-class parents punish their children for displaying aggressive and hostile behavior, their own

pattern of giving way to anger is likely to be a more powerful influence on their children than their attempts to discourage such behavior.

Here is an example of educational background and socio-economic status affecting the ways in which individuals respond to threat.

Let us say that two individuals, a Mr. Bolt and a Mr. Holt, both employed by the same company, lose their jobs on the same day. Mr. Bolt has a sixth-grade education; Mr. Holt is a college graduate. Mr. Bolt's first reaction is one of anger. He marches back to the shop, over to the foreman's office, engages in angry conversation with him, and is physically restrained from punching him on the nose. The plant guards escort him to the gate and tell him that he has spoiled all chances of ever being rehired. Mr. Bolt's next reaction is one of panic, and he goes to the nearest bar to spend his pay check on getting drunk.

Mr. Holt's reactions are quite different. His first feeling is one of concern for the future, as he wonders how he and his family will manage while he looks for another job. Then he feels somewhat irritated. The reasons for the terminated employment are clear enough: a reduction in business volume has led to the elimination of several positions. But he wonders why it was *he* who was fired, instead of several others in his office. Then he feels depressed, thinking that he is a failure. Thus one phase of anxiety is succeeded by another. Some of Mr. Holt's anxiety is expressed in negative ways. He becomes absent-minded, is irritable with his family, and smokes and drinks more than usual. At the same time, some of his anxiety leads to positive behavior. For instance, he sits down and does a cold and objective analysis of his financial and vocational situation, laying plans in order to guide his activities for the next few years.

Anger and fear are responses to situations that are perceived as clear-cut and definite. Mr. Bolt reacts to frustrating and threatening situations as though they were clear-cut or black-and-white. People are either for him or against him, and anyone who he sees as frustrating, threatening, or blocking him must be against him. Mr. Holt is less inclined to view situations in such black-and-white terms. Instead, he is likely to perceive them as complex, as involving ramifications that are not evident at first glance. It is difficult to respond with strong emotion to complex, ambiguous situations, because it is hard to tell what one should respond to. Mr. Holt does not know whether to blame the company, his immediate boss, himself, or the situation-in-general. Under such circumstances he is likely to react with anxiety. But Mr. Bolt is not likely to analyze the situation in terms of its various complexities. He has a strong need to hold someone responsible, and to him the foreman is the most logical person. Only when he is told that he has lost all chances of re-employment does he think of blaming himself, and the resulting anxiety is so painful that he looks for some escape.

The differences in the behavior of Mr. Bolt and Mr. Holt can be explained partly by the fact that they perceive the situation differently and partly by the kinds of reactions they have learned to make regarding threatening situations. Mr. Bolt has learned to perceive situations affecting his employment as being either for him or against him. Mr. Holt has learned to perceive them as involving many complexities, as problems that must be solved. Complexities in the employment situation only enrage and upset Mr. Bolt; he does not try to understand them, but strikes out against them. The same complexities arouse anxiety on the part of Mr. Holt, but he has learned to live with his anxieties, and, providing they are not too strong, they may even help stimulate problem-solving behavior.

"Normal anxiety." Although anxiety in its more intense forms is a painful experience and one that we will go to great lengths to avoid, there is a great deal to be said in favor of a moderate amount of anxiety. It is anxiety that leads us to plan for the future. It promotes concern for the rights and feelings of others and stimulates work on problems that would otherwise be ignored. May (1950) refers to this "healthy" form of anxiety as "normal anxiety," and distinguishes it from "neurotic anxiety"—a reaction which is disproportionate to the perceived threat and which may lead to various forms of irrational behavior. The person who is incapable of experiencing anxiety is likely to be a person who is little concerned about the rights and feelings of other people and the consequences of his actions. Hence a certain amount of normal anxiety is essential for adequate functioning.

There are various levels of response to anxiety. The problem-solving response is the healthiest, of course. When Mr. Holt sits down to lay plans for his future, he is responding sensibly to the promptings of normal anxiety. When his smoking goes up to four or five packs of cigarettes a day his behavior may be considered somewhat more neurotic and less rational, but it is, nevertheless, understandable. Heavy smoking is one of Mr. Holt's ways of dealing with more anxiety than he can easily handle. Anxiety, as we have noted, is a

painful emotion, and it is relieved to some degree if he smokes more frequently. There are, of course, many other ways of dealing with anxiety that would be less detrimental to his health. Perhaps he could spend more time watching television, working in the garden, or improving his tennis. Although there is nothing objectionable about these activities, they do not solve his chief problem—that of finding another job—any better than his increased smoking. Their chief contribution would be that of helping him to adjust to a difficult situation by distracting him and relieving some of his tension. Or he might cope with his anxiety (but not with his problem) by changing his perception of the situation: concluding, for example, that he was the victim of office politics.

Behavior mechanisms. The kinds of behavior that we commonly use to cope with anxiety in this indirect way are termed "behavior mechanisms" or "defense mechanisms." Such mechanisms do not eliminate the situation that is producing the anxiety, but they do help us reduce or cope with anxiety that is being produced. Mechanisms are "ego-defensive," in the sense that they protect our feeling of self-esteem and make us feel as though we do not need to make any real changes in ourselves. If Mr. Holt decides that he lost his job because of office politics, he is relieved of the necessity to blame himself or to do anything positive about getting a new job. He no longer has to be self-critical, but can think angry thoughts about the people who manipulate events and situations in the office. Or he may increase his consumption of cigarettes. Smoking is a familiar, comfortable behavior sequence for him. Anxiety can be lightened a little by initiating this oft-repeated and reassuring ritual. When he feels the need to "do something," but finds that there is really little he *can* do, smoking may meet the need for "something to do."

Everyday patterns of adjustment

The various mechanisms or modes of coping with anxiety and defending the self-concept have been classified by psychologists into some two dozen categories, each of which designates a different aspect or variety of behavior. These categories are not, however, mutually exclusive. Any given defensive action involves several different mechanisms. For instance, if Mr. Holt should tell a friend of his that he lost his job because of office politics, he might be unconsciously overlooking

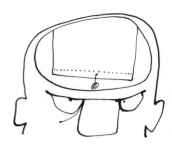

his own attempts to play politics (*repression*) and would be accusing someone else of doing something he was also guilty of doing (*projection*).

Although any system of classifying behavior mechanisms suffers from inexactitude and vagueness, we have tried to create some order by classifying them into two groups: those that seem to serve a self-deceptive function, and those characterized by the substitution of one kind of behavior for another.

Self-deceptive mechanisms. The behavior mechanisms discussed under this classification involve distortions in perception or reasoning. Essentially, they are ways in which we defend or maintain a chosen path of behavior by ignoring or denying or misinterpreting some aspects of reality. In other words, we develop a system of belief about ourselves or others that enables us to continue to think or behave in a certain way.

Repression. This mechanism consists of the unconscious forgetting of significant details of behavior, details that would be inconsistent with the self-picture we are trying to maintain. In the example just cited, Mr. Holt represses the memories of the times *he* has tried to play politics. He does not do this deliberately, that is, consciously. He merely behaves as though he never had any idea of playing politics. Feelings and memories that are inconsistent with our self-picture of the moment are likely to be repressed. To recognize them as part of our experience would introduce a note of ambiguity, and ambiguity would generate anxiety. Repression is basic to most other mechanisms in that it enables us to ignore the inconsistent, illogical, unrealistic qualities that are characteristic of a great deal of defensive behavior.

Not all kinds of forgetting are repression. Much forgetting occurs through the interference of new learning or through lack of reinforcement—the telephone number you used to have, the method of extracting square root, and the like. Some forgetting occurs deliberately—when, for example, you put some recurring and annoying thought "out of your mind." Psychologists call such deliberate forgetting *suppression,* to distinguish it from repression, which occurs unconsciously. According to psychoanalytic theory, facts that are embarrassing and guilt-laden are repressed from consciousness. But such a maneuver does not necessarily rid us of all unpleasantness. If the feeling of guilt is especially strong, we may con-

tinue to feel disturbed without knowing the reason why. If the resulting disturbance is severe and interferes with our ability to cope with everyday life, some form of psychotherapy may be needed to help us recover and identify the disturbing memory and accept it, that is, learn to face it and deal with it objectively and dispassionately.

Rationalization. Rationalization means, basically, "making reasonable." We are led to rationalize when our behavior is "unreasonable," when it does not "make sense" to us, because it is inconsistent with our self-picture.

One day, a week or so after Mr. Holt lost his job, he met a friend of his who said:
"Sorry to hear about the bad luck you had. The thought occurred to me: did you think of going over and talking to the people at Majestic? I understand they are expanding and will be doing some hiring."
To which Mr. Holt replied:
"I paid them a visit yesterday and looked them over, but I didn't like the set-up. The fellow I talked to sounded too smooth and slick to suit me. I had the feeling that I couldn't depend on him."

What Mr. Holt is saying, in effect, is: "I don't think I'd like to work for Majestic." To say that *they* do not want to hire *him* would be to admit something that would be damaging to his self-concept; hence he defends his feelings of self-esteem by implying that not working at Majestic is *his* choice, not theirs. Since such an implication is in keeping with a self-concept of being somewhat more of a free agent than he actually is, his statement "rationalizes" what would otherwise be an unacceptable situation: the fact that Majestic did not offer him a job. This is the "sour-grape" type of rationalizing—deciding that the desired goal is undesirable and hence not worth any further effort.

The converse of the "sour grape" attitude is the "sweet lemon," whereby the individual decides that the less desired accomplishment is best after all. The student who fails to win the short story contest says: "Even though I didn't make the grade, I'm glad I entered. It was good practice in writing, and I certainly learned a lot."

Rationalizing is more than simple "excuse-making" or similar conscious forms of blame-avoidance. When we rationalize, we are not aware that we are finding or inventing socially acceptable excuses for our behavior—the process is an unconscious one. Although our rationalizing may take the effect of explaining our behavior to other people, the chief purpose is not so much that of making ourselves "look good" to others, as it is that of preserving our self-esteem. In other words, we are primarily concerned about our *own* opinion of ourselves. With ordinary excuse-making, we are more concerned with protecting ourselves from the rejecting attitudes of other people, and we consciously search about for some plausible explanation for our behavior that has promise of being satisfying. Of course we may come to believe the excuse we fabricated, in which event it becomes a form of rationalizing.

Perceptual rigidity. There is a certain element of anxiety in facing new situations. We are not quite sure whether we shall be able to cope with them adequately; perhaps we will have to learn some new techniques or change our methods of procedure in some way or other. Unpredictability and the need for making changes are both characteristics that stimulate anxiety. One way to avoid such anxiety is to deny that there is anything new about the situation and to behave as though it is exactly like a situation previously encountered. (See Klein's research on page 140.) A common instance is the person whose parents were unwilling to permit any independence of thought and action. Perhaps he rebelled against them, or perhaps he always wanted to rebel but never could bring himself to do so. Now, as an adult, he reacts to every person in authority as though they were his parents. He is rebellious, disobedient, and quick to sense any move as an attempt to limit his rights and privileges. Each new authority figure is perceived in the same light; he makes no attempt to find out whether they actually are like his parents. Rebelling against persons in authority has now become a vital part of his personality and he perceives each authority figure as a threat in order to justify and to preserve this mode of conduct.

There is, of course, more to such behavior than mere stubbornness. Such individuals have personal needs that somehow are met by the feeling that one is the victim of persons in authority. The thought that persons in authority are always looking for ways to frustrate and punish is in some way important to the individual's self-picture.

We all employ perceptual rigidity to some degree. We find some security in assuming that new situations resemble previous ones. This feeling of security helps reduce our anxiety somewhat and enables us to use techniques and approaches that are at least familiar, if not always effective. But perceptual rigidity does limit our ability to perceive the elements in the new situation that are different, and thereby it reduces our capacity to learn.

Like other mechanisms, perceptual rigidity stems from our inability to tolerate ambiguity. Recognizing that a new situation is different arouses some doubt, some ambiguity as to what we should decide or how we should behave. A more mature approach, emotionally speaking, would be that of tolerating the ambiguity and its accompanying anxiety, recognizing the new elements in the situation, and devising new attitudes and approaches to deal with it.

Projection. Projection is the process of perceiving one's environment, and particularly other people, in terms of one's *own* (unconscious) needs, attitudes, and values. This tendency has been exploited in a large number of personality tests (called "projective tests") whereby the individual being tested is asked to interpret an ink blot or other kind of ambiguous stimulus. As we reported in Chapter 10, such replies can be analyzed in terms of his personality traits and his major emotional difficulties. The term "projection" is also used for a similar form of behavior: that of attributing one's own qualities to others. The following newspaper story is virtually a "classic example" of this kind of projection, showing the way in which one young man unconsciously "projected" his own personal characteristics onto a nonexistent robbery suspect.

When Robert M—— manager of the T—— Theatre reported a $400 holdup last January, he couldn't remember what the bandit looked like.

When he reported a second holdup Monday, of $575 in theatre receipts, he gave a full, and apparently accurate, description of the robber.

The investigating officers suddenly stared at M——. He fitted the description.

And today, flunking a lie detector test, he admitted that both holdups were faked to pay gambling debts.[1]

• When the term "projection" is used to identify a form of behavior mechanism, it refers to one particular variety of projecting behavior: the tendency to attribute our own faults to others. The person who wants to exploit others accuses them of wanting to exploit him; the person whose sexual yearnings are repressed but active thinks that others are "over-sexed"; the person who is most difficult to convince says that everyone else is stubborn. When a group of 67 clinical psychology students were asked to score some responses to a projective test in terms of the presence or absence of tension in certain areas of adjustment, they tended to score more tension in areas in which they themselves were experiencing difficulty, wholly unaware that their ratings were being biased by their personal problems. (Weingarten, 1949.)

Attributing our undesirable qualities to others would not in itself help us to avoid anxiety if it were not for the fact that the process enables us to *dissociate* ourselves from the traits in question. We talk to a student who has an argumentative, chip-on-the-shoulder air about him, and ask him how he likes college. He says that his main objection is that his fellow students are not friendly. Naturally, we wonder who is unfriendly—he or the other students? By projecting his unfriendliness on those around him, he is able to ignore it in himself. In effect, he dissociates himself from his own unfriendly qualities, which he then attributes to others.

Adjustment through substitute behavior. One way of reacting to frustration or conflict is to change our perception of the situation and decide that the threatening aspects are not there at all; hence that there is no need for anxiety. This is the method we have discussed in the preceding section. Another way of reacting is to find another goal to replace one that is unattainable or to substitute a problem that *can* be solved for one that is ambiguous or baffling.

Fantasy. Fantasy is one of the commonest forms of substitute behavior. We would like to escape from the tedious and demanding responsibilities that face us in our everyday life, but cir-

[1] *San Francisco Chronicle,* February 26, 1958, p. 2. Reprinted by permission.

Susan Greenburg

With children, fantasy often takes the form of highly imaginative role playing.

cumstances do not permit it. We cannot help thinking, however, how nice it would be if, instead of working, we were drifting in a canoe on some quiet lake, fishpole in hand, or basking in the sun on the sands of a bathing resort. Such day-dreaming is a form of wish-fulfillment. It is not as satisfying as a real vacation, but it momentarily reduces some of the dissatisfaction with the present. Fantasy may take the form of plans, as well as day-dreams. Perhaps we feel the need to "get away from it all" so strongly, that we begin to think of ways whereby the vacation trip can actually be accomplished. Usually such planning

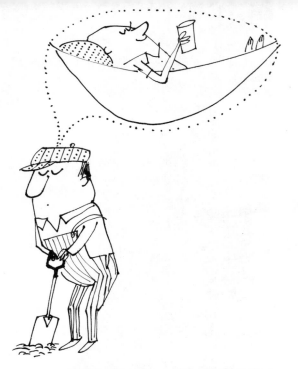

Similarly, the individual who is faced with a real or fancied psychological or social deficiency may try to compensate by developing other strengths. A member of a minority group may attempt to gain status by selecting a profession in which he can excel. A short person may feel that people look down on him because of his height and consequently may develop a pugnacious and aggressive pattern of behavior. A very tall person may feel that his height makes him conspicuous and consequently may cultivate a quiet, self-effacing manner. A minister's son may feel that he is tagged with the label of "goodness" and may try to impress the rest of the boys in his gang by out-swearing and out-fighting them.

The efforts of some individuals to achieve outstanding success in overcoming their handicaps are sometimes referred to as *over*compensation.

serves as a kind of substitute for the desired objective, but sometimes it may become a preliminary to the behavior that enables us to realize the desired goal.

Dreams that occur during sleep are another form of fantasy. Sometimes they provide a substitute for a desired goal. For example, a girl who is strongly attracted to a boy may dream that he is taking her to dinner in an expensive restaurant. Dreams may also provide wish-fulfillment in a negative way. A person who is afraid of losing his job and has been in a state of suspense and insecurity for several weeks or months may dream that he is walking near the edge of a cliff, is inexorably drawn to the brink, and finds himself slipping over the side in spite of all he can do. Such a dream symbolizes his feeling of helplessness and perhaps a wish that the ambiguous situation be resolved at all costs, even though the solution be unfavorable.

Analysis of dreams and other fantasy material offers an approach to studying personality and the emotional problems, inasmuch as the themes that appear are reflections or projections of our feelings, needs, attitudes, and conflicts.

Compensatory behavior. When a healthy organism develops some deficiency, its tendency is to try to make up or compensate for that deficiency in some way. A person who loses his sight will try to develop his auditory and tactual sensitivity. A person who is born without arms may develop a great deal of dexterity with his toes.

Examples often cited are Theodore Roosevelt, who was a physical weakling as a young man, but who became a national symbol for strength and vigorous action, and Helen Keller, who gained an international reputation as a writer, in spite of being born blind and deaf.

Sublimation. Thoughts and feelings that we consider to be unworthy of ourselves can be denied and repressed by developing forms of behavior that are strongly positive and socially acceptable. Instead of expressing our hostility toward others in the form of destructive acts or behavior which is socially disapproved, we can express it in some form of discreet competition, a form of behavior that meets with approval in our middle-class culture. The love-sick swain, who is prevented by his own moral code or by his fear of evoking the disapproval of others from expressing his sexual urges more directly, turns instead to the writing of poetry.

Although we generally approve of sublimation as a way of expressing undesirable motives, we should be aware that, like most other mechanisms, it operates unconsciously. It serves the purpose of keeping us unaware of the unwanted motives. The individual who uses sublimation as a mechanism would be surprised to find that he is really hostile or lustful, because the very effectiveness of the mechanism enables him to dissociate himself from those aspects of himself that he considers to be unworthy.

Reaction formation. This is a way of responding to unworthy motives by developing behavior that is the direct opposite. If the hostile individual develops a pattern of behavior that is characterized by extreme friendliness, and is thus able to deny to himself that he has any feelings of hostility, and if the love-sick youth would deny that he had any interest in girls at all and instead behaved hatefully toward them, they would be using the mechanism that is termed "reaction formation." Sublimation implies the acceptance of a substitute goal that is in the same general direction as the original motive; reaction formation implies a complete dissociation from anything remotely resembling the despised motive.

Displaced hostility. It very commonly happens that an individual is unable to express his hostile feelings toward the person or object that is the cause. He has the choice of swallowing his anger, turning it upon himself, sublimating it, or directing it against some person or object other than the source of the stimulus. In the last instance the anger is said to be "displaced." Here is an example of displacement which occurs and recurs in various forms in the folklore of different cultures:

A captain of a band of soldiers found fault with one of his lieutenants and criticized him in an insulting manner. Shortly thereafter the lieutenant encountered a sergeant whose method of saluting was not to his liking, so he gave him a tongue-lashing and finished by slapping his face. The sergeant, in his turn, sought out a private who had not completed an assignment properly and, after giving him a severe dressing down, knocked him down. The private returned to his task, which happened to be that of loading a donkey. As soon as the sergeant was out of sight, the private picked up a stick and began to beat the donkey.

Displaced hostility is a behavior pattern particularly characteristic of authoritarian settings. The individual who is the target for his superior's hostility and is unable to retaliate or defend himself must find some other way of expressing his frustration. The most likely target is a subordinate. Sometimes a group organized along authoritarian lines will select a low-status individual or a group to serve as a "scapegoat"—a target for the pent-up frustration and hostility that cannot be expressed within the group or toward superiors. Examples of scapegoating appear almost every day in the pages of the daily newspaper when, for example, politicians and other public figures blame recurring community problems on juvenile delinquents, the schools, the federal government, or whatever scapegoat happens to be available at the moment. Like other forms of displaced hostility, the scapegoat mechanism enables the individual to dissociate himself of all responsibility for his problems by laying them on the doorstep of some likely victim.

In the field of international politics, a recurring pattern is the tendency of the leaders of smaller nations to blame larger nations for whatever internal problem happens to be plaguing their country. The vulnerability of minority groups often makes them prime candidates for scapegoating. One of the most notable examples in recent years

is the persecution of the Jews by the Nazis in Germany.

Conformity. The patterns for our behavior mechanisms are to a large degree preselected for us by the norms of our culture. One culture teaches its members to sublimate hostility indirectly through cockfighting or bullfighting; another culture encourages its members to engage in competitive sports like polo, football, and dart-throwing; still another culture prescribes the vendetta or feud as a way of expressing hostility and aggression. The culture also prescribes the sequences of behavior that are to be used in attaining goals. To a large extent, it indicates which goals are legitimate and which are not.

The net result of this prescription is the elimination of much potential ambiguity and the consequent reduction in anxiety. All the individual has to do is to learn the goals that have been preselected by his culture and follow the prescribed sequence of actions that will lead to the desired goals. In actual practice, of course, anxiety is a frequent experience, because not all individuals adapt themselves equally well to the pattern prescribed by their culture, and the prescribed patterns do not fit all situations. Furthermore, the rapidly accelerating rate of change in the modern world means that patterns sometimes become outmoded faster than new ones can be developed.

Like other forms of adjustment, conformity is a learned process. As we grow and develop through childhood, adolescence, and adulthood, we are penalized for nonconformity and are able to gain acceptance and tolerance of others through our willingness to behave in terms of the expectations that they have for us. As we enter upon new social situations, we learn how to behave through a process of *identification*—through copying the behavior of others in the group. By identifying with the group and conforming to its norms we protect ourselves against rejection and consequent anxiety.

Conformity helps to eliminate ambiguity by providing us with models for our behavior. It always involves some sacrifice, however, because it forces us to give up individualistic or self-centered approaches to situations and problems in favor of the approaches prescribed by the group. On the one hand we may gain by eliminating friction, disturbance, ambiguity, and other anxiety-producing elements, but on the other hand

we run the risk of losing spontaneity, self-initiative, and creativity. The problem we face is how to participate in the group on a reasonably harmonious basis without sacrificing our identities as individuals. Unfortunately, many people cannot tolerate the normal anxiety that comes from even minor deviations from the patterns of thinking, feeling, and behaving that are characteristic of the groups to which they belong, and practice conformity to the extent of dissociating themselves from anything remotely resembling individuality. On the other hand, there are a few people who are made so anxious by the demands of society in the way of conformity that they develop a pattern of nonconformity that is as rigid and as sterile as the behavior of the most avowed conformists.

Less effective patterns of adjustment

Under this heading we shall discuss a number of patterns that are to a large extent extensions of mechanisms discussed in the pages immediately preceding, but which reflect more marked degrees of disturbance, disorientation, and maladjustment—hence their designation as "less effective." The patterns of behavior included in this section are characteristic of individuals who are encountering a greater or lesser degree of difficulty in their relations with others. In some instances, their mechanisms do not adequately protect them against anxiety; in other instances, the mechanisms protect them perhaps too well.

Regression. Under the stress of anxiety, it sometimes happens that we regress, that is, we return to forms of behavior that were satisfying or effective in the past but that are no longer appropriate to our present level of development. The six-year-old who has not sucked his thumb for some three years, takes up thumb-sucking again as he tries to cope with the strains and anxieties of the first days at school. The nine-year-old, who has not wet his bed since he was four, goes through a spell of bed-wetting when his parents talk of getting a divorce. In Chapter 5, we described what happened when a group of children, three and four years old, were first brought into a room and permitted to play with the interesting toys it contained and then taken to another part of the same room, where the toys were much less interesting. A barrier was erected between them and the interesting toys, so that the children could still see them but could not get close enough to touch them. As a result of this frustration, the behavior of the children regressed an average of seventeen months, that is, they began to display patterns of behavior characteristic of children seventeen months younger. (Barker, Dembo, Lewin, Wright, 1943.) A college student who encountered a number of rather acute problems of adjustment at school and at home began going around with a group of "hot-rod" boys two years her junior. When she was in elementary school she had been a tomboy, and under the stress of her difficulties she regressed to this earlier pattern of behavior.

Although regression is most common in childhood, it can also appear in adult life, as witness the "mothering" we like to receive when we are ill. Somewhat similar to regression is a behavior pattern called *fixation,* which is characterized by an inability to progress to more mature stages of behavior. The unmarried adult who lives with his parents, permits them to make his decisions for him, and generally maintains a "parent-child relationship" with them is an example of behavior that has been fixed at a less-than-adult level. Another example is the woman who is overdependent, can not function on an adult level, makes continual demands for protection and special consideration from those about her, and is unable to give the same kind of attention to others. In some ways, she is like a child who has never grown up.

These are neurotic patterns of behavior. They go far beyond the behavior-mechanism level of functioning. They are more than mere gestures designed to cope with a momentary increase in anxiety; they are a *way* of life. All of us regress occasionally and revert to childish behavior for short periods, but regression as a dominant and consistent pattern of life exceeds normal limits of adjustment behavior.

Behavior without choice. One of the threads that runs through a great deal of maladjustive behavior is the tendency to repeat certain kinds of behavior again and again, regardless of their inappropriateness. Individuals who are caught up in neurotic patterns of behavior have the feeling that they have no choice—that they are, in effect, *compelled* to behave as they do. The person who is chronically overdependent may even admit: "I know I'm being childish, but I just can't help it." There is even a "choiceless" element in the behavior mechanisms we employ in our everyday

life. The person who rationalizes, for example, feels *compelled* to give logical reasons for his illogical behavior. Certain habit patterns and sequences of behavior may incorporate this choiceless factor. Smoking is one of the commonest examples. The habitual smoker does not use smoking so much as a way of coping with everyday anxiety as he does to avoid the anxiety he would feel if he did *not* smoke. In its initial stages, smoking is to some degree a matter of choice: it may be a way of socializing or of expressing the feeling of having attained adult status. As they become thoroughly conditioned, physically and emotionally, to the ritual of smoking, smokers find that cutting down or eliminating tobacco produces an increase in tension; hence the question of whether or not to smoke becomes for them a "choiceless situation": they feel compelled to smoke to avoid the tension that would be caused by not smoking.

Alcoholism. The alcoholic, too, feels forced into a choiceless situation by his need for alcohol to reduce or relieve his tensions and anxieties. Alcoholism can be induced in animals by subjecting them to repeated fear-producing stimuli. Masserman and Yum (1946) found that cats who experienced mild electric shock or blasts of air as they were feeding came to prefer milk containing a 5 per cent solution of alcohol to plain milk.

The basis for human alcoholism is by no means clearly established. It may be that the metabolism of alcoholics is somewhat different from nonalcoholics, but even if this were so it would not prove that addiction is metabolically caused. The same may be said for personality patterns that appear to accompany alcoholism: did one cause the other or did they appear together? Cultural factors and early family background are apparently of some importance. Alcoholism is commoner among Americans of Irish descent than it is among those with Chinese, Jewish, or Italian backgrounds. Although drinking is not condoned by the Mormon religion, the small number of Mormons who do drink have a high proportion of problem drinkers. The attitudes that the subcultural group has toward drinking do seem to be an important determining factor as far as alcoholism is concerned. High rates of alcoholism appear to be associated with cultures that develop conflicting attitudes toward drinking. (Ullman, 1958.)

Narcotics. Drug addiction is a form of apparently choiceless behavior that bears some similarity to alcohol addiction. Persons addicted to certain drugs—particularly barbiturates and opiates—tend to develop a higher degree of physiological dependence on drugs, whereas the dependency factor in alcoholism seems to be largely emotional. The distinction between a dependence that is largely emotional and one that is both emotional and physical may be rather academic as far as the addicted individual is concerned. Certainly both types of addiction are cured only with difficulty.

As with alcoholism, personality and cultural patterns appear to be significant factors in drug addiction. Drug addicts are inclined to be bland, evasive individuals, who do not ordinarily "act out" their aggressive impulses against their environment. Fifty years ago drug addiction was more common among women than among men; today it is more common among men than among women. Although the range in educational and cultural background among addicts is great, the average amount of education is higher than that of the general population. It is almost entirely an urban phenomenon. A study of Malzberg (1949) in New York state found a somewhat higher tendency for persons with Jewish and Irish backgrounds to become addicted. Among the Jewish group, there were twice as many males as females; among the Irish group, there were almost three times as many females as males. Subjects with an Italian background consisted entirely of males. Although no one has satisfactorily identified and classified the cultural and personality factors that accompany drug addiction, these figures appear to indicate that addiction is a selective mechanism, that is, some individuals, because of their background and personality, are more likely to become addicted than others.

Gambling. Gambling is another form of behavior which, like alcohol and drug addiction, appears to have its choiceless aspects and thus dominates the life of its victims. The person addicted to gambling becomes just as undependable and as unpredictable as the confirmed alcoholic, as far as his responsibilities to his family and his employer are concerned. Once he has become addicted, he behaves as though he has no choice but to gamble, even though he may recognize the harm he is doing to himself, his family, and his associates. The gambler lives in a state of tension

and suspense, often masked by a façade of stoical calm (the well-known "poker face"). He cannot afford to relax, since he is continually planning or making bets, or raising funds to gamble or to pay off his debts. Just as many alcoholics hoard liquor in secret caches to tide them over a "dry period," the addicted gambler will maintain a reservoir of funds—his "betting money"—which he will not touch even for the pressing and urgent needs of his family and himself. Here is the summarized case history of an inveterate gambler:

L. M. was born in Russia of a wealthy and cultured urban family, the youngest of four children. The main attention of the family, especially that of the mother, was focused on the older children, who were guided toward successful professional careers. His mother died when he was 14; his father remarried shortly thereafter and moved away, leaving the boy to his own resources. The rigid discipline of the home collapsed with his mother's death, and he rebelled against the schooling she had imposed. He was apprenticed to a skilled craftsman, a move which the family regarded with embarrassment and disfavor. After a short period he embarked on a series of wanderings, arriving in the United States when he was 17.

In this country he became a skilled craftsman, periodically conducting his own business as an interior decorator and painting contractor. Within a short time, he fell in with a "sporting crowd," where he played the role of the cultured gentleman, often stressing with much pride the importance of his family connections in Russia. He was charming, witty, and unreliable, with strong feelings of resentment toward authority and resistant to any attempts to impose normal restraints on his behavior.

When he was 29 he married a girl of 18, who had experienced chronic feelings of insecurity in the large, lower-middle-class family in which she had grown up.

Partially because of this background and partially because she was the victim of an incurable illness, she attempted to impose upon her husband the same kind of discipline against which he had rebelled all his life. This only intensified his rebelliousness and irresponsibility. During this period he gambled steadily, neglected his wife, his children, and his business. The death of his wife, at the age of 31, seemed to provide him with an excuse to give up all idea of trying to succeed. Although he had periodic feelings of remorse for his neglect of his four children, he gambled continually, eventually giving up all pretense of legitimate employment. When interviewed by a sociologist, he was 83 years of age, living in a nursing home and prevented from gambling by the infirmities of age. He summed up his feelings about gambling by saying: "I don't know why I did it, but gambling is like a disease; I couldn't stop it even though I often wanted to." (Bloch, 1952.)

Hyperactivity. Not all forms of choiceless behavior are as socially disintegrative as are the forms of addictive behavior we have just reviewed. Hyperactivity, for example, is a trait that may lead to positive contributions of a social, as well as a personal, nature. However, the basis for hyperactivity is similar to that of the other forms of choiceless behavior: it is a device to shield the individual against anxiety. The hyperactive person involves himself in a multitude of activities and affairs to keep from facing what he fears are unsolvable problems: conflicts, feelings of inadequacy and inferiority, and the like. The hyperactive person usually admits that he is involved in too many activities, and that he has difficulty in finishing projects once he begins them, yet he is unable to resist the appeal of a new activity. It is almost as though he is compelled to overextend himself, just as the addict feels compelled to drink, take drugs, or gamble.

Shyness. Some people feel compelled to be shy. Even when they know that their best interests will be served by speaking out, they cannot bring themselves to do so. Shyness is especially prevalent during the adolescent and young-adult years, when individuals are learning to make adjustments to new roles and new self-expectations. Most people outgrow these earlier symptoms of shyness, particularly as they learn roles appropriate to adult status. There are some individuals, however, who are so easily panicked by anxiety and self-doubt that they are unable to develop more mature forms of behavior. Because they are shy, they fail to live up to their own expectations in a group setting. As they

brood over the humiliation resulting from such failures, they feel even more unworthy and inadequate. This in turn intensifies their feelings of inferiority and aggravates their shyness.

This "circular" type of interaction is rather characteristic of the more neurotic mechanisms. Although the individual employs the mechanism to avoid or reduce anxiety, it succeeds only temporarily or partially. He then feels ashamed of his "weakness" in falling back on such a despicable mechanism. The greater his guilt, the greater his anxiety, and the greater his anxiety, the greater the likelihood that he will use the mechanism.

Obsessive behavior. Obsessions are another variety of choiceless behavior. The obsessed person feels that he *must* make a certain association, commit a certain action, or think certain thoughts. Most of us have had the experience of being unable to get a certain tune or a certain idea out of our heads. On a more neurotic level, a person obsessed with cleanliness may feel compelled to wash his hands several times a day and may be distressed if circumstances do not permit him to do so. On a severely disturbed, that is, psychotic, level, an individual may be obsessed with the idea that he is a murderer, that someone is trying to poison him, or that some other kind of unlikely event is occurring.

Phobic behavior. Phobias are persistent, exaggerated fears. Many otherwise normal and healthy people have irrational fears about riding in elevators, looking down from the roof of tall buildings, getting hypodermic injections, and so forth. For most of us, such fears are a minor annoyance, perhaps even something to be joked about, but some people are so completely dominated by their phobias that they are unable to lead normal lives. The individual who must avoid open spaces or who is thrown into a panic whenever he rides in a moving vehicle finds that his capacity to cope with the everyday demands of life is much impaired.

Psychosomatic disorders. A large number of ailments are either caused or aggravated by anxiety. The individual who must cope with more psychological stress than he can readily handle in the form of direct expression or through some form of behavior mechanism may, as we indicated in Chapter 4, develop difficulties in bodily functioning.

In Chapter 7, we discussed the close relation-

Although most people would cross a railroad track if no train were in sight, it is conceivable that the crossing sign might make some overly anxious or neurotic people apprehensive to the degree that they would cross only with feelings of trepidation or impending disaster. Covering one's ears as a protection against the whistle of a train that is nowhere in sight or even in hearing distance would be a psychotic response.

ship between emotional behavior and body chemistry. By way of a brief review, the adrenals of persons who tend to express their frustration freely against their environment ("anger-out") secrete norepinephrine, a chemical that has little disturbing effect on the body, whereas the adrenals of people who react to frustration in terms of "anger-in" or "severe anxiety" secrete epinephrine, a chemical that has a stimulating and disturbing effect on the body. (Funkenstein, King, and Drolette, 1957.) Hence it follows that persons who have learned to react to frustration with the "anger-in" or the anxiety pattern, and who also have to cope with a great deal of frustration, would be more likely to suffer from psychosomatic disorders. This conclusion is supported by research conducted at the Mayo Clinic by Smith and Hightower (1948), who found that school teachers and religious workers (whose occupational roles do not permit free and open expression of hostility) were more than twice as likely to suffer from psychosomatic symptoms as were farmers and railroad engineers (whose occupational roles do permit free and open expression of hostility).

Psychotic patterns of behavior

In the first part of this chapter we discussed mechanisms that aid us more or less adequately in dealing with the anxieties and frustrations of everyday life. Next we took up varieties of behavior that are commonly used to cope with anxiety but whose effectiveness is limited—often they create more problems than they solve. In this section we shall discuss psychotic modes of behavior—behavior which is not only completely ineffective as a defense against anxiety (O'Kelly, 1949: 213), but which also interferes with adequate adjustment to life and its problems. The term "psychotic" implies the greatest degree of emotional disturbance. Persons who display psychotic behavior are to a considerable extent out of touch with reality and consequently are more or less unable to manage their own affairs. Because of this incompetence, and because of their need for psychiatric care and supervision, they are likely to be judged "insane" (a legal but not a psychological designation) and committed to a mental institution for treatment.

"Neurotic" is a term that is applied to behavior that shows some inability to function adequately, usually under stress of severe or chronic anxiety, for which some kind of psychological or psychiatric treatment is usually indicated. This does not mean that a person with severe or chronic neurosis is necessarily in danger of becoming psychotic; indeed, many psychologists are convinced that psychosis and neurosis are not merely different stages of emotional disturbance but are basically different kinds of mental illness that to some degree share the same symptoms. In fact, there is the evidence that the blood of individuals suffering from schizophrenia (one form of psychosis) contains substances not found in the blood of other persons.

"Normal" is the most difficult of the three terms to define, since normality covers such a tremendous range and variety of behavior, some of it effective and some of it not. There is no sharp dividing line between "normal" and "neurotic." Most people in a fast-moving, complex, and urbanized cultural environment develop some neurotic problems and probably could be helped at times by counseling or other forms of psychological assistance. In general, however, people considered "normal" are in good contact with reality and have a reasonable degree of success in dealing with their everyday affairs. Neurotic individuals generally are in contact with reality as well, but are more likely to make misinterpretations and distortions. Although they too are fairly competent in coping with the problems of everyday life, they tend to experience more difficulty in this respect. Relations with others at work, at home, or in social groups are more likely to be impaired. Although the neurotic person may need psychological help, he is generally considered to be competent to manage his own affairs, whereas the psychotic person usually is not.

The term "psychosis" covers a wide range of mental diseases that may be divided into two categories: organic and psychogenic. Organic psychoses are accompanied by and presumably caused by physical deterioration or destruction of some part of the nervous system, especially the brain itself. Psychogenic psychoses show no evidence of such deterioration and include schizophrenia, paranoid disturbances, and affective psychoses.

Schizophrenia. This is the commonest of the functional psychoses, accounting for two-thirds to three-quarters of the admissions in this category. Although there are many subvarieties of schizophrenia, the commonest characteristics are an apathy or indifference to reality and a dissociation of thoughts and ideas from normal emotions. In its less severe forms, the disorder is marked by neurotic symptoms, such as obsessions, compulsions, or bodily complaints. In its more severe forms there is withdrawal from reality, disintegration of thought processes, delusions and hallucina-

Joe Stalin's Superiority Complex

Ye though I Walk through the Valley of the shadow of death I Will fear No evil for the Lord is With Me. His Machine and his gun they comfort Me.

What Master of arts under the canopy of heaven has got broad enough shoulders to let the chips remain Where they fall?

Hitch your Wagon to a star.

Then if she answers No then on My Way I will go to be at I a lonely troopdoor.

P.S.

Joe Stalins Nieper has carried Hitlers account through to the black sea, Until and after all hell freezes over.

Two by four attorneys May Need to keep a case going over Joe E. Brown for the front, advertisement they receive.

Small deals stand in the Way of large projects.

A Mans pocket book has More Weight than himself.

Attorneys Would like to advance a settlement from the returns of a crap game With their daughter for an inherited romance.

(Coleman, 1950. Reprinted by permission.)

tions, distortion of emotional behavior, and disorganization of personal habits and normal controls. The excerpt from an article entitled "Joe Stalin's Superiority Complex" is an example of schizophrenic ideation. The recovery rate for schizophrenics is highly variable. Some patients respond readily to treatment; others remain in the hospital for years.

Paranoid disturbances. Paranoid reactions are characterized by systematic delusions of grandeur and/or persecution. Persons suffering from paranoid delusions often believe that someone is plotting against them or trying to kill them. Sometimes they are able to make their delusions sound very plausible. An Army captain in Hawaii during the days following Pearl Harbor believed that plantation owners were harboring enemy soldiers. His arguments were so convincing that his superiors transferred him to headquarters and placed him in charge of special investigative work. They became suspicious, however, when the persons he accused turned out to be completely loyal. When, finally, he reported that a man in army uniform had fired a service revolver at him, and investigation proved that his charge was completely baseless, he was placed in a hospital for observation and given a medical discharge from the service. Except for actions related to this para-

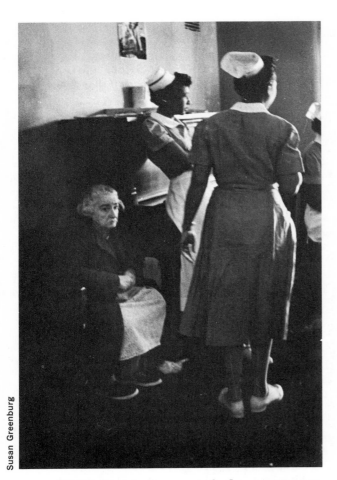

Susan Greenburg

Schizophrenia is one of the commonest forms of mental disorder.

noid delusion, his behavior was normal. (O'Kelly, 1949.)

Ordinarily, paranoid delusions are not nearly so convincing because they are likely to be associated with other forms of psychosis and hence are obviously ridiculous. Here is an example of schizophrenic behavior coupled with paranoid delusions:

S. E. was admitted to the hospital from the city jail, where he had been serving a sentence for "peddling without a license." The jail physician recommended psychiatric observation after the patient told him a story of being the Swedish ambassador to the United States who was traveling around the country in disguise to study "conditions." In appearance, S. E. was untidy and disheveled, a small man who appeared to be about forty-five years of age. He stated his age to be "six thousand and twelve," and said that he was the owner of the whole "continent of Sweden under God." He claimed that the medicine he was selling from door to door was made "from the innermost private essences of time without end, amen." For over a thou-

sand years, according to the patient, evil men had been trying to get his secret of perpetual life and even now were "operating on him." He said that he had discovered a super-radio with which he could tell where his enemies were and that at the proper time he would "order the armies into action" and give his whole fortune of several billion dollars to the support of "genuine Swedish Christianity." He maintained that he was not bothered by being placed in jail or being taken to the hospital, because his "super-ordered powers" would enable him to walk out through the thickest walls any time he chose.[1]

Affective psychoses. These disorders consist of extremes of mood or feeling, accompanied by severely disabling disturbances of behavior. Some patients fall into a state of extreme excitement and elation; others become extremely despondent and depressed; whereas still others swing from one extreme mood to the other. Affective disorders are more likely to respond to treatment than other psychoses. Often the attacks endure only a few months and may even terminate themselves spontaneously, without treatment. This type of psychosis is the only one that is commoner with middle- and upper-class persons.

Organic psychoses. Alcohol, syphilis, industrial chemicals, drugs, concussions and wounds, and the degenerative effects of old age may all prove to be damaging to brain tissue. Such damage results in behavior that is rather generally similar to the functional psychoses. For example, the behavior of an individual afflicted by *paresis,* a psychosis resulting from syphilitic infection, may resemble the behavior observed in some forms of schizophrenia, with a gradual withdrawal from the environment, accompanied by hallucinations and delusions. Some paretic patients develop an extreme depression, and others become expansive and elated, subject to grandiose delusions that resemble paranoia.

Interpersonal relations in psychosis. One of the characteristics of psychotic patients is a marked disturbance in their relationships with others, particularly relationships involving affectional ties. Murray and Cohen (1959) asked hospital patients in an orthopedic (that is, nonpsychiatric) ward, an "open" psychiatric ward, and a "locked" psychiatric ward to indicate which of the other patients they liked most, were most at

[1] Lawrence I. O'Kelly and Frederick A. Muckler, *Introduction to Psychopathology,* 2nd ed., copyrighted 1949, 1955 by Prentice-Hall, Inc., Englewood Cliffs, N. J., pp. 292–293. By permission of the publishers.

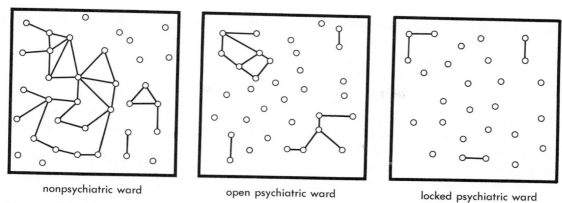

nonpsychiatric ward   open psychiatric ward   locked psychiatric ward

Figure 11-1. Positive reciprocal choices for three hospital ward groups showing the effects of different degrees of mental illness. (After Murray and Cohen, 1959.)

ease with, liked most to eat with, and to work with. As might be expected, patients in the non-psychiatric ward showed the greatest degree of friendliness and acceptance toward each other, as indicated by the large number of pairs of individuals who expressed feelings that were mutually positive. Patients in the open psychiatric wards showed a somewhat lower degree of positive feeling for one another, as was evidenced by fewer reciprocal choices, while patients in the locked ward reported the fewest reciprocal choices. In other words, the higher the degree of mental disturbance, the lower the degree of positive feelings towards others. Figure 11-1 shows how the three wards differed with respect to the number of reciprocal choices. In the nonpsychiatric ward, 74 per cent of the patients showed one or more positive reciprocal choices, as contrasted with 50 per cent in the open psychiatric ward and 25 per cent in the locked ward. Interestingly enough, the nonpsychiatric ward also showed the greatest number of *negative* reciprocations—26 per cent, contrasted with 6 per cent in the open psychiatric ward, and none in the locked ward. The point is that the nonpsychiatric patients showed a great deal more interpersonal interest and activity, all of which resulted in *both positive and negative* feelings, whereas the psychiatric patients showed varying degrees of apathy, depending on the severity of their illness.

Sociological factors in mental illness. The last decade has seen an increasing amount of research devoted to the identification of social factors related to various kinds of mental illness. Hollingshead and Redlich (1958), for example, carried on an extensive study of the mental health

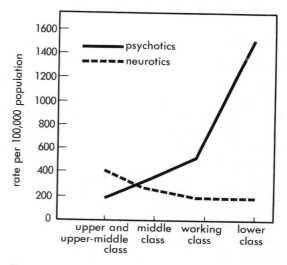

Figure 11-2. Prevalence of neurosis and psychosis in New Haven, Connecticut, according to social class. (After Hollingshead and Redlich, 1958.)

of New Haven, Connecticut, and found a marked relationship between social class (as characterized by educational and occupational level and residence area of individuals) and the incidence of psychosis and neurosis. Middle- and upper-class persons were more likely to develop neurotic symptoms of behavior, whereas lower-class individuals were more likely to develop forms of psychosis. (See Figure 11-2.) Perhaps there is a further relationship between this finding and that of Funkenstein, King, and Drolette (whose work was discussed in Chapter 7), who reported that students with upper-class backgrounds were more likely to show an "anger-in" reaction to stress. In other words, it would seem that people who have learned to contain their anger in the face of frustration are more likely to develop neurotic rather than psychotic symptoms.

The findings of Hollingshead and Redlich are also confirmed by Malzberg (1956), who analyzed the educational background of some 36,000 persons admitted to public and private mental hospitals in New York State from 1938 to 1941 and found that the greater the amount of education, the less the likelihood of psychosis. Individuals with no education showed the highest incidence of psychosis—almost double the rate for those with high school or college education. Individuals with six years or less of schooling were about 25 per cent more likely than those with high school or college education to be admitted with a diagnosis of some kind of psychogenic psychosis.

Psychotherapy

In its broadest sense, psychotherapy consists of the use of psychological techniques in order to help people with mental disorders or with problems of personal and social adjustment. It can be used to advantage with a wide range of problems, from that of the student who is having difficulty in making satisfactory grades to that of the catatonic schizophrenic patient who is unable to feed and clothe himself.

Psychotherapy may be concluded in one or two interviews or continue for months or years. The student who is having difficulty with his grades may talk over the problem with a psychologist once a week for a month or so and find that he has been helped considerably. Or it may turn out that the problem of poor grades is in turn related to some other very complex problem which requires more intensive therapy over a longer period of time. It is extremely likely that the catatonic schizophrenic patient will require intensive therapy over a relatively long period of time before he will begin to respond to treatment. Probably his psychotherapy will be accompanied by *somatotherapy*—physical treatment—such as the use of electric or insulin shock or the administration of some of the tranquilizing drugs, like chlorpromazine or reserpine. (The tendency today is for drug therapy to replace electric or insulin shock.) The use of the tranquilizing drugs helps reduce anxiety and make the patient who "cannot be reached" more available to psychotherapy.

Group therapy. Sometimes therapists work with patients in small groups. Most problems of adjustment directly or indirectly involve other people, and discussing them in a group setting under the supervision of a trained person can often help individuals develop new and more effective points of view toward their relations with others. Group therapy has the advantage of aiding an individual to discover that he is not alone in his problems, that other people have problems and feelings that are quite similar to his. This can be an important discovery, because it is very common to develop the feeling that no one has problems that are as bad as the ones that *we* must face. It is reassuring to learn that others have similar problems, experience similar antisocial impulses, and have made similar mistakes. Group therapy also gives the individual a chance to share his problems with the group and to share the problems of others. Such sharing may give him a feeling of release and thus help to reduce the feeling of guilt that is so frequently an obstacle to psychological improvement. At the same time he may become drawn out of himself by becoming involved in the task of helping other people solve their problems. Because of a past history of poor relations with persons in authority, some individuals have difficulty in accepting help from a psychotherapist but are more able to accept advice and criticism from the other members of a therapy group. Inasmuch as all members of the group have equal status, such an individual feels less threatened by the other members and is able to accept interpretation and advice that he could never accept in the setting of individual therapy. It is partly for this latter reason that group therapy is coming into greater use in prisons. A great many people are in prison because of their difficulty with persons in authority; hence they are able to learn a great deal through group therapy.

Play therapy. Problems of children can sometimes be successfully resolved through "play therapy." A child who is unwilling or unable to discuss his problems with an adult usually finds less difficulty in expressing himself through his play. In the therapy situation, he may use clay, paint, or other art materials as media for self-expression and for working off his tensions and anxieties, or he may resort to dramatic play, using dolls and household toys to act out the problems he is encountering in his relations with members of his family. For instance, a child who is troubled by

In modern mental institutions, education and vocational training not only form an important part of therapy but also give patients a chance to learn skills that will be useful when they return to the outside world.

mixed feelings of love and hostility toward his brother may treat a male doll with great tenderness for awhile and then abruptly throw it across the room. One preschool child made a figure of a man out of clay and then began to pull off pieces which he proceeded to smash, saying: "I am breaking my father's arms. I am breaking my father's legs." After a minute or so of this, he stopped, smiled, and said: "I am breaking my father all to pieces, but I still love him." Such experiences indicate that play therapy may be used as a way of diagnosing the problems of children, as well as of helping them develop more positive attitudes and behavior.

Occupational and recreational therapy. Most mental hospitals today provide opportunities for self-expression in various arts and crafts: weaving, woodworking, and ceramics are common examples. Many patients find that working with tools and raw material like clay and wood is a psychologically integrating experience, one that not only brings them into direct contact with reality in a very concrete form, but that also gives them an outlet for creativity. Recreational therapy also gives patients a chance to interact with others in a pleasant and socially stimulating way. Many hospitals also employ specialists to conduct educational programs that make it pos-

sible for patients to learn skills, like typing and accounting, and thus improve their employability and general competence.

Nondirective methods. One of the newer philosophies or modes of treatment is nondirective or client-centered therapy. Introduced by Carl Rogers (1942, 1951) during the early 1940's, the nondirective approach has stimulated a great deal of controversy among psychotherapists and counselors. Rogers criticized the traditional relationship between client (or patient) and therapist on the grounds that it actually interfered with the client's ability to improve. The chief aim of therapy, Rogers argued, is that of helping the client to help himself; hence it does little good for the therapist to do the job for him. The purpose of psychotherapy is that of aiding the client in achieving better insight and understanding of himself and his problems to the end that he becomes freer—better able to realize his own strengths and potentialities. For the therapist to interpose his own interpretations and advice, said Rogers, is to aggravate the client's feeling of helplessness and inadequacy.

Rogers proposed that therapists refrain from advice-giving and interpretation and instead bend their efforts to creating a permissive atmosphere, an atmosphere that gives the client the feeling

Play therapy gives children a chance to "act out" their problems.

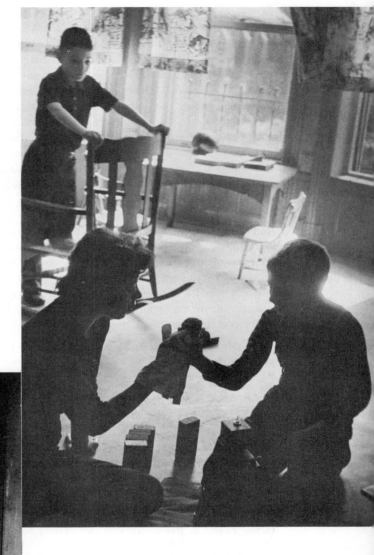

Photographs by Susan Greenburg.

of being accepted. The client should get the feeling that his thoughts, ideas, and feelings have value merely because they are his; he should not be expected to conform to the therapist's expectations or preconceptions. He should be free, in effect, to be himself. Such an atmosphere may be created by the way in which the therapist replies to the client's statements. Instead of directing or taking charge of the interview, he should attempt to reflect the "feeling content" of what the client has said, sometimes summarizing or restating but never evaluating, criticizing, or pointing out discrepancies in the client's statements.

Some of the differences between nondirective and other forms of therapy may be illustrated by the following excerpts from therapy interviews. The first excerpt is from the ninth interview of a patient in psychoanalytic therapy. She is showing concern about a leg operation. She arrives five minutes late for her appointment and walks slowly to the couch, without looking at her analyst:

PATIENT: I know that I am late and I ought to apologize but I can't. I really don't want to. (Lies down on couch. Pauses for several seconds before speaking.) Actually I'm feeling quite good today. I'm glad the surgeon said I won't have to give up smoking or wearing high-heel shoes. Those were the only two things that I was scared of. It would kill me if I had to give up those things. But now I know that I don't need to worry about those things any more. I can see that it really is better to face the facts than to keep on feeling afraid, like I felt before I went to the surgeon.

ANALYST: But I wonder if you really are facing the facts. You say that you were afraid only of those two things: having to give up smoking and wearing high heels. Last week, before you saw the surgeon, those certainly weren't the main things that you feared. The main fear you expressed was that he might tell you that you need an operation. And you were afraid that an operation might somehow lead to your losing your leg. Actually, it turns out that one of your fears has come true: your fear that you would need an operation was borne out by what the surgeon said.

PATIENT: Last week I did feel afraid of having an operation, but I don't feel that way any more. I'm looking forward to it. I think that I'm going to enjoy being in the hospital. They treat you like a baby, a dear little baby. That's what this operation means to me now. I know that I had been worried about my leg getting worse and having to be amputated. But now I know there's no danger of that at all. The operation is very simple and I'm going to have a really nice rest. Everyone will give me lots of affection. The whole thing will be a nice experience.

ANALYST: Do you really think that's true? Aren't you leaving out the unpleasant aspects of the operation?

PATIENT: Well, I know there will be some pain, of course, but I don't care about that. It won't be so bad, and everyone will feel sorry for me and treat me affectionately. I remember one of my neighbors went to the hospital for something or other, and when she came home she told me that she loved being in the hospital. She said she felt lonely at home alone all day all the time and she loved the attention she got at the hospital. I feel exactly the same way about it only I wouldn't admit it to anyone but you. I was surprised she admitted it to me. I'd hate to admit that I'm so lonely that I'd welcome an operation just to have contacts with people, but that is the way I feel. That's why I'm looking forward to it. I don't get enough satisfactions in other ways. I've told you all about that before.

ANALYST: Yes, and usually when you say that you don't get enough satisfactions it turns out to be a complaint directed against me and against this treatment.[1] (Janis, 1958: 65–66.)

The second excerpt, included here to illustrate nondirective methods, is from a third counseling interview with a young woman who has withdrawn from social contact with other people. (The letter "S" is used to represent the subject, and the letter "C" the counselor.)

S.: Well, in the first place, if I *were* to take a job right now I don't think it would be fair to the employer, I mean, I don't really think that it would be— when I'm in a rut like this. The point is, am I just raising that as a defense mechanism for not getting out? Or am I really thinking that it just wouldn't be fair? That's an important question to me.

C.: You feel that it wouldn't be fair, and at the same time there rises in your mind a question, are you just putting that up to keep from undertaking what would be a hard thing to do.

S.: That's right. (*Pause. Laughs.*) You shake your head. Is that all?

C.: You feel perhaps *I* should know the answers, then.

S.: That's right. Is it fair for an employee to go out and take a job that you feel, well, it may help you but it may not do very much for him? (*Pause.*) Is it justifiable?

C.: You feel you might be really cheating the employer by doing that.

S.: That's right. I've said that before. I know we've covered that once before. Uhuh. (*Long pause. Laughs.*) Well, what's the answer? Am I supposed to get the answers?

C.: You are wondering that, too, aren't you, whether maybe the answer is in you?

S.: In other words, I'd have to make a radical change before I . . . I'm supposed to change in attitude, and change in everything.

C.: You realize that it would mean a pretty radical shift if . . . uh . . . if you tried some of those things.

[1] Reprinted by permission.

s.: That's right. (*Long pause.*) I suppose it would be better for me, I mean, I probably wouldn't like it at first, but then maybe it would help me, wouldn't it? It would sort of force me to do things I don't want to do, I guess . . .[1] (Snyder, 1947:146–148.)

The nondirective approach to counseling and psychotherapy has been criticized by some psychologists on the grounds that it forces the psychotherapist to abdicate his responsibilities, and denies him the right to employ such techniques as psychodiagnostics, interpretations, and statements of emotional support even when the welfare of the patient would be materially benefited. When Rogers (1946) makes the statement: "Diagnostic knowledge and skill is not necessary for good therapy . . . ," some clinicians wonder whether he is not attacking the very basis of what they consider is the very heart of their professional competence. They feel that their diagnostic expertness is an important contribution to the therapeutic situation and that the Rogerian approach precludes their use of this expertness.

On the other hand, even the most outspoken of Rogers' critics concede that there is much in his method that makes sense, although they would claim that there is nothing especially new in the nondirective approach. A great many counselors feel that they already are using many of the nondirective techniques: the permissive, accepting approach to the client and the willingness to give the client a chance to find his own answers, for example. And they state that the nondirective therapist has no right to pre-empt the term "client-centered." *All* therapy, they say, is client-centered—that is, it is focused on the client and his problems and is for *his* benefit, not that of the therapist.

Although the philosophical differences between the nondirective and the directive schools of psychotherapy are wide enough to keep the controversy alive, one nevertheless gets the impression that practices and emphases in counseling and psychotherapy have moved in a nondirective and client-centered direction during the last two decades. Whether this change is due to the influence of the nondirective school, or whether the nondirective philosophy is merely symptomatic of an underlying trend in psychotherapeutic practice that was well under way before the appearance of Rogers' first book in this field, is difficult to say. In any event, an examination of actual prac-

tice appears to indicate that Rogers and his critics are not as far apart as their verbal disagreements might lead one to believe. (Fiedler, 1950, 1951.)

Specialists in psychotherapy. Everyone, as we noted previously, has need for help with emotional problems at some time or other in his life, although most of the ordinary problems of everyday life are solved without *professional* help. The student who feels that his math instructor "has it in for him" talks the matter over with some of the other students in the class and decides that there is nothing unique about his problem: they are *all* having difficulty in math. The couple whose first year of married life is marked by bitter quarrels and squabbles learns, after awhile, to adjust to each other's expectations and demands. The child who is upset almost to the point of tears by his first day in a new school finds that he feels much better about it after he has talked things over with his parents.

Not all problems work themselves out so easily, of course. Sometimes the individual who is faced by more anxiety than he can cope with finds that he has no one that he can turn to for help, or he finds that talking it over with parents and friends does not help. At this point he can decide that he might as well "live with the problem," since there is nothing he can do about it, or he can seek expert help.

If he seeks professional help, he will find it available in a number of different kinds of agencies. Most schools and colleges provide help for students who are experiencing difficulties with their academic work, in their choice of a career, or in their relations with people at home or at school. The background and training of the people supplying such assistance will vary from teachers who have an interest in counseling and who have taken a few courses in the field to persons with professional degrees in counseling or clinical psychology. Psychological help with everyday problems of life, both minor and severe, is also available from social workers in family service agencies.

When counselors in schools and family service agencies encounter problems that are beyond the range of their professional competence, they ordinarily refer clients to mental hygiene clinics or to psychotherapists in private practice. Three kinds of professional people work in clinics: psychiatrists, clinical psychologists, and psychiatric social workers. Psychiatrists have a degree in medi-

[1] Reprinted by permission.

Susan Greenburg

The psychiatric nurse plays a vital role in making the hospital a therapeutic environment.

cine, plus three years of advanced and specialized training in the diagnosis and treatment of nervous and mental disorders, two further years of experience, and have passed the examinations of the American Board of Psychiatry and Neurology. Clinical psychologists must have completed work in psychology leading to a graduate degree (preferably a Ph.D., but at least an M.A.) and including training in the general field of psychology, research methods, and psychodiagnostics, in addition to psychotherapy. Training in psychotherapy is provided through graduate seminars and supervised experience in clinical settings. The American Psychological Association helps maintain standards of training in clinical psychology by inspecting and certifying colleges and universities offering programs in clinical psychology. The American Board of Professional Examiners in Psychology functions as an arm of the Associa-

tion and examines individuals who wish to qualify for professional diplomas in clinical psychology. (See pages 15–18.) Psychiatric social workers are persons who have had a two-year course of training in a graduate school of social work leading to a master's degree. Like the psychiatrist and the clinical psychologist, the psychiatric social worker receives supervised training in psychotherapy, as well as in the special problems of the mentally disturbed patient.

In most clinics, people from these three professions work together in teams, interviewing the patient or the members of his family, collecting and analyzing pertinent facts. The team then comes together in a case conference and works out a plan of treatment. If the patient needs institutional care, he may be sent on to a mental hospital; if he is to be treated in the clinic, the team decides on an assignment of responsibility for his treatment.

Staffs of mental hospitals also include the three kinds of specialists named above, as well as psychiatric nurses—nurses with special training in dealing with mental patients. Some mental hospitals also provide specialized training for orderlies and other personnel, like occupational therapists and recreation workers. Today the trend is for all hospital personnel to become actively involved in the therapeutic process, in contrast to an emphasis on custodial care that was prevalent until quite recently.

Summary

In meeting frustrations and conflict, individuals experience a certain amount of threat and often work out inadequate solutions to such situations. Anxiety, depression, and irritability are common emotional reactions that are experienced until the problem is resolved by either adequate or inadequate behavior.

Anxiety is similar to fear, except that it is more diffuse and vague and often involves anticipation of future events. An ambiguous situation, for example, is more likely to arouse anxiety than fear. People are often more concerned about reducing the anxiety than in altering the situation that causes it. Anxiety is less primitive than fear and anger and is likely to be evoked by the frustration of socialized needs. The emotional response that we make to frustrating or conflictful situations is determined by our past learning. Individuals with better educational background and higher socio-economic status are more likely to react with anxiety than with fear and anger. Anxiety is not entirely bad; normal anxiety leads us to plan for the future, have concern for others, and work on the solution to various problems. The healthiest way to deal with anxiety is to attempt to solve the problem directly. Indirect solutions, called behavior mechanisms or defense mechanisms, help reduce the anxiety but leave the original problem unchanged.

Psychologists have classified these defense mechanisms into several categories, but we may divide them into those that serve a self-deceptive function and those that substitute one kind of behavior for another. Self-deceptive mechanisms involve distortions in perception or reasoning. Repression, the unconsciously motivated forgetting of threatening material, is the basic self-deceptive mechanism. Other nonrepressive forgetting occurs with the passage of time and with the deliberate or conscious suppression of an annoying thought. When behavior is inconsistent with our self-picture, we often rationalize; unconsciously, we make up an acceptable reason to explain what we did. A sour-grape rationalization is one in which a person decides that the goal was "really" undesirable, while a sweet-lemon rationalization involves the belief that the failure to attain the goal was all for the best. Excuse-making is a conscious process in which we are trying to explain our behavior to others, but in which self-deception is not involved. The anxiety evoked by a new situation may be reduced somewhat by perceptual rigidity in which we deny the differences and behave as though it is exactly like previous situations. A common example is the adult who reacts to all authority figures as though they were his parents. Projection is a mechanism whereby an individual perceives his own unconscious needs as if they were true of other people rather than himself.

Mechanisms that utilize substitute behavior rely on finding an alternate goal or a more easily solved problem. Fantasy is one of the most common substitute behavior techniques; any goal is obtainable in our daydreams or in the dreams we have while sleeping. A person with a real or imaginary deficiency may compensate for it by developing other areas of strength. Overcompensation refers to the attempt to achieve outstanding success in an area in spite of handicaps. Repressed

thoughts and feelings may gain expression in sublimated form. They are expressed in a disguised way in such socially acceptable forms as competition, art, poetry, etc. When behavior strongly expresses the opposite of unconscious motives, it is called "reaction formation." Our behavior mechanisms are to a large degree preselected for us by the norms of our culture. In varying degrees, we learn to conform to our culture and to identify with other members of the group. Either overconformity to the group or rigid nonconformity represent extreme reactions. Drives can be displaced onto substitute goals; for example, it may not be possible to direct one's hostility toward the real cause of it, but it may be displaced onto a less threatening individual. Displaced hostility in the form of scapegoating is especially apt to occur in an authoritarian setting.

There are other patterns of adjustment that represent more marked degrees of disturbance. When anxiety becomes acute, we may return to forms of behavior that were satisfying in the past but are no longer appropriate; this process is called "regression." Fixation is somewhat similar in that it is characterized by an inability to progress to more mature stages of behavior. Very often, the person who employs a behavior mechanism has the feeling that he is *compelled* to do so, that he has "no choice." One of the effects of alcohol is the reduction of anxiety, and some individuals feel compelled to use alcohol repeatedly to relieve their anxious feelings. Another, somewhat similar, maladjustment is drug addiction. Addiction to barbiturates and opiates leads to a physiological craving for the drugs, but the emotional dependence on other drugs and on alcohol can be equally strong so far as the individual is concerned. Gambling is another unconsciously motivated behavior that can come to dominate the life of its victims. Excessive shyness, a withdrawing sort of adjustment, is especially prevalent during adolescent and young adult years. Obsessions refer to thoughts that occur again and again to plague the individual. A special type of obsession is a strong, unreasonable fear (called a phobia) of some individual, object, or event. Psychosomatic disorders are physical ailments either caused or aggravated by anxiety.

The most serious form of maladjusted behavior is that known as psychosis. Psychoses can be organic in origin, but psychogenic psychoses have no known organic basis and may represent an extension of the less severe behavior mechanisms. The commonest psychotic category is schizophrenia, which most often involves apathy, indifference to reality, and a dissociation of thoughts and ideas from normal emotions. Paranoid reactions involve systematic delusions of grandeur and/or persecution. Affective psychoses consist of extremes of mood or feeling, accompanied by severely disabling disturbances in behavior. Alcohol, disease, industrial chemicals, drugs, injuries, and degeneration accompanying old age may all damage brain tissue and lead to psychotic behavior similar to functional psychoses, but these are termed organic psychoses. Psychotic individuals reveal a markedly disturbed relationship with other people, showing less positive and even less negative feeling toward others. Psychosis has been found to be most prevalent among lower-class individuals who have had little education.

Psychotherapy consists of the utilization of psychological techniques to help people alter their maladjusted behavior in favor of a more adequate adjustment. Therapy may take place with an individual or with small groups of individuals. With children, play therapy is the most common treatment method. Rogers' nondirective therapy is a somewhat controversial technique in which the therapist relies on acceptance and understanding to help the client find his own solutions rather than a more active intervention in the form of advice, diagnosis, or interpretation. Many therapists agree with the permissive, accepting, client-centered aspects of nondirective therapy, but disagree with Rogers' stand on diagnosis and interpretation. Psychotherapy may be given by psychiatrists (M.D.'s who have had specialized training and experience dealing with emotional disorders), clinical psychologists (persons with graduate degrees in psychology whose broad training in research skills and general psychology also includes special emphasis on abnormal behavior, psychodiagnosis, and psychotherapy), and psychiatric social workers (graduates in social work with special training in psychotherapy). Members of the three professions often work together in clinics and mental hospitals.

Questions

1. How do you typically react to severe frustration and conflict?

2. What is anxiety? Can you describe some situations that are more likely to evoke anxiety than fear or anger? How do individiuals learn to respond with anxiety rather than with other emotional feelings?

3. Choose some examples from your own experience to illustrate each type of defense mechanism.

4. Why do individuals develop defense mechanisms?

5. How do "neurotic" patterns of adjustment differ from "everyday" patterns of adjustment?

6. Can you suggest any similarities and any differences among the following behaviors: smoking cigarettes, drinking alcohol, using narcotics, and gambling?

7. Describe compulsive behavior and phobic behavior.

8. Why is psychotic behavior considered to be a less adequate form of adjustment than that represented by defense mechanisms?

9. What is the reason that social class and educational level are related to the type of maladjustment an individual develops?

10. Discuss some of the advantages and disadvantages of group psychotherapy.

11. How does nondirective psychotherapy differ from psychoanalytic therapy?

12. Describe the training of the various professional personnel who are qualified to offer psychotherapy.

Suggestions for further reading

Coleman, J. C., *Abnormal Psychology and Modern Life,* 2nd ed. Chicago: Scott, Foresman, 1956. A good standard textbook in the field of abnormal psychology.

Dollard, J., F. Auld, and A. M. White, *Steps in Psychotherapy.* New York: Macmillan, 1953. Contains transcriptions of several hours of psychotherapy, together with comments by the authors based on theories discussed in Dollard and Miller's book.

Dollard, J. and N. E. Miller, *Personality and Psychotherapy.* New York: McGraw-Hill, 1950. An analysis of the way in which neurotic patterns of behavior are learned, and how they are *unlearned* in psychotherapy.

Hamilton, M., *Psychosomatics*. New York: Wiley, 1955. A brief survey of the various psychosomatic disorders.

Hollingshead, A. B. and F. C. Redlich, *Social Class and Mental Illness*. New York: Wiley, 1958. A research study of sociological factors in the occurrence and treatment of mental illness in New Haven, Conn.

Leighton, A. H., J. A. Clausen, and R. N. Wilson, Editors, *Explorations in Social Psychiatry*. New York: Basic Books, 1957. A collection of papers dealing with mental illness considered from a socio-psychological point of view.

Lindgren, H. C., *Psychology of Personal and Social Adjustment*, 2nd ed. New York: American Book, 1959. Chapter 5 discusses defense and escape mechanisms.

May, R., *The Meaning of Anxiety*. New York: Ronald, 1950. A discussion of the psychological and philosophical aspects of anxiety.

Rogers, C. R., *Client-Centered Therapy*. Boston: Houghton Mifflin, 1951. A presentation of theory and research regarding client-centered or non-directive counseling and therapy.

Shaffer, L. F. and E. J. Shoben, Jr., *The Psychology of Adjustment*, 2nd ed. Boston: Houghton Mifflin, 1956. See Part 2: "Varieties of Adjustive Behavior."

Snyder, W. E., Editor, *Casebook of Non-Directive Counseling*. Boston: Houghton Mifflin, 1947. A presentation of excerpts from five cases together with editorial comments.

SOCIAL FACTORS IN BEHAVIOR

12

The social matrix of individual behavior

The individual and other people. Human behavior has many dimensions and levels, each of which is in itself a fascinating study. There are the abnormal and the normal variations of behavior; there is conscious behavior and behavior that lies beyond immediate awareness; there is group behavior and individual behavior. These are a few of the aspects that concern the behavioral scientist. So far in this book, we have been primarily concerned with aspects of *individual* behavior, as contrasted with *group* behavior. It is quite natural that we should begin our study of psychology with a consideration of individual behavior: the chief object of our concern is ourselves, and each of us is an individual.

But an understanding of human behavior that is based solely on what can be discovered about individuals is bound to be incomplete. In our previous discussions we have shown, in a number of different ways, that individuals are not separate phenomena, isolated in time and space, but are organisms that exist and develop in relationship to other organisms. The vital nature of this relationship was emphasized, for example, in our discussion of how the personality of the infant and child develops and responds to the emotional environment created by the significant individuals who populate the home and the school: parents and siblings, teachers and classmates. Therefore, at the present point in our study of psychology it should be clear that the kind of individuals we are today is to a large degree a product of the interaction we have experienced with other people.

267

It is somewhat disturbing to learn that so much of our behavior is determined by the attitudes and expectations of others.

It is perhaps easier to see how the interaction we experienced during our "formative years" made us what we are today than it is to see how our personalities are shaped and directed by our *current* relations with other people. In other words, we can see how our childhood relations with our father or mother or siblings are to some degree reflected in our basic attitudes, feelings, and values as adults, but it is harder to see how this process continues, how our self-concept continues to change in response to the attitudes and expectations of others. We tend to feel that it is *we* who determine "who we are," and the idea that much of our behavior is to a large degree predetermined by forces outside us and beyond our immediate perception can be somewhat disturbing, if not downright unbelievable.

In Chapter 6 we discussed some of the experiments of Asch (1952), who placed his subjects amid groups of accomplices who had been coached to give incorrect answers at various points in the experiment. The effect of group consensus on the behavior of the subjects was shown by the fact that about three-fourths of them conformed to the group norm and gave incorrect answers at least part of the time. About one-third of the subjects rather consistently went along with the rest of the group, regardless of whether the others were giving wrong answers or right ones.

In view of the fact that the misjudgments they were making were rather obvious ones (remember that a control group made virtually no errors on the same tasks), it would seem that many of us are most impressionable and vulnerable when we are functioning in a group context. Furthermore, when it comes to the apraisal of our talents, abilities, and personal qualities, we do not have access to anything as empirically verifiable as the length of a trio of lines. Hence we are highly dependent on the opinion of others in determining the kind of persons we are and in judging ourselves.

The self and the group

The question of identity. It is quite likely that we would not be so vulnerable and impressionable if it were not for the fact that other people are important to us, if they were not essential to our welfare. The hierarchy of basic needs (Maslow, 1954) that we discussed in previous chapters shows how closely our lives are involved with other people. The needs for love and for esteem very obviously draw us into relationships with others. Even the most basic needs—the needs to maintain physiological processes and a sense of security—are met more efficiently by pooling our resources with others. In a complex and civilized society, the satisfaction of *all* of each individual's basic needs requires collaboration and cooperation. Hence our very existence is inextricably involved with the lives of other people, and we find ourselves involved in group relationships irrespective of any reservations or any desires we may have to the contrary. Montagu (1950) asserts that a "social appetite"—a desire to be with others—is found throughout the entire range of living organisms: in fungi, bacteria, higher plants, and animals. In this respect, man differs from other forms of life only in the complexity of his social motives.

The unwanted self. The price we pay for this association with others is a loss of a great deal of our autonomy—our right to direct and govern ourselves, our right, in other words, to say "who we are." In effect, we give up some of our identity as autonomous individuals in exchange for the identity we receive from the group. For the most part, this surrender of identity takes place beyond the limits of our awareness, although it may be brought sharply and forceably to our attention when the group forces us to take on identities that are despised or are in other respects out of phase with our self-concepts. The young man who is arrested for stealing a car and who is sentenced to prison receives a new and unwanted identity as a "convict," an identity that is a natural consequence of his delinquency. Such an identity symbolizes the rejection of society, something that he probably does not wish to face. The child who is teased by his classmates by reason of his race, religion, or physical handicap likewise receives an un-

From his parents, each child learns the attitudes and behaviors that are typical of his culture, as well as many of the individual attitudes and behaviors that will characterize him for the rest of his life.

Jacques Lowe

wanted identity. Like the car thief, he is rejected and assigned to an "out-group."

Sometimes an identity is assigned without any intention of rejection but can nevertheless have an unsettling effect, if it is not in keeping with the individual's self-concept. Here is an example. An Englishwoman became ill as she was touring the United States and was admitted to a hospital. As she was being admitted, she said to the receptionist, with a note of pride: "I'm British, you know." The receptionist replied, comfortingly: "Don't worry, Honey, you'll get along all right. We get lots of foreigners here." Later, when the Englishwoman tried to understand why she had found the receptionist's remark disturbing, she decided that it was because she had never in her whole life had occasion to think of herself as a "foreigner." A foreigner is, of course, an outsider—a member of an "out-group." An even commoner example of being assigned an identity out of keeping with one's self-concept is that of the individual who is quite content to be an ordinary member of a group and who suddenly finds himself nominated to be its chairman. This can be an embarrassing as well as a flattering experience, because such an action usually denotes a high degree of group acceptance, and to reject the nomination might offend the group.

Such experiences are unsettling partly because we depend on others for confirmation of the concepts we have of ourselves, and when others suggest that they perceive us differently from the way we perceive ourselves, our self-assurance suffers a blow. Furthermore, there is the feeling that *we* would like to take the initiative in determining who we are, and the realization that we are so dependent on others for the main dimensions of our self-concept may come as a shock.

Group affiliations and the self-concept. One of the ways of testing the degree of this dependence is to ask someone to say who he is, to describe himself. He might say, for example:

I am Michael Redfern. I am a junior in art at Southern Methodist University. I am an American, a Texan, and a Democrat.

Another person might say:

I am Lois Marchand. I am 24 years old and single. I am an accountant for the federal government. I am a Catholic, a Republican, and a graduate of Lake College.

Note that when these individuals try to tell us who they are, they enumerate the groups with which they are affiliated. Even Miss Marchand's statement that she is twenty-four years old carries some implications of this sort. Being twenty-four is significant for self-identity in the sense that she expects herself to act and to be treated like other individuals twenty-four years old. Her mentioning this fact implies that she thinks of people twenty-four years old as having qualities and characteristics that distinguish them from individuals at other ages. Similarly, the references to "junior," "American," "Democrat," "accountant," "Catholic," "Republican," etc., imply some identification with the groups in question, some similarity with the other members of the groups. They also imply that there are differences between the individual being described and individuals who are not members of those groups.

How groups change personal characteristics of members. An interesting study of the ways in which groups shape the identities of their members was conducted by Muzafer and Carolyn Sherif (1953) and their associates. Twenty-four preadolescent boys from similar social backgrounds were brought together in a summer camp for an 18-day experiment. During the first stage of the experiment, the boys were allowed to mingle together and form friendships. In the second stage two groups were formed, and any friendships that had been formed were deliberately divided by assigning each member of each pair of friends to a different group. The groups were then permitted to develop identities of their own. During this stage, the experimenters bent every effort to help the groups build up solidarity and cohesiveness—the "we" feeling. The groups had very little contact with each other during the second stage but were brought together in a number of competitive situations during the third stage of the experiment. This stage was initiated by a series of athletic contests, in the course of which one of the groups, called the Bull Dogs, won all the honors, thanks largely to strong leadership and good organization. The experimenters then arranged that the Red Devils, the other group, would pick up their cake and ice cream first at dinner. Since half the desserts gave the appearance of having been damaged in transit, the Red Devils naturally took the portions that were in good shape, leaving the less desirable ones for the Bull Dogs. This incident, as might be expected, touched off a series of intergroup hostilities: fights, raids, name calling, and the like. In the final phase of the experiment, the experimenters tried, with but a minor degree of success, to counteract the divisive effects of the second and third stages of the experiment, to reconstitute the original group, and to restore friendly relations among the boys.

The observations that the Sherifs made during the course of the experiment show rather convincingly how groups may modify the behavior of their members, and how individuals depend on groups for a large measure of their identity. Even though the association with the groups lasted only a few days, a very strong "in-group" feeling was generated that had a marked effect on the feelings and general behavior of the boys. During the initial phase of the experiment, before the boys were divided into two groups, three of the boys, Hall, Miller, and Crane, formed a close alliance and even called themselves "The Three Musketeers." On one occasion a group of the boys on a hike decided to race to the top of a mountain. The race was won by Hall, Miller, and Crane, who "walked to the top abreast by mutual agreement, so that no one of them would arrive before the other two." (p. 245) On another occasion, all the other boys went out to play softball, but Hall, Miller, and Crane who went off to catch salamanders, saying: "When one of us doesn't do something, then none of us do it."

When the entire group of boys was divided into two groups, "The Three Musketeers" were split. Crane and Hall were assigned to the Bull Dogs, and Miller, to the Red Devils. Crane became the leader of the Bull Dogs, and Hall and Miller rose to positions of intermediate leadership in their respective groups. It might be expected, during the fourth and final stage of the experiment, when attempts were made to counteract the divisive effects of the second and third stages, that "The Three Musketeers" would renew the alliance they had made during the first phase. But instead there was a conflict between Hall and Miller, and the two boys got into a fight during the last days of camp. Crane, who had been especially close to Miller during the first phase of the experiment, egged Hall on and said later that if he had been doing the fighting he would have given Miller even more of the drubbing he deserved.

The point is that the association with their respective groups during the second and third phases of the experiment had given each of the three boys a new identity, an identity that was powerful enough to counteract any feeling of mutual attraction that they had felt earlier. In effect, they were no longer free to take up their friendship at the point at which it had been severed.

The experiment turned up other examples of identification. When a joint birthday party for a Red Devil and a Bull Dog was held during the fourth stage of the experiment, each of the boys except one contributed money toward the affair. The single exception was Lambert, a boy who had considerable difficulty in gaining status in the group to which he had been assigned (the Bull Dogs) during the second and third stages of the experiment. Lambert told the counselor that he was not going to chip in for a Red Devil and that, furthermore, he did not approve of the idea of the Red Devils coming to the party.

Masculinity and femininity

Masculine and feminine identification. The changes in identity experienced by the boys in the Sherifs' experiment were dramatic but hardly surprising. After all, preadolescents are relatively uninhibited in the expression of their feelings, and matters pertaining to group loyalty assume great and exciting proportions during this period of development. It is perhaps harder to perceive the less dramatic ways in which identity results from group affiliation. The identity we have as members of our respective sexes is a case in point. This identity is of course based on obvious physical differences, but this is only one aspect. Masculinity is more than "being a male," because we can recognize it in women who have rejected female roles and who have adopted the mannerisms usually associated with men. Common objects assume a "male" or a "female" quality. We look at a picture of rolling desert hills and decide: "That would look good in some man's den." Or we look at a picture of tropical birds painted in blazing color and decide: "Now that one would look good in a boudoir." French pastries and tea are "feminine;" steak and potatoes are "masculine." These are all associations that have grown up around the ideas of masculinity and femininity in our culture.

Sometimes the basis for assigning these characteristics is less obvious even though general agreement may be reached regarding the masculinity and femininity of an object. Look at Figure 12-1. Examine the figures and letters it contains and classify each of them as "masculine" or "feminine," circling "M" or "F" as the case may be. Then take a look at the bottom of page 274 and see how much you are in agreement with other people who have classified the same figures and letters. (Do this before you read further in this paragraph.) There is no logical or common-sense basis for saying that one number or letter is masculine and another feminine, unless it is that we have somehow learned to associate angularity with masculinity and roundedness with femininity. Masculinity in our culture is associated with such characteristics as aggressiveness, nonconformity, strength, dominance, and leadership, and femininity is associated with such characteristics as softness, submissiveness, charm, passivity, and sociability. There is, of course, a possibility that these personality traits may be due to biological factors, such as glandular secretions, or they may be predetermined by such factors as the greater size and strength of the adult male or the childbearing function of the adult female.

Figure 12-1. Which of these figures or letters is "masculine" and which is "feminine"? Indicate your decision by circling "M" or "F."

M F   M F   M F   M F

M F   M F   M F   M F

M F   M F

Masculine and feminine behavior in childhood. Such explanations of the difference in male and female personality patterns leave much to be desired. They do not account, for example, for the rather marked differences in personality between boys and girls during the elementary school years, when boys do not have the advantage of greater size, and when girls are not as yet involved in childbearing. Yet anyone who has worked with children is quite aware of the striking differences in behavior that distinguish boys from girls. Boys display more behavior problems, are likely to be more rebellious and nonconforming, and are more likely to encounter difficulties in reading. Girls, on the other hand, are likely to be more cooperative, and obedient, and less likely to display problem behavior. (Mullen, 1950.)

It seems quite likely, in the absence of any other supportable hypothesis, that boys and girls behave differently because they *learn* to behave differently. Boys learn to be active and rebellious, because adults *expect* them to be active and rebellious. Although we may disapprove of rebellious behavior, we say: "Ah, well, that's just like a boy." We may punish boys for rebellion, but our disapproval—as expressed through ridicule—is even greater if they attempt to take on behavior patterns reserved for girls. We say: "Don't cry, don't be such a sissy! *Boys* don't cry when they're hurt." As boys encounter attitudes of this sort, they gradually and unconsciously take on the behaviors and self-expectations that we associate with masculinity in our culture. With little girls, a similar phenomenon occurs: behavior that is acceptable for girls is rewarded and reinforced, and unacceptable behavior is discouraged.

We can check the validity of this hypothesis by examining the personality development of boys and girls in other cultures. Although boys are inclined to be dominant and girls submissive in most Western cultures, there are wide variations. European boys are, for example, more conforming and submissive than American boys, a fact that has led many a European to speak critically of American childrearing methods. (Olden, 1952.) Girls in England are expected to engage more vigorously and actively in sports. The "outdoor" type of girl who likes nothing better than a cross-country hike in rough weather is much more a British than an American ideal.

Cross-cultural studies of male and female behavior. Cross-cultural studies of the personal-

Certain attitudes toward children are standard in any culture and have a considerable effect on their behavior. Sex-linked attitudes and behavior are particularly crucial in our culture.

ity patterns of male and female adults also show that biological and physiological factors are not as significant as is popularly supposed. In a study of three primitive cultures in New Guinea, Mead (1935) found one culture, the Arapesh, in which both men and women are gentle, unaggressive, and mild; another culture, the Mundugumor, in which both men and women are aggressive, violent, and vengeful; and a third culture, the Tschambuli, in which men are charming, sensitive, and coquettish, and women are dominating, organizing, and aggressive, even taking the lead in initiating sex relations. In other words, both men and women in the Arapesh culture would be considered "feminine" by our standards; both men and women in the Mundugumor would be considered "masculine;" and the men and women in the Tschambuli would be considered to have reversed what we consider to be the normal male and female patterns of personality.

The learning of sex-linked patterns of behavior. The extent to which sex-linked behavior patterns are learned and may be modified is indicated by a study by Carey (1958), who developed a questionnaire designed to measure attitudes toward problem solving and which contained items like this: "I would rather have someone tell me the solution to a difficult problem than have to work it out myself." Men, she found, made higher scores than women on the questionnaire, indicating a more favorable attitude toward problem solving. When her subjects took a problem solving test, she found that men also received higher scores than women. In the next stage of the experiment, both men and women subjects participated in a group discussion designed to develop favorable attitudes toward problem solving, and in the final phase, they were given an additional set of problems to solve. Women made significant

increases in their scores on the problem solving test, but men did not. The implication of this study appears to be that sex-linked differences in problem solving ability can be reduced if women are encouraged to approach problem solving situations with more confidence.

The formation of personality

Uniqueness and similarity. The fact that our behavior is to a large extent predetermined by our association with other people should not cause us to lose sight of the more individual and unique aspects of our personalities. As Kluckhohn and Murray (1953: 53) put it, each of us resembles *all* other individuals, *some* other individuals, and *no* other individuals. We resemble *no* other persons to some degree because each of us is an individual, with a background of experiences that are like those of no other person—completely unique. We are like *all* other persons to the extent that we have the same needs to maintain ourselves as human beings, to grow and develop, to protect ourselves from dangers, to love and be loved, and to maintain social relations with other people. But the *ways* in which we meet these needs are determined partly by the culture, subculture, classes, and groups with which we identify and in which we have membership, as well as by the uniqueness of our experiences. Meeting these needs leads to our developing resemblances to *some* others, a process that consists largely of learning to conform to the expectations of others and of identifying with various groups and classes.

Social learning. The study of personality, as Rotter (1954: 86) explains it, is the study of learned behavior. Some of this learning may be self-initiating and autonomous, but most of it is *social* learning. It is through our interactions with others that we learn modes of behavior, attitudes,

The norms for men at this college call for informal dress and for relaxed, casual comportment.

and expectations that form the major dimensions of our personalities.

The search for meaning. In order for us to cope with the stimuli that are fed into our sensory systems, we have to have some basis for sorting them out, ignoring some and responding to others, and organizing the whole into some kind of interrelationship that has meaning for us and provides some kind of guide to action. Many psychologists have commented on man's preoccupation with a "search for meaning." (Bartlett, 1932; Cantril, 1950; Krech and Crutchfield, 1948; Newcomb, 1950.) By the term "meaning," we have reference to the perceived relationships among events, that is to say, among objects, persons, abstractions, occurrences, etc., particularly the relationship between an event and ourselves. An event has meaning for us according to our perception of the relationship it has to our needs, feelings, and experiences. As we pointed out in Chapter 6, we have a strong drive to achieve environmental stability and organize our perceptual processes in such a way as to attain that goal. The need for meaning has a high priority; since it is essential to safety and security, it would rank next to the need to maintain physiological proc-

esses on Maslow's hierarchy of needs. As Cantril (1950) says: "The search for meaning is essentially a search for greater surety and a wider inclusiveness of our assumptive worlds" (that is, the world based on our assumptions).

Some of our meanings are learned through direct experience (fire can burn you; a razor is sharp and can cut you), but most of them are learned from others (getting an "F" is a disgrace; gangsters are dangerous; cups, but not saucers, are for drinking purposes).

The cultural basis of meaning. The general structure or basic pattern by which we select and organize our percepts is derived from the culture in which we live. In America, when possessions are admired by others, such behavior is interpreted as a friendly gesture calling for an equally friendly response; in some Far Eastern cultures, it is necessary for the owner to give the admired object to the admirer. In America, growing up means, in part, "Make something of yourself," or "achieve status through your own efforts as much as possible"; in most other cultures, growing up is more likely to mean "follow the paths that older and wiser people have laid out for you." In America a panhandler or street beggar is perceived as someone who is too lazy to work and who prefers to live off the earnings of others. In Italy, the attitude is more that of "the poor are always with us," and the beggar is likely to be

Most people mark the figures and letters in Figure 12-1 as follows: masculine, 4, A, T, K, 7; feminine, S, 8, 9, 6, Q.

given a small coin or two. In North Africa and parts of Asia the beggar may not even be perceived.

It is, of course, easy for us to slip into the idea that our meanings are obviously better than those developed by other cultures. Because they are so thoroughly a part of ourselves, they seem "right" and "proper," just as some of the behavior that seems peculiar, awkward, or disgusting to us seems right and proper to people in other cultures.

The learning of meanings. The meanings we learn are the product of shared experiences, which in turn result in shared frames of reference. We learn the meaning of money—what it will buy, how it can be secured, and what our attitudes toward it should be—by participating in a great many interactions and transactions from childhood onward. As children, we went shopping innumerable times with our parents and watched them exchange money for goods. Money was given to us to spend; if we chose to save it, we were especially commended. We sat in on family arguments about money, and learned that financial deficit can be a very threatening and anxiety-provoking experience. People gave us money for small tasks, or neglected to pay us when we felt entitled to it. And so on and on, through childhood and adolescence, the meaning of money was built up in us. Hence today, when a colleague says: "We're always on hamburger during the last week before pay day," we nod in agreement, because we have learned that money is always something that is in short supply. But if another colleague should say, in reply: "Now, we don't have that trouble at all; *we* put 20 per cent of my salary into savings bonds each month," we look at him somewhat askance, for we obviously do not share the same attitudes, feelings, or patterns of behavior, when it comes to money.

Characteristics of groups

One of the strongest forces that holds individuals together in a group is a shared frame of reference. It was the shared frame of reference (which grew out of shared experiences) that evoked the strong loyalties and in-group feelings of the Bull Dogs and Red Devils in the experiment conducted by the Sherifs. Lambert, the Bull Dog member who refused to contribute to the birthday party held jointly for a Bull Dog and a Red Devil, found the frame of reference he had shared with his fellow Bull Dogs such a strong

influence that he could not perceive himself as having anything in common with a Red Devil. He had learned only too well to be "for" all Bull Dogs and "against" all Red Devils.

Norms. In Chapter 6 we described an experiment conducted by Sherif (1936) in which he asked individuals seated in a darkened room to observe the movement of a pinpoint of light. The light was actually stationary, but the subjects all reported some movement. When Sherif asked the subjects to report how far the light had moved, he found, over a series of 100 exposures, that each person tended to settle down to a narrow range of estimates (for example, 3 to 4 inches, or 6 to 7 inches). In other words, each subject developed an *individual norm* as the basis for his estimate.

In another part of the experiment, Sherif brought the same subjects together in groups of two or three and asked them to make estimates of the movement of the light. As the light was presented, each person announced his estimate of its movement and heard the other members of the group make their estimates. Although members of the group had reported rather widely divergent estimates when they had been tested independently, they now tended to reduce the differences and made their estimates more or less in conformity to a norm that was characteristic for each group.

Sherif reversed the procedure for a second group of individuals by testing them first in the group situation for a series of trials and then testing them individually. He found that the norm that characterized their estimates in the group setting persisted after they were no longer in the group. Figure 12-2 presents the records of the subjects in the two kinds of situations.

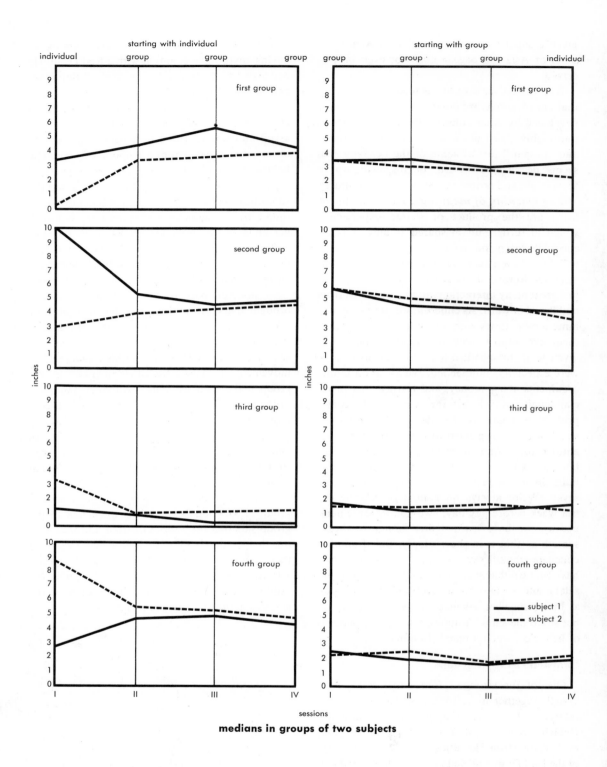

Figure 12-2. The amount of apparent movement in a fixed light reported by individuals in a darkened room under two kinds of conditions: alone and in a group. (Sherif, 1936. Reproduced by permission.)

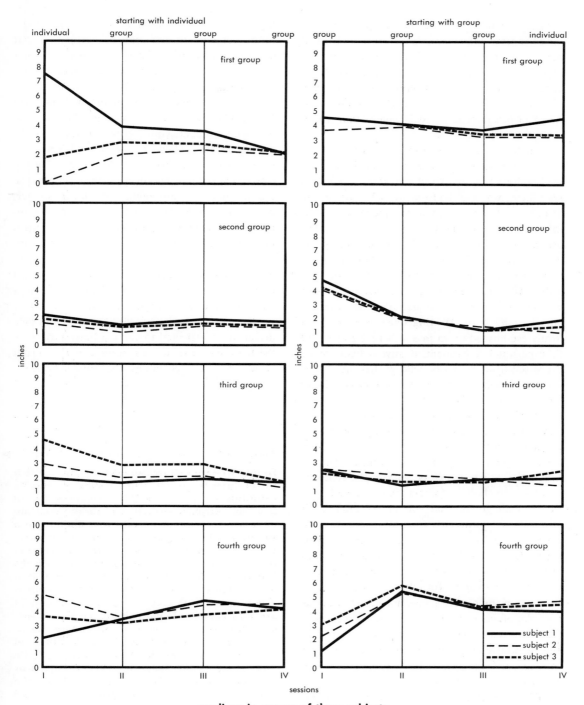

starting with individual

individual   group   group   group

first group

second group

third group

fourth group

starting with group

group   group   group   individual

first group

second group

third group

fourth group

subject 1
subject 2
subject 3

inches

inches

sessions

I   II   III   IV

medians in groups of three subjects

277

Sherif's study shows rather graphically how group norms take ascendancy over individual norms and how they develop as shared frames of reference out of shared experiences. As Newcomb (1950: 267) points out, norms produce "standard" meanings that facilitate communication and other forms of social interaction within a given group.

Sometimes norms result in a uniformity of behavior. In England, for example, people who are waiting for a bus are expected to stand in line and wait their turn, and the foreigner who goes to the head of the line may be told to "queue up." Waiting one's turn is the norm in America as well, but whether one forms a well-defined line or queue depends on the circumstances. In both England and America one is entitled to one's turn as a right, and resentment is expressed toward anyone who tries to enter a bus or get to a ticket window ahead of his turn. Waiting one's turn is not a firmly established norm in Southern Europe, and little personal resentment, if any, is likely to be expressed toward anyone who pushes into a bus ahead of others who have been waiting or elbows his way up to a ticket window.

Sometimes norms produce a variety of behaviors, all of them acceptable. Celebration of the Christmas holidays is a norm in America, but there is a great variety of ways in which it may be conducted. Some people emphasize the religious aspects of the holiday, others are concerned principally with giving, and still others think of it primarily in terms of Christmas decorations, parties, special music, or the exchange of greeting cards. Any of these forms of behavior is considered appropriate to the "spirit of Christmas." Some express their conformity to the norm by engaging in as many Christmas-linked behaviors as possible; others engage in only a few. Even non-Christians feel the pressure of the norm and often find themselves participating to some degree, if only as a defense against having to explain why they are not conforming.

Roles. Sometimes the behavior of individuals who share the same frame of reference varies in accordance with their positions within the group. A clergyman, a preschool child, a third-grade teacher, and a parent may all celebrate Christmas with approximately the same degree of interest and intensity but will do so in ways that are quite different. Some of these differences will be a function of the "positions" of each individual. The

term "position," as used in social psychology, refers not only to one's job or occupation, but also to a wide range of labels or designations that we use for organizing or standardizing certain perceptions about people. We all function as occupants of a number of different positions. Will Friedlander, for example, occupies the positions of college student, youngest son, part-time dishwasher in the college cafeteria, and volunteer typist for the local mental health society. During a given day, he may also occupy, for brief periods, the positions of automobile driver, customer, pedestrian, tennis player, member of a theater audience, and television watcher. For each of these positions there are roles: sets of behaviors that are expected of everyone occupying the position. In his position as a college student, Will is expected to attend class, take examinations, maintain a friendly attitude toward other students, work toward a degree, and so forth. As an automobile driver, he is expected to carry a license, observe the laws that other drivers observe, and to avoid accidents. The expectations that others have for

Figure 12-3. Posture as a Cultural Norm. ▶

In our Western culture, we take for granted that the postures we assume when resting or relaxing constitute the natural and normal ones for all mankind. Airplane cockpits and theatre seats are designed, for example, on the assumption that a sitting position with the base of the trunk about the same level as the knees is the natural and hence most comfortable one for the human body. But as these drawings indicate, what is restful in one culture is strained and awkward in another. The postures in the top row (1, 2, 3, 4, 5, 6, 7) are quite common in our culture, but the arm-on-shoulder postures of some of the western American Indians in the next row (8, 9, 10, 11) seem somewhat odd, while the Nilotic stance (12, 13, 14), found in the Sudan and Venezuela, seems extremely awkward. Most of the peoples in the world sit on the floor or on the ground, rather than on chairs, stools, or other raised areas. Arabs sit with their legs in more-or-less extended positions (15, 16, 17), while Southeast Asians prefer to sit cross-legged (18, 19, 20, 21, 22). Sedentary kneeling positions are favored by Japanese (23, 24, 25), while the deep squat (26, 27, 28, 29), so uncomfortable for persons in Western cultures, is the customary sitting position for at least one fourth of all mankind. (After Hewes, 1957.)

Susan Greenburg

Most people do not enjoy standing around in the cold rain, but under the impact of social forces, behavior can be altered to a marked degree, and what might ordinarily be highly distasteful may be tolerated or even enjoyed. These bandsmen came together in the first place because of a feeling of identity and loyalty to their school, a feeling that has been intensified through watching a football contest. Although the other spectators are on their way to warm rooms and dry clothing, the bandsmen linger to play the final hymn to their alma mater, a ritual that is part of the role of the college bandsmen attending a football game. This behavior is expected of them, and they have come to expect it of themselves.

him in these roles he also has for himself, and these expectations are activated or stimulated whenever he enters a situation calling for the enactment of a specified role. In his role of a customer, for instance, he is expected to wait his turn to be served; he is not expected to go behind the counter in search of merchandise; he is expected to thank the salesclerk for showing merchandise; and so forth. For Will's part, he expects salespeople to play *their* roles as prescribed by the culture.

A role may be a way of communicating, accomplishing certain goals, structuring a relationship, or resolving what might be an awkward situation. Here is an example of how roles help in social interaction.

Dr. Fafnir was attending a psychological convention in a hotel that was also host to a convention of

motion-picture theater owners. He wanted particularly to hear a certain paper that was to be given at 1:30 P.M. As he was going up in the elevator, he reached in his pocket for his program in order to verify the room number in which the paper was to be read. Then he realized that he had left the program at the restaurant. He thought he remembered the room as 408 and decided not to go back after the program. When he entered Room 408, however, there was no one there except a neatly dressed man who had evidently entered just before him. Dr. Fafnir immediately began to wonder whether he had been mistaken in the room number. He started to ask the other man and then hesitated. Was he a psychologist, a theater owner, or a stranger who had just wandered in? It was hard to say, because he was not wearing a badge. Then Dr. Fafnir decided that it was silly to hesitate and asked: "Is this where the session on subliminal perception is to be held?" The stranger said that this was the room, that he was scheduled to read the first paper, but that the session was not due to start for 20 minutes. At this point Dr. Fafnir realized that the starting time for the session was 2:00, instead of 1:30. However, he felt it was a stroke of luck, because it gave him a chance to talk with the author of the paper he had come to hear.

In the incident, Dr. Fafnir hesitated before talking to the stranger because he was not sure whether his communication would be understood. Only a psychologist would be likely to understand a question about subliminal perception. The discovery that the stranger was a psychologist, however, opened up a whole range of shared meanings and frames of reference that facilitated the flow of communication and made the further sharing of meanings possible.

The learning of roles has particular importance for adolescents and young adults. This is a period of life when individuals are faced with the necessity of learning the roles that will be theirs during their adult years. The problem of selecting appropriate occupational roles is a difficult one for some persons. Many young people have difficulties, too, with shyness. The learning of social roles helps to reduce anxiety because they enable one to know what to expect and what to do next. A great deal of the shyness and embarrassment experienced by adolescents and young adults when they are speaking before a group is the result of uncertainty as to what one should say or do next. They wonder: "Will I say something inappropriate? Will I make a ridiculous mistake? Will I be able to say anything at all?" As they become more experienced in speaking before groups, they develop better defined roles and expectations for themselves as speakers. They know what they should say next, they anticipate some of the reactions of their audience, and a great deal of the uncertainty is gone. The situation has more meaning, more structure, more predictability, and therefore arouses less anxiety.

Reference groups. Groups whose norms and standards serve as a model for our behavior are called "reference groups," because we "refer" to them or keep them in mind in ordering our behavior. The Bull Dogs and the Red Devils were reference groups for the boys in the summer-camp experiment of the Sherifs. However, it is not necessary to be an actual member of a group in order to use its norms as a point of reference. It quite commonly happens that an individual has a strong feeling of identity with a group that he admires and perhaps even idolizes, and which would not accept him as a member. The star

players in the National and American baseball leagues serve as reference groups for a great many boys, some of whom go to great lengths in copying the mannerisms of their favorite players. Movie and television personalities form a reference group for many teenagers and even some adults, who consciously or unconsciously pattern their dress, language, and general behavior according to the models this group provides. Jazz musicians also form a reference group for many individuals.

George Bonner, a college junior, has a large collection of jazz records. He and his friends spend several evenings a week in taverns frequented by jazz musicians in order to be close to the individuals whose work they admire. This admiration also takes the form of copying the language and dress of the jazz artists, much to the annoyance of George's parents, who heartily disapprove of his companions, his dress, his manner of speech, and his general attitude toward life. The more his parents disapprove, the more George feels drawn toward jazz. Jazz musicians, he feels, are the only really free and genuinely creative people there are. His deepest regret is that he himself has no musical talent that would enable him to participate more actively in the production of jazz, but for the most part he is content to worship at the shrine of jazz and to copy the behavior of the reference group that he admires so completely but of which he can never become a member.

George's parents often say that they do not see what he gets out of his association with jazz musicians. They point out that he derives nothing of practical value from the relationship and hence should give it up for something that would "do him more good." What they do not see, of course, is that George has a deep sense of identity with jazz musicians—he "identifies" with them. His relationship to jazz and its artists constitute a significant dimension of his self-concept—who he is.

Jazz musicians form a reference group for many individuals.

The social matrix of individual behavior | 281

Homeostasis and self-structure. In its broadest sense, knowing who we are is of immense benefit to the operation of our homeostatic processes. These processes, as we have noted, serve the function of keeping our physiological self in a state of healthy balance. It is obvious, too, that our health would be impaired if we were continually in a state of panic, indecision, or anxiety. Knowing who we are—what roles to play, what is expected of us, whom we resemble—helps us to decide what it is we must do to maintain or improve our situation, defend ourselves, and achieve a measure of self-expression. The world is a less threatening place because we know what to ignore and what to watch out for—we do not have to be continually mobilized for defensive action against every little occurrence, because we are able to figure out what it means in terms of our perceived self.

Hebb (1955) suggests that one of the chief contributions of a culture is that of protecting the individual from stimuli that are potentially disturbing. He points out that it is easy for us to say that we are not afraid of being alone in the dark because our civilization is organized in such a way that we seldom, if ever, are left alone in the dark, completely isolated from others. We can regard the superstitious fear that primitive people have for the dead with amused tolerance largely because our own culture insulates us against contact with the dead. As a protection against such potentially disturbing stimulation, our culture creates for us a social environment consisting of many layers of stimulation patterns, patterns on which we learn to depend, patterns that help stimulate and reinforce the feelings, attitudes, and the general behavior that are not only characteristic of people in our culture but which also have a psychologically homeostatic effect on our behavior, in the sense that they keep us from being upset, emotionally overstimulated or understimulated, and anxious. In Chapter 6 we mentioned the experiments conducted by Hebb and his associates in which individuals were isolated from virtually all contact with the outside world. Even during periods of isolation lasting only two or three days, subjects developed rather marked disorientation, indicating how important the familiar stimulus patterns of our social environment are in helping us maintain psychological integrity and balance.

Group life and "the self." A few pages back, we raised the question of why groups are necessary to us—why it is that we are willing to surrender so much of our freedom and autonomy in exchange for the acceptance and support that others can give us. What we have tried to show is that our association with others, and particularly with groups, helps us to determine something most vital to human existence: our self-concept—who we are. To be sure, we may not like who we are and we may want to be something better than we are, but the fact that we have some self-knowledge is a datum of great psychological value. Not being sure of one's identity can be upsetting and anxiety-arousing. The individual who moves from one social environment to another, a change that often calls for different roles and expectations, commonly experiences an increase in anxiety. For example, the person who leaves civil life and enters military service encounters a new pattern of expectations, norms, and standards. He finds that he is not "the same old Charlie Gladstone," but "Private Gladstone." The change in label symbolizes deep and significant changes in what is expected of him. It is quite common for new recruits to go through an initial period of anxiety—as expressed through some degree of depression, irritability, distractibility, or tension—while they reorient themselves and reorganize their self-concepts and self-expectations in response to the demands of the new environment. Even if an individual resists becoming the kind of person he thinks the military organization wants him to become, his very resistance will bring about changes in his self-structure.

The movement into new social settings is a phenomenon that inevitably accompanies growth in social maturity. The child moves out of the family into the school and the peer group; the adolescent and young adult move from a school setting into employment; the single person moves into marriage and family life. Although each of these moves is a positive one and may be the occasion for celebration (for example, graduation and marriage), it is also the occasion for some anxiety and insecurity, as the individuals concerned are faced with the need to make adjustments and learn new roles. In effect, each individual finds that the old self-concepts and expectations do not quite fit the new situation and that he must shape a new identity to fit the new roles he is learning.

In contrast to older, more tradition-bound societies, the American culture is characterized by a great deal more changing from one social scene to another. Moving from one neighborhood to another and even from one geographical region to another is much more common here than in most countries. There is also much more "vertical mobility"—more changing from one social level to another. Such changes in social level are more possible in an "open society," where freedom of movement from one group or class to another is permitted and even expected. The open society is more characteristic of newer countries, as for example those in the Western Hemisphere and in parts of Africa, whereas the closed society is more characteristic of the older countries of Europe and Asia. To be sure, an open society does stimulate anxiety, because the individual who is moving from one subculture to another is often unsure of his status—that is, he does not know whether he "really belongs" in the group he came from or the group he hopes to get into. He is less sure of "who he is," as it were. Furthermore, there is always the fear that he may fail and, as a consequence, slip back to the level from which he began his ascent. The closed society, on the other hand, fosters feelings of security by assigning each individual to the status and roles he is to retain all his life. The closed society is structurally more stable but less flexible; furthermore, it tends to reduce opportunities for individual self-expression. The "self-made man" is rather more characteristic of the "free society" than the closed society.

Status. The degree of acceptance that is accorded us by others constitutes what is termed "status." It is commonly associated with a given position. In the Bull Dog group, a boy named Crane achieved the highest status. When the experimenters made a sociogram or chart of friendship choices made by members of the group, they found that Crane was chosen by eight out of the eleven members of the group. The boys also expressed their attitude toward him by deferring to him in decision making. Here is an example:

When a whole watermelon was given to the group, the boys thought that the counselor should cut it. He replied that it was their melon. After about three minutes, Thomson . . . offered to do it. The group

shouted "No!" Evans . . . offered to cut it but did not move to do so. Then Wood, at the bottom of the [status] hierarchy, stepped up and took the knife. At this, Hall . . . grabbed the knife and handed it to Crane. Crane cut the melon, saying "You guys who yell the loudest will get yours last." (M. and C. Sherif, 1953: 253. Reprinted by permission.)

Status is a function of the perceived value the individual has for a group. This value may be of a practical nature, such as the value of a leader or an expert technician, but may also consist of any attribute that the group thinks important. A person may have high status because he is a popular entertainer, a good conversationalist, or the possessor of a handsome physique.

In our culture, status tends to be something that is earned or attained through individual efforts. An individual achieves professional status by devoting his time, energy, and intelligence to attending college and graduate school. He achieves managerial status by devoting himself to his job, by taking responsibilities upon himself, by producing more than is required of him, by maintaining pleasant relations with his associates, etc. We may attain leadership status in the groups in which we hold membership by volunteering for committee work, spending a great deal of time on activities of the organization, speaking up during meetings, and the like. Status in older cultures tends to be a matter of assignment—it is more a matter of "who you are," rather than "what you have done."

What we have been saying is, of course, only *relatively* true of our culture. Higher levels of status are more readily attainable by those who work to reach them than is true of older cultures, but it is also true that a great many people achieve high status on the basis of having been born into the "right families." A large-scale survey by Warner and Abegglen (1955) of the social origins of executives in large American business firms indicates the relative importance of "earned success" as contrasted with "inherited success." As Table 12-1 indicates, a disproportionately high number of the executives had fathers who were members of the professional-managerial class. Their families were obviously able to aid them by seeing that they received the kind of educational and social background that a modern business executive needs. It is of course impossible to determine the extent to which families were influential in having their sons appointed to positions of importance, but undoubtedly such support was helpful to many. However, the data contained in Table 12-1 also show that between 1928 and 1952, the proportion of executives who were the sons of laborers, clerks, and salesmen increased. Warner and Abegglen point out, furthermore, that the total number of laborers, farmers, and lower-level white collar workers in the general population decreased 7 per cent between 1900 and 1920 but that the proportion of business leaders from this background increased 5 per cent between 1928 and 1952. During these same periods, the proportion of business and professional workers in the population increased 7 per cent, but the proportion of business leaders from this background decreased 5 per cent. In other words, although an increasing number of men were the sons of business and professional workers, fewer *business leaders* were drawn from this group; and although fewer men were the sons of laborers, white collar workers, and farmers, more leaders were drawn from this group. These data seem to point to the possibility that the barriers between socio-economic classes in America are becoming weaker and that the trend toward an "open society" is continuing.

Social class

Ever since civilized societies began there has probably been a general awareness that the behavior of people differed in accordance with their social class. Persons in lower classes tend to think

Table 12–1 Percentages of American business leaders coming from various backgrounds in 1928 and 1952. (After Warner and Abegglen, 1955.)

Occupation of Father	1928	1952	1952 vs. 1928: Differences in Percentage
Unskilled or semi-skilled laborer	2	5	3
Skilled laborer	9	10	1
Clerk or salesman	5	8	3
Minor executive	7	11	4
Major executive	17	15	−2
Owner, small business	20	18	−2
Owner, large business	14	8	−6
Professional	13	14	1
Farmer	12	9	−3
Other	1	2	1

of themselves as warm-hearted, generous, practical, loyal, industrious, and deserving, and of upper-class persons as degenerate, cold, self-serving, lazy, impractical, and unreliable. For their part, persons in upper classes tend to think of themselves as cultured, discriminating, reserved, enlightened, and intelligent, and to think of lower-class persons as stupid, rude, dirty, boorish, unreliable, and degenerate. All of these pictures are obviously prejudiced, but the tendency of each group has been to behave as though they were in fact true. The question is, of course, whether there are any discernible differences in the general behavior (and hence in the personality patterns) of people at various socio-economic levels of society.

The "Yankee City" study. It is only in recent years that social scientists have conducted much research with respect to social status. They have found that it is possible to identify several different levels or classes of society, not merely on the basis of income or wealth, but on the basis of behavior patterns. Contrary to what is popularly believed, income is not the sole criterion that differentiates the classes. Other bases of classification are equally if not more important. Warner and Lunt (1941), in their study of a New England town, to which they gave the name "Yankee City," found that the income of some of the individuals who had the highest social status was lower than the income of most of the people in the classes immediately below them. And it is not unusual to find people in the lower social classes (for example, bulldozer operators) whose annual income exceeds that of many middle-class individuals (for example, ministers, social workers, and laboratory technicians). Although the social status of garbage collectors is usually rated as rather low, their income for the year 1958 in San Francisco exceeded the nationwide average for college professors, whose social status is fairly high.

In their research, Warner and his associates found that the residents of Yankee City used a number of different criteria in assigning social status to one another. One criterion was the occupation or profession of the individual, status being based on a scale that ranked the unskilled and the chronically unemployed at the bottom and persons in professional and managerial occupations at the top. The *kind* of income also reflected social status. It was ranked on a scale that started with hourly wages at the bottom and then ranged through salaries on weekly, monthly and annual basis, to income received from investments and property at the top. Also important as indices of status were education, family, informal and formal social relationships, and the area of town in which one lived.

Using these criteria, Warner constructed a social status scale consisting of six categories or classes. The proportion of residents of Yankee City that fell into each class is indicated by Figure 12-4. As he studied the individuals identified with each class, Warner found further differences in their behavior. For example, the magazines and newspapers read by upper classes were different from those read by the middle classes, and these, in turn, differed from those read by the lower classes. There were also differences in the churches they attended and in the ways in which they spent their leisure time.

Social-class differences in childrearing practices. A number of other research studies have confirmed the existence of behavioral differences between social classes. One study conducted by Ericson and widely publicized by Davis and Havighurst (1947) reported significant differences in childrearing practices on the part of middle- and lower-class mothers in Chicago. Other research by Maccoby and others (1954) also reports significant differences in childrearing between middle- and lower-class mothers. The results obtained by Ericson and Maccoby are somewhat in disagreement, the former finding that lower-class mothers were permissive and the latter finding them more restrictive and punitive. The differences in their findings may

result from the fact that Ericson's study was done in Chicago in the early 1940's, whereas Maccoby's study was done in Boston, 10 years later. In other words, it is possible that the norms for rearing children differ in these two cities, and it may be that during the intervening period the middle-class norm has shifted in the direction of permissiveness in accordance with the recommendations of people who write for women's magazines.

Social class and authoritarian attitudes. MacKinnon and Centers (1956) found that there was a rather close relationship between social class and attitudes as measured by a scale of authoritarian beliefs, individuals identifying themselves as "upper class" and "middle class" being the least authoritarian and those identifying themselves as "working class" being the most authoritarian. (See Table 12-2.) Inasmuch as authoritarian attitudes are characterized by a lack of permissiveness and a tendency to use reward and punishment as means of control, the findings of MacKinnon and Centers seem consistent with Maccoby's results. Further confirmation may be found in the opinion polls of high school students that have been conducted by Remmers (1950 *et seq.*) over a number of years. When replies were classified according to the income and education of the parents, it was found that democratic, permissive, and politically liberal attitudes tended to be associated with higher levels of income and education. Table 12-3 shows how attitudes and behavior vary according to the education and income of the family.

A poll conducted by *Fortune* (Cantril and Strunk, 1951) in 1946 showed a direct relation-

Figure 12-4. The class structure of Yankee City. (After Warner and Lunt, 1941.)

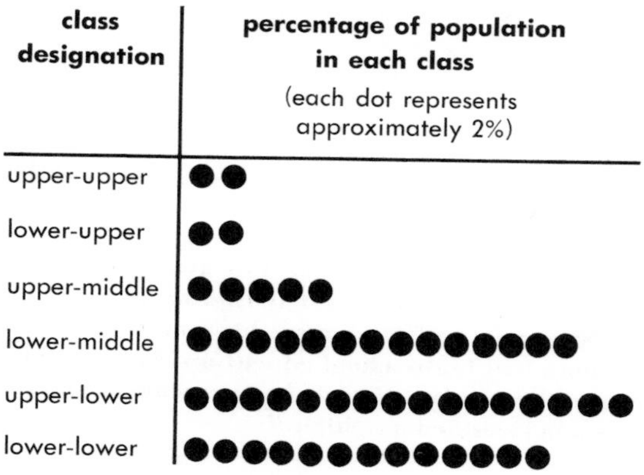

class designation	percentage of population in each class (each dot represents approximately 2%)
upper-upper	●●
lower-upper	●●
upper-middle	●●●●●
lower-middle	●●●●●●●●●●●●
upper-lower	●●●●●●●●●●●●●●●
lower-lower	●●●●●●●●●●●

Table 12–2 Differences in authoritarian attitudes among social classes. (After MacKinnon and Centers, 1956.)

Social Class	Number of Respondents	Per Cent "Authoritarians" *	Per Cent "Equalitarians" †
Upper Class	27	30	70
Middle Class	224	42	58
Working Class	195	62	38
Lower Class	8	50	50

* i.e., giving replies tending in the "authoritarian" direction of an attitude scale.

† i.e., giving replies tending in the "equalitarian" or "democratic" direction of an attitude scale.

Table 12–3 High-school students' replies to various questions classified according to parental education and income. (After Remmers *et al.*, 1950, 1951, 1952, 1953, 1957.)

Questionnaire Item	Mother's Education			Family's Income		
	Grade School	High School	College	Low	Medium	High
Percentage believing that if the United Nations decides that all atomic bombs should be destroyed the United States should agree:	52 *	56 *	58 *	52 *	—	61 *
Percentage believing that the true American way of life is disappearing so fast that force may be necessary to preserve it:	31	22	18	36	23	23
Percentage agreeing that persons committing sex crimes should receive medical treatment rather than punishment:	68	69	74	61	71	69
Percentage agreeing that obedience and proper respect for authority should be the very first requirements of a good citizen:	69	64	60	69	66	59
Percentage agreeing that an insult to our honor should always be punished:	25	23	18	25	23	23
Percentage who say that children whose manners are not good should be spanked:	41	34	29	46	35	34
Percentage who say that obedience and respect for authority are the most important virtues that children can learn:	83	75	66	79	74	69
Percentage saying that children need more discipline:	72	65	63	67	66	66
Percentage saying that some criminals are so bad they shouldn't be permitted to have a lawyer:	19	15	10	20	14	12
Percentage agreeing that a large mass of people are incapable of determining what is and what is not good for them:	56	48	45	51	49	42
Percentage agreeing that there will always be strong groups and weak groups, and that it is best that the strong continue to dominate the weak:	24	19	16	23	19	17
Percentage agreeing that it is a mistake to trust any nation till we are completely sure of them:	63	55	52	66	57	52
Percentage who feel that all juvenile delinquents should be sent to reform schools:	19	12	16	21	15	13
Percentage feeling that their parents should demand that they come home one hour after the ending of an important prom:	27	19	18	33	21	18
Percentage watching television five hours or more a day:	25	21	19	22	23	20
Percentage watching opera or symphonic concerts on television:	15	20	31	14	19	21
Percentage going to the movies more than once a week:	16	13	11	18	13	14

* Figures consist of percentages of students in each category who gave the reply indicated. Read the first line as follows: The reply that the United States should agree to the destruction of all atomic bombs, if the United Nations so decides, was given by 52 per cent of students whose mothers had grade-school education, 56 per cent of those whose mothers had high-school education, 58 per cent of those whose mothers had college education, 52 per cent of those whose family income was classified as "low," and 61 per cent of those whose family income was classified as "high."

ship between the education of respondents and their admiration of World War II military leaders. Persons with grade-school education were much more likely to prefer authoritarian leaders like Generals MacArthur and Patton, whereas college-educated persons were much more likely to prefer Generals Eisenhower and Marshall, leaders cast in a more democratic mold. (See Table 12-4.)

Middle-class culture in America. The dominant class in the American culture is the middle class. Most people are inclined to identify themselves with this class, even those who presumably would be classed otherwise by social scientists. (Kahl and Davis: 1955.) According to Loeb (1953), the middle class is a kind of a "core group" in the American culture, with persons in lower classes working toward achieving the values and behaviors of this "core group," and upper-class individuals modifying the culture of the "core group." Loeb also states that the behavior and values of persons in the highest and the lowest classes tends to vary from one community to another throughout the country, but that the behavior and values of the middle-class group tends to be rather consistent. The standards and values that are consistent with middle-class culture are propagated, disseminated, and, to a certain extent, actually taught by the mass media—radio, television, cinema, newspapers, and magazines—as well as by the schools and churches.

Middle-class culture is, in a manner of speaking, our "official culture." The middle-class culture, according to Loeb, is centered around the home. It emphasizes conformity to the official rules for proper behavior, an avoidance of open aggressiveness, little or no display of emotionality (except on ritualized occasions, such as birth, marriage, and death); cleanliness and tidiness; and the ownership of economic goods, land, and, naturally, one's own home. As one moves from the middle class into the upper-middle class, one learns to break some of the rules laid down in the core culture. Loeb uses attitudes toward garlic as an example. In the core culture, garlic tends to be avoided, because it is thought to be characteristic of certain lower-class ethnic groups. But people in the higher status levels find that garlic can be an interesting and satisfying ingredient in cooking. Hence people moving from the lower classes into the core culture learn to give up spicier diets for blander ones, and those who move from the core culture into the upper classes learn to enjoy a spicier diet.

One of the dominant patterns of behavior in the core culture is that of inhibiting or at least postponing the gratification of impulses. According to Loeb, one of the tasks of the upper-middle-class individual is to find acceptable ways to gratify his impulses, and thus it is that he learns how to break some of the rules laid down in the core culture.

The existence of different patterns or expectations with respect to feelings and attitudes makes the transition from one class level to another a difficult one. The lower-class youth who aspires to middle-class status finds his parents' attitudes and general way of life unacceptable. As he moves into a middle-class circle, he is likely to grow away from his family. This is likely to create conflict aggravated by bitterness and guilt, for although he is drawn to his family by feelings of loyalty, he is at the same time repelled by their lower-class mannerisms. For their part, his family accuses him of being ungrateful and snobbish. To a somewhat lesser degree a similar situation obtains for young people who are moving from a middle-class to an upper-middle-class environment. Although middle-class families are more tolerant of social mobility and are more aware of the kind of price to be paid, it is not unusual for tensions and anxieties to be aggravated. As one moves from one status level into another, one encounters new expectations, new attitudes, and new ways of playing familiar roles. One's self-concept undergoes some change, and this change is accompanied by changes in values. Changes of this sort quite understandably produce feelings of

Table 12–4 Military officers most admired in January, 1946, according to a nationwide poll by *Fortune.*

Officer	Percentage of Respondents "Admiring Most," Classified According to Educational Background		
	Grade School	High School	College
Douglas MacArthur	44.5	36.4	24.1
Dwight Eisenhower	28.0	41.0	51.5
George Patton	6.4	5.7	4.9
George Marshall	1.4	2.2	5.7
Others, no answer, and wrong answer	19.7	14.7	13.8

insecurity; there are bound to be times when the individual is not sure what behavior is appropriate to a given situation or when he displays behavior that is inappropriate to the new status level. And when parents see their adult sons and daughters expressing attitudes and behaving in ways that are in direct contrast to what they have always considered to be the "right" ways to think and act, it is quite understandable why they should be critical.

The attitudes and values that we get from the culture and social class with which we identify are a part of us. They become integrated into the expectations we develop for ourselves and others, and they guide and direct our behavior in countless ways. For the most part, we are unaware of the extent to which our everyday behavior is affected by the norms and patterns that are prescribed for us by culture and group; hence it is easy for us to fall into the error of believing, as "common sense" leads us to believe, that each of us is completely free to decide what he shall or shall not do.

Summary

Human beings are not isolated organisms; rather, most of our behavior takes place in relationship to other human beings. Our self-concept is not only the outcome of past interpersonal relationships, but it is also continually changing in response to the attitudes and expectations of others.

In a complex society the satisfaction of all of an individual's basic needs requires the collaboration and cooperation of others. We must pay for this association with a loss of some of our autonomy. When others give us a negative evaluation, our self-esteem suffers both because of the evaluation and because of the realization of our dependency on others. When an individual tries to identify himself, he tends to do so in terms of group affiliations. An experiment with twenty-four preadolescent boys at a summer camp gave striking evidence of the way in which group membership can influence personal characteristics.

One type of group identification that influences each of us is our identity as a member of one or the other sex. It seems likely that sex differences in behavior patterns are for the most part *learned* and only to a minor degree biologically determined. Parents' attitudes toward children differ according to the sex of the child. These differences are expressed in the way in which parents respond to the child's behavior. The learned nature of masculinity and feminity becomes apparent when we study other cultures and find wide divergencies from our concept of the "natural" behavior of the two sexes.

Although each individual's personality is to some extent unique, he also shares many qualities with other members of his culture and a few qualities with all of mankind. Most of our learning takes place in a social context. Man seems to be preoccupied with a search for meaning among the stimuli that impinge on his receptors. Some meanings are learned by direct experience, but most are learned from others in one's culture. It is easy for us to decide that the meanings supplied by our own culture are the right and proper ones. The particular meanings that we learn are also learned by many others in our culture and constitute frames of reference that we share with them.

One of the strongest forces holding group members together is a shared frame of reference. Group norms tend to have ascendancy over individual norms; they produce standard meanings and shared frames of reference that facilitate group interaction. Norms sometimes produce a uniformity of behavior, but at other times a variety of behaviors are permissible within certain limits. An individual's position within a group determines the roles he is to play. Roles can be very helpful in facilitating social interaction by reducing ambiguities. Adolescents and young adults face special problems in role selection and in learning to play the roles of adult life. A reference group is one whose norms and standards serve as a model for our behavior, even if we are not an actual member of that group. Our homeostatic processes function more easily when we know what roles to play, what is expected of us, who we are. Our culture functions to protect us against the disruption caused by potentially disturbing stimuli.

When a person changes his social environment, anxiety is commonly experienced because new roles and expectations are involved. America is characterized by a continually changing social environment. We change our neighborhood, geographical location, and even social class. Ours is an open society in which vertical mobility in terms of social standing is characteristic. Our status is determined by the degree of acceptance that is accorded to us by others. In our culture, status tends to be earned by individual effort, whereas status in older cultures is more likely to be assigned. Of course, even in our more open society, the chances of success are partially dependent on the socio-economic status of one's parents.

The behavior of individuals is somewhat influenced by their social-class membership. Income is not the main determinant of class standing; determinants that are more significant include occupation, kind of income, education, family, social relationships, and location of one's home. People in different classes tend to have different patterns of behavior. For example, lower-class and middle-class mothers tend to differ in their child-rearing practices, and upper- and middle-class individuals tend to be less authoritarian than those in the working class. The middle class is dominant in America, and its attitudes and values are disseminated by the schools, churches, and the mass media. The existence of different patterns or expectations with respect to feelings and attitudes makes the transition from one class level to another difficult. We are not usually aware of the behavior norms prescribed for us by culture and group and consequently tend to believe that we are freer than we actually are in deciding what we shall or shall not do.

Questions

1. In what ways are your values, attitudes, and decisions determined or influenced by group pressure?
2. Who are you? What sort of identity do you have? What effect does membership in various groups have on your identity?
3. What conclusions and implications can you draw from the Sherif and Sherif experiment with the Bull Dogs and Red Devils?
4. How do individuals learn their masculine and feminine roles in our culture? Could you teach a female child to be masculine and a male child to be feminine? If you were successful, what sort of problems would the children encounter?
5. In what way do you share some of your personality characteristics with all other individuals, some other individuals, and no other individuals?

6. Is your reaction to a television program any different when you are alone and when you are with others? If so, how is it different and why?
7. How many roles did you play during the past week? List them and describe their differences.
8. Describe some reference groups and how they influence the behavior of individuals.
9. What are some of the disturbing aspects of changing from the role of high school senior to that of college freshman?
10. In what ways is status achieved in elementary school, in high school, in college, and in adult life? Are there differences for men and women?
11. How is social class determined? In what way are social-class differences related to attitudes, personality factors, and childrearing practices?

Suggestions for further reading

Bendix, R. and S. M. Lipset, Editors, *Class, Status, and Power*. Glencoe, Ill.: Free Press, 1953. A book of readings concerned with sociological and psychological factors in social stratification.

Bossard, J. H. S., *The Sociology of Child Development,* rev. ed. New York: Harper, 1954. Stimulating and readable. See the chapters dealing with class and status differentials.

Hollingshead, A. B., *Elmtown's Youth*. New York: Wiley, 1949. A study of the social-class structure as it affected the lives of teenagers in a small Midwestern town.

Kluckhohn, C., *Mirror for Man*. New York: McGraw-Hill, 1949. How culture affects human behavior. Written by an anthropologist for lay readers.

Kluckhohn, C., H. A. Murray, and D. M. Schneider, Editors, *Personality in Nature, Society, and Culture,* rev. ed. New York: Knopf, 1953. A book of readings dealing with the social processes that contribute to the development of personality.

Maccoby, E. E., T. M. Newcomb, and E. L. Hartley, Editors, *Readings in Social Psychology*. New York: Holt, 1958. See sections on interpersonal influence, socialization of the child, social stratification, and role and role conflict.

Mead, M., *Sex and Temperament in Three Primitive Societies*. New York: Morrow, 1935. How the norms of a culture may alter behavior that other cultures consider to be typical of one sex or the other. Also published in pocket edition as a Mentor Book by the New American Library of World Literature, New York.

Newcomb, T. M., *Social Psychology*. New York: Dryden, 1950. See sections on social norms and roles, individual personality, and group membership.

Sargent, S. S. and R. C. Williamson, *Social Psychology: An Introduction to the Study of Human Relations,* 2nd ed. New York: Ronald, 1958. The first half of the book deals with the processes of socialization.

Sherif, M. and C., *Groups in Harmony and Tension*. New York: Harper, 1953. The second part of the book reports the research with the Red Devils and Bull Dogs discussed in this chapter.

13

Communication

The essential human process. Communication is at the same time one of the most vexatious and one of the most marvelous inventions of man. It is the very life blood of human interaction: it is the means whereby interaction takes place. We may feel that we communicate very badly—fumble for words, have trouble in expressing what we really mean—yet we are unable to conduct our daily affairs and maintain our existence as members of society without some attempt at communication. Our ability to convey meaning through the use of symbols is one of the qualities that distinguishes us from the other animals. Whereas animals can communicate some of the simpler facts of the immediate present—danger, hostility, sexual desire, hunger, and the like—they cannot communicate the events of the past or the probabilities of the future. Some of the higher animals, cats, rats, monkeys, etc., can learn to respond to a narrow range of symbols. Some animals can even learn to manipulate symbols. In Chapter 5, we mentioned the research of Wolfe (1936) who was able to teach chimpanzees to work for poker chips, save them, and use them in a vending machine to obtain water and food. But the ability of animals to abstract and to organize their experience symbolically is severely limited.

Man's ability to communicate and manipulate the symbols of communication has enabled him to develop complex social structures and relationships, modify his environment, and develop self-awareness. Through communication we learn the expectations that others have for us. Since our concept of ourselves is to a very large extent gov-

Here are two kinds of behavior that sometimes go unrecognized as forms of communication: voting, a process whereby the electorate communicates its approval or disapproval of candidates and policies;

and the gesture, which may communicate meaning more effectively than the spoken word.

erned by these expectations, communication makes it possible for us to find out who we are and thus develop our self-concepts. Communication thus seems to be *the essential human process* —the process that enables us to become human.

In our everyday affairs, we tend to overlook the vital part that communication plays in our lives, partly because we take it for granted and partly because we are inclined to be preoccupied with the aspect that appears to give us the most difficulty—the problem of getting our ideas, feelings, and desires across to other people. Most of us would like to succeed in this better than we do. Hence we invest much time and energy in learning how to express ourselves more clearly in speaking and writing. Communication, as it ordi-

narily appears to us, is a conscious process whereby we transmit information to others by such oral or written methods as face-to-face conversation, letter, telephone, telegraph, or messenger.

Communication as a social process. Communication viewed by psychologists and other social scientists, however, is a far more extensive process. It includes not only the techniques of self-expression, but every other method or dimension of transmitting, receiving, exchanging, or perceiving meaning. It includes all aspects of "communication behavior," whether active or passive, verbal or nonverbal, with or without awareness. It includes personal, face-to-face communication, as well as mass communication as exemplified by

Communication permits individuals to develop shared meanings and frames of reference that serve to bind them together in a group relationship and enable them to distinguish between their group and other groups. A political campaign offers many opportunities to observe this dual phenomenon.

Susan Greenburg

television, cinema, newspapers, and magazines.

Communication welds the links that hold the human group and each of its various divisions and subdivisions together. The kind of relationships we develop with others depends on our ability to communicate with them and their ability to communicate with us. Our ability to identify ourselves as members of a group depends on the communicative relationship we have with the group. Our status as members depends on our ability to find out what is expected of us, as well as on our ability to inform others what we are doing to maintain our membership in the group. Here is an example:

Scott Todd is a member of a group or class of people called Republicans. He keeps informed of what other Republicans are doing by reading political articles in current periodicals, talking with other Republicans, attending occasional meetings of party members, and listening to Republican speeches on television and radio. The Republican party is for him both a reference group and a membership group. He communicates his sense of membership by making an occasional financial contribution, by registering as a Republican voter, and, when he is making a statement on a political issue to persons of unknown political affiliation, by saying: "Of course, as a Republican, I'm inclined to think . . ." Because of such behavior, other people are able to identify him as a Republican, and Mr. Todd is able to identify himself and maintain his concept of himself as a Republican. Seen in a framework of party affiliation, his behavior makes sense—that is, communicates meaning—both to himself and to others.

Communication plays a double role for Republicans, as well as other groups, in the sense that it enables them to develop shared meanings and frames of reference that draw them together in common cause and give them a common base of identity. At the same time, it enables them to differentiate themselves from the members of other parties. "He talks like a Republican," we say, or "He sounds like a Democrat to me." Communication can thus be used to underscore similarities or differences. "You say you're a Democrat, but some of the things you say sound more like a Republican to me." (In other words, "You're not *my* idea of a Democrat.")

Communication and shared frames of reference. In the preceding chapter we discussed shared frames of reference as the basis for developing norms. Communication is also a vital part of the development of norms and is dependent for its effectiveness on shared frames of reference. Two students are engaged in an argument about democracy. Suddenly one of them stops and says: "I don't think we are talking about the same thing. Before we go any further we better have a definition of 'democracy.' You tell me what 'democracy' means to you, and I'll tell you what it means to me." What he is saying, in effect, is: "You and I are not able to communicate because we are not using a common frame of reference."

The way in which communication and the development of norms are based on shared frames of reference is illustrated by the attitudes toward garlic we discussed in the previous chapter. (Loeb, 1953.) A person of lower-middle-class (LM) status, dining in the home of an upper-middle-class (UM) individual, might be puzzled by the use of garlic in the cooking. In his frame of reference, garlic is associated with lower-class families—first- and second-generation Americans, say, from Poland, Italy, or Greece. He cannot understand why an UM family would use a lower-class ingredient like garlic in cooking. The UM family, however, favors a spicier diet than that found in most LM homes. If the LM person continues to associate with UM individuals (which means that he is probably rising in social status), he learns that the spicy foods of Central and Southern Europe have a favored position in the diets of UM individuals, and he modifies his own preferences accordingly. This learning takes place as the result of participating in or listening in on conversations dealing with the preparation of food or the kind of food to be found in restaurants favored by UM individuals. Or the LM individual may read about the use of garlic in the UM magazines he has begun to read as a result of his association with UM persons. Such communication informs him of the UM norm regarding the use of garlic and enables him to develop a frame of reference which he shares with UM individuals, and, as his frame of reference toward garlic changes, he is able to accept a pro-garlic norm and to dissociate himself from the norm that rejects its use.

The attitude toward the use of garlic in cooking is in itself an unimportant segment of behavior. It is, however, one of a large number of ways whereby a group expresses its "life style." European ways have a much stronger attraction for the UM individual in America than for LM persons. However, it is not enough to sense this affinity: it must be expressed in some way. Hence the UM develops a style of life that has a distinct European flavor. Not only does he seek out and serve European dishes at his table, he buys European cars, drinks wine with his meals, expresses a preference for European movies, and wears articles of clothing that are imported or that have a European cut.

Levels of communication

Communication among nations. The UM person who displays this kind of behavior is generally not aware that he thereby communicates something of his self-concept and group identity. Such communication is largely unconscious—beyond the limits of awareness. To be sure, people who express a preference for foreign motion pictures are aware of their preferences, but they are less likely to be aware that such a preference communicates something. The meaning communicated by such behavior is implicit rather than explicit.

Communication that takes place among nations also takes place on various levels of awareness. Let us say that our Department of State sends the government of a certain Asiatic country a rather disapproving note, stating that the latter has not been living up to certain treaty obligations. This is an example of conscious, verbal, and highly formal communication. Such modes of communication have at least two levels of meaning: one that may be deduced from the wording of the note, and another "hidden meaning" that is prescribed by diplomatic convention or that may actually be communicated by informal exchanges between the representatives of the governments. The second meaning of the note may be something like this: "This is official notice that you are violating our agreement, but we understand why you are doing it and will do nothing further to stop you." Or it may mean: "This is to put you on warning that you can expect no more favors from us till you take steps to correct the situation." Since the second kind of meaning is tacit, rather than explicit and obvious, the receivers of the note are left in a position to respond to it or ignore it, whichever appears more appropriate.

About the same time, an association of farmers in the Midwest sends an invitation to the farmers of the same Asiatic country, inviting them for a visit and stating that they would like to promote good will and understanding between the two countries by talking over common problems in a friendly, informal atmosphere. This communication is somewhat less formal than the diplomatic note, but like the note, it too communicates on two levels, one explicit and obvious, and the other subtle and less obvious. In this instance, the meanings on the second level may not be recognized by the individuals initiating the communication. They may be aware only of the desire to make a gesture of good will. The Asians, however, may be more concerned with the more obscure motives lying behind the invitation. They may wonder, for instance: "Do these Americans really want to exchange ideas with us, treating us as equals, or do they really want to show us how much better their farming methods are than ours?" It is of course possible that the invitation was prompted by *both* motives. Very likely the members of the association are more aware of the need to be friendly than of the need to impress others, because the first meaning is more consistent with their self-concept than the second. The co-existence of two such different motives is not at all unusual, for it is very common for both a selfish and an altruistic need to be satisfied with a single behavioral act.

In analyzing communication, it is also important to keep the "perceptual set" of the receiver of the communication in mind. (See Chapter 6 for a discussion of "perceptual set.") If the perceptual set of the Asians is favorable, they may very likely avoid making a negative interpretation of the invitation, but if it is hostile, they will ignore any of the altruistic motives underlying the invitation and will claim that Americans want

visitors only in order to belittle them. If the Asians do choose the latter course of action, the members of the farm association may suffer a bad case of injured feelings, being unaware of any needs to show off and not expecting that their invitation could be interpreted in this way. Such an interpretation would be inconsistent with their self-concept: they see themselves as friendly and helpful and are unaware of any need to show off their accomplishments to an admiring audience.

Let us say that while the Asians are deciding how they will respond to these two communications, the formal note and the invitation from the Midwestern farmers, a hurricane followed by a flood devastates one of the provinces of the country. Within a few days, large quantities of food, clothing, and medical supplies are collected in the United States and are sent on their way by boat and plane. Since such behavior has symbolic value in addition to the more obvious economic implications, it can be considered as a form of nonverbal communication.

The three examples we have given demonstrate three kinds of communication, each of which has a primary level that is explicit and obvious and may be superficial, as well as a secondary level that is implicit, less obvious, and largely unconscious. The diplomatic note represents a highly formalized and ritualized verbal communication at the highest level of abstraction. This note presumably states our "official policy" and may serve as an indirect way of communicating certain "unofficial policies." The behavior of the farm association may be somewhat at variance with both the official and unofficial policies of the State Department and may communicate something quite different. The donation of needed supplies may also communicate feelings that vary from those expressed by the government. The members of the Department of State may say: "The invitation of the farmers association and the donation of supplies have nothing to do with our policy of disapproval." This may of course be quite a proper interpretation, but it is also very likely that the government and people of the Asian country will say: "The Americans do not mean what they say in this rather stiff diplomatic note. The invitation of the farm association and the donation of these supplies sound as though Americans are much more friendly than their State Department makes them out to be." And this, too, may be a proper interpretation.

Although the problem of communication between individuals from different cultures can be resolved to some degree by the learning of languages, there are many concepts in each culture that are not easily communicated and that ofttimes defy translation.

Inconsistencies in interpersonal behavior. The situation we have described is somewhat analogous to the behavior of individuals who say one thing and do another.

The Ames family drove a small foreign car and praised its virtues to the skies. Nothing could excel it, they said, in maneuverability, convenience, and economy. But after they had owned it for nine months, they traded it in on a middle-priced American car. They explained this unexpected move by saying that a dealer had made them a trade-in offer that they couldn't afford to turn down.

To hear Mr. Sardi talk, you would think he trusted no one. He is always making wry and bitter comments on the inability of other people to fulfill their responsibilities and do the right thing. Yet he is exceedingly generous in giving his time and money to any person who needs help and to any project that appears to have merit. Such behavior communicates an accepting attitude toward others that is at complete variance with his verbalizations.

As we try to interpret the verbal and nonverbal behavior of people like the Ames family and Mr. Sardi, we are tempted to dismiss them impatiently by saying: "You can't trust people like that: they obviously don't mean what they say." However, such an attitude overlooks the point that their statements may be quite sincere. Furthermore, we can understand them better as individuals if we recognize that the differences between their verbal and their nonverbal behavior are due to their attempts to respond to motives that are somewhat at variance with one another. The important point is to remember that in attempting to understand the behavior of others, both individuals and groups, we should not base our interpretation on only one level of communication.

Levels of communication in different cultures. Very often the implicit meaning of a communication is recognized as more significant than the explicit meaning. The statement: "You must come over and see us some time" sounds like an invitation, but in our culture it is not. What such a statement actually means depends on the situation in which it occurs, but it usually is interpreted as one of those friendly noises like "How are you?" and "Nice weather we are having," that people make toward one another in a social context. If people in our culture *really* want to be visited they name a specific time when they would like to be visited—"How about next Sunday evening?" or "Are you free Saturday?" or the like.

Such differences between explicit and implicit meanings are seldom troublesome in the cultural context in which they originate, where everyone understands that the apparently obvious meaning is not the real one. But embarrassing problems can occur when individuals come from different cultural backgrounds. According to Shouby (1951) Arabs do not expect that their statements will be taken literally and are inclined to speak forcefully, overstressing as a matter of course. If an Arab were not to exaggerate, other Arabs would think that he meant the opposite. Non-Arabs are confused by this tendency to exaggerate, just as Arabs often fail to realize that the matter-of-fact way of speaking used by most Northern Europeans can be taken more or less at face value. Many Arabs will therefore interpret a simple "No" as indirectly expressed consent and encouragement.

Shouby describes the predicament of an English girl who complained that her Arab friend was bothering her with his attentions and protestations of love, refusing to take "No" for an answer, even though she had made it perfectly clear that she had absolutely no interest in him. For his part, the Arab protested that the English girl was encouraging him to make love to her, although he had shown only a modest degree of interest and admiration. According to their own concepts of their behavior, each was being honest and above-board, yet each was unaware of the differences between Arab overassertion and exaggeration and British tact and understatement.

Interpersonal communication

Communication and social learning. Learning to be a functioning member of one's society is an enormously complex and intricate process. It is partly because this process is so complex and involved that it takes so long to grow up in civilized cultures. As we pointed out in Chapter 3, full participation in the adult culture in civilized societies is ordinarily withheld until the early or middle twenties, whereas in many primitive cultures, children are ready to assume adult roles during the middle teen years. The adult in a civilized society is ordinarily expected to play a wide variety of complex roles. Not only must the adolescent learn these roles but he must also learn which roles are appropriate for which situations. Communication is involved in learning the roles, and the roles themselves communicate a sense of adult status and an acceptance of the norms prescribed by society.

Communication is also involved in the changes that take place in motivation with each succeeding stage of development. Using Maslow's (1954) hierarchy of needs as our frame of reference,[1] we can see that the needs at the lowest level (physiological processes and safety) can be met with a maximum of physical action and a minimum of communication. The higher-level needs (self-esteem, creativity) call for much more communication, and the order of their appearance roughly parallels the development of communication skills. With each succeeding level of maturity, the characteristics of our goals tend to shift in the direction of abstraction. The goals of childhood are more likely to involve the physical processes: being cuddled, engaging in large-muscle activity, eating sweets, being swung in Father's arms, and the like. As we become mature, we learn to extend the pleasures gained from these satisfactions by discussion, comparison, and reminiscence, and as we become less concerned with our physical needs, our communication becomes directed toward goals that grow out

[1] See Chapter 2, pages 45–50.

Suzanne Szasz

Imitation plays an important part in the learning of communication techniques.

of our interaction with others. The activities of adults are likely to be directed toward such intangible goals as economic success, appreciation of one's efforts, making a favorable impression on others, community service, and the like. Working toward these goals involves a great deal of communication; success or failure in meeting some of these goals consists entirely of the kind of communication that is directed toward one.

Empathic communication. A few pages back we pointed out that communication takes place on at least two levels—one that is explicit and obvious and another that is implicit, subtle, and sometimes unconscious. A great deal of the communication that is directed by adults toward the problem of helping young people learn adult roles is heavily loaded with meaning at the implicit level. Indeed the more emotionally laden meanings at the implicit level may be more significant than the meaning at the explicit level. Most teenagers eventually learn that "Don't you ever use language like that again!" means "Don't use such language where I can hear it." Or, when the teenager hears his father use the forbidden words with vigorous effect, he begins to understand that what is meant is "Don't use language like that till you are an adult," or perhaps even "When you use language that is only supposed to be used by adult men, I become aware of the fact that you are growing up and I don't want to be reminded of that."

The ability to look beyond what people are saying and respond to what they are really trying to communicate is a task that calls for empathy. Empathy, as we described it in Chapter 3, is the ability to be aware of the feelings and attitudes of other people. It is an especially important ability when it comes to social learning. Success in social learning depends on the ability to sense the expectations of other people. Very often these expectations are expressed through meanings that people cannot or will not put into words, but instead prefer to communicate indirectly—often through what is *not* said or done.

As we proceed through the various stages of maturity, our ability to benefit from empathic communication tends to develop along with our social maturation. Normally, the more important an individual is to our personal welfare, the better able we are to communicate with him empathically. We become "experts," so to speak, in predicting what his reaction will be to this or that situation, or this or that statement, and we learn to order our behavior accordingly.

Our awareness of the feelings and attitudes of others probably operates most acutely with respect to our peers, the people we perceive as most similar to us. It is with these people that we share the greater number of frames of reference. The better able we are to put ourselves in the place of another person, the better able we are to empathize with him. Hence, if we should see an instructor hand a paper to a friend of ours and say a few words that bring a smile to his face, we know that our friend is being complimented and is responding by showing pleasure. We do not even have to hear what is being said, for we know, empathically, what is going on. Since we, too, are students, we can imagine what it is like to have an instructor praise a paper.

Empathic communication and anxiety. The ability to learn in a classroom situation depends in part on the student's ability to empathize with the instructor. Cohn (1951) found that students best able to predict the instructor's responses on a personality test also tended to make the best grades. The empathic bond that exists between student and instructor can of course be weakened if the student is overly anxious and consequently misperceives the instructor's frame of reference. Anxiety narrows our perceptual scope. When we are anxious, we are likely to focus on aspects of behavior that appear to have threatening possibilities as far as we are concerned. The student who is worried about his grade remembers the instructor's saying that the forthcoming examination is an important one, and he studies the material to be covered by the examination thoroughly and diligently, giving careful attention to each name and date that might come up in the test, forgetting that the instructor also said: "This test will be concerned with broad theoretical principles and not with minor details."

Somehow, relations between people of unequal status seem to be fraught with anxiety, another reason why we find it easier to empathize with our peers. To put this in other terms, democratic relationships—relationships based on equal status—help facilitate and improve communication, whereas autocratic relationships—relationships based on inequalities in status—tend to impede communication. For instance, White and Lippitt (1953) found, in their study of groups functioning under various modes of leadership, that "work-minded conversation" occurred more frequently under democratic than autocratic leadership.

The difficulties of communication between persons of different levels of status are often aggravated by hostile attitudes. As Lindgren (1954) pointed out in his review of problems faced by leaders and other persons in authority, our culture tends to foster hostile feelings—sometimes conscious, sometimes unconscious—toward persons of higher status. The way in which hostility interferes with communication has also been studied by Newcomb (1947), who proposed a hypothetical construct he termed "autistic hostility." An attitude that is initially hostile toward a certain person, he said, leads to a restriction of communication and contact, which in turn serves to preserve the hostile attitude by preventing the acquisition of data that would help correct it. The importance of first impressions has also been demonstrated by Kelley (1950), who prepared several college classes in economics for a substitute instructor by giving them a mimeographed description. Half of the students in each section received a description that stated that the instruc-

tor was "a very warm person," and the other half were informed that he was "a rather cold person." Kelley noted that the students who had been informed that the instructor was a "warm" person participated more actively in the class discussion.

Stereotypes in communication

How stereotypes develop. In discussing the possible reactions of the Asian country to our communications, we used the term "perceptual set," a predisposition to respond to or perceive certain events in a certain way. When such perceptual sets result in fixed concepts, the result may be referred to as "stereotypes," particularly when they involve other persons or groups. When we employ stereotypes we are, in effect, not responding so much to the "real" person or persons as we are to a picture of him that exists in our minds. Some stereotypes, such as those experimentally developed by Kelley, are based on first impressions. The students in Kelley's experiment based their stereotypes on mimeographed descriptions, but in real life they may be produced by a wide variety of elements. If an individual reminds us through his manner, tone of voice, or general appearance, of our favorite uncle, we are inclined to assume that he, too, is a likeable person. But if he reminds us of an employer who was gruff and inconsiderate, we may use these im-

pressions as a basis for forming a negative stereotype. In either event, the resulting stereotype will be a predetermining factor in our behavior toward the individual.

Personalized patterns of need may also influence the kinds of stereotypes we develop. The person who is inclined to be overly dependent on others is likely to develop a response set in which the statements and general behavior of others are evaluated in terms of whether dependency is encouraged or discouraged. Some insecure people are prone to regard others in a disparaging way; others seem to "have a chip on their shoulder"—always looking for an argument.

A very common source of stereotypes is the culture that teaches us which ethnic groups (Mexicans, Negroes, Jews, Asiatics, or whatever) are "crafty and likely to take advantage of you," "lazy and good-natured," "dirty and undependable," and the like. Some of these stereotypes have a very powerful psychological appeal, and we are reluctant to give them up even when we meet individuals who do not conform to the stereotypes we hold for the ethnic group in question. We "explain" these contradictions by saying: "Yes, but he's an exception; he's not like the other ethnics." This rationalization enables us to accept the individual concerned as a person, without disturbing the stereotypes we hold for the ethnic group of which he is a member.

Stereotypes and defensive behavior. Haire and Grunes (1950) found that the introduction of concepts at variance with a stereotype had a confusing effect on subjects. They asked one group of college students to write descriptive paragraphs about an individual who was characterized by the following phrases:

Works on an assembly line in a factory
Reads the sports page in the newspaper
Goes to the movies once or twice a month
Has average height
Cracks jokes
Strong
Active

Another group of students was given the same set of descriptive phrases, except that the word "intelligent" was inserted after the phrase "cracks jokes." This second group of students had some difficulty writing a paragraph that would describe this individual, because the idea that an assembly-line worker could be intelligent was at variance with the stereotype they had for this kind of person. Hence some of them felt called upon to explain just why an intelligent person would be working on a factory assembly line— he was only doing it temporarily, or he was a foreman, etc. Some said that he "wasn't *very* intelligent," and others ignored the word altogether.

A study of the ways in which people defend their stereotypes was described by Kendall and Wolf (1949). Interviewers asked 160 non-Jewish working-class men to comment on 4 cartoons. Each of the cartoons depicted a "Mr. Biggott" making a statement that indicated an exaggerated degree of ethnic prejudice. In one cartoon, somewhat similar to the above, Mr. Biggott is telling a person who is obviously an American Indian: "I'm sorry Mr. Eaglefeather, but our company's policy is to employ 100% Americans only." Approximately two-thirds of the subjects missed the point of the cartoons entirely, and the remaining third misinterpreted the satirical aspect of the cartoons and thought they were designed to create bad feeling among ethnic groups and to intensify prejudices. Most of those who misunderstood the cartoons also had a considerable degree of ethnic prejudice, but were unaware of this fact. The interviewers found that the reactions of prejudiced individuals went through a number of stages when they were confronted by the cartoons. At first there was a considerable degree of understanding and even a feeling of identification with Mr. Biggott. This was followed by an attempt to escape from this identification—by saying, for instance, that Mr. Biggott was probably a Jew or a foreigner. The subjects then seemed to lose their initial understanding of the cartoon and to end up by misunderstanding it entirely.

What the studies by Haire and Grunes and by Kendall and Wolf seem to indicate is that we tend to perceive our stereotypes as rather important parts of ourselves, because when they are threatened in any way (by contradictory information or by ridicule) we take steps to defend them. In effect, we behave as though we are defending ourselves. When one of the subjects in the Mr.

Biggott study was asked what he thought the intent of the artist was, he said: "I don't know—trying to make a chump out of me, maybe."

Stereotypes: Are they good or bad? Because of the active campaigns against ethnic and religious prejudice in recent years, a great many educated people are quick to condemn the common tendency to use stereotypes. This is quite understandable, in view of the extent to which the uncritical use and acceptance of stereotypes may interfere with our understanding of the behavior of other people, as well as of ourselves. However, without the use of stereotypes, interaction with other people would become so complex as to be well-nigh impossible. A stereotype is, after all, a short cut. It is a way of abstracting a number of behavioral qualities, organizing them into a pattern of expectations and responding to the person as though he were the pattern. We walk up to a policeman in a strange city and ask him where a certain street is, assuming (1) that he will know, and (2) that he will be willing to help us. Our stereotype for policemen includes the belief that they know their city and that they are willing to help strangers. This happens to be a stereotype that has a high degree of validity. We buy a tablecloth in a department store, take it home, and find it is the wrong size. We take it back to the store where we bought it, confident that it will be exchanged or that our money will be refunded. We are able to do this because our stereotype of department stores includes the expectation that merchandise is returnable if not satisfactory. This is another stereotype that has some validity.

However, these are stereotypes that involve rather well-structured roles, stereotypes that are not only based on accurate knowledge of the groups concerned but which also lead to accurate predictions. A great deal of our trouble with stereotypes stems from the lack of adequate and accurate data on which many of them are based. This deficiency leads us to construct stereotypes that are invalid—that is, stereotypes that cause us to make inaccurate predictions about behavior. Some adults are inclined to regard all teenagers as actual or potential delinquents, basing this stereotype on rumor, prejudice, and rather lurid newspaper stories. Such a stereotype owes its existence largely to the fact that the adults in question do not know teenagers very intimately and do not allow themselves to get to know them. A similar situation obtains with respect to the stereotypes we hold regarding certain ethnic groups. Even though we may see members of these groups every day, we still build a social wall between us and them that prevents our getting to know them as people.

Stereotypes may lead to "circular behavior." One of the great dangers in stereotypes is the great influence they may have on the behavior of the person who is the subject of the stereotype. A stereotype is a kind of expectation, and the person who is stereotyped is bound to feel some social pressure forcing him into behavior consistent with the stereotype. In his discussion of interpersonal factors in personality, Leary (1957) points out how people use various roles in a reciprocal way. Not only does helpless, trustful behavior tend to "pull" assisting behavior from others, but strong, masterful behavior tends to "pull" trustful, dependent behavior. Leary uses this rather wry anecdote to illustrate the way in which we tend to "pull" the kind of behavior we want from others:

We recall the psychology professor who had developed at some length the thesis that teachers or psychotherapists should not give answers but should stimulate the student or the patient to seek the answers himself. "Don't let them become dependent on you; make them think for themselves." As soon as the lecture was over, a graduate student (well-trained to the dependency reflex) rushed up with a question: "In my undergraduate teaching section the students are continually asking me to solve their personal problems and demanding answers. What shall I do?" Pausing only to clear his throat, the professor reflexly responded: "Yes, you'll always find your students tending to trap you into solving their problems for them—the problems that they should work out for themselves. Now what I'd do if I were you is, first, I'd get them to . . ." [1]

This anecdote illustrates the "circular" behavior that often results from stereotypes. The student sees professors as persons to whom students should turn for the solution of problems. This leads him to play a certain role with respect to the professor. The role behavior he expresses evokes reciprocal role behavior on the part of the professor, which in turn reinforces the behavior of the student. The role each plays stimulates and reinforces the role behavior of the other, thus producing a "circular" form of interaction. Even

[1] Reprinted by permission.

though both professor and student are intellectually aware that the traditional and stereotyped authority-dependency relationship between teachers and students does not help students to learn how to think and act for themselves, the stereotypes have become so much a part of their everyday thinking that they are unaware of any inconsistency between their stated positions and their social behavior—that is, between the two levels of communication they are employing.

Feedback

Feedback defined. The interchange between the student and the professor also illustrates the way in which we insulate our stereotypes against being modified by pertinent data. Each of the two individuals knows that there are more effective ways for students and professors to interact, but they are successfully able to keep this knowledge from interfering with the integrity of their stereotypes. Similarly, we reject information that is not in keeping with our stereotypes regarding minority groups, members of the opposite sex, foreigners, teenagers, or any of the other conventional and traditional targets of prejudice.

One of the ways whereby we can break down or modify stereotypes and correct our false impressions is through a process called "feedback," a term psychologists have borrowed from the field of electronics.[1] Feedback occurs when energy representing data or behavior is fed into a system that has been arranged to feed back information as to the effect that the data or behavior has had on the system. (See Figure 13-1.) Controls based on feedback—thermostats—can be used to keep

[1] The scientific study of the regulation, control, and feedback of information in electrical circuits, machines, persons, and social groups is termed *cybernetics.* (See Wiener, 1950.)

the temperature of a room within a narrow range. Similar controls can also be used to keep a guided missile on the track of a shifting target. The radar impulses the missile sends out bring back information that is fed into its direction center and used to correct its course. In Chapter 4, the role of feedback in the functioning of the nervous system was discussed.

Feedback in social situations. Translating this process into social behavior, an individual who uses feedback can take steps to get information regarding the reaction he has on other people and can use this information to adjust his frame of reference and his behavior as he interacts with them. The management of a certain manufacturing plant may wish to try out a new wage-incentive plan but is not sure how employees will receive it. Industrial psychologists can be used to provide feedback through interviewing workers and getting their reaction to the proposal. An instructor can have his class fill out anonymous evaluation blanks to find out how his teaching efforts are being received. A discussion leader can have the members of the group fill out "post-meeting reaction sheets" at the end of each discussion period.

Feedback and two-way communication. Feedback deserves a great deal more attention than it commonly receives. Our usual concerns with communication, as we noted at the start of this chapter, are directed toward its production, rather than its reception, that is, we are preoccupied with learning how to speak and write properly, rather than with finding out how well we are understood. We seem to see communication not so much as a process of cooperative interaction, but as a form of competition in which success depends on facility in self-expression.

The individual who is interested in utilizing

Figure 13-1. Diagram showing the operation of feedback.

The system operates as follows: A stimulus affects a receptor; the message of the receptor is then transmitted to some controlling apparatus and thence to an effector that gives the response, which is then communicated back to the receptor as a new stimulus in such a way that the system is self-regulating. (After von Bertalanffy, 1955.)

Education may be viewed as a communicative process in which examinations serve as one form of feedback.

feedback will find himself becoming more concerned with the broader dimensions of communication. Although he may still be interested in self-expression, he will find himself doing more listening and interpreting and less talking. In order to make sense out of the data that are being fed back to him, he will have to give more time and attention to developing an understanding of the frames of reference used by others. To be sure, what he learns through feedback will make communication appear much more complicated, but the truth of the matter is that communication is a far more complex and difficult process than most of us are aware.

Correcting distortions in frames of reference. Feedback may also help in clearing up major differences in frames of reference, differences which are bound to interfere with effective communication. Let us say that the political representatives of country "A" approach the government of country "B" and ask for a sizable loan. There is bound to be difficulty if the representatives of country "A" think of the "loan" as a polite word for "gift" or "subsidy," while the leaders of country "B" think of "loan" as "some-thing that will be repaid." If the representatives of the two countries have an opportunity to interact on an informal basis, they may generate and receive enough feedback to discover that the use of the word "loan" is causing difficulty and thus are able to make adjustments in their frames of reference. Such a process of course assumes a certain flexibility. If the leaders of country "B" say, in effect: "If you want a subsidy, *ask* for a subsidy; if you want a loan, you had better count on paying it back with interest," a breakdown in communication may ensue. Perhaps the representatives of country "A" wish to preserve their self-esteem—"face," as it is sometimes called—by calling the subsidy a "loan." If there is no chance to preserve self-esteem, then they are not interested in negotiating further. If country "B" needs the political or military support of country "A" and thus stands to gain by helping to insure the latter's financial solvency, then its representatives stand to lose by not being flexible. It takes flexibility to be willing to admit that one's frame of reference may be interfering with communication and to set about making adjustments in it through feedback.

Hanging someone in effigy is a symbolic way of communicating hostility, even when it is done in fun. These students are expressing their feelings toward city officials who have resorted to strong legal measures in order to collect unpaid parking ticket fines.

Symbols

Symbolic behavior. Many of the difficulties that occur in communication are produced by the rigidity of our attitudes regarding the use and meaning of words, as well as of other forms of symbols. To many an insecure person, there is a certain "magic" power in symbols, a certain something that is beyond reality. Under such circumstances, symbols become more important than their referents—what they stand for. As Ogden and Richards (1927) put it:

At all levels of intellectual performance there are persons found to whom any suggestion that they change their symbols comes, and must come, as a suggestion that they should recant their beliefs. For such people to talk differently is to think differently, because their words are essential members of the contexts of their references.[1]

Words, rituals, and other forms of symbols or symbolic behavior have a strong attraction for the anxious person—for the person in search of security—because they have an eternal, unchangeable quality that is almost irresistible. People may change their feelings about one another, but words like "love," "loyalty," and "fidelity" never change. Women, scenery, horses, and paintings can express beauty in varying degrees in different settings, but the *word* "beauty" is the same wherever it appears. Because of the static quality of words, it is all too easy to take the next step of assuming that the reality they represent is equally static. Hence the long and fruitless arguments over what words like "beauty," "love," and "democracy" *really* mean. The difficulty here is that we forget that static and never-changing symbols represent a dynamic and ever-changing reality, a reality whose meaning differs according to each individual's frame of reference.

It is man's ability to invent and manipulate words and other symbols that has enabled him to master his physical environment, to develop his ever-increasing potentials, and, at the same time, to saddle himself with such widely differentiated difficulties as economic depressions, race prejudice, and misunderstandings of all sorts. The perfections and imperfections of language and other symbolic behavior produce both benefits and calamities.

Symbolic behavior operates essentially on the principle that it is possible to use a sound or a gesture or a sign to signify a thing, person, act, condition, quality, or even another symbol. This is the process of abstracting: letting a symbol represent something. This is a tremendous advantage. It is much simpler to shout: "Look out, George, there's a car coming!" than it is to dash out into the highway and drag George from the path of the automobile, assuming we could get there in time.

Symbols as abstractions. But there is a major difficulty in the use of symbolic behavior. We can so readily forget that we are dealing with symbols and not with reality. We forget that *symbols are not things* and in fact have no *inherent* connection with the things or events they are supposed to represent. The connection between the word "toast" and a slightly scorched

[1] Reprinted by permission.

piece of bread exists only by common agreement. It is a connection that can be dissolved or altered by those participating in the communicative act. We can decide, for example, that we will use the word "shingle" instead of "toast" to refer to the same object. Or we can decide that we shall use the word "toast" to refer to a color of a new model of sports car that we are trying to sell. Yet in spite of the fact that we can "make and break" words and other symbols at will or by common consent, and in spite of the fact that the reality they represent has certain qualities of instability and unpredictibility, we become so dependent on the accuracy of symbols that we feel cheated and let down whenever they turn out not to be reliable.

Professor Eames sent his student assistant to his office to get a "brown book," which he had left on the desk. The assistant came back puzzled; he could find no brown book. Professor Eames was positive he had left the book on his desk; he left the class and came back triumphantly, bearing the book in question. However, he was irritated: Why hadn't that stupid assistant been able to see a book that was lying there in plain sight? The explanation, of course, is that Professor Eames is color-blind and sees what most of us call a "green book" as a "brown book." He is irritated because the symbol "brown" is to him literally a *part* of the book in question, whereas his assistant is puzzled because he is not a party to the connection that Professor Eames has made between the symbol "brown" and the book.

Or, take the case of Mr. Abel, who has just rented a cabin at a motor court. He goes into the bathroom to wash his hands and turns on the tap marked "hot." The water gushes out, but it is cold. He is annoyed. Later, he turns on the tap marked "cold," and the water is boiling hot. We do not blame Mr. Abel for being irritated and resentful. It is as though someone has tricked him. The world of reality does not, for the moment, correspond to the world of symbols.

Consider, too, the experience of the New Yorker who stopped at a small town and tried to make some purchases. He had nothing smaller than a hundred-dollar bill. The storekeepers had never seen a hundred-dollar bill before and hence would not accept it. Like Mr. Abel and Professor Eames, the New Yorker was angry and resentful. His money *ought* to have value, but in this situation it does not. The relationship between symbol and reality depends on common consent. Evidently he and the villagers do not share the same frame of reference in this respect.

Abstractions of abstractions. The examples we have used in the preceding paragraphs deal with referents which are rather specific and concerning which there would be rather good agreement. But the words that cause us the most difficulty are those which have referents which are themselves abstractions. Consider such words as "self-defense," "reasonable profit," and "malicious intent." Since their referents are so abstract and ambiguous it is difficult to get people to find common agreement as to what the words mean. Most of the world's wars have been fought at least ostensibly in defense of symbolic abstractions.

Even though language can be misleading and divisive, it possesses tremendous advantages over nonlinguistic or prelinguistic methods of communication. Through the use of language man can become the heir to the past; he does not have to experience each event personally in order to gain understanding and knowledge, for *he can learn through the accumulated experience of others.* And this is the great difference between savage and civilized man—it is not that savages lack intelligence, but that civilized man has inherited a more complex and more adaptable culture. The culture we inherit enables us to broaden our understanding of human experience. It also provides us with symbols that can be manipulated to create devices and techniques which in turn can be used to control our physical and social environment.

Manipulation of symbols. However, we are not all equally skilled in the use of symbols. Those of us who are most able to manipulate symbols—lawyers, executives, financiers, and educated persons in general—are the ones who are most able to control their environment, further their own destinies, and manipulate others. Those who are least able to manipulate symbols—usually persons of little education—are those who are less able to protect themselves from the more abstract dangers of their environment and are more likely to be exploited by the symbol wielders. The social and psychological distance is great between those most able to manipulate symbols and those least able. This distance not only creates difficulties in communication, but fosters a feeling of mutual distrust. Some of this distrust is based on misunderstanding, but grows out of the fact that some individuals in business make a practice of exploiting people with little education.

The use of symbols in scientific research.
Although the manipulation of symbols can be used to exploit others, most of the time its purpose is more constructive. It is on the manipulation of symbols, for example, that the whole fabric of scientific research is erected. Generally speaking, symbols are used more effectively by scientists than they are by laymen. Perhaps this comes about because there is less disagreement among scientists with regard to the meaning of the symbols they use, or perhaps they are more cautious and meticulous about the ways in which they manipulate them. Furthermore, the general principle that underlies scientific endeavor is an unselfish one, the furthering of scientific knowledge. Hence there is less danger of scientists becoming personally involved in the symbols they use or in manipulating them to promote personal ends.

Science moves forward by a process of organizing existing knowledge into general principles or laws. Occurrences which hitherto appeared to be separate and unrelated are seen to have similar origin. An example of this is the phenemenon of oxidation. Centuries ago, man considered the decaying of wood, the rusting of iron, and the burning of oil to be unrelated processes; now we realize that they are similar, that is, they are changes produced by the chemical union of various elements with oxygen. This discovery, and others like it, would have been impossible if we had not developed systems of symbols that could be used to classify and analyze various phenomena and to communicate the results to others.

Science also moves forward by recognizing differences hitherto ignored. For instance, centuries ago we were unable to distinguish any functional patterns in the behavior of persons afflicted by emotional, mental, or nervous disorders. Today, we are able to make discriminations among mental patients suffering from brain damage, those who are the victims of schizophrenia, those who are in the grip of a severe depression, and so forth. Such classifications not only are useful in identifying the symptoms associated with each type of disorder, but also they may aid us in determining the kind of treatment indicated and the probability of cure.

The development of scientific terminology.
Scientists are often accused of trying to confuse or confound laymen by developing new terminology, thus making their work appear more complex and abstract than it actually is. In this, the scientist is faced with a dilemma. If he develops new terms, he is accused of trying to confuse or impress his audience. On the other hand, if he uses familiar words, their very familiarity may conceal the fact that they have been given unfamiliar meanings. Hence the preference is for developing new terms, rather than for developing new meanings for familiar words.

As each new branch of science has progressed, it has developed a vocabulary of its own to identify the principles and relationships that are important to its particular brand of understanding, to aid scientists in communicating with one another, and to assist in further investigations. The more highly developed a science becomes, the more likely it is to develop an elaborate and complex terminology—an inevitable outgrowth of the attempts of research workers to express themselves precisely, to differentiate, to classify, to generalize, and to express new concepts.

In this respect, scientists are only following pre-existing patterns, for as civilizations have become more complex and elaborate, their modes of expression have become more complex and elaborate. Indeed, so essential are verbal techniques in coping with the problems of our complex culture, that the ability to use these techniques can be used as a measure of intellectual functioning. The more symbols an individual can recognize and use, and the greater his ability to manipulate them, the higher his level of intelligence. Some intelligence tests measure this ability with the use of a series of problems, ranging from the simple and concrete to the complicated and abstract. Another approach is that of measuring the size of the individual's vocabulary. As a matter of fact, vocabulary size can be taken as the best single measure of intellectual ability.

Symbolic behavior and delinquency. It is of more than passing interest to find that there is a close relationship between an individual's ability to cope with his environment and his ability to function linguistically. For example, juvenile delinquents very commonly are retarded in reading, writing, and vocabulary development. When Glueck and Glueck (1950) compared 500 delinquent with 500 nondelinquent boys, they found that the delinquents had more problems with the symbolic aspects of life. They had greater difficulty in school, for instance, and had lower verbal intelligence than did the nondelinquents, although the two groups were quite similar in nonverbal intelligence. In general, the delinquents appeared to be possessed by a great deal of restless energy and were less able to tolerate frustration than were the nondelinquents. Most of us are able to express feelings of frustration in some symbolic way—by arguing or griping, modifying our goals, throwing ourselves into our work with greater energy, or by using such behavior mechanisms as daydreaming, rationalizing, projection, etc. In the Gluecks' study, the nondelinquents were more inclined to use such mechanisms than the delinquents. After all, the chief value of such mechanisms is symbolic, and the delinquent quickly becomes impatient and dissatisfied with symbolic expression, preferring to express his frustration in some direct form of hostile aggression. His approach to life resembles that of the "person of action" described by Ruesch (1957: 120–123). Such a person, says Ruesch, has difficulty in saying: "I dislike you." Instead, he has to communicate his feelings of dislike by hitting someone or breaking a window. Although he may correctly gauge the mood of another person, he has no words to express his own feelings and is unable to make use of second-hand knowledge about other people.

The difficulties encountered by delinquents in dealing with the symbolic and abstract aspects of life are also indicated by a study of Barndt and Johnson (1955), who found that nondelinquent boys were much more "future-oriented" than delinquent boys. Since the future exists only as an abstraction and not as a reality, it can be approached only through symbolic means. The making of plans for the future, for example, involves a great deal of symbol manipulation, an ability in which delinquents tend to be deficient.

Communication and psychopathology. In view of the fact that communication is such an essential process in coping with life and its problems and in getting along with others and even ourselves, it is hardly surprising that emotional disturbances would affect our ability to communicate. When we are upset, our voices are strained and tense, we have difficulty in expressing ourselves adequately, we are likely to misinterpret what others are saying, and even the quality of our handwriting may deteriorate. If we are deeply disturbed, trying to communicate may even seem to be hopeless or impossible.

The communicative ability of the chronically

Susan Greenburg

Workers in each branch of scientific endeavor have access to a vocabulary of symbols that enables them to conduct research and to communicate with one another.

disturbed individual—the neurotic and the psychotic—will likewise reflect the degree of disturbance. The attempts of the psychiatric patient to communicate—*how* he communicates, as well as *what* he is trying to communicate—are indicative of the amount and kind of disturbance. In fact, Ruesch and Bateson (1951) have proposed that disturbances in communication are more than mere indicators of mental illness, that psychosis and neurosis are in themselves stages of difficulty in communication. The essence of neurosis and psychosis is seen by Ruesch and Bateson to consist of the inability of the individual to express thoughts, wishes, and feelings adequately and to understand the thoughts, wishes, and feelings expressed by others. In short, they see the neurotic or psychotic individual as one who has more than the usual difficulty in interpreting himself to the world and in interpreting the world to himself. Thus, psychotherapy, according to Ruesch and Bateson, becomes a process aimed at improving or restoring the patient's ability to communicate.

Summary

Communication is the means whereby human interaction takes place. Man's ability to communicate and manipulate symbols makes possible civilization as we know it. Communication includes all types of human interaction; thus, the kind of relationships we develop with others depends on our ability to communicate with one another. Effective communication between two individuals depends on their sharing a common frame of reference.

There is more than one level at which communication takes place; one level is explicit, conscious, and verbal, whereas other levels are implicit, unconscious, and often nonverbal. Nations communicate on several levels of awareness as well as individuals. The meaning ascribed to a message is also influenced to a great extent by the perceptual set of the receiver. Often the inconsistencies in an individual's verbal and nonverbal behavior are a result of conflicting motives that are being expressed at different communication levels. Communication between individuals from different cultures is often hampered by misunderstanding about implicit as opposed to explicit meanings.

Learning to be a functioning member of one's society is a complex process that involves communication at each step. One aspect of empathic behavior is the ability to understand the implicit as well as the explicit meanings in the communications of others. Empathic communication is more likely to occur in nonanxious situations, such as between peers, than in anxious situations such as between individuals having different status. The difficulties of communication between persons of different status levels are often aggravated by hostility.

Perceptual sets that result in fixed concepts are termed "stereotypes." Personalized patterns of needs, such as overdependency, may influence the kinds of stereotypes we develop, but other stereotypes are learned from our culture. Stereotypes may become so much a part of us that we react defensively if we are presented with information contrary to the stereotypes we hold or if they are ridiculed in any way. Essentially, a stereotype is a way of abstracting behavioral qualities and responding to an individual as if he were the abstraction; some stereotypes are valid and useful whereas others are inaccurate and not only interfere with understanding but also may reinforce ethnic prejudice. Often the existence of a stereotype will lead the stereotyped person to behave in the expected fashion and thus lend support to the stereotype in a circular way.

When the effect of behavior is perceived and can thus have an influence on further behavior, we term the process "feedback." The more we know about the response that our behavior evokes in others the more effective our behavior can become. Feedback can enable us to understand and correct discrepancies between our frame of reference and that of others.

Words and other symbols are incorrectly regarded as real things by many people, and this rigid attitude leads to communication difficulties. Symbols and symbolic behavior seem to offer security to many anxious people, but they forget that symbols are only abstractions. The ability to manipulate symbols is a great asset in our complex society, but this manipulation often leads the uneducated to mistrust and feel hostility toward the educated. In science, the use of symbols is of vital importance. Scientific laws are constructed by the symbolic processes of making abstractions and generalizations about obtained data. Scientific terminology is complex and confusing to the layman, but these new symbols are necessary because they refer to new concepts for which the use of familiar symbols would be even more confusing. There seems to be a close relationship between an individual's ability to cope with his environment and his ability to deal effectively with symbols. Delinquents are found to be deficient in linguistic functions; neurotic and psychotic individuals have difficulty in communicating. It is possible to conceive of psychotherapy as a process aimed at improving or restoring the ability to communicate.

Questions

1. In what ways have you been engaged in the process of communication during the past 24 hours?

2. Can you think of any instances in which communication might be faulty because the individuals involved did not have a common frame of reference?

3. Find several newspaper examples of communication between nations (diplomatic notes, speeches, etc.). Can you find more than one level of communication in these messages?

4. Why might an individual's verbal behavior and his nonverbal behavior be inconsistent?

5. Make a list of statements and questions (such as "How are you?") which cannot be taken literally and which might be baffling to an individual from another culture.

6. Think of a few recent conversations that you held with a friend, parent, stranger, etc. Are there any discrepancies between explicit and implicit meanings in either your statements or those of the other person?

7. What effect does anxiety have on communication?

8. Describe some of the stereotypes to which you adhere. Which ones do you think are valid and which are probably false?

9. Give some examples of feedback in interpersonal interaction.

10. What sort of problems arise when individuals begin thinking of symbols as being equal to the things they represent?

11. Discuss some of the uses and misuses of symbols.

12. What is the relationship between the ability to engage in symbolic behavior and such behavioral difficulties as delinquency, neurosis, and psychosis?

Suggestions for further reading

Brown, R., *Words and Things: An Introduction to Language*. Glencoe, Ill.: Free Press, 1958. A well-written review of the psychological aspects of language.

Hartley, E. L. and R. E., *Fundamentals of Social Psychology*. New York: Knopf, 1952. A standard textbook in social psychology, organized around communication.

Hayakawa, S. I., *Language in Thought and Action*. New York: Harcourt, Brace, 1949. A stimulating discussion, written for a lay audience, of the uses and misuses of words and other symbols.

Lindgren, H. C., *Meaning: Antidote to Anxiety*. New York: Nelson, 1956. An analysis of the relationship between anxiety and meaning. Written for a lay audience.

Maccoby, E. E., T. M. Newcomb, and E. L. Hartley, Editors, *Readings in Social Psychology,* 3rd ed. New York: Holt, 1958. See sections dealing with language, stereotypes, communcation, and opinion change.

Osgood, C. E., G. J. Suci, and P. H. Tannenbaum, *The Measurement of Meaning*. Urbana: University of Illinois Press, 1957. Presentation of a statistical approach to analyzing the relationship among words. Fairly technical.

Ruesch, J., *Disturbed Communication*. New York: Norton, 1957. An exploration of the relationship between the behavior of neurotic and psychotic patients and their modes of communication.

Skinner, B. F., *Verbal Behavior*. New York: Appleton-Century-Crofts, 1957. An analysis of language from the standpoint of the experimental psychologist.

Rollie McKenna

14 Group processes

The effect of the group on communication.
Although it is communication that makes it possible for human beings to relate to each other and
to develop and maintain groups, this does not
necessarily imply that communication is the same
in all kinds of group contexts. Face-to-face communication with one individual involves skills and
problems that are quite different than those that
are involved in speaking to a group of friends or
in speaking to an audience of a hundred strangers.
For one thing, it is generally easier to empathize
with one person than with a half dozen or a hundred, and with intimates rather than strangers.
Furthermore, we are more likely to be less anxious with friends than strangers and consequently
find communication easier and freer.

Although most of us are aware of the greater
difficulties we encounter when we try to communicate in the context of a larger group, we are less
likely to be aware of the pervasive effect different
group contexts have on behavior generally.

Guy Levitt is a member of a hiking club that organizes an outing every Sunday into some nearby
natural area. However, with traffic becoming increasingly heavy, it is taking more and more time to
get to the areas where the hikes are being conducted.
Guy would like to have some hikes scheduled for
Saturday as an experiment. Not only would traffic
be lighter, but it might be possible to hike longer
distances and camp overnight. This would change the
pattern of activities that have been customary at the
club for some years. Guy feels strongly about his
proposal and talks it over with some of the other
members. They tell him that his idea is worth trying
and that they will support it. At the next meeting,
Guy puts forth his proposal. A number of the older
members are quite critical, saying that the Sunday

hike is something they look forward to all week and that they have organized their lives around it. It just wouldn't be the same if it took place on Saturday or was turned into an overnight camping expedition. Guy expected some opposition but he was quite put out when some of the members who said they would support him concurred with his critics. He felt that his friends had let him down, became bitter, and resigned from the club.

Guy Levitt's experience of having people say one thing in face-to-face interview and something quite different in the context of a larger group is not an unusual one. When it occurs, we may be puzzled and perhaps embittered, as Guy was, because we are unaware that quite different forces impinge on the individual in the smaller group, as contrasted with the larger group. Not only are the communicative relationships different, but the whole situation is perceived as different. If outward behavior were the only criterion, one might say that they are "not the same people" in the larger group setting. They have different expectations for themselves, there are different roles to play, and the status relationships are different. Since they are responding to different internal and external stimuli, and the motivational field is different, it is hardly surprising that their behavior should be different. One of the several studies that contrast behavior within the group with behavior outside its context is that conducted by Dashiell (1935), who found that students brought together on a group completed more problems than they did working in isolation.

Developmental stages in group awareness. Like most other forms of human behavior, our responses to the "group phenomenon" must be learned. As children, we must first become aware that there is such a thing as a group. We have to learn through repeated experiences that interacting with several persons separately and individually is not the same as interacting with them in a group. As we pointed out in Chapter 2, preschool children tend to have only a limited awareness of the differences between relationships with groups and relationships with individuals. Hence they are relatively unable to behave as members of a group and instead relate to each other as individuals. When they are in the same room with a number of other children their behavior tends to be self-oriented rather than group-oriented. A dozen or so nursery-school children together in a room are an "aggregate" or a "collection" of individuals rather than a group, and they be-

have as individuals rather than as group members. It is relatively difficult to get them to "do things together" or to "think as a group," because "groupness" is not yet very much of a factor in their awareness, and hence is not an important factor in their behavior.

During the primary grades, children begin to become more aware of the various facets of group life. They see various kinds of groups in action—football and baseball teams, birthday parties, congregations, and audiences. At the same time they are subjected to a great deal of pressure on the part of adults to display behavior that is less individualistic and more group-oriented. Gradually they learn group roles through such activities as group singing, group games, and even rudimentary committee work. During these years they are not very effective discussants because they are more concerned with expressing themselves than they are with listening to the other members of the group. They have not yet learned the discipline of group membership.

During the prepuberal years, group relations begin to be a more important force in the child's life. He derives pleasure out of Scout activities, he learns how to cooperate with other children (quite a different skill from learning how to "cooperate" with an adult), he begins to think of himself as a member of certain groups—a citizen of his country, a member of his church, one of an ethnic group, and so forth, and he becomes aware of groups other than his own. Differences that arise from group participation and membership are very much on his mind, and he is likely to complain: "Adults can get away with anything," (recognizing the differences between adults as a group and children as a group), or, "The kids on the next block won't play with me; they say I don't belong to their gang."

Group relationships during the adolescent years may become so important for some individuals that they may try to submerge their identities in one or more groups. Some adolescents engage in a kind of "flight from self": they feel restless and insecure when alone, away from members of the peer group; they display an intense loyalty to the group and whatever it stands for; they suppress or repress ideas of their own that may conflict with the norms of the group. Such behavior is, at least in the American culture, largely a stage in psycho-social development, a way of separating oneself from dependence on the family. A greater or lesser degree of subordination to the group may be an unavoidable part of learning some of the self-discipline that is necessary in a complex, urbanized culture like ours. Unfortunately, many individuals are unable to proceed beyond this stage of development to the point where they are able to think and act for themselves. They remain, as Riesman (1950) would call them, largely "other-directed." The extent to which we are able to maintain a balance between our responsibilities to ourselves as self-respecting individuals, and to the groups of which we are members, is to some degree a reflection of the degree of social and emotional maturity we have attained.

Types of groups. The relationships among group members will differ according to the nature, purpose, structure, size, and degree of intimacy of the group. Cooley (1909) distinguished between *primary* and *secondary* groups. Primary groups are face-to-face groups, so called because they are characteristic of the relationships that first appear in the life of a child. Common practice has been, however, to use the term "primary group" to apply to any group characterized by more-or-less intimate, face-to-face relationships: families, basketball teams, adolescent cliques, and the like. It is within the context of such groups that we find the deepest satisfactions and the most provoking frustrations, inasmuch as such groups are more closely involved in the satisfaction of our more basic needs (biological processes, security, love). Secondary groups are characterized by relationships that are less personal and intimate, and more abstract, intellectualized, and indirect. One's profession, school, social class, and political party are examples of secondary groups. To be sure, we can become emotionally involved in the defense of these groups or in pursuit of their goals, but such involvement is usually directed toward an abstract idea or symbol of the group, rather than toward its individual members.

Here is an example of the way in which membership in various groups affects the life and the behavior of one individual:

Mr. Francine is a Latin teacher at the Washington Township High School. He is a member of the local chapter of the state teachers association, the Kiwanis, and the American Classical Association. The first two organizations are primary groups, because Mr. Francine has been a member since he came to town sixteen years ago and he is on a "first-name basis" with the

other members. The American Classical Association is a secondary group. Although it holds meetings once a year, Mr. Francine has never attended. He keeps in touch with the organization by paying his dues and receiving its journal.

The groups that Mr. Francine belongs to can be characterized as formal or informal. Although his relationships with the other members of the teachers association and the Kiwanis are quite informal, they are, nonetheless, formal organizations. They have a rather definite structure, are more or less permanent, and have fairly well-defined goals and purposes. The teaching staff at the Washington Township High School is also a formal group, as are the American Classical Association and Mr. Francine's family. Here is an example of an informal group:

The other day, while walking to school, Mr. Francine noticed a neighbor trying to start his car. After a short discussion, the two of them decided that the battery was dead. Just at that moment Mr. Francine noticed two more neighbors coming down the street, so he called to them to help him give the car a push. After they had pushed the car a half block, it had gained enough speed to get the engine going. The driver of the car shouted "Thank you" and the three neighbors shouted back an "O.K." and then went their separate ways to work.

Every group has one or more purposes. Some purposes are simple and obvious, like the task of getting a neighbor's car started. The purposes of the teachers' organization to which Mr. Francine belongs are those of promoting the welfare of teachers, of the education profession generally, and of the children who attend the schools. But some of the members receive a "secondary gain" from their participation in the organization. They find that they have much in common with the other members and enjoy socializing at their monthly meetings. In order to heighten their enjoyment of one another's company, they have been instrumental in having meetings take place in a restaurant. Meeting together around a dinner table helps increase the feeling of relatedness and informality.

After analyzing the behavior of individuals in small groups, Carter (1954) came to the conclusion that three factors could account for their behavior:

Factor 1. *Individual prominence and personal achievement.* This factor covers the various kinds of behavior we engage in in order to get others to recognize us as outstanding, and to attain goals

The people in this group are working on a specific problem: church finance. However, such activity meets a variety of additional needs for each member of the group, some of which are personal and some of which are group-oriented.

that are self-oriented, rather than group-oriented.

Factor 2. *Aiding attainment by group.* This factor includes behavior that is intended to help the group attain the goals it has set for itself.

Factor 3. *Sociability.* Under this heading are included the various kinds of behavior oriented toward establishing and maintaining cordial and mutually satisfying relations with other people.

A person may participate in a group, of course, hoping to achieve all three of the purposes or needs that are implied in these factors, playing first one role and then another, in order to satisfy the need that has priority. But these three kinds of behavior are to a large degree antithetical. Behavior under Factor 1, for example, is aimed at building up the individual at the expense of other group members, whereas helping the group attain its goals requires self-denial. Socialization among people who are trying to compete with one another becomes, at best, a strained affair, and a marked emphasis on socialization will interfere with the more serious work of the group.

Meeting needs in a group context. Very likely all three of Carter's factors are related to individual members' personal needs for security, esteem, creativity and self-expression, and acceptance, and, as far as each member is personally concerned, the group exists for the purpose of helping meet his individual needs.

Mr. Francine and his colleagues participate in the local teachers organization because they need such a group to advance their economic welfare, help them professionally, and provide an opportunity for informal socialization. Their evaluation of the success of this group will undoubtedly depend on the extent to which they feel the organization is meeting their needs. However, to say that a group exists solely to meet the needs of its individual members may be too limiting a statement. Perhaps it can be said that people *enter* groups in order to meet certain personal needs, but once a group is formed, it may develop needs of its own, over and beyond the personal needs of the individual members.

When Mr. Francine joined the teachers' organization, the thought of doing committee work had never occurred to him. If it had, he probably would have thought the prospect neither very attractive nor very interesting. Yet, now, as one of the more senior members of the organization, he has had to spend as many as one or two nights a week serving on various committees. Although he complains about the seemingly endless chore of committee work, he would not vote to eliminate it. He recognizes that committees provide the best way of accomplishing certain objectives of the association, and, since he has a strong feeling of identification with the association, and hence with its goals, he feels some responsibility for helping it function adequately.

It is, of course, possible for the needs of a group to reach such levels that they assume more importance than individual needs. This may occur during periods of emergency or disaster, when a nation or community makes great demands on its members, requiring them to make personal sacrifices or to take risks involving possible injury or death. The subordination of individual needs is routine policy in totalitarian states, as the term "totalitarian" implies.

Although we are inclined to think of the subordination of individual needs as being instigated solely by states and other organizations, a great deal of such subordination is initiated by individuals themselves. Many persons, as Hoffer (1951) points out, have a driving compulsion to merge their identity with that of some group or ideology. Hoffer believes that such behavior is largely motivated by a feeling of personal worthlessness. Such individuals feel that the only way in which they can gain any self-respect, value, or importance is by dedicating or sacrificing themselves to, or otherwise becoming immersed in, some "cause" or movement. The more the "cause" demands of them, the more it strips them of their right to think for themselves, the greater its attractiveness for such individuals. Hoffer makes the point that a way of life characterized by extreme self-denial is bound to have its greatest appeal to individuals who for one reason or another feel rejected by the dominant groups in their society and hence feel as though they have nothing to lose by surrendering to a "cause" that demands everything of them.

The problem of keeping a balance between group needs and individual needs is a difficult one. As we shall see, the individual who is preoccupied with meeting his own needs may impair the cohesiveness and general effectiveness of a group, but the chronic subordination of individual needs leads to a dead-level conformity and other-directedness, as well as to a stifling of independent thinking and creativity.

Factors related to group effectiveness

The ability of any group to achieve its goals is dependent on a number of conditions or factors. Here are some of the major ones: morale, cohesiveness, climate, leadership, and structure.

Group morale. When we say that the members of a group have high morale, we mean that they accept the goals of the group and are optimistic about the chances for attaining these goals; hence they are willing to invest something of themselves in the group, collaborating with other members in an effort to achieve common purposes. The members of a group that has poor morale may be pessimistic, cynical, apathetic, resentful, or simply unable to take the goals of the group seriously.

An instance of the latter condition is the behavior of the high-school sophomores who had promised to clean up the school auditorium after a Halloween dance. The faculty sponsor of the class said that he would help them as soon as the faculty meeting was over, but the meeting ran a half hour overtime. The students had started to clean up the trash in an orderly fashion, but when the sponsor failed to appear, some of the leaders of the group started throwing pumpkins at one another. Then the others followed suit. When the sponsor finally did appear, he was able to restore order only with the greatest difficulty. As he sought to restrain some of the more destructive students, they called him a "spoil sport," accusing him of interfering with their fun.

Because we are inclined to tolerate and applaud humor and attempts at humor, we tend to overlook the fact that many attempts to be funny are a mask for hostility and destructiveness and may be detrimental to the effective functioning of a group.

When the morale of a group is low, members are inclined to withhold participation, sabotage the efforts of the group, or try to change the goals of the group or the methods of attaining the goals. If they are involved in several groups, they will be likely to channel their energies into those groups that have the highest morale—that is, those which promise the greater potential satisfaction.

It should not be assumed, however, that morale is the only important factor in group behavior. During World War II and the years immediately following, the Morale Division of the U.S. Strategic Bombing Survey (1947), under the direction of Rensis Likert, studied the effects of bombing on the morale of the German people. This was done by analyzing captured civilian mail, interviewing persons escaping from Germany, and interviewing civilians after the war. Researchers found that morale had been rather markedly lowered by the bombing. It produced apathy, weariness, a sense of defeat, and a realization that the war was lost. Relatively light bombing was as damaging to morale as was repeated, heavy pounding. But production and absentee records at German factories and the extent of subversive activity, that is, activity favorable to the Allied powers, showed that this lowered morale did not interfere to any great extent with the war effort of the German people until the closing months of the war, when it probably contributed to the total collapse of German productive capacity. Evidently the actual behavior of the German civilian was more affected by his traditional attitudes toward leader and group, rather than by his expectations with regard to the eventual success of the collective war effort.

People in a democracy are inclined to be outspoken and openly critical when they are inconvenienced, or when their personal comfort is adversely affected. Perhaps it is for this reason that we often assume that inconvenience and discomfort are detrimental to morale. However, a study by Katz and Hyman (1947) of American shipyards during World War II found little relationship between living conditions and morale. The workers at two shipyards located in the same New England town had to contend with inade-

The use of force against a group carries implications of psychological threat, which in turn may serve to increase the cohesiveness of the group.

quate housing, difficult transportation, inadequate recreation facilities, and hostile community attitudes toward newcomers, but morale and production were high in one yard and low in the other. In the first yard, 38 per cent of the workers had thought of quitting, as contrasted with 56 per cent in the second yard. The average time required to complete a ship in the first yard was 76 days, compared to 207 days in the second yard. The researchers found that the most important determiners of morale were those centered in the work situation: opportunities for promotion, conditions of work, quality of supervision, and psychological rewards for work accomplished. It is hardly surprising that only 20 per cent of the workers interviewed in the second shipyard expressed confidence in management, as contrasted with 67 per cent in the first yard. There are, of course, perfectly good humanitarian reasons why off-the-job frustrations and discomforts should be eliminated, but we should not assume that such elimination will necessarily improve morale or production.

Group cohesiveness. Cohesiveness is the mutual attraction that members of a group have for one another or that the group and its activities have for its members. Cohesiveness is some-

times used synonymously with "morale," but morale, strictly speaking, refers to the *tasks* of the group: cleaning up after a dance, winning a war, building ships, or whatever. Morale has an individual quality, in that the morale of a total group depends on the morale of its members. It is also possible to speak of the morale of an individual. For example, a student may be working below his potential because his morale is low—that is, he doubts whether his efforts will produce any worthwhile results.

The morale and the cohesiveness of a group are closely related. High morale heightens the attractiveness of the group for individual members, and as members find satisfactions in working together on common problems, their confidence in the group increases. High cohesiveness produces a certain task-orientation that is basic to good morale. Exline (1957) found, when he assigned subjects to congenial or noncongenial groups, persons in congenial groups were more accurate in perceiving task-oriented behavior. Other studies that have been made of groups solving problems through discussion methods indicate that the greater the cohesiveness of a group, the greater its effectiveness. (Marquis, 1951; Back, 1951.)

An increase in cohesiveness is not, however,

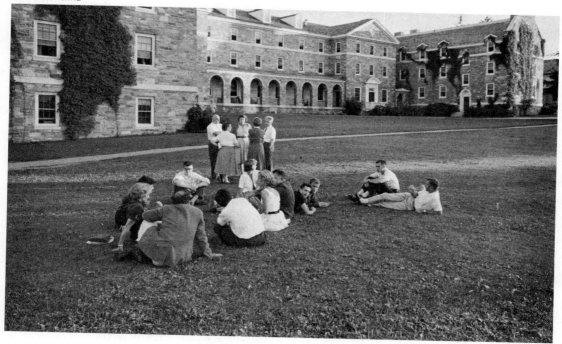

The atmosphere in these groups is one of easy informality.

invariably accompanied by an increase in productivity or effectiveness. Lanzetta, Haefner, Langham, and Axelrod (1954) compared the behavior of groups of ROTC students required to solve problems under "threat" or "nonthreat" conditions. (The quality of "threat" was introduced by telling the students that the results of their efforts would become a part of their ROTC records.) Members of groups functioning under conditions of "threat" developed behavior that would result in a reduction of tension and friction within the group and a higher degree of group acceptance—that is, behavior calculated to increase the level of cohesiveness within the group. Such behavior would not be unexpected; members of groups quite commonly defend themselves against external threats by strengthening the bonds within the group. In this experiment, however, the "threat" groups were not as effective as were the members of the less cohesive "nonthreat" groups. The latter were more forceful, assertive, and active in their attack on the task problem, whereas "threat" groups were less efficient, less adaptable, and varied more in their effectiveness.

Group climate. The terms "morale" and "cohesiveness" may be used to describe certain emotional aspects of group life in terms of the attitudes and behavior of its members. We can also describe the emotional factors operating within a group in terms of their being characteristic of a certain kind of *atmosphere* or *climate*. The atmosphere of a group is its general psychological or emotional state as of a given moment. We can speak of an atmosphere as characterized by indecision, discouragement, or hostility. When a certain kind of atmosphere *generally* prevails in a certain group, it can be referred to as its climate. Group members will tend to behave in terms of their perception of the prevailing atmosphere or climate. Here is an example of how climate and

atmosphere may affect the behavior of discussion groups in college classrooms:

Mr. Follis noticed that his eight o'clock section in Current Economic Problems had quite a different discussion pattern than his ten o'clock section. With the eight o'clock group, all he had to do was to ask: "Are there any questions this morning?" and the group would be off on a lively discussion. His only problem was that of seeing that the group was not dominated by two or three students who seemed to have more to say than the others. Starting a discussion was much harder in the ten o'clock section, and Mr. Follis often had to prod the class with leading questions to get it under way. Even so, the ten o'clock class did not appear to want to talk very long on any issue. It seemed as though they did not have anything to say. The explanation did not lie in their competence in economics: both classes seemed to be fairly evenly matched as far as examination grades were concerned. The people in the ten o'clock group, however, were definitely shyer and less sure of themselves. There were more older students in the eight o'clock class, and their willingness to speak up seemed to encourage the younger students. In spite of the general willingness to participate, there were times, however, when discussion lagged even in the eight o'clock class. For instance, when Mr. Follis announced that a mid-term examination had been scheduled for the following week, there was a flurry of questions as to what the test would cover, whether it was to be objective or essay, and so forth. Then there was no discussion for a minute or two, whereupon it started more slowly and tentatively than it usually did. After about ten minutes, however, it was going as well as ever.

The differences in the behavior of these two groups appear to be due, at least in part, to differences in climate. The eight o'clock group had developed a climate that was more conducive to the give and take of ideas, whereas the climate of the ten o'clock group had an opposite effect. Very likely there was more anxiety and insecurity in the ten o'clock class. Mr. Follis changed the atmosphere in his eight o'clock section when he announced the examination. The anxiety level of the group was raised, the discussion slowed down and stopped, but after a few minutes the effect was dissipated, as the group re-established the climate it was accustomed to.

The kind of climate that exists in a group is to a large degree a function of the expectations of the members. The eight o'clock group had come to expect a lively discussion, whereas the members of the ten o'clock group had come to expect that they would have little to say and would say that rather poorly. They knew that their instructor was disappointed in them, and they had come to anticipate his disappointment. Climate, then, has a kind of circular or reciprocating effect: it tends to produce the kind of behavior that perpetuates it.

The two classes we have described were groups that were to some degree instrumental in producing the kind of climate that governed their behavior. Most groups, however, are rather strongly dependent on their leaders to initiate the atmosphere that becomes the climate of the group. The classical study of the effect of social climate was conducted by Lewin, Lippitt, and White (1939), using 4 groups of 11-year-old boys. Each group was under the supervision of an adult leader for 7 weeks, whereupon a different leader was assigned to the group for 7 more weeks. A third and final period of 7 weeks was under the supervision of still another leader. The three leaders played different roles with each of the clubs they supervised, with the result that the research workers had a chance to observe the behavior of the clubs under three different philosophies of leadership: autocratic, democratic, and *laissez-faire*.

Autocratic leaders were instructed to prescribe club activities and procedures as much as possible. The techniques to be used in the activities undertaken by each group were communicated one step at a time, in order that the boys would be in the dark with respect to future steps. Democratic leaders were asked to play the role of discussion leaders, helping the boys to come to group decisions. Advice, when requested, was to be given in terms of alternatives. Everyone in the group was to be free to work with whomever he chose, whereas in the autocratic situation, each boy was told whom he was to work with. As much as possible, the democratic leader was to be a regular group member in spirit, without doing much of the work. The *laissez-faire* leader was asked to play a passive, inactive role, giving advice and help only on request.

The researchers found that autocratic leadership produced two kinds of climates: one aggressive and one apathetic, the aggressive climate being characterized by rebellious behavior, and the apathetic climate being characterized by extreme dependence on the leader and a low capacity for initiating group action. The *laissez-faire* climate produced the largest amount of disorganization and the lowest amount of time spent in constructive work on the group projects. As contrasted with the democratic situation, the *laissez-faire* produced more discontent, more hostility, and less friendliness. The democratic climate was characterized by a high level of friendliness among the group members and toward the leader. The level of work was satisfactory, although there was some loafing and some play that lowered production. Somewhat more time was spent in work under autocratic leadership, but when the leader was out of the room, task-orientation dropped markedly, whereas the boys kept on working when their democratic or *laissez-faire* leaders were out of the room.

Leadership

The role of the leader. The person who plays the role of leader in a group is obviously in a key position. As we have seen from the study by Lewin, Lippitt, and White, he is able to exert an important influence on group climate. Even in a group where a democratic climate prevails, the leader is often in a position to influence the attitudes and behavior of the group members in many ways, directly or indirectly. By the very nature of his position, the leader sets the pace and mood of the group, serves as a major source of stimulation, and initiates and directs communication within the group. The leader's position enables him also to develop an understanding of group opinion that is more accurate than that of most of the other group members. (Chowdhry and Newcomb, 1952; Greer, Galanter, and Nordlie, 1954.)

Much of the power exerted by a leader depends on how the group perceives him and how he perceives his role, and to some degree, these perceptions are related to the theory of leadership that is held. Basically, there are two major theories that attempt to explain leadership, that is, how individuals get to be leaders. According to one theory, certain individuals are bound to rise to the top because they have the proper combinations of the proper qualities. The aristocratic version of this theory, which still has some hold on our thinking, maintains that the qualities of leadership are inborn—inherited—whereas the democratic version holds that the qualities of leadership can be learned, and that anyone who has the opportunity and the desire may learn them. If we subscribe to the theory that a leader is a person who has a certain combination of qualities, we also seem likely to assume that there is a chronic scarcity of leaders. We say, for example, "What we need is more leaders like So-and-So," implying that we could use more leaders if we had them, but that there are no more to be had, because an insufficient number were born or trained.

The second theory of leadership has it that leaders are produced by certain situations. When a situation arises that calls for leadership, the person who happens to be in a strategic position will find himself in the possession of power and will be under some internal and external pressure to use that power in various ways, that is, he will be under pressure to behave like a leader. If this theory is followed to its logical conclusion, we must assume that the potential supply of leaders is inexhaustible, because each new situation will produce its own leader; if a capable leader is not already available, then one will appear.

The proponents of the first theory would claim that Napoleon arose to his position of leadership because he was the kind of person who was bound to be a leader under any circumstances, whereas the proponents of the second theory would claim that his rise to the position of supreme dictator was the result of a series of situations and circumstances which were bound to propel him in the proper direction.

Research supporting different theories of leadership. Actually, research supports both theories to some degree. There is a tendency for people who play leadership roles in one situation to play them in other situations. A study done by Williams and Leavitt (1947) showed that Marine Corps officer candidates who had been identified by their fellows and peers as leaders also demonstrated superior leadership after they graduated from officer candidate school and went out into active service. It is very likely that an individual who has successful experiences as a leader in one situation is likely to expect leaderlike behavior of himself in other situations. When he takes on leadership roles (that is, behaves like a leader), there is a tendency for others to perceive him as a leader. As Leary (1957) would put it, leaderlike behavior tends to "pull" followerlike behavior from the other members of the group.

This behavioral consistency on the part of persons with leadership experience was noted by Bass, Klubeck, and Wurster (1953) who found that persons who emerged as leaders in a "leaderless group discussion" were also likely to play leadership roles in real life. Research by Ames (1955) produced much the same results, but Ames also found that there were a number of individuals who received high leadership scores in the leaderless group discussion test but who had not played leadership roles previously. Such a finding seems to indicate that the supply of available "leadership talent" is larger than is popularly supposed.

The situational theory of leadership receives support from the research of Bavelas (1951) and Leavitt (1951), who experimented with the problem-solving effectiveness of small groups. Each group of 5 individuals was organized according to one of the patterns displayed in Figure 14-1. Each circle in the diagrams represents an individual, and the lines represent open channels of communication. Communication was limited to written notes and could take place only through the indicated channels. (Baffles were set up between subjects so that they could not even see one another.) Each of the arrangements diagrammed in Figure 14-1 was tested with 5 different groups of subjects. When each group had gone through 15 problems, the members were asked a number of questions, including these: "Did your group have a leader? If so, who?" Only about half the people who worked in the "circle" type of group identified a leader, and those they named were distributed among each of the positions in the circle, whereas almost all those who worked in the "wheel" type of group were able to recognize a leader, for they unanimously named the person occupying the position at the center of the group. As may be seen from the data reported in Figure 14-1, the persons at the center of each

kind of group tended to be most frequently mentioned as the leader. It appears, therefore, that the person whose position gives him the most power—that is, whose position enables and requires him to initiate, receive, and coordinate the largest number of communications—is most likely to be perceived as a leader.

Leadership and communication. There is, of course, much more to leadership than the power to control communication. An effective leader usually has some strong sense of identity with the group he leads, and the members of the group tend to identify, in turn, with him. This sense of mutual identity enables the leader to work on behalf of the group, both within the context of the group and outside of it—that is, it enables him to represent the group to other individuals and groups. An effective leader is also likely to be concerned about the administrative aspects of the group: organizing and reorganizing its structure, supervising its activities, planning activities for the future, making assignments and re-assignments, and so forth. However, both mutual identity and administrative efficiency are highly dependent on the effectiveness of communication in the group. Where the communication is effective, group members and leaders are able to understand each other better, and hurt feelings and frustrations, instead of being denied expression and allowed to simmer, are freely ventilated and openly discussed. One of the difficulties with groups organized on autocratic or authoritarian principles is that although the communication flows readily from the leader to the followers, there is no provision for feedback. Essentially, the underlying idea of the autocratic arrangement

Figure 14-1. Structures of experimental groups used in problem-solving experiment. (After Bavelas, 1951; Leavitt, 1951.)

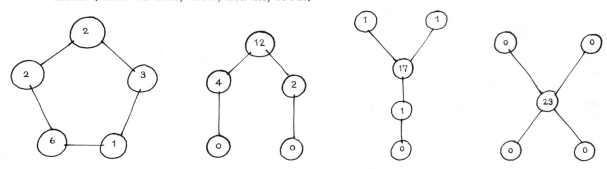

Figures in the circles show the number of times the persons in that position were perceived as leaders by the members of the group.

is this: what the leader has to say is important because *he is important,* but what the followers have to say is not important because *they are not important.*

Of the four types of groups used by Bavelas and Leavitt, the "circle" appears to be most conducive to democratic relationships, because each member has an equal opportunity to initiate, receive, and share communication, whereas the "wheel" type of group provides for the most centralized control and the least sharing of communication. When the participants in the four types of groups were asked how they felt about taking part in the work of their group, the members of the circle group expressed far more satisfaction than did the members in the less central positions of the other groups. The members located at the ends of the "spokes of the wheel" reported the least satisfaction. Research conducted by Leavitt (1951) and Smith and analyzed by Bavelas and Barrett (1951), using three patterns of groups, shows an inverted relationship between satisfaction and productivity. As Figure 14-2 shows, the "democratic" circle arrangement resulted in the highest morale but the least production, whereas the autocratic "wheel" arrangement resulted in the lowest morale but the best production. From the standpoint of production, the greatest advantage of the circle arrangement was its greater flexibility.

Leavitt (1951) explained the differences in satisfaction in terms of the amount of independence permitted by the structure of the group. In a culture like ours, he pointed out, needs for autonomy, recognition, and achievement are strong, hence it is to be expected that peripheral or "fringe" positions in the group (which by their very location limit opportunities for communication and freedom of action) would prove dissatisfying to their occupants. As the more democratic "circle" arrangement had no peripheral positions, it produced the highest degree of satisfaction. With respect to the differences in performance between the "democratic" and the "autocratic" arrangements in groups, some studies by Shaw (1954a, 1954b) suggest that the kind of task undertaken by the group may be important. When groups were assigned more difficult problems, groups in a "wheel" arrangement took longer than those arranged as "circles." It may be that more difficult tasks require a greater degree of independent thinking and are consequently performed more effectively in a democratic atmosphere.

The relationship between communication and group morale and cohesiveness is also demonstrated by a study of work stoppages in fifty business organizations during the two years after the outbreak of the Korean War. The companies were grouped on the basis of their labor-relations programs, including efforts to improve communication. Companies in Group A had well-developed programs; companies in Group B did little or nothing in this respect. The differences in the amount of communication attempted by the

Figure 14-2. Characteristics of three kinds of problem-solving groups. (After Bavelas and Barrett, 1951.)

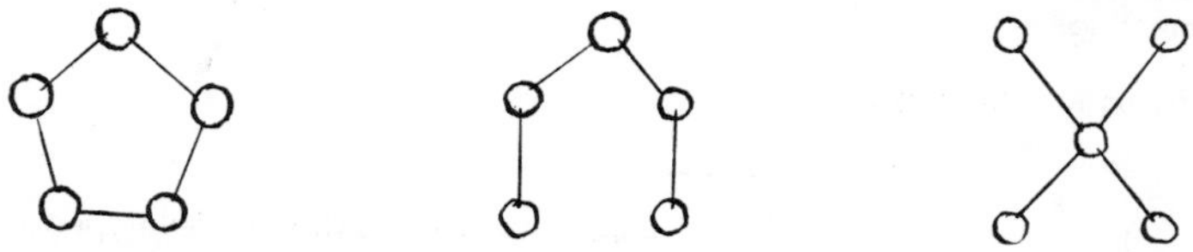

Characteristic	"Circle"	"Chain"	"Wheel"
Speed	slow	fast	very fast
Accuracy	poor	good	very good
Organization	no stable form of organization	slowly emerging but stable organization	almost immediate and stable organization
Emergence of Leader	none	marked	very pronounced
Morale	good	poor	very poor
Adaptation to Sudden Changes in Task	very good	poor	poor

firms in Group A and B and their experience with respect to labor strife are shown in Figure 14-3. As the data indicate, the companies that attempted the greater amount of communication had fewer strikes and thus presumably had a higher proportion of satisfied workers.

The need to share leadership. One of the chief differences between autocratic or authoritarian leaders and democratic leaders is their attitude toward the development of leadership on the part of group members. The autocratic leader is inclined to regard the attempts of his followers to lead as challenges to his authority, as attempts to compete with him. The authoritarian system, with its highly organized and highly centralized structure, is likely to be threatened and shaken by the appearance of new authority figures in competition with the established leadership. Hence, in order to maintain the group structure as it is,

the leadership is bound to attack and suppress those who are unwilling or unable to accept subordinate positions or wait their turn for promotion, thus signifying their acceptance of the established system.

The democratic approach is that of sharing leadership and power and encouraging group members to play leadership roles from time to time. The most effective leader, according to Gordon (1951) "is one who can create the conditions by which he will actually lose the leadership." Such an attitude is basic to the kind of group atmosphere in which members are really free to communicate.

In a leader-dominated group, the members are likely to look to the leader for cues as to their behavior; they do not think of solutions to the problems with which the group is faced because it is the leader's task to create solutions. If a mem-

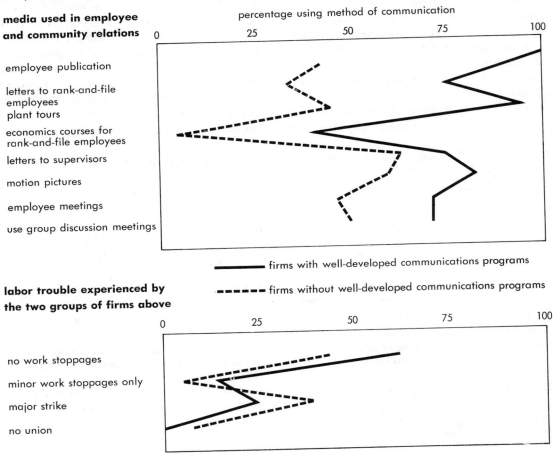

Figure 14-3. Differences in amount of communication initiated by two groups of companies and labor trouble experienced. (*Public Opinion Index for Industry,* Oct., 1952. Reproduced by permission of Opinion Research Corporation.)

ber makes a suggestion, he is likely to do so apologetically or truculently, depending on his attitude toward the leader. Neither attitude is conducive to free communication and the production of creative ideas. However, in groups where the leadership is passed from one person to another, as opportunities and circumstances arise, members feel freer to put forth ideas and solutions. In the Lewin, Lippitt, and White experiment we discussed, the groups under autocratic leaders were more likely to disintegrate when the leader left the room, because all authority had been centered in the leader, and in his absence there was no one who could take his place. In groups where the democratic climate prevailed, work continued because members were free to exercise leadership and initiative, and each one felt personally responsible toward maintaining an orderly and effective group. In groups where there is free and equal participation, members are more likely to take responsibility for their own behavior; in groups that are dominated by leaders, members are more likely to pass responsibility for their behavior on to their leaders.

Some autocratic individuals apparently function quite effectively as leaders: their groups are productive and efficient, morale is good, and cohesiveness is strong. Such results depend on the psychological maturity of the leader, the general effectiveness of the organization and structure of the group, and the willingness of the group members to accept an authoritarian setting. The cultural background of the members is very important, individuals from traditional cultures generally preferring a clearly defined structure with a definite hierarchy. Individuals with such cultural backgrounds would expect the leader to behave in authoritarian ways and would feel anxious and uncomfortable if he tried to share leadership and responsibility as is done in groups organized along democratic lines. Americans who try to introduce democratic methods into groups of people with authoritarian backgrounds often find that the procedures and assumptions that appear "natural and normal" to them appear "weak," "foolish," "unnecessary," and "inefficient" to others. Haythorn (1956) conducted an interesting study of the compatibility between the attitudes of small groups and those of their leaders. He assigned subjects to groups on the basis of their replies to a questionnaire measuring attitudes toward au-

thoritarian and democratic beliefs and practices. He found that authoritarian leaders worked best with groups having an authoritarian orientation, whereas democratic groups functioned more effectively under democratic leaders. When democratic leaders were assigned to authoritarian groups, and authoritarian leaders to democratic groups, groups came into conflict with the leader, were less cooperative, and suffered from lowered morale.

Social distance and leadership. One of the dilemmas that a leader in a democratic culture must face is that of deciding whether he will merge his personality with the group and become "one of the gang" or whether he will remain somewhat aloof in order to perform his rather unique functions and roles more adequately. This is a problem that is not easily resolved. The research we have cited up to the present point in our discussion seems to indicate that the decision should rest on whether the chief aim is group solidarity or whether it is efficiency in production. Some further light is shed by a study conducted by Hollander and Webb (1955) who studied the choices made by naval aviation cadets each of whom had been asked to list those classmates who, in his opinion, were most qualified to act as leaders, those whom he could depend on most if he were leader (that is, who were good followers), and those he preferred as friends. The results showed that those cadets selected as leaders were also likely to be selected as followers. There was some tendency to select friends as leaders or followers, but it was not a strong one. The important point, as far as our present discussion is concerned, is that leaders and friends were perceived as being somewhat different people. This implies a certain tendency to expect different qualities from leaders than are expected from friends.

Fiedler (1958) reviewed a number of studies comparing successful and unsuccessful surveying teams, high-school basketball teams, bomber and tank crews, open-hearth steel furnace gangs, and staffs of farm supply stores. In general, the successful groups differed from the unsuccessful in their attitudes toward their leaders. In the successful groups, the leader was well-liked, but was perceived as socially distant, that is, apart, from the rest of the group. Fiedler concluded that the person who leads groups that are involved in accomplishing some kind of task should be someone who is psychologically distant. Presumably, he said, such an attitude enables the leader to be more objective in his dealings with the group. Since he is less involved, he is able to maintain better discipline and more businesslike work relations. However, he felt that groups involved in other activities, such as policy-making, might call for different attitudes on the part of the leader.

Ghiselli and Lodahl (1958) report results which to some degree support Fiedler's conclusions. They assigned groups of four students each the task of operating a complicated model railroad system. Success was evaluated in terms of the number of times in a three-minute interval two trains could be run in opposite directions around the system. When subjects were given paper-and-pencil tests on supervisory ability and their approach to making decisions, it was found that neither the average amount of these traits possessed by each group nor the amount possessed by the highest scorer in the group was related to any degree to success in the assigned task. The researchers did find, however, that the most successful groups each possessed one individual who had a markedly higher score in decision-making than the other members of the group.

Although studies of this type are far from conclusive, they do raise the possibility that different kinds of group tasks may call for different kinds of leadership. They also point to the need for further research into the kinds of group structures, group climates, attitudes, and leadership that will produce the best results with the kinds of problems with which we are faced today.

Competition and cooperation

Competitive climates and group functioning. Another subject that has aroused much controversy is the question of whether competition should be encouraged or eliminated. Although competition tends to stimulate greater individual productivity (Hurlock, 1927), it also tends to lower the cohesiveness of a group. Some individuals, too, become easily discouraged by competitive situations, preferring not to attempt a task rather than fail at it.

Although competition is popularly assumed to be a dominant theme in human living, its position varies from one culture to another (Mead, 1937). In some societies like the BaThonga of Africa, the Zuñi Indians of the American Southwest, and the Eskimos, there is very little competition. Even in our own society the degree of competitiveness varies from one area of life to another. In general, attitudes and feelings that are group-oriented lead to cooperative behavior. Competition is a self-oriented, rather than a group-oriented approach, and as such, its effects are inclined to be divisive and disintegrative, rather than cohesive.

An experiment by Mintz (1951) illustrates with graphic effect how competition breaks down cooperative patterns within the group. A number of paper cones attached to strings were placed in a large glass bottle, and groups of subjects were given the task of getting the cones out of the bottle by pulling on strings. Cooperation was essential because the narrowness of the bottle neck meant that only one could be drawn out at a time. Any attempt to draw out more than one cone at a time caused them to jam up in the neck of the bottle, as Figure 14-4 illustrates. Under competitive conditions, subjects were promised rewards ranging from 10 to 25 cents for successfully removing their cones before they were wet by the rising level of water within the bottle. If they failed, they were to pay fines ranging from 1 to 5 cents. Under "no-reward" conditions, the subjects were told that the experiment would measure their ability to cooperate with each other. Serious "traffic jams" developed in well over half the trials

Figure 14-4. Cross section of the glass bottle used in experiment in competition and cooperation, showing two cones jammed together in the bottle neck. (After Mintz, 1951.)

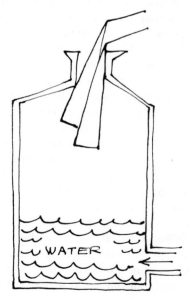

conducted under "reward-and-fine" conditions. Some of the groups that were able to function adequately under "no-reward" conditions were unable to get all their cones out of the bottle under the competitive or "reward-and-fine" conditions. The point is that when individuals became preoccupied with their personal welfare, they were unable to cooperate with the other members of the group, even though their chances for success depended on the cooperation of the group.

The divisive effects of competition on group behavior are also demonstrated by an experiment conducted by Grossack (1954), who assigned small groups of students a problem which they were to work on by means of writing messages to one another. Some of the students were told that the performance of the entire group would be rated; others were told that the performance of each individual would be rated. Grossack found that students who were encouraged to cooperate (that is, who were told that the performance of the *group* would be rated) were more inclined to develop cohesiveness in their group than those who were encouraged to compete (that is, who were told that they would be rated as individuals). Furthermore, in the "cooperative" group, attempts at communication were more successful.

Group structure

Sociometric analysis of group structure. It is possible to analyze the cohesiveness of a group by means of a device or technique known as *sociometry*. Each member of a group is asked to indicate which other members he would choose to work with, go to a show with, sit next to, serve on a committee with, or the like, and which members he would not choose. From these data, a diagram or chart can be constructed, showing the choices and rejections of the group. Figure 14-5 consists of a sociometric chart, showing the choices and rejections made by the members of two squadrons of naval aviators who were asked to indicate the men they would like to have fly beside them and those they would not like to have fly beside them. There were 23 acceptances and only 4 rejections within Squadron A, a high-morale group, but 19 acceptances and 17 rejections within Squadron B, a low-morale group. The officers in Squadron A evidently preferred members of their own group, because officers from other squadrons were mentioned only in terms of rejection, whereas 4 members of Squad-

ron B preferred the members of other squadrons for flying mates. There are two well-defined cliques, or exclusive subgroups, in Squadron B, whereas the sociogram for Squadron A shows no cliques, its members being bound together by "chains of acceptance" that link each member of the group and include the commanding officer and the executive officer.

It is plain to see why the morale of Squadron A would be higher than that of Squadron B. Evidently the members of Squadron A were better able to cooperate with each other. Very likely, too, the communication among members of Squadron A and between the members and their

Figure 14-5. Sociograms of two naval air squadrons. (After Jenkins, 1948.)

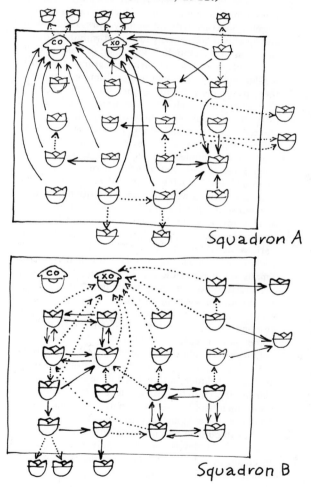

Each circle represents an officer; CO is the commanding officer of the squadron and XO is the executive officer. Solid lines represent choices; dotted lines represent rejections; and arrows indicate the direction of the choice or rejection.

leaders functioned more effectively. (Jenkins, 1948.)

Inclusive and exclusive groups. Generally speaking, the more cohesive a group is, the more satisfying it is to its members. Hence there is a strong tendency for group members to become emotionally invested in groups that they find to be congenial and satisfying and to find ways of making these groups more cohesive. One way of doing this is to expand the scope of activity of the group.

For example, at one time the members of the Southside Community Church used to linger on the steps and in the foyer of the church after the service in order to chat for a few minutes. Then they decided that these conversations could take place under more congenial circumstances, so they arranged for coffee to be served in the church school assembly hall. The church had a number of voluntary organizations, largely concerned with missionary work, fund raising, and other activities closely identified with the religious functions of the church. They began to hold an occasional meeting or so, featuring programs devoted to secular matters of rather general interest. In time, these programs grew in number until they were organized by the church administration into a large scale program of adult education. Hobby clubs also increased in number and scope. Before the church began to expand its activities, few members devoted more than a couple of hours a week to activities involving the church, but as a result of the expansion there are relatively few members who do not spend at least 4 hours a week in some kind of church activity, and some spend 25 hours a week and more.

This involvement is supported by much mutual encouragement to participate more actively in the various activities of the church. Members of the photography club solicit members for their club from among the congregation at large, and they, in turn, are urged to do work for the annual church fair and to attend the evening programs sponsored by the adult education committee. Some of the members respond favorably to this continual pressure to become more deeply and extensively involved in the activities of the church, but others, who are engaged in volunteer activities outside the church or who prefer their own solitude, are inclined to resist. The leadership of the church professes to be much concerned about members whose participation is limited to attendance at religious services, and there is a great deal of discussion and planning with respect to ways and means of "involving" these individuals. They are, in effect, perceived as a threat to the solidarity and cohesiveness of the group.[1]

[1] Festinger and Thibaut (1951) have been able to demonstrate experimentally that the more the behavior of group members differs from the expectations of the majority of the group, the greater the efforts of this majority to get them to conform.

What we have been describing is the behavior of an *inclusive group,* a group whose satisfaction in group activity is heightened by expanding the activities of the group and by recruiting and enlisting other members. This eagerness to expand and share the activities of a group is largely characteristic of free and open societies—societies, that is, which emphasize individual equality and freedom of personal movement.

The mirror image of the inclusive group is the *exclusive group,* a group whose satisfaction in group activity is heightened by excluding would-be members or by making it difficult for them to become members. Most communities that have been established for a generation or more have at least one formal or informal group composed of members of the elite. Sometimes the group is a literary society, sometimes it operates a hunting lodge, very often its chief occupation is conversation. College fraternities and sororities tend to be groups that are more or less exclusive groups. Groups of this sort not only provide their members with opportunities to communicate with their social peers, but also their exclusiveness produces a heightened feeling of status and importance.

There is some evidence to indicate that the difficulties encountered in being accepted as a member of a group heighten the value of the group to the would-be member. Aronson and Mills (1959) found that students who had to go through an embarrassing experience in order to become members of a discussion group thought more highly of the group than did members whose initiation involved little or no difficulty or disturbance. The authors interpreted their findings as indicating that the person who experiences a painful initiation is inclined to be convinced that membership in the group is worth the price he has paid and consequently tends to ignore some of the negative features or deficiencies of the group he has joined and to overestimate its attractiveness.

Being a member of a group enables us, as we have noted previously, to share feelings, norms, and frames of reference with others. In other words, it enables us to *feel similar* to others, the "others" in this case being members of the group. However, group membership also enables us to *feel different* from others, the "others" in *this* case being those who are not members of the group. Both kinds of feelings are important for the maintenance of our self-concept. On the one

On some college campuses, freshmen are expected to "prove themselves" in a traditional clash with sophomores. Such experiences have the result of giving membership in the student bodies of these colleges a higher psychological value than it might otherwise possess. The psychological value of membership in a given college may also be elevated through admission requirements that eliminate all but a small percentage of applicants, or by grading standards that eliminate the majority of lower classmen through academic failure.

hand, we want reassurance that we are to some degree like other people, but on the other hand, we want reassurance that we are different from others. Our membership in groups tells us, in effect, whom we resemble and whom we do not resemble. A person who is an accountant knows that in terms of his professional interests, at least, he resembles other accountants but does not resemble lawyers, farmers, grocery clerks, and social workers. A member of an electrician's union may see himself as having something in common with the other members of the union, but as being different from employers and from electricians who are not union members. In a way, there is a "figure-and-ground" relationship between membership and nonmembership, with the group being the figure and the rest of the population being the ground. The more important a group is to us, the greater our emotional involvement and investment in it, the more likely we are to perceive a difference between members and nonmembers.

The formation of exclusive groups tends to be characteristic of older, more authoritarian so-

cieties. The older a community or a society is, the more likely it is to become socially stratified. Individuals are more likely to be assigned to relatively fixed positions in the social structure, and freedom of social movement is thereby reduced. Exclusive societies serve the purpose of preserving and maintaining existing stratification, just as inclusive societies tend to cut across stratification.

Even in the most democratic societies there is inevitably some problem with regard to exclusiveness. The idea that some groups are better than others is incompatible with the principle of individual equality that is basic to democratic relationships. Yet there is a need for individuals to define their self-concepts in terms of identifying with groups that set some limits on their membership or their activities. Being an accountant would not have much meaning if anyone who wished could become an accountant merely by calling himself an accountant or if accountants had no well-defined functions and responsibilities—if there were, in other words, no psycho-social boundaries between accountants and nonaccountants. In order to preserve these important distinctions, accountants form organizations and get colleges and universities to set up special curricula as a way of specifying who accountants are, what they do, and what is necessary to become an accountant. These regulations and specifications help accountants communicate to the world at large their sense of professional identity, in order that others may have certain expectations for accountants and will accord them a measure of respect with regard to their competencies.

The problem in a democratic society, then, is not so much the elimination of exclusive groups, but the elimination of membership requirements that are based on aristocratic standards, that is, the idea that some people are born better or more worthy than others. The fact that we have not been able to eliminate aristocratic attitudes of social superiority and inferiority in our more or less democratic society is demonstrated by the existence of restrictions that make it difficult for the members of some racial or religious groups to participate on an equal basis in the competition for positions of status and power. These restrictions are, in turn, based on prejudices—deep-seated and irrational beliefs in the inherent intellectual and/or moral superiority of certain groups, as contrasted with the inferiority of others. Such prejudice has the effect of creating an impenetrable barrier between groups. In rigidly organized, autocratic societies, such barriers between groups are perhaps a necessary feature to maintaining the continuity of the social structure, but they are antithetical to the functioning of a democratic society, which depends on "openness" and accessibility—freedom of movement and freedom of communication among and within individuals and groups.

Summary

Communication is different in different group contexts because many aspects of the situation are different. Children tend to be self-oriented and must go through a learning process in order to respond as part of a group. Group relationships become increasingly important in preadolescent and adolescent years; mature individuals must learn to maintain a balance between responsibilities to self and to the group. Groups can be divided into the primary, or face-to-face, type and the secondary type. Many of our needs are met in group context, but often the group itself has needs which may become more important than individual needs.

Whether or not a group achieves its goals depends on several factors. High morale (an optimistic feeling about the group's chance of success) is helpful to a group. The factors that influence morale are not simply such things as physical comfort; rather, psychological rewards appear to be more important. Groups whose members have high mutual attraction are cohesive, and this quality may or may not increase productivity. The general psychological or emotional state of the group is termed its climate. Group climate seems to depend in large measure on the expectations of group members. The type of leadership (autocratic, democratic, or *laissez-faire*) also has a large influence on group climate.

The leader plays a key role in a group. There are two theories to explain the emergence of leadership: one explains it in terms of the personal qualities of the leader and the other explains it in terms of the situation that calls for or develops leadership. Actually, research evidence supports both theories. The type of communication between the leader and the group, and also among group members is somewhat different in autocratic and democratic situations. Research with small groups working on simple tasks shows some tendency for democratic arrangements to have higher morale and greater flexibility and for autocratic arrangements to have greater productivity. However, the personalities of the group members and the nature of the task also help to determine the relative effectiveness of different types of groups. Democratic leaders are much more willing than autocratic leaders to develop leadership within the group and to share this function. Several studies have found that successful leaders tend to be well-liked by the group but are also perceived by group members as socially distant.

Group-oriented attitudes and feelings lead to cooperative behavior whereas a self-oriented approach leads to competitive behavior. Competition tends to interfere with the performance of the group and to stifle cooperation, even when individual success is dependent on it.

Sociometry is a technique whereby group cohesiveness may be analyzed. Each member of a group is asked to choose other members of the group on some basis, whereupon the pattern of choices is plotted on a sociogram. An inclusive group is one that tries to expand by recruiting and enlisting new members in order to share the activities of the group. An exclusive group is one that excludes others and makes membership difficult to achieve in order to heighten the members' status and feeling of importance. The second type of group is more common in older, more authoritarian societies. Exclusive groups can also function in a democratic way to distinguish differences among groups (such as professions), and this need not imply social differences or individual inequality.

Questions

1. Is communication within a group of ten friends any different from communication between those same individuals two at a time? Why?

2. In what groups did you participate as you were growing up? What influence do you suppose they had on your behavior?

3. Give several examples of primary and secondary groups. How do they differ?

4. Using Carter's three factors as a basis, discuss the behavior of yourself and others in some small group of which you are a member.

5. In what ways do college fraternities and sororities meet the needs of their members, and in what ways do these groups have needs of their own?

6. What are some of the factors that influence the effectiveness of a group?

7. Describe and discuss the meaning of the Lewin, Lippitt, and White study of social climate with respect to situations at work and in the classroom.

8. What are the two major theories of leadership. Which do you believe and why?

9. Discuss some of the advantages and disadvantages of authoritarian leadership.

10. What are the effects of competition and cooperation on group performance?

11. Of what use are sociograms in analyzing the behavior of groups?

Suggestions for further reading

Cartwright, D. and A. Zander, Editors, *Group Dynamics: Research and Theory*. Evanston, Ill.: Row Peterson, 1953. A book of readings, dealing with such aspects of group functioning as cohesiveness, problem-solving, structure, and leadership.

Gardner, E. F. and G. G. Thompson, *Social Relations and Morale in Small Groups*. New York: Appleton-Century-Crofts, 1956. A report of research using sociometric methods to study interaction among college fraternity groups at Syracuse University.

Gordon, T., *Group-Centered Leadership*. Boston: Houghton Mifflin, 1955. Application of democratic principles to group functioning.

Gouldner, A. W., Editor, *Studies in Leadership: Leadership and Democratic Action*. New York: Harper, 1950. A collection of readings. See especially the section devoted to authoritarian and democratic leaders.

Hare, P., E. F. Borgatta, and R. F. Bales, Editors, *Small Groups: Studies in Social Interaction*. New York: Knopf, 1955. A selected group of papers dealing with theory and research in group processes.

Lindgren, H. C., *Effective Leadership in Human Relations*. New York: Nelson, 1954. A discussion of the problems encountered by leaders in attempting to cope with the hostile feelings generated by their subordinates. Written for lay readers.

Maccoby, E. E., T. M. Newcomb, and E. L. Hartley, Editors, *Readings in Social Psychology*, 3rd ed. New York: Holt, 1958. See sections on leadership, group structure, and group process.

Sargent, S. S. and R. C. Williamson, *Social Psychology: An Introduction to the Study of Human Relations*, 2nd ed. New York: Ronald, 1958. See the section dealing with interpersonal relations and the chapter dealing with group dynamics.

Sherif, M. and C. W., *An Outline of Social Psychology*, rev. ed. New York: Harper, 1956. Most of the chapters in this book are relevant to the subject matter of this chapter.

Thelen, H. A., *Dynamics of Groups at Work*. Chicago: University of Chicago Press, 1954. Describes six different types of working and learning groups and analyzes the underlying processes.

PART SEVEN

APPLYING PSYCHOLOGY TO HUMAN PROBLEMS

Susan Greenburg

15

Selecting and learning occupational roles

Work occupies a position of great importance in our middle-class system of values. The man who lacks gainful employment is likely to be perceived and to perceive himself as being somewhat out on the margin of social acceptability. There is something "incomplete" about being unemployed; a man must be gainfully employed if he is to be considered a fully functioning member of society.

Certain psychological needs are likely to be expressed through work. The male adult finds it a major outlet for self-expression and creativity, and, with the growing equality of the sexes, gainful employment is playing a more important part in the lives of women as well. The occupational role also provides a major route to active participation in the social group. And, as we shall see, there is a close relationship between our personal values and the kind of occupation we select.

Psychological motives in work. Money is popularly assumed to be the chief motive in work. The teacher shortage is blamed on the low salaries paid to teachers, with the implication that if salaries were to be raised, the shortage would disappear. And the dual phenomenon of the gradual disappearance of the general medical practitioner and the increase in the number of medical specialists is often attributed to the higher fees that specialists can command.

There is no doubt that there is a kind of rough relationship between income and occupational status. People in professional and managerial positions tend to earn more than skilled craftsmen like boilermakers and stone masons, and

Although all jobs provide some way of meeting needs for self-expression, opportunities for self-expression are more readily recognizable in some fields, like commercial photography

skilled workers earn more than the unskilled. Inasmuch as a college education is an essential preliminary step to entering the professions and, to a large extent, the managerial ranks, it might appear that the decisions of students to attend college and to go on to graduate school are based primarily on the desire to improve earning capacity.

However, a survey of a nationwide cross section of college students, conducted by Rosenberg and others (1957), indicates that their vocational interests are not focused on making money. As Table 15-1 shows, the largest majority of students are principally concerned with finding an occupation that provides an outlet for self-expression. When the same students were asked to indicate which one of the characteristics listed in Table

15-1 was of the *greatest* importance to them, 27 per cent chose "Provide an opportunity to use my special abilities or talents," and only 10 per cent chose "Provide me with a chance to earn a great deal of money."

The secondary importance of money in the framework of occupational values is also confirmed by the research of Morse and Weiss (1955), who polled a nationwide sample of 401 employed men, asking them a number of questions about their attitudes toward work. Their opening question was: "If by some chance you inherited enough money to live comfortably without working, do you think you would work anyway or not?" Only 20 per cent said they would not work. The 80 per cent who said they would work were asked why. Their answers, as shown

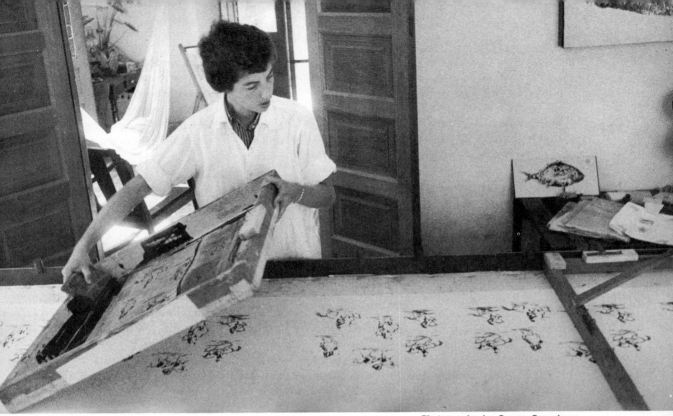

Photographs by Susan Greenburg

and textile design, than in others.

Table 15–1 Rating of "Requirements for Ideal Job or Career" by 4585 college students. (After Rosenberg, 1957.)

Requirement	Highly Important	Medium Importance	Little or No Importance, Irrelevant, or Distasteful
Provide an opportunity to use my special abilities or aptitudes	78%	20%	2%
Provide me with a chance to earn a good deal of money	39	48	13
Permit me to be creative and original	48	39	13
Give me social status and prestige	26	53	21
Give me an opportunity to work with people rather than things	44	36	20
Enable me to look forward to a stable, secure future	61	31	8
Leave me relatively free of supervision by others	38	48	14
Give me a chance to exercise leadership	32	53	15
Provide me with adventure	16	40	44
Give me an opportunity to be helpful to others	43	44	13

in Table 15-2, are a kind of catalog of the needs people satisfy in their work. Most of the negative reasons, and even some of the positive ones, indicate how much of the self-concept is wrapped up in the job. Many of these men reacted to the prospect of giving up their job as though they were being asked to give up a part of themselves.

When Morse and Weiss asked the same group what they would miss most if they stopped working, many of them expressed their answers in emotional terms. Life would not *feel* the same for them. A large proportion mentioned the relationship they had with other people, indicating the importance of work as a way of social participation. Their replies, as shown in Table 15-3, provide further clues as to the importance of the self in attitudes toward work.

The need to work is not present in the same strength at all ages. When Morse and Weiss analyzed their data with respect to age, they found that 90 per cent of the men aged 21 to 34 preferred to work, even if they had sufficient funds to live comfortably, as contrasted with only 61 per cent of the men aged 55 to 64. However, 82 per cent of the men aged 65 and over said that they would prefer to work. There were also differences with respect to social class. When the men were asked why they preferred to continue working, middle-class members (professional, managerial, and sales) were inclined to give reasons reflecting a sense of interest or accomplishment, whereas farmers and members of the working class were inclined to give as their reason the need to keep occupied.

The replies given by respondents in the study by Morse and Weiss also give clues as to some of the anxiety that we would experience if we were unable to work. Evidently the work we do makes a contribution to our lives that would sorely be missed. Part of this contribution is made to our self-concept, that is, our involvement in an occupation is to some extent "who we are." When we fill out blanks applying for credit, passports, or admission to a social organization, we are asked almost invariably to state our occupation. Our occupation is not only a role, a way of expressing ourselves and communicating with the world, but it is also an index, a classification that enables others to make assumptions and to develop expectations about us, rightly or wrongly. One of these assumptions has to do with social status.

Occupational roles and social status. In the American culture, occupation is perhaps the best single indicator of social status. (Kornhauser,

Table 15-2 Why men would wish to continue working (even though they had enough money to live comfortably without working). (After Morse and Weiss, 1955.)

	Percentage
Positive reasons	
Enjoy the kind of work	9
To be associated with people	1
To keep occupied (interested)	32
Justifies my existence	5
Gives feeling of self-respect	5
Keeps individual healthy, good for person	10
Other	1
Total positive reasons	63
Negative reasons	
Without work, would:	
Feel lost, go crazy	14
Feel useless	2
Feel bored	4
Not know what to do with my time, can't be idle	10
Habit, inertia	6
To keep out of trouble	1
Total negative reasons	37

Table 15-3 What men would miss most if they did not work. (After Morse and Weiss, 1955.)

	Percentage
General feeling	
Feeling of living, belonging, being a part of something	3
Feeling of doing something important, worthwhile, feeling of self-respect	9
Feeling of interest, being interested	5
Feeling of doing something, would be restless	25
Total expressing general feeling	42
Specific things missed	
The kind of work I do	12
The people I know through or at work, the friends, the contacts	31
Regular routine	6
Money	2
Other	1
Total mentioning specific things that would be missed	52
Would miss nothing	6

Being without a job not only cuts an individual off from a regular source of income, but it also serves to cut him off from society to some degree. Not only does the unemployed worker miss the social participation he enjoys with his fellow employees, but he also suffers a certain loss of identity, since his self-concept is to a greater or lesser extent derived from his job.

1953.) More than any other variable, it is an index to educational and family background, intelligence, income, and the various patterns of attitudes and beliefs that we have learned to associate with the various social levels. For example, Folsom and Sobolewski (1957) asked students to rank a number of occupations on the basis of social status. A week later, they were asked to estimate the average annual income for individuals in each of the professions. The relationship between the social status assigned to the occupations and the estimated income was fairly high, between .64 and .74.

From time to time during the last thirty years, researchers have been checking the way in which people rate a list of twenty-five occupations according to social status. On each occasion, the rankings have been quite consistent, ranging from banker, physician, and lawyer at the top, to janitor, hodcarrier, and ditchdigger at the bottom. (Deeg and Paterson, 1947.) When Canter (1956) compared these ratings with the intelligence test

scores made by individuals from the occupations on the list during their Army service in World War II, he found the correlation to be very high: .92.

In a culture where occupational role plays such a dominant part in each individual's life, it is to be expected that the process of selecting and preparing for an occupation will result in some anxiety. It becomes a major concern in secondary school and college.

Dynamics of occupational choice. Occupational choice, is, in effect, a way of implementing a self-concept. (Super, 1957.) It is a process whereby a person is called upon to state rather specifically: "I am this or that kind of person." For individuals who have not completely thought through this problem, choosing an occupation thus becomes a time for self-analysis and self-discovery, a time for finding some of the answers to the question: "Who am I?"

The student who has not made an occupational choice often confesses to a sense of confusion.

He may say, for example: "I haven't the remotest idea of what I want to do. I've looked into two or three likely professions, but they don't seem to be at all what I would really like." Such students may even feel a kind of anxiety in their inability to make a choice, and a few may even experience a mild degree of panic. This is quite understandable, in view of the degree to which an individual in our culture derives a sense of identity from his occupation. Not to have made a vocational choice is, in a sense, like being an incomplete person. Some students even try to deal with this problem by making arbitrary or random choices of a major in order to resolve what for them is a perplexing problem.

Actually, however, even the most occupationally confused person has made some choices. His problem, as Tyler (1959) points out, is essentially that of becoming aware of the choices he *has* made. These choices may not necessarily be *directly* related to this or that occupation, but they have a significant bearing on the kind of occupation eventually chosen. The individual, for example, who is restless when he is cooped up within four walls, has in effect made a choice that eliminates indoor jobs. The individual who is very "security conscious" has in effect eliminated occupations, like selling, characterized by a variable income. The most significant choices, Tyler says, are the negative ones. Each negative choice eliminates a whole category of jobs, but the number of different kinds of jobs is so extensive (over 30,000), that even a large list of "dislikes" would leave some occupational areas available for choice.

An important factor to be considered, however, is the change that takes place with maturity. When Lindgren, Mather, Harries, and Beronio (1959) presented college students with a list of occupations with unpleasant connotations (for example, garbage collector, undertaker's assistant) and asked them to indicate which ones they would be unwilling to accept under any circumstances, students in their teens rejected a significantly higher number than did students in their twenties. The fact that the "rejecting attitudes" which are characteristic of teenagers are not limited to the vocational area is suggested by the rather high correlations the authors found between the number of rejected items on the occupational list and the number of rejections on a list of foods.

A relationship between vocational choice and maturity is also suggested by a study conducted by Small (1953), who found that the choices of better-adjusted boys aged 15 to 19 were more realistic than those of emotionally disturbed boys the same age. Interestingly, he also found that the *second* vocational choice of better-adjusted boys was less realistic than their first choice, whereas the second choice of disturbed boys tended to be more realistic than their first choice.

Some students seem to be less prepared than others for the task of self-discovery and self-analysis that is an important part of realistic vocational choice, and the extent to which they are prepared to make a choice is often reflected in the kind of success attained in college. The individual who, because of psychological immaturity or conflicting interests and value patterns, is unable to make a decision, is less likely to achieve adequate grades and is more likely to drop out of college. This is quite understandable: the student who has no readily definable objective, who does not know, in effect, why he is in college at all, will tend to lack the motivation necessary to maintain an acceptable academic record and will repeatedly ask himself whether college is worth the effort.

People who have not made an occupational choice are somewhat more inclined to look upon work as a source of economic security, prestige, or financial return, whereas those who have made definite or tentative choices are more inclined to see work as a means for self-expression or for helping others, according to research done by Miller (1956). In other words, people who had made an occupational choice were more inclined to see work in terms of intrinsic rewards—satisfactions to be derived from *participation in the work itself*—in contrast to the extrinsic rewards that come *as a result of employment.*

None of this should, of course, be taken to indicate that students who have not chosen an occupation will improve their chances for academic survival or for eventual occupational satisfaction by making an immediate and arbitrary decision as to an occupation. There are usually very valid and cogent reasons why a given student has not been able to make a choice. For some students, the best decision might be that of trying a number of different college courses in an attempt to find a congenial occupational pattern; for others, the best solution might be that of dropping out of college and working for a few years until a decision is reached. However, any student can benefit from the improved understanding of himself and the occupational world that may be gained through vocational counseling.

Vocational counseling. Not very many years ago, the student who was perplexed and confounded by vocational indecision, who could not decide whether to make an arbitrary choice, drop out of college for a while, or spend a year or so trying out various combinations of college courses, was forced to make such decisions entirely on his own. Sometimes he had the help of faculty advisers who were well meaning but professionally unprepared for the task of providing students with the kind of information needed for choosing an occupation. Today, most colleges and universities of any size have student personnel departments staffed by people with training in the field of vocational counseling. The function of these counselors is, generally speaking, not that of deciding what choices a student should make, but rather that of helping him arrive at a decision of his own. They can help a student explore various aspects of the world of work, administer aptitude and interest tests, interpret the results, provide him with occupational information, and inform him concerning the alternatives that face him. Even students who have already made vocational choices may benefit from counseling. There are many who make choices that are inappropriate and are likely to lead to failure and frustration.

To expand somewhat on the idea suggested by Tyler (1959), it is the task of the counselor to help students discover two kinds of choices that have already been made: (1) the choices they have made for themselves by virtue of their patterns of likes and dislikes, and (2) the choices that have been made for them by the requirements of various occupational fields and their individual patterns of abilities. Here is an example of how a counselor might help a college student identify some of the choices that have already been made —choices that he therefore does not have to make:

George Reinecke is concerned because he cannot make a decision between the fields of engineering and business administration. As his counselor goes over his test scores and his academic records, he shows George a rather consistent pattern of low-average grades in mathematics and science which is related to below-average interests in mechanical, scientific, and engineering activities. The fact that George's scores on the college aptitude tests are average for college students means, perhaps, that he could finish the engineering curriculum if his motivation were high enough. But the counselor wonders, on the basis of the past record and the low measured interests in engineering and allied fields, if George were not *already* developing in a direction that led away from engineering, rather than toward it. The pattern of aptitudes and interests that George displays is dissimilar from the kinds of patterns that lead to success and satisfaction in engineering. By becoming the kind of person he is, George has unwittingly made decisions that have eliminated engineering as a possible occupational field.

"Faith in people" as a variable. When Rosenberg and others (1957) conducted the nationwide poll of college students referred to previously, they asked a number of questions in order to assess the students' "faith in people": questions as to whether people could be trusted, whether people would generally prefer to help others or look out for themselves, and the like. On the basis of the replies, the researchers classified the respondents as having "high faith in people" or "medium and low faith in people." The careers preferred by these two groups are reported in Table 15-4. Persons having a high degree of faith in people are more likely to choose social work, personnel work, and teaching—occupations in which success is more dependent on willingness of other people to "do the right thing." It is hardly surprising to find that advertising, business, and sales rank at the bottom of the list, in view of the fact that much of their work is involved in developing and carrying out strategies whereby others may be manipulated in the interests and to the advantage of the manipulator. In any event, as Rosenberg points out, faith in people is seldom the factor that *completely* de-

Susan Greenburg

Social work is one of the occupations selected by persons with a high degree of "faith in people."

Table 15–4   Relationship between choice of a career and "faith in people." (After Rosenberg, 1957.)

Career Selected	Percentage of Students with High "Faith in People"	Percentage of Students with Low "Faith in People"
Social Work	62	38
Personnel Work	59	41
Teaching	56	44
Science	51	49
Government	50	50
Farming	45	55
Art	43	57
Hotel Management	41	59
Medicine	40	60
Journalism–Drama	39	61
Architecture	39	61
Law	39	61
Engineering	36	64
Advertising–Public Relations	36	64
Business–Finance	34	66
Sales–Promotion	22	78

termines an individual's choice of an occupation, but it may attract people toward certain kinds of work and steer them away from other kinds. Individuals with a high level of faith in people may, for instance, shy away from business or sales-promotion because they feel that the requirements of the job may run counter to their basic feelings about others. Similarly, the person who is "tough-minded," who feels that people in trouble should help themselves, and who feels that they have "only themselves to blame," is less likely to be attracted to careers of the social-welfare variety.

In another part of his study, Rosenberg shows the effect that personal values have on the selection of occupations. He classified Cornell University students in 1950 both as to their occupational choice and the kind of values they expected from their future career. He found that students who expressed what he called "people-oriented" values tended to select occupations which also were "people-oriented." There was, however, a large minority of individuals whose values and occupational choices were inconsistent. When

Rosenberg polled these same students two years later, he found that the size of this "inconsistent" group had decreased. In general, they tended to change their occupational choice to make it conform with their value pattern, rather than their value pattern to conform with occupational choice, indicating a certain tendency for values to predetermine vocational choice.

Interest tests. During the years that have elapsed since World War I, psychologists have been identifying and classifying value patterns in an effort to determine their effect on vocational choice and on success in school and on the job. One of the earliest of these efforts was the Allport-Vernon Study of Values, still used today, which measures the degree to which individuals prefer aesthetic, religious, economic, political, social, or theoretical values. Today, the use of the Study of Values is largely restricted to research, most vocational counselors preferring to use the Kuder Preference Record or the Strong Vocational Interest Blank for men or for women.

The research of E. K. Strong, Jr. (1943), with

his Vocational Interest Blank, showed that people employed in a given occupation tend to have a characteristic pattern of likes and dislikes that is different from individuals in other occupations. Strong has developed scoring keys based on the response patterns for some 40 different occupations for men and 25 for women. This makes it possible to score the responses of an individual in terms of the extent to which they resemble the response patterns of successful individuals in the occupations for which keys have been developed. An individual who scores in the "A" area of the engineer's scale, for example, has interests that are similar to at least one-third of the engineers who have taken the test, whereas if he scores in the "C" area of the same scale, his interests are similar to only two per cent of the same group. If he plans to go into engineering and has an "A" score, he should find engineering a congenial occupation and will be less likely to change to a different career. On the other hand, if he has a "C" score in engineering and persists in trying to enter the field, he is likely to lose interest and enter some other occupation.

A study by Saddler (1949) shows that students who remain in the engineering curriculum tend to have a different pattern of Strong test scores than those who drop out. As Figure 15-1 (page 342) shows, not only do the students who leave engineering have lower scores on the engineering scale, but also their scores on all the other occupational scales in Group II (the science-mathematics group) tend to be lower. Possible sources of their dissatisfaction with engineering are indicated by their higher scores in social-welfare (Group V), business (Groups VII, VIII, and IX), and linguistic (Group X) types of occupations. Strong's research also indicates that the scores made on his test are predictive to some degree of grades in certain preprofessional curricula, and in one instance—life insurance selling—they are even predictive of financial success.

Other research also verifies the existence of different patterns of interest characterizing people in different professions. Dickinson (1954), for example, asked male college seniors to rank the factors they thought would be important in selecting a job. The differences between seniors intending to go into business and those intending to go into teaching were especially marked. Students intending to go into accounting, business administration, and sales rated *opportunity for advancement* higher than the average for the group, whereas those intending to go into education marked it lower. The education group marked *human relations* (good relations with supervisors and co-workers) as being more important, but the business administration group thought it was less important. The accounting group tended to rate *working conditions* (good hours, pleasant surroundings) as less important than the average senior, whereas the education group ranked the same factor as being more important. The education group also ranked *job security* higher than most seniors, whereas students intending to go into accounting or business administration majors tended to rank *type of work* (work which is interesting and liked by employee) lower than most seniors.

Factors that predetermine occupational choice. There are other factors, in addition to interests, that help predetermine the choice of a career. Women have some difficulty in entering most of the professional fields. Few fields are absolutely closed to them, but prejudice against their sex is so strong that they have difficulty in entering or making progress in fields that are traditionally male. Restrictions created by prejudice also make it difficult for members of certain racial and religious groups to enter or make progress in a large number of occupations. The physically handicapped, discharged mental patients, and exconvicts also find the barriers of prejudice raised against them.

However, there are factors other than prejudice that help to predetermine vocational choice. Rosenberg, in the study cited previously, found that students from families in upper economic brackets were more likely to select business and the "free professions" (medicine and law), whereas students from lower economic levels were more inclined to choose the salaried professions of engineering, teaching, social work, and science. (See Table 15-5, page 344.) The part that religious background may play in occupational choice is shown by the tendency of Catholics and the members of the more "fundamentalist" Protestant sects to choose occupations outside the field of science. (Roe, 1956.)

The importance of the college years

Most students have made some kind of a vocational choice before they enter college. Although many of them will make one or more changes be-

Figure 15-1. Vocational interests of engineering students who remained in engineering and those who changed their majors (as measured by Strong Vocational Interest Blank). (After Saddler, 1949.)

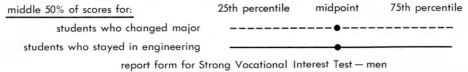

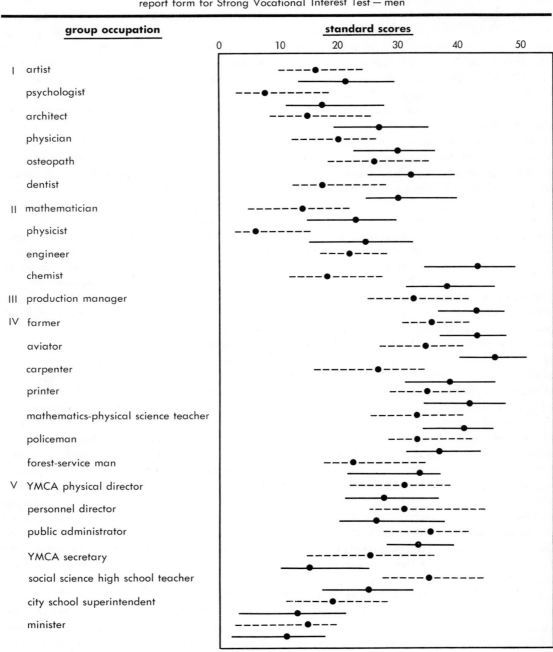

group occupation

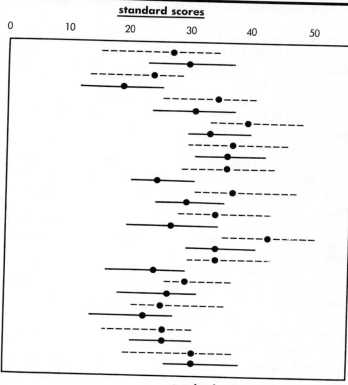

VI	musician
VII	C.P.A.
VIII	accountant
	office man
	purchasing agent
	banker
	mortician
IX	sales manager
	real estate salesman
	life insurance salesman
X	advertising man
	lawyer
	author-journalist
XI	president-manufacturing concern

standard scores

0   10   20   30   40   50

interest-factor scales

interest maturity

occupational level

masculinity-femininity

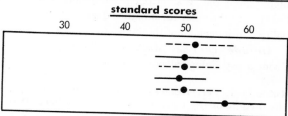

standard scores

30   40   50   60

fore they complete their training and seek employment, they are inclined to look upon college as one of the final phases in the process of carrying out the choice they have made. For other students, the college years are admittedly a period of search and definition, a period in which they must not only select a career but also must complete the academic preparation that it requires.

Differences between high school and college. It is probably a truism to state that few students entering college life have any awareness of the problems that lie ahead of them. A great many students, for instance, make the more or less tacit assumption that college is a great deal like high school, that it is, in fact, a kind of continuation of high school with somewhat more freedom and glamor. There is some basis for such an assumption: in general, people who are successful in high school do tend to be successful in college and *vice versa,* although there are numerous exceptions. But it does not take very many weeks of college for the average freshman to realize that there are many differences. For one thing, the psychological climate is quite different. College students are subject to much less personal supervision, but they are expected to take a greater degree of personal responsibility for their actions; few allowances are made if they neglect their assignments. The college population is a select one, intellectually speaking. The student who earned "A's" in high school usually has to struggle to keep from dropping below a "B" in college; the "B" student in high school has to work hard for his "C" average in college; and the dropout rate is highest among those who got through high school on "C's." College assignments are heavy, and they call for a higher degree of originality and independent thinking.

Attitude changes during college years. From a psychological point of view, one of the most interesting aspects of college life is the lasting effect it has on the attitudes and behavior of those who have completed even a few years of college work. Poll takers, for example, find that they must create a separate category for the responses of college-educated people, since they are likely to react differently from the general population. They also tend to differ in buying habits, in the amount and kind of material they read, and in their participation in community affairs. It is difficult, of course, to determine how much of this behavior is the result of college experiences and how much is due to the influence of other variables. However, research by Sanford and others (1956) does appear to indicate that rather a fundamental reorganization of the personality tends to take place during the college years. When freshmen and seniors at Vassar were compared in terms of their responses to a battery of psychological tests, seniors were found to be more tolerant and flexible, more inclined to do their own thinking, more realistic and self-confident, more inclined to reject traditional values, and less cynical about people. A group of alumnae who took the same tests scored higher than the freshmen in these traits, but somewhat lower than seniors. The view that is sometimes expressed that college students become more alike in their general attitudes as a result of attending college was challenged by Webster (1958). Using some of the measures employed in the Vassar study, he compared the reactions of a number of groups of students at various stages in college and found that seniors were generally less homogeneous and less conforming than freshmen. Seniors were, however, more consistent than freshmen in their greater tolerance for nonconforming behavior and ideas.

Research by Newcomb (1943, 1952) describes the marked change that took place in the attitudes

Table 15–5 Percentages of students choosing certain occupational fields, classified according to the income of their fathers. (After Rosenberg, 1957.)

Occupational Choice	Father's Income				
	Under $7,500	7,500– 10,000	10,000– 20,000	20,000– 30,000	Over 30,000
Business and the "free professions" (law and medicine)	38	42	56	68	71
Some salaried professions (engineering, social work, science, teaching)	45	32	26	21	16
Other occupations	17	26	18	11	13

and beliefs of the students of Bennington College during their four-year stay at the college, a change brought about partly through contact with the norms of the student group and partly through the influence of the faculty. Jones (1956) reports on studies made at the University of Buffalo that demonstrated the kind of changes that may occur in the attitudes of college-educated people. Freshmen were asked to indicate the extent to which they agreed or disagreed with a set of statements. Twenty years later, they were again asked to record their attitudes. Researchers found that there was no relationship between the degree of dogmatism expressed as a freshman and that expressed twenty years later. However, there was a greater tendency for those who had been less successful vocationally to be more rigid, that is, to have maintained the same attitudes over a twenty-year period.

College experiences and vocational success. College students are often concerned about the relationship between vocational success and such variables as college grades, part-time employment, and activity in campus affairs. The data here are rather confusing, and no clear pattern emerges. Havemann and West (1952) found, in a survey of more than 9000 college graduates, that there was a significant but negative relationship between the income earned after graduation and the amount of time devoted to self-support in college. The average income in 1947 of those graduates who had to earn more than half their college expenses was $4831, as contrasted with $4995 for those who had to earn less than half their expenses, and $5276 for those who did not have to work at all. However, it is quite likely that these differences reflect the help given by the family both *before and after* graduation—that is, the family that can pay all the expenses of a college student is also likely to help him get a better-paying job. And as the data in Table 15-5 indicated, there is a tendency for students from wealthier families to go into business and the better-paying professions.

College grades and extracurricular activities. Havemann and West also show that there is a relationship between grades and income. In business, law, medicine, dentistry, and the scientific fields, male graduates who were "A" students tend to earn more than those who were "B" students, who, in turn, earn more than those who were "C" and "D" students. Male teachers, clergymen, artists, and government employees who were "A" students earn on the average, markedly more than "B" students, who, in turn, earn about the same as "C" and "D" students. There is little difference between grades and earnings of women employed in the field of business. Women who were "A" students do much better than those who were "B", "C", and "D" students in the fields of medicine, law, dentistry, science, teaching, and the fine arts, whereas in government work, both "A" and "B" students do better than "C" and "D" students.

The relationship between grades and income is also confirmed in the research reported by Jones (1956). College grades were the best predictors of income twenty years later for graduates in the field of science (including medicine). College aptitude tests also predicted income to a slight degree for this professional group, but there was a small negative correlation between extracurricular activity and income (indicating that there was a slight tendency for scientists and physicians who had been active in campus affairs to earn somewhat less and those who had been inactive to earn somewhat more). The best predictor for income in the field of the social services (including law), however, was extracurricular activity—in other words, graduates in these fields who had been active in campus affairs when they were students tended to have the highest income, and those who had been inactive tended to earn less. There was no relationship between income and ability as measured by college entrance test scores for this group, but there was a slight relationship between income and grades. The best predictor of income for the field of education was the college aptitude test, but both grades and extracurricular activity had some slight predictive value. Grades were of no value in predicting income in the field of business, but aptitude test scores showed a slight negative correlation (the higher the score, the less the income; the lower the score the more the income). Extracurricular activity had moderate predictive value. As far as business and law were concerned, *leadership* in extracurricular activities was even more significant than mere participation: it proved to be an excellent predictor for social service and law and a fair predictor in business.

There was very little relationship between the amount of extracurricular activity and college grades among the students included in Jones'

Susan Greenburg

Leadership in extracurricular activities—not mere participation—is predictive of success in most of the occupations college students enter after graduation.

research. However, 33 per cent of the most important student leaders made a "B" average or better, a level attained by only 10 per cent of the student body as a whole. On the other hand, nearly a quarter of the top leaders barely graduated from college. Twenty years later, almost 90 per cent of those who had been most active as student leaders reported themselves as being "very satisfied" with their work, but only 50 per cent of those who had been inactive in campus affairs reported themselves as being "very satisfied." About half the men who had been the most outstanding leaders on the campus were earning $15,000 or more when Jones made his survey in 1955. This was a level attained by only one quarter of the entire group of alumni.

It would appear from the foregoing data that the factors that make for future vocational success vary with the individual and the field he has chosen for his speciality. There is some relationship between grades and success, but there are many exceptions. In general, "A" students in *any* vocational field tend to do better than their classmates, but the advantages of being a "B" student varies from negligible to considerable,

depending on the vocational field. Participation in extracurricular activities evidently is not as important as playing *leadership* roles in campus groups, but even here, participation was of no importance to future scientists, who seemed to be better off if they achieved high grades and avoided campus affairs.

Very likely there are few students who consciously decide to become campus leaders or "A" students, just as there are few students who decide to get high or low scores on the college entrance test. Such behavior is a function of ability, opportunity, and the way in which a student perceives himself and his environment. As the perceptions of the environment and the self shift, behavior changes accordingly. There are, as we have said, likely to be changes in attitudes and perceptions during the college years, but these changes seldom occur so dramatically that the individual is made aware of them. Although some individuals change rather radically during this period, others change only a little. But underneath the change, there is a tendency for personalities to maintain a relatively high degree of consistency. The student who comes to college with a preference for research as opposed to socializing will probably maintain this basic approach through his college career. He may change some of his attitudes toward life and may develop somewhat broader interests, but he will probably maintain his basic orientation toward research. He will continue to get his deepest satisfactions from science, and, if he has the kind of ability that produces top grades, he is likely to move to the top of his profession during the years that follow the completion of his graduate work.

The individual who enjoyed manipulating social situations and exercising of power as a student leader in high school will probably continue this kind of behavior in college. He, too, may broaden his interests and change some of his attitudes, but his basic personality pattern is likely to be unchanged. The chances are that he will be attracted to social service, law, or business (according to Jones' data) and will go on to find a high level of satisfaction and financial return in his work.

"Under-achievers" and "over-achievers." The point is that individuals who have well-defined patterns of behavior tend to continue these patterns, particularly as they are rewarded and reinforced by their experiences in college and after graduation. Individuals who are less sure of themselves, who do not know why they are in college, who have no firm convictions regarding one vocational field or another, are less likely to find satisfying, reinforcing experiences both in college and in later life. In this connection, Jones compared the records of a group of bright students who had made poor grades ("under-achievers") with a group of students who had made below-average scores on the college entrance test, but who had made better-than-average grades ("over-achievers"). During their college years, the "under-achievers" barely maintained passing grades, while the "over-achievers" made decided gains. The "under-achievers" were quite active in campus affairs and more than half of them became leaders, while only a quarter of the "over-achievers" showed any leadership. However, twenty years later the "over-achievers" had a median income of $12,500, as contrasted with $10,803 for the "under-achievers." Almost 90 per cent of the "over-achievers" stated that they felt "very satisfied" in their work, as against less than half of the "under-achievers." These differences are even more impressive when one considers the fact that the "over-achievers" tended

Students who were leaders in high school tend to continue to display leadership patterns in college.

to come from lower socio-economic levels and hence were less likely to have the advantages of family assistance enjoyed by the "under-achievers."

Some research by Shaw and Brown (1957) sheds further light on the background of under-achievers. They found that under-achieving, bright college students did as well on achievement tests—that is, had learned as much subject matter—as students who received higher grades. However, they differed from the more successful students in that they came from smaller towns. Evidently, growing up in a larger city tends to give students an advantage, as far as getting superior grades in college is concerned.

One of the factors involved in grade getting was explored by Gilmore (1958), who studied the tendencies of college students to recall failures or successes. Freshmen students in psychology were presented with 20 paper-and-pencil problems, each of which had to be completed within 2 minutes. Ten of the tasks could easily be accomplished within the time limit; the other 10 appeared easy, but actually had no solution. The students were then asked if they could recall any of the tasks in the experiment. Those students who tended to recall more failures than successes turned out to have higher grade-point averages at the end of the semester. Contrary to popular belief, it appears that students who are more concerned about their failures than their successes tend to get better grades.

What a college degree means. Whatever else a college degree symbolizes, it does indicate to the employer that the holder has been able to persist for four years in the completion of a self-assigned task in spite of frustrations, disappointments, and distractions. The assumption is made that he can handle problems and assignments of a fairly abstract nature and that he has at least some of the qualifications for the performance of supervisory or administrative roles.

The college graduate, too, makes certain assumptions. He expects to attain a higher level of occupational status than would have been possible had he not acquired a college degree. He expects that this status will carry with it some degree of financial security or higher income or both. He expects that the job he enters will enable him to use his abilities and capacities, and this in turn implies some responsibility, as well as some freedom, to do his own thinking and planning—freedom, that is, from close supervision.

To a steadily increasing degree, college graduates are seeking this combination of security, income, status, and opportunity in large organizations, either in business and industry or in governmental agencies. These organizations and agencies have grown larger and more complex with each succeeding decade. As organizations increase in size and complexity, administrative problems are created that call for the services of a new professional group: the specialists in management. Because college-educated individuals are as a rule better qualified for such positions, either as a result of special training or because of their general educational background, they have been actively recruited by these large organizations. Even lawyers and physicians, members of what Rosenberg terms the "free professions," are increasingly becoming the salaried employees of large business and government organizations. Another factor that increases the attractiveness of employment in large organizations is the rather widespread belief, not without foundation, that opportunities for advancement are better in larger organizations than in smaller ones. There is the feeling that among the many positions in a large organization, one has a better chance of finding the kind of work for which one is best suited.

The staffing of positions at the higher levels of business and government has had a number of side effects. It has helped to perpetuate a pattern of hiring college graduates for supervisory positions, thus eliminating, or at least reducing, the proportion of promotions of individuals with less education from the lower ranks. This practice has naturally aroused some resentment on the part of employees on the lower levels, who often fail to see how a college degree helps make one a better supervisor or administrator. There is a danger,

too, that the increasing educational homogeneity of management personnel may serve to widen the already sizable gap between the supervisor and the supervised. As Roethlisberger (1941) points out, there is a general breakdown in communication between the college-educated managers and engineers in industry and the less well-educated persons they supervise. In other words, college-educated people are more or less comfortable communicating with each other on a fairly high level of abstraction, but have difficulty in communicating with those who function on less abstract levels. According to Whyte (1955) these difficulties in communication are aggravated by the fact that management is unaware that the frames of reference it is using are not shared by labor.

Work as a source of satisfaction and dissatisfaction

Vocational satisfaction. Do college graduates find whatever it is they are seeking in their work? A large number of studies indicates that in general they do achieve a high degree of vocational satisfaction. The commonly reported tendency is for a higher proportion of individuals in "white-collar" work, professions, and other middle-class occupations to report themselves as "very satisfied" with their work, as contrasted with lower percentages for "blue-collar" workers —those employed in unskilled, semi-skilled, and skilled trades. These differences may be due, at least in part, to the degree of involvement in one's work. Dubin (1956) did a questionnaire study of some 1200 workers employed in Midwestern manufacturing plants and found that only 24 per cent could be considered job-oriented in their interests. Although relationships at work are a major source of social stimulation for a great many professional and business people, only 9 per cent of the factory workers in Dubin's study saw their important primary social relationships as taking place at work.

Differences among "white-collar" workers. Even among white-collar workers, however, the degree of satisfaction differs from one occupational group to another. Jones found, in the study cited previously, the following percentages of professional workers reporting themselves as "very satisfied": education, 65 per cent; social service and law, 58 per cent; and business management, 53 per cent. Similar differences were also found by

Morse and Weiss (1955): 54 per cent of the professional group reported themselves "very satisfied," in contrast with 46 per cent of the sales group and only 23 of the managerial group. Jones found that scientists who had been the best students showed the highest percentage of satisfaction, but two-thirds of those who had barely passed in science and law were not satisfied. In social science and business there was no tendency for the best students to be more satisfied.

The data collected by Havemann and West (1952) tend to support the thesis that people in the professions, and particularly in the sciences, are more satisfied. When the researchers asked respondents whether they wished they had taken a different major in college, only 9 per cent of those who had gone to medical school responded in the affirmative, as contrasted with 25 per cent of the total group of graduates. Nineteen per cent of the graduates who had majored in engineering were dissatisfied, but most of them merely wished they had studied a different branch of engineering. Although 24 per cent of graduates in the fields of science and mathematics reported themselves dissatisfied with their field, they, too, were inclined to wish that they had taken another branch of science. On the other hand, the percentages of dissatisfaction were 30 per cent or more among those who had majored in social science, business administration, history, the humanities, and pharmacy. The dissatisfied people who had majored in the social sciences most often wished that they had gone into business administration, the dissatisfied business administrators most often mentioned engineering as a preferred field, and the others were most likely to mention medicine.

It appears, then, that among college-educated people the highest percentages of satisfied individuals will be found in the scientific and medical professions, with the lowest percentages reported by those in business. Some clues as to this difference are provided by Havemann and West, who report that only 40 per cent of humanities and social science men graduates enter the field of their choice. A great many of them end up in business, where 24 per cent of humanities graduates and 31 per cent of social studies graduates were holding down rank-and-file jobs. For a good many of these individuals, such jobs were undoubtedly below their level of aspiration and out of phase with their self-concepts. It is quite understandable why they should report dissatisfaction. Havemann and West state that men who major in social science and the humanities are less likely to have a clear picture of where they are going, vocationally, than those who major in science, law, and engineering. When they wind up in business, a field that provides the most job opportunities, they do not do as well as those who have special training—very likely because they never really planned to go into business and are never quite satisfied with the jobs they get.

Sources of vocational dissatisfaction. A great deal of the work in large organizations, both in government and in business, allows little opportunity for independence and initiative. Answers to problems encountered in work are to be found in the rules and regulations, and larger issues are resolved by appeal to authority. Hence it is understandable why many college-educated people doing such work do not encounter the opportunities for self-fulfillment they had hoped for. Even people in the professions commonly find that their work is much more routine and tedious than they had expected.

Another difficulty arises from conflicts in role. Individuals in the "free professions," such as law, medicine, and dentistry, must play the dual role of professional practitioner, whose chief interest is in the welfare of the client or patient, and that of the entrepreneur or businessman, whose success is measured in terms of the amount of income he receives. Sometimes these roles come into conflict with each other, as, for example, when one must decide whether to spend a great deal of time on a "charity case" that promises little financial return or to put it aside in favor of more lucrative cases. Role-conflict is also experienced by the teacher who wishes to maintain an encouraging, nonthreatening relationship with his students, as a way of fostering independent thinking and intellectual self-development, but who finds that the warm and accepting emotional climate he has so carefully built up in his classroom is destroyed during the examination period when he shifts over to the role of the critic, judge, and giver of grades. In some ways, his conflict is analogous to that encountered by the members of the "free professions," that is, in his role of helping patients, clients, or students, the professional person uses his expertness, but not his power (defined here as the ability to manipulate others, to *make* them perform certain acts), whereas in the role of busi-

nessman or judge, he becomes involved in the use of power.

Wispé (1955) describes a similar conflict experienced by life-insurance salesmen. According to the insurance agents he contacted, a good salesman should be "aggressive" and "hard-hitting." "Sympathy" appeared to have no place in their picture of a successful salesman. When Wispé asked the agents who among their colleagues they would choose to help them in making their daily sales quotas, they tended to name individuals who were aggressive and who were lacking in sympathy. But when he asked them who they would choose as a house guest, they tended to select colleagues who were sympathetic, rather than those who were good salesmen and aggressive. As Wispé points out, the dilemma for these individuals lies in the conflict between wanting to be accepted, and wanting to be successful salesmen. Yet the choices they made among their colleagues indicated that the qualities that make a person successful as an insurance salesman prevent his being chosen as a friend. In his occupational role, a salesman should be aggressive and hard-hitting, but off the job he should be sympathetic and understanding. Such a built-in inconsistency produces conflict, since few individuals can play such diametrically opposed roles successfully. Wispé suggests that the conflict is resolved by the fact that the salesmen are aware that it is more important to be successful than to be accepted.

The more we are aware of conflict in our roles, the more anxiety we are likely to experience. Shall we play roles in which we minister to the needs of others, largely on their terms? Shall we play roles in which our own needs have priority, or shall we play impersonal roles as members of a professional group or an organization, performing the functions that are in keeping with our assigned or prescribed duties? Usually, we try to work out roles that satisfy as many needs and functions as possible. Very often this results in roles that are not well-defined, roles that present us with unresolved dilemmas. For example, Wispé and Thayer (1957) interviewed life-insurance agents and their assistant district managers and found that the latter expressed considerably more anxiety than the former. The researchers attributed this difference to the fact that there was a great agreement as to the functions (the role) of the agents, but little agreement as to the functions of the assistant managers.

Conflicts between occupational roles and family roles. A very common source of dissatisfaction and anxiety arises from conflicting demands of occupational life and home life, from mutual inconsistencies in our vocational roles and the roles we play as spouse, parent, and homemaker.

Let us take the case of Leonard Drachma, who is a junior executive in a large oil company. Several times he has had to give up or postpone a planned holiday with his family because some emergency arose in his office. On one occasion he had to spend two weeks taking a special course in human relations at company headquarters in a distant city while his wife was in the last stages of pregnancy. Each time Mr. Drachma has been promoted, he has had to sell his house, pack up the family and move to another part of the country where the new position was located. This occurred on the average of once every four years, while the Drachma children were growing up. It is not easy for adults to make the adjustment of leaving friends and familiar surroundings and arrive as strangers in another city; it is infinitely harder on children. Mr. Drachma knows this, yet his loyalty to his job is such that he has no choice. However, he has paid a price for this loyalty in terms of family quarrels, children's behavior problems, tensions, and guilt feelings.

Dr. Bernice Cesta is a wife, a mother, and an anesthesiologist. Her husband is a surgeon. Her problem is more difficult than Mr. Drachma's, because our culture expects a man to give his work his first claim on his time, whereas a mother is expected to give her primary attention to her family. But as a physician,

her loyalty is owed primarily to her patients. Hence the dilemma. Nor would this dilemma be easily resolved by a decision to leave her profession and devote full time to her family, for she would always feel cut off from a legitimate source of self-expression, kept from playing the role of the professional person by accident of having been born a woman. Instead, Dr. Cesta makes a rather skillful compromise of playing both the professional role and the family role. Nevertheless, she cannot avoid the conflicts, worries, and guilt feelings that arise when the two sets of roles come into conflict.

There is a strong likelihood that the conflict between job and family has been somewhat aggravated today by a growing tendency to place family before the job. When Rosenberg (1957) asked students at Cornell "What three things or activities in your life do you expect will give you the most satisfaction?", they were much more likely to say "family relationships" instead of "my career or occupation." (See Table 15-6.) During the years since World War II, employers have complained, from time to time, about the reluctance of young people to become personally involved in their work, to develop enthusiasm and drive. It may well be that much of the interest formerly devoted to the job has shifted to the family. On the other hand, it may be that the tendency of organizations to become more complex and jobs to become more specialized and restricted in their scope has led employees to seek

Table 15–6   Anticipated major life satisfactions of college men and women. (After Rosenberg, 1957.)

"What three things or activities in your life do you expect will give you the most satisfaction?"	Percentage Naming as			
	First Choice		Second Choice	
	Men	Women	Men	Women
Your career or occupation	25	8	52	40
Family relationships	62	83	26	12
Recreational activities	6	2	12	25
Religious beliefs or activities	3	6	5	13
Participation as citizen in community affairs	1	1	3	12
Participation in activities directed toward national or international betterment	1	1	2	3
Number of students responding	2007	749	2007	749

off-the-job outlets for creativity and self-expression: homemaking, childrearing, recreation involving the whole family, and community betterment. As work becomes less of a challenge to the individual, he may be tempted to turn his talents and his interests elsewhere.

Summary

Work occupies an extremely important position in our middle-class system of values. Money is generally thought to be the primary motive behind work, but surveys have found that many other motives are actually more important. Most people indicate that they would continue working even if they had sufficient money to make work unnecessary. One reason for the importance of work is that our occupation contributes a large proportion of our self-concept: it is an important role that we play, and it constitutes a classification that communicates a good deal about us. In the American culture, occupation is perhaps the best single indicator of social status.

In the light of these various considerations, it is not surprising that the process of selecting and preparing for an occupation usually results in some anxiety. Some aspects of vocational choice are involved in the basic concepts that a person holds about the kind of person he is and is not, and the kind of life he desires to live. With increasing maturity, there are often changes in these concepts and decisions. The person who has chosen an occupation is more likely to do well in school and more likely to see work in terms of intrinsic rewards instead of extrinsic ones. Vocational counseling, which is provided by most colleges and universities, helps students to arrive at

their own decisions. Among the variables that seem important in choosing a vocation is that of high as opposed to low faith in other people and the extent to which an individual is "people-oriented." A person's pattern of interests is related to vocational choice and vocational success, and several interest tests have been developed to measure this variable. One of the most successful is the Strong Vocational Interest Blank, which compares the likes and dislikes of the testee with those of successful individuals in several occupations. There are other factors that help determine occupational choice, for example, prejudices against various groups (women, certain ethnic groups, etc.) restrict vocational opportunities for many persons. There are also relationships between an individual's socio-economic level and the type of occupation he is likely to choose.

The college years are extremely important ones, and few students are aware of the psychological aspects of this period. The college population is a select one, and the student is expected to show more personal responsibility and greater originality and independent thinking, than is expected in high school. It has been found that college life has a lasting effect on the attitudes and behavior of those involved. The relationship between vocational success and such variables as grades, part-time employment, and extracurricular activity is somewhat confusing. The various relationships (whether positive, negative, or zero) depend primarily on the occupation being studied. Individuals who have well-defined patterns of behavior in college tend to continue these patterns, particularly if they are reinforced by college and postcollege experiences. Studies have found that over-achievers (low entrance-test scores but high grades) are less likely to be leaders in college, to make more money afterward, to feel more satisfied in their work, to come from a lower socio-economic level than under-achievers (high entrance-test scores, low grades). Students who are more concerned about failures than successes tend to get better grades.

Graduation from college has become increasingly important in our society, and more and more positions in various large organizations and agencies are staffed by college graduates. It has been found that "white-collar" workers tend to be more satisfied with their work than "blue-collar" workers. Among "white-collar" workers, those in the professions (particularly the sciences) tend to be the most satisfied and those in business the least satisfied. One barrier to vocational satisfaction is the lack of opportunity in large organizations for independence and initiative. Role conflicts also lead to vocational problems. The conflict between the demands of occupational life and home life creates many difficulties. There is some evidence that interest has been steadily shifting from job-centered activities to family-and-home-centered activities in the years since World War II.

Questions

1. What occupation do you plan to enter? Why? How do your reasons compare with those of others given in research studies?

2. How is occupational role related to social status?

3. What are the different ways in which individuals go about choosing a vocation? What are their relative advantages and disadvantages?

4. Do you think your "faith in people" is consistent with your chosen career?

5. How was the Strong Vocational Interest Blank developed? What does a high score on one of the occupational scales mean? What does a low score mean?

6. Did you find college any different from high school? In what way? How did you react to the differences?

7. What are some of the effects of college education on various aspects of behavior?

8. What is the relationship between college grades and later financial success? Why do you suppose the answer is different for different occupations?

9. How do college over-achievers compare with under-achievers?

10. Would you prefer to work for a large organization, a small organization, or for yourself? Why?

11. Discuss some of the sources of vocational dissatisfaction.

Suggestions for further reading

Heyns, R. W., *The Psychology of Personal Adjustment*. New York: Holt, 1958. See Chapter 13, "Adjustment to College."

Lehner, G. F. J. and E. Kube, *The Dynamics of Personal Adjustment*. New York: Prentice-Hall, 1955. See Chapter 10, "School Adjustments," and Chapter 12, "Career and Job Adjustment."

Lindgren, H. C., *Psychology of Personal and Social Adjustment*, 2nd ed. New York: American Book, 1959. Chapters 12 through 16 deal with problems of vocational adjustment, choosing an occupation, and getting an education.

Pressey, S. L. and R. G. Kuhlen, *Psychological Development through the Life Span*. New York: Harper, 1957. See chapters dealing with education and "the work life."

Roe, A., *The Making of a Scientist*. New York: Dodd Mead, 1953. A study of the psychological factors that lead individuals to select and enter scientific professions.

Roe, A., *The Psychology of Occupations*. New York: Wiley, 1956. A discussion of research and theory bearing on occupations and the people who follow them.

Rosenberg, M., *Occupations and Values*. Glencoe, Ill.: Free Press, 1957. A report of the research that has been referred to in the present chapter.

Strong, E. K., Jr., *Vocational Interests of Men and Women*. Stanford: Stanford University Press, 1943. An extensive review of the research underlying the Strong Vocational Interest Blanks for Men and Women.

Super, D. E., *Appraising Vocational Fitness*. New York: Harper, 1949. A textbook discussing the merits and shortcomings of the tests used by vocational counselors and personnel workers.

Super, D. E., *The Psychology of Careers*. New York: Harper, 1957. An analysis of the factors involved in vocational choice and occupational adjustment.

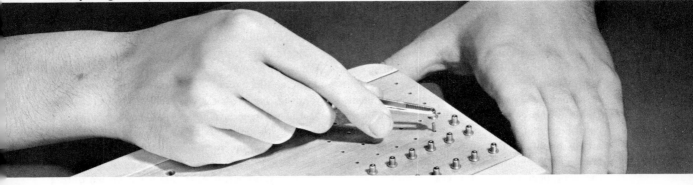

16

Psychology in business and industry

The use of science in industry. A number of factors have contributed to the success and the rapid expansion of American business and industry during the last hundred years or so. One of the most important of these is the practical, problem-centered approach of the individuals who have been managing and directing American business. In other words, these people have tended to view the production and distribution of goods as a series of problems to be solved: processes to be made more efficient and markets to be created or expanded. During the early years of the industrial era, managers relied largely on their own common sense and ingenuity to develop the answers to their problems, as well as on the growing number of inventions and scientific discoveries. However, as products, processes, and industrial organizations became more complex, and as managers began to encounter problems that were beyond the scope of their competence, they came more and more to rely on the help of the scientist.

At first, the relationship between the problems to be solved and the contributions of science was rather clear and obvious. A company concerned with the producing and refining of oil, for instance, needed the expert assistance of geologists and chemists—geologists to help locate sources of crude oil, and chemists to develop and supervise refining processes. And industries of all sorts found themselves hiring an ever larger number of engineers, who in turn looked to physics and chemistry to help them with the problems they encountered. The vast and complex technology that

355

serves us today in the production of goods and services is the result of the application of scientific findings to industrial problems.

Growth of industrial psychology. Today, the major problems of business and industry are not technological, but psychological—problems of human behavior, rather than problems of mechanical and chemical behavior. Perhaps it can be argued that since the problems of production are as much human as they are mechanical, psychological problems must have been present from the very beginning of the era of industrial expansion. However, inasmuch as the behavioral sciences, including psychology, are rather new ones, it is only in recent years that it has been at all possible to approach problems from a psychological point of view.

It is very difficult to determine the extent to which the leaders of business and industry are aware of the psychological nature of their problems. A glance through the contents of a magazine like *Business Week* will show how many of the problems that management currently faces involve incentives, morale, selection and placement, relations with labor, communication, and interpersonal relations. Although the occasional appearance of phrases like "human relations," "motivation research," and "depth interview" indicates that there is some inclination to view problems in terms of their psychological aspects, the general nature of the discussion appears to indicate that businessmen, like most laymen, are rather inclined to take a "common-sense," rather than a scientific, point of view regarding human behavior. Nevertheless, there is other evidence to indicate that psychology and psychologists are making some headway in this field. Figure 16-1 shows how the membership of the Division of Industrial and Business Psychology of the American Psychological Association has grown during the years between 1948 and 1957. The growth of this group reflects the increase in the interest that employers are showing in industrial psychology, as well as the increase in the interest that psychologists are displaying in the problems of business and industry. A recent survey by McCollom (1959) shows that at least 1000 psychologists are employed full time in industry, as contrasted with less than two dozen some 30 years ago.

Differing objectives of psychology and business. Although this mutual interest has resulted in an extremely rapid increase in the number of industrial psychologists, most business firms make no use of psychologists or any form of psychological services. When Lester (1954) made a survey of hiring practices in the Trenton,

Figure 16-1. Growth in the membership of the Division of Industrial and Business Psychology of the American Psychological Association as contrasted with the total divisional membership of the APA. (After Hildreth, 1958.)

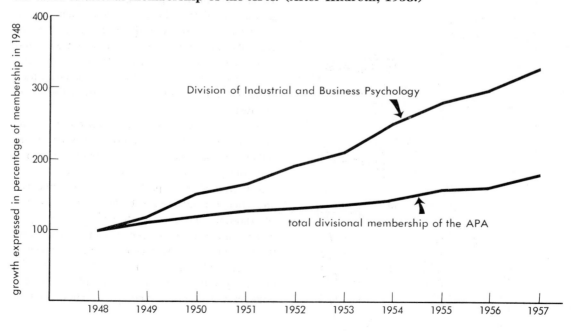

N. J., area, he found that there was very little attempt to make use of techniques used or recommended by psychologists. Malm (1955) found similar results when he surveyed practices in the San Francisco Bay area.

One factor that undoubtedly retards the growth of industrial psychology is the different orientation possessed by psychologists and employers. In general, the values and interests of psychologists are different from those possessed by the leaders of business and industry. For instance, psychologists, as classified by the Strong Vocational Interest Blank for Men, tend to have interests that are more similar to those that are characteristic of artists, architects, physicians, dentists, osteopaths, and veterinarians (the "free professions"), whereas the interests of the personnel of business and industry classify themselves into four groups: those having to do with organization and structure (accountants, office workers, bankers); sales; production management; and top management. Generally speaking, persons scoring high on the psychologists' scale of the Strong test tend to score low in the four fields just mentioned.[1] The leaders of business and industry may be concerned with long-range goals, such as service to the public and making the world a better place in which to live, but at the same time they tend to be preoccupied with the attainment of such short-range goals as operating at a profit, expanding production and sales, cutting costs, and maintaining patterns of behavior that seem to be satisfactory from a business point of view. In addition to their research interests, psychologists are more likely to be interested in the long-range goals of human welfare, which are consistent with such short-range goals as promoting morale, job satisfaction, democratic relationships, and the like. A great many managers feel that these short-range goals are important, too, but they would want to be sure that the attainment of such goals also had economic outcomes. For example, a president of a manufacturing concern is much more likely to be interested in improving the communication in his organization if it can be shown that the present arrangement interferes with production and that the proposed changes will improve efficiency and raise profits. The psychol-

ogist, on the other hand, may see improved communication as something that is part of better morale, increased satisfaction, and better human relationships. To him, improved communication is something that is desirable because it promotes human welfare, irrespective of any increases it may yield in production and profits.

American business men commonly pride themselves on their ability to solve problems through prompt, decisive action. Here is another potential source of difficulty. The psychologist, as a behavioral scientist, prefers to study a problem from a number of different angles before making even a diagnosis, let alone making a recommendation as to how it might be solved. He prefers to withhold judgment until he has accumulated sufficient data, a process that may take weeks and months, if not years. He knows that hasty research runs the risk of being bad research. But often the problems that crop up in everyday business and industrial operations cannot wait for lengthy research: they must be dealt with as they occur. This frequently means that suggestions for their solution must be made on the basis of "working hypotheses" (informed guesses) based on theory and on research done on similar problems in other situations. Such a procedure is likely to be distasteful to the careful scientist, necessary though it may be.

To a large extent, the psychological problems encountered in business and industry are not greatly different from those encountered in other areas of human endeavor. Whether we attempt to apply psychological principles and methods to education, psychotherapy, military affairs, personnel management, or production, we encounter the same kinds of difficulties: there never seems to be enough time to do the research necessary to arrive at ideal solutions to the problems at hand. Furthermore, the skills used by psychologists in the various applied fields are basically similar: the interview, the questionnaire, the group discussion, the methods of appraisal and evaluation. There are few techniques used in industrial psychology that are not used in other fields of psychology. What makes the major difference is the setting in which psychology is practiced.

Selection

The employer's relationship with his employees begins with the hiring process. If several applicants present themselves for a single position,

[1] The correlations between the psychologists' scale and scales for occupational specialities in business and industry range from $-.17$ (production manager) to $-.75$ (banker). (Strong, 1943.)

the employer must decide which one is the best potential producer. Most employers tend to use common-sense methods in making such decisions. If a job calls for mechanical skill, an employer will quite obviously look for a person who has experience and a sufficient amount of the requisite skill. But if several persons possessing similar experience and the right kind and amount of skill are available, the employer must then turn to other criteria. Some employers consciously or unconsciously make their hiring decisions on criteria that have no relationship to job success. One employer may prefer high school graduates to nongraduates for routine, unskilled work, because they are "superior." Another employer may refuse to hire anyone who has more education than he does. Still another employer may insist that all his employees be aggressive and "masculine" in appearance and manner. The importance of appearance is indicated by the fact that few employers are willing to hire anyone without a personal interview. Often a less qualified person who has been interviewed is hired in preference to a well-qualified person who is represented only by his papers, that is, the record of his experience, his letters of recommendation, and so forth.

In general, personal qualifications are weighted very heavily. Among several applicants, all of whom possess the minimum skill and background required, the individual who makes the best personal impression stands the best chance of being hired. Many a man has been hired because he had a ready smile, a firm handshake, and looked his prospective employer straight in the eye. We have been so conditioned by our culture to respond favorably to such cues that we have difficulty in looking beyond these more or less superficial aspects of behavior for more tangible evidence of employability and personal worth. What employers are continually seeking, however, is someone who will "fit into" the organization and will not become a center of disturbance and discord. The importance of personal qualities is indicated by the fact that the vast majority of firings are based not on lack of occupational skills, but on interpersonal difficulties. And many a person with substandard skills is kept on the job because he is pleasant and agreeable and gets along so well with his fellow employees and his employer.

The problem of selection is therefore a two-fold one: that of finding people with sufficient training, skill, and experience, on the one hand, and

acceptable personal qualities on the other. Larger companies rather generally make their decisions on the basis of application blanks, references, and personal interviews. The applicant very commonly applies at the personnel office of the company, fills out some kind of an application blank, lists his references, and is interviewed by the personnel manager, or, in a large company, by a personnel specialist. If he appears to be a good employment risk, he is usually referred for final decision to the foreman or supervisor under whom he will be working. The personnel department performs what is called a "staff" function—it recruits applicants, conducts initial interviews, maintains records, and may supply information and advice on request. Actual hiring and firing are "line" functions and are the responsibility of foremen or supervisors.

The psychologist who is employed by business and industry is most likely to be assigned to the personnel department. His is a "staff" function—primarily that of providing information and advice to his employers. His information may be gathered from the administration of tests to applicants, from interviews, and from research of various kinds. In a large company that has a well-developed program of psychological services, the psychologist may actually participate in the decisions regarding applicants. For example, he may recommend the elimination of some applicants on the basis of unsatisfactory test scores.

Developing a selection program. It takes time, patience, and, of course, money to develop an effective selection program along psychological lines. Let us say that a psychologist has the task of developing a selection program for gas- and electric-meter readers. His first task is to study the job for which applicants are to be selected. Perhaps he will talk to meter readers about their job and follow them around while they go about their work. He will certainly want to talk to the people who supervise this work and ask them what factors they believe lead to successful or unsuccessful meter reading. He may ask them to indicate the workers that are the most effective and those who are the least effective, in order that he can watch them at work. He will ask such questions as these: "What are the chief problems in meter reading: Inaccuracy? Inability to read a sufficient number of meters in a working day? Turnover of personnel? Getting meter readers to keep accurate and readable records?"

As a result of this exploratory work, the psychologist will put together a battery of tests that appear to measure the factors that are important for effective meter-reading. He may decide that intelligence is a factor, in which event he will include a test of intelligence. He may decide that the ability to read dials is important, in which event he may devise a test whereby the applicant is required to read sets of dials that resemble the dials on gas and electric meters. On the other hand, he may decide that it is not as important for applicants to *know* how to read dials as it is for them to *learn* how to read them, in which case he wants to be sure that he has a test that measures learning ability. He may conclude that one of the chief problems is that of turnover, in which event, he may select a personality test that he believes will measure the traits associated with the willingness to remain on routine jobs for long periods of time. Or he may hypothesize that certain biographical items (as revealed by the application blank) will predict the number of months or years that meter-readers will remain with meter reading.

The psychologist's next step will be that of checking his proposed measures against the behavior of the persons currently employed as meter readers, by having them take the tests and by examining their personnel records. Perhaps he will find that persons rated "most successful" as meter readers will be from the middle range of intelligence scores, whereas those rated as "least successful" come from upper and lower ranges. And perhaps he will find that successful and unsuccessful meter readers can be identified by a certain interest test, but cannot be identified by personality tests. It may be, too, that he will find two or three items of biographical data (perhaps amount of schooling, marital status, and number of previous jobs) will be related to success in meter reading.

After the psychologist has reviewed and evaluated his data, he may end up with a few tests and a few items on the application blank that are related to success in meter reading. But his work is not finished. He must now see whether the combination of test scores and biographical items actually will predict the *future performance* of applicants for meter-reading jobs. Ideally, in order to give his combination of measures a fair trial, he should test and hire every applicant over an extended period of time. In actual practice, it

is usually impractical and too expensive to conduct such an extensive survey; hence the research must concern itself with those who actually are selected and hired. Very likely the psychologist will find that some of the tests and biographical items will predict success and some will not. Perhaps those tests and items that are related to success will improve the efficiency of the selection appreciably. If they do not, the psychologist must begin his task again.

What devices like batteries of psychological tests actually do is to improve the "batting average" of the company's hiring. When a company employs a person, it is, in effect, predicting that he will be successful on the job for which he is hired. If the company bases its decisions to hire on the information provided by a properly developed battery of tests, the efficiency of its predictions is improved in the sense that the proportion of effective employees hired should be increased and the proportion of ineffective employees should be decreased.

The way in which psychological test scores may be used to improve selection is demonstrated in Figure 16-2. The scale at the left of the figure represents scores made on a psychological test, and the scale at the bottom represents the ratings made by supervisors. Each dot represents a workman. The data show that if no one had been hired with a score of less than 85, applicants A, B, C, and G would have been eliminated. Of these

Figure 16-2. The use of cutting scores on psychological tests in the selection of workers. (After Maier, 1955.)

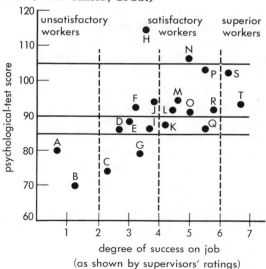

four, A and B turned out to be unsatisfactory, and C and G were satisfactory, but below average. If the "cutting score" had been set at 90, applicants D, E, I, K, and Q would have been eliminated in addition to the four already named. All of these workers turned out to be satisfactory, but none is superior, and three out of the five are below average. Furthermore, of the workers scoring 90 or over who would have been hired, all are satisfactory or superior, none is unsatisfactory, and only three are below average. Where the "cutting score" should be set depends, of course, on a number of factors: how many workers are needed, how much production is expected, and so forth. Under some conditions it may be desirable to set the cutting score low and risk hiring a few unsatisfactory workers; under other conditions it may be desirable to set the cutting score high and eliminate some potentially satisfactory and above-average workers in order to ensure hiring as high a proportion of superior workers as possible.

Intelligence tests. Intelligence tests of various kinds are included in most of the batteries of psychological tests used for selection purposes. Often their true nature is disguised by such terms as "adaptibility test," "classification test," or "general aptitude test." People are understandably quite sensitive about being "shown up" as unintelligent, and the use of words other than "intelligence" or "mental ability" in the title probably protects some egos that might be bruised and perhaps helps reduce anxieties somewhat.

One obvious basis for including intelligence tests in selection batteries is the assumption that "the more intelligent the employee or worker, the better." However, the actual value of such tests varies considerably. The data reported in Figure 16-3 show that they are more likely to be helpful in selecting skilled workers, supervisors, clerical workers, and salesmen, but to be of no value in selecting unskilled workers and sales clerks. One study of the selection of clerical workers in a life insurance company showed a tendency for applicants scoring high on intelligence tests to leave the job after a few months. (Kriedt and Gadel, 1953.) However, the authors stated that irrespective of the results of their study, they felt it desirable to hire some applicants demonstrating a high level of intelligence in order to have individuals on hand that could be promoted to supervisory positions.

In general, the more the amount of preparation and training required for a job and the more complex the job, the more likely intelligence is to be a factor in job success. Indeed, one of the most defensible arguments in favor of including intelligence tests in selection batteries is the need to train the applicants that one hires. The longer and more complex the training required for the job, the more likely intelligence is to be an important factor. During World War II, all the armed services made extensive use of intelligence tests (termed "General Classificaton Tests") for the purpose of selecting and assigning personnel for various kinds of training. High scores were demanded of recruits slated for electronics schools, whereas recruits with low scores were assigned to general duty or were given short periods of training in relatively simple operations. In general, scores made on general classification tests proved to be excellent predictors of success in training schools.

Special aptitude tests. Although there is an infinite variety of tests that are used to measure special aptitudes, the most commonly used types are those that measure various clerical aptitudes and those that measure various factors involved in mechanical work.

The basic factor contributing to success in clerical work appears to be perceptual speed—the ability to check verbal and numerical symbols accurately and rapidly. (Super, 1949.) This factor can be measured by tests like the Minnesota Vocational Test for Clerical Workers, which includes items like the following:

Numbers

5493218 ___ 5493218
87387 ___ 87378
22014896 ___ 22013896
935905437 ___ 9359905437

Names

G. Fredrick Boone ___ G. Frederic Boone
French & Maddison ___ French & Maddison
New Jersey RR. ___ New Jersey RR.
Clark Travel Agency ___ Clarke Travel Agency

The test taker is told to place a check mark on the line between each pair that is exactly the same and to complete the test as fast as possible without making mistakes.

Although the scores made on this test are significantly affected by the experience of the individuals taking the test, it has proved to be a good predictor of success in various kinds of clerical work. Other tests that have been used with varying degrees of success measure skills in copying, filing, typing, sorting, computation, and the like.

There are two main types of mechanical aptitude tests: manipulative and paper-and-pencil. Manipulative tests are used to measure speed and accuracy in such operations as placing and turning, the use of fingers and tweezers in fine operations, the matching and fitting of odd shapes, and the execution of common mechanical problems, the assembly and disassembly of faucets, locks, and so forth. Generally speaking, the usefulness of such tests is quite limited. That is, they can be used to predict success at certain specific mechanical tasks, usually of a low order of complexity and skill, but are less valid when used to predict success in a wide range of jobs. The Minnesota Rate of Manipulation Test is, for example, an excellent predictor of success for wrappers and packers but rather poor for success in assembly work. (Cronbach, 1949.) Apparently there is no single factor that is basic to success in manipulative work—at least, if there is, it has not as yet been isolated and measured.

The paper-and-pencil tests used to measure mechanical aptitude are concerned with such

Figure 16-3. Average correlations between intelligence-test scores and job performance in selected occupations. (After Ghiselli and Brown, 1955.)

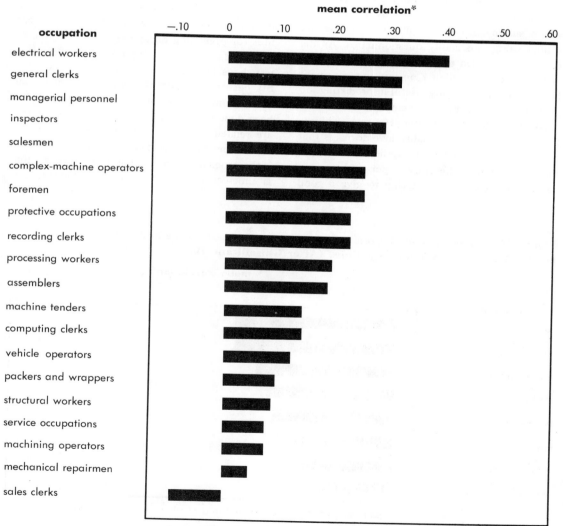

*composites of correlations found in a number of different studies

widely varied skills as the ability to perceive spatial relations, dotting and tracing, the understanding of mechanical principles, blueprint reading, and mechanical knowledge. Generally speaking, these tests are better at predicting success in training situations than they are in predicting success on the job. However, one study of aircraft factory workers, using the Bennett Test of Mechanical Comprehension, reported rather substantial validity coefficients. (Shuman, 1945.)

Personality tests. Because of the great importance played by emotional factors in job success, it was only natural that industrial psychologists should turn to personality tests in search of predictive measures. The device most commonly used is the personality questionnaire, which we discussed in Chapter 10.

The ability of such inventories to predict occupational success is indicated by Figure 16-4, which summarizes the results of 113 research studies using personality questionnaires. As the data indicate, such tests are most useful in predicting success in selling. Contrary to what might be expected, they are less useful in predicting job performance for supervisory employees.

As we stated in Chapter 10, one problem that is peculiar to personality inventories is that of "faking." A number of studies have shown that people reply differently to personality questionnaires when they are trying to give a good

report of themselves. Hence it is possible to find that a certain personality test discriminates rather well between effective and ineffective employees (who, since they are already employed have relatively little to gain by faking) but is of little use in identifying applicants that will turn out to be good or poor workers. The tendency of an applicant to slant his replies in an attempt to present a favorable picture of himself may not necessarily be a conscious attempt to fool the employer: the knowledge that one's fate rests on one's replies would in itself be enough to produce a consistent bias.

In an attempt to find tests whose results cannot be compromised by conscious or unconscious faking, industrial psychologists have turned to projective tests like the Rorschach inkblot test, Murray's Thematic Apperception Test (TAT), and the various forms of sentence-completion tests. Although it is possible that research with these tests may in the future provide valid measures for predicting occupational success, the results so far have been disappointing. Projective tests have been used with some success to identify personality patterns characteristic of certain occupational groups, but very little research has been done with respect to measuring factors that are related to occupational success and failure. One of the difficulties in conducting such research is the problem of scoring the tests, a process that is time-consuming and complex. Another dif-

Figure 16-4. Average correlations between personality-test scores and job performance for selected occupations. (After Ghiselli and Barthol, 1953.)

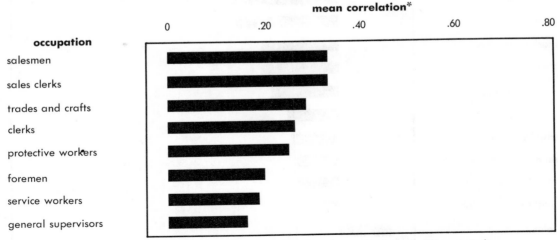

*composites of correlations found in a number of different studies

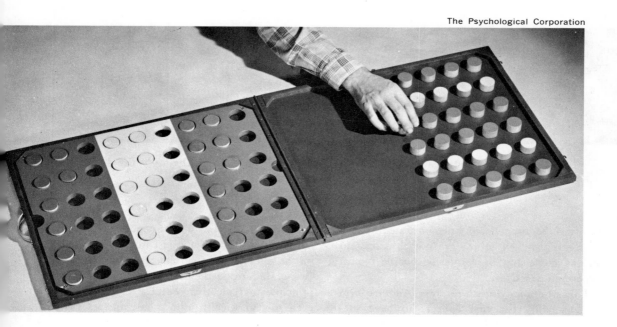

The Stromberg Dexterity Test and

the Crawford Small Parts Dexterity Test are examples of manipulative tests.

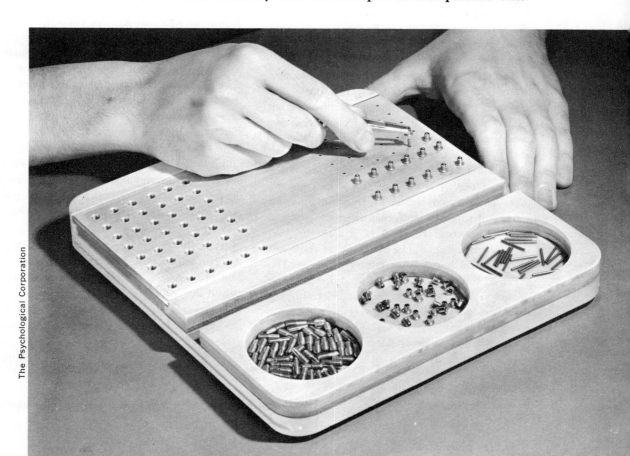

In these pictures four candidates are being evaluated through the leaderless group discussion method.

ficulty is the low reliability demonstrated by projective tests—their scores are not as consistent and as stable as those produced by the typical paper-and-pencil test.

Forced-choice questionnaires. Another form of personality test that appears to have successfully eliminated faking is the forced-choice type. The test taker is presented with a series of pairs of adjectives or descriptive phrases and is asked to indicate which one of each pair is most applicable to him. Here are some sample items:

>___energetic : ambitious___
>___loyal : dependable___
>___noisy : arrogant___
>___affected : moody___

As may be seen from these pairs, there is nothing to give the respondent any clue as to which choice is desirable: in the first two pairs, both choices are favorable; in the second two pairs, both choices are unfavorable.

This technique has been used with some success in the Jurgensen Classification Inventory. Researchers report very good results with salesmen, moderate results with bakeshop managers, and poor results with industrial supervisors. (Jurgensen, 1944; Pred, 1948; Knauft, 1949.) Ghiselli and Barthol (1956) found eighteen pairs of adjectives (four of which are reproduced above) that distinguished between successful and unsuccessful supervisors. Jurgensen maintains that each employment situation is unique and that keys for his test should be based on the responses of successful and unsuccessful employees. The expense, time, and effort required for such an operation do not of course make tests like Jurgensen's very attractive to employers who hire only a few employees or who are looking for simple, low-cost ways to improve selection.

One of the advantages of the forced-choice method is that results do not depend on any preconceived notions of the test maker, but rather on the association of certain responses with success or failure on the job. This is an important principle to remember, because employers and even psychologically trained test makers sometimes have in mind certain personal qualities that they are sure are related to job success. However, even the most logically conceived hypotheses may turn out to be invalid. For instance, when a series of studies was conducted with respect to mental health and production in a British factory, no relationship was found between the two variables. Hence, if a measure of mental health had been included in the selection battery, it would have added nothing of value and would have been a waste of time and money, as far as the prediction of worker productivity was concerned. (Lewis, 1953.)

This does not, of course, mean that employers or psychologists should ignore their hunches in developing selection instruments, but it does mean that hypotheses must be checked against actual results if they are to form an acceptable basis for selection. Often such hunches do provide useful items for selection instruments. For example, McGuire (1956) constructed a personality inventory intended to discriminate safe drivers from accident-prone drivers, selecting items on the hypothesis that accident-prone drivers would display attitudes of irresponsibility, rebelliousness, overt hostility, and egocentricity. The resulting test correctly identified between 60 and 70 per cent of a group of individuals who had been involved in recent accidents.

Interest tests. Most interest inventories are subject to the same criticism that we have made of personality questionnaires: they can be easily faked. This does not prevent their being useful in-

struments in vocational counseling, but it does raise a question with respect to their validity in situations where something is to be gained by displaying one kind of interest in preference to another. E. K. Strong's Vocational Interest Blank for Men (see Chapter 15) is somewhat less subject to faking than are other interest tests. It has proved to be of considerable value in predicting success in selling, particularly in the field of life insurance. Figure 16-5 shows some of the relationships that have been found between interest test results and success in various occupations.

Situational tests. The idea of trying an applicant out in actual work situation did not, of course, originate with the industrial psychologist. Since the dawn of civilization employers have made their decisions to hire or reject an applicant after watching him complete a trial task or two. In recent years this approach has sometimes been standardized for use in hiring skilled craftsmen, whereby each applicant is assigned one or more tasks to be completed in a given amount of time. The completed work is then rated according to a schedule.

Although situational tests can sometimes be effectively employed with certain tasks that are quite specific and that have measurable outcomes, they cannot be readily applied to jobs that involve all kinds of unpredictable variables, particularly jobs that involve working with people. During World War II, the Office of Strategic Services needed a number of persons to carry on military intelligence work, sabotage in enemy territory, and various other kinds of secret and highly dangerous operations. In order to select individuals who would be able to handle difficult assignments with maximum effectiveness, psychologists devised a number of "stress situations." One task required candidates to move a heavy, eight-foot log and themselves over two walls that were ten feet high and eight feet apart, separated by an imaginary bottomless chasm. In another situation, each candidate was required to assemble the framework of a five-foot hollow cube out of poles and spools with the "help" of two assistants who had been coached to sabotage his efforts through heckling and feigned stupidity. (OSS Assessment Staff, 1948.) The behavior of candidates in such situations was observed by psychologists who pooled their observations and came to an agreement on the probable performance of each candidate. As might be expected, it proved to be most

Figure 16-5. Average correlations between interest-test scores and job performance for selected occupations. (After Ghiselli and Brown, 1955.)

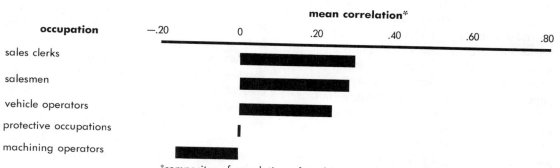

*composites of correlations found in a number of different studies

difficult to check up on the validity of these predictions, partly because it was impossible to predict the kinds of situations and the amount of
stress each candidate would encounter.

One of the methods used by the OSS assessment
personnel was the leaderless group-discussion
technique. Candidates were assembled and asked
to carry on an undirected discussion for a stated
period of time, while observers rated them in
terms of the amount and kind of leadership behavior they displayed. This method has been
found to yield reliable results, although evidence
as to its ability to predict success on the job is still
rather scanty.

The problem of criteria. In general, the simpler the job and the more predictable the job situation, the easier it is to construct or select tests that
are valid predictors of success. For simple jobs,
the task of measuring success or failure is relatively easy, once the essential features of the job
have been identified. Typical criteria of success
are: quantity and quality of production and lon-
gevity or the ability to "stay hired." One of the
problems in devising measures to predict success
in supervisory and professional occupations has
been the difficulty of agreeing upon what it is that
constitutes success. What is it, for example, that
characterizes the successful teacher? Is it the
amount of material that his students learn? Is it
his ability to impress administrators or students
with his competence? Or is it possible at all to
identify the qualities that are characteristic of
teaching success? So far, the three most commonly
used methods of measuring teaching success are
pupil gain (the amount learned by students as
measured by achievement tests), supervisory ratings (whereby administrators or supervisors assign ratings based on their general impression of
the competence of each teacher), and pupil ratings (whereby pupils anonymously rate the competence of their teachers). Pupil gain is subject to
criticism because the intellectual potential and
general teachability of classes vary widely and
because achievement tests measure only a part of
what the school is attempting to teach. Supervisor's ratings tend to lack reliability. Ratings by
pupils are the most reliable measure, but are
subject to criticism because teachers and administrators have difficulty in accepting the idea that
pupils are competent to judge teaching effectiveness. Because of the difficulty in identifying and
measuring competence in teaching, it is hardly

surprising that none of the attempts to predict
teaching effectiveness—personality inventories, attitude scales, grades received in teacher training,
or professors' ratings—have met with any consistent success. It so happens that there have been
more attempts to predict success in teaching than
in any other professional field, but there is every
reason to believe that similar discouraging results
would be obtained in other fields as well.

Supervision and management

Personnel development. An increasing number of the psychologists employed in business and
industry today are engaged in organizing and conducting courses with such titles as "Management
and Morale" and "Human Relations in Industry"
for supervisors and other management personnel.
The work of these specialists has attracted so
much attention that industrial psychology has
become, in the eyes of many people, identified
with human relations training, even though a substantial proportion of industrial psychologists still
is primarily concerned with selection.

The main impetus to the "human relations"
movement in industrial psychology came during
World War II. Because manpower was in exceedingly short supply, problems of meeting demands
for increased production obviously could not be
met by selecting the workers with the best potential and rejecting the rest. Hence managements
were forced to find other ways of improving
efficiency and raising production.

The Hawthorne study. The solution to these
problems lay in some research that had been done
during the late 1920's at the Hawthorne Works
of the Western Electric Company, located near
Chicago. In its initial stages, research at the
Hawthorne plant was concerned with measuring
the effect of illumination on production. Researchers experimented with various levels of illumination but found no consistent relationship between
the amount of light and the amount of production.
Indeed, there was a tendency in some of the experimental groups for production to go up regardless of whether the amount of light was increased or decreased. From these studies, it became evident that factors other than illumination
were playing a significant part in production.

A second series of experiments was undertaken
in order to identify some of the correlates of production. A group of girls whose task was that of

Foremen, supervisors, and other intermediate leaders tend to follow patterns of interpersonal behavior initiated by top management.

assembling small relays was isolated from a larger group of 100 workers and placed under close observation. During the period of the experiment the production of the group was recorded under conditions that varied as to the number of hours worked, the number and length of rest periods, and the basis of computing wages. Again, no relationship was found between working conditions and production. Production increased regardless of whether the girls put in more time on the job or less, whether they had more rest periods or fewer, or none at all. Although there was a relationship between increased income and increased production, the total increase in production could be only partially attributed to this factor. Hence the experimenters were forced to cast about for other explanations of this phenomenon. An examination of the detailed records that had been kept as a part of this research revealed that employee *attitudes* were the significant factor. Further research indicated that these attitudes were in turn very much influenced by the attitude and general behavior of the supervisors. It was evident that the kind of supervision that was taking place in the experimental situation was much more effective than the supervision elsewhere in the plant. In the experimental situation, the girls were free to talk and make suggestions, a condition that did not prevail elsewhere in the plant. Furthermore, the research worker who was present for the purpose of making observations was relaxed and friendly—not at all like the usual stereotype of a supervisor. The special status of the girls bolstered their feeling of importance and helped their morale. There is no question but that they found their work more enjoyable than did other similar employees in the plant. (Roethlisberger and Dickson, 1939.)

"Human relations" training. One of the outcomes of the application of research findings like the results of the Hawthorne studies to the industrial problems of World War II has been the development of training programs in "human relations" for supervisory workers. Although these programs vary a great deal in quality, many of them are excellent both as to content and methodology. The best of the programs attempt to help supervisors gain an understanding of the underlying motives of human behavior and the dynamics of groups. The approach is usually problem-centered, and the various ways of dealing with problems are "role-played" in order to test out solutions and to give supervisors practice in developing better relationships with their subordinates.

Although such training programs are a definite step forward, they are by no means the entire solution to the problem. In many organizations, any potential value from such training programs is almost completely nullified by the negative attitudes and behavior of top management. It does little good to train a supervisor or a foreman in more enlightened and humane approaches to personnel problems when he is required to carry out policies initiated by top management that are diametrically opposed to what he has learned in human relations training sessions. Furthermore, the supervisor who has been taught the wisdom of involving his subordinates in the formulation of decisions that affect them is understandably reluctant to follow through on this procedure when top management refuses to involve *him* in decisions. As we pointed out in Chapter 14, behavior in a group setting is conditioned by the emotional climate of the group, which, in turn, is to a large degree created by the group's leaders. Hence, if the top leadership in the group is creating an authoritarian climate, the attempts of intermediate leaders to create a democratic counter-climate will make little progress.

The International Harvester study. The difficulty of improving human relations in an industrial organization by training supervisors in better practices in human relations is illustrated by an experimental program conducted by the Personnel Research Board of the Ohio State University for the International Harvester Co. (Fleishman, Harris, and Burtt, 1955.) Researchers classified supervisory behavior into two types: "initiating structure" and "consideration." Examples of "initiating structure" are: emphasizing the meeting of deadlines, seeing to it that supervised individuals work up to their capacities, criticizing poor work, and deciding in detail what shall be done and how it shall be done. "Consideration" was characterized by such behavior as: giving in when others disagree, expressing appreciation when someone does a good job, stressing the importance of high morale, and putting subordinates at their ease when talking to them. In other words, "initiating structure" behavior was characterized by authoritarian or autocratic attitudes, whereas "consideration" was characterized by democratic attitudes and was consistent with a "human relations" point of view.

When researchers examined the behavior of foremen who had taken part in a two weeks' training course devoted largely to the improvement of human relations, they found no consistent pattern of improvement. Indeed, the on-the-job behavior of some of the foremen worsened, as far as "consideration" was concerned. Further investigation showed that the behavior of foremen was actually dependent on the behavior of their own supervisors. A supervisor who was considerate tended to have foremen who felt and acted the same way, and a supervisor who was "tough" tended to have foremen whose behavior was characterized by "initiating structure." The investigators concluded that the chief target of human-relations training programs should be top management. Favorable leadership climate, they decided, could spread *down* the status hierarchy in an industrial organization, but could not spread *up*.

They also questioned "the often stated proposal that good morale leads directly to increased efficiency." Structure-initiating behavior, they found, tended to be characteristic of production departments (for example assembly lines), where foremen are under pressure to get work out in a limited time, whereas in nonproduction departments (for example, maintenance and supply) foremen were more inclined to get the job done by creating a friendly atmosphere and by considerate behavior, with little emphasis on work methods, standards, and structuring of work activities. Very likely the amount of emphasis on efficiency or morale is governed to some degree by the demands of the situation.

The dichotomy between efficiency and morale is also illustrated by a study of military leadership conducted by Duryea and Greer (1956). Leaders who showed more of a tendency toward structure-initiation tended to have lower morale in their groups but were rated higher by their superiors, whereas leaders who showed a higher degree of consideration received lower ratings from their superiors but had higher morale in their groups. This effect was especially pronounced in military companies, where the size of the group is around one hundred, as contrasted with platoons, where the size of the group is about twenty. However, the researchers were unable to find any evidence that one kind of leader was any more effective than the other. There was no relationship, for example, between either of the two kinds of leadership behavior and the number of men AWOL or on sick call or the scores the men made on tests of military information.

Ambiguities in the supervisor's role. An important problem that impedes the development of democratic relationships between the supervisor and the supervised is the ambiguous nature of the supervisor's self-expectancies. Many foremen and other supervisory workers feel a strong sense of identity with their subordinates: because they work closely with them and have an understanding of their problems, they are inclined to feel sympathetic toward them. On the other hand, supervisory employees are also a part of management, and consequently are likely to identify their interests and needs with management. Hence when an issue arises that requires action favoring either the worker or management but not both, many foremen and supervisors feel drawn both ways. Such a conflict naturally aggravates feelings of anxiety and insecurity. Because of such ambivalent feelings and conflicts in loyalty, and because the supervisory employee is not completely accepted by top management or by labor, he feels a sense of isolation both from top management and the people he supervises. What many supervisors would like to do is to take matters into their own hands and work out some kind of compromise between the needs of workers and the needs of management, but generally speaking, they do not have that kind of power. Indeed, one of the most difficult aspects of supervision is the need to accept a situation in which one possesses the maximum of responsibility and the minimum of power. That is, the supervisor is expected to get results, but is seldom given the power that is needed to produce the results that are expected.

Some industrial and personnel psychologists believe that the best way to introduce "human relations" into business and industry is to start at the top. Their approach is that of providing a counseling service for top managerial personnel with the purpose of broadening management's understanding of the psychological problems that grow out of operating business and manufacturing establishments. If their re-education of top management succeeds, the psychologists move on to middle management of the same organization, repeating the same process. Although this approach to "human relations" in business and industry has had little formal evaluation so far, the underlying principles and the general intent seem sound, considered in the light of research in group processes. (Glaser, 1958.)

Engineering psychology

The chief preoccupation of industrial psychologists, as we have described it in the preceding pages, is that of helping man to find ways of meeting his needs more effectively in an industrial society. To a large extent, this has meant helping man to adapt himself to the machine. The "efficiency experts" of the early years of the present century approached this problem in an intellectualized fashion, largely unconcerned with the possible importance of any emotional factors.

The best known of the early figures in this field are F. B. Gilbreth (1911) and F. W. Taylor (1911). Gilbreth developed an ingenious system of symbols which he used to analyze the motions involved in various industrial tasks. By studying such matters as position of worker and methods of handling materials, he was able to eliminate a great deal of waste motion. For example, by reorganizing the work pattern, he was able to reduce the number of motions required in bricklaying from eighteen to five and thus increased the number of bricks that could be laid from 120 to 350 an hour. Taylor attempted to improve efficiency by such methods as incentive pay (higher pay for higher production). However, workers do not respond to financial incentives as favorably as management personnel expect them to. They quite commonly fear that if they raise production in order to earn higher amounts of incentive pay, management will cut the rate per unit and they will end up by working twice as hard for just as much pay as they originally received. Consequently, the efforts of "efficiency experts" are often thwarted by tacit agreements among workers to limit production to what they consider to be a normal day's work. (Whyte, 1955.)

The emphasis in recent years has been less on improving efficiency by adapting man to the machine, but has been rather on finding ways to adapt the machine to man, by applying the methods and the findings of experimental psychology to such problems as the design of tasks, human-operated equipment, and systems involving the interaction of men and machines. Much of this research has concerned itself with the conventional areas of experimental psychology: vision, hearing, perception, and learning.

World War II gave great impetus to this branch of psychology because it produced a great variety of problems involving the use of unfamiliar equipment. In two models of aircraft, for example, pulling a similar lever in the same direction produced opposite and in one case potentially fatal results. The multiplicity of dials and gauges that had to be under the constant observation of the aircraft pilot also contributed to the probability of errors in judgment.

Some of the research in this field has concerned itself with producing a set of eight instrument control knobs, no one of which would be confused with the others. (Jenkins, 1952.) Research with dial shapes resulted in the finding that the "open-window" type produced the least amount of error. (Sleight, 1948.)

Engineering psychology is by no means confined to problems posed by the military agencies and production engineers. Almost any segment of business and industry can find problems for the experimental psychologist. For example, Baldwin and Nielsen (1956) conducted a study of color-television images and found that the green image was more important than the red and blue images in producing a picture that was

Engineering psychologists are included among the specialists who study the behavior of men engaged in high-speed, high-altitude flight.

judged sharp by viewers. They were able to tell the television industry that the maximum in sharpness could be achieved by assigning about two-thirds of the total bandwidth to the green picture, thus making possible a saving of 50 per cent in bandwidth without loss in picture sharpness.

Other research in this field has concerned itself with the convenient and efficient arrangement of working space, the physical comfort of the worker, and the development of task patterns to eliminate monotony, boredom, and fatigue.

Research like that done at the Hawthorne Works shows that changes in the physical environment of employees will not necessarily produce desired changes in efficiency and production.

Hence it appears that the amount of improvement that can be produced through re-engineering is limited. Nevertheless, the appearance of engineering psychology as a field of research at least raises the possibility that the job can be adapted, as well as the man.

At the present time, the largest number of engineering psychologists are employed in military work, either working directly for one of the branches of the Department of Defense, or working for a contracting organization, like the Systems Research Laboratory of the RAND Corporation. The RAND Corporation ("RAND" stands for "research and development") was under the U.S. Government during World War II, but has since been operated as a private, nonprofit corporation. By 1958 its Systems Research Laboratory had a staff of over one hundred psychologists, engaged in developing and testing complex systems of machines and men, with particular emphasis on problems of communication, feedback, and the transmittal of information. Systems research development has been concerned largely with the problems of producing the optimal organization for minimizing the amount of error in any system of machines and men. Although most of the work so far has been limited to small systems, such as radar warning systems and fire-control (that is, artillery) systems, the data accumulated by these psychologists—classified under the headings of communication theory, information theory, organization theory, and the like—hold the promise of producing principles and concepts that may improve the effectiveness of larger organizations. Because of the great range and variety of problems encountered by researchers in this field, their work has taken on a decidedly interdisciplinary character, ranging into physics, engineering, linguistics, mathematics, and sociology, in addition to psychology. (Haire, 1959.)

Public opinion sampling and market research

The need to study opinions and attitudes.

One of the most important ingredients in the success of any large-scale undertaking, public or private, is accurate information. For instance, the most efficient production methods are useless if management is incorrectly informed as to the quantity and quality of available raw materials. A government agency needs to have some idea of the number of individuals who will be applying for benefits under a new law in order to be able to process applications promptly. And a manufacturing business needs to have information regarding the buying attitudes of the public. Indeed, in most large-scale business operations today, few new products are launched unless the manufacturer has had some indication of whether they will be favorably received.

As it is seldom feasible to contact all potential users of a new product, the information needed by the manufacturer is ordinarily secured by polling a sample of the buying public. (See Chapter 8 for a discussion of sampling.) Such methods can also be used to sample public opinion regarding national and local issues.

Organizations that commission the taking of polls are interested in how individuals will behave under a given set of circumstances—whether they will buy a certain product, how they will vote at a forthcoming election, whether they will prefer this or that kind of packaging. The tendency to behave this or that way toward a given class of objects or issues is what is termed an *attitude*. An individual may or may not be aware of the attitude he has toward the product or the issue under consideration, but if asked about his attitude, he will usually venture an *opinion* as to his probable reaction if the occasion to act should arise.

Motivation research. Unfortunately, opinions are not always reliable indices to the behavior that will actually take place under a given set of circumstances; hence pollsters have tried to devise questions and methods of probing into basic attitudes without getting the subject to commit himself on an opinion. This probing into more-or-less unconscious motives is sometimes called "motivation research." Sometimes projective devices are used to tap motives that are beyond immediate awareness. When Sanford (1951) asked 963 respondents in the course of an hour-long interview what they worried about, 159 mentioned family problems, and only one mentioned sex or "love life." But when he presented them with a simple drawing, like the one depicted in Figure 16-6, and asked them how the person in the drawing would reply to a question regarding the problem that was on his mind, 130 mentioned family problems and 30 mentioned "love life." The point

Figure 16-6. Drawing used as a projective device in attitude surveying. (Sanford, 1951.)

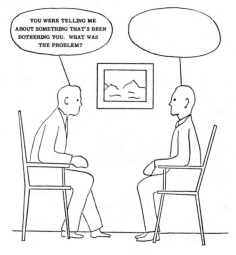

is that the respondents found it easier to talk about intimate and personal matters when they could project them onto a figure in a cartoon than they could in responding to a direct question put to them by an interviewer.

Another approach used to probe into the more basic attitudes that could predetermine future behavior is the *open-end question,* a device which does not require a specific reply, like "yes" or "no," but which permits the respondent to answer in his own words. The *depth interview* probes even deeper into the unconscious motivation of the respondent. By letting him ramble and discuss a wide variety of subjects more or less of his own choosing, the interviewer gathers information that would elude him under direct questioning.

The advantages and disadvantages of asking direct questions in a poll versus such methods as using projective devices or depth interview are much like the advantages and disadvantages of personality questionnaires and projective tests. The direct questions take less time and produce data that are more readily quantifiable and hence can be readily processed. However, they do not take into account the more-or-less unconscious motives that may be a more dependable index to the individual's future behavior. Projective devices and depth interviews take a great deal of time (hence are much more expensive) and produce data that may provide clues to the individual's unconscious motivational patterns but may also lead to conclusions of dubious validity.

Sampling problems. The second question—who should be polled—is one of sampling. Since it is never possible to poll every person whose attitude may be important, the pollster tries to build a sample that is representative of the group he is interested in. If he is interested in assessing the potential market for new automobiles, he will limit his sample to people who are able to drive and own cars. If 20 per cent of the new car market is in California, 20 per cent of his sample must be Californians. If his product is a child's atlas, he *may* try to secure the reaction of children to his product, but even more probably he will approach parents and teachers—the individuals who will actually be in a position to buy the book when it appears on the market.

Variables that are commonly taken account of in building a sample are geographical and rural-urban distribution, socio-economic status, education, age, and sex. If the sample is to be truly rep-

resentative of a broad group, such as the persons who will be voting at the next election, care must be taken not to have over-representation of better educated people and those in professional or managerial occupations. The *Literary Digest* poll of 1936 erred badly in predicting the presidential election because its ballots went out to telephone subscribers, who were more representative of middle and upper socio-economic groups. Although the sampling in the 1948 pre-election polls was conducted more scientifically, the fact that middle-class people are more accessible and respond more readily to polling produced data that led the pollsters to exaggerate the expected size of the Republican vote. Although the error was only six percentage points, it was large enough, in a close election, to result in a wrong prediction.

Laymen are sometimes concerned because the voting behavior of millions of people is predicted on the basis of polling a few thousand. Actually, if the right questions are asked in the right way of a truly representative sample, it is possible to achieve a high degree of accuracy. Table 16-1 shows how close estimates from surveys based on five thousand respondents came to matching estimates based on manufacturers' records. The two estimates are close enough to indicate the high

Table 16–1 Estimates based on surveys of households and farms compared with estimates based on other sources. (After Noyes and Hilgard, 1946.)

	Estimates Based on Surveys * (millions)	Estimates Based on Industry and Government Sources (millions)
Homes with electric irons	29.2	26.0
Homes with washing machines	17.7	18.4
Homes with refrigerators	20.6	19.9
Motor trucks on farms	1.3	1.1
Mowing machines on farms	2.7	2.8
Cream separators on farms	1.7	1.8
Tractors on farms	2.0	1.9

* The first survey (Nov. 1943) covered 5000 homes; the second (Feb. 1944) covered 2678 farm operators.

degree of validity that can be obtained by polling small samples.

Exaggerated claims. Laymen sometimes take the opposite attitude—that of ascribing a certain omniscience to polls—and frequently express fear that unscrupulous manufacturers are using depth interviews and other esoteric methods to get information that can be used to force helpless consumers to buy whatever the manufacturer wants them to buy. Somehow the general public seems to equate "psychology" with "magic," and feels that whoever has "psychology" on his side has some kind of magical power. The furor in 1958 over subliminal advertising is a case in point. The immediate cause of the controversy was the announcement by Vickary that he had been able to increase soft drink and popcorn sales in a motion-picture theatre when the words "Eat Popcorn" and "Drink Coca-Cola" were flashed on the screen of a motion picture theatre with exposures of ⅓₀₀₀ of a second. (See discussion of subliminal perception on pp. 136–137.) This statement touched off claims and counterclaims, with the Federal Communications Commission being asked to protect the nation's viewers against being exploited by this presumably "irresistible psychological device." The cause for alarm was, however, virtually baseless. A review of relevant research showed that other attempts made under adequately controlled conditions to influence the behavior of subjects subliminally had produced inconclusive results. (McConnell, Cutler, McNeil, 1958.) The absence of conclusive findings raises a question as to whether it is at all possible to influence buying behavior subliminally. During recent years, a number of statements have appeared in the popular press making rather extravagant claims as to the ability of psychologists in the employ of large business concerns to manipulate and exploit the helpless consuming public. Unfortunately, such statements only help to reinforce the idea in the public mind that psychology is a form of necromancy instead of a behavioral science.

Summary

One of the reasons why American business and industry have been able to expand so rapidly is that the production and distribution of goods have been viewed as a series of problems to be solved. As the problems have become increasingly complex and specialized, scientists have been called upon for help. Although today problems of human behavior are the most difficult ones to solve, relatively few business and industrial leaders are aware of the psychological nature of such problems. Nevertheless, the field of industrial psychology has grown rapidly since World War II. One difficulty in this field is that of the differences between psychologists and business leaders in their values, interests, methods, and objectives.

Employee selection is one problem to which industrial psychologists apply their skills. Employers are often influenced by the appearance of a prospective employee, as well as his training, skill, and experience. The psychologist's job is that of obtaining information about both the ability and the personal qualities of applicants in order to form a basis for decisions about hiring. Ideally, research should be conducted to develop a selection program for each type of position; in such research, the job is carefully studied, a preliminary test battery is set up to measure the variables that may be related to job success, the test scores of successful and unsuccessful employees are compared, and those tests that are predictive of success are retained in a selection battery. Such batteries are then useful in improving the "batting average" of the company's hiring procedure. Intelligence tests are included in many selection batteries, but their value as predictors depends on the job in question. In general, the more the amount of preparation and training required for a job, and the more complex the job, the more likely intelligence is to be a factor in job success. Special aptitude tests have been developed to predict performance in various occupations. Personality tests have also been used in several selection batteries; for example, they have proven to be of some value in predicting selling ability. Faking is an ever-present problem, when personality and interest tests are used for this purpose, and more sophisticated approaches to personality measurement have attempted to overcome this problem. Situational tests of various types are also valuable in selection procedures. One major difficulty in effective employee selection is that of defining the criteria of successful job performance. In general, the simpler the job and the more predictable the job situation, the easier it is to construct or select tests that are valid predictors of success.

The skills of industrial psychologists are also

useful in devising ways to improve supervisory and managerial practices, but employers have been slow to utilize psychologists for this purpose. Psychologists, too, have been slow in developing these techniques. For one thing, they have been hampered by the fact that the results are not as readily quantifiable as they are in selection situations. The Hawthorne study of the 1920's was one of the first to identify the very important relationship between employee attitude and productivity. A result of such research has been the development of training programs in "human relations" for supervisory workers. A difficulty with such programs is that the training of foremen in democratic practices is of little value if top management holds contradictory attitudes. It has been found that a favorable social climate can spread down the status hierarchy, but not up. A factor that sometimes impedes the development of democratic relationships between the supervisor and his supervisees is the conflict between his tendencies to identify both with his subordinates and with management. In a sense, he is somewhat isolated from both groups.

At the beginning of this century, efficiency experts began to find ways to reduce waste motion in order to increase the productivity of employees. These efforts were often thwarted by tacit agreements among workers to limit production and avoid possible exploitation. In recent years, engineering psychologists have been working on the task of finding ways to adapt the machine to man. It is vitally important to discover the simplest and most effective ways to design and place levers, dials, push buttons, etc., on our increasingly complex equipment. In recent years there has been much activity in developing more effective systems composed of men and machines.

Accurate information about the public is essential to the success of any large-scale undertaking. Public opinion is measured by polling carefully selected samples of the population. Individual attitudes concerning products, political candidates, and national issues are important to ascertain, but their measurement presents various difficulties. Most people will, if asked, readily make a guess as to their probable reaction to various events. Because such opinions are not always reliable indices to behavior, attempts are being made to get at the more or less unconscious motives of individuals. "Motivation research" is the term used to identify this approach, which makes use of projective tests, open-end questions, depth interviews, and so on. The problem of validity in these methods is as yet unsolved. The sampling problem is also an extremely important one. The pollster tries to make sure that the sample is representative of the group in which he is interested. Some people tend to discount the results of polls, but they have actually proven to be quite accurate predictors when conducted properly. On the other hand, there are individuals who go to the opposite extreme and fear the omniscience and omnipotence of psychologists using polls and motivation research. Actually neither extreme viewpoint is justified; such techniques have been quite useful, but psychologists are not omniscient, nor are their techniques infallible.

Questions

1. Why is there any need for psychologists in the world of business and industry?
2. How do the objectives of the average businessman and the average psychologist differ?
3. Why do employers tend to insist on a personal interview before hiring a prospective employee? What are the advantages and disadvantages of this procedure?
4. Describe how you would go about developing a selection program for used-car salesmen.
5. What are the various types of tests that psychologists have used in employee selection? What sort of results have been obtained?

6. What criteria of success would you suggest for the following occupations: real-estate salesman, physician, truck driver, congressman?
7. Discuss the findings and implications of the Hawthorne study.
8. How is leadership behavior in industry related to morale and productivity?
9. What sort of problems are handled by engineering psychologists?
10. If you had developed a new product for the home, how would you determine: (a) its potential appeal to the public; (b) what name to give it; and (c) the sort of advertising campaign that would be most influential?

Suggestions for further reading

Calhoon, R. P., E. W. Noland, and A. M. Whitehall, *Cases on Human Relations in Management.* New York: McGraw-Hill, 1958. Presentation of a number of problem situations for analysis and discussion.

Katz, D., D. Cartwright, S. Eldersveld, and A. McC. Lee, Editors, *Public Opinion and Propaganda.* New York: Dryden, 1954. Although principally concerned with the measurement and manipulation of political opinion, much of the book has relevance to advertising and opinion research in industry.

Leavitt, H. J., *Managerial Psychology.* Chicago: University of Chicago Press, 1958. A book written to explain the principles of social psychology and personality theory to supervisory and executive personnel.

Maier, N. R. F., *Principles of Human Relations: Applications to Management.* New York: Wiley, 1952. Presents some of the ways whereby decisions can be shared, morale raised, and communication improved. Includes case material.

Roethlisberger, F. J. and W. J. Dickson, *Management and the Worker.* Cambridge, Mass.: Harvard University Press, 1939. Contains a report of the Hawthorne Study and a discussion of the application of the findings to management policy.

Shartle, C. L., *Executive Performance and Leadership.* Englewood Cliffs, N. J.: Prentice-Hall, 1956. A discussion of psychological factors in the practical problems faced by executives and administrators.

Stagner, R., *The Psychology of Industrial Conflict.* New York: Wiley, 1956. Application of concepts drawn from social psychology and personality theory to the understanding of industrial conflict.

Stone, C. H. and W. E. Kendall, *Effective Personnel Selection Procedures.* Englewood Cliffs, N. J.: Prentice-Hall, 1956. Discussion of techniques of recruiting, interviewing, and selecting employees.

Viteles, M. S., *Motivation and Morale in Industry.* New York: Norton, 1953. A thorough-going review of the research relevant to this topic.

Here are five good texts in industrial psychology:

Blum, M. L., *Industrial Psychology and Its Social Foundations,* rev. ed. New York: Harper, 1956.

Ghiselli, E. E. and C. W. Brown, *Personnel and Industrial Psychology,* 2nd ed. New York: McGraw-Hill, 1955.

Maier, N. R. F., *Psychology in Industry,* 2nd ed. Boston: Houghton Mifflin, 1955.

Ryan, T. A. and P. C. Smith, *Principles of Industrial Psychology.* New York: Ronald, 1954.

Smith, H. C., *Psychology of Industrial Behavior,* New York: McGraw-Hill, 1955.

Psychology
and
world affairs

17

The prevention of war. How often have we heard the words: "Why can't the people of the world get together? Why do they always have to be fighting one another?"

The desire for world peace has a universal appeal; it resulted in the formation of the League of Nations after World War I, and the United Nations in 1945. Nations exchange diplomatic missions to keep channels of communication open and thus reduce the chances for international friction that could lead to armed conflict. And many if not most military alliances are entered into for the ostensible reason of preventing war. It is difficult to assess the usefulness of these attempts at international cooperation in preventing war— that is, we know how many wars they were *un*able to prevent, but we do not know how many wars they *did* prevent. The incontrovertible fact is, of course, that our efforts up to the present time have not been completely successful. Something more is needed, something that goes beyond international organizations, diplomatic exchanges, and military alliances.

The international situation is to some degree analogous (but not identical) to situations in our home communities. On the international level we would like to eliminate a large-scale form of social pathology—war—and on the local scene we would like to eliminate social pathology on a smaller scale—social pathology that takes the form of crime and delinquency. Our treatment of these two kinds of pathology, war and delinquency, is also similar. Our general tendency is to regard the problem of peace both in our home communities and among nations largely as a problem calling for legal measures, backed up by force. On the local level, we try to keep crime and delinquency under control by having the right kind of laws and a good law-enforcement agency; on the international level, we attempt to avoid wars by legal instruments in the form of treaties and other international agreements and by maintaining a strong military establishment.

Or, our "common sense" may tell us that peace at home and abroad may be secured and maintained by good will, that people who "want to do the right thing" will not break laws or will not start wars. On the home front we try to inculcate certain values in our children and young people so that they will become "people of good will," while on the international front we initiate various kinds of behavior—diplomatic negotiations, exchanges of persons, gifts and loans of money, and so forth—in the hope that the people of other nations will be assured of our good will toward them and will react with good will toward us. Interestingly, the two approaches are based on diametrically opposed assumptions: the good-will approach assumes that people can be trusted; the law-enforcement-military approach assumes that they cannot.

Psychological factors in international relations. Although the behavioral scientist might endorse either the military-legal and the good-will approaches to international peace-making, he would still have reservations about depending completely on them, because each appears to be based on an assumed simplicity in human behavior that does not check with the facts as he knows them. Like most other approaches to solving human problems that are based on "common-sense" principles, they are composed partly of a realistic understanding of human behavior and partly of wishful thinking. Let us take the good-will approach as an example. Although it is true that human beings tend to behave in accordance with the communicated expectations of others and to respond favorably to gestures of good will, at the same time they also respond to other stimuli, stimuli that might be present in the situation but that may be perceived by one set of individuals, but not another. In the give and take of international relations, examples of this turn up almost daily.

An economically advanced nation (which we shall call "Omega") may offer to send expert technicians to help the farmers in an economically underdeveloped country (which we shall call "Omicron"). Omicron may reject the offer with some coolness, perhaps because it is interested in developing its industrial potential and is less interested in developing its agriculture. In the status hierarchy of nations, industrialized countries have

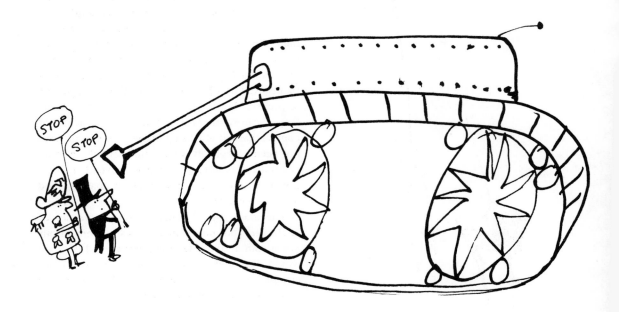

International expressions of good will may take the form of medical aid to children. These pictures show work being done in Guatemala to combat malnutrition and in Burma to combat malaria under the direction of the United Nations Children's Fund (UNICEF) and the World Health Organization (WHO).

higher prestige than countries whose resources are largely agricultural. Almost every underdeveloped country, it appears, longs for its own steel mill. Perhaps Omicron has been asking Omega for help in developing its industrial potential, and perhaps negotiations were not progressing because experts in Omega felt that building a steel mill in Omicron would be economically unfeasible. But to show that they are sympathetic to Omicron's problems, they generously offered to send the agricultural experts. The people in Omicron, instead of responding positively to this gesture of good will, feel offended. Here they have been aspiring to the status of an industrial nation, and Omega has not only refused to give them the help they requested, but is apparently attempting to keep them in their despised status as an agricultural nation. The offer of agricultural experts is interpreted by Omicron as meaning: "Do not aspire to higher status, but be content to remain an agricultural nation. You should accept the fact that you will never have as high status as we have here in Omega."

As we have pointed out previously, the difficulty with common-sense theories of human be-

havior is that they lead us to ignore the importance of emotional factors in human behavior, or, for that matter, any facts that contradict the theory we happen to be using at the time. We behave internationally much as we do interpersonally: we adopt a certain frame of reference based on "common-sense" principles, accept it as reality, and act accordingly; then, if results do not work out as expected, we rationalize. We blame the stupidity of people in other countries, the ineptness of our leaders, our own lack of courage—anything and everything except our theories of human behavior. It never seems to occur to us that the theories of human behavior on which we base our frame of reference are at fault. Sometimes we are willing even to go to war to keep from changing our basic assumptions.

If we adhere to a naive and oversimplified good-will approach in our relations with other nations, an approach based on the assumption that our good intentions should be as obvious to other nations as they are to ourselves, we will undoubtedly encounter disappointments and may slip into the opposite and equally unrealistic extreme in our attitudes. We may, for example, become cynical and fatalistic, saying: "What's the use—there always will be wars. The only answer is to make ourselves strong enough so that any nation will think twice before attacking."

"Common-sense" attitudes toward social pathology. Such a feeling of discouragement is analogous to the pessimism that was prevalent in previous centuries regarding disease. Although specific remedies were known for a few ailments, a common attitude was: "It is the lot of mankind to suffer, and nothing can be done about it. Perhaps it is God's will." And a number of medical scientists had to suffer persecution and harassment because an ignorant populace thought they were acting contrary to the will of God. In many parts of the world today such fatalism regarding disease still exists.

The alleviation of social pathology also provides analogies. The traditional attitude, which is still widespread, is that criminal and delinquent acts are committed only by people who are inherently bad. The world, according to such a theory, is divided into good people and bad people, and bad people are the ones who will commit crimes if they are not restrained by the forces of law and order. According to this theory, when the perpetrators of delinquent acts are caught, they should be severely punished, in order to serve as an example and thus to deter the criminal tendencies of others. People who hold this theory believe that some crime will be committed in spite of these deterrents, and there is little that good people can do except to defend themselves by such measures as carrying sidearms, hiring guards and special police, and locking up or executing the bad people who break the law.

We have in the past been able to hold such "common-sense" theories because we were innocent of any understanding of individual differences. We had little awareness, for instance, that differences among individuals were not differences of kind (that is, there are not two classes of people, one "good" and the other "bad") but of degree (each of us has tendencies toward both "good" and "bad" behavior). We were generally unaware that when we were legislating against delinquency, we were legislating against ourselves. Although a great many writers and philosophers have for centuries pointed out the flaws in the reasoning that so artificially separated the "good" from the "bad," the general weight of public opinion and behavior supported the "common-sense," legalistic approach to delinquency and criminal behavior.

Common sense also held that there were certain crimes that were "natural," that could not be eliminated by law. Dueling, wife-beating, feuding, and cruelty to children are a few of the crimes that have been characterized at various times as completely "natural"—as behavior that could never be eliminated or controlled by law. Yet it is significant that as we have progressed in our understanding of human behavior, we have been able to reduce the incidence of such crimes to a very marked degree. There are, of course, many other forms of social pathology that we have had less success in controlling or eliminating; and because of such failures we sometimes forget our successes.

There is still a substantial residue of feeling that criminal behavior is inevitable and calls for drastic treatment, but the attitude of the general public has swung to a more liberal point of view. Although our attitude still tends to be somewhat punitive, we are more inclined today than we were a generation ago to be interested in rehabilitating adult and juvenile delinquents instead of merely locking them up. Our present-day parole and probation systems are based on the idea that law-breakers *can* learn more acceptable patterns of behavior. This change in the methods of treating delinquents has been brought about partly

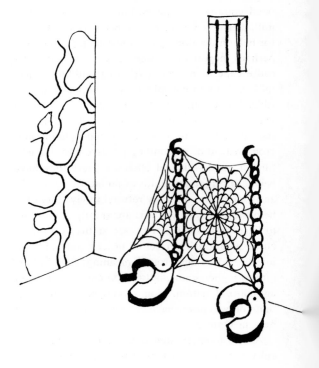

through the spread of more humane attitudes and partly through a greater psychological understanding of criminal behavior itself. There is much more that we need to know about the causes and control of such behavior, but what we have learned so far has enabled us to obtain results that are encouraging.

Understanding the causes of war. So far, our understanding of the dynamics of international behavior has lagged behind our psychological understanding of individual behavior, but the modest progress we have made so far in individual behavior gives us cause for encouragement with respect to international behavior. Perhaps one approach to such understanding is to recognize and identify some of the basic similarity between the kinds of pathology that appear in individuals —neurosis, psychosis, and delinquency—and the pathology that appears in groups—mob violence, wars, and ethnic prejudice. As Chisholm (1946) stated in his William Alanson White Memorial Lecture:

> The necessity to fight wars . . . is as much a pathological psychiatric symptom as is a phobia or the antisocial behavior of a criminal who has been dominated by a stern and unreasonable father.

John Dewey (1939) also put his finger on a significant aspect of the relationship between individual and group pathology:

> The serious threat to our democracy is not the existence of foreign totalitarian states. It is the existence within our own personal attitudes and within our own institutions of conditions similar to those which have given a victory to external authority, discipline, uniformity, and dependence upon The Leader in foreign countries.

Political scientists, too, are becoming aware of the close connection between international and personal levels of behavior. In a recent textbook, Haas and Whiting (1956) criticize the common-sense point of view that the policies of nations are dictated or predetermined by "immutable injunctions of geography, principle, and power." Instead, they say, the behavior of nations is a product of shifting attitudes, aims, and policies occurring *within* each country. "Only an examination of the motives of men and groups of men can make clear the tangled pattern of international relations."

In essence, our problem in dealing with pathology both at the personal and the community level, as well as the international level, has been that of moving from an irrational, prescientific (or common-sense) approach to human behavior to an approach that uses the findings of scientific research. Much of the research that is helping to broaden and deepen our understanding is interdisciplinary. The research of cultural anthropologists helps to point up similarities and differences among cultures, which in turn aids in communication among individuals in different cultures. The data produced through economic research provide useful information as to the problems faced by people in various countries. Sociologists describe and classify the institutions and structures of society and identify changes that are taking place in various societies. Although psychologists were at one time principally interested in the motivation and behavior of individuals, in recent years they have produced a great deal of research in the field of group behavior. Other behavioral scientists who are making contributions to a better understanding are trained in the disciplines of political science, education, and psychiatry.

The understanding of behavior means, among other things, the ability to view a given action from a number of different aspects. Let us return to the problem of the difficult relations between the two nations, Omega and Omicron, which we mentioned earlier in this chapter. The resident of Omega who takes a common-sense or a legalistic point of view is very clearly baffled by the hostile attitude of Omicron to the offer of expert agricultural assistance. He is also perplexed and irritated by the insistence of Omicron that it be helped to build a steel mill, a project that is economically unfeasible.

The behavioral scientist living in Omega may feel a sense of personal irritation at what appears to be the stubborn and unrealistic behavior of the Omicron government, but if he has any kind of broad, interdisciplinary background, he will counsel against taking any precipitous and impulsive action. Because he is aware of the inherent complexities of any behavioral act, he knows that there are many forces operating to produce what seems like an illogical, ungrateful form of behavior. Perhaps he can draw on the work of cultural anthropologists who have studied the people of Omicron and who can shed some light on their characteristic reactions and patterns of behavior. Perhaps, too, he can help conduct an opinion poll that will help clarify the problem that has grown up between the two countries. Or perhaps, through his understanding of human motivation, he can trace the emotional development of what seems to be an irrational attitude on the part of the people of Omicron. If the government of Omega is fortunate enough to have hired him as a consultant, he may be able to explain some of the problems in the situation to the members of the government so that they, too, may see the behavior of the Omicron government as something other than stupidity and ingratitude.

At this stage in the development of the human species, it is difficult to tell what kinds of action nations or international organizations should undertake to promote international understanding and world peace. Perhaps the best that can be done at present is to approach the problem both boldly and tentatively—*boldly,* because our past failures argue for the search for new and different approaches, and experimenting with new and untried methods takes courage; and *tentatively,* because it is necessary to be flexible, to be able to withdraw and try other approaches when it is evident that one has made a mistake and that a certain solution which seemed promising is creating additional difficulties.

The role of psychologists and other behavioral scientists in international affairs should be that of conducting research into the nature of human behavior; developing theories and working hypotheses that can be used by those who are trying to improve international understanding and cooperation; and translating research findings, theories, and working hypotheses into concepts that laymen can understand and use. An additional role, and one that is unfortunately an uncomfortable one for most behavioral scientists, is that of the publicist—the person who tries to develop public attitudes that are tolerant and supportive toward behavioral scientists and their research and are more receptive to the application of the methods and findings of science to problems of everyday life and international relations. In the last hundred years there has been a steady increase in the receptivity of the general public to the contributions of the natural and physical sciences, but the behavioral sciences have not been able to share equally in this acceptance. However, as we have tried to show in the two preceding chapters, a significant degree of progress has been made. Psychological principles are even beginning to be recognized by courts of law. The decision of the Supreme Court of the United States in 1954 to outlaw racial segregation in the schools was based

in part on the research findings of psychologists and other behavioral scientists.

Of the several roles outlined for the behavioral scientist in the preceding paragraph, those of the research worker and theory builder are clearly the most important. The roles of consultant and publicist are ones which must of necessity be incidental to the main job of finding the answers to questions about human behavior. As a matter of fact, it is very often the scientific amateur, the interested and enlightened layman, who is the first to see how psychological principles or research findings can be applied to everyday behavior, and it is very likely that behavioral scientists must continue to depend on such persons to make the applications that will solve the problems of international cooperation and world peace. Hence in the remainder of this chapter we shall be concerned principally with some of the psychological theory and research that has some relevance to international understanding.

Cross-cultural research. One obvious area for research consists of the differences and similarities that exist among peoples of various cultures. Such research can be justified on the grounds that the more information we have regarding the values and behavior patterns of people in other countries, the more intelligently we can behave toward them.

Recent years have seen a notable increase in the number of cross-cultural studies, some of them quite ingenious. Anderson and Anderson (1956) prepared a series of "incomplete stories" designed to bring out differences in values of preadolescent children in various countries. One story, entitled "The Lost Meat," tells of a boy named Michael whose mother sent him to the store to buy a pound of wieners. Instead of coming home directly, he stopped to play for a few minutes. While he was playing, a dog got into the package and ran away with half of them, whereupon Michael wrapped up the remainder and took them home. After the children had read the story, they were asked: "What did Michael say to his mother?" This question is of course a projective device designed to find out what the respondent would himself do in a similar situation. The data, as shown in Table 17-1, confirm the authors' hypothesis to the effect that children in more authoritarian cultures would be inclined to say that Michael would tell a lie, whereas children in a more democratic culture, being less afraid of their parents, would be inclined to say that he told the truth. One of the problems of cross-cultural research, however, is that it sometimes raises new questions that call for further research. Although the German children in this experiment were more inclined than American children to say that Michael would lie, the difference between southern Germany (Karlsruhe and Munich) and northern Germany (Hamburg) is much greater than the difference between northern Germany and the United States.

The findings of an isolated piece of research like the one described above have limited application, of course, but they have some implications that are worth careful consideration. For instance, they suggest that people in different cultures have different methods of resolving threatening situations. Further research is necessary in order to see whether attitudes toward telling the truth are homogeneous in their respective cultures. Research is also needed to determine what factors produce the differences in attitude. It is not enough to find out that, say, southern Germans are less conscientious than Americans, Finns, and northern Germans about telling the truth. It is also important to find out how truth telling fits in with the larger value system of southern Germans. Without such understanding, we are likely to develop a moralistic attitude toward southern Germans, forgetting that we have to share a portion of the world with them and must hence work out some pattern of mutual acceptance and coexistence.

Another area of cross-cultural research consists of the attitudes which individuals in one country have toward citizens of another country. One team of researchers, using both direct questions and projective techniques, explored the feelings that adolescent and preadolescent Mexicans have toward Americans, that is, toward citizens of the United States. When the children were asked: "If you were not a Mexican, who would you like to be?", the nationality most commonly named was American. In response to another question, approximately two-thirds of the children said that they would like to be an American. However, when the children responded to projective tests designed to assess their underlying feelings toward Americans, it became clear that although they felt that Americans were superior to Mexicans socioeconomically and physically, they also felt that Americans were inferior intellectually and ethically. The researchers concluded that Mexicans unconsciously regard Americans as figures of authority, but representing an authority that is not acceptable. This attitude, the researchers said, produces feelings of hostility which appear in the form of jokes, criticism, and scorn directed toward whatever positive values Americans attempt to represent. (Davila et al., 1956.)

These are two examples of the kind of research aimed at contributing to our fund of information about value systems and attitudes in various cultures. We should not leap to the conculsion, however, that the increased availability of information, important as it may be, will in itself promote better relationships among peoples of different cultures. One study in the field of industrial psychology shows that there is no relationship, for example, between the attitudes of employees and how much

Table 17–1 Percentages of replies made by preadolescent children in four countries coded as "telling truth" or "telling lie" in "The Lost Meat" story. (After Anderson and Anderson, 1956.)

City and Country	Sample Size	Percentage * of Replies Coded as	
		"Michael Tells the Truth"	"Michael Tells a Lie"
Knoxville, USA	217	64	19
Birmingham, USA	398	58	31
Hamburg, Germany	281	53	44
Helsinki, Finland	209	50	32
Karlsruhe, Germany	257	39	50
Mexico City, Mexico	333	37	45
Munich, Germany	165	35	64

* Percentages do not add up to 100 per cent for each city, since there were other ways of resolving the problem than having Michael tell the truth or tell a lie.

they know about the company they work for. (Perry and Mahoney, 1955.) It seems likely that a similar generalization would hold true with respect to intercultural attitudes. Smith (1955) attempted to answer the question: "Do intercultural experiences affect attitudes?" He queried 183 secondary and college students who had visited Europe and found that basic attitudes were not changed significantly. The best predictors of each individual's response to his experience were his previous attitudes. Although individuals whose initial attitudes were moderately "conservative" were inclined to develop attitudes that were more world-minded, individuals who were exceptionally nationalistic and prejudiced tended to become even more nationalistic and prejudiced as a result of the experience. Such studies show that the problem of developing favorable intercultural attitudes is an exceedingly complicated one—a problem that will not be resolved merely by having people in different countries get to know each other better. One reassuring finding in the Smith study, however, was his discovery that those persons who established close personal ties with Europeans during their trip were more likely to engage in internationally oriented activities on their return.

Frustration, hostility, and aggressive behavior. One obvious cause of war is the development of hostility. When frustration and emotional conflict build up more hostility in a people than they can contain, they are likely to find some way to express it. Sometimes a dictator will deliberately permit or encourage armed aggression against another nation, perhaps out of fear that so much hostility, if not expressed, could be directed toward the government in the form of a revolt or a coup d'etat. Or sometimes a minority group may be designated to serve as the scapegoat—for example, the Jews in Germany under the Nazis. Usually people who are experiencing widespread frustration cannot readily identify its real causes. In a complex and ever-changing world, difficulties are likely to be the result of a number of different factors operating together. Even when one factor predominates, it is often not readily recognizable. For instance, the people in a certain country may become very restive because an inflation of the currency has resulted in sharply increased prices. Since wages tend to lag behind prices, this means that the wage-earner finds that his wages buy less. Because the dynamics of inflation are difficult to

understand, and because inflation is after all an abstraction, the wage-earner tends to direct his hostility at something or someone real and tangible—usually, the merchant who raises the prices or the employer who is reluctant to raise wages. If he is eventually successful in getting his wages raised, this has the immediate and short-range effect of increasing the amount of spending power, which then helps to bid up prices to new and higher levels. The situation has a certain built-in frustration potential which is well-nigh inescapable.

The inflation spiral is but one of the many active foci of mass frustration in the world. The hostility that is generated in such foci may spill over into international relations or may interact with other sources of frustration. The everyday give-and-take of international relations provides ample opportunity for the people of any nation to feel misunderstood, manipulated, deprived, cheated, insulted, ignored, or whatever. Any national population that is at all sensitive and has a low tolerance for frustration has almost daily cause to become enraged at the kind of treatment it is experiencing at the hands of other nations.

The point is that frustration and hostility are unavoidable by-products of both the internal affairs of nations and international relations. What people decide to do about these frustrations is a function of their national character, their culture and traditions, their generalized frames of reference, and the characteristics of the situation at hand. One nation adopts an attitude of philosophical resignation; another maintains that it is "common sense" to stand up for one's rights and not get "pushed around"; still another nation believes in being adroit and devious and depending on skill in negotiation. And some nations attempt all three approaches simultaneously.

Although such maneuvers appear to work most of the time, a study of history, both recent and remote, shows that they will work only up to a point. Inevitably, hostility spills over and armed conflict supplants diplomatic debates. The question is: What suggestions can we find in psychological research that will help us improve on "common sense"?

A psychological understanding of hostility. To begin with, the psychologist takes a different point of view toward hostility than the layman does. The layman is likely to regard hostility as "good" or "bad," depending on his cultural values, as well as on the situation in which he finds him-

Marc Riboud, Magnum

The psychologist who is interested in behavior on national and international levels must inevitably become concerned with the problems that relate to the nature, expression, and control of group hostility and aggression.

self. Although our own hostility is generally perceived as "good" (because it is "righteous" and "justified"), the hostility that is directed *against* us is "bad." In some cultures, however, there are strong tendencies to deny or repress hostility or to avoid situations that would generate hostility. Members of such societies would therefore regard *any* hostility—even if self-generated—as "bad."

The psychologist who is undertaking research into the causes of hostility does not regard it as "good" or "bad," but merely as a form of behavior that is the inevitable and natural result of frustration. Presumably, if the amount of frustration were reduced, there would be a consequent reduction in hostility, but the problem is not as simple as that. Some individuals seem to experience more frustration than others do. Perhaps the amount of frustration experienced is a function of perceptual factors: Does the chronically frustrated person (or cultural group) tend to *perceive* more frustration than others do? Are there certain personality traits or conditions that predispose one to perceive or experience frustration? What is the relationship between level of aspiration and tendencies to per-

ceive one's experiences as frustrating? These are some of the problems that psychologists have been investigating in recent years. Clinical research has indicated that there are people whose personality patterns or self-structures lead them to anticipate more than normal amounts of frustration. Whether there are more of such people in some cultures than in others is a problem that has not been adequately explored.

Catharsis as a means of coping with hostility. Assuming that research eventually will demonstrate that the people of certain nations are more prone to perceive their experience as frustrating, of what value are such findings? Coping with hostility is an everyday experience for many psychologists. Clinical, counseling, and school psychologists take it as a matter of course that some of their clients are going to manifest a high degree of hostility. Sometimes the appearance of hostility is welcomed, particularly if the person undergoing treatment has been apathetic or discouraged. A show of hostility may indicate an increase in morale—it can mean, for example, that the individual feels that he has a chance to do something about a difficult situation. If a client

Psychology and world affairs | 385

feels hostile, it is the generally accepted role of the counselor to help the individual *express* his hostility, rather than to encourage him to ignore it, forget it, or push it from consciousness. This attitude of accepting a person's hostility and encouraging him to express it is part of a larger attitude that psychologists have toward counseling or psychotherapy—namely, that it should be an opportunity for *catharsis,* an opportunity for the free expression of feelings of hostility, anxiety, fear, and guilt.

Anyone who has had the experience of "talking out" his problems with a sympathetic listener or who has helped another person do the same is aware of the therapeutic effect of catharsis. Although such experiences are an everyday occurrence, we often forget them when we have to deal with an angry person. Perhaps our own anxiety or hostility is raised by the intensity of his emotion; at any rate, we tend to deal with angry persons in an angry way. One question is: Is the clinical experience of psychologists confirmed by research?

Here is one study that seems to provide such confirmation. Feshbach (1955) conducted a study whereby the hostility of a number of college classes was aroused by an experimenter who adopted an authoritarian, arrogant manner, and who made a number of derogatory remarks about the motivation, ability, and level of maturity of the group. He stated, for example, ". . . if you will try to look beyond your limited horizons, your cooperation will be useful. In other words, I'd like you to act like adults rather than adolescents." Another group was not insulted, but received a friendly introduction, designed to gain their confidence. The classes of insulted students received one of two kinds of treatment: either they were asked to write stories about four cards selected from the Thematic Apperception Test (TAT) or they were given a series of aptitude tests that provided no opportunity for self-expression. Then all students were given an eight-item attitude questionnaire. The results, as Table 17-2 shows, indicate that the group that had the friendly reception (the Non-Insult Group) had relatively little hostility toward the experiment or the experimenter. As might be expected, the two "insulted" groups showed a much higher degree of hostility, but the students who had a chance to

Table 17–2 Percentage of subjects giving hostile responses to an attitude questionnaire, after being subjected to three different conditions. (After Feshbach, 1955.)

Question	Response	Groups		
		Non-insult	Insult TAT	Insult Control
1. How much did you like participating in the study just conducted?	*Very irritated,* or *extremely irritated.*	0	9	25
2. How worth while was it to participate in the study just recently conducted?	*Considerable waste of time,* or *complete waste of time.*	6	16	20
3. If you were asked by the Experimenter to volunteer for another study he was conducting, would you volunteer?	*Probably not,* or *definitely not.*	6	33	50
4. In your opinion, how much of a contribution will this study make to the field of psychology?	*Very little* or *none.*	12	26	30
5. In your opinion, how competent was the psychologist who conducted the experiment in which you participated?	*Very incompetent,* or *extremely incompetent.*	4	22	36
6. What is your reaction now to the psychologist who conducted this experiment? How much do you like or dislike him?	*Dislike very much.*	0	42	57
7. Is there anything you disliked about the experiment?	*Yes.*	42	73	82
8. Several experiments are going to be conducted by the psychology department. Are you willing to volunteer?	*No.*	56	56	66

express themselves in the projective test (the Insult-TAT Group) showed a somewhat lower degree of hostility than the group that had no such opportunity (the Insult-Control Group). In other words, the opportunity to express hostile feelings through fantasy (that is, through writing stories for the TAT pictures), helped to reduce the amount of hostility. Or, to put the matter the other way around, the *lack* of opportunity to find an outlet for hostile feelings either increased the amount of hostility or permitted it to remain at a high level. It is significant to note, too, that the amount of hostility expressed toward the experimenter (Items 3, 5, and 6) is greater than that expressed toward the experimental situation (Items 2 and 4), and it is in the attitude toward the experimenter that we also find the greater reduction in hostility with the TAT group.

An experiment like this does not, of course, provide us with any kind of a definitive answer to the problem of what to do about hostility on an international level. It does, however, confirm clinical observations about the desirability of permitting hostile persons to communicate their hostility. Generally speaking, it is better for society if hostility is expressed through fantasy than if it is expressed through some kind of aggressive or destructive behavior. Although our "common sense" may tell us that crime stories, as they appear in television, in the movies, and in comic books, stimulate delinquent behavior, it may be that they actually serve as a kind of a deterrent, through providing an outlet via fantasy for hostile and aggressive impulses. Certainly the research that has been done so far finds no evidence that comic books have any bad influence on behavior.[1] (Lewin, 1953.)

As far as international relations are concerned, a great deal of research must be undertaken be-fore we can determine whether fantasy or any other more or less harmless outlet can be employed to reduce hostile and aggressive tendencies within and among nations. In the meantime, it may be well to keep in mind, as a kind of working hypothesis, that it may be healthier to recognize the existence of hostility and to help people find some way of expressing it harmlessly than to repress it or act as though it does not exist.

It would be better, of course, if people expressed their hostility through some sort of sublimation—through fighting disease, replacing slum areas with decent housing, battling poverty, and the like—but we must remember that "anger-in" types of response to frustration, such as sublimation, have to be learned. A cultural group whose behavior is characterized by the "anger-out" type of response cannot readily convert its way of life to an "anger-in" pattern without major changes in cultural values. If such changes come at all, they come slowly.

Prejudice as a source of chronic hostility. An obvious approach to dealing with the problem of chronic hostility is that of getting at its source. Presumably if some of the factors causing hostility could be controlled or eliminated, there would be less of it to cope with.

The particular kind of hostility that concerns us

example, Frederic Wertham, a psychiatrist, led a crusade against comic books and wrote *Seduction of the Innocent,* a book that achieved nationwide recognition as a best seller. Research in this field so far, however, has failed to reveal a shred of evidence that reading comic books causes delinquency or even that delinquents read more comic books than nondelinquents. This is an example of the way in which common-sense formulations take on the status of accepted truths, and, as such, are perceived to be immune from questioning or experimental verification. People think that such "truths" are so obvious that contradictory evidence is ignored or dismissed as obviously incorrect or biased.

---

[1] This finding is particularly interesting because it is so much at variance with common sense, which assumes a "natural" correlation between *reading* about violence and *engaging* in acts of violence. Indeed a good many well-intentioned people, deeply concerned about increases in juvenile delinquency, have fallen into the trap of assuming that the simultaneous increases in crimes of violence and the publication of crime comic books pointed to a cause-and-effect relationship between the two. Even persons whose scientific training should have taught them to be cautious about assuming cause-and-effect relationships unsubstantiated by adequate research findings have been led, by the intensity of their feelings, to take stands that are incompatible with scientific attitudes. For

Authoritarian attitudes tend to be characterized by a willingness to tolerate or to engage in drastic or violent actions against outgroup members. When such attitudes are coupled with an intense ethnic prejudice, as they often are, they may lead to such incidents as the bombing of this synagogue in Atlanta in 1958.

here is the hostility that one national or ethnic group feels towards other groups. The word "hostility" is etymologically related to the words "host," "guest," and "hospitality": all are words that have something to do with people from outside the primary group—strangers. Both "hostility" and "hospitality" share the same Indo-European root but during the course of linguistic and cultural history moved in opposite directions. The point is that both friendliness and unfriendliness toward outsiders are attitudes that have ancient origins. To overgeneralize for a moment, let us say that it is the primitive and immature aspects of our personalities that lead us to react to the unfamiliar with fear or anger, whereas it is the civilized, gregarious, and mature aspect that leads us to react to the new and unfamiliar with curiosity and acceptance.

What concerns us, then, in our efforts to eliminate or reduce hostility at its source, are those attitudes or feelings that lead us to perceive stran-

gers as threatening, that is, to respond to all outsiders with fear or anger or both. What is it that leads us to "pre-judge" outsiders—to be prejudiced against other ethnic groups? In other words, what are the causes of ethnic prejudice?

During the early 1940's a rather large-scale research study was conducted on the Berkeley campus of the University of California, under the direction of Adorno, Frenkel-Brunswik, Levinson, and Sanford (1950), for the purpose of testing the hypothesis that attitudes and personality traits of the following types were interrelated (that is, individuals who possessed one would tend to possess the others):

ethnic prejudice: the tendency to regard members of other ethnic groups with fear and/or hostility.
ethnocentrism: the tendency to exaggerate the virtues of one's own ethnic group.
authoritarianism: a preference for social arrangements with a clearly defined power structure, with subordinates properly submissive to their "betters."
conventionalism: a superficial and rigid adherence to conventional values and behavior.
rigidity: the inability to solve new problems or old problems in new settings.

Although there were a number of methodological flaws in the Berkeley study, the data it produced do seem to indicate that there is at least a fair degree of interrelationship among the factors listed. Furthermore, studies conducted subsequently have partially confirmed its findings. Solomon (1951), for example, found that people who had a high degree of ethnic prejudice tended also to have rigid patterns of thinking and were likely to encounter difficulty in using the scientific method in dealing with unfamiliar problems. He noticed a tendency for rigid individuals to have difficulty in perceiving relationships among isolated pieces of data. Because of this difficulty, they were unable to see how the pieces could be combined in solving problems.

Authoritarian attitudes: The F scale. One of the measures developed as part of the Berkeley study was a scale of authoritarian attitudes, commonly known as the "F scale" ("F" standing for "fascistic attitudes"), a scale positively correlated with the "E scale," a scale measuring ethnocentric attitudes—that is, ethnic prejudice. The F scale has been used in a large number of research studies during the last decade. Siegel (1956) examined the relationship between F-scale scores, scores made on a 50-item questionnaire of "manifest hostility," and Rorschach responses presumably indicative of hostility. The three tests were administered to a group of university students and to 57 veterans receiving out-patient treatment at a mental hygiene clinic. He found a significant intercorrelation for all three measures for the veteran group, although only the F scale and the "manifest hostility" scale were significantly correlated for the university group. Haiman (1955) devised a 10-item scale designed to distinguish between group-centered and leader-centered attitudes. His scale proved to have a high degree of correlation with the F scale, thus showing that the attitudes measured by the F scale were related to tendencies to defer to authority figures.

A number of studies have raised the question, however, of whether the F scale might be measuring something other than the complex of attitudes, values, and personality traits identified by the Berkeley group. Davids' study (1956) is only one of several that show a negative relationship between "authoritarianism" and intelligence (that is, the higher the intelligence, the lower the authoritarianism), and the studies by MacKinnon and Centers (1956) and by Remmers (1947 et seq.) discussed in Chapter 12 of this book appear to indicate that the more the education and the higher the social status, the less the amount of authoritarianism. Furthermore, Remmers' data show that both ethnic prejudice and authoritarian attitudes are more characteristic of high school students whose parents have less education and lower income. Table 17-3 shows the relationship of ethnic prejudice to socio-economic background. Such research seems to indicate that education helps to reduce the amount of prejudice. Indeed, the research conducted by Remmers and his associates shows a small but steady reduction in the

Table 17-3 Relationship between ethnic prejudice and socio-economic backgrounds of students. (After Horton, Mainer, and Remmers, 1953.)

Question	Mother's Education			Family's Income		
	Grade School	High School	College	Low	Medium	High
1. Percentage agreeing that people of different races should not dance together.	36 *	28 *	26 *	40 *	29 *	32 *
2. Percentage agreeing that swimming pools should admit people of all races and nationalities, to swim in the same pool.	33	38	49	27	40	41
3. Percentage agreeing that there should be laws against marriage between persons of different races.	40	30	27	41	33	32
4. Percentage agreeing that hotels are right in refusing to admit people of certain races or nationalities.	29	26	17	39	23	28
5. Percentage agreeing that pupils of all races and nationalities should attend school together everywhere in this country.	49	56	64	37	59	54
6. Percentage agreeing that there are people of some races and nationalities who are by nature less capable of advancement.	52	57	38	59	44	42
7. Percentage agreeing that any kind of people —no matter what race or national origin— can become 100% Americans.	72	79	81	62	79	77
8. Percentage agreeing that all theatres should admit people of all races and nationalities and allow them to sit anywhere they want.	52	60	71	42	62	60

* Figures consist of percentages of students in each category who gave the reply indicated. Read the first line as follows: The reply that people of different races should not dance together was given by 36 per cent of students whose mothers had grade school education, 28 per cent of those whose mothers had high school education, 26 per cent of those whose mothers had college education, 40 per cent of those whose family income was classified as "low," 29 per cent of those whose family income was classified as "medium," and 32 per cent of those whose family income was classified as "high."

amount of ethnic prejudice and authoritarian attitudes expressed by students with each succeeding year of high school. Similar results were found by Plant (1958), whose research showed that students at San Jose State College had a lower degree of ethnocentrism (as measured by the E scale) as seniors than as freshmen.

Pitfalls in questionnaire studies. It might be well to point out a major deficiency in studies based on results obtained through questionnaires. Such data lead one to make the all-too-easy assumption that attitudes expressed on questionnaires are a *direct* reflection of "real-life" behavior. A number of studies show, however, that such an assumption does not necessarily follow. LaPiere (1934), for example, toured the United States accompanied by a Chinese student and his wife, traveling some 10,000 miles. During this period they stopped at 66 establishments providing sleeping accommodations and 194 restaurants. Only once were they refused service, and even then it was not clear whether the basis of the refusal was the fact that LaPiere's traveling companions were Chinese. At the end of his travels, LaPiere circularized the same establishments with a questionnaire asking whether the proprietors would accept members of the Chinese race as guests in their establishments. Replies were received from about half of the total number of establishments. Over 90 per cent of the respondents said they did not serve Chinese.

Although studies like that of LaPiere raise questions about tendencies to take questionnaires at face value, they should not be interpreted to mean that questionnaires are useless. What is needed is more research comparing questionnaire results with everyday behavior. Such studies are difficult to conduct, very largely because of the complex problem of securing agreement among judges as to the significance of social behavior. In other words, it is easier to classify questionnaire responses than actual interpersonal behavior.

Nevertheless, questionnaire results that confirm rather well-substantiated hypotheses do take on a certain degree of validity. McGranahan (1946) found, for example, that German youth were more inclined than American youth to give replies to questionnaires that were indicative of prejudice and authoritarian attitudes. Among the German youth, those sympathetic to the Nazi party tended to be more authoritarian and prejudiced than the others. In a study of the behavior of groups, Hay-thorn (1958) found that leaders scoring high on the F scale were likely to behave in more authoritarian ways than leaders scoring low.

To return to the question we raised at the beginning of this section, the many questionnaire studies that have been conducted in this area lead us to believe that ethnic prejudice may be related to a number of personality traits—rigidity and authoritarianism, for example. Very likely such attitudes are the result of childhood training, as the Berkeley group suggest, although other research appears to indicate that education and socio-economic status may also be important variables. There is, however, a need to exercise caution in interpreting the results of studies that depend so heavily on questionnaires, in view of the obvious need to check their validity further against "real-life" behavior.

Psychological factors in propaganda

Throughout the world today there are a number of organizations and agencies that are working to reduce hostility and ethnic prejudice within and among nations. Because such attitudes are to a large extent a traditional part of most cultures, the task of counteracting them is one that calls for the utmost skill in the use of propaganda techniques.

Attitudes toward propaganda. Perhaps the use of the word "propaganda" in this context seems somewhat odd. If so, it is because of the common tendency to think of propaganda as an attempt to influence opinion through the use of falsehood or half-truths. The behavioral scientist, however, considers *any* deliberate attempt to influence attitudes and behavior as propaganda. Seen in this light, a great many kinds of activities turn out to be propagandistic. All forms of advertising are, of course, propaganda, because they are aimed at influencing buyer behavior. All sermons read from the pulpit are propaganda, because they are aimed at producing changes in thought and action. All forms of educational endeavor must become involved in propaganda to some degree: if education does not make some changes in the behavior of students, it has failed.

Regarding propaganda objectively provides a considerable advantage. Instead of being preoccupied with whether an attempt at communication is "bad" (and therefore "propaganda," in the layman's sense of the word) we can devote ourselves to analyzing it to determine whether there is any obvious or hidden attempt to influence our attitudes or actions. Perhaps we will find that what seems to be a simple bit of useful information is actually a very subtle device intending to prejudice us for or against a certain institution, group, or kind of behavior. Perhaps after examining the motives behind the propaganda, we will decide that there are advantages in changing our attitudes or behavior, or perhaps we will decide that we should take some kind of defensive action to resist the effects of the propaganda. In any event, a detached and objective attitude toward propaganda enables us to behave in ways that are to our best advantage.

Inevitably, we all become involved in propaganda. Everyone attempts, some time or other, to influence other people. Even behavioral scientists, preoccupied as they are with research and other scientific endeavor, find that they must engage in propaganda for the things they believe in. They have to propagandize for their own branch of science, for the time, money, and even the right to do research, for better working conditions for behavioral scientists, and for a more favorable attitude on the part of the general public toward the behavioral sciences. And sometimes, wittingly or unwittingly, they become involved in propaganda for social progress and world peace.

The "Psychologists' Manifesto." A year before the end of World War II, a group of American psychologists drew up a statement embodying the following principles, each of which was elaborated in some detail:

1. War can be avoided: war is not born in men; it is built into men.
2. In planning for permanent peace, the coming generation should be the primary focus of attention.
3. Racial, national, and group hatreds can, to a considerable degree, be controlled.
4. Condescension toward "inferior" groups destroys our chances for a lasting peace.
5. Liberated and enemy peoples must participate in planning their own destiny.
6. The confusion of defeated people will call for clarity and consistency in the application of rewards and punishments.
7. If properly administered, relief and rehabilitation can lead to self-reliance and cooperation; if improperly, to resentment and hatred.
8. The root-desires of the common people of all lands are the safest guide to framing a peace.
9. The trend of human relationships is toward ever wider units of collective security.
10. Commitments *now* may prevent postwar apathy and reaction. (Murphy, 1945.)

This statement was circulated among the psychologists of the country with the request that they endorse it in order that it be presented at the national psychological convention a month later. Sixty per cent of the psychologists replied, and 99 per cent of those replying endorsed the statement.

The obvious purpose of this "Psychologists' Manifesto," as it was called, was that of communicating to the world at large the attitudes of the psychological profession toward the problems of the day. It is doubtful, however, that so large a number of psychologists would have endorsed the statement if they felt that its purpose was solely that of communication. What led them to endorse the manifesto was the possibility of *influencing* the opinions (and hence the behavior) of people who were in a position to make decisions on these issues. The chief purpose of the manifesto, in other words, was that of propaganda.

The point is that psychologists are inclined to have the kind of values that lead them to become involved, directly or indirectly, in attempts to propagandize for world peace, international cooperation, or any significant step to promote human welfare. Klineberg (1956) describes the psychologist who is at all interested or involved in international affairs as a person who believes that "international cooperation is better than conflict, peace better than war; he is in favor of a higher standard of living, a lower death rate, universal education, although he would like these introduced with as little disruption as possible of indigenous cultures; he is against ethnic prejudice and discrimination; he supports women's claims to equality." These values, to be sure, may seem obvious—to be in favor of them might seem like being "against sin." However, we should keep in mind that many people in this country do not support one or more of these values, and in many cultures such values are rejected or are relegated to positions of minor importance. A psychologist who holds these values is likely to behave in ways that implement them. He donates money to CARE; joins a local mental health organization that is a branch of a national organization, which is in turn affiliated with an international organization; and describes the pathological aspects of ethnic prejudice to his psychology classes.

If international cooperation is to replace armed conflict as a pattern of behavior, such a change will not occur of itself. If it does occur, it will be

Posters serve as important propaganda vehicles in Europe and particularly in Italy, where the readership of newspapers and other periodicals is low. These photographs depict various attempts to influence political behavior and attitudes.

Photographs by Lindgren

This poster advertises the fact that the United States is making substantial contributions (evidently from its agricultural surpluses) to provide a school lunch program for Italian children.

This poster points to the Communist Party of Italy's "thirty-six years of struggle, heroism, and success in the cause of liberty, social justice, and peace." Citizens are urged to "join the Italian Communist Party, a sure guide to the Italian approach to socialism."

The center poster publicizes former President Eisenhower's plea for "open skies for peace." The other two commemorate agreements among Western European nations to share in the benefits of atomic development and to work for the elimination of trade barriers.

These two posters highlight the political battle between the major party in Italy, the Christian Democrats, and the Communist-oriented bloc. The poster on the left is entitled "Three-Ring Circus" and shows Khrushchev juggling accusations and eulogies of Stalin with Togliatti, the head of the Italian Communist Party, while the latter receives support from Nenni, the leader of the left-wing socialists. The one on the right shows Nenni headed for a party congress in Venice, with "his feet in both stirrups"—that is, "democracy" and "communism."

aided at least in part by propaganda favoring more enlightened methods of resolving tensions and difficulties. And such propaganda will be needed if only to counteract the effects of other propaganda aimed at bringing about violent and drastic solutions to world problems. Krech and Crutchfield (1948: 455) point out that people in a crisis situation cannot stand ambiguity for very long. During a crisis, few people are immune to propaganda that urges some kind of drastic action. And no one who expects to have any influence on decisions that affect human destiny can afford to dissociate himself from the use of propaganda. Hence the problem that faces any individual or group interested in promoting international cooperation and world peace is not whether to engage in propaganda, but how. What methods of propaganda, in other words, are the most effective?

Fear-arousing propaganda. The "common-sense" approach to the problem of influencing others is a direct one: tell them. In other words, if you want people to use peaceful instead of warlike methods of resolving problems, you must tell them the advantages of the peaceful methods and the disadvantages of the warlike methods; you must praise the peaceful methods in glowing terms; and you must describe the consequences of war in horrible detail.

This direct approach as a way of influencing others has considerable appeal and has been used extensively. The Nazi film depicting the horrors of blitzkrieg in Poland was shown in the motion picture theaters of countries to the west of Germany and presumably had a demoralizing effect on the population, thus helping to make the subsequent conquest of these countries a relatively easy matter. If anything, however, it had the opposite results in Britain, where German attempts to produce panic apparently had the effect of stiffening resistance, instead of weakening it. As this is written, well-known scientists, philosophers, and other intellectual leaders are involved in efforts to prevent the further development of atomic weapons. Some of these leaders have been using the direct approach, that is, they have been painting in lurid colors the horrors of atomic war, in the apparent hope that the people of the world will be frightened into taking measures to stop the development of atomic weapons or to take steps that will eliminate war altogether as a means of resolving international conflict. So far their efforts have not been successful.

Some research by Janis and Feshbach (1953) suggests a reason why propaganda based on fear may not produce the expected results. Freshman students in a large high school were divided into four groups of fifty on a random basis. Three of the groups were subjected to one of three different propaganda treatments regarding the care of the teeth; the fourth group served as a "control" or check on the results obtained with the other three. Each of the first three groups sat through a 15-minute lecture supplemented by a number of slides, which were projected on the screen in a prearranged sequence. One group was subjected to a "strong appeal," in which the fear-arousing stimuli were at a maximum; the second group received the "moderate appeal;" and the third group was subjected to a "minimal appeal." The "strong appeal" emphasized the painful consequences of tooth decay, diseased gums, and other dangers that can result from improper dental hygiene. As students looked at the highly realistic and vivid photographs of tooth decay and mouth infections, they were told:

If you ever develop an infection of this kind from improper care of your teeth, it will be an extremely serious matter because these infections are really dangerous. They can spread to your eyes, or your heart, or your joints and cause secondary infections which may lead to diseases such as arthritic paralysis, kidney damage, or total blindness.

Table 17–4 Percentages of students conforming to dental-hygiene recommendations, grouped according to the kind of propaganda to which they were subjected. (After Janis and Feshbach, 1953.)

Type of Change	Strong Appeal	Moderate Appeal	Minimal Appeal	Control Group
Increased conformity	28	44	50	22
Decreased conformity	20	22	14	22
No change	52	34	36	36
Net change in conformity	+8	+22	+36	0

The "moderate appeal" described the dangerous consequences of improper oral hygiene in a more factual way, using impersonal language, and using photographs of milder pathology than those shown with the "strong appeal." The "minimal appeal" presented a limited discussion of unfavorable consequences in a purely factual style, accompanied by x-ray pictures, diagrams of cavities, and photographs of perfectly healthy teeth.

According to common sense, the group subjected to the "strong appeal" should have showed the greatest change in behavior in the desired direction, but a follow-up by the researchers demonstrated that such was not the case. As Table 17-4 shows, the "minimal appeal" produced the best results, and the "strong appeal" the poorest. This difference occurred in spite of the fact that students found the "strong appeal" more interesting and more provocative of worry.

A week after the groups were subjected to the propaganda, the investigators subjected them to a form of counter-propaganda, to test the stability of the attitudes generated as a result of the initial dosage of propaganda. The first lecture had made a particular point that it was important to use the "proper" kind of toothbrush. In the counter-propaganda phase of the experiment, a statement was read to the students as follows:

A well-known dentist recently made the following statement: Some dentists, including a number of so-called "experts" on dental hygiene, claim it is important to use a special type of toothbrush in order to clean the teeth properly. But from my own experience, I believe there is no sound basis for that idea. My honest opinion, as a dentist, is that it does not matter what kind of toothbrush a person uses. Any sort of toothbrush that is sold in a drugstore will help keep your teeth clean and healthy—if you use it regularly.

The results, as shown in Table 17-5, indicate that although all the groups subjected to the initial propaganda were inclined to resist the counter-propaganda, the greatest resistance was shown by the group to which the "minimal appeal" had been made.

The greater effectiveness of a more subdued approach to opinion change is also confirmed by a study made by the Information and Education Division of the U.S. War Department (1947) during World War II. Researchers found that it was easier to change the viewpoint of persons initially opposed to a certain proposition, if propaganda included the arguments against the proposition, as well as the arguments in favor of it. The method is not without its dangers, however. Individuals who had not graduated from high school and who were already favorably disposed to the point of view supported by the propaganda tended to react more positively to a one-sided presentation and were actually dissuaded to some extent by a presentation of arguments on both sides. Persons who had graduated from high school tended to react more favorably to propaganda that presented both sides, regardless of their initial attitudes.

The extent to which an individual's receptivity to various appeals is conditioned by his attitudinal patterns is indicated by a study conducted by Roden (1958), who devised an ingenious way of measuring the success of various kinds of propaganda. College students were asked to make contributions of their time in addressing envelopes for an Easter Seal drive. Some groups heard an appeal made by a fellow student (peer appeal); other groups heard an appeal made by a person introduced as the "Associate Dean of Education" (prestige appeal); and still other groups heard an appeal made by the Dean of Men, whose contact with the student body was largely punitive in nature (fear appeal). The greatest response was secured from students who were at the highest or the lowest ranges of the F scale, with students in the middle ranges being less responsive. However, low-authoritarian students tended to respond more favorably to the peer appeal and the prestige

Table 17–5 Percentages of students agreeing with counter-propaganda, grouped according to the kind of propaganda to which they were initially subjected. (After Janis and Feshbach, 1953.)

Type of Change	Strong Appeal	Moderate Appeal	Minimal Appeal	Control Group
More agreement	30	28	14	44
Less agreement	38	42	54	24
No change	32	30	32	32
Net change	−8	−14	−40	+20

appeal, whereas high-authoritarian students were more likely to respond to the fear appeal.

Changing behavior through "group decision." So far, we have considered only "direct" attempts to influence behavior and have not considered the effectiveness of other, less direct approaches. Some research conducted under the direction of Lewin (1947) produced results that seem to indicate that group decision is a more effective molder of behavior than the more conventional method of "telling people what to do," a finding that has been confirmed by more recent studies. (Kipnis, 1958; Levine and Butler, 1952.) One of the studies reported by Lewin deals with attempts to change the buying habits of housewives during World War II. Because of meat shortages, government authorities urged that the cheaper cuts of meat—sweetbreads, beef hearts, and kidneys—be purchased in preference to the more popular cuts. Accordingly, three groups of housewives were subjected to propaganda in the form of lectures emphasizing the vitamin and mineral content of the meats, the low price, and the need to support the war effort. Preparation of the meats was discussed, and mimeographed recipes distributed. The lecturer was able to arouse interest by telling the women of the success she had with using the meats in question with her own family.

Three other groups conducted discussions about "housewives like themselves" who would encounter obstacles in introducing such meats to their families. At the end of the meeting, the women were asked by a show of hands to indicate who would be willing to try one of the meats the following week.

A follow-up showed that only 3 per cent of the women who heard the lectures actually served one of the meats, as contrasted with 32 per cent of those who had participated in the group decision. A similar experiment aimed at getting mothers to use more milk also demonstrated the greater effectiveness of group decision over lecture. Another experiment compared the relative effectiveness of group decision with individual instruction. The state hospital in Iowa City had been trying to get mothers to give their babies orange juice and cod liver oil, but without much success. When the group decision method was tried, it produced results far better than the hospital had been achieving with individual instruction.

The principle here seems to be that people are more likely to follow through on decisions they have made themselves, in preference to advice or information given them by others. This principle is a difficult one to follow, partly because it runs counter to the natural desire of the propagandist to be *sure* that his message is received and believed by his audience, and partly because the mechanics of group decision are very much more complex. Superficially, they seem less efficient. Somehow, broadcasting one's message through the mass media seems more effective and more satisfying than the slower, more tedious job of sitting down with small groups of people and getting them to participate in a discussion, even though the latter method may be the most efficient in the long run.

This is not to say that group discussion methods are the ideal approach for opinion change. Very little research has been done outside America, although reports of its use have come in from other countries. One hears, for example, that the Chinese Communist government has made massive use of group discussion techniques in promoting the acceptance of its program on the Chinese mainland. So far, most of our research has dealt with changing opinions that are only moderately controversial—opinions that do not have a central position in the value systems of the individuals concerned. Nevertheless, the research conducted by Lewin and his associates indicates a new area in the field of opinion change that may have implications for those interested in human progress.

One obvious difficulty of using group decision methods to promote the cause of international cooperation and world peace is this: if the decision of a group is to have any meaning for them, it must be made by the members of the group with a minimum of advice-giving or any other kind of manipulation from outside agencies. Therefore, any attempt to use group decisions runs the risk of having the participants decide on steps that lead away from the desired goal rather than toward it. However, the willingness to take such a risk is consistent with the kind of values most psychologists subscribe to, because they believe, as we indicated previously, that people should participate in planning their own destiny.

Political participation. One of the key problems in any movement toward world peace is that of getting people to participate in decision-making activity. An obstacle to such participation is the common feeling, "What can *I* do?" Although psychologists have not developed any solutions to

The resolution of intercultural and international problems inevitably involves the interaction of individuals in small groups.

the problem of how to involve the apathetic citizen in decisions that affect the destiny of the world, some clues may be provided by studies of the dynamics of participation.

Douvan and Walker (1956) studied the attitudes of a sample of employed persons in Detroit and found a consistent relationship between the individual's sense of effectiveness in public affairs and his feeling of competence in personal affairs. People who were optimistic about their chances for being promoted were, for example, more inclined to feel that the average citizen has considerable influence on government decisions.

Mussen and Wyszynski (1952) asked 156 students at the University of Wisconsin to reply to a 10-item questionnaire. When they classified the students according to their activity in political affairs, they found some interesting personality differences between those most active (for example, members of Young Democrat or Young Republican groups) and those who expressed no interest in politics. Some of the replies indicating the most significant differences between the two groups are listed in Table 17-6. Politically active students are more self-critical, but they also are more inclined to be concerned about the rights of other people.

A review of their replies indicates a rather active "social conscience." As contrasted with inactive students, they seem to be more interested in intellectual activities and less concerned about the more superficial aspects of social conformity. In short, they seem to resemble the creative individuals described at the end of Chapter 9. Although the research initiated by Mussen and Wyszynski needs to be replicated with larger samples drawn from less restricted populations, their findings do seem to provide clues to the attitudes that are basic to the kind of participation and involvement that will be needed if the goals of international cooperation and world peace are to be attained.

Although our chances for international cooperation and world peace will to a large extent depend on the presence of certain positive emotional factors, such as a willingness to find nonviolent ways of resolving international problems, nevertheless a certain degree of intellectual competence and breadth seems also to be an important corollary. The findings reported by Mussen and Wyszynski deserve serious consideration only because they are confirmed by other research studies (many of which are reported

Table 17–6 Comparison of 45 politically active and 37 politically apathetic college students on the basis of selected replies to ten "projective questions." (After Mussen and Wyszynski, 1952.)

Questions and Types of Replies	Percentage Replying as Indicated *	
	Politically Active	Politically Apathetic
1. *What moods or feelings are most unpleasant to you?*		
Disappointment in self due to failure to exercise capabilities	24	8
General self-blame and reproach	27	16
Feelings of rejection	18	5
Exploitation of, or discrimination against, others	13	3
Loneliness; fear of being alone	4	14
Feelings of being victimized	7	14
2. *What desires do you have difficulty in controlling?*		
Expressing aggression against intolerance	11	5
Escape studies; quit school	7	27
3. *What great people do you admire most?*		
Social scientists and liberal figures	33	11
Industrial leaders	11	3
4. *What could drive a person nuts?*		
Inability to adjust to situations or to face reality	18	0
Generalized worry; indecision	2	16
5. *What are the worst crimes a person could commit?*		
Crimes against society; discrimination; exploitation	18	3
Aggressive; physical attack	7	19
6. *What experiences do you find most embarrassing?*		
Being personally responsible for mistakes	20	8
Social slips; violations of rules of etiquette	9	30
7. *If you had only six months to live, how would you spend your time?*		
Social contribution	22	5
Social events; having a good time	7	22
8. *What things give you the greatest feeling of awe?*		
Intellectual, aesthetic, scientific achievements	38	16
Mass emotion; people unified	18	5
Being recognized and loved	13	5
9. *As a parent, what would you try most to instill in your child?*		
Intellectual, aesthetic, and social values	38	6
Social consciousness	33	8
Striving for maturity and independence	20	5
Ability to love and be loved	9	24
Good manners and obedience	13	43
Good morals	29	51
10. *If you could change your parents in any way you wanted, what changes would you make?*		
Greater happiness	38	19
More social consciousness and tolerance	16	5
Denial of need to change; parents perfect	7	31

* Replies for most questions add up to less than 100 per cent because only those replies that discriminated at a statistically significant level between politically active and apathetic students are given. Replies to other questions add up to more than 100 per cent because some students gave more than one response.

throughout this book), showing a fair but consistent degree of correlation between the willingness to respect the rights of others and the amount of education. This is not to say that education is a cure-all for the world's ills, but it does raise the hope that the people of the world can be educated into finding better solutions to their problems than seem to be available today. It is understandable, of course, that informed people might make better decisions than uninformed people, and the steadily rising level of literacy in most parts of the world increases the potential number of informed individuals. If international cooperation and world peace become more substantial realities than they are at present, it will be because they have been initiated and supported by informed and educated people throughout the entire world.

Furthermore, any program aimed at increasing the level of information and education can succeed only if it is based on a sound understanding of human behavior. And it is the development of this understanding that is the primary goal of psychology. So far, psychology has provided us with few definitive answers to international problems, but it has made a substantial beginning in constructing theories and in developing methods that may contribute to the understanding that is needed.

Summary

In spite of a universal desire for world peace, wars have occurred with such frequency that it becomes obvious that their prevention requires more than hope, international organizations, diplomatic exchanges, or military alliances. We tend to handle both international and local social pathology (war and crime and delinquency) in the same way and with equal lack of success. A "common-sense" attitude toward social pathology leaves us with a fatalistic notion about human nature and the inevitability of wars. Behavioral scientists would like to see a more objective, flexible, research-oriented approach to these problems. As this approach grows in importance, psychologists and other behavioral scientists find themselves in the familiar roles of research worker and theorist and in the unfamiliar role of publicist.

One avenue of study has been cross-cultural research, which explores the differences and similarities among peoples of the world. The discovery of basic attitudes and of feelings toward other nationalities, for example, could be extremely helpful in understanding some aspects of international relations. Psychological studies of the frustration-aggression relationship give us many clues about some of the underlying causes of aggressive pathologies like war, scapegoating, and prejudice. Psychologists approach this problem by trying to identify many causes of frustration, by learning why some individuals are more sensitive to frustration, and by helping individuals to find acceptable ways of expressing hostile feelings. It is known that hostility is reduced by the process of expressing one's feelings verbally to an accepting listener, by engaging in hostile fantasy, and by learning to take part in sublimated aggressive activities. Because prejudice is a widespread and chronic source of interpersonal hostility, psychologists have devoted a good deal of effort toward understanding its causes. Studies have found that ethnic prejudice, ethnocentrism, authoritarianism, conventionalism, and rigidity tend to go together. This cluster of attitudes and behavior is also related to manifest hostility, a tendency to defer to authority figures, lower intelligence, less education, and lower social status. It should be noted that whenever a questionnaire approach to attitudes is employed, it is important to find out just how these attitudes are related to everyday behavior.

Bad connotations aside, propaganda refers to any deliberate attempt to influence opinion and behavior for whatever reason. We all become involved in propaganda in one way or another. Since World War II, psychologists have been quite active in propagandizing for world peace, international cooperation, and other steps to promote human welfare. Research on propaganda techniques has revealed that one's approach is extremely important in determining whether or not the desired message influences the audience. In a study concerning dental hygiene, for example, a minimal appeal was more effective than stronger appeals. Presenting both sides of the argument appears to be effective, especially with educated people. Personality factors are important; low authoritarian individuals tend to respond to peer appeal, whereas high-authoritarian individuals respond to a fear appeal. A wide variety of studies have shown the effectiveness of group decision in changing behavior; people seem to be more likely to follow through on decisions that they themselves made.

One of the key problems in promoting world peace is getting people to participate in political activities and thus to have an influence on important decision making. It has been found that individuals who feel competent in their personal affairs are more likely to feel a sense of effectiveness in public affairs. Research studies are beginning to supply cues to the basic attitudes underlying the kind of individual involvement that is necessary for achieving the goals of international cooperation and world peace.

Questions

1. What is wrong with the military-legal and the good-will approaches to local and international social pathology?

2. Give your opinion of the statement, "There will always be wars."

3. Is there anything wrong with the classification of people into "good" and "bad"?

4. Select some recent event of international hostility from the newspapers. Contrast a "common-sense" interpretation of the event with the possible interpretations of behavioral scientists.

5. How might psychological theory and research aid international understanding?

6. What is the relationship between frustration and war? What are the implications of this relationship in terms of recent national and international events?

7. In what way are frustration, prejudice, rigidity, and hostility interrelated?

8. Select examples of advertisements, newspaper articles, political speeches, etc., and indicate in what ways propaganda is involved in each. What do you guess about the effectiveness of each, and why?

9. Can you think of any familiar situations in which group discussion and group decision might be superior to a more autocratic approach?

10. What can you personally do to promote world peace?

Suggestions for further reading

Cook, L. and E., *Intergroup Education.* New York: McGraw-Hill, 1954. Discusses research in the field of ethnic prejudice and describes some of the ways in which prejudice may be eliminated or reduced.

Katz, D., D. Cartwright, S. Eldersveld, and A. McC. Lee, Editors, *Public Opinion and Propaganda.* New York: Dryden, 1954. How attitudes may be measured and manipulated. A book of readings compiled for the Society for the Psychological Study of Social Issues.

Maccoby, E. E., T. M. Newcomb, and E. L. Hartley, Editors, *Readings in Social Psychology,* 3rd ed. New York: Holt, 1958. See Section 13, "Intergroup tension, prejudice," which contains a brief summary of the University of California studies on the authoritarian personality.

Schramm, W., Editor, *The Process and Effects of Mass Communication.* Urbana: University of Illinois Press, 1954. See the final section in this collection of papers: "Special problems of achieving an effect with international communications."

Chisholm, B., *Prescription for Survival.* New York: Columbia University Press, 1957. A series of four essays dealing with the importance of personal mental health as a factor in peace and world survival. The author is an internationally known psychiatrist and was formerly Director-General of the World Health Organization, an agency of the United Nations.

GLOSSARY

This glossary contains definitions of the technical words used in this book, as well as some common words that have special meaning in a psychological context. Meanings listed here are restricted to the way in which the terms are used in this textbook; some of the terms have different meanings in other psychological and nonpsychological contexts. For fuller discussions of the meanings of these and other terms used in psychology, students are referred to *A Comprehensive Dictionary of Psychological and Psychoanalytical Terms,* by Horace B. English and Ava C. English. (New York: Longmans Green, 1957.)

adolescence: The period of human life beginning with puberty and ending at the attainment of maturity.

adjustment: The relationship between an individual and his environment through which his needs are satisfied in accordance with social demands.

adrenalin: One of the hormones produced by the adrenal medulla. It is secreted during strongly emotional states.

affective reaction: A psychotic behavior that involves severe disturbances of mood ranging from severe depression to extreme elation. Sometimes called manic-depressive psychosis.

Allport-Vernon Study of Values: A test designed to measure an individual's relative interest in theoretical, social, religious, esthetic, economic, and political matters.

American Psychological Association or APA: The professional association to which most American psychologists belong. It is concerned with the communication of research findings, setting professional standards, maintaining public relations, and, in general, furthering the science and the profession of psychology.

analysand: An individual who is undergoing psychoanalysis.

anthropology: The science that studies man's bodily characteristics, social customs, and language.

antisocial: Hostile to society and its codes of behavior.

antisocial personality: A personality disorder characterized by impulsiveness, lack of anxiety and guilt, difficulties with society, and absence of close interpersonal ties.

anxiety: An unpleasant emotional state, similar to fear, directed toward a somewhat vague source, often in the future.

aptitude: The ability to acquire a certain skill, given opportunity for training.

Army General Classification Test or AGCT: An intelligence test used in the U.S. Army during and after World War II.

artifact: An object that is man-made, rather than natural.

asocial: Indifferent to or unaware of social rules and values.

attention: The selection of a given stimulus or set of stimuli for perception—a process that involves a narrowing of one's perceptual range.

attitude: An enduring, acquired predisposition to behave in a particular way toward a given object or class of objects.

authoritarianism: A way of controlling others in which one person gives orders, prescribes techniques, and makes judgments without permitting others to take part in the process of decision.

autistic: A tendency for a person's thoughts to be determined by wishes, fantasies, and personal meanings rather than by reality.

autokinetic effect: The apparent movement of a stationary dot of light in a darkened room.

average: The arithmetical average is the same as the mean—the sum of all the values divided by the number of cases.

basal metabolism test: A procedure that measures the rate at which a person produces heat while resting, but awake. It is an index to the energy necessary for minimum functioning.

behavior: Any act performed by an organism.

behavioral science: Any science that studies the behavior of man and other animals using the methods of the natural sciences. Included are psychology, social anthropology, and sociology.

behavior mechanism: See "defense mechanism."

bimodal: A distribution having two modes.

brain waves: Spontaneous fluctuations in the brain's electrical activity.

California Psychological Inventory or CPI: An empirically derived personality inventory that measures various aspects of functioning in interpersonal situations.

castration: The removal of the testicles or of both testicles and penis.

catatonic: Pertaining to a form of schizophrenia characterized by stupor, negativism, muttering, waxy flexibility, catalepsy, or excessive excitement.

catharsis: In psychological treatment, the reduction of anxiety and tension by discussing frankly one's feelings and reliving conflictful incidents from the past.

chance: The likelihood that an event will occur in accordance with the theory of probability.

clinical psychology: A branch of psychology concerned with diagnosis, treatment, prevention, and research in the field of mental, behavior, or personality disorders.

clinician: A professional person whose work involves the diagnosis and treatment of physical and mental disorders: commonly used in reference to clinical psychologists and psychiatrists.

closure: The Gestalt principle that behavior or mental processes tend toward a finished, stable, or closed state.

cognitive map: In Tolman's learning theory, a hypothesized cognitive representation of the way in which a particular goal may be attained.

communication: The transmission and reception of meaning by symbolic means.

comparative psychology: The branch of psychology concerned with the study of animal behavior and the comparison of the behavior of different species.

compensation: Behavior that attempts to make up for some lack or the loss of some valued physical or psychological characteristic.

compulsive: Characterized by a tendency to repeat a certain behavior over and over in a ritualistic way, regardless of its inappropriateness. The term is generally applied to personality characteristics that involve overconcern for neatness, cleanliness, orderliness, precision, and conformity.

conditioned response: The response elicited by the new (conditioned) stimulus in a conditioning process.

conditioned stimulus: The new stimulus in a conditioning process that originally did not elicit the desired response.

conditioning: The learning process in which a response comes to be elicited by a new stimulus through repeated pairings of that stimulus with another stimulus that already elicits the response.

conflict: The simultaneous arousal of two or more incompatible drives.

conformity: The tendency for attitudes or behavior to be molded or guided by patterns or standards of others.

conscious: Pertaining to the process of being aware of or being able to verbalize feelings, perceptions, attitudes, etc.

constancy: The tendency for objects to be perceived as retaining a normal appearance relatively independent of their actual stimulus quality in a given situation.

control group: In an experiment, those subjects who are treated in an identical way to the experimental group, except that they are not exposed to the experimental conditions.

correlation: A measure of the relationship of two or more variables.

counseling psychology: The branch of psychology that specializes in helping individuals solve personal problems such as academic, social, or vocational difficulties.

contiguous conditioning: In Guthrie's learning theory, the connection between a stimulus and a response that takes place any time the two occur simultaneously, reinforcement being unnecessary.

cretin: An individual who suffered a marked thyroid deficiency in early life that has resulted in mental and physical retardation.

culture: (1) The way in which a society prescribes that its members shall function, and (2) the material aspects of that society. Culture includes the social institutions, factual knowledge, beliefs, artistic creations, morals, customs, shared habits, and the material implements of a group of people.

cutting score: A point in a series of ranked scores that is used to separate the scores of individuals who should receive one kind of treatment (for example, admission to college) from those who should receive another kind of treatment (such as refusal of admission to college).

defense mechanism: An unconsciously motivated behavior that functions to prevent or reduce anxiety by either self-deception or substitute behavior.

delirium tremens: An accutely confused state precipitated by alcohol and characterized by anxiety, tremor, delusions, and hallucinations.

delusion: An incorrect belief held despite contradictory evidence.

dependency: Reliance on others for emotional support or for help in making decisions and carrying out activities.

developmental psychology: The branch of psychology concerned with the physical and psychological development of organisms.

displacement: The substitution of one goal object for another as the target of a particular response.

Doctor of Education or Ed.D.: The highest academic degree conferred by schools of education. It is held by many educational administrators, college teachers, and psychologists.

Doctor of Philosophy or Ph.D.: The highest academic degree conferred by universities. For psychologists, it involves three to five years of advanced study and training past the A.B., and a demonstration of the ability to carry out original experimental research to serve as the basis for a doctoral dissertation.

dream: Sequences of mental images that occur during sleep.

drive: A hypothetical state of an organism that is aroused by internal or external stimuli and leads to behavior.

dynamometer: An instrument that measures the intensity of muscular pressure such as the strength of an individual's grip.

educational psychology: That branch of psychology concerned with the study of educational problems.

ego: In psychoanalysis, those mainly conscious aspects of behavior that involve perception of reality, thought, and the integration of psychological functions.

electric shock therapy: A method sometimes used to treat mental disorders. An electric current is passed through the brain to induce convulsions.

electrodermal response or EDR: The charges in the electrical conductivity of the skin as a result of minute changes in the amount of moisture present. The EDR is used as a measure of emotional response. Also known as psychogalvanic response and galvanic skin response.

electroencephalogram: A record of brain waves made by placing electrodes on the cranium and recording the changes of electrical potential.

emotion: A complex feeling-state accompanied by characteristic behavioral and visceral activities.

empathy: The ability to perceive the reactions and feelings of other individuals.

empirical: Based on factual investigation.

endocrine glands: The ductless glands that secrete hormones directly into the blood stream.

engineering psychology: The branch of industrial psychology concerned with the relationship between man's behavior and the design of his tools and machines.

environment: All of the conditions external to an organism capable of influencing it.

epinephrine: Often used as a synonym for adrenalin.

erogenous: Giving rise to sexual feelings.

ethnic prejudice: A bias, often hostile in nature, directed toward members of a group that has well-defined cultural and/or biological characteristics.

ethnocentrism: A tendency to believe that one's own ethnic or national group is superior.

experiment: An arrangement of conditions under which phenomena may be observed, with the aim of determining the relationship between or among the phenomena.

experimental group: In an experiment, those subjects who are exposed to a specified condition to determine whether one variable being studied has any effect on the second variable being studied.

experimental psychology: Broadly, all branches of psychology that use the experimental method. As ordinarily used, the term refers to that branch of psychology concerned with basic or "pure" laboratory research.

extinction: The progressive decrease in the strength of a conditioned response that results when the conditioned stimulus is no longer rewarded or reinforced.

extrasensory perception or ESP: Perception of stimuli that is presumed to take place without the use of any of the known senses.

extravert: An individual whose pattern of interests is centered outside of himself, in the physical and social environment.

feedback: A process whereby an individual gets a sensory report of the effect of his behavior and can thus modify the behavior when necessary.

fetus: The human embryo after the third month of pregnancy.

fixation: Behavior which remains at an earlier developmental level.

fixed-interval reinforcement: Intermittant reinforcement that occurs after a given interval of time.

fixed-ratio reinforcement: Intermittent reinforcement that occurs after a given number of responses.

folklore: The remaining elements of earlier legends, stories, rules of conduct, beliefs, etc., that still exist in a given culture.

free association: A sequence of words or ideas in which each response is the stimulus for the next response, without any imposed structure or direction.

frequency distribution: An array of values, ranging from the highest to the lowest, together with a report of the number of times each value occurred.

frustration: The blocking of goal-directed activity. Also the emotional state aroused by such blockage.

functional autonomy: The tendency of a secondary drive to become independent of the primary drive with which it originated.

galvanic skin response or GSR: The changes in the electrical conductivity of the skin as a result of minute changes in the amount of moisture present. The GSR is used as a measure of emotional response. Also known as psychogalvanic response and electrodermal response.

general psychology: A branch of psychology concerned with synthesizing or generalizing principles common to all branches of psychology. Also, the branch of psychology concerned with studying behavioral characteristics of individuals in general.

Gestalt: A German word meaning form, configuration, or pattern. It is applied to a school or theory of psychology that emphasizes the functioning of wholes as opposed to parts.

group: Two or more individuals who have some quality in common.

habit: An acquired behavior sequence that is relatively enduring.

hallucination: An incorrect perception unique to the individual concerned and which may represent a distortion of an actual object or mere fantasy.

heredity: biological influences transmitted from parent to child that determine various characteristics of the child.

heterosexuality: The tendency to be attracted to members of the opposite sex.

homeostasis: The process of maintaining a state of constancy or equilibrium of bodily processes.

homosexuality: The tendency to seek sexual gratification from members of one's own sex.

hormone: A chemical substance secreted by an organ of the body, which, when transported to some other organ, produces there a specific effect.

hypnosis: An induced state characterized by a heightened degree of readiness to respond to the suggestions of the hypnotist.

hypothesis: A tentative and untested explanation of a given set of data.

id: In psychoanalysis, those unconsciously motivated aspects of behavior that involve impersonal, instinctual strivings for immediate gratification.

identification: Adopting as one's own the values, beliefs, and behaviors of another person or group.

idiot: A mentally defective individual with an IQ below 25. Such individuals are usually unable to protect themselves against even simple dangers and often are unable to learn speech.

illusion: An incorrect perception of an object that is usually shared by others presented with the same stimulus.

imbecile: A mentally defective individual with an IQ in the range of 25–49. Such individuals are usually capable of simple learning but are unable to earn a living.

industrial psychology: The branch of psychology that deals with the problems of business and industry either from an experimental or an applied approach.

infancy: Usually, the first year of human life.

inhibition: The act of holding back a response even though the usual stimulus is present.

innate: Pertains to differences in structure or behavior that are not the result of environmental influences.

inner-directed: The tendency to be guided in values, beliefs, and actions by one's own internalized principles.

insight: The process whereby a solution, meaning, or understanding of a situation is gained; or, the understanding that is gained.

instinct: A set of responses elicited in most members of a given species even when the opportunities for learning the responses are absent.

insulin-shock: The injection of insulin to produce convulsions—a method used in treating some forms of mental disorder.

intelligence: The hypothesized characteristic measured by an intelligence test and defined in terms of (1) ability to deal with abstract concepts, (2) ability to learn, and (3) ability to adapt to new situations.

intelligence quotient or IQ: An index of an individual's intellectual development, determined by dividing his mental age by his chronological age and multiplying the result by 100.

introvert: An individual whose pattern of interests is turned inward.

Ishihari test: A series of color plates that test for color blindness.

kinesthesis: The sense that informs us of our bodily movements.

Kuder Preference Record: A test that measures a person's relative preferences among ten areas of interest.

kurtosis: The extent to which a frequency distribution is flat or peaked.

laissez-faire: The type of leadership in which the leader exercises a minimum of control, guidance, and assistance.

law: A statement or description of the way a given class of events occur, supported by a considerable amount of evidence.

layman: An individual who is not professionally trained in the subject under discussion.

learning: The processes that bring about relatively enduring behavioral changes as the result of experience.

learning dilemma: A problem situation in which previously learned responses are ineffective.

learning set: An approach to problems that reveals that the organism has acquired a tendency to attempt to learn in such a situation.

level of aspiration: The standard an individual sets and uses to judge the success or failure of his performance.

libido: In Freudian terminology, the energy that underlies all of man's life strivings. Usually used to refer to the drive for sexual gratification.

life space: All of the phenomena that constitute reality for an individual or group and exert an influence on its behavior.

life style: In Adlerian theory, the behavior that an individual characteristically uses to deal with his inadequacies and inferiorities.

limen: Threshold.

maladjustment: Chronic failure in adjustment.

masochism: The deriving of pleasure from being mistreated, punished, or humiliated. Also, the tendency to invite such treatment.

masturbation: The attainment of sexual gratification through manual or other mechanical stimulation of the genital organs.

maturation: The developmental changes that take place in all normal members of the species when a suitable environment is provided.

maturity: That state that characterizes the adults of a species.

mean: The average, obtained by dividing the sum of all the scores by the total number of cases.

median: The value of the midmost case in a series of cases. Half of the cases fall above the median and half below it.

menarche: A female's first menstruation.

mental age: A given child's level of ability, expressed in terms of the age at which the *average* child attains that level of ability. For example, an average child of 12 has a mental age of 12.

mental defective: A term used to describe an individual who is academically, vocationally, and socially handicapped by intellectual limitations, and who consequently must be provided with a sheltered environment.

mental illness: A general term referring to any severely disordered behavior.

mind: A hypothetical construct that refers to the organized system of all mental activities.

Minnesota Multiphasic Personality Inventory or MMPI: An empirically derived personality inventory that measures behavior along the dimensions of various diagnostic categories of abnormal behavior.

mode: The most common value in a series—the value which has the largest number of cases.

mood: An emotional state of relatively low intensity that recurs or is maintained for a period of time.

morale: The prevailing attitude of the individuals in a group with respect to confidence in the group, confidence about their group role, loyalty to the group, and desire to work for the group.

moron: A mentally defective individual with an IQ in the range of 50–69, usually capable of holding a job and earning his own living.

motivation: An hypothesized process that energizes responses and determines their direction.

narcotic: A drug that induces drowsiness, stupor, or deep sleep.

need: (1) A deficiency or lack of something the organism requires for minimal or optimal functioning, (2) the tension produced by this deficiency. Often used synonymously with *drive* and *motive,* but with specialized distinctions (for example, need for love, status needs).

nerve: A bundle of neurons.

nervous breakdown: A layman's term somewhat vague in meaning but which usually refers to the onset and course of any severe mental disorder.

neurology: The science that deals with the structure and function of the nervous system.

neuron: The single cell that is the basic unit of nerve tissue.

neuropsychiatry. A medical specialty dealing with physiological and psychological aspects of mental disorder.

neurosis: A psychological disorder, less severe than psychosis, characterized by anxiety, physical symptoms, obsessions, fears, or severely repressive forgetting.

nondirective: A technique and a theory of psychotherapy in which the responsibility for treatment and care rests with the client. The therapist avoids probing questions, interpretations, suggestions, etc., and instead concentrates on creating an accepting atmosphere and reflecting the feeling and content of the client's statements.

nonsense syllable: A pronounceable, but meaningless combination of letters used in experimental work where it is important to control familiarity with the stimulus.

norm. The usual (hence expected) performance of a given group.

normal: Conforming to the usual or average.

normal distribution: A bell-shaped curve found when an infinite number of cases are studied, and the variation is subject to chance. The greatest frequency is in the middle of the distribution with a gradual tapering toward each extreme.

obsessive: Characterized by tendencies to have a recurring thought or thoughts that may disrupt an individual's regular activity.

Oedipus complex: In psychoanalytic theory, the unconscious sexual attraction of an individual to the parent of the opposite sex. The term is used for both sexes, but the desire of a girl for her father is sometimes designated as the Electra complex.

operant behavior: Behavior for which the stimulus conditions are not known, and which is identified by its effect on the environment.

operant conditioning: The procedure whereby an organism learns to respond to a situation with a behavior or series of behaviors which lead to a reward or are reinforced.

operational definition: A way of defining a term by specifying the operations or behavior that may be used to measure or identify it.

other-directed: The tendency to be guided in one's values, beliefs, and actions by other individuals.

ovariectomy: The removal of the ovaries.

overcompensation: An exaggerated attempt to make up for some lack or loss of physical or psychological characteristic. (Often used instead of *compensation*.)

paranoid reaction: A psychotic behavior characterized by systematic delusions of persecution and/or grandeur.

pathological: Characterized by the presence of disease, defect, abnormality, or disorder.

peer: Any person who is considered to be an equal, usually of the same age.

percentile: One of the dividing points in a distribution of ranked scores divided into 100 parts with an equal number of cases in each part. Percentile scores are numbered from the bottom up, from 1 to 99. Each percentile point indicates the percentage of cases falling below that point.

perception: A hypothetical internal event controlled primarily by the stimulation of the sense organs. Perception is inferred from the nature of the stimulus and the succeeding behavior.

perceptual defense: Changes in perceptual threshold or distortions of threatening stimuli that serve a protective function as far as the ego or self is concerned.

personality: The relatively enduring ways of behaving that characterize each individual.

phenomenological field: Everything experienced by an organism at any given moment.

phi phenomenon: The tendency to perceive motion when stationary stimuli are flashed in rapid succession.

phobia: Excessive, unreasonable fear of some object or situation.

physiological psychology: That branch of psychology concerned with the relationship between physiological processes and behavior.

pilot study: A small-scale experiment designed to try out methods and to explore the feasibility of conducting a more extensive experiment.

placebo: A preparation, often used in research, that contains no medicine and is given to subjects who believe they are receiving treatment.

poll: A survey of a number of individuals with respect to their attitudes on a given subject.

polygraph: An apparatus that is able to record several responses simultaneously on a revolving drum.

preadolescence: The two years of human life preceding puberty, usually about ages 10 to 12.

preconscious: Mental processes not present in consciousness at a given moment, but which are easily available to consciousness when needed.

probability: The likelihood of the occurrence of an event.

projection: (1) A defense mechanism in which one's own unconscious motives and attitudes are attributed to others. (2) A tendency to interpret ambiguous stimuli in terms of one's own needs and interests.

projective test: A test that employs a relatively unstructured, ambiguous stimulus to which the subject responds with a minimum of restrictions.

propaganda: Any deliberate attempt by an individual or group to influence the attitudes or behavior of other individuals or groups.

psychiatric nursing: The branch of nursing involving special training in the care of mental patients.

psychiatric social work: The branch of social work that deals with individuals having mental disorders and with their families. The activity involves both social case work and psychotherapy.

psychiatry: The medical specialty that deals with the prevention, diagnosis, treatment, and care of mental disorders.

psychoanalysis: A term used to refer either to the personality theories developed by Freud and his followers or the psychotherapeutic technique that applies such theories.

psychodiagnosis: Any procedure designed to discover the underlying causes of behavior.

psychogalvanic response or PGR: The changes in the electrical conductivity of the skin as a result of minute changes in the amount of moisture present. The PGR is used as a measure of emotional response. Also known as electrodermal response and galvanic skin response.

psychology: A branch of science that deals with the behavior of humans and other animals.

psychopath: Either a person who is classified as an antisocial personality, or a person suffering from any mental disorder.

psychopathic: Pertaining to any mental disorder.

psychosis: A very severe mental disorder that usually leads to hospitalization. Specific psychoses include schizophrenia, paranoia, and affective psychosis.

psychosomatic: Pertaining to disorders having physical symptoms that are caused, at least in part, by psychological factors.

psychotherapy: Any process in which psychological techniques are used to bring about changes in disordered or disturbed behavior.

puberty: The developmental period at which the sexual organs become capable of functioning. It is marked by the beginning of menstruation in females and the appearance of pigmented pubic hair in males.

Q sort: A personality measurement in which a series of statements are sorted into piles that indicate the extent to which each statement is descriptive of the subject.

quartile deviation: A rough measure of the variability of a frequency distribution. It is equal to half the distance between the first and third quartiles.

questionnaire: A device that presents a series of questions on a given topic.

random: Occurring by chance.

range: In a distribution of scores, the distance from the highest to the lowest value.

rating scale: A paper-and-pencil device used by a rater to estimate the degree to which a given trait or quality characterizes the rated individual.

rationalization: The defense mechanism in which plausible reasons for one's behavior are unconsciously put forward in place of the real, less acceptable reasons.

raw score: The score originally obtained on a test before it has been treated or interpreted statistically.

reaction formation: A defense mechanism in which the behavior is exactly opposite to the unconscious motive.

reference group: A group with which an individual identifies himself and whose standards and norms he uses as a guide to his own behavior.

reflex: An unlearned stimulus-response connection involving relatively simple behavior.

regression: A return to an earlier, less-mature form of behavior that was once satisfactory.

reinforcement: Any condition, such as drive reduction, that increases the probability of a stimulus evoking a response that resulted in that condition.

reliability: The extent to which a test is consistent and dependable in measurement.

repression: An unconscious process characterized by the selective forgetting of material that is anxiety-provoking or threatening.

research: A systematic attempt to solve a certain problem or group of problems and to identify the principles which govern it. The term primarily is used to indicate first-hand observation of data, as in experiments.

respondent behavior: Behavior that occurs in response to a known stimulus.

response: Any muscular or glandular activity that depends on stimulation.

response hierarchy: A group of responses arranged in order of decreasing probability of their being elicited by a given stimulus.

reward: A reinforcement.

rigidity: A tendency to persist in the same attitudes and behavior even when they are no longer appropriate because of changes in the situation.

role: The expected behavior of an individual who occupies a particular position in a group.

Rorschach test: A projective approach to personality measurement in which subjects respond to ink blots reproduced on ten cards.

sadism: The tendency to associate pleasure or sexual satisfaction with the pain or discomfiture of another person.

sample: A portion of a total population that is taken as representative of the entire population.

scatter diagram: A chart used to compare the scores on one variable with those on another. Constructing such a diagram is a preliminary step in the computation of a correlation coefficient.

schizophrenia: A psychotic reaction involving severe disturbances in reality contact, interpersonal relationships, and thought processes. It is characterized by withdrawal, apathy, and autistic thinking.

school psychologist: A person who uses psychological techniques and concepts in dealing with school problems. His duties may include diagnostic testing, pupil placement, counseling, and psychotherapy.

self: That portion of the total field that an individual perceives as having relation to his own identity: "me," "I," "myself."

self-actualization: The development of one's capacities and talents, as facilitated by self-understanding, self-acceptance, and an integration of one's motives.

sense organ: Any organ which is sensitive to the activity of stimuli.

sensory adaptation: A change in the responsiveness of a sense organ as the result of continued stimulation.

sentence completion test: A personality test in which the subject is asked to supply a word or phrase to complete an unfinished sentence.

set: A condition in which an organism is predisposed toward a certain perception or a certain response.

sib or sibling: A brother or sister.

sign-Gestalt: In Tolman's learning theory, a complex object to which the organism reacts with the expectation that certain behavior will achieve a particular goal.

significance: In statistics, the probability that the score, value, or difference obtained did not occur by chance alone.

situational test: A test in which an individual's response to a problem in real life or in a simulated situation is observed.

skewness: The extent to which a frequency curve is nonsymmetrical because of an unequal division of cases on either side of the mode.

social class: A division of society made up of individuals having approximately the same status in terms of occupation, income, neighborhood characteristics, education, etc.

socialization: The processes by which a child learns to behave like others in his culture.

social psychology: A branch of psychology concerned with the study of the behavior of individuals and groups in a social setting.

sociogram: A diagram depicting the type and number of interactions, choices, or rejections among individuals in a group.

sociology: The science that deals with man's group life and his social organization.

somatotherapy: The treatment of mental disorders with physical means, for example, drugs, insulin or electric shock, brain surgery, etc.

spontaneous recovery: The return of an extinguished conditioned response after a period of rest.

standard deviation: A measure of variability of a distribution, obtained by summing the squared differences from the mean, dividing by the number of measures, and extracting the square root of the result. In a normal distribution, 68.2 per cent of the scores fall within one standard deviation above and below the mean.

standardization group: The group of individuals used in establishing the norms of a test.

Stanford-Binet test: An intelligence test patterned after the original Binet-Simon scale and revised in 1937 by Terman and Merrill.

static sensitivity: The sense that informs us of our location or movement in space.

statistical psychology: The branch of psychology that specializes in the development and application of statistical principles to psychological data.

statistics: The mathematical science concerned with gathering, processing, and analyzing numerical data in any field.

status: The position and degree of acceptance given to an individual by others.

stereotype: A rigid, oversimplified, or biased perception of individuals or social groups.

stimulus: A change in physical energy that causes physiological activity in a sense organ.

stimulus generalization: The tendency for stimuli that are perceived as similar to an original stimulus to evoke the same response evoked by the original stimulus.

Strong Vocational Interest Blank: A test that measures the similarities between an individual's pattern of interests and the patterns that are typical of a number of different occupational groups.

subject: A person or a lower animal whose behavior is studied in an experiment.

sublimation: The achievement of drive satisfaction by the substitution of socially acceptable behavior and goals for the original ones.

subliminal: Pertaining to stimuli that lie below the measured threshold of perception.

superego: In psychoanalysis, moral standards and values that become incorporated as an integral part of the individual's behavior and which are learned first from parents and later from society itself.

suppression: The conscious process of withholding from expression unwanted thoughts, feelings, and impulses.

temperament: The general emotional responsiveness of individuals.

test: A set of standardized, controlled stimuli that elicit a measurable sample of behavior from an individual.

Thematic Apperception Test or TAT: A projective approach to personality measurement in which a person is asked to make up stories to go with the pictures reproduced on a series of twenty cards.

theory: A general principle, supported by data, proposed to explain a given phenomenon.

threat: A stimulus, real or imaginary, perceived by an individual as a sign of impending danger, injury, embarrassment, or discomfiture.

threshold: The point at which a stimulus is just able to elicit a response. A difference threshold is the point at which one stimulus just differs from another to a degree sufficient to elicit a differential response.

tonus: A continuing state of slight tension present in healthy muscles when they are not in active movement.

trait: An enduring personality characteristic in which individuals vary from one another.

tranquilizer: One of a variety of drugs used in treating mental disorders. When used in mental illness, these drugs act to reduce anxiety, hostility, fear, and tension, and help make the patient more responsive to psychotherapy.

transfer: Either a positive or a negative effect on the ability to perform a certain behavior as a consequence of previous learning.

trial-and-error learning: Learning in which the correct response to a problem is achieved only by chance.

twins, fraternal: Twins that develop from two separate eggs; in effect, siblings that happen to be born at the same time.

twins, identical: Twins that develop from the splitting of a single egg, which thus gives them the same inherited characteristics.

type: A pattern of personality and/or physical characteristics into which individuals may be categorized.

unconditioned response: The response elicited by the original stimulus in a conditioning process.

unconditioned stimulus: The original stimulus, in a conditioning process, that elicits the desired response before the learning trials begin.

unconscious: A quality characteristic of mental processes and other forms of behavior that lie beyond the limits of awareness and which cannot readily be brought to awareness.

validity: The extent to which a test measures what it purports to measure.

variable: Any characteristic that may appear in changed amount or quality in different instances.

variable-interval reinforcement: Intermittent reinforcement that occurs randomly.

Wechsler Adult Intelligence Scale or WAIS: An adult intelligence test that yields measures of both performance and verbal intelligence; a revision of the Wechsler-Bellevue Scale.

Wechsler Intelligence Scale for Children or WISC: An intelligence test for children that yields measures of both performance and verbal intelligence.

REFERENCES

Works cited in this book are listed alphabetically by author and year of publication. Numbers in boldface following each citation refer to the text pages on which the works are cited.

Abegglen, J. C., *see* Warner and Abegglen (1955).

Adorno, T. W., E. Frenkel-Brunswik, D. J. Levinson, and R. N. Sanford (1950), *The authoritarian personality*. N. Y.: Harper. **388**

Allee, W. C., N. Collias, and C. Z. Lutherman (1939), Modification of the social order in flocks of hens by the injection of testosterone propionate. *Physiol. Zool.*, 12:412–40. **58**

Allen, L., *see* Honzik, et al. (1948).

Allport, F. H. (1955), *Theories of perception and the concept of structure*. N. Y.: Wiley. **134, 151**

Allport, G. W. (1937), *Personality*. N. Y.: Holt. **112**

American Psychological Assn. (1954), Technical recommendations for psychological tests and diagnostic techniques. *Psychol. Bull.*, 51:201–38. **188, 191**

American Psychological Assn. (1960 et seq.), *Directory*. Washington: Amer. Psychol. Assn. **26**

Ames, R. (1955), Leaderless group discussion and experience in group leadership. *Calif. J. educ. Res.*, 6:166–69. **320**

Anastasi, A. (1954), Psychological testing. N. Y.: Macmillan. **232**

Anastasi, A. (1956), Intelligence and family size. *Psychol. Rev.*, 53:187–209. **183**

Anastasi, A., and J. P. Foley, Jr. (1949), *Differential psychology*, rev. ed. N. Y.: Macmillan. **214**

Anderson, H., and G. Anderson (1956), Cultural reactions to conflict: a study of adolescent children in seven countries, in G. M. Gilbert, ed., *Psychological approaches to intergroup and international understanding, a symposium of the Third Interamerican Congress of Psychology*. Austin, Tex.: Hogg Foundation for Mental Hygiene. **383**

Angell, G. W. (1949), The effect of immediate knowledge of quiz results on final examination scores in freshman chemistry. *J. educ. Res.*, 42: 391–94. **120**

Applezweig, M. H., and G. Moeller (1958), *Conforming behavior and personality variables*. Group Psychol. Branch, Off. Naval Res., Tech. Rep. No. 8. **234**

Aronson, E., and J. Mills (1959), The effect of severity of initiation on liking for a group. *J. abnorm. soc. Psychol.*, 59:177–81. **326**

Asch, S. E. (1952), *Social psychology*. Englewood Cliffs, N. J.: Prentice-Hall. **268**

Asch, S. E. (1955), Opinions and social pressure. *Scient. Amer.*, 193(5):31–35. **148**

Asch, S. E. (1956), Studies of independence and submission to group pressure: 1. A minority of one against a unanimous majority. *Psychol. Monogr.*, 70: No. 416. **147, 212**

Assessment Staff of the U.S. Office of Strategic Services (1948), *Assessment of men.* N. Y.: Rinehart. **199**

Atkinson, J. W., and A. C. Raphelson (1956), Individual differences in motivation and behavior in particular situations. *J. Pers.,* 24:349–63. **232**

Atkinson, J. W., *see also* McClelland et al. (1953).

Auld, F., *see* Dollard et al. (1953).

Ax, A. F. (1953), The physiological differentiation between fear and anger in humans. *Psychosom. Med.,* 15:433–42. **96, 163**

Axelrod, H., *see* Lanzetta et al. (1954).

Azrin, N. H., and O. R. Lindsley (1956), The reinforcement of cooperation between children. *J. abnorm. soc. Psychol.,* 52:100–102. **114**

Back, K. W. (1951), Influence through social communication. *J. abnorm. soc. Psychol.,* 46:9–23. **316**

Back, K., *see also* Festinger et al. (1950).

Baker, C. T., *see* Sontag et al. (1955) and (1958).

Baldwin, A. L. (1955), *Behavior and development in childhood.* N. Y.: Holt. **51**

Baldwin, A. L., J. Kalhorn, and F. H. Breese (1945), Patterns of parent behavior. *Psychol. Monogr.,* 58: No. 268. **43**

Baldwin, A. L., *see also* McClelland et al. (1958).

Baldwin, M. W., and G. Nielsen (1956), Subjective sharpness of simulated color television pictures. *J. Opt. Soc. Amer.,* 46:681–85. **369**

Bales, R. F., *see* P. Hare et al. (1955).

Barbe, W. B. (1956), Career achievement of gifted students. *Personnel guid. J.,* 34:356–59. **202**

Bard, P., and V. B. Mountcastle (1947), Some forebrain mechanisms involved in the expression of rage with special reference to suppression of angry behavior. *Res. Publ. Assn. nerv. ment. Dis.,* 27: 362–404. **96**

Barker, R., T. Dembo, and K. Lewin (1941), Frustration and regression: an experiment with young children. *Univ. Iowa Stud. Child Welfare.* 18: No. 1. **118**

Barker, R. G., T. Dembo, and K. Lewin (1943), Frustration and regression, in Barker, Kounin, and Wright, eds., *Child behavior and development.* N. Y.: McGraw-Hill. **246**

Barndt, R. J., and D. M. Johnson (1955), Time orientation in delinquents. *J. abnorm. soc. Psychol.,* 51:343–45. **307**

Barrett, D., *see* Bavelas and Barrett (1951).

Barron, F. (1958), The psychology of imagination. *Scient. Amer.,* 199(3):150–66. **14, 212**

Barthol, R. P., *see* Ghiselli and Barthol (1953) and (1956).

Bartlett, F. C. (1932), *Remembering.* Cambridge, England: Cambridge Univ. Press. **127, 274**

Bass, B. M., S. Klubeck, and C. R. Wurster (1953), Factors influencing reliability and validity of leaderless group discussion assessment. *J. appl. Psychol.* 37:26–30. **319**

Bass, B. M., *see also* Flint and Bass (1958).

Bateson, G., and M. Mead (1942), *The Balinese character.* N. Y.: Academy of Sciences. **36, 155**

Bateson, G., *see also* Ruesch and Bateson (1951).

Baughman, E. E. (1951), Rorschach scores as a function of examiner difference. *J. proj. Tech.,* 15: 243–49. **232**

Bavelas, A. (1951), Communication patterns in task-oriented groups, in Lerner and Lasswell, eds., *The policy sciences.* Stanford: Stanford Univ. Press. **320**

Bavelas, A., and D. Barrett (1951), An experimental approach to organizational communication. *Personnel,* 27:366–71. **321**

Bayley, N., and M. H. Oden (1955), The maintenance of intellectual ability in gifted adults. *J. Gerontol.,* 10:91–107. **209**

Beach, F. (1958), *Hormones and behavior.* N. Y.: Hoeber. **104**

Bellows, R. T. (1939), Time factors in water drinking in dogs. *Amer. J. Physiol.,* 125:87–97. **95**

Bender, L. (1950), Anxiety in disturbed children, in Hoch and Zubin, eds., *Anxiety.* N. Y.: Grune and Stratton. **45**

Bendix, R., and S. M. Lipset, eds. (1953), *Class, status, and power.* Glencoe, Ill.: Free Press. **289**

Bevan, W., *see* Secord et al. (1956).

Bexton, W. H., W. Heron, and T. H. Scott (1954), Effects of decreased variation in the sensory environment. *Canad. J. Psychol.,* 8:70–76. **206**

Binet, A. (1909), *Les idées modernes sur les enfants.* Paris: E. Flammarion. **199**

Blake, R. R., and G. V. Ramsey (1951), *Perception: an approach to personality.* N. Y.: Ronald. **151**

Bloch, H. (1952), *Disorganization: personal and social.* N. Y.: Knopf. **248**

Blum, M. L. (1956), *Industrial psychology and its social foundation,* rev. ed. N. Y.: Harper. **375**

Bobbitt, J. M. (1942), An experimental study of the phenomenon of closure as a threshold function. *J. exp. Psychol.,* 30:273–94. **134**

Borgatta, E. F., *see* P. Hare et al. (1955).

Boring, E. G., *see* Holway and Boring (1941).

Bossard, J. H. S. (1954), *The sociology of child development,* rev. ed. N. Y.: Harper. **51, 289**

Bowers, A. M., *see* Healy et al. (1930).

Bowers, W. H. (1952), An appraisal of worker characteristics as related to age. *J. appl. Psychol.,* 36:296–300. **73**

Bowlby, J. (1951), *Maternal care and mental health.* Geneva: World Health Organization. **45**

Brackbill, Y. (1958), Extinction of the smiling response in infants as a function of reinforcement schedule. *Child Develpm.,* 29:115–24. **120**

Bradway, K. P., C. W. Thompson, and R. B. Cravens (1958), Preschool IQs after twenty-five years. *J. educ. Psychol.,* 49:278–81. **209**

Brady, J. V. (1958), Ulcers in executive monkeys. *Scient. Amer.,* 199(4):95–100. **99**

Brand, H., ed. (1954), *The study of personality.* N. Y.: Wiley. **236**

Breese, F. H., *see* Baldwin et al. (1945).

Bridges, K. M. B. (1932), Emotional development in early infancy. *Child Develpm.,* 3:324–34. **163, 168**

Britt, S. H. (1940), Pedestrian conformity to a traffic regulation. *J. abnorm. soc. Psychol.,* 35:114–19. **180**

Brobeck, J. R. (1946), Mechanism of the development of obesity in animals with hypothalamic lesions. *Physiol. Rev.,* 26:541–59. **94**

Bronfenbrenner, U., *see* McClelland et al. (1958).

Bronner, A. F., *see* Healy et al. (1930).

Brooks, J. (1957), The little ad that isn't there. *Consumer Rep.,* 23: No. 1. **137**

Brose, I. D. J. (1953), *Design for decision.* N. Y.: Macmillan. **191**

Brown, C. W., *see* Ghiselli and Brown (1955).

Brown, D. J., *see* Shaw and Brown (1957).

Brown, R. (1958), *Words and things: an introduction to language.* Glencoe, Ill.: Free Press. **309**

Bruce, P. (1958), Relationship of self-acceptance to other variables with sixth grade children oriented in self-understanding. *J. educ. Psychol.,* 49:229–38. **225**

Bruce, R. W. (1933), Conditions of transfer of training. *J. exp. Psychol.,* 16:343–61. **123**

Bruner, J. S., and C. C. Goodman (1947), Value and need as organizing factors in perception. *J. abnorm. soc. Psychol.,* 42:33–44. **146**

Bruner, J. S., and R. Tagiuri (1954), The perception of people, in G. Lindzey, ed., *Handbook of social psychology.* Cambridge: Addison-Wesley. **218**

Bruner, J. S., *see also* Postman et al. (1948).

Bugelski, R., *see* Miller and Bugelski (1948).

Burtt, H. E., *see* Fleishman et al. (1955).

Butler, J., *see* Levine and Butler (1952).

Byrne, D. (1956), The relationship between humor and the expression of hostility. *J. abnorm. soc. Psychol.,* 53:84–89. **176**

Byrne, D. (1957), *Response to humor as a function of drive arousal and psychological defenses.* Unpublished doctoral dissertation, Stanford University. **184**

Byrne, D. (1959), The effect of a subliminal food stimulus on verbal responses. *J. appl. Psychol.,* 43:249–52. **137**

Calhoon, R. P., E. W. Noland, and A. M. Whitehall (1958), *Cases on human relations in management.* N. Y.: McGraw-Hill. **375**

Cannon, W. B. (1939), *The wisdom of the body.* N. Y.: Norton. **104**

Cannon, W. B., and A. L. Washburn (1912), An explanation of hunger. *Amer. J. Physiol.,* 29:441–54. **94**

Canter, R. R. (1956), Intelligence and the social status of occupations. *Personnel guid. J.,* 34:258–60. **337**

Cantril, H. (1950), *The "why" of man's experience.* N. Y.: Macmillan. **26, 274**

Cantril, H., and M. Strunk (1951), *Public opinion, 1935–46.* Princeton: Princeton Univ. Press. **285**

Carey, G. L. (1958), Sex differences in problem-solving performance as a function of attitude differences. *J. abnorm. soc. Psychol.,* 56:256–60. **273**

Carlson, A. J., *see* Wangensteen and Carlson (1931), and Luckhardt and Carlson (1915).

Carmichael, L., ed. (1954), *Manual of child psychology,* 2nd ed. N. Y.: Wiley. **51**

Carmichael, L. (1957), *Basic psychology: a study of the modern healthy mind.* N. Y.: Random House. **14, 26, 171**

Carpenter, B. (1954), Birthplaces and schools of experimental and clinical psychologists. *Amer. Psychologist,* 9:637–39. **22**

Carter, L. F. (1954), Recording and evaluating the performance of individuals as members of small groups. *Personnel Psychol.,* 7:477–84. **313**

Cartwright, D., and A. Zander, eds. (1953), *Group dynamics: research and theory.* Evanston, Ill.: Row, Peterson. **329**

Cartwright, D., *see also* D. Katz, et al. (1954).

Cattell, J. McK. (1927), *American men of science,* 4th ed. Garrison, N. Y.: Science Press. **37**

Cattell, R. B. (1946), *Description and measurement of personality.* Yonkers: World Book. **226**

Centers, R., *see* MacKinnon and Centers (1956).

Chambers, A. S., and R. N. Zabarenko (1956), Effects of glutamic acid and social stimulation in mental deficiency. *J. abnorm. soc. Psychol.,* 53:315–20. **48**

Charles, D. C. (1953), Ability and accomplishment of persons earlier judged mentally deficient. *Genet. psychol. Monogr.,* 47:3–71. **210**

Chein, I., *see* R. Levine et al. (1942).

Child, I. L. (1950), The relation of somatotype to self-ratings on Sheldon's temperamental traits. *J. Pers.,* 18:440–53. **98**

Child, I. L., *see also* Whiting and Child (1953).

Chisholm, H. B. (1946), The re-establishment of peacetime society. *Psychiatry,* 9:3–20. **381**

Chisholm, H. B. (1957), *Prescription for survival.* N. Y.: Columbia Univ. Press. **400**

Chowdhry, K., and T. M. Newcomb (1952), The relative abilities of leaders and non-leaders to estimate opinions of their own groups. *J. abnorm. soc. Psychol.,* 47:51–57. **319**

Clark, B., M. L. Johnson, and R. E. Dreher (1946), The effect of sunlight on dark adaptation. *Amer. J. Ophthal.,* 29:828–36. **132**

Clark, K. E. (1957), *America's psychologists: a survey of a growing profession.* Washington: Amer. Psychol. Assn. **15, 24, 26**

Clark, R. A., *see* McClelland et al. (1953).

Clausen, J. A., *see* Leighton et al. (1957).

Cleveland, S. W., *see* Fisher and Cleveland (1956).

Cohen, M., *see* Murray and Cohen (1959).

Cohn, T. S. (1951), A study of nonintellective factors in grade getting. Unpublished paper presented at annual convention of Western Psychol. Assn. **298**

Coleman, J. C. (1956), *Abnormal psychology in modern life,* rev. ed. Chicago: Scott, Foresman. **251, 262**

Collias, N., *see* Allee et al. (1939).

Combs, A. W., *see* Snygg and Combs (1959).

Conant, J. B. (1951), *Science and common sense.* New Haven: Yale Univ. Press. **13**

Conger, J. J., *see* Sawrey et al. (1956).

Conrad, H. S., *see* H. E. Jones and Conrad (1953).

Cook, L., and E. Cook (1954), *Intergroup education.* N. Y.: McGraw-Hill. **400**

Cooley, C. H. (1909), *Social organization.* N. Y.: Scribner. **313**

Courts, F. A. (1939), Relations between experimentally induced muscular tension and memorization. *J. exp. Psychol.,* 25:235–56. **124**

Coyne, J. W., H. E. King, J. Zubin, and C. Landis (1943), Accuracy of recognition of subliminal auditory stimuli. *J. exp. Psychol.,* 33:508–13. **137**

Craighill, P. G., *see* Sarason et al. (1952).

Cravens, R. B., *see* Bradway et al. (1958).

Cronbach, L. J. (1949), *Essentials of psychological testing.* N. Y.: Harper. **194, 361**

Cronbach, L. J. (1960), *Essentials of psychological testing,* rev. ed. N. Y.: Harper. **214**

Crutchfield, R. S. (1955), Conformity and character. *Amer. Psychologist,* 10:191–98. **212**

Crutchfield, R. S., *see also* Krech and Crutchfield (1948).

Culbertson, F. M. (1957), Modification of an emotionally held attitude through role playing. *J. abnorm. soc. Psychol.,* 54:230–33. **125**

Cutler, R. L., *see* McConnell et al. (1958).

Dashiell, J. F. (1935), Experimental studies of the influence of social situations on the behavior of individual human adults, in C. Murchison, ed., *Handbook of social psychology*. Worcester, Mass.: Clark Univ. Press. **312**

Davids, A. (1956), The influence of ego-involvement on relations between authoritarianism and intolerance of ambiguity. *J. consult. Psychol.*, 20: 179–84. **389**

Davidson, C., and E. L. Demuth (1945), Disturbances in sleep mechanism: a clinicopathologic study. I. Lesions at the cortical level. *Arch. Neurol. Psychiat. (Chicago)*, 53:399–406. **96**

Davidson, K., *see* Fox et al. (1958).

Davila, G., et al. (1956), Image of Americans in the Mexican child, in G. M. Gilbert, ed., *Psychological approaches to intergroup and international understanding, a symposium of the Third Interamerican Congress of Psychology*. Austin, Tex.: Hogg Foundation for Mental Hygiene. **383**

Davis, A. (1948), *Social-class influences upon learning*. Cambridge: Harvard Univ. Press. **239**

Davis, A., and R. J. Havighurst (1947), *The father of the man*. Boston: Houghton Mifflin. **285**

Davis, J. A., *see* Kahl and Davis (1955).

Deeg, M. E., and D. G. Paterson (1947), Changes in social status of occupations. *Occupations*, 25: 205–08. **337**

Dekker, E., H. E. Pelser, and J. Groen (1957), Conditioning as a cause of asthmatic attacks. *J. psychosom. Res.*, 2:97–108. **80**

Delgado, J. M. R., W. W. Roberts, and N. E. Miller (1954), Learning motivated by electrical stimulation of the brain. *Amer. J. Physiol.*, 179:587–93. **96**

Dembo, T., *see* Barker et al. (1941) and (1943).

Demuth, E. L., *see* Davidson and Demuth (1945).

Dennis, W. (1943), The Hopi child, in Barker, Kounin, and Wright, eds., *Child behavior and development*. N. Y.: McGraw-Hill. **32**

Denny, M. R., Jr. (1957), Learning through stimulus satiation. *J. exp. Psychol.*, 54:62–64. **113**

Denny, R., *see* Riesman et al. (1950).

Dewey, J. (1929), *The quest for certainty*. N. Y.: Minton, Balch. **13**

Dewey, J. (1939), *Freedom and culture*. N. Y.: Putnam. **381**

Dickinson, C. (1954), Ratings of job factors by those choosing various occupational groups. *J. counsel. Psychol.*, 1:188–89. **341**

Dickson, W. J., *see* Roethlisberger and Dickson (1939).

Diethelm, O., and D. J. Simons (1945), Electroencephalographic findings in psychopathic personalities. *J. nerv. ment. Dis.*, 102:611–14. **98**

Dollard, J., and N. E. Miller (1950), *Personality and psychotherapy*. N. Y.: McGraw-Hill. **107, 127, 262**

Dollard, J., F. Auld, and A. M. White (1953), *Steps in psychotherapy*. N. Y.: Macmillan. **262**

Dollard, J., *see also* Miller and Dollard (1941).

Douvan, E., and A. M. Walker (1956), The sense of effectiveness in public affairs. *Psychol. Monogr.*, 70: No. 22. **397**

Downing, W. L., *see* Lotsof and Downing (1956).

Dreher, R. E., *see* Clark et al. (1946).

Dreikurs, R. (1948), *The challenge of parenthood*. N. Y.: Duell, Sloan, and Pearce. **37**

Dreikurs, R. (1950), *Fundamentals of Adlerian psychology*. N. Y.: Greenberg. **236**

Drolette, M. E., *see* Funkenstein et al. (1957).

Dubin, R. (1956), Industrial workers' worlds: a study of the "central life interests" of industrial workers. *Soc. Probl.*, 3:131–42. **349**

DuBois, C. (1944), *The people of Alor*. Minneapolis: Univ. of Minnesota Press. **232**

Dudek, S., *see* Symonds and Dudek (1956).

Dunbar, H. F. (1954), *Emotions and bodily changes*, 4th ed. N. Y.: Columbia Univ. Press. **104**

Duryea, R. A., and G. D. Greer, Jr. (1956), The leader behavior description technique applied to Army basic training companies and platoons. Unpublished paper presented at the annual convention of the Western Psychological Assn. **368**

Dykman, R. A., E. K. Heimann, and W. A. Kerr (1952), Lifetime worry patterns of three diverse cultural groups. *J. soc. Psychol.*, 35:91–100. **72**

Dymond, R. F., *see* Rogers and Dymond (1954).

Eccles, J. C. (1958), The physiology of imagination. *Scient. Amer.*, 199(3):135–46. **91**

Edwards, A. L. (1958), *Statistical analysis*, rev. ed. N. Y.: Rinehart. **191**

Ekman, G. (1951), On the number and definition of dimensions in Kretschmer's and Sheldon's constitutional systems, in Ekman et al., eds., *Essays in psychology dedicated to David Katz*. Uppsala: Almqvist and Wiksells. **225**

Eldersveld, S., *see* D. Katz et al. (1954).

Ellis, H. (1926), *A study of British genius*, rev. ed. Boston: Houghton Mifflin. **37**

Ellis, W. D. (1938), *A sourcebook of Gestalt psychology*. N. Y.: Harcourt, Brace. **151**

Emmons, W. H., *see* Simon and Emmons (1956).

English, H. B., and A. C. English (1958), *A comprehensive dictionary of psychological and psychoanalytical terms*. N. Y.: Longmans, Green. **7, 401**

Eriksen, C. W., *see* Lazarus et al. (1951).

Erikson, E. H. (1950), *Childhood and society*. N. Y.: Norton. **51**

Estes, W. K. (1958), Stimulus-response theory of drive, in M. Jones, ed., *1958 Nebraska symposium on motivation*. Lincoln: Univ. of Nebraska Press. **107**

Exline, R. V. (1957), Group climate as a factor in the relevance and accuracy of social perception. *J. abnorm. soc. Psychol.*, 55:382–88. **316**

Fairweather, G. W., *see* Moran et al. (1956).

Faust, M. W. (1960), Developmental maturity as a determinant in prestige of adolescent girls. *Child Develpm.*, 31:173–84. **57**

Feshbach, S. (1955), The drive-reducing function of fantasy behavior. *J. abnorm. soc. Psychol.*, 50:3–11. **386**

Feshbach, S., *see also* Janis and Feshbach (1953).

Festinger, L. (1957), *A theory of cognitive dissonance*. Evanston, Ill.: Row, Peterson. **101**

Festinger, L., S. Schachter, and K. Back (1950), *Social pressures in informal groups: a study of a housing project*. N. Y.: Harper. **8**

Fiedler, F. E. (1950), A comparison of therapeutic relationships in psychoanalytic, nondirective, and Adlerian therapy. *J. consult. Psychol.*, 14:436–45. **259**

Fiedler, F. E. (1951), Factor analyses of psychoanalytic, nondirective, and Adlerian therapeutic relationships. *J. consult. Psychol.*, 15:32–38. **259**

Fiedler, F. E. (1958), Interpersonal perception and group effectiveness, in Tagiuri and Petrullo, eds., *Person perception and interpersonal behavior.* Stanford: Stanford Univ. Press. **323**

Finger, F. W. (1942), The effect of varying conditions of reinforcement upon a simple running response. *J. exp. Psychol.,* 30:53–68. **120**

Fisher, S., and S. W. Cleveland (1956), Relation of body image to site of cancer. *Psychosom. Med.,* 18:304–09. **100**

Fisher, S., *see also* Moran et al. (1956).

Fiske, D. W. (1944), A study of relationships to somatotype. *J. appl. Psychol.,* 28:504–19. **98**

Flavell, J. H. (1956), Abstract thinking and social behavior in schizophrenia. *J. abnorm. soc. Psychol.,* 52:208–11. **183**

Fleishman, E. A., E. F. Harris, and H. E. Burtt (1955), *Leadership and supervision in industry.* Bureau of Educ. Res., Ohio State Univ., Monogr. No. 33. **368**

Flint, A. W., and B. M. Bass (1958), Comparison of the construct validities of three objective measures of successful leadership behavior, in *Behavior in Groups,* Office of Naval Res. Tech. Rep. No. 17. **201**

Foley, J. P., Jr., *see* Anastasi and Foley (1949).

Folsom, W. W., and E. Sobelewski (1957), Income and social status of occupations. *Personnel guid. J.,* 36:277–78. **337**

Fonda, C. P., *see* Lazarus et al. (1951).

Fox, C., K. Davidson, F. Lighthall, R. Waite, and S. B. Sarason (1958), Human figure drawings of high and low anxious children. *Child Develpm.,* 29:297–301. **233**

Frank, L. K. (1939), Projective methods for the study of personality. *J. Pers.,* 8:389–413. **223**

Freeman, F. N., *see* Newman et al. (1937).

Freeman, F. S. (1955), *Theory and practice of psychological testing,* rev. ed. N. Y.: Holt. **214**

Frenkel-Brunswik, E., *see* Adorno et al. (1950).

Friedman, M. (1958), Speech given before the 1958 meeting of the American Heart Assn. in San Francisco. **100**

Friedman, M., and R. H. Rosenman (1959), Association of specific overt behavior patterns with blood and cardiovascular findings. *J. Amer. Med. Assn.,* 169:1286–96. **100**

Fromm, E. (1947), *Man for himself.* N. Y.: Rinehart. **236**

Funkenstein, D. H., S. H. King, and M. E. Drolette (1957), *The mastery of stress.* Cambridge: Harvard Univ. Press. **166, 171, 239, 250, 253**

Gadel, M. S., *see* Kriedt and Gadel (1953).

Galanter, E. H., *see* Greer et al. (1954).

Gardner, E. F., and G. G. Thompson (1956), *Social relations and morale in small groups.* N. Y.: Appleton-Century-Crofts. **329**

Gates, A. I., *see* Harrell et al. (1955) and (1956).

Geldard, F. A. (1953), *The human senses.* N. Y.: Wiley. **151**

Gesell, A. (1954), The ontogenesis of infant behavior, in L. Carmichael, ed., *Manual of child psychology,* 2nd ed. N. Y.: Wiley. **38**

Ghiselli, E. E., and R. P. Barthol (1953), The validity of personality inventories in the selection of employees. *J. appl. Psychol.,* 37:18–20. **362**

Ghiselli, E. E., and R. P. Barthol (1956), Role perceptions of successful and unsuccessful supervisors. *J. appl. Psychol.,* 40:241–44. **364**

Ghiselli, E. E., and C. W. Brown (1955), *Personnel and industrial psychology,* 2nd ed. N. Y.: McGraw-Hill. **361, 365, 375**

Ghiselli, E. E., and T. M. Lodahl (1958), Patterns of managerial traits and group effectiveness. *J. abnorm. soc. Psychol.,* 57:67–75. **324**

Gilbreth, F. B. (1911), *Motion study.* Princeton, N. J.: Van Nostrand. **369**

Gillin, J. (1948), Personality formation from the comparative cultural point of view, in Kluckhohn and Murray, eds., *Personality in nature, society, and culture.* N. Y.: Knopf. **36**

Gilmore, J. L. (1958), The relation of success and failure recall preference to academic performance in college. Unpublished research presented at annual convention of Western Psychol. Assn. **348**

Glaser, E. M. (1958), Psychological consultation with executives: a clinical approach. *Amer. Psychologist,* 13:486–89. **369**

Glazer, N., *see* Riesman et al. (1950).

Glueck, S., and E. Glueck (1950), *Unravelling juvenile delinquency.* N. Y.: Commonwealth Fund. **44, 306**

Goodman, C. C., *see* Bruner and Goodman (1947).

Gordon, H. (1923), *Mental and scholastic tests among retarded children.* London: Board of Educ., Educ. Pamphlet No. 44. **203**

Gordon, T. (1951), Group-centered leadership and administration, in C. R. Rogers, *Client-centered therapy.* Boston: Houghton Mifflin. **322**

Gordon, T. (1955), *Group-centered leadership.* Boston: Houghton Mifflin. **329**

Gouldner, A. W., ed. (1950), *Studies in leadership: leadership and democratic action.* N. Y.: Harper. **329**

Greenspoon, J. (1955), The reinforcing effect of two spoken sounds on the frequency of two responses. *Amer. J. Psychol.,* 68:409–16. **124**

Greer, F. L., E. H. Galanter, and P. G. Nordlie (1954), Interpersonal knowledge and individual and group effectiveness. *J. abnorm. soc. Psychol.,* 49:411–14. **319**

Greer, G. D., Jr., *see* Duryea and Greer (1956) and Palmer and Greer (1956).

Groen, J., *see* Dekker et al. (1957).

Grossack, M. M. (1954), Some effects of cooperation and competition on small group behavior. *J. abnorm. soc. Psychol.,* 49:341–48. **325**

Grunes, W. F., *see* Haire and Grunes (1950).

Gump, P., and J. S. Kounin (1957), Effects of teachers' methods of controlling misconduct upon kindergarten children. Unpublished paper read at annual convention of Amer. Psychol. Assn. **44**

Guthrie, E. R. (1935), *The psychology of learning.* N. Y.: Harper. **127**

Guthrie, E. R., and G. P. Horton (1946), *Cats in a puzzle box.* N. Y.: Rinehart. **119**

Haas, E. B., and A. S. Whiting (1956), *Dynamics of international relations.* N. Y.: McGraw-Hill. **381**

Haefner, D., *see* Lanzetta et al. (1954).

Haiman, F. S. (1955), A measurement of authoritarian attitudes toward discussion leadership. *Quart. J. Speech,* 41:140–44. **389**

Haire, M. (1959), Psychological problems relevant to business and industry. *Psychol. Bull.,* 56:169–94. **371**

Haire, M., and W. F. Grunes (1950), Perceptual defenses: processes protecting an organized perception of another personality. *Hum. Relat.*, 3: 403–12. **300**

Hall, C. S., and G. Lindzey (1957), *Theories of personality.* N. Y.: Wiley. **219, 236**

Hall, W. B. (1958), The development of a technique for assessing esthetic predispositions and its application to a sample of professional research scientists. Unpublished paper read at annual convention of Western Psychol. Assn. **Facing p. 212**

Haller, A. O., *see* Sewell et al. (1957).

Hamilton, M. (1955), *Psychosomatics.* N. Y.: Wiley. **262**

Hare, P., E. F. Borgatta, and R. F. Bales (1955), *Small groups: studies in social interaction.* N. Y.: Knopf. **329**

Harlow, H. F. (1949), The formation of learning sets. *Psychol. Rev.*, 56:51–65. **115**

Harlow, H. F. (1958), The nature of love. *Amer. Psychologist,* 13:673–85. **20**

Harrell, R. F., E. Woodyard, and A. I. Gates (1955), *The effect of mothers' diets on the intelligence of offspring.* N. Y.: Columbia Univ. Press. **100**

Harrell, R. F., E. Woodyard, and A. I. Gates (1956), The influence of vitamin supplementation of the diets of pregnant and lactating women on the intelligence of their offspring. *Metabolism,* 5:555–62. **100**

Harris, D. B. (1957), A scale for measuring attitudes of social responsibility in children. *J. abnorm. soc. Psychol.*, 55:322–26. **62**

Harris, E. F., *see* Fleishman et al. (1955).

Hartley, E. L., and R. E. Hartley (1952), *Fundamentals of social psychology.* N. Y.: Knopf. **309**

Hartley, E. L., *see also* E. E. Maccoby et al. (1958).

Havemann, E., and P. S. West (1952), *They went to college.* N. Y.: Harcourt, Brace. **345, 349**

Havighurst, R. J. (1953), *Human development and education.* N. Y.: Longmans, Green. **55, 69**

Havighurst, R. J., *see also* Davis and Havighurst (1947).

Hay, E. N. (1943), Predicting success in machine bookkeeping. *J. appl. Psychol.*, 27:483–93. **153**

Hayakawa, S. I. (1949), *Language in thought and action.* N. Y.: Harcourt, Brace. **309**

Haythorn, W. (1956), The effects of varying combinations of authoritarian and equalitarian leaders and followers. *J. abnorm. soc. Psychol.*, 52:210–19. **323, 390**

Healy, W., A. F. Bronner, and A. M. Bowers (1930), *The structure and meaning of psychoanalysis.* N. Y.: Knopf. **221**

Heath, R. W., M. H. Maier, H. H. Remmers, and D. G. Rodgers (1957), High school students look at science. Report of Poll No. 50. *Purdue Opinion Panel,* 17(1). **7**

Heathers, G. (1955), Emotional dependence and independence in nursery school play. *J. genet. Psychol.*, 87:37–87. **40**

Hebb, D. O. (1949), *The organization of behavior.* N. Y.: Wiley. **104, 156, 171**

Hebb, D. O. (1955), The mammal and his environment. *Amer. J. Psychiat.*, 111:826–31. **170, 206, 282**

Hebb, D. O. (1958), *A textbook of psychology.* Philadelphia: Saunders. **162**

Heimann, E. K., *see* Dykman et al. (1952).

Helper, M. M. (1958), Parental evaluation of children and children's self-evaluations. *J. abnorm. soc. Psychol.*, 56:190–94. **49**

Heron, W., *see* Bexton et al. (1954).

Hertzman, M., *see* Witkin et al. (1954).

Hewes, G. W. (1957), The anthropology of posture. *Scient. Amer.*, 196(2):122–32. **279**

Heyns, R. W. (1958), *The psychology of personal adjustment.* N. Y.: Holt. **171, 353**

Hightower, N. C., *see* Smith and Hightower (1948).

Hildreth, G., *see* Rohde and Hildreth (1947).

Hildreth, H. M. (1958), Growth of divisions in the American Psychological Assn. Unpublished research in the files of the APA Central Office. **356**

Hilgard, E. R. (1951), The role of learning in perception, in Blake and Ramsey, eds., *Perception, an approach to personality.* N. Y.: Ronald. **130, 134**

Hilgard, E. R. (1956), *Theories of learning,* 2nd ed. N. Y.: Appleton-Century-Crofts. **127**

Hilgard, E. R., *see also* Noyes and Hilgard (1946).

Hinkle, L. E., Jr., and H. G. Wolff (1957), Health and the social environment: experimental investigations, in Leighton et al., eds., *Explorations in social psychiatry.* N. Y.: Basic Books. **98**

Hoffer, E. (1951), *The true believer.* N. Y.: Harper. **314**

Hollander, E. P., and W. B. Webb (1955), Leadership, followership, and friendship: an analysis of peer nominations. *J. abnorm. soc. Psychol.*, 50: 163–67. **323**

Hollingshead, A. B. (1949), *Elmtown's youth.* N. Y.: Wiley. **289**

Hollingshead, A. B., and F. C. Redlich (1958), *Social class and mental illness.* N. Y.: Wiley. **253, 263**

Hollingworth, H. L. (1913), *Advertising and selling: principles of appeal and response.* N. Y.: Appleton-Century-Crofts. **137**

Holmes, J. A. (1958), Spelling disability as a functional analogue of repression: a psycho-physiological experiment in education. Unpublished paper delivered before the annual convention of the Amer. Educ. Res. Assn. **124**

Holway, A. H., and E. G. Boring (1941), Determinants of apparent visual size with distance variant. *Amer. J. Psychol.*, 54:21–37. **135**

Holzinger, K. J., *see* Newman et al. (1937).

Honzik, M. P., J. W. Macfarlane, and L. Allen (1948), The stability of mental test performance between 2 and 18 years. *J. exp. Educ.*, 17:309–24. **207**

Horney, K. (1937), *The neurotic personality of our time.* N. Y.: Norton. **236**

Horney, K. (1945), *Our inner conflicts.* N. Y.: Norton. **163**

Horst, P., *see* Strother et al. (1957).

Horton, G. P., *see* Guthrie and Horton (1946).

Horton, R. E., R. E. Mainer, and H. H. Remmers (1953), Candidates and issues of the 1952 election as seen six months later. *Purdue Opinion Panel,* Purdue Univ., 12(3): Poll No. 35. **389**

Horton, R. E., *see also* Remmers et al. (1952).

Hoskins, R. G. (1946), *The biology of schizophrenia.* N. Y.: Norton. **98**

Hovland, C. I., and R. R. Sears (1940), Minor studies in aggression: VI. Correlation of lynchings with economic indices. *J. Psychol.*, 9:301–10. **183**

Huff, D. (1954), *How to lie with statistics.* N. Y.: Norton. **191**

Hull, C. L. (1943), *Principles of behavior.* N. Y.: Appleton-Century-Crofts. **118**

Hurley, J. R. (1957), Achievement imagery and motivational instructions as determinants of verbal learning. *J. Pers.*, 25:274–82. **232**

Hurlock, E. B. (1927), The use of group rivalry as an incentive. *J. abnorm. soc. Psychol.*, 22:278–90. **324**

Hyman, H., *see* Katz and Hyman (1947).

Information and Education Division, U.S. War Dept. (1947), The effects of presenting "one side" versus "both sides" in changing opinions on a controversial subject, in Newcomb and Hartley, eds., *Readings in social psychology*. N. Y.: Holt. **395**

Irion, A. L., *see* McGeoch and Irion (1952).

James, W. (1890), *The principles of psychology* N. Y.: Holt. **222**

Janis, I. L. (1958), *Psychological stress*. N. Y.: Wiley. **258**

Janis, I. L., and S. Feshbach (1953), Effects of fear-arousing communications. *J. abnorm. soc. Psychol.*, 48:78–92. **394**

Jenkins, J. G. (1948), Nominating technique as a method of evaluating air group morale. *J. Aviation Med.*, 19:12–19. **325**

Jenkins, W. O. (1952), The tactual discrimination of shapes for coding aircraft-type controls, in M. L. Blum, ed., *Readings in experimental industrial psychology*. N. Y.: Prentice-Hall. **369**

Jersild, A. (1957), *The psychology of adolescence*. N. Y.: Macmillan. **76**

Johnson, H. M., T. H. Swan, and G. E. Weigand (1930), In what position do healthy people sleep? *J. Amer. Med. Assn.*, 94:2058–68. **95**

Johnson, M. L., *see* Clark et al. (1946).

Jones, E. S. (1956), *College graduates and their later success*. Univ. of Buffalo Studies, 22(4). **345, 347, 349**

Jones, H. E. (1943), *Development in adolescence: approaches to the study of the individual*. N. Y.: Appleton-Century-Crofts. **56**

Jones, H. E. (1954), The environment and mental development, in L. Carmichael, ed., *Manual of child psychology*, 2nd ed. N. Y.: Wiley. **37**

Jones, H. E., and H. S. Conrad (1933), The growth and decline of intelligence: a study of a homogeneous group between the ages of ten and sixty. *Genet. psychol. Monogr.*, 13:233–98. **209**

Jones, M. C., and P. H. Mussen (1958), Self-conceptions, motivations, and interpersonal attitudes of early- and late-maturing girls. *Child Develpm.*, 29:491–502. **57**

Joseph, A., *see* Kaplan et al. (1956).

Judd, C. H. (1908), The relation of special training to general intelligence. *Educ. Rev.*, 36:28–42. **120**

Jurgensen, C. E. (1944), Report on the "Classification Inventory," a personality test for industrial use. *J. appl. Psychol.*, 28:445–60. **364**

Kahl, J. A., and J. A. Davis (1955), A comparison of indexes of socio-economic status. *Amer. sociol. Rev.*, 20:317–25. **287**

Kalhorn, J., *see* Baldwin et al. (1945).

Kalish, D., *see* Tolman et al. (1946).

Kallmann, F. J. (1946), The genetic theory of schizophrenia. *Amer. J. Psychiat.*, 103:309–22. **98**

Kaplan, B., M. A. Rickers-Ovsiankina, and A. Joseph (1956), An attempt to sort Rorschach records from four cultures. *J. proj. Tech.*, 20:172–80. **232**

Karli, P. (1956), The Norway rat's killing response to the white mouse: an experimental analysis. *Behaviour*, 10:81–101. **155**

Karolchuck, P. A., and L. Worell (1956), Achievement motivation and learning. *J. abnorm. soc. Psychol.*, 53:255–56. **232**

Katz, B., *see* Secord et al. (1956).

Katz, D., D. Cartwright, S. Eldersveld, and A. McC. Lee (1954), *Public opinion and propaganda*. N. Y.: Dryden. **375, 400**

Katz, D., and H. Hyman (1947), Morale in war industries, in Newcomb and Hartley, eds., *Readings in social psychology*. N. Y.: Holt. **315**

Keliher, A. V. (1938), *Life and growth*. N. Y.: Appleton-Century-Crofts. **57**

Kelley, H. H. (1950), The warm-cold variable in first impressions of persons. *J. Pers.*, 18:431–39. **298**

Kendall, P. L., and K. Wolf (1949), The analysis of deviant cases in communications research, in Lazarsfeld and Stanton, eds., *Communications research, 1948–1949*. N. Y.: Harper. **300**

Kendall, W. E., *see* Stone and Kendall (1956).

Kerr, W. A., *see* Van Zelst and Kerr (1951), Tobolski and Kerr (1952), and Dykman et al. (1952).

Ketchel, R., *see* Spence et al. (1956).

Key, C. B., *see* Sherman and Key (1932).

King, H. E., *see* Coyne et al. (1943).

King, S. H., *see* Funkenstein et al. (1957).

Kinsey, A. C., et al. (1948), *Sexual behavior in the human male*. Philadelphia: Saunders. **66**

Kinsey, A. C., et al. (1953), *Sexual behavior in the human female*. Philadelphia: Saunders. **66**

Kipnis, D. (1958), The effects of leadership style and leadership power upon the inducement of an attitude change. *J. abnorm. soc. Psychol.*, 57:173–80. **396**

Klein, G. S. (1951), The personal world through perception, in Blake and Ramsey, eds., *Perception, an approach to personality*. N. Y.: Ronald. **139, 140**

Klein, G. S., *see also* G. J. W. Smith et al. (1959).

Klineberg, O. (1956), The role of the psychologist in international affairs. *J. soc. Issues*, Supplement No. 9. **391**

Klubeck, S., *see* Bass et al. (1953).

Kluckhohn, C. (1949), *Mirror for man*. N. Y.: McGraw-Hill. **33, 36, 289**

Kluckhohn, C., H. A. Murray, and D. M. Schneider, eds. (1953), *Personality in nature, society, and culture*, rev. ed. N. Y.: Knopf. **273, 289**

Knauft, E. B. (1949), A selection battery for bake-shop managers. *J. appl. Psychol.*, 33:304–15. **364**

Koch, H. L. (1955), Some personality correlates of sex, sibling position, and sex of sibling among five- and six-year-old children. *Genet. psychol. Monogr.*, 52:3–50. **38**

Koffka, K. (1935), *Principles of Gestalt psychology*. N. Y.: Harcourt, Brace. **223**

Köhler, W. (1925), *The mentality of apes*. N. Y.: Harcourt, Brace. **114, 127**

Köhler, W. (1958), The present situation in brain physiology. *Amer. Psychologist*, 13:150–54. **87**

Kornhauser, R. R. (1953), The Warner approach to social stratification, in Bendix and Lipset, eds.,

Class, status, and power. Glencoe, Ill.: Free Press. **336**

Kounin, J. S., *see* Gump and Kounin (1957).

Krech, D., and R. S. Crutchfield (1948), *Theory and problems of social psychology.* N. Y.: McGraw-Hill. **274, 394**

Krechevsky, I. (1937), Brain mechanisms and variability: II. Variability when no learning is involved. *J. comp. Psychol.,* 23:139–63. **113**

Kretschmer, E. (1925), *Physique and character.* N. Y.: Harcourt, Brace. **225**

Kriedt, P. H., and M. S. Gadel (1953), Prediction of turnover among clerical workers. *J. appl. Psychol.,* 37:338–40. **360**

Kube, E., *see* Lehner and Kube (1955).

Kuhlen, R. G., *see* Pressey and Kuhlen (1957).

Laird, D. A. (1932), How the consumer estimates quality by subconscious sensory impressions. *J. appl. Psychol.,* 16:241–46. **137**

Landis, C., *see* Coyne et al. (1943).

Landis, J. T. (1957), Physical and mental emotional changes accompanying the menstrual cycle. *Proc. Pacific Sociol. Soc.; Res. Stud. State Coll. of Washington,* 25 (2):155–62. **97**

Langer, W. C. (1943), *Psychology and human living.* N. Y.: Appleton-Century-Crofts. **236**

Langham, P., *see* Lanzetta et al. (1954).

Lanzetta, J. T., D. Haefner, P. Langham, and H. Axelrod (1954), Some effects of situational threat on group behavior. *J. abnorm. soc. Psychol.,* 49:445–53. **317**

LaPiere, R. (1934), Attitudes vs. actions. *Soc. Forces,* 13:230–37. **390**

Lawrence, M. (1949), *Studies in human behavior.* Princeton: Princeton Univ. Press. **135, 151**

Lazarus, R. S., C. W. Eriksen, and C. P. Fonda (1951), Personality dynamics and auditory perceptual recognition. *J. Pers.,* 19:471–82. **141**

Leary, T. (1957), *Interpersonal diagnosis of personality.* N. Y.: Ronald. **301, 319**

Leavitt, H. J. (1951), Some effects of certain communication patterns on group performance. *J. abnorm. soc. Psychol.,* 46:38–50. **320**

Leavitt, H. J. (1958), *Managerial psychology.* Chicago: Univ. of Chicago Press. **375**

Leavitt, H. J., *see also* Williams and Leavitt (1947).

Lee, A. McC., *see* D. Katz et al. (1954).

Leeper, R. W. (1948), A motivational theory of emotion to replace "emotion as a disorganized response." *Psychol. Bull.,* 55:5–21. **162**

Lehman, H. C. (1953), *Age and achievement.* Princeton: Princeton Univ. Press. **73**

Lehner, G. F. J., and E. Kube (1955), *The dynamics of personal adjustment.* Englewood Cliffs, N. J.: Prentice-Hall. **353**

Leighton, A. H., J. A. Clausen, and R. N. Wilson, eds. (1957), *Explorations in social psychiatry.* N. Y.: Basic Books. **282**

Lenkoski, L. D., *see* Pilot and Lenkoski (1957).

Lester, R. A. (1954), *Hiring practices and labor competition.* Princeton: Princeton Univ. Press. **356**

Levin, H., *see* Sears et al. (1957).

Levine, J. M., and J. Butler (1952), Lecture vs. group discussion in changing behavior. *J. appl. Psychol.,* 36:29–33. **125, 396**

Levine, R., I. Chein, and G. Murphy (1942), The relation of the intensity of a need to the amount

of perceptual distortion: a preliminary report. *J. Psychol.,* 13:283–93. **147**

Levinson, D. J., *see* Adorno et al. (1950).

Levy, D. M. (1942), Psychosomatic studies of some aspects of maternal behavior. *Psychosom. Med.,* 4:223–27. **97**

Levy, J., and R. L. Monroe (1938), *The happy family.* N. Y.: Knopf. **76**

Lewin, H. S. (1953), Facts and fears about the comics. *Nation's Schools,* 52:46–48. **387**

Lewin, K. (1935), *A dynamic theory of personality.* N. Y.: McGraw-Hill. **160, 223**

Lewin, K. (1947), Group decision and social change, in Newcomb and Hartley, eds., *Readings in social psychology.* N. Y.: Holt. **396**

Lewin, K., R. Lippitt, and R. K. White (1939), Patterns of aggressive behavior in experimentally created "climates." *J. soc. Psychol.,* 10:271–99. **318, 323**

Lewin, K., *see also* Barker et al. (1941) and (1943).

Lewis, A. (1953), Research in occupational psychiatry. *Folia psychiatrica, neurologica et neurochirurgica Neerlandica,* 56:779–86. **364**

Lewis, H. B., *see* Witkin et al. (1954).

Liddell, H. S. (1954), Conditioning and emotions. *Scient. Amer.,* 190(1):48–57. **239**

Lighthall, F., *see* Fox et al. (1958).

Lindgren, H. C. (1953), Sociometric study of leadership. Unpublished research in the files of the senior author. **181**

Lindgren, H. C. (1954), *Effective leadership in human relations.* N. Y.: Nelson. **298, 329**

Lindgren, H. C. (1956), *Meaning: antidote to anxiety.* N. Y.: Nelson. **309**

Lindgren, H. C. (1959), *Psychology of personal and social adjustment,* rev. ed. N. Y.: American Book. **171, 263**

Lindgren, H. C., and F. Lindgren (1960), Expressed attitudes of American and Canadian teachers toward authority. *Psychol. Rep.,* 7:51–54. **234**

Lindgren, H. C., F. J. Mather, P. Harries, and D. Beronio (1959), Rejections of foods and occupations. Unpublished research in the files of the senior author. **338**

Lindsley, O. R., *see* Azrin and Lindsley (1956).

Lindzey, G., *see* Hall and Lindzey (1957).

Lippitt, R., *see* Lewin, Lippitt, and White (1939) and White and Lippitt (1953).

Lipset, S. M., *see* Bendix and Lipset (1953).

Lodahl, T. M., *see* Ghiselli and Lodahl (1958) and Moon and Lodahl (1956).

Loeb, M. B. (1953), Implications of status differentiation for personal and social development. *Harvard educ. Rev.,* 23:168–74. **287, 294**

Lotsof, E. J., and W. L. Downing (1956), Two measures of anxiety. *J. consult. Psychol.,* 20:170. **183**

Lowell, E. L., *see* McClelland et al. (1953).

Luckhardt, A. B., and A. J. Carlson (1915), Contributions to the physiology of the stomach: XVII. On the chemical control of the gastric hunger mechanism. *Amer. J. Physiol.,* 36:37–46. **94**

Lutherman, C. Z., *see* Allee et al. (1939).

Maccoby, E. E., et al. (1954), Methods of child-rearing in two social classes, in Martin and Stendler, eds., *Readings in child development.* N. Y.: Harcourt, Brace. **285**

Maccoby, E. E., T. M. Newcomb, and E. L. Hartley, eds. (1958), *Readings in social psychology,* 3rd ed. N. Y.: Holt. **309, 329, 400**

Maccoby, E. E., *see also* Sears et al. (1957).

Macfarlane, J. W., *see* Honzik et al. (1948).

Machover, K., *see* Witkin et al. (1954).

MacKinnon, W. J., and R. Centers (1956), Authoritarianism and urban stratification. *Amer. J. Sociol.,* 61:610–20. **285, 389**

Mahoney, T. A., *see* Perry and Mahoney (1955).

Maier, M. H., *see* Heath et al. (1957).

Maier, N. R. F. (1949), *Frustration.* N. Y.: McGraw-Hill. **239**

Maier, N. R. F. (1952), *Principles of human relations: applications to management.* N. Y.: Wiley. **375**

Maier, N. R. F. (1955), *Psychology in industry,* 2nd ed. Boston: Houghton Mifflin. **359, 375**

Mainer, R. E., *see* R. E. Horton et al. (1953).

Malinowski, B. (1927), *Sex and repression in savage society.* N. Y.: Harcourt, Brace. **222**

Malm, F. T. (1955), Hiring procedures and selection standards in the San Francisco Bay Area. *Ind. Labor Relations Rev.,* 8:231–52. **357**

Malzberg, B. (1949), A statistical study of some characteristics of drug addicts. *Ment. Hyg. News* (N. Y. State Dept. Ment. Hyg.), 20(June):4–8. **248**

Malzberg, B. (1956), Education and mental disease in New York State. *Ment. Hyg.* (*N. Y.*), 40:177–95. **74, 254**

Mandler, G., *see* Sarason et al. (1952).

Marquis, D. G., et al. (1951), A social psychological study of the decision-making conference, in H. Guetzkow, ed., *Groups, leadership, and men.* New Brunswick, N. J.: Rutgers Univ. Press. **316**

Martin, W. E., and C. B. Stendler, eds. (1954), *Readings in child development.* N. Y.: Harcourt, Brace. **51**

Martin, W. E., and C. B. Stendler (1959), *Child development,* rev. ed. N. Y.: Harcourt, Brace. **51**

Maslow, A. H. (1954), *Motivation and personality.* N. Y.: Harper. **45, 54, 154, 268, 274, 297**

Maslow, A. H., and N. L. Mintz (1956), Effects of esthetic surroundings: I. Initial short-term effects of three esthetic conditions upon perceiving "energy" and "well-being" in faces. *J. Psychol.,* 41:247–54. **146**

Mason, H. L., *see* R. D. Williams et al. (1940).

Masserman, J. H., and K. S. Yum (1946), An analysis of the influence of alcohol on experimental neurosis in cats. *Psychosom. Med.,* 8:36–52. **247**

May, R. (1950), *The meaning of anxiety.* N. Y.: Ronald. **240, 263**

McArthur, C. (1956), Personalities of first and second children. *Psychiatry,* 19:47–54. **37, 48**

McCarthy, D. (1954), Language development in children, in L. Carmichael, ed., *Manual of child psychology,* 2nd ed. N. Y.: Wiley. **32**

McClelland, D. C., ed. (1955), *Studies in motivation.* N. Y.: Appleton-Century-Crofts. **171**

McClelland, D. C., J. W. Atkinson, R. A. Clark, and E. L. Lowell (1953), *The achievement motive.* N. Y.: Appleton-Century-Crofts. **214, 232**

McClelland, D. C., A. L. Baldwin, U. Bronfenbrenner, and F. L. Strodtbeck (1958), *Talent and society: new perspectives in the identification of talent.* Princeton: Van Nostrand. **214**

McCollom, I. N. (1959), Psychologists in industry in the United States. *Amer. Psychologist,* 14:704–08. **356**

McConnell, J. V., R. L. Cutler, and E. B. McNeil (1958), Subliminal stimulation: an overview. *Amer. Psychologist,* 13:229–42. **151, 373**

McConnell, R. A., *see* Schmeidler and McConnell (1958).

McGeoch, J. A., and A. L. Irion (1952), *The psychology of human learning.* N. Y.: Longmans, Green. **111, 120**

McGinnies, E., *see* Postman et al. (1948).

McGranahan, D. V. (1946), A comparison of social attitudes among American and German youth. *J. abnorm. soc. Psychol.,* 41:245–56. **390**

McGuire, F. L. (1956), The safe-driver inventory. *U.S. Armed Forces med. J.,* 7:1249–64. **364**

McNeil, E. B., *see* McConnell et al. (1958).

McNemar, Q. (1955), *Psychological statistics,* 2nd ed. N. Y.: Wiley. **183, 184, 191**

Mead, M. (1935), *Sex and temperament in three primitive societies.* N. Y.: Morrow. **273, 289**

Mead, M., ed (1937), *Competition and cooperation among primitive peoples.* N. Y.: McGraw-Hill. **324**

Mead, M., *see also* Bateson and Mead (1942).

Meissner, P. B., *see* Witkin et al. (1954).

Melzack, R., and W. R. Thompson (1956), Effects of early experience on social behavior. *Canad. J. Psychol.,* 10:82–90. **206**

Merrill, M. A. (1938), Significance of IQ's on the revised Stanford-Binet scales. *J. educ. Psychol.,* 29:641–51. **195**

Merrill, M. A., *see also* Terman and Merrill (1937).

Miles, C. C., and W. R. Miles (1932), The correlation of intelligence scores and chronological age from early to late maturity. *Amer. J. Psychol.,* 44:44–78. **209**

Miller, C. H. (1956), Occupational choice and values. *Personnel guid. J.,* 35:244–46. **338**

Miller, N. E. (1948), Theory and experiment relating psychoanalytic displacement to stimulus-response generalization. *J. abnorm. soc. Psychol.,* 43:155–78. **227**

Miller, N. E., and R. Bugelski (1948), Minor studies of aggression: II. The influence of frustrations imposed by the in-group on attitudes expressed toward out-groups. *J. Psychol.,* 25:437–42. **227**

Miller, N. E., and J. Dollard (1941), *Social learning and imitation.* New Haven: Yale Univ. Press. **116**

Miller, N. E., *see also* Dollard and Miller (1950) and Delgado et al. (1954).

Mills, J., *see* Aronson and Mills (1959).

Milner, P., *see* Olds and Milner (1954).

Mintz, A. (1951), Non-adaptive group behavior. *J. abnorm. soc. Psychol.,* 46:150–59. **324**

Mintz, N. L. (1956), Effects of esthetic surroundings: II. Prolonged and repeated experience in a "beautiful" and an "ugly" room. *J. Psychol.,* 41:459–66. **146**

Mintz, N. L., *see also* Maslow and Mintz (1956).

Mirsky, I. A., *see* Weiner et al. (1957).

Moeller, G., *see* Applezweig and Moeller (1958).

Mohandessi, K., and P. J. Runkel (1958), Some socioeconomic correlates of academic aptitude. *J. educ. Psychol.,* 49:47–52. **206**

Monroe, R. L. (1955), *Schools of psychoanalytic thought.* N. Y.: Dryden. **236**

Monroe, R. L., *see also* Levy and Monroe (1938).

Montagu, M. F. Ashley (1950), *On being human.* N. Y.: Henry Schuman. **268**

Montagu, M. F. Ashley (1953), *Darwin, competition, and cooperation*. N. Y.: Henry Schuman. **156**

Moon, L. E., and T. M. Lodahl (1956), The reinforcing effect of changes in illumination on lever-pressing in the monkey. *Amer. J. Psychol.*, 69:288–90. **114**

Moran, L. J., G. W. Fairweather, S. Fisher, and R. B. Morton (1956), Psychological concomitants to rate of recovery from tuberculosis. *J. consult. Psychol.*, 20:199–203. **183**

Morgan, C. T., and E. Stellar (1950), *Physiological psychology*, 2nd ed. N. Y.: McGraw-Hill. **94, 95, 104**

Morse, N. C., and R. S. Weiss (1955), The function and meaning of work and the job. *Amer. sociol. Rev.*, 20:191–98. **324, 349**

Morton, R. B., *see* Moran et al. (1956).

Mountcastle, V. B., *see* Bard and Mountcastle (1947).

Muckler, F. A., *see* O'Kelly and Muckler (1955).

Mullahy, P. (1948), *Oedipus, myth and complex*. N. Y.: Nelson. **236**

Mullen, F. A. (1952), Truancy and classroom disorder as a symptom of personality problems. *J. educ. Psychol.*, 41:97–109. **272**

Munn, N. L. (1946), *Psychology*. Boston: Houghton Mifflin. **80**

Munn, N. L. (1957), The evolution of mind. *Scient. Amer.*, 196(6):140–50. **115**

Murphy, G., ed. (1945), *Human nature and enduring peace*. Boston: Houghton Mifflin. **391**

Murphy, G. (1947), *Personality: a biosocial approach to origins and structure*. N. Y.: Harper. **236**

Murphy, G. (1949), *Historical introduction to modern psychology*. N. Y.: Harcourt, Brace. **26**

Murphy, G., *see also* R. Levine et al. (1942).

Murray, E. J., and M. Cohen (1959), Mental illness, milieu therapy, and social organization in ward groups. *J. abnorm. soc. Psychol.*, 58:58–64. **252**

Murray, H. A. (1933), The effect of fear upon estimates of the maliciousness of other personalities. *J. soc. Psychol.*, 4:310–29. **147**

Murray, H. A., *see also* Kluckhohn et al. (1953).

Mussen, P. H., and A. B. Wyszynski (1952), Personality and political participation. *Hum. Relat.*, 5:65–82. **397**

Mussen, P. H., *see also* M. C. Jones and Mussen (1958).

Nelson, V. L., *see* Sontag et al. (1955) and (1958).

Newcomb, T. M. (1943), *Personality and social change*. N. Y.: Dryden. **344**

Newcomb, T. M. (1947), Autistic hostility and social reality. *Hum. Rel.*, 1:68–86. **298**

Newcomb, T. M. (1950), *Social psychology*. N. Y.: Dryden. **274, 278, 289**

Newcomb, T. M. (1952), Attitude development as a function of reference groups: the Bennington study, in Swanson, Newcomb, and Hartley, eds., *Readings in social psychology*, rev. ed. N. Y.: Holt. **344**

Newcomb, T. M., *see also* Chowdhry and Newcomb (1952) and Maccoby et al. (1958).

Newman, H. H., F. N. Freeman, and K. J. Holzinger (1937), *Twins: a study of heredity and environment*. Chicago: Univ. Chicago Press. **203**

Nielsen, G., *see* Baldwin and Nielsen (1956).

Noland, E. W., *see* Calhoon et al. (1958).

Nordlie, P. G., *see* Greer et al. (1954).

Noyes, C. E., and E. R. Hilgard (1946), Surveys of consumer requirements, in A. B. Blankenship, ed., *How to conduct consumer and opinion research*. N. Y.: Harper. **372**

Oden, M. H., *see* Bayley and Oden (1955).

Office of Strategic Services, Assessment Staff (1948), *Assessment of men*. N. Y.: Rinehart. **365**

Ogden, C. K., and I. A. Richards (1927), *The meaning of meaning*. N. Y.: Harcourt, Brace. **304**

Ogg, E. (1955), *Psychologists in action*. Public Affairs Pamphlet No. 229. N. Y.: Public Affairs Committee. **16, 26**

O'Kelly, L. I. (1949), *An introduction to psychopathology*. Englewood Cliffs, N. J.: Prentice-Hall. **250, 252**

O'Kelly, L. I., and F. A. Muckler (1955), *Introduction to psychopathology*, 2nd ed. Englewood Cliffs, N. J.: Prentice-Hall. **252**

Olden, C. (1952), Notes on child-rearing in America, in *Psychoanalytic study of the child*, vol. 7. N. Y.: International Universities Press. **272**

Olds, J., and P. Milner (1954), Positive reinforcement produced by electrical stimulation of septal area and other regions of rat brains. *J. comp. physiol. Psychol.*, 47:419–27. **96**

Opinion Research Corp. (1952), Industrial relations: policy and action. *Public Opinion Index for Industry*, 10(10). **322**

Ort, R. S. (1950), A study of role conflicts as related to happiness in marriage. *J. abnorm. soc. Psychol.*, 45:691–99. **70**

Osgood, C. E., C. J. Suci, and P. H. Tannenbaum (1957), *The measurement of meaning*. Urbana: Univ. of Illinois Press. **309**

Owens, W. A. (1953), Age and mental abilities: a longitudinal study. *Genet. psychol. Monogr.*, 48:3–54. **73, 209**

Palmer, D., and G. D. Greer (1956), An analysis of certain determinants, characteristics, and covariates of basic trainee leadership sociometric data. Unpublished paper delivered at annual convention of Western Psychol. Assn. **201**

Parten, M. L. (1932), Social participation among preschool children. *J. abnorm. soc. Psychol.*, 27:243–69. **39**

Paterson, D. G., *see* Deeg and Paterson (1947).

Pavlov, I. P. (1927), *Conditioned reflexes*. London: Oxford Univ. Press. **110**

Pearson, G. H. J. (1949), *Emotional disorders of children*. N. Y.: Norton. **159**

Peck, R. M., and L. H. Storms (1956), Validity of the Marsh-Hilliard-Liechti MMPI sexual deviation scale in a state hospital population. *J. consult. Psychol.*, 20:133–36. **183**

Pelser, H. E., *see* Dekker et al. (1957).

Penfield, W. and T. Rasmussen (1950), *The cerebral cortex of man*. N. Y.: Macmillan. **104**

Perry, D., and T. A. Mahoney (1955), In-plant communications and employee morale. *Personnel Psychol.*, 8:339–46. **384**

Pfeiffer, J. (1955), *The human brain*. N. Y.: Harper. **104**

Pilot, M. L., and L. D. Lenkoski (1957), Duodenal ulcer in one of identical twins. *Psychosom. Med.*, 19:221–27. **80**

Pinneau, S. R. (1955a), The infantile disorders of hospitalism and anaclitic depression. *Psychol. Bull.*, 52:429–52. **45**

Pinneau, S. R. (1955b), Reply to Dr. Spitz. *Psychol. Bull.*, 52:459–62. **45**

Plant, W. T. (1958), Changes in ethnocentrism associated with a four-year college education. *J. educ. Psychol.*, 49:162–65. **390**

Podolsky, A. (1955), The chemical brew of criminal behavior. *J. crim. Law Criminol.*, 45:675–78. **92**

Postman, L., J. S. Bruner, and E. McGinnies (1948), Personal values as selective factors in perception. *J. abnorm. soc. Psychol.*, 43:142–54. **146**

Powell, M. (1955), Age and sex differences in degree of conflict within certain areas of psychological adjustment. *Psychol. Monogr.*, 69: No. 387. **67**

Pred, G. D. (1948), *A comparison of the test performance of "good" and "poor" industrial supervisors.* Unpublished master's thesis, Purdue Univ. **364**

Pressey, S. L., and R. G. Kuhlen (1957), *Psychological development through the life span.* N. Y.: Harper. **76, 353**

Radke, M. J. (1946), *The relation of parental authority to children's behavior and attitudes.* Minneapolis: Univ. of Minn. Press. **43**

Radler, D. H., *see* Remmers and Radler (1957).

Rafferty, J. E., *see* Rotter and Rafferty (1950).

Ramsey, G. V., *see* Blake and Ramsey (1951).

Ransom, S. W. (1939), Somnolence caused by hypothalamic lesions in the monkey. *Arch. Neurol. Psychiat.*, 41:1–23. **95**

Raphelson, A. C., *see* Atkinson and Raphelson (1956).

Rasmussen, T., *see* Penfield and Rasmussen (1950).

Redlich, F. C., *see* Hollingshead and Redlich (1958).

Reiser, M. F., *see* Weiner et al. (1957).

Remmers, H. H., et al. (1947 et seq.), *Purdue Opinion Panels.* Lafayette, Ind.: Division of Educational Research, Purdue Univ. **285, 389**

Remmers, H. H., R. E. Horton, and B. B. Scarborough (1952), Youth views purposes, practices, and procedures in education. Report of Poll No. 31. *Purdue Opinion Panel.* 11(2). **59**

Remmers, H. H., and D. H. Radler (1957), *The American teenager.* Indianapolis: Bobbs-Merrill. **63, 67, 76**

Remmers, H. H., *see also* Heath et al. (1957) and Horton et al. (1953).

Rensch, B. (1957), The intelligence of elephants. *Scient. Amer.*, 196(2):44–49. **121**

Reymert, M. L., ed. (1950), *Feelings and emotions.* N. Y.: McGraw-Hill. **171**

Ribble, M. A. (1943), *The rights of infants.* N. Y.: Columbia Univ. Press. **45**

Richards, I. A., *see* Ogden and Richards (1927).

Rickers-Ovsiankina, M. A., *see* Kaplan et al. (1956).

Riesman, D., N. Glazer, and R. Denny (1950), *The lonely crowd.* New Haven: Yale Univ. Press. **55, 210**

Ritchie, B. F., *see* Tolman et al. (1946).

Roberts, H. V., *see* Wallis and Roberts (1956).

Roberts, W. W., *see* Delgado et al. (1954).

Rock, J. (1958), Repetition and learning. *Scient. Amer.*, 199(2): 68–72. **11**

Roden, A. (1958), Stimulus, residual, and background in contributing behavior. Unpublished research paper read at annual convention of Amer. Educ. Res. Assn. **395**

Rodgers, D. G., *see* Heath et al. (1957).

Roe, A. (1953), *The making of a scientist.* N. Y.: Dodd, Mead. **353**

Roe, A. (1956), *The psychology of occupations.* N. Y.: Wiley. **341, 353**

Roethlisberger, F. J. (1941), *Management and morale.* Cambridge: Harvard Univ. Press. **349**

Roethlisberger, F. J., and W. J. Dickson (1939), *Management and the worker.* Cambridge: Harvard Univ. Press. **367, 375**

Rogers, C. R. (1942), *Counseling and psychotherapy.* Boston: Houghton Mifflin. **255**

Rogers, C. R. (1951), *Client-centered therapy.* Boston: Houghton Mifflin. **125, 127, 147, 255, 263**

Rogers, C. R. (1952), Personal thoughts on teaching and learning. Speech before the Harvard Conference on "Classroom approaches to influencing human behavior." **124**

Rogers, C. R., and R. F. Dymond, eds. (1954), *Psychotherapy and personality change.* Chicago: Univ. of Chicago Press. **224, 236**

Rohde, A. R., and G. Hildreth (1947), *Sentence completions test.* N. Y.: Psychological Corp. **230**

Rosenberg, M., et al. (1957), *Occupations and values.* Glencoe, Ill.: Free Press. **334, 339, 351, 353**

Rosenman, R. H., *see* Friedman and Rosenman (1959).

Rosenzweig, S. (1948), *Rosenzweig Picture-Frustration Test.* St. Louis: S. Rosenzweig. **230**

Rotter, J. B. (1954), *Social learning and clinical psychology.* Englewood Cliffs, N. J.: Prentice-Hall. **273**

Rotter, J. B., and J. E. Rafferty (1950), *The Rotter Incomplete Sentence Blank.* N. Y.: Psychological Corp. **230**

Ruesch, J. (1957), *Disturbed communication.* N. Y.: Norton. **307, 309**

Ruesch, J., and G. Bateson (1951), *Communication: the social matrix of psychiatry.* N. Y.: Norton. **307**

Runkel, P. J., *see* Mohandessi and Runkel (1958).

Ryan, T. A., and P. C. Smith (1954), *Principles of industrial psychology.* N. Y.: Ronald. **375**

Saddler, L. E. (1949), *A comparison of students remaining in an engineering curriculum and students transferring from engineering to other curricula.* Unpublished doctoral dissertation. Univ. of Missouri. **341**

Sanford, F. H. (1951), The use of a projective technique in attitude surveying. *Publ. opin. Quart.*, 14:697–709. **371**

Sanford, F. H. (1952), Annual report of the Executive Secretary. *Amer. Psychologist,* 7:686–96. **15**

Sanford, R. N., et al. (1956), Personality development during the college years. *J. soc. Issues,* 12(4). **344**

Sanford, R. N., *see also* Adorno et al. (1950).

Sarason, S. B., G. Mandler, and P. G. Craighill (1952), The effect of differential instructions on anxiety and learning. *J. abnorm. soc. Psychol.*, 47:561–65. **123**

Sarason, S. B., *see also* Fox et al. (1958).

Sargent, S. S., and R. C. Williamson (1958), *Social psychology: an introduction to the study of human relations.* N. Y.: Ronald. **289, 329**

Sauer, E. G. F. (1958), Celestial navigation by birds. *Scient. Amer.,* 199(2):42–47. **130**

Sawrey, W. L., J. J. Conger, and E. S. Turrell (1956), An experimental investigation of the role of psychological factors in the production of gastric ulcers in rats. *J. comp. physiol. Psychol.,* 49:457–61. **117**

Sawrey, W. L., and J. D. Weisz (1956), An experimental method of producing gastric ulcers. *J. comp. physiol. Psychol.,* 49:269–70. **117**

Schachter, S., *see also* Festinger et al. (1950).

Schaie, K. W., *see* Strother et al. (1957).

Scarborough, B. B., *see* Remmers et al. (1952).

Schifferes, J. J. (1960), *Essentials of healthier living.* N. Y.: Wiley. **83, 85, 89**

Schmeidler, G. R., and R. A. McConnell (1958), *ESP and personality patterns.* New Haven: Yale Univ. Press. **139**

Schneider, D. M., *see* Kluckhohn et al. (1953).

Schramm, W., ed. (1954), *The process and effects of mass communication.* Urbana: Univ. of Illinois Press. **400**

Scott, T. H., *see* Bexton et al. (1954).

Sears, R. R., E. E. Maccoby, and H. Levin (1957), *Patterns of child rearing.* Evanston: Row, Peterson. **66**

Sears, R. R., *see also* Hovland and Sears (1940).

Secord, P. F., W. Bevan, and B. Katz (1956), The Negro stereotype and perceptual accentuation. *J. abnorm. soc. Psychol.,* 53:78–83. **112**

Senden, M. V. (1932), *Raum- und Gestaltauffassung bei operierten Blindgeborenen vor und nach Operation.* Leipzig: Barth. **131**

Sewell, W. H., A. O. Haller, and M. A. Straus (1957), Social status and educational and occupational aspiration. *Amer. sociol. Rev.,* 22:67–73. **210**

Shaffer, L. F. (1953), Of whose certainty I cannot doubt. *Amer. Psychologist,* 8:608–23. **22**

Shaffer, L. F., and E. J. Shoben, Jr. (1956), *The psychology of adjustment.* Boston: Houghton Mifflin. **98, 171, 263**

Shartle, C. L. (1956), *Executive performance and leadership.* Englewood Cliffs, N. J.: Prentice-Hall. **375**

Shaw, M. C., and D. J. Brown (1957), Scholastic underachievement of bright college students. *Personnel guid. J.,* 36:195–99. **347**

Shaw, M. E. (1954a), Some effects of problem complexity upon problem solution efficiency in different communication nets. *J. exp. Psychol.,* 48:211–17. **321**

Shaw, M. E. (1954b), Some effects of unequal distribution of information upon group performance in various communication nets. *J. abnorm. soc. Psychol.,* 49:547–53. **321**

Sheldon, W. H. (1954), *Atlas of men: a guide for somatotyping the adult male at all ages.* N. Y.: Harper. **225**

Sheldon, W. H., and S. S. Stevens (1942), *The varieties of temperament.* N. Y.: Harper. **98, 225**

Sheldon, W. H., S. S. Stevens, and W. B. Tucker (1940), *The varieties of human physique.* N. Y.: Harper. **98, 225**

Sherif, M. (1935), A study of some social factors in perception. *Arch. Psychol.,* 27: No. 187. **147**

Sherif, M. (1936), *The psychology of social norms.* N. Y.: Harper. **275, 276**

Sherif, M., and C. Sherif (1953), *Groups in harmony and tension.* N. Y.: Harper. **270, 275, 281, 283, 289**

Sherif, M., and C. Sherif (1956), *An outline of social psychology.* N. Y.: Harper. **329**

Sherman, M., and C. B. Key (1932), The intelligence of isolated mountain children. *Child Develpm.,* 3:279–90. **203**

Shoben, E. J., Jr. (1949), The assessment of parental attitudes in relation to child adjustment. *Genet. psychol. Monogr.,* 39:101–48. **44**

Shoben, E. J., Jr., *see also* Shaffer and Shoben (1956).

Shouby, A. (1951), The influence of the Arabic language on the psychology of the Arabs. *Middle East J.,* 5:284–303. **296**

Shuman, J. T. (1945), Value of aptitude tests for factory workers in the aircraft engine and propeller industries. *J. appl. Psychol.,* 29:156–60. **362**

Shuttleworth, F. K. (1939), The physical and mental growth of girls and boys six to nineteen in relation to age at maximum growth. *Monogr. Soc. Res. Child Develpm.,* 4: No. 3. **56**

Sidis, B. (1898), *The psychology of suggestion.* N. Y.: Appleton-Century-Crofts. **137**

Siegel, S. M. (1956), The relationship of hostility to authoritarianism. *J. abnorm. soc. Psychol.,* 52: 368–72. **388**

Siipola, E. M. (1935), A study of some effects of preparatory set. *Psychol. Monogr.,* 46: No. 210. **143**

Simon, S. W., and W. H. Emmons (1956), Responses to material presented during various levels of sleep. *J. exp. Psychol.,* 51:89–97. **12**

Simons, D. J., *see* Diethelm and Simons (1945).

Skinner, B. F. (1953), *Science and human behavior.* N. Y.: Macmillan. **26**

Skinner, B. F. (1957), *Verbal behavior.* N. Y.: Appleton-Century-Crofts. **309**

Sleight, R. B. (1948), The effect of instrument dial shape upon legibility. *J. appl. Psychol.,* 32:170–88. **369**

Small, L. (1953), Personality determinants of vocational choice. *Psychol. Monogr.,* 67: No. 351. **338**

Smith, B. F., *see* R. D. Williams et al. (1940).

Smith, G. J. W., D. P. Spence, and G. S. Klein (1959), Subliminal effects of verbal stimuli. *J. abnorm. soc. Psychol.,* 59:167–76. **137**

Smith, H. C. (1955), *Psychology of industrial behavior.* N. Y.: McGraw-Hill. **375**

Smith, H. L., and N. C. Hightower (1948), Incidence of functional disease (neurosis) among patients of various occupations. *Occup. Med.,* 5:182–85. **250**

Smith, H. P. (1955), Do intercultural experiences affect attitudes? *J. abnorm. soc. Psychol.,* 51:469–77. **384**

Smith, M. W. (1952), Evidences of potentialities of older workers in a manufacturing company. *Personnel Psychol.,* 5:11–18. **73**

Smith, P. C., *see* Ryan and Smith (1954).

Snider, R. S. (1958), The cerebellum. *Scient. Amer.,* 199(2):84–90. **90**

Snyder, W. U. (1947), *Casebook of nondirective counseling.* Boston: Houghton Mifflin. **258, 263**

Snygg, D., and A. W. Combs (1959), *Individual behavior,* rev. ed. N. Y.: Harper. **222, 236**

Sobelewski, E., *see* Folsom and Sobelewski (1957).

Solomon, M. D. (1951), *The personality factor of rigidity as an element in the teaching of the scientific method.* Unpublished doctoral dissertation, Michigan State College. **388**

Sontag, L. W., C. T. Baker, and V. L. Nelson (1955), Personality as a determinant of performance. *Amer. J. Orthopsychiat.,* 22:534–41. **209**

Sontag, L. W., C. T. Baker, and V. L. Nelson (1958), Mental growth and personality development: a longitudinal study. *Soc. Res. Child Develpm. Monogr.,* 23: No. 68. **207**

Spence, D. P., *see* G. J. W. Smith et al. (1959).

Spence, K. W., J. A. Taylor, and R. Ketchel (1956), Anxiety (drive) level and degree of competition in paired-associates learning. *J. exp. Psychol.,* 52:306–10. **123**

Spitz, R. A. (1945), Hospitalism. An inquiry into the genesis of psychiatric conditions in early childhood. *Psychoanalyt. Stud. Child,* 1:53–74. **45**

Spitz, R. A. (1946a), The smiling response: a contribution to the ontogenesis of social relations. *Genet. Psychol. Monogr.,* 34:57–125. **31**

Spitz, R. A. (1946b), Hospitalism: a follow-up report on investigation described in Volume 1, 1945. *Psychoanalyt. Stud. Child,* 2:113–17. **45**

Stagner, R. (1956), *The psychology of industrial conflict.* N. Y.: Wiley. **375**

Stellar, E., *see* Morgan and Stellar (1950).

Stendler, C. B., *see* Martin and Stendler (1954) and (1959).

Stevens, S. S., ed. (1951), *Handbook of experimental psychology.* N. Y.: Wiley. **104**

Stevens, S. S., *see also* Sheldon et al. (1940) and Sheldon and Stevens (1942).

Stewart, N. (1947), A.G.C.T. scores of army personnel grouped by occupations. *Occupations,* 26:5–41. **202**

Stewart, R. G. (1958a), Can psychologists measure driving attitudes? *Educ. psychol. Measmt.,* 18:63–73. **6**

Stewart, R. G. (1958b), Reported driving speeds and opinions on speed and traffic law enforcement. *Educ. psychol. Measmt.,* 18:409–15. **6**

Stone, C. H., and W. E. Kendall (1956), *Effective personnel selection procedures.* Englewood Cliffs, N. J.: Prentice-Hall. **375**

Storms, L. H., *see* Peck and Storms (1956).

Stott, L. H. (1951), The problem of evaluating family success. *Marriage fam. Living,* 13:149–53. **71**

Stouffer, G. A., Jr. (1952), Behavior problems of children as viewed by teachers and mental hygienists. *Ment. Hyg. (N. Y.),* 36:271–85. **43**

Strang, R. (1957), *The adolescent views himself.* N. Y.: McGraw-Hill. **76**

Straus, M. A., *see* Sewell et al. (1957).

Strodtbeck, F. L., *see* McClelland et al. (1958).

Strong, E. K., Jr. (1943), *Vocational interests of men and women.* Stanford: Stanford Univ. Press. **23, 183, 340, 353, 357, 365**

Strother, C. R., K. W. Schaie, and P. Horst (1957), The relationship between advanced age and mental abilities. *J. abnorm. soc. Psychol.,* 55:166–70. **74**

Strunk, M., *see* Cantril and Strunk (1951).

Suci, C. J., *see* Osgood et al. (1957).

Sullivan, H. S. (1953), *The interpersonal theory of psychiatry.* N. Y.: Norton. **236**

Super, D. E. (1949), *Appraising vocational fitness by means of psychological tests.* N. Y.: Harper. **353, 360**

Super, D. E. (1955), *Opportunities in psychology.*

N. Y.: Vocational Guidance Manuals, Inc. **22, 26**

Super, D. E. (1957), *The psychology of careers.* N. Y.: Harper. **337, 353**

Swan, T. H., *see* Johnson et al. (1930).

Symonds, P. M. (1951), *The ego and the self.* N. Y.: Appleton-Century-Crofts. **236**

Symonds, P. M., and S. Dudek (1956), Use of Rorschach in the diagnosis of teacher effectiveness. *J. proj. Tech.,* 20:227–34. **232**

Tagiuri, R., *see* Bruner and Tagiuri (1954).

Tannenbaum, P. H., *see* Osgood et al. (1957).

Tasch, R. J. (1952), The role of the father in the family. *J. exp. Educ.,* 20:319–61. **69**

Taylor, F. W. (1911), *The principles of scientific management.* N. Y.: Harper. **369**

Taylor, J. A. (1953), A personality scale of manifest anxiety. *J. abnorm. soc. Psychol.,* 48:285–90. **123**

Taylor, J. A., *see also* Spence et al. (1956).

Terman, L. M., et al. (1925), *Genetic studies of genius. Vol. 1. The mental and physical traits of a thousand gifted children.* Stanford: Stanford Univ. Press. **37**

Terman, L. M., et al. (1938), *Psychological factors in marital happiness.* N. Y.: McGraw-Hill. **70**

Terman, L. M., and M. A. Merrill (1937), *Measuring intelligence.* Boston: Houghton Mifflin. **183**

Thaler, M., *see* Weiner et al. (1957).

Thayer, P. W., *see* Wispé and Thayer (1957).

Thelen, H. A. (1954), *Dynamics of groups at work.* Chicago: Univ. of Chicago Press. **329**

Thompson, C. (1950), *Psychoanalysis: evolution and development.* N. Y.: Nelson. **236**

Thompson, G. G., *see* Gardner and Thompson (1956).

Thomson, C. W., *see* Bradway et al. (1958).

Thorndike, E. L. (1920), Intelligence and its uses. *Harper's Magazine,* 140:227–35. **199**

Thorndike, E. L. (1924), Mental discipline in high school studies. *J. educ. Psychol.,* 15:1–22, 83–98. **123**

Thorndike, R. L. (1954), The psychological value systems of psychologists. *Amer. Psychologist,* 9:787–89. **16, 22**

Thornton, G. R. (1944), The effect of wearing glasses upon judgments of personality traits of persons seen briefly. *J. appl. Psychol.,* 28:203–07. **140**

Tinbergen, N. (1948), Social releases and the experimental method required for their study. *Wilson Bull.,* 60:6–51. **130**

Tinbergen, N. (1951), *The study of instinct.* London: Oxford Univ. Press. **130**

Tobolski, F. P., and W. A. Kerr (1952), Predictive value of the Empathy Test in automobile salesmanship. *J. appl. Psychol.,* 36:10–11. **183**

Tolman, E. C. (1932), *Purposive behavior in animals and man.* N. Y.: Appleton-Century-Crofts. **127**

Tolman, E. C., B. F. Ritchie, and D. Kalish (1946), Studies in spatial learning. II. Place learning versus response learning. *J. exp. Psychol.,* 36:221–29. **119**

Tsang, J. C. (1938), Hunger motivation in gastrectomized rats. *J. comp. Psychol.,* 26:1–17. **94**

Tuddenham, R. D. (1948), Soldier intelligence in World Wars I and II. *Amer. Psychol.,* 3:54–56. **203**

Tucker, W. B., *see* Sheldon et al. (1940).

Turrell, E. S., *see* Sawrey et al. (1956).

Tyler, L. E. (1956), *The psychology of human differences.* N. Y.: Appleton-Century-Crofts. **214, 225**

Tyler, L. E. (1959), Toward a workable psychology of individuality. *Amer. Psychologist,* 14:75–81. **338**

Ullman, A. D. (1958), Sociocultural backgrounds of alcoholism. *Ann. Amer. Acad. Pol. Soc. Sci.,* 315:48–54. **247**

Ulrich, J. L. (1915), The distribution of effort in learning in white rats. *Behav. Monogr.,* 2: No. 5. **120**

Underwood, B. J. (1949), *Experimental psychology.* N. Y.: Appleton-Century-Crofts. **112**

U.S. Strategic Bombing Survey (1947), *The effects of strategic bombing on German morale.* Washington: Govt. Printing Office. **315**

Van Zelst, R. H., and W. A. Kerr (1951), Reported lifetime worry experiences of Illinois building trades union leaders. *Personnel Psychol.,* 4:151–59. **72**

Verplanck, W. (1955), The control of the content of conversation: reinforcement of statements of opinion. *J. abnorm. soc. Psychol.,* 51:668–76. **124**

Viteles, M. S. (1953), *Motivation and morale in industry.* N. Y.: Norton. **375**

von Bertalanffy, L. (1955), General system theory. *Main currents in modern thought,* 11(4):75–83. **302**

von Bertalanffy, L. (1956), Some considerations on growth in its physical and mental aspects. *Merrill-Palmer Quart.,* 3:13–23. **50**

Von Frisch, K. (1955), *The dancing bees.* N. Y.: Harcourt, Brace. **130**

Waite, R., *see* Fox et al. (1958).

Walker, A. M., *see* Douvan and Walker (1956).

Wallis, W. A., and H. V. Roberts (1956), *Statistics: a new approach.* Glencoe, Ill.: Free Press. **191**

Wangensteen, O. H., and A. J. Carlson (1931), Hunger sensations in a patient after total gastrectomy. *Proc. Soc. Exp. Biol.,* 29:545–47. **94**

Wapner, S., *see* Witkin et al. (1954).

Warnath, C. F. (1955), The relation of family cohesiveness and adolescent independence to social effectiveness. *Marriage fam. Living,* 17:346–48. **61**

Warner, L. (1952), A second survey of psychological opinion on E.S.P. *J. Parapsychol.,* 16:284–95. **135**

Warner, W. L., and J. C. Abeggin (1955), *Big business leaders in America.* N. Y.: Harper. **283**

Warner, W. L., and P. S. Lunt (1941), *The social life of a modern community.* New Haven: Yale Univ. Press. **284**

Washburn, A. L., *see* Cannon and Washburn (1912).

Watson, G. (1957), Some personality differences in children related to strict or permissive parental discipline. *J. Psychol.,* 44:227–49. **43**

Watson, J. B. (1924), *Psychology from the standpoint of a behaviorist,* 2nd ed. Philadelphia: Lippincott. **112**

Watson, R. I. (1959), *Psychology of the child.* N. Y.: Wiley. **51**

Wattenberg, W. W. (1955), *The adolescent years.* N. Y.: Harcourt, Brace. **76**

Webb, W. B., *see* Hollander and Webb (1955).

Webster, H. (1958), Changes in attitude during college. *J. educ. Psychol.,* 49:109–17. **344**

Wechsler, D. (1958), *The measurement of adult intelligence,* 4th ed. Baltimore: Williams and Wilkins. **196, 209, 214**

Weigand, G. E., *see* H. M. Johnson et al. (1930).

Weiner, H., M. Thaler, M. F. Reiser, and I. A. Mirsky (1957), Etiology of duodenal ulcer. 1. Relation of specific psychological characteristics to rate of gastric secretion (serum pepsinogen). *Psychosom. Med.,* 19:1–10. **82**

Weingarten, E. M. (1949), A study of selective perception in clinical judgment. *J. Pers.,* 17:360–406. **243**

Weiss, R. S., *see* Morse and Weiss (1955).

Weisz, J. D. (1957), The etiology of experimental gastric ulceration. *Psychosom. Med.,* 19:61–73. **117**

Weisz, J. D., *see also* Sawrey and Weisz (1956).

Wheeler, L. R. (1942), A comparative study of the intelligence of East Tennessee mountain children. *J. educ. Psychol.,* 33:321–34. **203**

White, A. M., *see* Dollard et al. (1953).

White, R. K., and R. Lippitt (1953), Leader behavior and member reaction in three "social climates," in Cartwright and Zander, eds., *Group dynamics: research and theory.* Evanston: Row, Peterson. **298**

White, R. K., *see also* Lewin, Lippitt, and White (1939).

White, R. W. (1952), *Lives in progress: a study of the natural growth of personality.* N. Y.: Dryden. **76**

Whitehall, A. M., *see* Calhoon et al. (1958).

Whiting, A. S., *see* Haas and Whiting (1956).

Whiting, J. W. M., and I. L. Child (1953), *Child training and personality.* New Haven: Yale Univ. Press. **43**

Whyte, W. F. (1955), *Money and motivation.* N. Y.: Harper. **218, 349, 369**

Whyte, W. W., Jr. (1956), *The organization man.* N. Y.: Simon and Schuster. **69**

Wickman, E. W. (1928), *Children's behavior and teachers' attitudes.* N. Y.: Commonwealth Fund. **43**

Widdowson, E. M. (1951), Mental contentment and physical growth. *The Lancet,* 260:1316–18. **45**

Wiener, N. (1950), *The human use of human beings: cybernetics and society.* Boston: Houghton Mifflin. **302**

Wilder, R. M., *see* R. D. Williams et al. (1940).

Williams, A. C. (1938), Perception of subliminal visual stimuli. *J. Psychol.,* 6:187–99. **137**

Williams, R. D., H. L. Mason, R. M. Wilder, and B. F. Smith (1940), Observations on induced thiamin (vitamin B$_1$) deficiency in man. *Arch. Intern. Med.,* 66:785–99. **100**

Williams, S. B., and H. J. Leavitt (1947), Group opinion as a predictor of military leadership. *J. consult. Psychol.,* 11:283–91. **183, 319**

Williamson, R. C., *see* Sargent and Williamson (1958).

Wilson, R. N., *see* Leighton et al. (1957).

Wispé, L. G. (1955), A sociometric analysis of conflicting role-expectancies. *Amer. J. Sociol.,* 61:134–37. **350**

Wispé, L. G., and P. W. Thayer (1957), Role ambiguity and anxiety in an occupational group. *J. soc. Psychol.*, 46:41–48. **350**

Witkin, H. A., H. B. Lewis, M. Hertzman, K. Machover, P. B. Meissner, and S. Wapner (1954), *Personality through perception*. N. Y.: Harper. **143, 151**

Wolf, K., *see* Kendall and Wolf (1949).

Wolfe, J. B. (1936), Effectiveness of token-rewards for chimpanzees. *Comp. Psychol. Monogr.*, 12: No. 60. **110, 291**

Wolff, H. G., *see* Hinkle and Wolff (1957).

Wolfle, D. (1955), Comparisons between psychologists and other professional groups. *Amer. Psychologist*, 10:231–37. **15**

Woodworth, R. S. (1941), Heredity and environment: a critical survey of recently published material on twins and foster children. *Soc. Sci. Res. Coun. Bull.*, No. 47. **203**

Woodyard, E., *see* Harrell et al. (1955) and (1956).

Worell, L., *see* Karolchuck and Worell (1956).

Wurster, C. R., *see* Bass et al. (1953).

Wyszynski, A. B., *see* Mussen and Wyszynski (1952).

Youden, W. J. (1950), Normal curve. *Amer. Statistician,* 4:11. **178**

Yum, K. S., *see* Masserman and Yum (1946).

Zabarenko, R. N., *see* Chambers and Zabarenko (1956).

Zander, A., *see* Cartwright and Zander (1953).

Zubin, J., *see* Coyne et al. (1943).

INDEX

Items preceded by an asterisk (*) are also to be found in the Glossary, pp. 401–407. Authors whose works are cited in the text are to be found in the References, just preceding this section.

abstractions, 304–305
achievement, need for, 210–212
Adler, A., 222
*adolescence, 53–67
  anxiety during, 64–66
  awareness of others during, 61–62
  empathy in, 62
  independence in, 59–60
  self-concern in, 62–64
adolescents, closeness to parents, 61
  early- and late-maturing, 56–58
  relations with parents and peers, 58–65
adulthood, emotional problems of, 71–73
alcohol, 100–101
alcoholism, 247
*Allport-Vernon Study of Values, 340
ambiguity tolerance, 394
American Board of Professional Examiners in Psychology (ABEPP), 15, 260
American Board of Psychiatry and Neurology, 260
American Council on Education Psychological Examination for College Freshmen (ACE), 201
*American Psychological Association (APA), 15, 195, 260, 356
anger, 96
anger-in and anger-out patterns, 96, 166–168, 387
*anxiety, 166–168, 223, 233, 238–240
  in adolescence, 64–66
  and cultural differences, 65–66
  and learning, 123–124
  learning as a factor in, 239–240
  nature of, 238–239
  "normal," 240
  and sex roles, 64–65
  and social class, 239
  and empathy, 298–299
Arabs, 296
Arapesh, 273
Army Alpha and Beta tests, 73, 195–196, 209
*Army General Classification Test (AGCT), 201–202, 360
*attention, 143
attitudes, authoritarian, 285–287, 388
*authoritarian, see attitudes, climate, culture, leadership
autocratic, see climate, leadership
awareness, behavior without, 7–8, 218
  learning without, 124

Balinese, 34–36, 155
basic needs, 45–50, 54, 67–68, 154, 268, 274, 297
Ba Thonga, 324
*behavior, analyzed, 106–110
  causal approach to, 9
  defensive, 300

behavior (cont.), goal-directed, 113, 154
  inconsistencies in, 296
  during infancy, 30–33
  prediction of, 9–10
  primitive aspects of, 30–31
  social factors in, 267–329
  symbolic, 304–307
behavior mechanisms, 240–246
behavior patterns, consistency of, 38–39
*behavioral science, 7
Bennett Test of Mechanical Comprehension, 362
Binet, A., 194, 199
birth order, effects of, 37–38
blue-collar workers, 349–350
body types, 98
bombing, effects of, 315
brain, 86–89
  diagram of, 89, 90
brain waves, 91
business and industry, psychology in, 355–375

*California Personality Inventory (CPI), 228–229
California Test of Personality, 228
cancer, 100
*catharsis, 385
central tendency, measures of, 177
Charcot, J. M., 11, 219
child development, 29–52
childrearing, social-class differences in, 285
children, disciplining of, 44–45
  first-born, 37–38, 48
  psychological needs of, 45–50
children's play, 118
Christmas, 278
clerical tests, 360
client-centered therapy, 255–259
climate, autocratic, democratic, and laissez-faire, 318
  group, 317–19, 323
*clinical psychology, 18, 259–260
cohesiveness, 316–317
college, attitude changes during, 344–345
  extracurricular activities in, 345–347
  importance to vocational success, 345
  leadership in, 345–347
college degree, meaning of, 348–349
color blindness, 140
comic books, 387
"common sense," 121, 123, 135, 162, 219, 221, 226, 387
  and science, 6–9, 11, 14
*communication, 291–309
  and competitiveness, 325
  effect of groups on, 311–312
  empathic, 297–299

communication (*cont.*), in industry, 321–322, 349
  levels of, 296–297
  between management and labor, 218
  among nations, 294–295
  and psychopathology, 307
  and shared frames of reference, 294
  and social learning, 297
  and status differences, 298
communication nets, 320–321
*compensation, 244
competition, 324–325
*compulsive behavior, 247, 249
*conditioning, 110–111
*conflict, 160–162
  reactions to, 237–238
*conformity, 246
  effects of, 212
cooperation, 324–325
correlation coefficient, 182–184
counseling, vocational, 339
Crawford Small Parts Dexterity Test, 363
creativity, 50, 210–212
cross-cultural research, 272–273, 382–384
cultural differences, 156–158, 232, 247
culture, effect on children, 33–39
cultures, authoritarian, 382–383
cutting scores, 359
cybernetics, 302

defensive behavior, 300
delinquency, juvenile, 44
  and symbolic behavior, 306–307
democratic conditions, and childrearing, 43–44
  and learning, 124–125
dental hygiene, 394–395
depth interview, 372
depth perception, 132–133
Descartes, R., 96
development, in adolescence, 56–58
  in infancy and childhood, 29–52
developmental stages, 297, 312–313
developmental tasks, in adolescence, 55–56
  in adulthood, 68–69
discrimination, 112
displaced hostility, 245–256
dreams, 244
drives, 94–96, 106–109, 154–155
drugs, 101–102

ear, diagram of, 85
*ego, 220–222
Eisenhower, D. D., 287, 393
*electrodermal response, 124
*electroencephalograph, 91, 93
elimination, 95
emotional behavior, 162–170
  and blood chemistry, 166–167
  as motivation, 162–163
  perceptual changes in, 169
  physiological aspects of, 163–168
*empathy, 62, 297–299
engineering psychology, 369–371
environmental stability, 134–135
*epinephrine, 166–168, 250
Eskimos, 324
*ethnocentrism, 387–390
experimental methodology, 11–14
*extinction, 111–112
extracurricular activities, 345–347

*extrasensory perception (ESP), 139
*extravert, 225–226
eye, cross section of, 83

failure, tendency to recall, 348
"faith in people," 339–340
family roles, 351–352
fantasy, 243–244
  as outlet for hostility, 386–387
fear, 96
*feedback, 89–90, 302–303
femininity, 271–273
Finland, 382–383
first-born children, 37–38, 48
*fixation, 247
forced-choice questionnaires, 364
Fortune poll, 285–287
*frequency distribution, 176
Freud, S., 219–222
*frustration, 113, 384
  reactions to, 237–238
F scale, 388–390
future-orientation, 307

gambling, 248–249
garlic, 287, 294
Germans, 382–383, 390
*Gestalt, 133–134
Gestalt psychology, 219
glands, 92–94
goal-directed behavior, 113
grades, 345–347
group awareness, 312–313
group behavior, factors in, 313–314
group climate, 317–319
group decisions, 396
group discussion, 396
group dynamics, 367–368
group life in childhood, 40–41
group membership, 270
group processes, 311–329
group structure, 325–326
group therapy, 254
*groups, characteristics of, 275–284
  inclusive and exclusive, 326–328
  meeting needs in, 314–315
  primary and secondary, 313–314
  reference, 281
  types of, 313
Guthrie, E. R., 118–119

*habits, 158
Hawthorne study, 366–367, 370
hearing, 83–85
*homeostasis, 50, 94
  and self-structure, 282
Hopi Indians, 32–33
hostility, 384–388
  toward authority, 234
Hull, C., 226
human relations training in industry, 366–368
humor, 315
hunger, 94
Huxley, A., 12
hyperactivity, 249
*hypotheses, development of, 10
  testing of, 11–12

*id, 220–221
identification with parents, 42

identity, 268–273, 282
*illusions, 135–136
imitation, 115–116
in-group feeling, 271
in-groups, 326–328
Incomplete Sentences Blank, 230
independence in adolescence, 59–60
industrial psychology, 355–375
inflation, economic, 384
Information and Education Division, U.S. War
    Dept., 395
*insight, 114–115
*instinct, 130–131, 155
Institute of Child Welfare, Univ. of California, 56–
    59
Institute of Human Relations, Yale Univ., 226
Institute of Personality Assessment and Research,
    14, 212
instruction, 116
*intelligence, 193–210
    changes in, 207–210
    inherited factors in, 203–207
    varieties of, 199–203
intelligence testing, *see* mental testing
intercultural attitudes, 382–384
interest tests, *see* tests, interest
international relations, 377–400
*introvert, 225–226
IQ, computation of, 195
    meaning of, 194–195

James, W., 11
Janet, P., 219
jazz, 281
job satisfaction, 349–350
Jung, C. G., 222, 225
Jurgensen Classification Inventory, 364
juvenile delinquency, 387

kinesthesis, 84–86
Koffka, K., 219
Köhler, W., 134, 219
*kurtosis, 180–181

labor strife, 321–322
Latin, 123
leader, role of, 319
leaderless group discussion, 364–366
leaders, authoritarian, 390
leadership, 319–325
    authoritarian, 320–323
    autocratic, 318, 320–323
    and communication, 320–322
    democratic, 318, 320–323
    laissez-faire, 318
    need to share, 322–323
    patterns of, 368
    and social distance, 323–324
    theories of, 319–320
*learning, 105–127
    and anxiety, 123–124
    without awareness, 124
    beginnings of, 31–32
    through imitation, 115–116
    through insight, 114–115
    and performance, 116–117
    and practice, 120
    during sleep, 11–12
    social, 33–41, 273–274, 297
    to talk, 32

learning (*cont.*), testing for, 119–120
    transfer of, 121–123
    trial-and-error, 114
    whole vs. part, 120
*learning dilemma, 113–114
    unresolved, 117–118
life satisfactions of college students, 352
light, refraction of, 82
Literary Digest, 372

MacArthur, D., 287
Manifest Anxiety Scale (MAS), 123
marital adjustment, problems of, 69–71
marriage and the family, 68–71
Marshall, G. C., 287
masculinity, 271–273
*maturation, 32–33
maturers, early and late, 56–58
McDougall, W., 219
*mean, 177
meaning, 120, 274–275, 278
*median, 177
menstruation, effects on behavior, 97–98
mental hygiene, 237–263
*mental illness, 246–260
    sociological factors in, 253–254
mental testing, 193–210, 360
    Binet scales, 194–195
    clinical use of, 196–199
    group tests, 195–196
    validity of, 201–203
Mexico, 382–383
middle-class culture, 287–288, 294
military psychology, 369–370
mind vs. body, 96–97
*Minnesota Multiphasic Personality Inventory
    (MMPI), 228–229
Minnesota Rate of Manipulation Test, 361
Minnesota Vocational Test for Clerical Workers,
    360
*mode, 177
monkeys, emotional needs of, 20–21
*morale, 315–317, 325–326, 368
*motivation, 153–162, 297
    biological factors in, 154–155
    conflicts in, 160–162
    emotional factors in, 162
    levels of, 154
    social, 155–156
    unconscious, 158–159
"motivation research," 371–372
motor activities, 89–92
Mundugumor, 273
muscles, voluntary and involuntary, 91–92

Napoleon, 319
narcotic addiction, 102, 248
*needs, in adolescence, 54–55
    in adulthood, 67–68
    basic, 45–50, 54–55, 67–68, 154, 268, 274, 297
    esteem, 48–49, 54
    homeostatic, 50
    for love, 45–48
    physiological, 94–95
    self-actualization, 49–50, 54–55
Neo-Freudians, 222
nervous system, 86–91
*neurosis, 221, 307
neurotic behavior, defined, 250–251
*nondirective therapy, 255–259

nor-epinephrine, 166–168, 250
normal curve, 178–180
normality, defined, 228–229, 251
*norms, 275–279, 281
nutrition, 100

*obsessive behavior, 249
occupational choice, 337–339
occupational roles, 336–337, 351–352
occupational status, 336–337
occupational therapy, 255
*Oedipus complex, 221–222
Office of Strategic Services (OSS), 365–366
old age, problems of, 73–74
open-end questions, 372
open society, 283
*operant conditioning, 114, 119, 124
*other-directedness, 55, 313
Otis, A. S., 195
out-groups, 326–328
over-achievers in college, 347

pain, 84, 105
paranoia, 223
*paranoid behavior, 251–252
parental expectations, 37–38
Patton, G., 287
*perception, 129–151
    as influenced by anxiety, 223
    defects in, 139–140
    depth, 132–133
    as influenced by drives, 147
    extrasensory (ESP), 139
    factors influencing, 143–149
    individual differences in, 139–143
    innate patterns of, 130–132
    as organized experience, 133–134
    physiological aspects of, 82–86
    selective, 159–160
    as influenced by social pressures, 147–149
    subliminal, 136–137, 373
    as influenced by surroundings, 146
    as influenced by values, 146
*perceptual defense, 141
perceptual rigidity, 242
perceptual set, 143–146, 295
permissiveness with children, 43–45
*personality, 217–236
    cultural factors in, 222
    development of, in children, 33–39
    implicit theories of, 217–227
    measurement of, 227–234
    psychoanalytic theories of, 220–222
    S-R theories of, 226–227
    theories of, 217–227
    trait theories of, 226
    types of, 225–226
    uniqueness of, 273
personality questionnaires, 227–229
Personnel Research Board, Ohio State Univ., 368
*phi phenomenon, 136
phobic behavior, 249
physiological processes, 79–104
    effect on psychological processes, 80–82, 97–102
play, 39–41, 118
play therapy, 254, 256–257
pleasure drive, 96
political participation, 396–399
posture, as cultural norm, 278–279
practice, 120

prejudice, 387–388
probability, 185–187
problem-solving behavior, 273
*projection, 242–243
*projective tests, 229–234, 371–372
*propaganda, 390–396
    fear-arousing, 394–395
    posters, 392–393
*psychiatric social workers, 259–260
psychiatrists, 259–260
*psychoanalysis, 220–222
psychoanalytic theories, 220–222, 227
psychoanalytic therapy, 258
*psychodiagnosis, 227–234, 259
psychologists, interests of, 22–24
    training of, 15
    values of, 17–22
    where employed, 16
Psychologists' Manifesto, 391
*psychology, and "common sense," 6–9
    defined and described, 3–26
    fields of, 16–22
    as perceived by laymen, 3–6
    as "magic," 4–5
    as manipulation, 3–4
    as a pioneering discipline, 14
    as a profession, 14–24
    as perceived by psychologists, 5–6
    as a science, 6–14
psychopathology, and communication, 307
psychoses, 252, 307
psychosomatic disorders, 80, 99–100, 249–250
psychotherapists, 219–220
*psychotherapy, 254–260
    and communication, 307
psychotic behavior, 250–254
    interpersonal relations in, 252–253
public opinion polling, 371
punishment, of adults, 380
    of children, 42–45

Q-sort, 223–224

RAND Corporation, 370–371
Rank, O., 222
*rationalization, 241–242
*reaction formation, 245
recall, 120
recreational therapy, 255
reference, frames of, 275, 294, 303
*reference groups, 281
*regression, 246–247
*reinforcement, of behavior, 106–110
    schedules of, 120–121
relationship, measures of, 182–184
*reliability of tests, 189
*repression, 241
*research, scientific, 11–14
*response, 109
*roles, 278–281, 297, 301
    conflict in, 350–352
    selecting occupational, 333–353
*Rorschach test, 229–232
Rosenzweig Picture-Frustration (P-F) Test, 230–231
Russia, 11

Safe-Driver Inventory, 364
safety campaigns, 6
sampling, 185

sampling (*cont.*), problems in polling, 372
satisfactions, 156–158
scapegoating, 245–246
*schizophrenia, 98, 251
science, and ambiguity, 14
    attitudes of high school students toward, 7
    behavioral, 7
    and "common sense," 6–9
    and controversy, 13–14
    use of in industry, 355–356
scientific attitudes, 12–14
scientific methods, 12–14
selection, in industry, 357–366
selective perception, 159–160
*self, 222–224
    acceptance of, 225
    and group, 268–271, 282–283
    unwanted, 268–270
self-concept, 222–224, 327
    and group membership, 270
    and occupational role, 337–339
self-ideal, 224–225
self-structure, 282
*sensory adaptation, 132
sensory deprivation, 137–139
*sentence completion test, 230
*set, perceptual, 143–146
sex drive, 95
sex roles, 271–273
    and anxiety, 64–67
    in childhood, 272
sexual adjustment, problems of, 66–67
shyness, 249, 281
*significance, statistical, 186–187
*situational tests, 365–366
*skewness, 180–181
skin senses, 84
Skinner, B. F., 114, 119
sleep, 95–96
sleep learning, 11–12
smell, 84
smiling response in infants, 31–32
Smith, S. L., 321
smoking, 101, 158, 247
social appetite, 268
*social class, 54, 65–66, 71–72, 239, 253–254, 284–288, 389
social distance, 323–324
social influences on intelligence, 206
social learning, 273–274, 297
social pathology, 377–382
social pressure, 147–149
socialization in children, 31–38
sociometry, 252–253, 325–326
*somatotherapy, 254
spelling, 124
spicy foods, attitudes toward, 287, 294
*standard deviation, 178–179
standardization of tests, 187
*Stanford-Binet test, 195–196
*statistics, 175–191
    of description, 176–184
    of inference, 185–187
    use of in testing, 187–189
*status, 283–284
    differences in, 298
    occupational, 336–337
    social, 336–337
*stereotypes, 299–302
*stimulus, 106–110

Stromberg Dexterity Test, 363
*Strong Vocational Interest Blank, 23, 183, 340–343, 353, 357, 365
Study of Values, 340
*sublimation, 244–245
*subliminal perception, 136–137, 373
Sullivan, H. S., 222
*superego, 220–221
supervisors, roles of, 368–369
*suppression, 241
sweat glands, 123–124
Swift, Jonathan, 115
symbolic behavior, 304–307
Systems Research Laboratory, 370–371

taste, 84
teachers' attitudes toward children, 43
Terman, L. M., 194–196
terminology, scientific, 306
"terrible two's," 41–42
*tests, 187–189
    intelligence, *see* mental testing
    interest, 340–343, 364–365
    manipulative, 361–363
    personality, 227–234, 362–364
    situational, 365–366
    special aptitude, 360–362
    use of in industry, 357–366
*Thematic Apperception Test (TAT), 229–232, 362, 386–387
thirst, 94–95
*threat, psychological, 317
time-and-motion study, 369
Tolman, E. C., 119
totalitarianism, 314–315
*traits, personality, 226
*trial-and-error, 114
Trobiand Islanders, 222
Tschambuli, 273
Tuaregs, 53–54

ulcers, 80–82, 99, 117
unconscious motivation, 158–160, 268
under-achievers in college, 347
UNICEF, 379
uniqueness of personality, 273

*validity of tests, 187–188
variability, measures of, 178–179
Vicary, J. M., 137, 373
vision, 82–83

war, prevention of, 377–378
    understanding causes of, 381–382
Wechsler, D., 196
*Wechsler Intelligence Scales, 196–199
Welsh Figure Preference Test, 211
Wertham, F., 387
Wertheimer, M., 219
Western Electric Co., 366–367
white-collar workers, 349–350
witnesses, unreliability of, 8
work, attitudes toward, 334–336
    motivation in, 333–336
World Health Organization (WHO), 379
Wundt, W., 11

Yankee City, 284–285

Zimmerman, R. R., 20–21
Zuñi Indians, 33, 324